ADVANCE PRAISE

With this stirring, brilliant, and comprehensive look at the history of the Latino civil rights movement through the lens of immigration, Charles Kamasaki cements his legacy as one of the most knowledgeable and effective advocates for the Hispanic community over the last forty years. And if there was a "Game of Thrones" about how IRCA passed, this book would be the script!
 —Janet Murguía, President and CEO, UnidosUS

Charles Kamasaki provides us with a poignant, evocative, and timely look into the national debate on immigration. We couldn't be luckier for this book. In *Immigration Reform: The Corpse That Will Not Die*, Kamasaki traces the roots of the perpetual racial divide by inviting us into a front row seat to a pivotal moment when he helped shape the comprehensive, bipartisan immigration reform widely known as IRCA in 1986. At a time when these issues loom even larger, dominated by anger, xenophobia, nativism—emotions underscored by the siren call for a Wall—*Immigration Reform* is a must read. It provides valuable lessons on how we got here and how to get out of the logjam that's challenging the core foundation of a nation of immigrants.
 —Alfredo Corchado, Border-Mexico Correspondent
  for the *Dallas Morning News*

Charles Kamasaki's archly titled *Immigration Reform: The Corpse that Will Not Die* is compelling history for any American trying to understand the ever-expanding policy pothole that is our broken immigration system—and the polarizing politics that have paralyzed progress. It is a timely reflection on the web of contingencies that often inform the fate of national issues. For reform advocates who have been struggling for decades to enshrine a more inclusive vision of America in our immigration laws, it provides encouragement to keep fighting and important insights about the need for an all of the above approach to securing landmark legislation: crafty inside lobbying, street heat in communities across the country, fresh communication and policy strategies, lawmakers willing to put real skin in the game, openness to compromise, and an unwavering moral compass. Amidst one of the most relentless attacks on immigrants and immigration in a generation, these words of wisdom from a legend in the field provide a hopeful reminder that reform is not dead—and will not die.
 —Marshall Fitz, Managing Director, Immigration,
  The Emerson Collective

Charles Kamasaki has painstakingly written a book that provides invaluable insight into the labyrinthian process of enacting major social legislation: original intent, coalition building, public engagement, leadership personalities, the interplay of ideals and compromises. And because the legislation he chronicles involves the contentious subject of immigration, the book goes far beyond a narrative of lawmaking. Kamasaki captures the evolution of public attitudes, the human and economic costs, and the hardening positions that have transformed immigration into one of the most conflictive issues in modern America. This is legislative history intertwined with social history in one powerful volume.

—Henry Cisneros, Chairman, *Cityview*, and former Secretary of U.S. Housing and Urban Development.

Immigration Reform: The Corpse That Will Not Die is a timely and important achievement! Immigration policy remains one of our most vexing national issues. Kamasaki offers an insightful analysis of the factors that helped produce the nation's last comprehensive immigration act 30 years ago. However, its greater contribution may be in what it says about the challenges facing us today. The fact that the story is viewed through the lens of the Latino civil rights movement makes the book even more significant. Bravo!

—Wade Henderson, Immediate Past President, The Leadership Conference on Civil and Human Rights

What Americans don't know about how immigration policy is made could fill a book. Finally, that book—about how the "corpse" of immigration reform once rose from the dead and could be revived again—has been written, by someone who knows where all the bodies are buried. *The* definitive chronicle of immigration reform; destined to be a classic legislative case study.

—Raul Yzaguirre, President Emeritus, UnidosUS (formerly NCLR)

From his role in the cast of the drama, Charles Kamasaki gives us a masterful, sweeping account of the enactment in 1986 of landmark immigration legislation that reverberates through our immigration debates today. His telling—in highly readable, storytelling style—connects major American cultural and political themes, from U.S.-Mexican relations to the origins of key social justice movements to the influence of southern lawmakers in American politics, with the nation's immigration history. But ultimately, the book shows how history and change are about the individuals who are in the fray and what they do to get to "yes" from deeply different places. Would that such actors were on the stage again today.

—Doris Meissner, former INS Commissioner and Director, US Migration Policy, Migration Policy Institute

Who gets to be a citizen of America and who gets to decide is a defining challenge for our nation. The immigration policy debate continues to roil our politics and our elections, and some believe it is our country's most difficult policy issue to resolve. This book is the origin story of this modern-day showdown. Written by a warrior who was in the room at every stage, and who, along with his fellow advocates, helped shape one of modern America's monumental and improbable legislative breakthroughs, this book offers a remarkable view into the dynamics of the immigration reform debate, the challenges of making legislative sausage, and the forces that compete and cooperate to produce either political paralysis or, this case, historic change.

    —**Frank Sharry, Executive Director, America's Voice**

In this deeply researched and beautifully written insider account of the Immigration Reform and Control Act of 1986, Charles Kamasaki has formulated a clear, compelling narrative that is highly relevant to the ongoing struggle to advance immigrants' rights today. Everyone who is engaged in the debate about the future of immigration reform should read this book.

    —**Anthony D. Romero, Executive Director, American Civil Liberties Union**

Essential reading for anyone who is at all curious about how the country's always-challenging immigration debate got to where it is. In this account, expertly told by an acute observer of policy and the humans who shape it, you will learn about history, about race, and about how our democracy works almost before you realize that it's happening. No journalist should attempt to cover immigration without reading this book!

    —**Cecilia, Muñoz, Vice President, *New America*, and former Director of
    the White House Domestic Policy Council under President Obama**

Nearly everyone regards the US immigration system as "broken," yet the nation is so divided on the subject that it seemingly can't be fixed. It's the "corpse that will not die" of Charles Kamasaki's magisterial recounting of dozens of failed attempts to bring it alive. Yet, in 1986, Congress and the Reagan administration did pass a comprehensive immigration reform—pushed by a small group of activists who succeeded against all odds. Kamasaki was at the center of that struggle and tells in detail how it happened. His tale is instructive for current-day leaders and citizens: if reform could happen three decades ago, why not now?

    —**Mort Kondracke, American political commentator and journalist**

Charles Kamasaki's book *Immigration Reform* is both a rare insider's view on how the country's last major immigration reform got done in Congress—with unique insight on how outside groups shape major policy changes—and a masterful feat of storytelling, engaging and enjoyable from beginning to end. He seamlessly weaves together the interests, the politics, and the personalities that shaped the reform effort in a way that makes it both a great story and an essential historical account that has important lessons for today's immigration debates.

—Andrew Selee, PhD, President, Migration Policy Institute (MPI)

Kamasaki tells a compelling and true story of American politics through the eyes of a participant, the mind of a scholar, and the voice of a novelist. He transports the reader with vivid portrayals of people and moments as a historic reform debate unfolded in the Congress, and the country. If readers want to understand the fundamental character of the politics of immigration then and now, how Washington can fail repeatedly yet still rise to achieve historic reforms, and how the 1980s illuminate paths ahead in the Age of Trump—then read this book. Trust me. I was there.

—Rick Swartz, Founder, National Immigration Forum

Charles Kamasaki masterfully describes the power of agricultural employers and rural legislators to obstruct and shape immigration reform and the creative responses of advocates for farmworkers. The book demonstrates the pivotal role in the 1986 immigration bill of the compromise on a "Special Agricultural Worker" program, legalizing 1.1 million undocumented farmworkers, and changes in the agricultural guest worker program. Its trenchant analysis informs the current and centuries-long struggles over agribusiness's recruitment of foreign citizens to harvest its crops and the economic and political status of farmworkers."

—Bruce Goldstein, Executive Director, Farmworker Justice

IMMIGRATION REFORM

IMMIGRATION REFORM

THE
CORPSE
THAT WILL
NOT DIE

Charles Kamasaki

MANDEL VILAR PRESS

This book is typeset in Sabon MT Pro. The paper used in this book meets the minimum requirements of ANSI/NISO Z39.48-1992 (R1997). ∞

Cover photo/illustration by Sophie Appel

Publisher's Cataloging-in-Publication Data
Names: Kamasaki, Charles, author.
Title: Immigration reform : the corpse that will not die / Charles Kamasaki.
Description: Simsbury, Connecticut : Mandel Vilar Press, [2019] | Includes bibliographical
    references and index.
Identifiers: ISBN 9781942134558 | ISBN 9781942134565 (ebook)
Subjects: LCSH: United States. Immigration Reform and Control Act of 1986. | Emigration and
    immigration law—United States. | United States—Emigration and immigration—Government
    policy.
Classification: LCC KF4819 .K36 2019 (print) | LCC KF4819 (ebook) | DDC 342.73082—dc23

Printed in the United States of America
19 20 21 22 23 24 25 26 27 / 9   8 7 6 5 4 3 2 1

The opinions expressed herein are those of the author, and may not necessarily represent the views of UnidosUS, the Migration Policy Institute, or any of the book project's funders.

Mandel Vilar Press
19 Oxford Court, Simsbury, Connecticut 06070
www.americasforconservation.org | www.mvpress.org

CONTENTS

CHAPTER 9

Reflections   391

An Inconclusive Conclusion   •   Lessons

POLICY PRIMERS

CAST OF CHARACTERS (1983–1990)

THE GROUP

Phyllis Eisen, Vice President, National Immigration, Refugee and Citizenship Forum

Wade Henderson, Legislative Counsel, American Civil Liberties Union

Charles Kamasaki, Director of Policy Analysis, National Council of La Raza

Warren Leiden, Executive Director, American Immigration Lawyers Association

J. Michael Myers, Washington Representative, Church World Service

Dale Frederick "Rick" Swartz, President, National Immigration, Refugee and Citizenship Forum

Arnoldo Torres, National Executive Director, League of United Latin American Citizens

Joseph Michael "Joe" Treviño, Deputy Executive Director, League of United Latin American Citizens

COLLEAGUES AND ALLIES

Muzaffar Chishti, Director, Immigration Project, International Ladies' Garment Workers' Union

Monsignor Nicholas DiMarzio, Director, Migration & Refugee Services, US Catholic Conference

Martha Escutia, Legislative Director, National Council of La Raza

Richard Fajardo, Staff Attorney, Mexican American Legal Defense and Educational Fund

Emily Gantz McKay, Vice President, National Council of La Raza

Morton Halperin, Director, Washington Office, American Civil Liberties Union

Antonia Hernández, Regional Counsel, Mexican American Legal Defense and Educational Fund

Michael Hooper, Executive Director, National Coalition for Haitian Refugees
Dolores Huerta, Vice President, United Farm Workers of America
Wells Klein, Executive Director, American Council for Nationalities Service
Cecilia Muñoz, Senior Immigration Policy Analyst, National Council of La Raza
Joy Olson, Policy Associate, Church World Service
Dan Purtell, Immigration Policy Fellow/Policy Associate, National Council of La Raza
Gary Rubin, Deputy Director of National Affairs, American Jewish Committee
Frank Sharry, Executive Director, National Immigration Forum
Dianne Stewart, Policy Associate, Texas State Office of Federal Affairs
Carol Wolchok, Staff Attorney, American Civil Liberties Union
Raul Yzaguírre, President, National Council of La Raza

LAWMAKERS

Representative Howard Berman (D-CA)
Representative Hamilton Fish (R-NY)
Representative Barney Frank (D-MA)
Representative Robert García (D-NY)
Senator Edward Kennedy (D-MA)
Representative Daniel Lungren (R-CA)
Representative Romano "Ron" Mazzoli (D-KY)
Representative John Joseph "Joe" Moakley (D-MA)
Representative Peter Rodino (D-NJ)
Representative Edward Roybal (D-CA)
Representative Esteban Torres (D-CA)
Senator Alan Simpson (R-WY)

OTHERS

Roger Conner, Executive Director, Federation for American Immigration Reform
Garner James "Jim" Cline, House Judiciary Committee
Lynnette R. Conway, House Subcommittee on Immigration, Refugees and International Law
Richard Day, Senate Subcommittee on Immigration and Refugees
Arthur P. "Skip" Endres, House Judiciary Committee
Carl Hampe, Senate Subcommittee on Immigration and Refugees
Albert Jacquez, Rep. Esteban Torres (D-CA)
Brenda Pillors, Reps. Shirley Chisholm (D-NY) and Edolphus Towns (D-NY)
John Tanton, Founder, Federation for American Immigration Reform

AUTHOR'S NOTE

I mmigration Reform: The Corpse That Will Not Die is about the Immigration Reform Act of 1986, known among insiders as "IRCA," the last "comprehensive immigration reform" enacted into law. It is not principally a "policy book" that analyzes various alternatives and concludes with a recommended solution. Nor is it purely a "process book" that studies legislative procedure. It doesn't purport to be a "complete" history of recent immigration policy debates. Its story is deeply intertwined with racial politics, but it isn't exactly a book about "race." And it's certainly not a thorough examination of nonprofit organizational roles in shaping immigration policy. Rather, the book is about IRCA's "life and times," its forebears, birth, near-death, struggle to achieve its mission in the real world, progeny, and legacies. To be sure, this "biography" touches on public policy, the legislative process, historical milestones in US immigration policy, and the evolution of various groups' actions on immigration. But mostly this book tries to tell a story, or to be more precise, a series of stories, behind the historical summaries or headlines by which most Americans learn of or follow any law.

This isn't exactly the book I intended to write. I went into the project fully expecting to cover the role of The Group, a small coalition of public interest lobbyists that I was a member of that played a key role in shaping and then implementing IRCA. I expected, as well, to trace the trajectories of the major Latino civil rights organizations, one of which is still my employer, engaged in that debate. I wanted to address the legislative process itself through the lens of IRCA, its predecessors, and its successors, and the roles of key lawmakers in shaping those bills. And the relationship between racial politics and immigration policy was a part of the story that couldn't be ignored. After five years of research, countless rewrites, pursuit of various tangents, and forays down numerous blind alleys, those stories remain a core part of this book.

Other stories jumped out at me, such as the growth of two sets of movements—one focused on immigrant rights and another determined to restrict, even reverse immigration—both with roots in the IRCA era, now deeply embedded in opposing political parties. Their existence may be a given in contemporary discourse, but it seemed to me that an initial inquiry into the origins of these movements and their influence on the two major political parties, was a story worth telling, if nothing else to catalyze future, deeper scholarly pursuits.

The story I least expected was that of the emergence of the concept of comprehensive immigration reform as first embodied in IRCA, an inanimate object consisting of thousands of words printed in black ink on white paper, as an almost humanlike character. It was born with the legislative equivalent of a silver spoon in its mouth, carefully nurtured by elites in both parties, blessed by almost universally positive press, brought into the world in the hands of two capable sponsors, and seemed destined to become a legislative and policy juggernaut. But then it was bruised, battered, bloodied, and even buried on multiple occasions, only to rise up, Lazarus-like, barely staggering over the legislative finish line and onto the president's desk. Even its immediate progeny, a follow-on bill passed four years later, seemingly first had to endure two ritual deaths before being resuscitated.

Whether viewed simply as millions of characters on the printed page, a combination of often disparate policy proposals, the product of gifted but flawed lawmakers working the gears of the legislative machinery, a set of noble ideas embodying the aspirations of millions of immigrants already in the country and millions more who wish to enter—or according to its most vociferous critics, a disaster of monumental proportions amounting to "genocide" of white American culture—the idea of definitive comprehensive reform legislation that can "solve" the immigration issue, is, truly, a "corpse" that refuses to die. If nothing else, I hope readers of this chronicle will come away understanding how and why "comprehensive immigration reform" has become and will remain a near-perpetual topic of political debate for the foreseeable future.

A final note about how I chose to portray my own role in this book. I was a direct participant in many events of the IRCA era and the debates that followed. I have vivid memories of what was a deeply formative period in my personal and professional life. In various drafts of this manuscript, I tried using a first person, memoirish tone for certain incidents or activities that included my participation. But the more I wrote the less appropriate it felt to use the personal pronoun *I* to describe my own role. In my mind's eye, the individual being written about was someone else, not just younger but quite different in many other ways from the person I've become.

Odd as it may seem to friends and colleagues who read pieces of the manuscript and suggested otherwise, switching self-references to the more formal third person resulted in something of a breakthrough. Describing my younger self in the third person made it far easier for my current self to view events from a distance, to be more accountable as a writer and tell the story the reader deserves to read, which is certainly not the version that the 1980s-era Kamasaki might have preferred. Hard lessons that Kamasaki learns were more easily, and I hope honestly, presented when I could imagine myself lecturing "him" on how much he still had to learn.

CKK
April 15, 2018
Weslaco, Texas

IMMIGRATION
REFORM

INTRODUCTION

Washington is like a roaring river. And in the river there are thousands
of logs, each one a different policy idea. And on each log, there are
thousands of ants. Most logs break apart. Others wash ashore, or get
stuck in a log jam. Once in a while, a log makes it all the way to sea. And
each ant on that log thinks she's the one who steered it there.
—MORTON H. HALPERIN[1]

The Immigration Reform and Control Act of 1986 began, in Mort Halperin's classic metaphor quoted above, as one "log" in the roaring river that as well as any other captures the often chaotic legislative process in the nation's capital. Halperin's metaphor affirms a core truth about policy making in Washington: most of those involved in enacting legislation tend to exaggerate their roles. Part of this is simple human nature: our egos tend to see and interpret events through the prism of our own actions, not fully aware of how others might've been equally or even more impactful. People want and need to be the heroes of their own stories.

The metaphor reveals another core truth about policy making: large structural forces often years, decades, or even centuries in the making shape the course of events as much or more than the decisions or actions of mere mortals. In nature, the paths of logs in a river are generally determined by accident, such as where and when the log falls into a river, and how it interacts with largely preestablished boundaries like the shape of the river's banks, its gradient, the volume of water carried, or the location of midstream boulders washed into the waterway centuries ago. Inevitable forces of nature gradually change a stream's course, and major natural disasters can alter a river's path quickly. Routine events that occur by happenstance, such as a storm that accelerates the water's flow, or random human acts such as a single farmer felling a tree that happens to

1

fall into the river at a certain angle, can splinter some logs apart or divert off course others that once seemed destined to reach the sea.

Similarly, major policy reforms to address long-standing, well-known problems become actionable due to the confluence of several, often predetermined, factors—the state of the economy, cultural trends, the nation's demographics, and a shifting of the political winds—with "precipitating events" such as a scandal, acts of violence, or natural disaster. Within those structural forces and acts of God, people—the ants on the metaphorical logs—do matter. In most stories about legislation, the best known and most prominent ants—storied lawmakers, powerful presidents, influential businesses, or in a few cases potent interest group leaders—are cast as protagonists, successfully steering their legislative log from a tributary on a mountain hillside all the way to the sea. These ants are actually more akin to large ant colonies, and come replete with swarms of staff, institutional support, and perhaps as important, media storytellers who chronicle the events, ensuring that future generations of ants are informed of the officials' historic roles.

But there are other ants on those logs, including small groups speaking for constituencies that typically are underrepresented in the policy process. Most don't affect the course of the log they're on, and their impact is frequently cancelled out by ants representing other interests. But amid the river's swirling, often unpredictable microcurrents, even minute changes in direction can push one log ashore and keep another in the main stream. If enough ants get together, read the currents, anticipate obstacles, and time their movements precisely enough—think of the sailing maneuver known as *heeling*, where members of a crew weighing a total of a few hundred pounds lean over the boat's railing to alter the speed and balance of yachts weighing several tons—they can influence the log's course and direction.

One of this book's stories is told from the perspective of a small group of ants—nonprofit advocates rarely featured in "standard" legislative chronicles. A key faction that first delayed, then shaped, and later helped implement the legislation was a tiny coalition of nonprofit lobbyists from Latino, civil liberties, legal, and religious organizations calling itself The Group. All were members of a new pro-immigrant umbrella organization, the National Immigration, Refugee and Citizenship Forum, now known as the National Immigration Forum, that audaciously positioned itself as a counterweight to the Select Commission on Immigration and Refugee Policy, the "blue ribbon" government commission charged with drafting the outlines of what became IRCA. Members of The Group often saw themselves and were perceived as a single unit, although they had diverse backgrounds and faced many personal and organizational tensions. When confronted by a legislative juggernaut that seemed certain to pass, the advocates organized against the bill using some tools and tactics that even today would be considered unconventional, even extreme. But in a largely untold story, The Group evolved from unyielding opponents to active participants in shaping, even facilitating passage of the final bill in 1986.

Another story involves the bill's lengthy antecedents and tortured path to enactment. Efforts to pass legislation cracking down on unauthorized immigration sponsored by liberal Democrats Peter Rodino of New Jersey and Massachusetts senator Edward "Ted" Kennedy twice passed the House but died in the Senate in the 1970s, the victim of opposition from agribusiness interests. A third attempt, which for the first time linked tougher enforcement with a "legalization" or "amnesty" program for undocumented immigrants already in the United States, was never brought to a vote in the Democratic-controlled House in 1976. Even if it had been, it wouldn't have had a chance of passing a Senate dominated by an ideological working majority largely content with the *status quo*, and agricultural interests that demanded a temporary worker program as their price for reform. In the waning days of the Carter administration, an unusually potent government commission began crafting the outline of major reform legislation, a product eagerly awaited by elites heralding its report. IRCA was shaped by celebrated legislators such as Rodino and Wyoming Republican senator Alan Simpson, the two principal sponsors of the final version of the legislation. One of the bill's original main authors, centrist Democrat Romano Mazzoli of Kentucky, was nudged to the sidelines during the final stages of the debate, but persevered to play a statesmanlike role in the legislation's eventual passage, while Ted Kennedy, among the most accomplished legislators of the modern era, was mainly a supporting actor.

Although its core policy provisions—new enforcement measures, an amnesty program for some undocumented immigrants, and some form of temporary worker program—were endorsed by four successive administrations and had passed at least one house of Congress a half-dozen times over a dozen years, the bill had to be rescued by the introduction of a completely new idea into the debate. That legislative innovation was drafted by an unlikely trio of legislators: Reps. Leon Panetta and Howard Berman, both California Democrats but representing opposing interests, and New York Democrat Charles Schumer. Republican Dan Lungren, a powerful supporter of the legislation, was so put off by the new innovation that he led an effort to kill the bill, but eventually acceded to its enactment. Another key lawmaker, Democratic Rep. Esteban Torres, also of California, started off as one of the bill's strongest opponents, but later delivered the votes leading to its passage. The venerable Rep. Edward Roybal, founder of the Congressional Hispanic Caucus, began the debate working hand-in-hand with The Group as the leader of the opposition, was shunted aside, but later reemerged to play an unexpectedly crucial role.

A third story involves IRCA's progeny, highly consequential follow-on legislation known as the Immigration Act of 1990, which established the system that doubled legal immigration from its 1980s levels and set the precedent for the Deferred Action for Childhood Arrivals (DACA) program and similar initiatives announced two decades later by the Obama administration. Crusty Massachusetts congressman Joe Moakley, an unlikely champion for Central American refugees, tried mightily but failed to include in IRCA his own measure protecting those fleeing violence in the region. He eventually prevailed in the 1990 Act after a dramatic confrontation with Simpson in the proverbial smoke-filled room.

Two of IRCA's most important stories have yet to be completed. The bill connected two vastly different pro-immigrant movements. Before IRCA, what might've been called the immigrant rights movement was dominated by mostly sectarian service organizations, all led by white men with stronger ties to European immigrants from previous generations than to the "new immigration" from Latin America and Asia. These venerable organizations and their leaders, many from elite families, did most of their business in quiet meetings with government officials with whom they shared old-school ties and social networks. During the IRCA debate, Latino civil rights leaders and a small group of advocates arose, most members of the new National Immigration Forum, to represent immigrant interests. As IRCA was implemented, the immigrant rights movement began an evolution into its current manifestation. The modern immigrant rights movement is now a robust, well-resourced, even crowded field, with no fewer than six major national pro-immigrant advocacy networks, mainly immigrant-led, wholly dedicated to advancing the interests of what will soon become the largest wave of immigrants in the nation's history. Most have a powerful focus on community organizing; all are aggressive and unafraid, and they do much of their work through protests and demonstrations in the streets. The demise of the old guard and the rise of the Young Turks of the immigrant rights movement is explained in large part by the IRCA debate and its aftermath.

At the same time, a somewhat inchoate yet indisputably powerful set of immigration reform opponents began to coalesce within the Republican Party, eventually exemplified by the candidacy of Donald Trump. A key strand of this modern anti-immigrant movement has its roots in the 1960s-era push for population control, while another is closely linked with adherents of neoclassical economics historically associated with organized labor. They later joined with what might be called traditional nativists, including those with white nationalist ties and others linked to the Tea Party. Powerful enough to exercise veto power over the GOP's natural inclination to support open markets and the attendant labor mobility that almost inevitably results, developments during the IRCA debate explain the origins of this increasingly ascendant wing of the Party of Lincoln. These new movements' full stories have yet to be written, but if immigration reform is to be resuscitated in the near future, these new sources of power based outside of the nation's capital arguably will have as much to say about its contents as any.

There are other stories developing that we can barely see the outlines of today. Future debates may well be shaped by unforeseen and unpredictable developments, both here and abroad. For example, for obvious reasons immigration policy and the status of the US economy have long been inextricably linked. Yet longstanding rules and ratios that policy makers have relied on to manage the economy—such as the "fact" that low unemployment would inevitably lead to wage increases—no longer seem to hold. And advances in artificial intelligence and robotics seem to portend massive changes in the shape of the domestic labor market, with unknown consequences for immigration policy. Similarly, unforeseen events abroad inevitably shape the nation's immigration policy and politics. For example, unexpected outflows from Cuba and Haiti in the late 1970s served as a precipitating event that led IRCA, and few predicted in 2003 that the Iraq War would lead to a refugee crisis in Europe a decade later. In this broader context, no set of domestic reforms, no matter how well designed, is likely to produce an immigration policy guaranteed to be both workable and sustainable over several decades. For these reasons alone, one might expect ongoing debates over immigration policy well into the future.

But in this story, the passions in immigration debates originate from unresolved and still highly contested questions of American identity. People of Mexican descent were first subjected to the jurisdiction of the US by conquest, and what some call an "original sin" of occupation, which resulted in conditions akin to the Jim Crow South. Only later did these questions manifest themselves in immigration policy, a phenomenon that arguably continues through the modern era. For the foreseeable future, the vast majority of immigrants will be people of color, so the interaction between immigration policy and the question of American identity is unmistakable. It's unclear when, or even whether, a consensus on the essence of American identity will emerge. Until then, our nation can expect a continuing—some might say never-ending—debate on immigration reform.

The cliché that "history may not repeat itself but often rhymes," frequently but perhaps mistakenly attributed to Mark Twain, befits the story of immigration reform. Economic restructuring and uncertainty marked the IRCA era, as did the fallout from unpredictable and unforeseen international developments. While only rarely explicitly articulated in congressional debates, the question of race—and the impact of the entry of large numbers of Latino immigrants on American identity—was omnipresent. Yet lawmakers and interest groups in that era managed to overcome deep economic anxiety, unanticipated global events, and the American public's profound ambivalence about the demographic changes associated with immigration to enact comprehensive reform legislation, along with a follow-on capstone bill, but only after the measures failed before they succeeded. None of the parties engaged in the debate—lawmakers, interest groups, or pundits—were entirely satisfied with the policies enacted, and reforms didn't always produce the substantive outcomes their sponsors intended. These are perhaps the enduring lessons of IRCA's story: major reforms are hard, require compromise, often fail at first, and then when enacted produce only incremental advances.

A core lesson of this book is that various immigration reform proposals from across the political spectrum—logs in Halperin's metaphor—will be major subjects of public discourse into the future as far as the eye can see. Much deserved attention will be drawn to logs occupied by major politicians—ant queens that bring with them whole colonies of staff, institutional supporters, and media admirers who help them navigate the policy river's treacherous currents. But during those future debates, smaller groups of ants, some representing nonprofit organizations, will also be on those logs. If the story of IRCA's enactment means anything at all, what those ants choose to do can shape the substance, timing, and implementation of future reforms. In Margaret Mead's immortal words, "Never doubt that a small group of thoughtful, committed citizens can change the world; indeed, it's the only thing that ever has."

CHAPTER 1

A Meeting and a Movement

A MEETING: SPRING 1984

The Group was nervous. Several of them had battled against the immigration reform bill for two long years and against a "blue ribbon" government commission seemingly intent on producing proposals they opposed for three years before that. Although the members of The Group represented divergent interests and came from vastly different backgrounds, they were united by a belief, an almost religious conviction, that they alone were responsible for shielding vulnerable, exploited immigrant communities from a potentially disastrous set of policies masquerading as reform. But the bonds between them were deeper than simple agreement on public policy. Like soldiers defending their position from wave after wave of attacks from superior forces, they were battle-hardened veterans; and like those who've shared foxholes, their relationships were deeply loyal, in some ways more loyal to each other than to the organizations that employed them. They all felt they were fighting for a cause bigger than themselves.

They'd survived a near-death experience, when the Simpson-Mazzoli immigration reform bill they opposed came close to passage at the end of the previous Congress. The bill, named after chief sponsors Republican senator Alan Simpson of Wyoming and Kentucky Democratic congressman Romano Mazzoli, was widely perceived as both good policy and good politics inside the Beltway, the multi-laned Interstate 495 that surrounds Washington, DC. It had origins in a major government commission, enjoyed wide support among elite opinion leaders, and attracted energetic, capable sponsors like the wise-cracking Simpson, already a media darling, and the hard-working, intellectual Mazzoli. The issue seemed to be one whose time had come.

As they mingled in the hallway outside of the office of Rep. Barney Frank, the nonprofit lobbyists exchanged greetings in hushed, quiet tones. For The Group, this was a serious, solemn occasion. The meeting with Frank, an unlikely but potentially valuable ally, could prove crucial to their strategy of disrupting the bill's inexorable momentum. It had passed the Senate by an overwhelming margin in 1982 and had died on the House floor in a special lame duck session that year. The bill had passed the Senate again early in 1983 and appeared poised for passage by the House in early 1984. Hundreds of newspaper editorial boards had endorsed the bill in one form or another, some chastising The Group, sometimes by name, for obstructing the bill's passage. Congressional staff that previously had welcomed them into their offices to discuss the issues or coordinate strategy were now too busy to meet, some even looking the other way when approached in congressional hearing rooms or cafeterias, seemingly afraid to be seen with The Group or even to acknowledge them publicly.

The Group needed a game changer, something to alter the fundamental dynamics of the legislative landscape. Because delaying tactics alone seemed insufficient to stop Simpson-Mazzoli this time, League of United Latin American Citizens (LULAC) executive director Arnoldo Torres, The Group's unofficial leader, had come up with an audacious ploy to derail the bill: to draft their own alternative legislation. In his mind, nothing less than a credible legislative alternative to Simpson-Mazzoli was required to shift the unfavorable political dynamics they faced. The old Capitol Hill adage was "You can't beat something with nothing," and Torres was determined to come up with "something." For months The Group had been meeting several evenings a week, debating and drafting their alternative bill. After sometimes cooperative, often difficult meetings, Rep. Edward Roybal of California, the founder of the Congressional Hispanic Caucus, had introduced "their" bill. If Barney Frank, a key supporter of Simpson-Mazzoli and an emerging force in Congress, could be persuaded to cosponsor, or at a minimum say some good things about their bill, it would be a crucial first step in affirming their new strategy.

The Group had no illusions that their bill would pass intact. But at worst they thought the introduction of a plausible alternative could buy time—they could request hearings on the bill for example, and possibly even convince one or more committees to formally consider their bill. This process could consume months, possibly even a year or more. And if they could mount a credible campaign for their ideas, it was likely that key provisions of their bill could be attached as amendments to Simpson-Mazzoli, thus improving the final product if, in the end, it passed. Even if the worst happened, and their proposals were dismissed, they would gain a powerful talking point: that they had tried in good faith to compromise, had been refused, and thus had no choice but to fall back into an opposition mode.

After keeping The Group waiting for several minutes, Rep. Frank's top aide Doug Kahn stuck his head into the hallway and called them in. Typically, when constituents, interest groups, or guests walked into a House member's office, the representative stood and greeted them as they entered. This degree of personal hospitality reflected the fact that representatives are on the ballot every two years—they're always "in cycle"—and thus with rare exceptions they try to be "regular folks." By contrast, in the more august Senate, guests usually were assembled and waited before the senator was ushered in through a side door. As The Group entered his inner office, Frank stayed seated behind his desk, reading the newspaper, puffing away on a cigar, great wafts of smoke billowing around him. He didn't even acknowledge The Group's presence as he flipped the newspaper pages, one by one. He was a fast reader, but he *was* reading, grunting or commenting sotto voce on the news of the day, as they waited. "Bullshit!," Frank whispered to himself, scanning one headline.

The Group seated itself roughly in order of seniority. Torres took the chair closest to Frank's desk. Next to him was Wade Henderson, American Civil Liberties Union (ACLU) legislative counsel and a seasoned lobbyist. Warren Leiden, executive director of the American Immigration Lawyers Association, and The Group's technical expert on immigration law, was next, along with the National Council of Churches' Michael Myers, who represented the refugee resettlement organizations likely to play a huge role in processing undocumented immigrants if a legalization or "amnesty" program was enacted. Bringing up the rear were Torres's deputy, Joe Treviño* and Charles Kamasaki, policy analysis director of the National Council of La Raza, the junior member of The Group.[1]

Brash, smart, mercurial, and intense, Arnoldo Torres was, in 1984, the most visible and outspoken Hispanic advocate in DC, often to the consternation of his more senior Latino organizational peers. He approached his mission of advancing Latino interests with almost religious fervor, combined with more than the usual amount of sanctimony. Torres's ascendancy to the top tier of Latino advocacy on the issue of immigration policy inside the Beltway was, in many ways, anomalous. For one thing, Torres represented what traditionally had been among the most conservative of the major Hispanic civil rights organizations—it was no accident that the last word in LULAC's name was "citizens," a term historically meant to distinguish LULAC's more elite business-

---

* Joseph Michael Treviño, then deputy executive director of LULAC, had been known to friends and family as "Michael" much of his life; because Torres always referred to him as "Joe," the rest of The Group knew him by that name as well. Although "J. Michael" Treviño went on to have a successful career first with Gulf Oil Company and later as a management consultant, he is referred to in this text as "Joe," the name most of his colleagues in immigration advocacy circles called him and knew him by in the 1980s.

oriented constituency from the poorer, less educated Latino immigrants. And although LULAC was known for its "work within the system" ethos whose leaders invariably were respectful of those holding high office, Torres was often provocative, saying things to elected officials that they rarely heard from others. It wasn't so much that he intended to be discourteous; he was someone who thought of himself as scrupulously honest, who might've been characterized in centuries past as "carrying his heart on his tongue."[2]

There was little in Torres's past to suggest that he'd become a national Hispanic leader. After graduating from the University of the Pacific, he served for two years in the Legislative Analyst's Office of the California State Assembly—something like a combination of the Congressional Research Service and the Congressional Budget Office in Washington, DC—a prestigious post to be sure, but a unit normally populated by studious introverts and bureaucrats, not firebrands. In one respect Torres looked the part; he was perfectly coiffed and beautifully dressed, and looked like a GQ model. Joe Treviño confided to his colleagues his amazement that, "Arnold has one closet of just shirts, all pressed, organized by color. He has another whole closet full of suits, divided by color and weight." Nonetheless, Treviño emphasized, Torres was no "dandy"; he'd played on both the varsity soccer and intramural rugby teams in college, and had no shortage of physical courage and toughness.[3]

Torres didn't smoke, drink, or curse, and made sure everyone around him knew it. He hated the smell of smoke. Although many in The Group were pack-a-day-plus smokers, at a time when even congressional hearing rooms had ashtrays available, they never smoked in meetings with Torres present. It was clear that Frank's unmistakable display of keeping The Group waiting, while leisurely reading and smoking, was irritating Torres. The Group waited, quietly at first, for several minutes that felt like an eternity before Torres quietly cleared his throat. Torres had a habit of throat clearing at least once during every conversation; whether this was a physical problem or just a nervous habit was never clear to even his closest friends and colleagues.

Frank noted the interruption, peered over the top of his newspaper at Torres for a few seconds, and then promptly resumed reading. Barney Frank was not your typical congressman. Brilliant, witty, and loquacious, Frank was first elected to Congress in 1980, winning the seat previously held by the liberal Catholic priest, Rep. Robert Drinan. Having crushed longtime incumbent Republican Margaret Heckler in 1982 when redistricting forced them to run against each other, he was on a roll. Frank was, together with classmate Charles Schumer (D-NY), one of the hottest young stars in Congress on the Judiciary Committee, which had jurisdiction over immigration issues. He was also already a major force on the Banking (now Financial Services) Committee, which he eventually chaired, twenty-five years later, in 2007. An unapologetic progressive on a wide range of issues, Frank was a key supporter of the Simpson-Mazzoli immigration bill, one who was being counted on to protect Mazzoli's vulnerable "left flank" in the Democratic-controlled House of Representatives.

There were widespread rumors among Capitol Hill insiders that Frank was gay. But in those more genteel times, members' sexual orientation was not a story often pursued by the mainstream press. National Council of La Raza (NCLR)'s* legislative director Martha Escutia once confessed that she had a "serious crush" on Frank. "Just look at him," she said as she swooned.[4] Indeed, Frank's persona was hardly consistent with gay stereotypes—he was a tough, unrelenting questioner of Reagan administration officials who deigned to come before either the Judiciary or Banking Committees unprepared, and woe to those on either side of the aisle who challenged him without bringing their A game. Democratic staffers occasionally dropped what they were doing and packed the hearing rooms where Frank was holding forth, just for the sheer joy of watching him in verbal combat. Even Frank's faint lisp, rather than detracting from his eloquence, seemed to make him a stronger and more compelling speaker, as he rattled off multiple arguments, cracking jokes and citing statistics, law cases, and classical literature, all at breakneck speed and without notes.

By now The Group had been kept waiting at least ten minutes inside the office, and perhaps ten minutes previously in the hallway, while Frank read, and smoked, and read some more. It was way past the awkward stage. Kamasaki had never before experienced the metaphorical "tension so thick it could be cut with a knife," but he felt it now. In the days before laptops, cell phones, or blackberries, the lobbyists had nothing to do but shuffle their papers, look at each other, and shrug their shoulders. The cigar smoke was now permeating the room. Torres cleared his throat again, possibly from his sensitivity to the smoke, or more likely due to impatience, loudly and unmistakably this time. Frank laid his paper aside. He put the cigar into an ashtray. He checked his watch. He took a couple of swigs of coffee. He glared at The Group for a few more seconds, and said, "OK, I've got fifteen minutes. Tell me what you got. Shoot!"[5]

The rest of the meeting was a blur, as the lobbyists, like lawyers before an appellate court, could barely get their arguments out before Frank peppered them with snide comments, probing questions, and point-by-point rebuttals, sometimes all in a single run-on sentence. As they attempted to answer the questions, as Supreme Court justices typically do Frank broke in, sometimes with more questions, other times with dismissive replies. Initially upset and taken aback that Frank first kept them waiting, gave them just a few minutes to make their case, and then interrupted them before they could even finish articulating

---

* NCLR is now UnidosUS.

their points, most felt relieved when the meeting ended, perhaps thirty minutes later.

Later, joined by Rick Swartz and Phyllis Eisen of the National Immigration, Refugee and Citizenship Forum, The Group recapped the week's events. At least a couple of times a week, and often for several nights in a row, The Group convened at the end of the day in the NCLR's small basement conference room, conveniently located on the "unit block" of F Street, just a few blocks from the Capitol, and centrally located between the coalition members' offices. It didn't hurt that the conference room had sliding doors to a patio that enabled smokers to indulge during breaks, and that the hotel restaurant around the corner was always open late. As the junior member of The Group, NCLR's Kamasaki was responsible for making sure there was a fresh pot of hot coffee available, completing menial tasks such as making copies, and performing what a colleague later called "the shit work."[6]

The Group hadn't gotten everything they had hoped for that week. Congressman Frank declined to even consider cosponsoring their alternative bill, but appeared intrigued by some of its substantive provisions, even asking questions about how certain proposals might work. Perhaps most important, while making it clear that he was unhappy with their consistent opposition to reform, he seemed genuinely interested in working with them to improve Simpson-Mazzoli, especially if that might assure passage of the legislation. While Frank would not be their public champion, he appeared willing to be a silent partner on certain issues.

Some three dozen other representatives, mostly avowed Simpson-Mazzoli opponents, had expressed their willingness to cosponsor the Roybal bill. Even some previously die-hard reform supporters appeared interested in carrying some of their provisions as amendments. Together with support they'd received from California Rep. Howard Berman, a reluctant opponent of the bill who had expressed willingness to negotiate on their behalf, and New York's congressman Charles Schumer, an immigration reform supporter who clearly coveted the role of a broker able to bring opposing sides together, Frank's somewhat benign position on their alternative might be enough to give them the leverage to either improve the Simpson-Mazzoli bill substantially, or at a minimum demonstrate that their opposition was sufficiently principled so that their fragile coalition of opponents could hang tough if required. The ACLU's Henderson typically cut to the heart of the issue by remarking, "Well, at least we met the 'laugh test,'" meaning that when asked to cosponsor their bill, Frank didn't break out laughing.

The meeting with Frank marked something of a turning point. In late 1983, The Group had intensely debated whether and how to change their posture from all-out opposition to the bill to something more nuanced. The Group already had decided to shift from the pure opposition approach they'd pursued previously to an "affirmative defense" strategy, meaning they'd offer their own bill, argue its superiority over the Simpson-Mazzoli construct, and in so doing at least implicitly communicate a willingness to negotiate over and potentially accede to passage of immigration reform. While rarely stated, they were now prepared to concede that reform was inevitable; at issue going forward were the details, but not enactment, of immigration reform.

Why this was such a difficult decision, and the consequences of this fateful shift for the millions of immigrants in the country then and the millions more to come, had their roots in events that had taken place decades earlier thousands of miles from the halls of Congress.

BIRTH OF A "RACE"

Under the Treaty of Guadalupe Hidalgo, which ended the Mexican–American War in 1848, most of what is now Texas, New Mexico, Arizona, California, Colorado, Utah, and Nevada was acquired by the US. Those remaining in the territories, including the Mexican-origin population, estimated to be about one hundred thousand, were declared American citizens.[7] Following the war, according to the conventional narrative, while there were might have been unfortunate examples of discrimination against Mexicans and Mexican Americans, these were "casual," even isolated, and never approached anything resembling that faced by African Americans.[8] In this narrative, Mexicans and other Latinos resemble "white ethnic" immigrants like the Italians and Southern Europeans of the late nineteenth and early twentieth centuries, destined to face only modest levels of temporary discrimination that eventually were overcome by the country's commitment to equality of opportunity. The notion that native-born Latinos faced significant ongoing discrimination was not widely accepted in progressive circles.[9]

Supported by a rich and growing body of scholarship, beginning in the 1960s, Latino advocates asserted that the conventional narrative was both ahistorical and inaccurate. The Treaty of Guadalupe Hidalgo supposedly guaranteed the rights of the new US citizens of Mexican origin, but these were widely and routinely violated. Scholars documented that Mexican Americans faced land grabs, job bias, housing and school segregation, physical violence, and political exclusion similar in scope to that faced by blacks in the Jim Crow South.[10] Some even asserted that lynching rates of Mexican Americans were of a similar order of magnitude as that of African Americans, a claim initially viewed as preposterous, but later confirmed by careful scholarship.[11] According to social scientists who study "racial boundaries," the dominant Anglo majority treated Mexicans, regardless of citizenship status, as an " 'internally colonized' group subject to discrimination while being 'racialized' as non-White."[12] The *Anglo* term, shortened from the "Anglo-Saxon" label originally applied to those of English, Irish, or Scottish descent, commonly came to include all "whites," an exclusionary label to describe anyone with European origins *except Latin Americans*.[13] And even the term *Anglo*, commonly used to distinguish white Americans from Mexicans, was based on an inaccurate racial myth.[14]

The academic response to the conventional narrative acknowledges that the white ethnics who arrived in the US in the late 1800s and early 1900s indeed faced substantial discrimination. For an entire generation, in some cases two, the racial positioning of Irish, Italians, Jews, and other immigrants from southern and eastern Europe was ambiguous and uncertain. As scholar David Roediger has documented, social scientists have used a number of terms to describe this semi-racialized status: *not-yet-white*, *situationally white*, *not quite white*, *offwhite*, and *conditionally white*.[15] But, if viewed as a lower class of white, they were, fundamentally, considered *white*. The Americanization movement of the Progressive Era in fact *assumed* that these immigrants could assimilate once they learned English and abandoned the cultural norms of their home countries. Later policies reinforced the inclusion of white ethnics in the American melting pot, but they largely excluded Latinos, as well as African Americans, from the mainstream. For example, the country's first labor laws and the Social Security system excluded domestic and agricultural workers that were "mainly black and brown," but covered the crafts and trades dominated by European immigrants and their progeny.[16]

Real estate professionals, who played a key role as enforcers of social norms, accepted that white ethnics would eventually assimilate. Thus, while Italian immigrants in large eastern cities were even more segregated than blacks in 1910, this was "completely reversed" by 1920.[17] Not so for negroes and Mexicans in the Midwest and Asians or Mexicans in the western US, who were generally excluded from housing in white neighborhoods by racial covenants and other discriminatory tactics until well after the civil rights era.[18] The post–World War II GI Bill's subsidized housing and education programs, from which essentially all African Americans and most Latinos were excluded by law or practice, completed this Americanization process. By the third generation, virtually all of the "white ethnics" were simply "white."[19]

In contrast, discrimination against Mexican immigrants, Mexican Americans, and other Latinos wasn't tied to a temporal characteristic like immigration status, according to scholars that have studied the issue. Nor was it purely racial, as was discrimination against blacks, based almost entirely on a simple, unchangeable factor like skin color. Instead it was based on *both* fluid attributes such as language, speech accent, or immigration status that might diminish with time *and* immutable traits such as surname, skin color, facial features, and physical traits that continue across generations. While not a racial group per se, Hispanics experienced manifestations of racism analogous to those faced by blacks, if perhaps not as systematic or expansive.[20]

Another tenet of Hispanic scholars that emerged in the late 1960s and 1970s, was the framing of the American Southwest as conquered, occupied, colonial territory. In his groundbreaking book, *Occupied America*, activist scholar Rodolfo Acuña famously framed the post-Mexican–American War era as an "occupation," in which the Anglo-American conquerors used the social and legal constructs of race to subjugate their Mexican-origin subjects, 90 percent of whom had indigenous blood.[21] In Acuña's framing, Mexican Americans were analogous to natives of European colonies: subjects but never full citizens of the nations of their colonial masters. A slightly permeable racial hierarchy developed in which Anglos at the top and lower class Mexicans at the bottom lived almost fully segregated lives, with small groups of upper-class Mexican-origin and mixed-race families occupying rungs in between. Some upper-class Mexicans, especially elites claiming pure Castillian or Spanish heritage sought with mixed success to disassociate themselves from "half-breed" *mexicanos* with indigenous heritage.[22] Under the "occupation," as described by David Montejano and Richard Flores, the idea of a "Mexican race," and a system to enforce it, was institutionalized "in the shadow of the Alamo."[23] Other scholars described:

> a system of ethnic or racial difference in which Mexicans are initially a barbarous enemy but later become incorporated as a racialized source of cheap labor. . . . A racial hierarchy, often hidden in discourse and popular thought, has emerged in which Mexicans are classified as separate and inferior; it perpetuates their treatment as subordinates . . . [even if a few] have risen to middle class status, intermarry, and even hold assimilationist dreams.[24]

In 1930, over 90 percent of South Texas schools were segregated; by the 1940s, the number of strictly Mexican school districts had grown to 122 across fifty-nine counties in the state.[25] Formal school segregation was also routine in California until successfully challenged in 1946 by *Mendez v. Westminister*, a case that served as a precedent for the more famous *Brown v. Board of Education* lawsuit shortly thereafter.[26] These weren't isolated examples; an authoritative study of schools in the five southwestern states in which the bulk of the Mexican-origin population lived found that 85 percent of such students attended strictly segregated schools in the mid-1930s.[27] A lasting effect of the concentration of Mexican Americans in poor neighborhoods from Texas to California, first imposed through legal segregation and later enforced through custom, ensured that their children attended schools with far fewer resources than their

Anglo peers. Because schools were financed mainly through local property taxes, per-pupil expenditures in Mexican schools were significantly lower, in some cases just a fraction of those in Anglo schools, a disparity that continues in the twenty-first century.[28]

Employment discrimination was rampant, with Mexican-origin workers relegated to agriculture, mining, railroad, industrial, and other manual work, where they typically were paid a "Mexican wage" that was 20–40 percent lower than that received by their Anglo counterparts.[29] Mexicans were routinely excluded from juries and policy-making roles in government institutions; many public facilities including swimming pools, parks, and playgrounds were segregated. Even if not always formally required by law, custom and practice enforced separation of Anglos and Mexicans by private businesses, exemplified by the ubiquitous signs on restaurants, bars, movie theaters, swimming pools and recreational facilities, and upper-end retail stores reading "No Dogs or Mexicans Allowed."[30]

Up through the 1970s, while strictly speaking not against the law and hardly unheard of, intergroup dating and marriage was frowned on. It was largely acceptable, if perhaps a bit distasteful, for Anglo men to date but not marry Latinas; the thinking seemed to be that if boys had to sow their wild oats, it was better for everyone if white girls were kept unsullied while Mexican girls were fair game. In the football-crazy state of Texas, where Mexican American high school stars were afforded quasi-white status, intergroup dating required complex arrangements. In 1961, the tiny South Texas Donna High School "miracle" state champions defeated a series of larger, richer, white upstate schools in games where they were taunted with epithets and jalapenos were thrown from the stands. A Mexican American star of that team, one of the few to date an Anglo girl, explained that to pull off an interracial date, "[One of] our Anglo buddies would take out the white girl, and I'd take out the Hispanic girl, and then we'd switch."[31] One exception to the cultural taboo against formal interracial relationships involved upper-class, landed Mexican American women, mostly fair-skinned, often with land grants and family lineage traceable back to Spanish nobility. Such women often "married up" in social status, while their Anglo husbands, few of whom had assets of their own, acquired wealth in the process. In the nineteenth and early twentieth centuries, these marriages preserved assets that, had they remained only *mexicano*-owned, would have been at risk from Anglo squatters and "Robber Barons."[32] The marriages produced upward mobility for a few mixed-race *mexicanos* with Anglo surnames in future generations, but were rare: in 1930, 97 percent of Mexican household heads had Mexican spouses, according to the Census, equivalent to the intermarriage rate among blacks.[33]

RACE WAR AND REPATRIATION

A more brutal manifestation of being "perpetually foreign" was the direct product of US immigration policy: the so-called "repatriation campaigns" in the 1920–1954 period. Even before then, frequent ad hoc efforts resulted in the expulsion of tens of thousands of Mexicans across the southern border. In 1856 the entire Mexican-origin population of Colorado County in southeast Texas was ordered to leave, and through the late nineteenth century across the state "harassment against Mexicans by Anglo-Americans was so severe that many were forced to abandon their homes."[34] Such discrimination seemed something of a deterrent to large-scale immigration; by 1900, perhaps half a million people of Mexican ancestry, only one hundred thousand of whom were foreign-born, lived in the US.[35] Then came the Mexican Revolution.

Running roughly from 1910 through 1920, to all but diehard scholars the war was a confusing mix of multiple factions in often shifting coalitions. To oversimplify, future Mexican presidents Victoriano Huerta and Venustanio Carranza, joined by Pancho Villa and Emiliano Zapata, revolted against the dictatorial president Porfirio Díaz. Díaz had succeeded the legendary Benito Juárez, one of the first indigenous heads of state in the Americas, who was widely credited with progressive reforms.[36] Thousands of Mexicans fled the violence in 1910, crossing the border into the US, sparking calls in the Anglo community for all Mexicans, regardless of citizenship status, to be expelled. One faction of Mexican revolutionaries was said to be exploiting the unrest to attempt a Mexican takeover of the American Southwest. In 1915, one of the alleged plot's leaders was arrested in McAllen, Texas, with a copy of a manifesto, known as *El Plan de San Diego*, which seemed to confirm the takeover threat. Some historians think the plan was a fraud because some Spanish phrases were "unidiomatic and wrong."[37] Others believe it was an authentic "expression of Mexican resistance to Anglo domination."[38] Regardless, *El Plan* was given credence when Carranza followers began guerilla raids into Texas. Later the infamous *bandido* Pancho Villa's raids in New Mexico prompted the US to send "a large military force under General John J. Pershing into northern Mexico in pursuit of Villa"; the two countries soon came to a peaceful settlement.[39] However, scholars wrote, "panic gripped Anglo-American society" in South Texas, resulting in a campaign of violence and forced repatriation where "as many as one-half of the Mexican residents of the lower Rio Grande Valley abandoned their homes."[40] Anglos widely feared and prepared for a "race war."[41]

In the end, sixty-two Anglo civilians and sixty-four US soldiers were killed in the raids and other violence in South Texas between 1915 and 1917, compared to some five thousand Mexican and Mexican American civilian deaths.[42] In

Brownsville, Texas, two hundred Mexicans were executed without trial by the Texas Rangers, local police, and private citizens; a Republican National Committee member later testified that "90% of those [executed] had committed no crime."[43] Of the total of five thousand victims of violence at Anglo hands, "more than 300 Mexicans or Mexican Americans were summarily executed" by public officials or vigilante groups, according to official federal government reports.[44] But until an exhibit opened at the Bullock Texas State History Museum in January 2016, no state agency ever publicly acknowledged that the violence against Mexicans and Mexican Americans had occurred. According to a group of academics and community activists that had lobbied for the exhibit:

> The dead included women and men, the aged and the young, long-time residents and recent arrivals. They were killed by strangers, sometimes by neighbors, some by vigilantes and other times at the hands of local law enforcement officers or Texas Rangers. Some were summarily executed after being taken captive, or shot under the flimsy pretext of trying to escape. Some were left in the open to rot, others desecrated by being burnt, being decapitated, or revealing evidence of other forms of torture or violation, such as having beer bottles rammed into their mouths. Extralegal executions became so common that a San Antonio reporter observed that "finding dead bodies of Mexicans, suspected for various reasons of being connected with the troubles, has reached a point where it creates little or no interest. It is only when a raid is reported or an [Anglo] American is killed that the ire of the people is aroused."[45]

Widespread violence, largely borne by those of Mexican origin, was "most intense in Texas, but it was commonplace throughout the southwest," scholars later wrote.[46]

Another form of violence involved a kind of immigration policy in reverse. Historians have documented at least four distinct repatriation campaigns affecting millions of US residents of Mexican descent in the twentieth century. As the economy slowed after World War I, the country's first broad-scale immigration laws were enacted.[47] Growers and businesses generally opposed the immigration controls called for by organized labor, but both sides agreed that *Mexicans*, a term assigned to both the US- and foreign-born, were an inferior race. The Texas State Federation of Labor adopted a resolution referring to "the peon Mexican" as "the greaser, a species of human invented by the Spaniards that ranked even lower than rattlesnakes."[48] The head of the Los Angeles County Department of Agriculture observed that "the oriental and Mexican" were ideally suited for stoop labor because "their crouching and bending habits are fully adapted, while the white is physically unable to adapt himself to them."[49] "Experts" such as esteemed Stanford University psychologist Lewis Terman wrote in 1916 that

Mexicans were genetically an "inferior race" whose deficiencies were "not correctable by education."[50]

Against a backdrop of high unemployment among veterans returning from World War I, in 1921 an estimated 150,000 residents of Mexican descent were summarily repatriated to Mexico from several states, including Colorado, Illinois, Missouri, Arizona, and Texas.[51] The departures were purportedly voluntary, but emigrants were pressured to leave, as scholars documented, often "cheated out of their wages and dumped across the border."[52] Mexican newspapers wrote that emigrants were brutally treated by authorities, and many were forced into "concentration camps," chained, and put into work parties before being pushed back across the Rio Grande.[53] Perhaps as much as one-fifth of the entire Mexican-origin population in the American Southwest was pushed out of the country.[54] Since many who left consisted of intact families, an unknown number of those repatriated were legal residents and US-born citizens.[55] Even those born in Mexico had entered the US before the imposition of formal immigration restrictions and thus could have asserted claims of lawful presence had they been given an opportunity, but few were afforded deportation hearings. They were told to leave, and so they left, although many were enticed to return to work the crops and fill other manual jobs in the following boom years.[56]

It was just the beginning. At the onset of the Depression in 1930, high unemployment and virulent nativism led to calls for another round of deportations. President Hoover's secretary of labor—head of the department in charge of border control before creation of the Immigration and Naturalization Service (INS) in 1933—called for increased immigration restrictions, with the goal of strengthening the country by making it "more homogeneous."[57] States and cities passed resolutions supporting mass removal of Mexicans. The American Federation of Labor, the American Legion, and the American Eugenics Society joined the call for repatriating Mexicans, a position largely supported by major newspapers. In what was dubbed Operation Deportation, sweeps of fields, factories, and neighborhoods began, mainly by a combination of federal, state and local law enforcement personnel, but private vigilante groups also participated. Little effort was made to distinguish between those lawfully present and those without legal status; everyone who "looked Mexican" found themselves at risk of being picked up and taken into custody.[58]

Some citizens and legal residents of Mexican origin who'd been abroad and returned to the US were summarily excluded at the border.[59] Foreshadowing the later roundup of Japanese Americans during World War II, many of those apprehended were unable to secure or sell their property at prices at anything approaching market value before being repatriated.[60] In many thousands of cases, families were separated, with some children remaining in the US and their siblings going to Mexico with one or both parents; one study estimated that for every deportee removed more than one dependent remained behind.[61] Future congressman Esteban Torres (D-CA) was only three years old when his father was deported; Torres never saw his father again.[62]

Before it was over, as many as two million people of Mexican origin were "returned" to Mexico during the 1930s, according to official government estimates, although this number is likely exaggerated.[63] The official tally by the Mexican government tracking those who received assistance from its consulates at some point in the process of being expelled was 422,831, but many repatriates were returned without contacting their government.[64] Noting that US officials had powerful incentives to inflate their numbers, while their Mexican counterparts missed many who were returned, historians Francisco Balderrama and Raymond Rodriguez, whose book *Decade of Betrayal* is the definitive account of the period, concluded that, "taking the middle ground, it is reasonable to estimate that the total number of repatriates was approximately one million."[65] They also estimated that about 60 percent of those expelled were US-born children, based on contemporary accounts and subsequent evidence.[66] Others placed the percentage of American citizens among those sent to Mexico as high as 75 percent.[67] Depending on which estimate is correct, at least one-fifth and perhaps one-third of the entire Mexican-origin population of the US was removed, in an incident that if it happened abroad today would be denounced as ethnic cleansing but few Americans have ever heard of.[68] The story is barely mentioned in textbooks; in a 2006 *USA Today* survey, four of the nine most widely used American history texts didn't mention Mexican repatriation, and only one devoted more than a half-page to the subject.[69]

The third repatriation campaign in 1947 isn't widely described in the literature, perhaps because it foreshadowed the far more notorious Operation Wetback a few years later.[70] The 1947 campaign removed 195,657 allegedly deportable aliens, according to official government reports.[71] It is unknown how many lawful residents or US citizens were affected by the campaign, nor does it appear that anyone ever bothered to find out.[72] In early 1954, with the economy in recession, there were more calls to crack down on Mexicans. Labor and Mexican American groups believed immigrants and temporary workers produced an excess supply of labor that undercut wages and working conditions for domestic workers, and the American GI Forum, an important Hispanic civil rights group, joined the Texas State Federation of Labor to produce "What Price Wetbacks?," a pamphlet that stated in part: "Truly, the American people are entitled to ask: 'What price wetbacks?' What is the price in terms of depressed wages for citizens of the US who have a right to a wage on which they can live according to American standards of living? The 25-cent hourly wage cannot support American citizens."[73]

Alleged job competition wasn't the only basis for growing calls for repatriation. State and local officials in the Southwest complained of alleged growing burdens on welfare programs. Media outlets decried the "Wetback Menace," attributing all manner of social ills—crime, prostitution, narcotics, and purported internal threats to security—to the growing population of "wetbacks."[74] Some growers warned of "Russian" or "Gestapo" tactics inherent in the coming crackdown.[75] But many quietly decided to cooperate with the enforcement effort to protect their public image and bolster support for the *bracero* temporary agricultural worker program.

In that era, "many citizens [and] legal residents did not have papers proving their citizenship, had lost their papers, or just never applied for citizenship."[76] Indeed, many Americans of the period had no "documentation" proving citizenship, but in the anti-Mexican fervor, it was almost exclusively those of Mexican origin who were expected to be able to prove their right to be in the country. There was a widespread sense that "the privileges of citizenship offered little of substance" to Latinos, given that even native-born citizens were at risk of summary deportation.[77] Negative portrayals of wetbacks were applied to all people of Mexican origin, regardless of immigration status. Sociologist Mae Ngai observed that the very "construction of the 'wetback' as a dangerous and criminal social pathogen fed the general racial stereotype 'Mexican.'"[78] Even social scientists of an era more tolerant of racial stereotypes than today found it noteworthy that among the Southwest's Anglo population in the 1950s: "No careful distinctions are made between illegal aliens and local citizens of Mexican descent. They are lumped together as 'Mexicans' and the characteristics that are observed among the wetbacks are by extension assigned to the local people."[79]

In June 1954, the government formally launched Operation Wetback, "a massive enforcement effort aimed at apprehending and deporting" unauthorized workers, especially but not limited to farm laborers, "conceived and executed as though it was a military operation."[80] Employing some 750 immigration, Border Patrol, and other federal law enforcement personnel supported by local police and backed by hundreds of planes, jeeps, cars, and buses, the operation apprehended and deported 170,000 people in its first three months.[81] By 1955, by one account between one and two million people were returned to Mexico, most without any semblance of due process.[82] Other scholars believe the actual number removed from the country, whether formally deported, departed "voluntarily" after arrest, or who fled in fear of apprehension, was substantially higher than the commonly accepted one million estimate, perhaps even as high as three million.[83]

Although no truly reliable estimate exists, many who were deported were lawful residents and US citizens.[84] The record includes numerous examples of wrongful arrest and detention of legal residents and American citizens, including detailed reports produced by the Independent Progressive Party and the Los Angeles Committee for the Protection of the Foreign Born.[85] Although the government dismissed them as coming from "radical groups"—a potent charge in the virulently anti-Communist fervor of the McCarthy era—it couldn't discredit complaints from supporters of Operation Wetback such as the American Legion, which protested that Mexican Americans had been subject to treatment "that no American citizen should have to stand for."[86] When a Mexican American woman inquired about her apprehended spouse, an officer responded, "We don't keep a record of their names. . . . If he was picked up on Monday, he was taken across the border Monday night."[87] Even INS commissioner Joseph Swing acknowledged in response to a congressional inquiry into mistreatment of American citizens that, "in such a large scale operation individual instances of an unfortunate nature will occur."[88] Privately, officials admitted that most arrested weren't given opportunities to assert claims that would've enabled them to stay, and it was "quite likely" that many "U.S. citizens had been inadvertently deported."[89] Left unstated was the government's threat that employers or civil rights groups that "interfered" in the roundup were threatened with prosecution for "harboring," which undoubtedly chilled efforts to protest the deportations or document abuses.[90]

For Mexican American advocates, Operation Wetback was a game changer. At a time when US leaders trumpeted American values of liberty, justice, equality, and the rule of law abroad, Mexican Americans noticed that legal immigrant status, and even citizenship, didn't protect them from being forcibly removed from their own country without due process. The same year the US Supreme Court declared in *Brown v. Board of Education* that racial segregation was unconstitutional and the black civil rights movement was building consciousness about the fundamental dignity of every human being, Mexicans were treated as disposable commodities: recruited during labor shortages to perform stoop labor at low wages, then forcibly removed, along with their American-born children, when no longer needed. Héctor P. García, founder and head of the American GI Forum, was profoundly disturbed by Operation Wetback, and subsequently reversed his previous position that had uniformly favored tougher immigration restrictions.[91] His epiphany foreshadowed by nearly two decades a period when virtually every Hispanic leader opposed policies that treated their community's workers as commodities, insisted on full due process rights in the enforcement of immigration laws, and embraced rather than excluded their foreign-born coethnics as part of their natural constituencies.

BRACEROS

Interspersed between the four major repatriations was the rise and fall of the infamous *bracero* agricultural worker program, initiated as a wartime emergency measure during World War II when millions of Americans served in the military and defense industries. In 1942, the US and Mexico agreed to permit the temporary entry of Mexican workers, mainly but not exclusively in agriculture, under contracts stipulating that *braceros* (literally "strong men") would receive adequate transportation, housing, and wages, as well as American government guarantees against discrimination; from 1942 to 1947, about 220,000 Mexican workers entered under this initial phase.[92] The program was extended several times; from 1948–1951 about four hundred thousand more workers entered the US.[93] An additional 4.2 million braceros entered over the 1951–1964 period before Congress ended the program in 1964.[94] It wasn't lost on anyone that a program intended as a wartime emergency measure continued for nearly two decades after the war, principally due to the political power of an agricultural industry that had, by its own admission, become dependent on the cheap labor of Mexican workers.[95]

The arrangement was fraught with problems from the beginning. Bracero workers, wrote critics, were "tied to their employer, they were tied to a specific occupation, wages were low . . . [and] they could not bring their spouse or children."[96] Denied the ability to leave an employer and find work elsewhere, braceros were subject to the whims of their sponsors. Many, perhaps most, were well treated by the standards of the era, especially outside agriculture; they worked on railroads, in steel mills, and in the converted auto factories producing weapons of war for the military. As the son of one bracero wrote, "Some towns . . . were so grateful they organized welcoming committees to meet the Mexicans as they got off buses and trains, even urging them to stay on and bring their families with them."[97] The program exerted a powerful "pull" factor in Mexico; as a former bracero recounted: "We all saw how the braceros came back with good clothes for their families and nice shoes. They said they suffered a lot in the United States, but I saw how much better they lived. I wanted to do the same. I thought to myself, 'God willing, I'm going to go to the United States too.' "[98]

As hundreds of thousands of others made their way north, labor advocates, the Mexican government, Latino civil rights organizations, and some workers themselves complained bitterly about mistreatment by growers and widespread discrimination in the society at large.[99] Mexico benefited from the program in many ways: by the 1950s, remittances mainly from braceros were its third-largest form of foreign exchange.[100] But the Mexican government tried hard to protect its nationals in the US. The Mexican Consul in McAllen, Texas, estimated that over half of the braceros in the region were paid 30–35 cents an hour instead of the 50 cent hourly rate they were owed.[101] One study found more than a third of the labor camps were substandard even by the lax standards of the era.[102] The Department of Labor found violations in about half of the eleven thousand formal complaints over a two-year period, although few workers were willing to risk deportation to complain.[103] As one former bracero said, the grower held all the cards: "The grower has little expense of recruitment; the government brings them practically to his gate. He gouges on wages. He works them twelve to fifteen hours a day, on Saturday and Sunday and holidays. If they complain or join a union, or do anything but work their ass off, *pfft*! He slams them back to Mexico."[104] Another practice condemned by labor and Hispanic advocates was when INS allowed entry of braceros or unauthorized workers but "miraculously appeared at the end of harvest season" just in time for growers to avoid paying wages owed to workers before their deportation.[105]

The US often imposed its will on its weaker southern neighbor in determining terms and conditions of the program. When the Mexican government took a harder line over an extension of the program in 1948 by demanding better wages and stronger worker and antidiscrimination protections, US officials opened the international bridge in El Paso, destroying Mexico's leverage by demonstrating a willingness to allow unauthorized workers to enter outside of the bracero program if the agreement was not renewed.[106] During another negotiation in 1954, the US again opened the border, resulting in bloody clashes as an embarrassed Mexican government deployed troops to try and prevent its citizens from crossing over to the US.[107]

Policy decisions to relax entry on a wholesale basis were matched by local arrangements that growers had with the INS. According to official government reports, often as the result of congressional pressure, INS officials "were instructed to defer apprehension of Mexicans employed on Texas farms where untimely removals would likely result in loss of crops."[108] So-called specials—workers with higher skills and more training—were given legal status by INS, as the agency had power to "exercise discretion" over enforcement priorities. INS actively assisted in "drying out" or "wringing out" unauthorized wetbacks, sometimes taking apprehended workers to the border, allowing them to set "one foot in Mexico" and returning them forthwith to their employers, this time as "legal" bracero workers.[109] In other cases INS simply permitted growers to retain special workers, even when it was known they were unauthorized.[110] In the Imperial Valley of California, a gentlemen's agreement allowed unauthorized workers to work while saving up money for a visa; once the required amount was accrued, the "worker would be taken to a nearby border immigration station, and his entry into the United States would be officially legalized."[111] So widespread were these arrangements that a presidential commission concluded in 1951 that they constituted the "dominant feature of the Mexican farm-labor program."[112] Nor were these acts of rogue government workers; according to contemporary observers, the Congress consciously facilitated the mass movement of workers from Mexico—both via the bracero program and through growing rates of illegal immigration—to accommodate their powerful agricultural constituents.[113]

One so-called special named Ricardo Ovilla benefited from these lax policies; according to Pulitzer Prize–winning journalist and author Dale Maharidge, in 1945 he "picked sugar beets, fixed track for the Great Northern Railroad, tended sheep, and worked next to German prisoners of war. After his *Bracero* papers expired, he was arrested by immigration authorities, but like so many Mexicans, his employer, a subsidiary of Sunkist Oranges, came to his rescue and pleaded his case. . . . The blessing by the corporation was enough to set things straight. Not only could he remain, but he was allowed to bring his family north in 1949."[114]

More than thirty years later, Ovilla's granddaughter Martha Escutia became an important player in shaping US immigration policy as legislative director of the NCLR. Like Ovilla, many braceros didn't return home. Some married US citizens or otherwise adjusted their status, but a number just "skipped" their contract, working illegally side-by-side with braceros.[115] As a result, the program actually increased illegal immigration substantially.[116]

These irregularities occurred in part because lawful entry was difficult for most prospective Mexican immigrants. Theoretically, legal immigration from Mexico and the Western Hemisphere was unrestricted up through the 1970s, but in practice many seeking to enter lawfully found it difficult and exceedingly unpleasant to do so. The cost of procuring a visa was prohibitive for most, and many applications were denied by the bureaucracy. A common basis for visa denials for Latin Americans was illiteracy; another was the likelihood that the immigrant could become a "public charge" reliant on public assistance.[117] There was a catch-22 quality to overcoming the public charge exclusion, since most immigrants from Mexico, historians wrote, "could not do this by demonstrating a job was waiting, because this would violate the [law's] prohibition against contract labor."[118] In addition, lower-income Mexican immigrants who came to the US on foot "were subjected to degrading treatment that others were not subjected to, such as delousing, having their hair shorn, inspection while naked, walking naked past medical officers, and fumigation of their belongings and clothes. Discriminatory treatment, and not the law, subjected only Mexican laborers to this type of inspection."[119]

When the bracero program finally ended twenty years later, it was no longer needed according to one scholar because, "the extralegal system that had grown alongside it had grown large and strong enough to fulfill the country's farm labor demand."[120] The combination of migration patterns established in the bracero program, bureaucratic and other barriers to legal immigration, and a largely unpoliced border fueled growing levels of unauthorized entry after World War II, but the Mexican immigrants had few institutions to protect their rights.

THE LEAGUE OF UNITED LATIN AMERICAN CITIZENS

The League of United Latin American Citizens was founded in Corpus Christi, Texas, on a cold, rainy February day in 1929.[121] Explicitly integrationist, aggressively assimilationist in orientation, LULAC was what one scholar calls the first manifestation of diverging identity between Mexican Americans and immigrant arrivals; League membership was limited to US citizens, and the organization actively encouraged their *mexicano* brethren to naturalize.[122] Its message resonated beyond Texas; in just three years LULAC councils were established in Arizona, Colorado, New Mexico, and California.[123] The high status of the business and professional people that comprised most of LULAC's members didn't protect them from the extensive discrimination and "rampant nativism" of the era; most of its members "saw themselves as crusaders, soldiers in the battle against" racial prejudice and injustice.[124] Over the next several decades, LULAC produced an enviable civil rights record, fighting and often winning battles against exclusion of Mexican Americans from juries and public accommodations, barriers to voting, and other forms of discrimination; LULAC members also played key roles in school desegregation lawsuits in both California and Texas.

In part because of the capricious way that states defined *race*, LULAC took different positions on the issue of whether Mexicans were *white*. In 1954, when Pete Hernandez, supported by LULAC, tried to overturn his conviction by an all-white jury from which Mexican Americans had been excluded, the State of Texas argued that Mexicans were white, and therefore he had been duly tried by a jury of his peers. Ironically, as scholar Ian Haney-Lopez noted, "at the very courthouse where Hernandez was tried, the restrooms were segregated: one was unmarked, and the other was labeled 'Colored Here' and 'Hombres Aqui.' "[125] After *Brown v. Board of Education*, the State of Texas again attempted to use the Census's official position that Mexicans were white against them, claiming to comply with desegregation orders by busing African American kids to Mexican schools and vice versa, while leaving Anglo schools untouched.[126] In those cases, LULAC and its successors argued that Mexican Americans should be considered to be distinct from whites. In other cases, LULAC argued that Mexican Americans were white in order to protect what few rights they had—including the right to naturalize, which until 1940 was reserved only to whites and blacks under the immigration laws.[127]

LULAC pioneered self-help educational programs—one of its early versions was said to have influenced the design of the Head Start program—sponsored scholarships, and conducted voter registration drives.[128] It also conferred considerable social status to its members; in segregated towns up through the 1970s LULAC's charity drives and galas were the centerpiece of upper-class Mexican American society, complete with *quinceñeras* and cotillions where LULACers' daughters were introduced to the community as they came of age. Together with the American GI Forum, it created "Project SER," representing both the Spanish verb "to be" as well as an acronym for service, employment, and redevelopment. Now called SER-National, it is one of the largest Latino direct-service organizations in the US, focused principally on workforce development.[129] Texas LULAC leader Pete Tijerina played an instrumental role in 1968 in founding the Mexican American Legal Defense and Educational Fund (MALDEF), a Mexican American counterpart to the National Association for the Advancement of Colored People (NAACP) Legal Defense and Educational Fund (LDF), which had been brought to prominence by the legendary lawyer and later supreme court justice Thurgood Marshall.[130]

LULAC and the American GI Forum bitterly protested labor abuses in the bracero program, as well as the high rates of illegal immigration associated with it. Some LULAC and American GI Forum leaders publicly supported the deportation and repatriation campaigns of the pre-1960 period, although others protested abusive treatment of Mexican immigrants in the repatriation efforts, and began to reassess their views on immigration in the wake of Operation Wetback.[131]

Many believed that immigrants reinforced negative stereotypes of Mexicans, so one way to reduce discrimination was to distinguish themselves from newcomers; said a LULAC member: "At the time we didn't want to say that we were Mexican American, not because we were ashamed—but we wanted to get away from the Mexican because everywhere you could see the signs saying 'No Dogs or Mexicans Allowed.' "[132] Or conversely, to emphasize the positive, one scholar explained that LULACers thought that if they "displayed accouterments of the dominant society" and underscored the Mexican American community's "gratitude and loyalty" to the US, they'd "become acceptable to the Anglo population and would no longer face discrimination and [white] supremacism."[133]

LULAC's substantive agenda, promoting full incorporation of Mexican Americans into American society through legal and policy reform, was similar to that of the NAACP, as was its chapter-based membership composed mainly of the community's upper class. However, unlike the NAACP, it eschewed large-scale protests, emphasizing instead the assertion of grievances through the legal and political system. It aggressively pursued "self-help" programs designed in part to "reassure the Anglo community that its members were not trying to organize an uprising or to radically disrupt" the existing social order.[134] And through the early 1960s, the strategy seemed to be working. By 1963, LULAC was formidable enough that its Texas State Convention attracted both President John F. Kennedy and Vice President Lyndon Johnson, already in campaign mode for the upcoming 1964 elections.[135] It was the most important Mexican American organization, a distinction that also made it a convenient target for the younger, more militant activists emerging in what was later known as the Chicano movement.

THE FOUR HORSEMEN

Much has been written about the Chicano movement, although precious little of it has pierced the consciousness of mainstream civil rights leaders and race-oriented scholars, much less reflected in historical or contemporary portrayals of Latinos. For some prominent Chicano scholar-activists, many of whom were participants in *el movimiento* as young students, the period is viewed with nostalgia, even reverence.[136] But like aspects of the Black Power ethos that for a time seemed to dominate the civil rights movement, it's the subject of both considerable interest and ambivalence in certain academic and activist circles, if largely unknown or forgotten, even among the Mexican American rank and file. And despite extensive scholarship, much about the Chicano movement remains a matter of both confusion and controversy.

Even the etymology of the term *Chicano* is controversial; some trace its roots to indigenous languages of Mesoamerica, while others believe its origins lie in the tendency of Mexican Americans to transfer *x* or *s* consonants into "ch" sounds, in effect turning "Mexicanos" into "Me-Chicanos." Used initially as a disparaging term for lower-class Mexicans, it emerged in the 1960s as an affirmative expression of cultural pride and solidarity.[137] The term also served as a dividing line between activists and the majority of Mexican Americans who weren't part of *el movimiento* because they were uncomfortable with the movement's ideology or tactics, afraid of retaliation from the Anglo establishment, or simply indifferent to politics. Much of the Chicano movement's strategy focused on energizing what activists saw as an excessively docile Mexican American population that accepted their condition, or attacking those like LULAC leaders who were seen as sellouts—"Tio Tacos," the movement equivalent of "Uncle Tom"—for adopting pro-assimilationist rhetoric that seemed to reject their cultural and racial heritage.[138]

The movement's backdrop was the turbulent 1960s and 1970s when American society was wracked by massive crosscurrents: national security crises early in the era that brought the US and Russia to the brink of nuclear war and the takeover of the US Embassy in Iran later on; passionate activist movements focused on civil rights, the Vietnam War, environmentalism, and feminism; the ascension of rock music, where clean-cut, safe pop acts were superseded by the hip-gyrating Elvis Presley, the long-haired "British Invasion" that included the Beatles and the Rolling Stones, and sensuous soul and R&B acts; social upheavals like the growth of a drug culture, a counterculture of societal dropouts exemplified by "hippies," and the sexual revolution. In the midst of the tumult of the late 1960s, the Chicano movement burst onto the scene, evolved, and then faded away in about a decade, barely a blip on the radar screens of the nation's major media and intelligentsia. Although it never achieved anything approaching the same traction as the Black Power movement, together with a distinct but spiritually related activism among Puerto Ricans in the Northeast, the movement reshaped the Latino community's public policy agenda well into the twenty-first century.[139] Activists and scholars often summarize this complex history through the contributions of the so-called four horsemen of *el movimiento*: César Chávez, Corky Gonzáles, Reies Lopez Tijerina, and José Ángel Gutiérrez.

The United Farm Workers' César Chávez is by far the best known. He began as an organizer for the California-based Community Service Organization (CSO), a grassroots group headed by Fred Ross and backed by Saul Alinsky, two of the more influential community organizers in recent US history. After CSO's leadership resisted his desire to organize farmworkers, Chávez left to form the National Farm Workers Association (NFWA), which evolved into the United Farm Workers of America (UFW).[140] Chávez consciously exploited images that resonated with his largely Mexican-origin constituency: his first strike in 1965 was called on September 16, coinciding with the launch of the Mexican independence movement from Spain, and the use of the black Aztec eagle against a red background on the organization's flag symbolized cultural pride. The UFW brought important innovations to the struggle, such as the use of music and *teatro* (community theater) to educate and build solidarity within the ranks, and boycotts and demonstrations that enabled students and others far from the fields to participate in the cause. Chávez's charisma and commitment, which included living in near-poverty and courting death several times in hunger strikes that brought nationwide attention to the plight of farmworkers, provided the larger Chicano movement with a dignified, ennobling face.[141]

Scholars note that Chávez, like other labor leaders in the 1960s, "opposed immigration from Mexico" because in his view immigration "built up labor surpluses that lowered wages and made it difficult to organize."[142] Union membership was open to all regardless of immigration status, but the UFW fought the growers' use of undocumented workers as strikebreakers, which in practice meant cooperating with the INS. It also led in 1973 to a still-controversial incident in Yuma, Arizona, where in the midst of a strike against citrus growers, UFW officials set up a so-called wet line along the border to prevent Mexican workers from crossing. Two dozen union members were arrested for illegally carrying weapons and assaulting immigrants, charges Chávez called exaggerated.[143] Some credible observers have said that Chávez has gotten "a bad rap" as a restrictionist on immigration, noting the UFW opposed strikebreakers, many of whom happened to be undocumented, but not based on immigration status.[144] But the UFW remained in the immigration restriction camp into the early 1980s.[145]

If for Chávez the class struggle trumped ethnic solidarity with Mexican immigrants, this was never true of Denver's Rodolfo "Corky" Gonzáles. Perhaps best known for his epic poem, "Yo Soy Joaquín" ("I am Joaquín"), Gonzáles was nothing if not ethnocentric. "Yo Soy Joaquín" promoted cultural pride, tracing the community's roots directly back to the advanced Aztec and Mayan civilizations of Mesoamerica, but equally to the Spanish conquistadors, glorifying the *mestisaje*, or mixture of races, that produced the *mestizo* blend that characterizes the vast majority of Mexicans. His Denver-based organization Crusade for Justice organized cultural events, set up "defense committees" to protect the *barrio* against drugs and gangs, and sponsored a bilingual school. But it was Gonzáles's aggressive rhetoric and philosophy that put him on the map: he pulled no punches, accusing Anglos of "cultural genocide against Chicanos."[146]

Gonzáles organized the National Chicano Liberation Youth Conference in March 1969, with heavy involvement of students from California universities, which under his guidance produced *El Plan Spiritual de Aztlan*, a clarion call for cultural separatism, including restitution for past discrimination, rejection of the two-party political system and "political liberation" through a Chicano political party, a national school walkout on September 16 of that year, and ominously to many, "self-defense against the occupying forces of the oppressor."[147] Many found Gonzáles's language extreme, but his vision of Chicanos "taking back" their land was metaphorical. Not so for the movement's third horseman, New Mexico's *El Tigre*, Reies Lopez Tijerina, a man intent on literally taking back some of the land he thought had been stolen from his people.

New Mexico was an unlikely setting for Chicano activism. Much of its predominantly fair-skinned *Hispano* population claimed "Spanish" descent, differentiating itself from *mexicanos* with indigenous blood, and many claimed "that their lands had been taken from them through deception and fraud."[148] After attempts to seek redress through the legal process failed, in the late 1950s Pentecostal preacher Reies Lopez Tijerina stepped into the void, reminding New Mexico's *Hispanos* of their patrician roots, that their territory came to their forbears through land grants from the Spanish Crown. *El Tigre*'s crusade came to a head in June 1967, when he and his followers attempted a "citizens' arrest" of an official who refused them a permit for a protest. In the resulting confrontation a county deputy and a prison guard were shot, Lopez Tijerina fled to the mountains, and the National Guard was called out to support federal, state, and county law enforcement in the largest manhunt in the state's history.[149] *El Tigre* was eventually arrested, acquitted of some charges and convicted of others, and was in and out of jail for some five years. Always a mystic and somewhat eccentric, his behavior became increasingly erratic after his release from prison in 1974; by the late 1970s he'd faded away from the movement.[150] But in his moment in the spotlight, Lopez Tijerina "seemed the epitome of the new Chicano leader" who represented "the *macho*, a real man who not only talked tough but backed up his words by taking the law into his own hands."[151] He was a true militant, inspirational to many but threatening to those, both *mexicano* and Anglo alike, who didn't identify with *Chicanismo*.

This new militancy paralleled developments among the era's black activists. As early as 1963, John Lewis, head of the Student Nonviolent Coordinating Committee (SNCC), a committed disciple of nonviolent action and himself a future congressman, was growing impatient. Before ascending to the podium to speak at the March on Washington, movement elders had to talk him out of attacking the pending civil rights bills as grossly inadequate.[152]

Lyndon Johnson's War on Poverty also turned out to be less than advertised, especially as its early implementation coincided with the growing US military escalation in Vietnam. It wasn't just a question of competing budget priorities, although in a fundamental sense it was a classic guns versus butter controversy. One "problem" was that the economy was growing too fast and in danger of overheating in 1965; unemployment had dropped to 4 percent, and Johnson's economic advisors worried about inflationary pressures that would require fiscal restraint. Fearing that Congress would, in Johnson's words, "give him the war but not the Great Society" programs, the administration deliberately held back the real costs of the war. As detailed by David Halberstam in *The Best and the Brightest* the official cost estimate for the war in 1966–1967 was $8 billion, although privately expenses were estimated to be $10 billion. The actual cost that year was $21 billion. The next year, the government officially pegged the war's cost at $21 billion and attacked critics who said it might reach $24 billion; the actual cost ended up at $27 billion, paralleling the $23 billion federal deficit that year. The war, or more precisely Johnson's failure to pay for it through a tax increase, both starved the War on Poverty and sowed the seeds of the runaway inflation that plagued the economy for more than a decade.[153]

After passage of the civil rights bills and the War on Poverty produced little discernible improvement, younger African American activists grew frustrated by the work-within-the-system ethos of the principal civil rights groups like the NAACP and the National Urban League. By the mid-1960s Black Power advocates Malcolm X, Stokely Carmichael, and H. Rap Brown gained both adherents and attention. He later moved away from explicitly advocating violence, but Malcolm X became "the face and the voice of a burgeoning black nationalist movement" by declaring the white man was "by nature, evil."[154] Brown, later convicted of burglary and murder in separate incidents, was chairman of SNCC in 1967, by which time it had abandoned its commitment to nonviolence; as that commitment waned, many thought the movement began losing its "moral catchet."[155] As Halberstam put it, by late 1967 and early 1968, "a sense of bitterness and hate seemed to pervade, and traditional civil rights leaders were pushed aside. . . . More alienated and scarred leaders . . . rose. They were protesting not just legal segregation, but the very structure of American life. The problem was not a Negro problem, they said, it was a White problem. They did not want In, they wanted Out."[156]

Just as African American voices were becoming more strident and Lopez Tijerina's land grant movement was reaching its zenith, a new effort began in San Antonio, led by the fourth horseman of the Chicano movement, José Ángel Gutiérrez, head of the Mexican American Youth Organization (MAYO). A graduate student at St. Mary's University, in 1967 Gutiérrez and fellow activists Mario Compeán, Ignacio "Nacho" Pérez, Willie Velasquez, and Juan Patlán began weekly discussions that eventually led to the formation of MAYO. The group rejected the "old guard" not just due to insufficient militancy but because on a purely practical level, they believed working within the system was ineffective; Gutiérrez said that the "passing of resolutions, signing of petitions, holding of conferences, voter registration and social activities . . . are ineffective and the results obtained through them are too meager."[157] Gutiérrez and his militant *compadres* "wanted to be the antithesis of LULAC and the G.I. Forum."[158]

But while they knew what they were against, at first they weren't clear on exactly what they were for. Like the diligent students they were, they adopted a demanding reading schedule, studying and then debating the tactics of Martin Luther King's Southern Christian Leadership Conference and those of the black militants. They traveled to California, Colorado, and New Mexico to learn firsthand about the strategies adopted by Chávez, Gonzáles, and Lopez Tijerina.[159] They engaged in long discussions—"rap sessions" in 1960s parlance—debating the merits of the approaches they'd studied. They settled on what some have called "pragmatic nationalism," seeking concrete substantive objectives through incendiary rhetoric and confrontational tactics that would result in repression from the Anglo establishment, thus politicizing and mobilizing the largely dormant Mexican American masses.[160]

Scholars believe MAYO's enduring legacy was instigating some thirty-nine school walkouts, or blowouts in the vernacular, in South Texas in the late 1960s to protest educational discrimination Mexican Americans had experienced for decades: substandard facilities; English-only rules, even on the playground; the absence of culturally relevant courses; and biased teachers who openly denigrated Mexican Americans.[161] It wasn't always the substantive questions that catalyzed student activism, but more mundane issues foremost on high school students' minds, such as the process for selecting cheerleaders and homecoming queens.[162] But these were not just angry, mindless protests. Recognizing that "boycotts would deprive schools of public funding based on average daily attendance," the formula used by the state to parcel out funding to local districts, the activists knew that the walkouts gave them leverage because they hit school officials right where it hurt most: in the pocketbook.[163]

The group fused activism with pragmatism. Using the federally funded (but state-administered) Volunteers in Service to America (VISTA) program, it built a cadre of organizers across South Texas. They created the Texas Institute for Educational Development (TIED), which provided health and education services to farmworkers and other low-income *mexicanos* in Texas. Together with the Southwest Council of La Raza, they formed the Mexican American Unity Council (MAUC), a community organization initially headed by Velazquez, to provide housing, job training, and economic development programs to San Antonio's *barrio* residents.[164] Gutiérrez briefly went on the payroll of MALDEF soon after the legal organization's founding in San Antonio in 1968. Except for Velasquez, who quickly moved on from MAUC to work full time on traditional voter empowerment work, this "mainstream" period didn't last long, although some observers argue that MAYO was far less militant than comparable black activists of the era, and was pragmatic in many respects.[165] But it didn't appear that way to everyone.

GUTIÉRREZ V. GONZÁLEZ

José Ángel Gutiérrez was often deliberately and excessively provocative, as in a 1969 press event, where he stated that one of MAYO's aims was to "eliminate the gringo." Pressed by a reporter to elaborate on the meaning of the phrase, Gutiérrez "explained": "You can eliminate an individual in various ways. *You can certainly kill him but that is not our intent at this moment*. You can remove the base of support that he operates from, be it economic, political, social. That is what we intend to do [emphasis added]."[166]

The quasi-denial with the "not our intent at this moment" qualifier, *might* have muddied the waters enough for the episode to fade away, but it didn't end there. The reporter wrote that when further pressed about killing gringos, Gutiérrez replied "if worst comes to worst and we have to resort to that means, it would be self-defense."[167] Supporters tried to put the statements "in context," noting that Gutiérrez had been the target of attempts on his life, and that his second statement *may* have referred to his personal situation. Perhaps, but given the opportunity to retract or walk back references to "eliminating" or "killing" gringos, Gutiérrez declined, instead qualifying the circumstances under which killing might be justified. Readers couldn't avoid the conclusion that Gutiérrez was, at a minimum, leaving the door open to violence against Anglos as a legitimate political strategy. Unsurprisingly, Gutiérrez and the causes he was associated with became the subject of widespread condemnation, which continues to this day.[168]

Attacks from the white establishment were to be expected, indeed were in some ways the point of Gutiérrez's strategy, but harsh criticism from the Mexican American middle class personified by San Antonio congressman Henry B. González (D-TX) proved more damaging. "Henry B" was a Golden Gloves boxer, had worked in naval intelligence during World War II, was elected to the San Antonio City Council in 1953, and, as state senator in 1957, "attracted national attention for holding the longest filibuster in the history of the Texas Legislature" against bills circumventing *Brown v. Board of Education*.[169] Elected to Congress in 1960, he was an old-fashioned liberal: a staunch critic of the bracero program, one of the only members of the Texas delegation in the House to vote for the 1960s civil rights bills, and an opponent of the "red-baiting" House Un-American Activities Committee. He was also, in the Mexican tradition, *muy macho*. Early in his career he "swatted" one Republican colleague, and even in his seventies delivered a one-punch knockout to a man in a San Antonio restaurant, both of whom had called him a Communist.[170] Reporters wrote, González "had an ego that demanded life-or-death combat [and] the heart of a philosopher" but "was often not in control of his own emotions."[171]

Never one to back down from a confrontation, "Henry B." was itching for a fight with the activists for reasons almost too numerous to list. He thought they were aligned with his local Mexican American political opponents. He believed some he had mentored, such as Velasquez, who had been an intern in his office, had abandoned him. And, no doubt, he felt threatened in the way the old guard always views Young Turks with suspicion. But his main beef was substantive: González fundamentally disagreed with their ethnocentric approach to politics.[172] A friend and sometime opponent said of González that he could be "meaner than a riled cat when he goes after you."[173] He lived up to this description and more as he went after everyone associated with MAYO with a vengeance, denouncing them on the House floor, trashing their supporters—especially the Ford Foundation, the major funder of the Southwest Council of La Raza, MALDEF, and the Mexican American Unity Council—in the press, and joining conservatives to pass legislation to reign in foundations that supported "radical" causes. González said the activists fomented "race hate," and MAYO's Juan Patlán responded in kind, accusing the congressman of "an alliance with the racists and Birchers who don't give a damn about the poor" to pass legislation to restrict the activities of foundation funders of the Latino groups.[174] The resulting Tax

Reform Act of 1969 forced the Ford Foundation to place more conditions on its funding, gave political cover for conservatives to cut off VISTA and other support to movement groups, and helped to change the Internal Revenue Service rules that nonprofit organizations and their funders had to adhere to when engaging in advocacy and voter registration activities.[175]

By late 1969, MAYO was falling apart and its leadership group scattered. Patlán went to the helm of Mexican American Unity Council, Nacho Pérez divided his time between MAUC and the Texas Institute for Educational Development, and Velasquez joined the Southwest Council of La Raza's staff to develop what later became the Southwest Voter Registration Education Project.[176] Gutiérrez and Compeán decided to build an ethnocentric political third party: Partido Nacional de La Raza Unida. They started in Gutiérrez's home town of Crystal City in South Texas, gained effective control of both the school board and the city council in 1970, and the effort spread to sixteen other predominantly Mexican American counties in the state, albeit with less success. In 1972, they shocked the Democratic Party establishment when the Raza Unida gubernatorial standard bearer Ramsey Muñiz, a handsome, articulate, and polished former Baylor University football player, forced a runoff between liberal Frances "Sissy" Farenthold and conservative Dolph Briscoe, when many progressives believed Farenthold had a chance at outright victory in a crowded Democratic primary field. A supporter of former Alabama governor George Wallace for the Democratic presidential nomination against George McGovern that year, Briscoe won the runoff and the general election, but with a slim four-point margin over a GOP opponent after Muñiz garnered more than 6 percent of the vote statewide.[177] Less successful Raza Unida efforts cropped up in other states, and Muñiz ran again for governor in 1974, winning a slightly smaller but still respectable share of the vote.

Velasquez rejected the ethnocentric third-party route to nurture the Southwest Voter Registration Education Project (SVREP), which became a highly accomplished nonprofit voter mobilization group closely allied with the Democratic Party. Although SVREP always maintained a clear focus as a Hispanic organization, Velasquez wryly noted that appeals on ethnic solidarity grounds weren't always effective but, "When we got Mexican American candidates saying, 'Vote for me and I'll pave the streets,' goddamit that's when the revolution [in voter registration] started."[178] A little over a decade later, the number of Mexican Americans registered to vote in Texas and California doubled, a development many credited mainly to Velasquez and his leadership of SVREP, along with MALDEF's litigation.[179]

Gutiérrez bitterly vied with Corky Gonzáles for national leadership of the Chicano movement. By 1977, with the Raza Unida party "in its death throes,"

Gutiérrez made what one scholar called "his final bid to remain a major player in Mexican American politics."[180] He organized the First National Chicano/ Latino Immigration Conference in San Antonio to respond to the Carter administration's immigration plan, which called for border controls and penalties on employers for hiring unauthorized workers. Gutiérrez's invitation letter framed the issues in stark terms: "The very same man Raza supported for the Presidency now seeks to deport us. The Carter Administration is designing a new immigration policy. We are the main targets. The phobia mongers insist our people, because of our numbers, birth rate, geographic spread and undocumented status threaten the very underpinnings of this society."[181]

The event attracted virtually "every major Mexican American organization in the country."[182] The more mainstream LULAC, American GI Forum, MALDEF, and NCLR joined some 1,500 activists from thirty states at the event. Like many *movimiento* gatherings of the era, it quickly degenerated due to "destructive, internecine conflicts"; according to one writer, during a "rambunctious ten hours of debate," several factions of socialists and communists walked out.[183] While accounts differ on whether a ten-point plan drafted by Gutiérrez was formally endorsed by remaining participants, the event was nevertheless notable.[184] Almost all remaining groups opposed Carter's tougher enforcement plan. There was also agreement on the need for "total amnesty of all undocumented workers."[185] This was a remarkable evolution from the almost unanimously restrictionist views of the community's recognized leaders in the 1930s through the 1950s, and differed even from the more equivocal and nuanced positions expressed by the succeeding generations of Mexican American advocates, scholars, and spokespeople into the late 1960s.[186] In the struggle between ethnocentrism—even the relatively mild version espoused by the mainstream Latino civil rights groups—versus the class-based ideology promoted by the left-leaning academics and organized labor that led inevitably to restrictionist immigration policies, the notion of standing by the community's coethnics, even those born abroad, won decisively.

In the 1978 Texas elections, MAYO cofounder Mario Compeán was the Raza Unida gubernatorial nominee, collecting only 15,000 votes, a dismal one-half of 1 percent of total votes cast. Paradoxically, even this helped Republican William Clements defeat incumbent Dolph Briscoe for the governorship and contributed to GOP senator John Tower's razor-thin 13,689 vote margin over Democrat Bob Krueger. Although the election marked the "death knell" of the Raza Unida in Texas, in a final parting shot to the Texas Democratic establishment it had finally, unequivocally, proven to be a spoiler in a statewide election contest. One scholar-activist wrote that by then the Chicano movement was "all but dead."[187] But among its legacies was a Mexican American leadership that was markedly ethnocentric and pro-immigrant in orientation.

LULAC STEPS UP

Stepping into the void created by the decline of the Chicano movement, to the surprise of many, was LULAC. Denigrated by the militants at the height of the movement, the league's leadership didn't support the radicals' tactics, or for that matter the sharper-edged activism in the black civil rights movement. Prior to the emergence of the Chicano movement, LULAC, it seemed, was on a "steady as she goes" course, committed to incremental progress through the mainstream political process; as one LULAC president had observed in 1963: "We have not sought solutions to problems by marching to Washington, Sit-ins, or picketing. . . . Mass meetings and mass gatherings often times lead to mass hysteria. This paves the way for emotional and irrational thinking which [are] not the criteria for clear thinking Americans. We have been taught to be courteous and highly respectful of all offices in our governmental pattern whether we agree with the individual serving in that office or not."[188]

But coming out of the late 1960s and early 1970s, when activism, organizing, and advocacy had propelled enactment of landmark civil rights legislation, launched the women's rights movement, and contributed to the end of the Vietnam War, business as usual wasn't an especially sexy strategy. It also dawned on the mainstream Mexican American leadership that the new civil rights laws and War on Poverty programs under the Johnson administration largely excluded their community. Never a particularly efficient enforcement agency to begin with, the Equal Employment Opportunity Commission was believed to be "ignoring Mexican problems"; in the same vein, LULAC president Alfred Hernandez decried the almost complete absence of Hispanic appointments in the Johnson administration, concluding that Mexican Americans were "Stepchildren in this Great Society."[189] LULAC official Carlos Truan, who later served in the Texas State Senate and on both the MALDEF and NCLR boards, argued that although "Latin Americans . . . constitute the ethnic group hardest hit by a chronic and unnecessary poverty in the Southwest," Mexican Americans were neglected in Great Society programs.[190]

LULAC itself was evolving. Its demand for equity in the War on Poverty and enforcement of the civil rights laws already reflected a shift from its traditional emphasis on individualism and self-help and concomitant distaste for government programs.[191] As Chicano scholar Ignacio M. García wrote, LULAC and the moderate American GI Forum: "had come to accept the reality that integration would take longer than anticipated and that programs based on race and national origin were an acceptable part of the equalization process that would lead to full integration. This was a concept they had rejected before as being segregationist in nature."[192]

LULAC's volunteer model with annual elections of officers led to constant turnover of its spokespeople, limiting its ability to build relationships with policy makers, advocacy partners, or funders.[193] As of the mid-1970s, its membership had receded for two decades and its visibility had been eclipsed by the eminently more quotable Chicano radicals.[194] But just as LULAC started a downward spiral, its fortunes were revived by a marked shift in a more activist direction spearheaded by the 1979 election of Ruben Bonilla as LULAC's thirty-eighth president.

The Corpus Christi–based Ruben Bonilla had long been active in LULAC as its former Texas state director and deputy director, and in state political circles as a successful attorney in private practice. Bonilla was credited by scholars with leading a "blossoming into a new era of aggressive political action" of the organization. Immediately after his election he issued a "scathing attack on the Carter Administration and its neglect of the Mexican American population."[195] He was especially interested in getting LULAC's message out through the mainstream media, and there he proved both skillful and tireless, gaining widespread press attention for the organization. With the comfortable income provided by his law practice, and a willingness to invest personal financial resources into his presidency, Bonilla attended "more national and international conferences than any other past national [LULAC] president."[196] By the end of his second term in 1981, LULAC membership was at an all-time high.[197]

Bonilla was a LULAC loyalist and had little use for the rhetoric espoused by Chicano activists—he believed in working through the system not overthrowing it—but it was impossible for him, impossible really for anyone in advocacy circles in Texas, not to have been influenced by the movement. He was quite close to Willie Velasquez; both believed that third parties like Raza Unida couldn't make it in the US political system.[198] But Bonilla could work with those he had differences with. He considered José Ángel Gutiérrez a friend, even after the many disparaging remarks that the activist had made about LULAC. One scholar observed that under Bonilla "the strident line of political action that came out of the Chicano Movement became internalized in LULAC—truly a dialectical synthesis between Mexican Americanism and Chicanismo."[199]

Bonilla was also comfortable in mainstream establishment circles. In 1976–1978 widespread reports of excessive police force against Latinos and blacks in Texas led to protests in Port Arthur, Houston, Dallas, and a half-dozen other cities. Then LULAC's state director, Ruben Bonilla worked with the Community Relations Service, the mediation arm of the Justice Department, in a series of convenings between Hispanic leaders and police chiefs across the state. With Bonilla's guidance, they "produced a sense of achievement beyond anything anticipated" by the Service's professional mediators, contributing to a marked reduction in tensions.[200] Along with San Antonio mayor Henry Cisneros, Indiana senator Dan Quayle, singer Donny Osmond, and football star Leroy Selmon, among others, Bonilla was named one of "10 Outstanding Young Americans" by the national Jaycees for his work in fighting police abuse.[201] He was a sought after speaker but also was keenly aware that no matter how eloquent he was, afterward some in the audience would "say 'who the hell was that Mexican anyway?' . . . [W]hen we turn our backs, they will wonder where a Mexican learned to speak like that."[202] A student of history who could rattle off with precision and detail the ebbs and flows, hypocrisies and inconsistencies in US immigration policy toward Mexicans, early in his tenure Bonilla criticized the Carter administration's immigration proposals, differentiating LULAC from the Democratic partisans that made up much of the community's most visible leadership.[203]

Bonilla believed it was important to open up a permanent LULAC office in the nation's capital to lobby Congress and the administration. In June 1979 he was introduced to Arnoldo Torres by José Longoria, who headed the LULAC National Educational Service Centers (LNESC) office in DC. Torres had just finished a master's program while working part time first for the National Congress of Hispanic American Citizens, or *El Congreso*, a Latino advocacy group, and later Democratic California senator John Tunney. Together with a previous stint as a Lyndon B. Johnson Fellow with Rep. Pete Stark (D-CA), his work in the Legislative Analyst's Office in the California legislature—only the second Latino ever hired to work in the prestigious unit—service on Tunney's (losing) reelection campaign, and an advanced degree, for a Hispanic of his generation Torres was unusually well qualified for a congressional liaison position.[204] Although before meeting the new LULAC president Torres had decided to head back to California to accept another job, he and Bonilla hit it off during their interview. Bonilla was impressed with Torres's credentials, but mostly liked that Torres had the proverbial "fire in the belly."[205] For his part Torres appreciated Bonilla's assurances that he would not be a micromanager. Bonilla offered Torres the job as LULAC's Washington representative on the spot, which was gratefully accepted. Both wanted LULAC to become a "presence in this city" so that lawmakers knew that Latinos "had an agenda, had opinions, and could contribute" to the policy process; to the young Torres, then just twenty-four, it was "a dream come true, a phenomenal opportunity to put an organization on the political map."[206]

Bonilla emphasized that as a newly elected LULAC president limited by the group's constitution to serving two annual terms, he had "only two years" to make his mark.[207] His message was clear: Torres was expected to move quickly. His new Washington representative, soon promoted to national executive director, almost immediately set up a series of meetings for Bonilla with top-level Carter administration officials and a coveted speaking appearance at the National Press Club.[208] Torres was hardly a shrinking violet himself, as his "confrontational and assertive style of leadership got him national media exposure and notoriety" on *The Phil Donahue Show*, then the top-rated daily television variety show, and conservative icon William F. Buckley's popular PBS's *Firing Line* program. Even scholar-activists associated with the Chicano movement, once LULAC's toughest critics, acknowledged the effectiveness of the group's two new leaders whose skills were closely aligned: noting both were "articulate, knowledgeable on the issues, and apt in the workings on the media."[209]

The backlash Gutiérrez and his *compadres* generated from Rep. Henry B. González, and LULAC's evolution toward a more activist frame in the 1970s were barely noticed outside the Southwest. To most of the country, Mexican Americans were still invisible, as noted by a researcher for the US Commission on Civil Rights: "The high drama and nationwide visibility of the [black] civil rights movement have tended to obscure the more localized protests of the Mexican American groups and the demands of their spokesmen that Mexican Americans achieve the full rights and responsibilities of citizenship, and become enabled to participate fully in American economic, political, and social life."[210]

Lack of national media coverage was certainly an issue, as was minimal philanthropic support for Latino institutions; when Equal Employment Opportunity Commission member Vicente Ximenes, whose role as chairman of the Cabinet Committee on Opportunities for Spanish-Speaking People made him the highest-ranking Hispanic in the Johnson administration, invited the nation's largest foundations to a meeting in 1968, only one showed up.[211]

THE COUNCIL

The one foundation with an interest in Mexican Americans in the 1960s was the Ford Foundation, whose director of national affairs was Paul Ylvisaker. Unusually for an elite leader of the period, Ylvisaker included Mexican Americans in his conception of "race"; in 1964 he awarded a grant to the University of California-Los Angeles to prepare a study, *The Mexican American People: The Nation's Second Largest Minority*, eventually released in 1970. In 1966 Ylvisaker attended a conference featuring discussion of a new book by Notre Dame University sociologist Julian Samora, *La Raza: Forgotten Americans.* He later met with conference participants who impressed him: scholar Samora, labor leader and activist Ernesto Galarza, and Herman Gallegos, a past organizer with the Community Service Organization who was, said expert observers, "highly respected for his strong organizational skills."[212] Ylvisaker retained the trio to develop recommendations to Ford for a grant-making portfolio focused on Mexican Americans, exhorting them to "go out and dream your dreams."[213]

Galarza, Gallegos, and Samora found that "fragmentation" among Mexican American organizations attributed to "the lack of resources to enable Chicano leaders to pick up the phone" to make long distance calls or travel for face-to-face meetings. They called for "ongoing technical assistance to help coordinate and strengthen the work of the local groups," complemented by "national advocacy on behalf of Mexican Americans."[214] The key recommendation was for an organization in the Southwest—a "council"—to link and support emerging *barrio*-based groups. In February 1968, the trio began a planning process that resulted in the Southwest Council of La Raza. The first financial support was from the National Council of Churches and the United Auto Workers, followed by a grant from the San Francisco-based Rosenberg Foundation. In June the Ford Foundation awarded the group a two-year, $630,000 operating grant (about $5.4 million in 2017 dollars), with the cofounders in leadership roles: Gallegos agreed to serve as executive director for a maximum of two years, with Samora joining the board and Galarza as a consultant.[215] The new council was notably intellectual in orientation: Galarza and Samora were accomplished scholars and Gallegos served as the movement's liaison to mainstream institutions; a journalist noted he had effortlessly "moved from neighborhood organizing in a San Jose barrio with César Chávez and Saul Alinsky to a directorship of the Pacific Telephone and Telegraph Company."[216]

The organization's founding in 1968 coincided with the assassinations of Rev. Martin Luther King in April and Robert F. Kennedy in June. In between, some 130 cities burned, with riots in Chicago, Baltimore, Kansas City, Wilmington, Detroit, Pittsburgh, Cincinnati, Louisville, and the nation's capital, where Black Power leader H. Rap Brown told an audience at St. Stephen's church to "get you some guns and burn this town down."[217] At the height of the turmoil, Southwest Council executive director Herman Gallegos and board member Henry Santiestévan, an AFL-CIO official who soon succeeded Gallegos, issued "A Call to La Raza for a Personal Pledge to Non-violence." Their manifesto emphasized their belief that "social justice can be peacefully achieved not only for La Raza but for all victims of poverty, deprivation, and alienation."[218] It placed the organization, like its established black counterparts the NAACP and the National Urban League, squarely within what some called "the moderate middle," focused on ending discrimination and promoting equality using conventional tactics like advocacy, voter registration, and social programs.[219] Their stance also presaged the merging of tough movement rhetoric attached to a largely mainstream agenda—the "dialectical synthesis"—that LULAC adopted under the leadership of Ruben Bonilla and Arnoldo Torres a decade later, albeit from far different starting points. The council's roots were decidedly left leaning, but it found itself in a center-left position as racial politics moved in a radical direction in the late 1960s and early 1970s; LULAC moved leftward from its moderate-conservative origins fifty years earlier.

The Southwest Council was headquartered in Phoenix, presumably neutral territory between the Chicano community's rival California- and Texas-based factions. The council's constituency—its first "affiliates"—included the Mexican American Unity Council in San Antonio; Chicanos Por La Causa in Phoenix; the Mexican American Community Programs Foundation and The East Los Angeles Community Union in Los Angeles; the Spanish-Speaking Unity Council in Oakland; and the Mission Development Council and the Organization for Business, Education and Community Advancement, which soon changed its name to Arriba Juntos, in San Francisco. The affiliates—mostly part of a cohort of groups called "community development corporations" that used sophisticated financial techniques to fight poverty—were on the whole highly successful.[220] Most are thriving today.

The Council was a "funding intermediary" between the Ford Foundation and the local groups, many of which initially lacked the requisite nonprofit 501(c)(3) tax status that the foundation required.[221] It was also the self-identified "hub" to support community groups springing up in Mexican American neighborhoods across the Southwest to fight poverty and discrimination, many with funds from the War on Poverty.[222] It sought to make a name for itself on the advocacy front, and in December 1972 executive director Henry Santiestévan proposed moving the organization's central office to the nation's capital; in 1973 the renamed National Council of La Raza opened its headquarters in Washington, DC, thinking this would both facilitate raising federal grants to fund its "hard programming" and establish a national advocacy presence.[223]

Before it could solidify this advocacy base, it was buffeted by internal struggles. Only a single woman was seated on the original NCLR twenty-six-member board; by 1971 the number had grown to three. Board member Graciela Olivárez demanded equal representation of women on the council's governing body; her proposal passed by a single vote in 1972.[224] Several male board members, including cofounder Julian Samora, voluntarily gave up their seats to accommodate the new female members required to achieve gender balance.[225] The open battle over gender was followed by a wrenching, personal schism between competing board factions with ties to organized labor, which was establishing the affinity group now known as the Labor Council for Latin American Advancement. At issue, in short, was who would be selected to head the labor group, and both leading candidates were on NCLR's board, exacerbating other factional conflicts.[226] With issues playing out as proxy battles between the two rivals, Santiestévan was caught in the middle; he decided to step down in order to "keep the frail craft that was the Council" from going under.[227] On an unseasonably cold, snowy day in Denver in June 1974, he was succeeded by Raul Yzaguírre, a reluctant candidate approved by the NCLR Board by a one-vote margin after an intrigue-filled search process.[228]

Yzaguírre was a longtime activist who as a teenager had organized school walkouts in his native San Juan, Texas, in the late 1950s, well before the MAYO-inspired blowouts a decade later, and had been elected to the board of the Texas state chapter of the American GI Forum at the age of sixteen. His military service brought him to the DC suburbs to work in the medical laboratory at Andrews Air Force Base. After an honorable discharge, while attending George Washington University, he organized a group called NOMAS (National Organization for Mexican American Services), whose principal distinction was to earn Yzaguírre a place as the first Hispanic member of the Leadership Conference on Civil Rights, the coalition that played a central role in passage of the historic civil rights bills in the 1960s.[229] He joined the Office of Economic Opportunity, the agency that administered the War on Poverty, and then founded a first-of-its-kind, Latino-owned consulting agency, Interstate Research Associates, whose clients included both NCLR and several of its affiliates.[230] He had turned the company over to partners and moved back to his native South Texas before accepting the NCLR job.[231]

Short and stocky, with a gravelly voice that retained a remnant of a *mexicano* accent, Yzaguírre wasn't the central casting version of a charismatic leader. His degree in general studies from George Washington University wasn't especially impressive. His organizing work as a teenager with the American GI Forum was dated; as of the mid-1970s, the venerable veteran-oriented civil rights group was on the decline. His stint in government and private consulting made him well known among Latino-led local community-based organizations, but these jobs also kept him out of what little political limelight shone on Latino leaders during the rise and fall of the Chicano movement. He acknowledged, with self-deprecating humor, that his group NOMAS's leaders in those days were "national advocates only in our own minds."[232] Still, as nonprofit management experts observed years later, the "thoughtful and soft spoken" Yzaguírre had a real presence, a "quiet power."[233]

Yzaguírre himself often struggled between contradictory impulses of militance and moderation. When angered, he could revert to his activist roots, spouting grievances against the Hispanic community by mainstream society in inflammatory terms. But upon reflection when counseling his own staff who expressed similar frustrations, he said something like: "We live in a democracy. Hispanics are a small minority. We cannot impose our will on the majority. Rather, we have to persuade them that it is in their interest to support us. The bigger the change we seek, the more people we have to persuade. Insulting them or calling them names isn't the best way to do that."[234]

The organization's political positioning reflected the belief that broad-scale, sustainable changes could only occur with substantial support among influential elites and the body politic. The council often took unpopular positions, such as supporting affirmative action and bilingual education, but Yzaguírre's advocacy strategies were designed to build support for its policy agenda in traditional ways: research and policy analysis, educating the public, and lobbying.

Over his first five and one-half years at the helm, NCLR's budget grew tenfold, from about $500,000 to nearly $5 million, including dozens of new federal grants and contracts, with the staff roster growing commensurately, from thirteen to about one hundred. Yzaguírre also recruited new constituents; by 1980, the affiliate base had grown from seventeen to over one hundred.[235] Two key senior staffers played a pivotal role in shaping the organization's policy agenda. One, Emily Gantz McKay, who'd worked with Yzaguírre often during his consulting days, had deep activist roots: her father was a Jewish immigrant committed to social justice and her mother was associated with the left-leaning, innovative Antioch College. After earning undergraduate and graduate degrees at Stanford, McKay worked for a consulting firm that advised a number of civil rights organizations, including NCLR, before joining the National Council staff in 1978. McKay played multiple leadership roles at NCLR, but her initial focus was on fundraising, as the group, in Yzaguírre's words, "wrote [funding] proposals as fast as we could."[236] McKay also drafted training curricula and then delivered the content in the field; the fundraising training programs she spearheaded were highly regarded.[237] She also wrote or edited all key organizational documents; Yzaguírre called her "the single most capable and productive human being I have ever known."[238]

The second, Michael Cortés, had worked for Yzaguírre at Interstate Research Associates, where he headed a national farmworker survey, then saw firsthand how policy advocacy worked when El Congreso's Manny Fierro used the study to gain federal funding for disabled farmworkers. After enrolling in a doctoral program in public policy in 1974, Cortés advised Yzaguírre that "NCLR needed a policy shop."[239] His advice dovetailed nicely with the NCLR executive's intent "to conduct research/advocacy to impact on the public policy needed to effectuate change."[240] In 1977, Yzaguírre convinced Cortés to leave school to head the group's new policy unit. NCLR initially focused on the Hispanic "data gap"— few agencies included Latinos when gathering or reporting data.[241] Even the Bureau of the Census, the official collector, keeper, and producer of the nation's vital statistics, was confused about how to treat Hispanics; as of 1969, as far as the Census was concerned, Mexican Americans, Puerto Ricans, Cubans, and other Latinos were "white," even though these groups were subject to substantial discrimination.[242] In 1974, the US Commission on Civil Rights criticized the classifications for obscuring discrimination against Latinos while undermining the ability of its advocates to press claims for policy reforms.[243]

The data issue was linked to another of the NCLR chief executive's passions: a "pan-Hispanic" community identity. The notion that those of Mexican, Puerto Rican, and Cuban descent could share a common identity was almost unheard of, and when raised, highly controversial. NCLR thought that this almost invisible minority needed a "critical mass" of numbers to command policy attention; around this time Louis Nuñez, head of the National Puerto Rican Coalition agreed, noting that for Latinos to achieve power and recognition, "it would have to be as one group . . . [not] as four or five groups, no matter what everyone would like."[244] But Yzaguírre wasn't just resigned to Latino panethnicity based on pragmatism alone, he believed in the concept on its merits; the issue wasn't so much how the diverse subgroups viewed themselves, he'd say, but how they were viewed by the majority society, noting that few white Americans made distinctions between Latino subgroups, and they were all subject to shared, negative stereotypes.[245] Yzaguírre argued for a pluralistic approach to Latino identity, where subgroups could retain their individual identities with a common bond: "We need to emphasize our Hispanic roots and treasure our differences— we're Mexican Americans, we're Hispanic, we're minority, we're American— and begin to see all of these concentric circles of relationships, not to be so isolated but to begin to define ourselves as a broader coalition."[246]

Yzaguírre was forced to move cautiously. Some vowed to oppose what they called Chicano imperialism: an attempt by majority Mexican Americans to impose their will on the smaller Puerto Rican and other Hispanic subgroups.[247] He also faced resistance from within, as one board member resigned rather than be a party to "diluting" the council's scarce resources on other Latino subgroups.[248] But in 1979, NCLR's board of directors formally "affirmed its role as an advocate for all Hispanics."[249] As documented by sociologist Cristina Mora, NCLR played a pivotal role in ensuring that the 1980 Census, and every decennial count since, asked every person surveyed whether they were "Hispanic." She wrote that NCLR "pioneered the notion of Hispanic panethnicity within the social movement field."[250] While many groups and institutions played important roles, Mora noted, it was under Yzaguírre's leadership that NCLR successfully "spearheaded the notion that Mexican Americans, Puerto Ricans, Cuban Americans [and other subgroups] could work together as one community."[251]

Yzaguírre viewed immigration policy mainly through a civil rights lens, believing that Hispanics disproportionately bore the brunt of enforcement efforts.[252] It was a tricky issue for a group with limited capacity: in the early1980s only three of its one hundred affiliates had immigration legal service programs.[253] In addition, researchers reported that the Latino leadership's support for immigrant rights wasn't shared by the rank and file, or by local grassroots activists, many associated with organized labor, who saw immigrant workers "as an economic threat and consumers of scarce public resources."[254] Still, Cortés noted, "immigration policy was never forgotten because one guy—my boss—refused to let me ignore it."[255] NCLR opposed Carter's immigration reform proposals in 1976, and testified against employer sanctions legislation.[256] NCLR also tried hard to form alliances with African American organizations to address a range of issues, including immigration policy.[257] As Cortés wrote, in the late 1970s: "The National Council of La Raza and its Latino allies helped persuade leaders of African-American organizations within the Leadership Conference [on Civil Rights] to caucus independently. They organized themselves into a "Black-Brown coalition" . . . [that] issued a joint statement opposing employer sanctions [penalties on employers for hiring undocumented workers]."[258]

But most black leaders of the era supported restrictive immigration policies; as EEOC chair, future congresswoman, and foremost black intellectual Eleanor Holmes Norton commented: "The Labor Department predicts there will be something approaching a labor shortage in this country by the mid-1980s. I do not expect the country to fill this shortage by going around the world looking for immigrants. I expect it to look inside. And that is when the rising education levels of blacks, and affirmative action programs . . . will really pay off."[259]

Under pressure from the AFL-CIO and from other black leaders, the African American groups in the Leadership Conference on Civil Rights soon reversed course and reverted back to their historical support for tough immigration enforcement. As a result, according to Cortés, "There was real anger and bitterness" among Latino civil rights organizations when a few years later the major black civil rights groups reemerged as a major voice for immigration restriction.[260]

In 1979, Yzaguírre became the first Hispanic to earn the prestigious Rockefeller Public Service Award, selected by the trustees of Princeton University, who described him as: "brave and angry enough to have come up through the ranks in the movement's chaotic days yet wise and statesmanlike enough to convert emotion into constructive action, he has orchestrated the fragmented energies of many local groups into a unified and powerful movement embracing the concerns of the national community of Hispanic Americans."[261]

Yzaguírre was also one of a small group of emerging Latino leaders highlighted by David Broder, perhaps the most respected political writer of the era, in his 1980 book, *Changing of the Guard*, about imminent shifts in power and leadership in the US.[262] There were other positive signs for the group. Cortés wrote that NCLR had proven an "attractive grantee for risk-averse [corporate and foundation] funders" with "little risk of the sorts of scandal and embarrassment that are anathema to organized philanthropy."[263] The Rockefeller Foundation—one of the major funders of civil rights and antipoverty organizations in the US—made a multiyear grant to support the council's public policy work in the fall of 1980.[264] By then Cortés had left for family reasons, and oversight over public policy went to Emily Gantz McKay, adding to her already prodigious fundraising, editing, and other roles at the organization. Francisco Garza, one of a tiny number of Latinos with an advanced degree in public policy earned at the prestigious LBJ School of Public Affairs, hired by Cortés as NCLR's legislative director, oversaw the group's lobbying activity across a half-dozen major priorities, including immigration policy.[265]

But just as NCLR seemed to find its footing, the election of Ronald Reagan in 1980 and the enactment of his major domestic budget cuts that reduced the group's funding signaled a major reversal of the group's fortunes. As the 1970s came to a close, LULAC seemed ascendant under the leadership of its new President Ruben Bonilla and Executive Director Arnoldo Torres while NCLR, facing massive budget cuts and painful staff layoffs, had a highly uncertain future.

CHAPTER 2

Storm Warnings

NODDING AND WINKING

T he perceived need in the 1980s for legislation to address unauthorized immigration came about from the convergence of multiple factors spanning many decades. Prior to the late 1800s, the US had no broad-based limits on immigration; to that point the law focused on discrete groups such as "enemy aliens," slaves and other "forced labor," or criminals and prostitutes.[1] A series of bills collectively known as the Chinese Exclusion Acts, whose intent was self-explanatory, was passed around the turn of the century, accompanied by a gentlemen's agreement with Japan, which "agreed to restrict the movement of its nationals to the American mainland in exchange for a commitment by the United States not to enact a Chinese-style exclusion."[2] In the 1920s, broad legislation was enacted that set yearly, per-country immigration quotas based on that nationality's portion of the US population, so-called "national origins quotas." For the next half-century, one journalist wrote, "the central principle of immigration policy was that America's new citizens should resemble its old ones."[3]

The Immigration and Nationality Act of 1952, called the McCarran–Walter Act after its sponsors Sen. Pat McCarran (D-NV) and Rep. Francis Walter (D-PA), continued restrictionist policy, with one exception. Supported by organized labor, Sen. Paul Douglas (D-IL) unsuccessfully proposed the imposition of penalties on employers of unauthorized immigrants. Instead, the final bill "made it unlawful to transport or harbor illegal aliens, but clarified that 'harboring' did *not* include employment," a clause known as the Texas Proviso after that state's agribusiness interests that insisted on its inclusion.[4] The cumulative effect of five decades under restrictive legislation, massive drops in demand for US visas from

Europe after World War II as the continent's economies recovered and the Iron Curtain limited emigration from the Soviet bloc, and "repatriations" of Mexicans combined with administrative barriers to Mexican immigrants meant that by the 1960s, the foreign-born population of the US was barely 5 percent, nearly its lowest point in history.

By then, the national origins quota system increasingly was viewed as racist and un-American in the context of a civil rights awakening and a world enmeshed in the process of decolonization; few public officials openly defended the system either domestically or abroad.[5] In 1958, then senator John F. Kennedy published *A Nation of Immigrants*, calling for elimination of the national origins quotas, and reaffirmed this view as president in July 1963.[6] After his assassination, Lyndon B. Johnson urged enactment of Kennedy's proposals immediately after passage of civil rights legislation. Congress followed his lead, and on October 4, 1965, President Johnson signed the Immigration and Nationality Act of 1965 into law at the foot of the Statue of Liberty, with both Edward and Robert Kennedy by his side.[7] The 1965 Act and a follow-on bill in 1968 replaced national origins quotas with ceilings on immigrants from the Eastern and Western Hemispheres; established a series of immigration "preferences" with 74 percent of visas set aside for family members of US residents, 20 percent for certain skills, and 6 percent for refugees; and permitted immediate family members of US citizens to enter outside the ceilings, a system largely still in place today.[8] The 1965 Act's future effects on legal immigration were largely attributable to the unlimited visas available to minor children, spouses, and parents of US citizens; what the law's critics call "chain migration" and defenders refer to as "family reunification." The *Washington Post* called Kennedy's proposal "the best immigration law within living memory," while the *New York Times* editorialized that its passage was an "act of justice and wisdom."[9] The public eventually agreed; according to Gallup polls, prior to the law's passage nearly three-fourths of Americans preferred either the same or lower levels of immigration, but after its enactment nearly 70 percent favored the new law.[10] Critics complained that previously, about 80 percent of the country's immigrants came from Europe, with less than 20 percent from Asia or Latin America, proportions that were reversed following passage of the 1965 Act. They believed that changing the demographic and racial makeup of the country was self-evidently harmful; others countered that growing diversity was a demonstrable strength.

Almost unnoticed was the law's effect on unlawful migration. In retrospect, it was one of a perfect storm of factors that made a massive increase in illegal entries at the southern border inevitable. Repatriation campaigns from 1920–1954 had removed millions of Mexican-origin citizens from the US; had they remained they could have petitioned for their immediate relatives through the legal immigration system but instead were relegated to extra-lawful means to reunify families. The end of the bracero program in 1964 eliminated the ability of farmworkers to legally enter on a temporary basis, but did nothing to quench demand for the workers.[11] And just as the US was closing the door to legal pathways Mexican workers had relied on for decades, internal developments in Mexico were pushing its growing population to look north for jobs. The Mexican fertility rate peaked in 1965, swelling the country's labor force.[12] At the same time, the country's economy weakened, beginning a series of currency devaluations.[13] The 1965 Act was the fourth element of this perfect storm, starting a process that eventually cut legal immigration visas for Mexico in half. Because the 1965 Act also failed to either close the Texas Proviso loophole or strengthen border enforcement, as Aristide Zolberg wrote, "There was every reason to anticipate . . . unauthorized entries to rise and reach unprecedented levels" but policy makers consciously chose to "bury their heads in the sand."[14]

Illegal entries across the southern US border grew rapidly. While an imperfect measure, INS apprehensions of unauthorized immigrants skyrocketed from less than 44,000 in 1964 to 870,000 in 1976, to over a million in 1977.[15] The public demanded that Congress "do something" about illegal immigration. That "something"—to repeal the Texas Proviso and penalize employers for hiring unauthorized workers—was first embodied in legislation sponsored by Rep. Peter Rodino (D-NJ), who as the chair of the House Immigration, Citizenship, and Nationality Subcommittee began holding hearings on the "illegal alien problem" in 1971. Rodino wasn't yet famous; it wasn't until three years later that as chair of the Judiciary Committee he would preside over the nationally televised impeachment proceedings of President Richard Nixon.

He was the child of Italian immigrants, raised in a bilingual household, and having been christened Pelegrino at his birth in 1909, his name was later changed to Peter. His father had come to his new country "with a tag on," meaning his passage to America had been paid by an employer or labor contractor. As described by author Joel Millman: "The tag was put inside the greenhorn's lapel or coat collar, and had to be hidden from inspectors at Ellis Island. It was revealed only after the immigrant was waved through, so that the contractor's representative, the factory foreman or whoever was sent to meet the new man at the dock, could identify him among the bewildered, blinking rabble. The practice was illegal, indentured servitude having been outlawed in 1855. But it was widespread nonetheless."[16]

It's no small irony that the father of Peter Rodino, who later led a decades-long crusade to toughen enforcement against unauthorized immigrants, originally entered the US unlawfully. His story was common. Critics of high immigration, such as the late conservative commentator Phyllis Schlafly, have argued that Hispanic immigrants are "not the same sort" as those that came before; she once cited composer Irving Berlin "as the kind of America-loving immigrant who supposedly no longer comes to the United States."[17] Berlin's family came to the US after fleeing a pogrom in their native Russia. Traveling without passports—and thus illegally—they reached Antwerp, Belgium, and from there went to Ellis Island, and entered the US under false names; had they been caught they, like Rodino's father, would have been considered "illegal immigrants." One scholar has noted that "the records of Ellis Island are filled with" similar stories of technically unlawful entries like those of Rodino's and Berlin's families.[18]

But even had they been apprehended, the Rodinos and Berlins likely would've been allowed to stay, covered by a "blanket amnesty" of sorts; as sociologist-historian Mae Ngai has noted, *all* of those who entered unlawfully in the early 1900s were protected from deportation after one to five years by statutes of limitations.[19] Subsequently, as Ngai has documented, "In the 1930s and 1940s, tens of thousands of people, overwhelmingly Europeans and Canadians were legalized" administratively after first having come to the US illegally.[20] The vast majority of illegal or fraudulent entries rarely came to the attention of their own families, much less the authorities. In an episode of scholar Henry Louis Gates's Public Broadcasting Service's 2014 television series *Finding Your Roots*, famed Harvard Law professor Alan Dershowitz was shown immigration documents he "had never seen before" of twenty-eight relatives, Polish Jews who entered the US fraudulently on the eve of World War II.[21] By contrast, Jews seeking to come to the US legally to escape the impending Holocaust—such as the father of Anne Frank, whose diary about living under Nazi occupation was required reading for generations of schoolchildren—were repeatedly denied entry, as recent scholarship has uncovered.[22]

Early in his career, Rodino was among other things an insurance salesman, factory worker, and employee of the Pennsylvania Railroad during the Depression. After working days and attending New Jersey Law School (which later became part of the Rutgers University system) at night, and then opening a law practice, Rodino ran unsuccessfully for the state assembly before enlisting in the army at the outbreak of World War II, serving in England, North Africa, and Italy, and winning the Bronze Star. He also earned decorations from the Republic of Italy for his postwar service as adjutant to the commanding general of Rome, a posting facilitated by his fluency in Italian. He lost his first race for Congress in 1946 but won on his second try in 1948.[23] Decades later, his official entry in the *Congressional Directory* still listed the *Cavaliere di Gran Croce of the Order of Al Merito della Republica* among numerous other honors; he was described as "a man proud of his awards."[24] He retained his seat as the district changed from "white ethnic" to majority African American, wrote experts, by being "an effective advocate of positions which black voters believe in . . . long before he had a black-majority constituency."[25]

Another critical constituency for urban Democrats was organized labor, which was agitating for measures to deal with the "illegal alien influx." Rodino was an unusually strong supporter of organized labor, with a 99 percent rating from the AFL-CIO.[26] Given labor's restrictionist leanings, it was natural that Rodino, chairman of the subcommittee with jurisdiction on the issue, in 1971 proposed legislation to repeal the Texas Proviso, thus making it unlawful for employers to hire unauthorized immigrants.[27] He presided over a series of hearings in 1971 and 1972, including six "field hearings outside of Washington, receiving testimony from some 200 witnesses," the vast majority of whom supported penalties on employers for hiring illegal immigrants.[28] But one witness, Anthony Bevilacqua, vice chancellor of the Diocese of Brooklyn who'd started the first local office for migration and refugees within the Catholic Church, introduced a new idea. At a hearing in March 1972, Bevilacqua made a startling call for "total amnesty" for unauthorized persons in the country, among the first prominent leaders to articulate a policy position that remained a controversial element of legislation for decades to come.[29]

Bevilacqua's plea wasn't reflected in legislation that moved to the House floor in 1972; Rodino's bill set up a system of graduated penalties, a warning for the first offense, then fines, and finally criminal penalties—sanctions—on employers that employed an unauthorized alien, a proposal henceforth known as employer sanctions. "Sanction" was an unfortunate label for the policy's proponents. Originating from a Latin word that meant "to render sacred or inviolable," for much of its history in English the term meant "to approve"; only in the twentieth century did it also come to mean "to penalize."[30] Unlike some other short-hand policy terms whose purposes are intuitively obvious—think minimum wage, Social Security, Medicare, or Head Start—*employer sanctions* is at best confusing. Proponents of the policy forever were hobbled by a label headlined by a "contranym" or an "autonym," a word that can be its own antonym.[31]

Terminology aside, replacing the Texas Proviso loophole with penalties against employers for hiring undocumented workers was controversial. Serious opposition came from the agricultural lobby, and conservatives attacked the proposal on libertarian grounds. Others, including Rep. Edward Roybal from California, pointed out that much illegal immigration from Mexico would have been lawful prior to the imposition of limits on Western Hemispheric migration initiated by the 1965 reforms; he called for raising legal immigration quotas for the "contiguous countries" of Canada and Mexico, eliminating incentives to enter illegally.[32] The argument that sanctioning employers for hiring unauthorized workers would cause employment discrimination was asserted by diverse opponents, including Rep. O. C. Fisher (D-TX), who'd voted against all of the civil rights bills in the House previously, and the only Puerto Rican representative,

Policy Primer: Employer Sanctions

"Employer sanctions" refer to a series of penalties on employers that "knowingly hire" people not authorized to work in the US. In theory, such sanctions reduce undocumented migration by shutting off the "magnet" of employment in two ways: (1) By deterring unauthorized entry because prospective undocumented immigrants would know they could not work legally; and (2) By encouraging existing unauthorized immigrants to return to their home countries for lack of stable employment prospects. The system eliminated the philosophical contradiction that existed prior to the Immigration Reform and Control Act of 1986, whereby it was illegal for people to enter or remain in the US without a visa, but entirely legal for employers to hire them.

Employer sanctions were designed to be implemented and enforced through what is known as a system of "employer verification," as follows:

- Each new hire would be required to demonstrate their identity and eligibility to work by producing one of several documents, including:
  o a "green card" or US passport, or similar document that demonstrates both identity (via a government-approved photo) and authorization to work (since "green cards" denote lawful permanent residence and passports are proof of American citizenship); OR
  o a document proving identity (like a state-issued driver's license or other government-issued ID with a photo), AND
  o a document providing eligibility to work (such as a work-authorized Social Security card or state-issued birth certificate).

- The employer would attest under penalty of perjury that the new hire had provided the requisite documents, and record the transaction on a government form required to be retained for three years.

During the IRCA era, the employer sanctions policy was:

- supported by the AFL-CIO and most of organized labor, some large business organizations such as the Business Roundtable, the NAACP, and advocates of immigration restriction such as the Federation for American Immigration Reform (FAIR)

- opposed by the US Chamber of Commerce as an unwarranted expansion of government authority that would increase costs on employers, and by Latino groups, some religious groups, and civil liberties advocates for fear the sanctions would lead to increased employment discrimination against lawful workers perceived to be "foreign"

Herman Badillo (D-NY), who warned that if the bill passed, "anyone who speaks with an accent and/or has the appearance of being Latin or Hispanic will be subject to questioning about their citizenship or immigration status."[33]

These concerns notwithstanding, with Congress rushing toward adjournment the bill passed by voice vote.[34] Rodino had few illusions that the Senate—where rural states were overrepresented in comparison to their larger urban counterparts and therefore was more favorable toward agricultural interests than the House—would act on the legislation. Sen. Ted Kennedy sponsored the companion bill in the Senate, where it died the expected, quiet death in the Judiciary Committee chaired by James Eastland (D-MS). Eastland was perhaps best known as one of the die-hard segregationists who filibustered against civil rights legislation in the 1950s and 1960s. Eastland opposed any legislation that could increase the government's power: his campaign literature bragged, "His record in slowing down, stalling, and even killing appointments and laws he considers against the best interests of the people is unsurpassed."[35] From his familiar perch as one of the "old bulls" that controlled the upper chamber's business, Eastland was, his colleagues said, "disengaged" from the formal work like attending hearings, passing bills, and making floor speeches. His energies were directed to his daily post-5:00 pm meetings, when "his people"—segregationists such as Southern Democrats Georgia's Richard Russell and South Carolina's Strom Thurmond and Republican leaders Everett Dirksen (R-IL) and Hugh Scott (R-PA)—came over to his office for a drink or two or three. "Everything that happened" in the Judiciary Committee, said one participant, was determined by these after-hours sessions.[36] A cotton farmer, Eastland was characterized by scholars as "a friend of the growers who opposed" the bill, and predictably declined to take any action on the legislation.[37]

Proponents of employer sanctions came back in 1973. Because Rodino had been elevated to the chairmanship of the full Judiciary Committee, the bill was managed by Rep. Joshua Eilberg (D-PA), the immigration subcommittee chair. During debate on the bill, Rep. Mario Biaggi (D-NY) became one of the first lawmakers to call for regularization of unauthorized immigrants; he asked for compassion for illegal aliens, citing a press release issued by Anthony Bevilacqua's Diocese of Brooklyn, which "urged measures that would regularize the status of illegal aliens by a certain date before the proposed [employer sanctions] legislation takes effect."[38] The Rodino-Eilberg employer sanctions bill passed by a vote of 297–63.[39] Under an open rule permitting unlimited amendments, the House adopted a major immigration reform bill in a matter of a few hours, perhaps the last time in its history that it would ever do so. But Eastland again declined to hold hearings, and blocked attempts by other senators to have the bill considered.[40]

FALSE STARTS

The nation was soon consumed by the climax of the scandal that had begun almost two years earlier when burglars with White House ties were caught inside the Democratic National Committee headquarters in the posh Watergate complex on the banks of the Potomac River. A month before consideration of the Rodino-Eilberg legislation, on May 17, 1973, the Senate Watergate Committee began its nationally televised hearings into the scandal.[41] The hearings made a folk hero of the committee's chair, North Carolina Democratic Sen. Sam Ervin, and would vault its ranking member, Tennessee Sen. Howard Baker into national prominence, as he summarized the core question, "What did the President know, and when did he know it?" But the Senate couldn't initiate formal measures to remove a sitting president; under the Constitution the upper body acts as a jury only if the House enacts an impeachment resolution. After the infamous October 1973 "Saturday Night Massacre" in which President Nixon instructed subordinates to fire Special Prosecutor Archibald Cox, twenty-two impeachment resolutions were introduced in the House and referred to the Judiciary Committee chaired by Peter Rodino.

Some expressed apprehension about Rodino's ability to manage the proceedings, suggesting that a special committee—with a different chairman—should be formed to handle the matter.[42] While humbled by the "awesome responsibility," Rodino insisted that his was the committee of jurisdiction and never backed down.[43] After wavering at first, Speaker Carl Albert (D-OK) allowed Rodino to handle the matter. Albert thought Rodino "a quiet man, of quiet talents," and that once the public saw the committee at work, it would see "that the members of Congress were not mediocrities or incompetents."[44] By early May 1974, the committee began public hearings on impeachment.[45] Rodino oversaw the process, noted close observers, with "great patience, caution, enormous energy, and fairness above all."[46] He labored to form a bipartisan coalition for impeachment, respectfully courting both Democratic and GOP swing voters on the committee.[47] He was aided by staff director Garner James "Jim" Cline, a holdover from Celler's staff.[48] Cline, who'd worked through law school as a Capitol elevator operator, had a brief moment in the spotlight when he called the roll of committee members as they voted on the impeachment question.[49] He was a player, if a somewhat mysterious one, on immigration policy for the next thirty years.

On the evening of July 24, 1974, on national television Rodino solemnly opened the committee's official consideration of articles of impeachment by invoking Roman "Emperor Justinian, from whose name the word 'justice' is derived," as providing the guiding principle over the body's work. The public watched as committee members debated the issues; especially impressive was

Rep. Barbara Jordan (D-TX), an African American who, with her trademark precise diction and impeccable logic laid out the case that the president had "counseled his aides to commit perjury, willfully disregarded the secrecy of grand jury proceedings, concealed surreptitious entry, and attempted to compromise a federal judge."[50] On July 27, the committee approved the first of three articles of impeachment that eventually passed, with six Republicans joining all twenty-one Democrats in recommending that the president be removed from office.[51] After the vote, which led to President Nixon's resignation two weeks later, Rodino went back to his office, and while discussing next steps with staffers, began shaking, broke into tears, and left the room to call his wife to tell her, "I pray we did the right thing. I hoped it didn't have to be this way."[52]

The national trauma brought on by the resignation of a sitting president almost, but not quite, brought action on immigration reform to a halt. Heeding Bevilacqua's call for "amnesty," Rodino and Eilberg, together with Senator Kennedy, drafted legislation "linking the employer sanctions idea with limited legalization and anti-discrimination provisions."[53] Their bill passed the Judiciary Committee in July 1975, but the sponsors decided not to move forward to the House floor. The committee's senior Republican, Rep. Robert McClory (R-IL), later indicated that Rodino had grown tired of moving legislation that the Senate failed to act on.[54] Still, the pairing of employer sanctions with some form of legalization established two critical policy lynchpins that characterized immigration reform legislation for decades to come. A harbinger of future events was Rodino's disinclination to move legislation in the House without first having some guarantee of Senate action, a development that would have a profound impact on future debates.

In 1975 Nixon's successor Gerald Ford's Domestic Council Committee on Illegal Aliens endorsed increased border enforcement, employer sanctions, and without providing specific details, some form of regularization for unauthorized immigrants in the US, declaring mass deportations both "inhumane and impractical . . . requiring police state [tactics] abhorrent to the American conscience."[55] Meanwhile, the *New York Times* reported that Eastland's immigration subcommittee had spent $2 million (about $ 9.5 million in 2017 dollars) over the previous decade without holding a single hearing or markup.[56] Eastland succumbed to pressure and actually introduced legislation and held a hearing, making it clear that he would not move a bill without a temporary worker program for agriculture.[57] But with Ford already a weak, unelected president further damaged by his unpopular pardon of President Nixon for Watergate-related offenses, progress on major immigration reform had to wait.[58] Still, Eastland formalized in proposed legislation a third critical lynchpin, together with enforcement and legalization, of "comprehensive" immigration reform: a "guestworker" program for agriculture.

One ostensibly "minor" bill did slip through just before Congress adjourned in 1976. The 1965 Act had not, as some hoped, resulted in an immediate reduction in legal immigration from Mexico, in part because hemispheric and per-country ceilings weren't applied to the Americas.[59] Subcommittee chair Eilberg had campaigned unsuccessfully for years to provide an equal number of visas and per-country limits to both Eastern and Western Hemispheres—despite higher demand for visas from the Americas generally—in effect completing the process begun in 1965. Eilberg's stalled bill also eliminated the long-standing informal custom that the immediate relatives of US citizens from Mexico would not be subject to deportation.[60] The bill would've remained dormant but for Eilberg's chance encounter with Manny Fierro, of El Congreso. As recounted by journalist Ellis Cose, Fierro told the lawmaker that if anything, immigration from Mexico should increase, suggesting "that maybe Eilberg should simply admit defeat and give up the fight for a Western Hemispheric" limit.[61]

Fierro's position was appropriate for a Hispanic advocate, given that Eilberg's bill would cut legal immigration from Mexico by more than half. At the time legal immigration from the US's southern neighbor averaged about sixty thousand annually, and was rising.[62] Nor was it the first time Eilberg had heard these views; Rep. Roybal and committee chair Rodino had both supported increased visas for Canada and Mexico.[63] Perceiving Fierro's statements as gloating, a dangerous tactic with a proud elected official, Eilberg responded "with a fury," promptly moving his bill through the House and personally walking over to the Senate to promote its passage; it was one of a flurry of bills passed "with dizzying speed" in the waning minutes of the Senate.[64] Gerald Ford reluctantly signed the bill, but according to historian Aristide Zolberg, the president: "criticized the rigid [per-country] ceiling provision and promised to submit legislation to increase the Mexican quota. Legal immigration from Mexico was immediately reduced by half, but given the ease of unauthorized entry, the consequences were obvious."[65]

Ford wasn't able to make good on his promise since he was defeated by Jimmy Carter later that year. Nor was there much interest from other policy makers to relieve growing backlogs of Mexicans seeking to legally enter the US, even though it seemed to Latino advocates that exceptions had been made for seemingly every other group—Europeans after World War II, Chinese after the Communist takeover there, Cubans fleeing Castro's dictatorship, Jews escaping the Soviet Union, and the initial trickle of Southeast Asian refugees finding their way to the country in numbers far exceeding official refugee quotas.[66]

One advocate who heard this story was future LULAC leader Arnoldo Torres, who'd worked briefly with Fierro at El Congreso. To Fierro's one-time protégé the incident showed that when it came to immigration the Mexican American community's interests were routinely undermined, with impunity, and that the "establishment" would punish those raising their voices to assert legitimate community interests. He thought it blatantly hypocritical for the government to engage in multiple repatriations, cut legal immigration from Mexico, end the bracero program without enforcing labor laws that could improve conditions for domestic workers, but turn around and complain about the entirely predictable increase in illegal Mexican immigration that followed.[67] The episode was an "outrageous" example of immigration legislation blatantly unfair to their community, enacted without fair consideration being given to Hispanic perspectives, and Torres "vowed never to let such a thing happen again."[68]

Seven months into his administration, without consulting with congressional or constituency group leaders, in 1977 President Carter proposed his own immigration reforms, including: (1) sanctions against employers engaged in a "pattern or practice" of hiring undocumented aliens and use of the Social Security card as the designated identification document for employee eligibility; (2) beefed-up Border Patrol forces at the Mexican border; and (3) an amnesty program granting permanent resident status for all aliens living in the country prior to 1970.[69]

Given the growing consensus among Latino advocates that employer sanctions would result in employment discrimination against their community and deepening unease with calls for tougher restrictions on immigration overall, out of the gate the "National Council of La Raza joined MALDEF, LULAC, the ACLU, church lobbies, and lawyers groups" to coordinate a vigorous lobbying campaign against the Carter proposals, one scholar wrote. They also called for a more generous legalization than Carter's, which excluded those who entered the US after 1970.[70]

The harsh public criticism of the Carter proposals from Hispanic groups was hurtful to INS commissioner Leonel Castillo, one of the president's highest-ranking Latinos. Castillo started his career as an activist fighting for more educational opportunity for minorities in Houston, eventually winning appointments to the boards of MALDEF, NCLR, and the National Urban League. In 1971, he was an unexpected winner of a race for the city comptroller, where he earned a reputation even among business groups that had opposed his election as a strong, sophisticated, and fiscally conservative manager of the city's finances. By 1976, he was a Carter delegate to the Democratic Convention, someone political experts thought might be "the first member of an ethnic minority group to be elected to statewide office" in Texas.[71] His INS post, a reporter wrote, required Commissioner Castillo to navigate: "criticism from fellow Hispanics, who feared he would 'sell them out' to secure his position, and the Anglos—including many in his own bureaucracy—who assumed he was in his job only to take care of 'his own people.'"[72]

But if anyone had the savvy and skill to pull it off, it seemed that Castillo, one of the few Mexican American politicians of his generation able to earn the support of both the activists and the establishment, might. Carter likely expected Castillo to manage or at least neutralize Latinos' advocacy on the Carter administration plan. But those hopes were dashed by their opposition to the Carter immigration proposals. Ironically, some Latino advocates viewed their opposition posture as purely "tactical," designed to give Castillo greater bargaining power to improve the plan as it went through further administration and congressional proceedings.[73] The plan was, in the vernacular, "dead on arrival"; Jerry Tinker, who staffed Ted Kennedy's immigration subcommittee, said of the proposals: "It was vintage Carter—no consultation with outside groups, no consultation with Congress. It was a mess and it wasn't going anywhere, which is exactly what we would have told the President had we been brought in ahead of time."[74]

For congressional leaders, "immigration, it seemed, was a no-win issue." Especially for Kennedy, contemplating a future run for the presidency, the issue of employer sanctions put him squarely in the crossfire between two constituencies, organized labor and Hispanics, that would form key parts of his political base.[75] But if immigration policy worried Kennedy, after introduction of his aborted proposals it was completely off President Carter's radar screen, garnering not a single mention in an otherwise extremely detailed diary of his time in office.[76]

In 1978 Kennedy, Rodino, and Eilberg prevailed on Congress to authorize and Carter to support creation of a Select Commission on Immigration and Refugee Policy, with a virtually unlimited mandate to review "the entire issue of immigration."[77] With the exception of the increasingly difficult question of refugee admissions, there was no legislative action on immigration issues until well after the Select Commission issued its report more than three years later.

THE COMMISSION

Punting a controversial issue to an advisory body is often the equivalent of sending the issue to the graveyard; the annals of policy making are filled with examples of commission reports that did nothing more than gather dust on bookshelves, often unread much less acted on.

This commission was different. It was chaired by Father Theodore "Ted" Hesburgh, head of Notre Dame University, past chairman of the US Commission on Civil Rights, and confidant of US presidents and foreign chiefs of state. Father Ted was perhaps the most respected public personage of his era. A man of rare political and intellectual gifts, he was simultaneously "the most influential priest in America," and one willing to "stand up to the Roman Catholic hierarchy," described as a recipient of "more than a dozen White House appointments under six presidents" who was "never awed by the power of the Oval Office."[78] Handsome, articulate, silver-haired but athletic and physically vigorous, the supremely self-confident Hesburgh was the very embodiment of the fair-minded "wise man," not just nonpartisan but seemingly above partisanship itself, required to untangle the thorny issue of immigration.

The Select Commission included four senators and four representatives from the congressional committees of jurisdiction, who were expected to turn its recommendations into legislation, and four Cabinet officials who were responsible for implementing a law and who, in theory, had substantive expertise. The Select Commission also included independent appointees including two Latinos and an Asian American, representatives of the ethnic groups most likely to be affected by a new law. The commission's members collectively presented to the public, and particularly opinion makers, an impressive, formidable aura of sober, thoughtful, expert opinion in an era when public opinion polls documented consistently higher levels of respect for government bodies than in recent years.[79]

Its executive director was Lawrence Fuchs, who headed a team of some fifty staff and consultants, many of whom were or would soon become highly respected experts in the field. Fuchs was an important player in his own right; a full professor in American studies at Brandeis University, he was especially well known as an expert on ethnic groups, having published the seminal work in the field, *American Ethnic Politics*, a decade earlier. And he was unusually well connected in elite circles; he once team-taught courses with Eleanor Roosevelt and later was an advisor on ethnic affairs to then senator John F. Kennedy just before his presidential run.[80] The son of an Austrian immigrant, Fuchs served as a navy medic during World War II, graduated from New York University, went to Harvard to pursue his doctorate, and began teaching at Brandeis; he soon became one of the most respected and popular professors on campus.[81] Fuchs was an avowed political pluralist—the term *multiculturalist* was not yet invented—with strong ties to ethnic groups, having once served on MALDEF's board of directors. He was thus a shrewd choice for those thinking of moving legislation in what was, in 1978 when he was selected, the Democratically controlled Congress. But Fuchs also appealed to moderate and conservative thinkers in both political parties; he was firmly opposed to racial preferences.[82]

Although the Select Commission's report was later than originally expected, released in late February 1981, at the beginning of the Reagan administration instead of during Carter's tenure, one cause of the delay was its apparent thoroughness and even-handedness. Fuchs and his staff produced dozens of briefing papers, and contracted with some forty scholars to conduct research and produce policy reports. Cabinet agencies produced special papers for the commission, as did the Library of Congress and the Bureau of the Census. The commission held a dozen formal hearings across the country to complement another two dozen invitation-only, often daylong working "consultations" with government officials and experts in DC. Learning from Carter's failure to touch base with key constituencies, Hesburgh and Fuchs, it seemed, followed a process to ensure that every conceivable interest had a fair shot at getting its views heard.

And both could be sticklers for process while also using creative consensus-building maneuvers. At the Select Commission, Hesburgh often began consideration of issues with informal straw votes followed by detailed discussions, then dispatched Fuchs to engage commissioners individually or in small groups to try and forge consensus. Early on it was decided that only the members themselves, and not staffers, were allowed to vote, which once forced Secretary of State Cyrus Vance to reschedule congressional testimony so he could vote at a commission meeting. Fuchs later correctly observed that this commission was not just substantively robust but "highly political," much more than the typical government "study commission."[83]

One highly sophisticated procedural step postponed final decisions until the end of the process, as commissioner Alan Simpson later noted, to ensure that decisions would not "go out to the troops" in pieces, protecting the commissioners from outside constituency pressures.[84] While meeting notices and agendas, official proceedings, and formal votes were all a matter of public record, much of the real action took place in dinner meetings closed to the public and the media. Hesburgh and Fuchs were highly skilled advocates, carefully building up the importance of the upcoming commission report in the press. Both were quoted in a *New York Times* article in May 1980 that focused on a number of potential new directions in immigration policy, and a later *Times* piece observed that the commission's extensive research already had made "a permanent contribution to the debate" and was the "most authoritative Government study of the issue."[85] Fuchs also reacted quickly to public criticism. When the ACLU warned that a new worker identification system being considered by the commission would be "tantamount to a domestic passport," Fuchs responded immediately by listing a series of safeguards to prevent abuses.[86]

Latino organizations complained that "they had not been adequately consulted" during the commission's deliberations.[87] Others charged that with its decision making behind closed doors, commissioners were free to "advocate positions they would not defend in public."[88] This was, of course, precisely the point. Hesburgh and Fuchs weren't interested in fractious public debates on individual parts of their proposal; they wanted to build support for their whole package. Indeed, as the commission began planning its final meeting on December 6 and 7, 1980, at an isolated rural retreat facility, according to researcher Rosanna Perotti's review of internal commission documents: "Hesburgh and Fuchs sought to have the meeting closed to the press and public ostensibly because national security matters would be discussed, but more pointedly to enable the commissioners to express themselves openly. Once there, participants agreed that having a closed meeting facilitated frankness. The press lobbied vigorously for an open meeting and got it on December 7; when commissioners could come to no agreement concerning numerical limitations [on legal immigration], they hammered it out at lunchtime—in private."[89]

The commission's official thirteen-volume final report, a single volume of which was about the size of a ream of paper in its original oversized printing with a red, white, and blue cover, offered 270 pages of "proceedings"—the choices presented to the commissioners, the details of each vote taken, and various exhibits including additional and dissenting views of a few members and summaries of the commission's contracts, hearings, and consultations. The House Judiciary Committee later produced a smaller, more manageable version of this document, known as a "committee print" of this "proceedings" report.[90] An even larger companion appendix included selected research studies and background papers; immediately it became the single most important reference document in the field, dog-eared copies of which could be found frequently on the shelves of academics, congressional staffers, and advocates alike. Of the thirteen volumes of the report, two were devoted to a complete rewriting of the Immigration and Nationality Act.[91]

But the commission's actual recommendations, while broad in scope, amounted to far less than a wholesale rewrite of the law. The direction of its recommendations was illustrated by Hesburgh's metaphor of "closing the back door to undocumented/illegal migration" while "opening the front door a little more to accommodate legal migration in the interests of the country."[92] The commission's measures to address illegal immigration, according to Fuchs, were analogous to a three-legged stool wherein each separate leg was crucial to the success of the overall policy: border enforcement, mainly through increased resources for the Border Patrol; employer sanctions: instituting a series of graduated penalties on employers for knowingly hiring unauthorized workers; and legalization of long-term undocumented residents of the US.

In addition to the three legs of Fuchs's symbolic stool, the commission proposed maintaining the existing legal immigration system, with a "flexible cap" of 350,000, together with an additional 500,000 visas over five years to reduce backlogs, producing what it believed would be a modest increase in legal entries. The panel pronounced itself opposed to a "large scale" guestworker program, but open to "slight expansion" of existing, so-called H-2 temporary worker provisions in current law, attempting to finesse the agricultural labor question that had dogged previous reform efforts. It supported modest procedural changes, such as reduced numbers of appeals, to crack down on a perceived increase in fraudulent or frivolous asylum claims. On the thorny question of how to ensure

Policy Primer: Legalization

Legalization, or "amnesty," refers to a policy to allow certain previously undocumented people to come forward and apply for regularization of their status. Legalization was often posited as a more humane alternative to mass deportation policies that would endanger the civil rights and civil liberties of lawful US residents. It was also designed to make future enforcement more effective by: (1) "wiping the slate clean" of much of the preexisting unauthorized population; and (2) providing law enforcement with data about methods of illicit entry and employment that could be used to target resources more effectively.

Eligibility for legalization was limited to undocumented immigrants that could demonstrate certain factors designed to ensure that only longer-term residents would qualify and to prevent the program from serving as an incentive to further unlawful migration, including:

- entry into the US prior to a cutoff date

- continuous residence, with minor exceptions, in the US since the cutoff date

- continuous physical presence in the US since the date of enactment of the statute

As ultimately enacted, with limited exceptions, successful applicants also could not otherwise be "excludable" under US law—for example, they could not be likely to become a "public charge"—could not have committed a felony or more than three misdemeanors, and had to either pass an English/civics test or be enrolled in a government-approved course. Applicants were required to pay a fee covering the cost of the program, complete an application demonstrating their eligibility, and be interviewed by a government official.

During the IRCA era, legalization was:

- supported by Hispanic groups, religious organizations, and much of organized labor

- opposed by advocates of immigration restriction such as the Federation for American Immigration Reform (FAIR)

the effectiveness of employer sanctions, the commission largely punted, calling merely for a "more secure system of identification" without specifying how employers were to distinguish between authorized and unauthorized workers, thus avoiding accusations that it was proposing a national identification system.[93]

Although any one individual leg of the three-legged stool might be opposed by one interest or another, the package taken as a whole appeared to be the triumph of moderation, and reflected careful political calculation as well. It leaned toward traditional labor liberals and immigration restrictionists by including border enforcement and employer sanctions, offered Hispanics and pro-immigration advocates a generous legalization program, and sought to satisfy those weary of a series of refugee crises with measures to reduce asylum abuse without excessively curtailing legal protections. It offered modest increases in legal immigration but addressed those who worried about demographic change with a new overall limit or cap on legal immigration. And, in the vernacular, the report "showed a little leg" on the issue of temporary workers, not revealing quite how far its congressional patrons would go to placate agriculture, but hinting that it would be far enough. The *New York Times* noted "a nearly unbroken chorus of favorable comments" on the commission's recommendations.[94] And if the commission's gravitas, weighty report, and fawning media coverage weren't enough, its timing was exquisite.

John Kingdon, one of the most influential of modern political scientists, wrote that major legislative reforms require the convergence of each of three streams—a problem stream, a policy stream, and sufficient political will. This meant that existence of solutions like the recommendations of the Select Commission ("policy stream") aren't actionable until something like a "precipitating event," brings a "problem stream" to public attention and forces politicians to act.[95] The 1979–1981 Cuban–Haitian boatlifts, in which some 130,000 Cubans and 40,000 Haitians came to Florida, was immigration reform's "precipitating event."

BOAT PEOPLE

The Cuban exodus began in 1980, when six dissidents entered the Peruvian embassy in Havana seeking asylum; the country's dictator Fidel Castro permitted them, and thousands of others, to leave the island. President Carter at first welcomed the "refugees seeking freedom from Communist domination" with an "open heart and open arms."[96] His aides tried to walk back the seemingly unlimited welcome, and Carter himself soon reversed course, demanding a more managed, orderly process, but in the words of one scholar "the damage was done."[97] Before it ended nearly 125,000 additional Marielitos, named after Mariel, the Cuban port from which most had exited, had arrived in South Florida.

Haitians had been leaving their own island dictatorship for decades; one esti-mate was that one-eighth (12.5 percent) of the population fled in the years the country was ruled by "Presidents-for-Life" François "Papa Doc" Duvalier begin-ning in 1957, and his son Jean-Claude "Baby Doc," who took over in 1971. Few Haitian emigres initially came to the US, opting to cross the land border to the Dominican Republic or for the short hop to the Bahamas. But as repression grew more brutal over time, and as their neighbors increased enforcement, increasing numbers came to the US; a few were able to enter legally, but many more were unauthorized.[98] Only a small number sought asylum; as of 1979, only 10,000 Haitians had applied for political asylum in the US, and little wonder, since only 55 of the claims had been granted.[99] Discrimination in the Dominican Republic, crackdowns in the Bahamas, and the apparent welcome afforded Mariel Cubans led more Haitians to try and enter the US "across 800 miles of hazardous ocean in flimsy sailboats."[100] By 1980, some 40,000 had arrived on US shores.[101]

The treatment of the two groups couldn't have been more different. As Fidel Castro came to power in 1958 through 1965, some 960,000 Cubans fled the island dictatorship for the US in several distinct waves. While virtually all were "paroled"—a temporary protection against deportation awarded at the discre-tion of the attorney general—per-country limits on legal immigration applied to the Americas in 1965 meant that except for the few immediate relatives of US citizens, only 20,000 could receive permanent resident status every year. Against the backdrop of the Cold War and the recent Cuban Missile Crisis, in 1966 Con-gress passed the Cuban Adjustment Act. The act codified parole status, meaning that although it remained theoretically discretionary, in practice almost no Cubans except convicted hardened criminals were ever denied entry or deported.[102] The act also allowed the government to "award permanent resi-dency to any Cuban who is paroled into and physically present for one year" in the US regardless of the per-country limits on legal immigration.[103] It was, schol-ars noted, "an open-ended entitlement [to permanent residence] for all Cubans" who reached US soil.[104]

By contrast, almost no Haitians were afforded legal status. Fearing "a flood of 'economic refugees,'" the INS set up procedures critics said were designed to "cur-tail severely the right to request asylum." The National Council of Churches sued the INS in 1976, demanding that the agency bring its rules into line with the United Nations conventions governing treatment of refugees. After losing in lower courts, and with the case set for consideration by the Supreme Court, in November 1977 the Service agreed to revise its regulations, but soon, legal scholars wrote, the "INS would once again, but with greater urgency, return to the enjoined practices."[105] As the influx grew, INS set up a special Haitian program; in 1978–1979, wrote one academic, the "INS processed thousands of Haitian cases through this program and rejected every single application." More litigation followed, culminating in

Haitian Refugee Center v. Civiletti in 1980, in which a federal judge found "a pattern of discrimination" against Haitians, in which the government "willfully and systematically violated" its own procedures.[106] Two Justice Department attorneys implementing the policy resigned, one for "reasons of conscience" and the other due to "moral doubts" about the INS's actions; one of them later said "the Haitians were singled out for discriminatory action in order to make an example out of them."[107] It was difficult to avoid the conclusion that the real basis for excluding Haitians was their race.[108]

But against a backdrop of stagflation—the deadly combination of economic stagnation and high inflation—and the Iranian hostage crisis, the influx to Florida felt like a national security crisis. Some observed the refugee crisis led directly to the defeat of President Carter in Florida in 1980, a crucial battleground state he'd carried four years earlier.[109] It wasn't responsible for Carter's loss—Ronald Reagan had a ten-point popular vote margin and an electoral college landslide and the dominant campaign was the Iranian hostage crisis—but politicians' sensitivity to the dangers potentially posed by appearing "soft" on immigration issues was certainly heightened as a result.

According to one student of the Select Commission on Immigration and Refugee Policy, in this atmosphere its "work gave the search for answers to the immigration dilemma the characteristics of a crusade—a crusade driven by ostensibly neutral parties."[110] The legislation it recommended was to be carried by the bipartisan team of Alan Simpson and Romano Mazzoli, new chairs of the Senate and House immigration subcommittees, two appealing, energetic, and serious legislators. In a world that appeared to be spinning out of control, the commission's recommendations and the bill it spawned seemed in Capitol Hill parlance a safe horse to ride to the rescue of the long-intractable issue of immigration policy.

THE BACKDROP

However, in those first early days of the Reagan presidency in 1981 immigration was hardly a first-tier policy question. Even in the context of the Cuban–Haitian refugee crisis, the Select Commission on Immigration and Refugee Policy faced serious competition as it tried to draw congressional attention to its report. President Reagan's new administration had swept into power barely a month before. Lines were being drawn in what became epic policy battles between Reagan—who ran on a now familiar but then novel supply-side economics platform calling for major cuts in federal tax rates and domestic spending programs—and the unapologetically liberal Massachusetts representative Thomas "Tip" O'Neill, Speaker of the House, who proudly opposed both the tax and budget reductions. O'Neill, who had ascended to the Speakership in 1977, had a difficult relationship with Jimmy Carter, who was known for his prickly interactions with Capitol Hill.[111] After the internecine squabbles with Carter, some sensed O'Neill was itching for a no-holds-barred partisan brawl on budget and tax policy to test the new Republican president's mettle.

The Speaker seemed to have the upper hand, given Democrats' 243–192 advantage in the House, even after Republicans had gained 33 seats in 1980. But appearances could be deceptive; nearly 50 Democratic "boll weevils," conservatives or moderates mainly from the South, heavily outnumbered liberal or moderate Republicans, mainly from the Northeast. There was a likely bipartisan ideological majority for much of Reagan's agenda, but with a caveat: the House leadership was solidly liberal and controlled scheduling of legislation and other institutional levers of power. Since Reagan's victory was accompanied by a Republican takeover of the Senate, the upper body seemed likely to go along with much, if not all, of Reagan's agenda.[112] Congressional consideration of the new president's budget and tax proposals was a conflict for the ages, a clash of ideology with real, substantive issues at stake involving two outsized personalities in Reagan and O'Neill.

The change in administration coincided with massive transition in the civil rights community. After a series of profoundly important Supreme Court wins and legislative victories in the 1950s and 1960s, policy progress stalled, and the civil rights establishment was on the defensive.[113] Personnel changes added to the civil rights community's discomfort. The head of the NAACP's Washington Bureau, Clarence Mitchell Jr., so prominent that he was called The 101st Senator, had retired a year earlier, succeeded by Althea Simmons, a longtime NAACP staffer trusted by the executive director Rev. Benjamin Hooks, himself a relatively new leader. Simmons had a powerful presence, but anyone who succeeded Mitchell had less stature in elite Washington circles than her legendary predecessor. Less than two years earlier, in 1979, another crucial player in the civil rights arena, the AFL-CIO, had undergone its own leadership change, as Lane Kirkland replaced George Meany, who'd headed the labor organization since the mid-1950s. Although certain elements of organized labor, like the rest of society, had been hostile to the advancement of minorities, by the 1980s the AFL-CIO was a dominant player in the civil rights movement. During the halcyon days of the movement unions provided the money, the political muscle, and organizational backing that pushed civil rights bills over the finish line; the AFL-CIO assigned its top lobbyists to support the effort, and even paid the salaries of key staff of certain civil rights groups.[114]

The changes played out within the Leadership Conference on Civil Rights, a broad-based coalition of civil rights, religious, and labor organizations; the literature of the epic civil rights battles of the 1960s is replete with references to LCCR's role, perhaps best described as providing the "inside lobbying game" in Washington to complement the "outside game" of the famous mass-protest organizations such as Martin Luther King's Southern Christian Leadership Conference (SCLC), James Farmer's Congress for Racial Equality (CORE), and John Lewis's Student Nonviolent Coordinating Committee (SNCC).[115] In addition to turnover of key players within its ranks, the coalition, which heretofore had focused mainly on the African American civil rights agenda, faced pressures from women's groups, Hispanic and Asian organizations, disability rights advocates, and others demanding a greater say in the civil rights agenda.[116] LCCR was undergoing its own transition, as its principals—general counsel Joseph Rauh from Americans for Democratic Action, cofounder and executive secretary Arnold Aronson of the National Community Relations Advisory Council (whose acronym NCRAC was pronounced "Knack-Rack" by insiders), and executive director Marvin Caplan from the AFL-CIO—retired or reduced their roles. Former Capitol Hill staffer Ralph G. Neas, who'd just emerged from a life-threatening bout with Guillain-Barré syndrome, a nervous system disorder, was taking the helm of the large and powerful but frequently unwieldy civil rights coalition.[117] Neas's first challenge was reauthorization of the Voting Rights Act, arguably the flagship legislative achievement of the civil rights movement during its glory days two decades earlier.

And that battle took place in the shadows of an earlier struggle between Latino and African American advocates. During the voting rights bill's previous extension in 1975, the law was extended to more areas with large Hispanic populations, and new "language assistance" provisions, including bilingual ballots for Latino and other voters not fully literate in English, were added. The NAACP's Clarence Mitchell thought the provisions might sink the whole bill, telling reporters that, "If you've got something that is working, you want to make sure you don't improve it out of existence."[118] He instead urged two separate bills, "one for blacks and one for Latinos, saying the groups would support each other's bills," an approach that assured the death of the new provisions covering Hispanics.[119] As described by LCCR executive director Caplan:

> The Hispanic Americans, represented by the National Council of La Raza, set off several bitter confrontations. Among their goals were the institution of bilingual education programs in the schools and their inclusion in the protections of the Voting Rights Act. The latter objective resulted in a head-on collision between La Raza representatives and Clarence Mitchell. . . . Things came to a head in an unforgettable and shocking moment, when Clarence lost his temper . . . and shouted: "Blacks were dying for the right to vote when *you people* couldn't decide whether you were Caucasians [emphasis added]."[120]

It was a clear case of people with good intentions but limited knowledge talking past each other. Mitchell likely had missed Latinos' perspective that their community was discriminated against for more than a century, not based solely on skin color—although many indigenous-looking Hispanics had been subject to such bias—but on characteristics such as surname, speech accent, and language. There had indeed been considerable debate within the Mexican American community about where they fit in a black–white racial paradigm created without taking them into account, a debate that to an extent continues today. But since the 1970s, MALDEF and NCLR, especially, had worked hard to position Latinos as allies of African Americans on civil rights issues. Mitchell probably was unaware of this history of Mexican American civil rights activism, given that even today few school textbooks cover this perspective.[121]

Latinos' position that discrimination against their community in the electoral process was sufficient to warrant protection under the Voting Rights Act was confirmed both by scholarly research and congressional findings.[122] But such was Mitchell's prestige that his opposition alone could have killed the new voting rights protections for Latinos. With help from the LCCR's "wise men"—executive director Caplan, general counsel Rauh, and executive secretary Arnold Aronson—the dispute was resolved in favor of Latinos, and ultimately they were covered by the 1975 Voting Rights Act extension. Mainly a behind-the-scenes player, Aronson was "quick witted, skilled at repartee" and an important strategist universally respected in civil rights circles; he was also completely unafraid of anyone. After John Kennedy's election in 1960, Aronson and the NAACP's Roy Wilkins met with him at the Carlyle in New York to urge quick action on civil rights; the president-elect responded, "Are you two out of your minds?" Aronson wasn't shy about expressing his own displeasure, remarking that while Kennedy ordered and ate a room service lunch during the meeting, "The son of a bitch didn't even offer us a cup of coffee."[123] That fearlessness led Aronson and Rauh to confront Mitchell, persuading him to back off. NCLR president Raul Yzaguírre credited Aronson for the 1975 Act's coverage of Latinos, noting, "He stood up for our community when it was unfashionable to do so."[124] But the incident also embedded in Yzaguírre's psyche the notion that within the LCCR, Hispanic issues often were an afterthought, a perspective he painfully and publicly expressed fifteen years later at the LCCR's fortieth anniversary dinner over an internal dispute over immigration policy.[125]

The entire Voting Rights Act had to be reauthorized again in 1982; as a concession to opponents, the previous 1975 extension was good for only seven years, compared to the original act's ten-year authorization. A group of largely untested leaders, many of whom had never worked together before, were charged with preserving the act, and thus the legacy of Thurgood Marshall, Martin Luther King, and others who had brought down the barriers of segregation and state-sanctioned discrimination that had stained so much of America's past.[126] It remained to be seen whether the fragile coalition would hold together, given the tension and history of misunderstanding between Latinos and African Americans, the bill's two principal beneficiaries.

With epic battles over the federal budget, tax policy, and civil rights, as well as Cold War tensions, it seemed unlikely that a second-tier issue like immigration, which had not undergone a significant legislative reform since 1965, eventually would become a major focus of three successive Congresses. But policy entrepreneurs Alan Simpson and Romano Mazzoli were determined to enact the third immigration reform in the twentieth century. They eventually succeeded, but only after a bloody, six-year battle with members of a new organization, eventually named the National Immigration, Refugee and Citizenship Forum.*

BIRTH OF A MOVEMENT

On February 26, 1981, as winter began a slow turn toward spring in the nation's capital, a press conference was held to announce a new organization. In a city where dozens of press conferences, few of which actually involve real news, are held on a daily basis, the event wasn't noteworthy. Announcing a new organization in Washington, DC, where allegedly new groups often are made up of the usual suspects sporting a different letterhead or have deceptive names designed to confuse more than illuminate, wouldn't ordinarily draw much attention anyway. The organization sported a more-than-a-little-awkward name of the National Forum on Immigration and Refugee Policy. It had no budget, no IRS-approved nonprofit tax status, and a single volunteer staffer, founder Dale Frederick "Rick" Swartz, then on the payroll of the Alien Rights Project of the Washington Lawyers Committee for Civil Rights and Urban Affairs.

The new group wasn't a coalition, because its members didn't have a shared policy agenda. Nor was it an advocacy organization; its bylaws included the explicit disclaimer that it would "not speak for its members" on policy issues. Its stated purpose was to "stimulate and coordinate systematic, policy focused working relationships and communications networks that span the range of issues, interests and disciplines involved in immigration, refugee and related foreign policy matters."[127] The collection of disparate interests with a vague mission and structure may not have appeared ready for prime time, but Swartz hoped his Forum would catalyze an "immigrants' rights" field, analogous to the civil rights field that had passed landmark legislation in the 1960s.[128]

In his early thirties, Rick Swartz had no shortage of vision or audacity. Raised in a comfortable, upper-middle-class household, Swartz was both an

---

* Now known simply as the National Immigration Forum.

exceptional student and a high school baseball star. He recalled anti-Semitic slurs on the baseball diamond from players who mistakenly assumed his last name was the more common, often Jewish Schwartz; the taunts and epithets provided him at least modest insight about what it must feel like to be discriminated against, he believed. He adopted what turned out to be a lifelong "activist orientation" toward social justice issues in college at Amherst; after graduating from the University of Chicago Law School, in 1975 he landed a coveted position in the pro bono department at Hogan and Hartson, one of the largest and most influential law firms in Washington, DC. An irony of the profession is that the most prestigious law firms attract the best students but then assign them to do the legal equivalent of manual labor. Although well compensated, junior associates at the firms work notoriously long hours on arcane technical matters. Legal ethics require all lawyers to perform some free legal assistance, a mandate often honored in the breach, but major firms take this responsibility seriously. While they do grunt work for paying clients, associates in the typical pro bono case are deeply engaged in strategy and tactics, sometimes on matters that reach the Supreme Court. Swartz received an extraordinary grounding on issues at the nexus of race and the law, serving on the legal teams representing the NAACP and MALDEF, distinguishing himself such that he received several unprecedented extensions of the normal tenure in the pro bono division. But Swartz thought his future lay in the public interest arena, and he found work at the Lawyer's Committee.[129]

The press conference announcing formation of the National Forum on Immigration and Refugee Policy didn't make much news, although it was mentioned at the very bottom of a *New York Times* article covering the generally favorable reaction to the Select Commission's report. The *Times* quoted Swartz as warning: "Many of us have strong objections to the commission's recommendations and analysis, but we are, in effect, holding our fire. We want to study it very carefully, and where we disagree, we want to offer well reasoned alternatives."[130]

It would have been unlikely to think a new, not-quite coalition with a cumbersome moniker and an ambiguous, largely undefined purpose could challenge legislation endorsed by the Select Commission that had the support of the vast majority of the nation's opinion leaders. But such was Swartz's vision that he successfully positioned the two dozen members of his brand-new organization as the principal counterweight to the Select Commission.

Three years earlier, in 1978, as a new staffer at the Alien Rights Project, Swartz found himself in a small network of activist attorneys focused on treatment of Haitian refugees, including Ira Gollobin, the "godfather" of the modern immigration bar, a private attorney who'd cofounded the leftist National Lawyers Guild, and was then general counsel of both the National Council of

Churches and the American Committee for the Protection of the Foreign Born, the national office of its Los Angeles-based affiliate that had been one of the few organizations to protest against Operation Wetback. Another was Ira Kurzban, a Miami-based attorney in private practice who would go on to literally write the book on immigration law: the first edition of *Kurzban's Immigration Law Sourcebook* was published in 1990; its fourteenth edition was released in 2014.[131] The network also included Peter Schey, an immigrant from South Africa, still among the most prominent and prolific litigators in the field.[132] Together, and sometimes separately, over 1977–1981, they filed a series of lawsuits against the government's treatment of Haitian refugees that according to one scholar "prevailed in nearly every case."[133]

Swartz, who because of his DC base was the point man for larger policy discussions, negotiated with the Carter administration's decision makers on Haiti, briefed the Reagan transition team on immigration and refugee issues, and formed close relationships with Rep. Shirley Chisholm (D-NY), DC delegate Walter Fauntroy, the Rev. Jesse Jackson, and others concerned about treatment of Haitian refugees. This led the Congressional Black Caucus into "its first major foray into foreign affairs and migration policy," Swartz recalled, as he evolved from a "lawyer's lawyer, organizing *pro bono* litigation to getting more involved in policy debates," and liking the shift more and more.[134] As his policy work brought him in contact with advocates for Hispanics, Asians, and other immigrant communities, he saw that they shared a common interest in promoting more welcoming policies and attitudes toward newcomers in general.[135]

The intense, chain-smoking Swartz saw a vacuum, since there was no equivalent to the Leadership Conference on Civil Rights: an "organization of organizations" for the immigration field.[136] He found many kindred spirits. "We realized we needed a broader umbrella," said one early Forum member, "one that would be better organized, not to speak with a single voice, but to unify various ragtag groups that supported immigrant rights."[137] Initial members attending its seminal February 1981 press conference included Muzaffar Chishti, director of the immigration project at the International Ladies' Garment Workers' Union, representing Jay Mazur, the Forum's acting chairman and a rising power within the union; Phyllis Eisen, government affairs director at Zero Population Growth; Michael Myers of Church World Service; Ron Gibbs, representing the City of Chicago; Pat Craig, who headed the legislative affairs unit for the National Association of Counties; Gary Rubin, deputy national affairs director of the American Jewish Committee; the American Friends Service Committee's Aurora Camacho DeSchmidt; Norman Hill of the A. Philip Randolph Institute; Michael Hooper from the Lawyers Committee for International Human Rights; and Antonia Hernández, director of MALDEF's office in DC.[138] But this was just the beginning.

Soon, the Forum's leaders were deeply engaged in merger negotiations with the American Immigration and Citizenship Conference. AICC, whose members included some of the old-line, "white ethnic" organizations with roots going back to World War I and before, was a venerable institution. It had played a major role in eliminating the discriminatory national origins quota system in 1965, its conferences featured luminaries such as Sen. Ted Kennedy as keynote speakers, and its fundraising events earned coverage in the *New York Times.*[139] But its membership had fallen from a high of over ninety in the 1960s to perhaps fifty in the early 1980s, as the inflow of immigrants and refugees from war-ravaged Europe slowed.[140] AICC had several powerful attractions for the emerging Forum. One was purely administrative; it already had nonprofit tax-exempt status. Many of its members continued to be important players in the immigration and refugee field and Swartz was eager to gain its membership *en masse*, which was much more efficient than recruiting each individually.

AICC's central role in the immigration field remained extraordinarily valuable symbolically. Among its board members were the most recognized figures in the "old guard," such as scholar Read Lewis, an attorney who'd worked with the settlement house movement and was a cofounder of *Common Ground* magazine, one of the first American publications to concentrate on questions of ethnicity.[141] *Common Ground* published numerous influential articles, including "The Democratic War Effort" by Eleanor Roosevelt, praising the role of immigrants in World War II, and Langston Hughes's "White Folks Do the Funniest Things," a satirical piece on the irrationality of discrimination, which was subsequently widely syndicated.[142] AICC was a direct link to Horace Kallen and other original framers of the cultural pluralism school that fought the "Know Nothing" political party's virulent nativism from the Civil War through the turn of the century.[143] Gaining its imprimatur would allow the new Forum to trace its lineage directly back to the original cultural pluralists, whose vision had triumphed in the 1965 immigration act.

Some pieces fell into place quickly. Swartz was an impressive presence, combining powerful analytical and public speaking skills with strong passion; he was an effective proselytizer, able to discuss both politics and policy with an insider's knowledge. San Antonio mayor Henry Cisneros, probably the most important Hispanic politician of his generation, later referred to Swartz as "my go-to guy on immigration."[144] Conservative commentators observed that even in meetings of Wall Street whizzes, Swartz was often "the smartest guy in the room."[145] But he was neither detail-oriented nor especially patient. Although few AICC members disputed that merging with the upstart Forum would strengthen pro-immigrant forces at a critical moment, some found Swartz too pushy, in too much of a hurry; negotiating the merger's details thus fell to Muzaffar Chishti of the International Ladies' Garment Workers' Union (ILGWU).[146]

Chishti, of a Muslim family who grew up in the disputed northern Indian province of Kashmir, came to the US as a foreign student. Having received a law degree in India, he completed his master's in law at Cornell in 1975 and, still feeling himself insufficiently educated, was intending to attend graduate school at Tufts when a chance encounter with a former Indian ambassador to the United Nations led to a referral for a job interview with Jay Mazur, then the assistant manager of an ILGWU local in New York. Chishti took a part-time job with Mazur while going to graduate school at Columbia. When he completed his master's in 1980, the union agreed to sponsor Chishti to work full time, mainly on collective bargaining and contract issues. Years later, Mazur said of Chishti, "He had three [advanced] degrees and I only paid him $300 per week. I thought 'What a bargain, only a hundred bucks a degree!'"

Mazur was moving up the union hierarchy rapidly, and assigned Chishti to cover immigration, as the heavily immigrant union—a single local in New York had twenty-eight thousand predominantly Chinese immigrant workers—was beset with INS raids and labor disputes with clear immigration overtones. Mazur needed a framework to support his pro-immigrant instincts. "I want nothing less than unconditional amnesty" for undocumented immigrants, he demanded of fellow Jewish Labor Committee members, as they prepared their formal positions for the Select Commission; he assigned Chishti to draft a policy paper on its behalf. Chishti "lucked out" when he crossed paths with Roger Waldinger, an ILGWU organizer who was pursuing a PhD at Harvard and was working for MIT economist Michael Piore, who was developing a then-groundbreaking analytical framework positing the existence of "dual labor markets" in which few unauthorized workers competed with domestic workers for jobs. Both Waldinger and his mentor Piore later became among the most influential scholars in the field.[147]

Previous neoclassical economists generally viewed the economy through the lens of a single, unified job market. Under this rubric, expansion of the supply of workers via immigration, or for that matter increased entry of women into the labor force, produces higher unemployment, lower wages, or both. Because "loose" labor markets strengthened employers' bargaining powers and weakened those of workers, high immigration inevitably harmed domestic workers, according to conventional neoclassical theorists. Moreover, conventional labor economists thought illegal immigration especially harmed downscale workers; since unauthorized workers lack the ability to complain about mistreatment, the theory went, they'd typically work for lower wages and worse working conditions than domestic workers, lowering labor standards for everyone else.[148] Tougher restrictions on immigration were thus seen by traditional economists as something of an affirmative action program for minorities and other disadvantaged workers in the US.[149]

By contrast, Piore was a leader of a then-nascent, eventually dominant group of economists that posited the existence of both primary job markets characterized by stable employment, high wages, and upward mobility, and secondary job markets with high turnover, low wages, and little or no upward mobility.[150] In this dual labor market, immigrants that typically filled the lower-tier secondary jobs not only didn't compete with natives holding the upper-tier positions, but actually helped create or retain the primary jobs. The framework rung true with Mazur's and Chishti's experience in the northeastern garment industry, from which factories were then moving, first to the Deep South where wages were lower, and then to Mexico and the far east, areas with even cheaper labor. In their experience, few natives were willing to work in the garment factories, which had first introduced the term *sweatshop* into the English vocabulary. The immigrants working long hours for low wages on the factory floor were, they thought, helping retain the industry's related middle-class supervisory, managerial, and sales jobs, most of which were held by white, often Jewish Americans in the Northeast, that would otherwise leave the US.

For Chishti, the new theoretical framework was "a godsend." Relying heavily on Waldinger's analysis, Chishti's paper on behalf of the Jewish Labor Committee broke with organized labor's traditional support for tougher immigration policy and instead recommended legalization of undocumented workers and a more careful, nuanced approach to enforcement. Although Mazur didn't yet speak for the union—he was named secretary-treasurer in 1983 and ascended to the top job in 1986—his rejection of restrictionism both contributed to and reflected a growing trend within the garment workers and other unions with large immigrant memberships. An article produced by the union's top leadership called for a "generous amnesty," suggested that employer sanctions "will not serve as an effective deterrent to the future hiring of illegal aliens," and called for greater foreign aid and promotion of human rights abroad.[151] This stance brought Mazur and Chishti into broader immigration advocacy circles, where they kept running into Swartz and his allies, and Mazur was recruited to serve as the new group's interim chairman.[152]

In part because he had done some contract negotiation work for the union, "Muz"—which Swartz would pronounce like "moose"—Chishti was tasked with completing the final stages of the AICC-Forum merger, which meant participating in a series of meetings with Ruth Casselman, president and founder of AICC then in her eighties, and with Read Lewis, then in his nineties and AICC's treasurer. Both were icons in the field; Casselman was a huge player in the 1965 immigration reforms, and Lewis was connected to the settlement house and pluralism movements of the last great wave of immigration around the turn of the twentieth century. Casselman had herself overseen the joining of the two predecessor groups that formed the AICC and knew that a merger was all but inevitable; besides, according to Chishti she'd apparently "taken a shine to Swartz."[153] Lewis initially resisted. After a series of negotiations, often at Casselman's Park Avenue apartment, Lewis conceded, but insisted that the term *citizenship* be included in the new organization's name, because in his mind the immigration debate was about having a broad, inclusive definition of the term. Thus was born the National Immigration, Refugee and *Citizenship* Forum.[154]

Once the merger—really a takeover of the old AICC by the new Forum—was completed in June 1982, Jay Mazur was only too happy to be relieved of his "interim chair" position as his union responsibilities grew. AICC board chair Charles Keely, a demographer at the Population Council, was the obvious pick to become the first chair of the Forum's board of directors, with Ruth Casselman awarded an honorary president role while Read Lewis was named honorary treasurer.[155] Not only was Keely strongly associated with AICC as a longtime board member, he was a highly respected immigration researcher and policy analyst in his own right. His work, which included policy reports that unlike many academic tomes were highly readable and accessible, suggested a keen understanding of the politics, and not just the academic research, in the field.[156] Naturally calm and unexcitable, Keely provided an essential steadying force during the Forum's critical formative years, from its founding through 1984.

THE OLD GUARD

As Swartz, Chishti, and Keely filled out the rest of the board, Wells Klein, head of the American Council for Nationalities Service (ACNS), who became the Forum's chair in 1984, was a natural and eventually consequential choice. Klein, then in his mid-fifties, had become prominent in the refugee resettlement arena since taking over ACNS in 1975. Klein's father Philip was a social work professor at Columbia. His mother, the former Alice Campbell, was of the "Vermont Campbells," a prominent family in the state. It was said that many in her aristocratic family felt she had married beneath her when she wed Philip, who was, despite strong academic credentials, the son of poor Jewish immigrants.[157] The younger Klein was the perfect product of the union: a connoisseur of good food and drink, collector of fine oriental rugs, and, as befitting one "to the manor born," both deeply committed to social justice and a bit of a swashbuckler, always on the lookout for the next adventure.[158] After naval service in World War II and degrees from Sarah Lawrence and Columbia, he began working with CARE, the humanitarian organization, rising in the mid-1950s to become mission chief in Saigon. At the height of the Vietnam War in the late 1960s, he took over and resuscitated International Social Service (ISS), a nonprofit agency specializing in cross-border adoptions. When he moved to ACNS, he took ISS's

American branch with him, an example of what admirers called his entrepreneurialism and critics saw as empire building.

ACNS's roots were in the massive Eastern European migrations at the turn of the twentieth century, when it supported settlement houses to help the new immigrants integrate into American society. It experienced an uptick in growth following World War II, when it helped resettle a new wave of refugees and immigrants fleeing war-ravaged Europe. ACNS once had been the publisher of *Common Ground*, the groundbreaking quarterly journal co-founded by AICC's Read Lewis.[159] But like many old-line refugee organizations, ACNS had been in a steady decline since the early 1950s. Even as the national organization suffered, its local member agencies, including International Institutes and Traveler's Aid groups, thrived amid the changing demographics, serving the post-1965 inflow of Latinos and Asians through legal assistance, English classes, job training, and other programs.

Around the time Klein took the helm of ACNS, Saigon fell to the North Vietnamese and its allies, marking the beginning of a vast flow of refugees out of Southeast Asia; eventually, over 1.4 million were resettled in the US.[160] Klein foresaw that two political forces in the US that typically opposed each other would converge to encourage acceptance of a large portion of these refugees. Pro-war hawks, many holding powerful government positions, were conservative on migration but felt obligated to save Vietnamese allies who'd supported the US, while antiwar doves were predisposed to accept refugees on humanitarian grounds, despite their opposition to the war. Klein was well connected with both camps. Contacts he had made with State Department officials and lawmakers while with CARE, and in brief stints as a consultant to the Senate refugee subcommittee, gave him easy access to those deciding how the new refugee flow into the US was managed.[161] His social work background and old-school elite connections gave ACNS both professional standing and back-channel clout, and his group's network of member organizations was well-prepared to help new arrivals, including many deeply traumatized by the war and its aftermath, adapt to life in the US. With only about 12 percent of the total refugee flow, ACNS wasn't the largest resettlement agency. The Catholic Church's vast network of social service agencies, which resettled about 40 percent of the refugees, held that distinction, with other sectarian groups like Church World Service, the Hebrew Immigrant Aid Society, Lutheran Immigration and Refugee Service, the National Association of Evangelicals, and the nonsectarian International Rescue Committee playing important roles. But Klein soon was viewed by many as the "first among equals" in the small, tight-knit resettlement world, cutting deals allocating territory, the number of refugees served, and funding among the groups.[162]

Early, largely ad hoc meetings among the resettlement groups in 1975–1976 were fraught with tension, with large individual and institutional egos, not to mention millions of dollars, at stake. But the agencies' shared interests—protecting the maximum number of refugees from harm and easing their transition into US society while, not incidentally, maximizing the resources to process them—overcame their differences. By 1979, the process of allocating refugees (and therefore funding) among the groups had evolved into a routine, twice-weekly cooperative "auction," with an atmosphere that a visiting reporter described as "lighthearted, with much joshing and swapping of case histories among the representatives."[163]

Klein took the lead in negotiating the terms of resettlement with government officials, including the amounts the agencies were paid for their services. His finance skill served not just ACNS but all the groups known collectively as VOLAGs, an acronym for voluntary agencies, a designation that distinguished them from the international nongovernmental organizations (NGOs) or the community-based organizations (CBOs) most often applied to purely domestic groups. The VOLAGs were well compensated by the government for processing, relocating, and housing the newcomers, and providing English, job training, and other services to facilitate the refugees' transition into US society.[164] In 1979, about one-third of the way through the fifteen-year Indochinese resettlement effort, nine resettlement groups divided up $30 million in annual State Department grants for "reception and placement," equivalent to over $108 million in 2017 dollars, not counting additional State Department funds for transportation and grants from other federal and state agencies for English classes, job training, and other kinds of services.[165]

Klein built ACNS into a financial and programmatic powerhouse. The steady flow of refugees enabled ACNS to pass through funding to its member agencies, strengthening the national organization's ties to its field infrastructure. By streamlining the agency's program overhead, with support from his longtime operations director Christine Gaffney, Klein generated operating surpluses, giving it substantial discretionary income. With ACNS Klein inherited *Interpreter Releases*, which despite its odd name serves as the field's preeminent journal, covering legal and policy developments on immigration and refugee matters. He soon sold the publication for a tidy sum to the Thomson Reuters publishing empire.[166] He expanded an effort begun originally through ISS to resettle Vietnamese children, especially orphans and "Amer-asian" children fathered by American GIs, an initiative Klein was especially passionate about.[167] By the early 1980s, when many nonprofits were reeling from a double whammy of Reagan-era budget cuts and recession-induced drops in private giving, ACNS was building a balance sheet that became the envy of all but the largest US nonprofits.[168] Klein worried that ACNS itself, with its strongly European origins, couldn't represent the newer Asian and Latino immigrants, but he wanted to play a leadership role in doing so and saw the value of an entity like Swartz's Forum to serve as a bridge to the newcomers' organizations.[169]

In turn, Klein appealed to Swartz, although the relationship was not without complications. Swartz saw Klein as a link to the old guard that had been the dominant domestic players on migration matters and still attracted the bulk of the resources spent by government and foundations in the field. Swartz thought he might benefit from Klein's legendary business acumen, and it certainly didn't hurt that ACNS provided the first $10,000 contribution to fund the fledgling Forum effort.[170] But Swartz also closely identified with small, refugee-led groups called mutual assistance associations, who feared that Klein and others of his generation would resist sharing their power and influence; Swartz was happy to advise them in ways they could outmaneuver their patrons, a role that the old guard might've been suspicious of.[171]

GUYS AND GALS

Another presence at the Forum's founding would play an even larger role in shaping future immigration policy. J. Michael Myers—always Michael, never Mike among friends—was in 1981 the Washington representative of Church World Service, the immigration and refugee arm of the National Council of Churches, the association of mainline Protestant denominations in the US. He was the son of Baptist missionaries and had grown up in Vietnam; even close associates were taken aback to hear the blond-haired, blue-eyed Myers, whose English had a trace of a Southern accent from his parents' Mississippi heritage, addressing visiting Vietnamese dignitaries or restaurant waitstaff in rapid-fire, fluent Vietnamese.[172] He joined Church World Service in the mid-1970s while attending Columbia, in part because of the growing demand for his language skills as the flow of Indochinese refugees began.[173]

Church World Service was housed in New York at the famed, and in some circles infamous God Box, the imposing nineteen-story building on Riverside Drive where the national offices of the major Protestant faiths were headquartered and that, before growth of the evangelical churches and concomitant decline of the mainstream denominations, had pretensions of being the "Protestant Vatican."[174] It wasn't a household name but CWS had cachet in immigration and refugee circles. While part of the old guard of VOLAGs, it was guided by a philosophy of empowering those it resettled; its materials stated that CWS "recognized early on that to be successful, projects and programs must come from the people themselves, not be imposed by others."[175] Its executive director Dale DeHaan had staffed Ted Kennedy on immigration issues, and served in the Carter administration as the United Nations deputy high commissioner for refugees, the most prestigious post reserved for US appointees. The Kennedy connection was important, as was the moral authority of the Protestants, who had many member churches in every state and congressional district. But the organization's most valuable asset was Myers, who began coming to DC in the 1980s to work on refugee issues, and years later joined Kennedy's staff in 1987, and subsequently was tabbed by the *Washington Post* as "one of the most powerful staffers on Capitol Hill."[176] Like others at the Forum's press conference, Myers had a Haiti connection; when the National Council of Churches filed lawsuits challenging the INS's failure to afford Haitians due process, Myers provided the complementary DC-based advocacy.[177]

Of medium height and medium build, a colleague observed that Myers, "didn't always have a lot to say, but when he did say something you paid attention."[178] Unlike most Hill staffers in charge of refugee policy, he hadn't just read about Indochina, he'd grown up there. Myers didn't learn about refugees' hardships by parachuting in on a quick visit, he'd lived the experience. His background lent him unique authenticity, but he also had the common touch in dealing with people, coming off as a straight shooter, if perhaps also as a bit of a boy scout. Myers generally kept a low press profile, although he often appeared in church-related publications that kept his constituency informed about and mobilized support for refugee protection.[179] In contrast to many Beltway insiders who can't wait to hear themselves speak or to read their names in the paper, Myers was an unusually good listener who preferred to work behind the scenes.

Present at the initial Forum press conference, off to the side cracking jokes and making snide comments about others present, were Michael S. Hooper and Brenda Pillors. Everyone loved Mike Hooper. Born to very traditional British parents, tall, rail-thin, with an unruly quasi-Afro hair style and wire-rimmed glasses, Hooper came off concurrently as both an unusually hyper hippie and as a happy mad scientist type, in constant motion, always rushing in from or off to the next meeting with a wad of telephone message slips in hand. Starting his career as an organizer for César Chávez's United Farm Workers in the early 1970s, then earning a law degree from Northeastern University, Hooper directed the Haiti project of the Lawyers Committee for Human Rights. His fluency in French and Haitian Creole made him the natural point man for a series of fact-finding missions sponsored by various assemblages of human rights organizations to the island dictatorship, and he produced a steady stream of reports documenting in sometimes gruesome detail the massive scope of human rights abuses in Haiti.[180]

Hooper's wealth of relationships on the island gave him a unique degree of stateside authority on all things Haitian. If many advocates felt deeply about the treatment of Haitian refugees, none matched Hooper's passion for the people of Haiti, individually and collectively. An advocate who accompanied him to a gathering of human rights advocates on the island thought the experience was what it must be like to be part of a rock star's crew, as Hooper literally was mobbed by those seeking to get a word with him. It seemed as if Hooper was the human face of all that was good about America.[181] He didn't act like a Yankee lawyer collecting facts to buttress his predetermined arguments; he listened more than preached, studied more than lectured, and demonstrated a sincere curiosity about the culture and history of the island. He acted as if on borrowed time, following a brutal schedule that involved flying between his New York base to DC, South Florida, Port-au-Prince, back to DC, and then home again many times a year; unbeknown to all but his closest friends, as it turned out Hooper literally *was* on borrowed time. He'd been diagnosed with a malignant melanoma—associates thought that the many days in the sun organizing farmworkers combined with his countless field trips to Haiti must have contributed to the light-complexioned lawyer's disease—which he had removed in 1982, but which eventually led to an untimely, early death.[182]

Hooper's principal activity was formation of the National Emergency Coalition on Haitian Refugees, incorporated a year later after dropping the qualifier "Emergency," since the issue was going to be around for a while. The coalition's executive committee, chaired by Anthony Bevilacqua, by then bishop of Pittsburgh, read like a "who's who" of the refugee and civil rights fields: Dale DeHaan of Church World Service, Don Hohl of the US Catholic Conference, and Wells Klein of ACNS, representing refugee resettlement groups; Benjamin Hooks and John Jacob, CEOs of the NAACP and National Urban League, respectively; Rabbi Marc Tanenbaum of the American Jewish Committee; Lane Kirkland of the AFL-CIO; Rep. Shirley Chisholm (D-NY); Wade Henderson of the American Civil Liberties Union; Joseph Rauh of the Leadership Conference on Civil Rights; prominent immigration lawyer Ira Gollobin, and several Haitian leaders, including Rev. Gerard Jean-Juste of the Haitian Refugee Center, the lead plaintiff in much of the important Haitian litigation.[183] With overlapping memberships and constituencies, the Haitian coalition and the immigration forum grew up together.

A felicitous by-product of the Haitian organizing effort was strengthening of the connections between immigration advocates and the African American civil rights leadership. The A. Philip Randolph Institute was headed by Bayard Rustin, a seminal figure in the civil rights movement, and his deputy Norman Hill. Rustin was perhaps best known as the man who "made the trains run on time" in the civil rights movement; he organized the first Freedom Rides in 1947 and the 1963 March on Washington that featured Martin Luther King's epochal "I Have a Dream" speech. Rustin largely delegated non-Haiti immigration issues to his chief deputy Norman Hill, who represented the institute on the board of the Forum, and for a brief period served as interim cochair.[184] The imprimatur of the A. Philip Randolph Institute was vital to the Forum at a time when tensions, often linked to immigration policy, emerged between the established African American groups and newer Latino civil rights organizations.

But of far greater consequence was how the Haiti work linked the immigrant advocates to Rep. Shirley Chisholm (D-NY), who chaired the Congressional Black Caucus's Immigration Task Force. It is difficult to overstate the respect that Shirley Chisholm, the first black woman elected to Congress, had among "underdog" constituencies on Capitol Hill. A few knew of her only through her quixotic campaign for the 1972 Democratic presidential nomination, which was privately derided even by many of her colleagues in the Black Caucus.

Chisholm could be an easy target. While an articulate, deft phrase maker, she had a strange voice, sometimes sounding as if she had a mouthful of marbles. But those who privately made fun of the congresswoman and her presidential run were always reticent to go against her in public; the seven-term representative was "a determined fighter . . . with a tough, discipline-minded streak."[185] She was described by one admirer as a "feisty, intelligent, compassioned, dark-complexioned woman born of [West Indian] parents."[186] While true enough, the description still seems inadequate; she somehow synthesized both parts of her heritage—her immigrant background and upbringing in the tough Brownsville section of Brooklyn—emerging as a fierce warrior for the underprivileged. Decades later Chisholm earned a place on a list of "The Most Underrated Politicians in History" alongside such notables as several former US presidents, the Greek philosopher Cicero, and Lee Kuan Yew, the founding father of Singapore.[187] She was also posthumously awarded a Presidential Medal of Freedom in 2015, when President Barack Obama summed up her character by saying, "Shirley Chisholm had guts."[188] She also had a deep reservoir of compassion. During her 1972 presidential run, segregationist candidate George Wallace was shot and gravely wounded by a would-be assassin. Chisholm interrupted her campaign to visit the former Alabama governor's hospital room, explaining that in a democracy, it was important to both show sympathy and respect even, perhaps especially, to those with whom you disagreed vehemently.[189]

But perhaps her most underrated contribution to the field would come through her staffer, Brenda Pillors, a Californian with a PhD in criminal justice who had come to Washington in 1977 as a Congressional Black Caucus Fellow, and then found a job with Rep. Chisholm.[190] Handsome, almost stately in appearance and manner in formal settings, in private Pillors was funny, earthy, and tough; she didn't suffer fools, and was always ready with a wisecrack at an opponent's flaws or colleague's foibles. She was also, according to her close friend Barbara Lee, then an aide to Congressman Ron Dellums and a future representative herself, "Solid as a rock . . . humble, caring, wise and considerate."[191] But mostly, Pillors was a *worker*; she performed everything from mundane administrative tasks like obtaining rooms on Capitol Hill for the Forum's press conferences to connecting the largely unknown advocates in the Forum to the wide network of former Chisholm staffers in other congressional offices.[192]

Another founding Forum board member with a Haiti connection was Gary Rubin of the American Jewish Committee. Founded in 1906 by prominent Jewish Americans to "prevent the infraction of the civil and religious rights of Jews in any part of the world," the AJC was, according to the *New York Times*, "the dean of Jewish organizations in the United States."[193] It was the most centrist of the major Jewish groups, generally left of the political center, but never *too* far left. The group's leadership viewed their dual identities as Jews and as Americans as "more than compatible," had strongly supported civil rights legislation and the expansion of legal immigration, but at the same time "viewed the methods of mass protest with disfavor."[194] The AJC's *amicus curiae* brief supporting integration of schools was quoted by Chief Justice Earl Warren in his opinion in *Brown v. Board of Education*, and the group was an active supporter of the civil rights movement in the 1960s. However, AJC split with African American groups on the question of "race conscious" affirmative action remedies and other issues a decade later.[195] AJC was the publisher of *Commentary*, an influential journal that had started as politically liberal in 1947 but over time had moved right, eventually becoming what some viewed as a mouthpiece for so-called neoconservatives.

Notwithstanding its occasional centrist impulses, with Rubin as its lead staffer on the issue, the AJC was unambiguously pro-immigrant in the 1980s. Rubin had once worked for Wells Klein at ACNS, helping to beat back congressional attempts to staunch the growing flow from Southeast Asia. After returning to New York from a series of advocacy meetings in DC, one of his colleagues remembers Rubin saying, "Man, I love this stuff," noting that he had clearly caught the "Beltway Bug."[196] He was perfectly suited for a career in public policy, combining, accordingly to Swartz, "a steel-trap mind with a smiling personality." Rubin was also fond of noting that "Jews have the story of Exodus in our blood," instinctively sympathetic to refugees fleeing persecution and immigrants seeking a better life in a strange country.[197]

Phyllis Eisen offered similar credibility with the environmental movement, at the time trending toward supporting tougher restrictions on immigration. A former schoolteacher, Eisen was policy director for Zero Population Growth,* lobbying on family planning and population issues, and also oversaw the organization's work on immigration policy.[198] ZPG was cofounded in 1968 by uber environmentalist Paul Erlich following his massive bestseller, *The Population Bomb*. Erlich was wildly popular among progressives and in the mainstream

---

* Known today as Population Connection.

media, earning multiple appearances on Johnny Carson's *Tonight Show*, with its millions of television viewers. However, in some circles there was discomfort about ZPG's supposed insensitivity to "third-world countries" abroad and minorities at home, who tended to have higher birthrates than their European, white counterparts.[199]

Although nominally representing ZPG at the Forum's early organizing meetings, Eisen was increasingly uncomfortable with the nativist tone of some inside her organization. As this feeling took hold, Eisen heard Swartz at a presentation on Haitian refugees, and was "swept off her feet" by "his charisma, his passion, and commitment."[200] She began actively plotting with Swartz about the idea of an "organization of organizations" to work on immigration policy, and they worked together on the group's original funding proposal to the Ford Foundation. Swartz valued Eisen's ties to the environmental movement as well as her "energy, her understanding of the big picture, and her ability to talk to everybody."[201] She left ZPG in 1982 to join Swartz as vice president of the Forum. Eisen, a single mother and networker extraordinaire, seemingly knew everyone involved in immigration refugee policy; more importantly, she knew almost everything *about* them. When asked about an elected official, Swartz described their policy positions or political inclinations; Eisen could discuss the subject's favorite restaurants and hangouts, their hobbies and passions, their kids, and their personal affairs, extramarital and otherwise. Inside the Beltway, where relationships matter above all else, Eisen had unique insight into just about every one of the myriad personalities who might have had a say in shaping immigration legislation.

She gathered much of her intelligence from monthly lunches with other women involved in immigration issues. At a time when most debates on most issues were dominated by men, Eisen was de facto organizer of a small but highly influential network of women in key positions in the then-tiny immigration policy field. The group included Doris Meissner, who served in several top government posts including as acting commissioner at the INS through the Carter and Reagan years; Joyce Vialet of the Congressional Research Service, the leading expert in immigration policy on Capitol Hill; Marion "Muffie" Houstoun, a Labor Department official and seminal researcher in the field; Jane O'Grady, the AFL-CIO's legendary lobbyist who played important roles in the passage of every civil rights bill in the previous two decades; several congressional staff; and, every once in a while, MALDEF's Antonia Hernández.

While much of the lunch conversation was social, the women inevitably shared information and debated the issues, and Eisen was an exquisitely skilled listener. "People always said I talked a lot, and maybe I did," she said years later, "but what I really did was listen a lot. You learn a lot more by listening."[202] The women also shared a powerful bond.

Capitol Hill in the 1980s was very much a "boys club," replete with sexual innuendo, locker room humor, frequent outright propositions, and other behavior that today easily would qualify as a hostile environment to the thousands of young women in executive agencies, congressional offices, law firms, trade associations, and nonprofits working in "government relations." A few years earlier, when Patricia Schroeder (D-CO) and Ron Dellums (D-CA), an African American, were elected, Armed Services Committee chair F. Edward Hebert (D-LA) tried but failed to block their appointment to his panel. As Schroeder noted later, Hebert responded by announcing: "while he might not be able to control the makeup of the committee, he could damn well control the number of chairs in his hearing room. . . . He said that women and blacks were worth only half of one 'regular' member, so he added only one seat to the committee room and made me and Ron share it. Nobody else objected, and nobody offered to scrounge up another chair."[203]

This wasn't shocking coming from Hebert, who'd first been elected to the House in 1940, but the failure of others to come to Schroeder's or Dellums's defense showed how deeply entrenched such attitudes were. Working in this ecosystem required women with considerable grit; the always immaculately dressed and somewhat matronly Eisen was perfectly capable of dropping a well-chosen profanity of her own to make a point. She was known in later years to describe a particularly difficult negotiating encounter as a "Five Fucks Meeting," where the real give and take couldn't begin until each side had first dropped at least five F-bombs on the other to emphasize how strongly they felt about the issue in question.[204]

The Forum leaders were a powerful combination. Swartz brought analytical skills and a litigator's intensity to the partnership; Eisen was a positive, ebullient presence, smoothing over controversies her colleague was disinclined to address. Swartz was an impressive speaker who performed at a high level in the public eye. Eisen worked behind the scenes, cheerful and enthusiastic, something of a mother hen to the intensively competitive young men associated with the Forum and a supportive friend to the women, all of whom faced gender-based professional challenges common to that era.

A STEEL FIST IN A VELVET GLOVE

One woman at the unveiling of the Forum was in the early stages of a distinguished career of overcoming such challenges herself. Antonia Hernández represented MALDEF, and her organization's membership added substantial credibility to the new Forum. While LULAC was the nation's oldest and largest Hispanic civil rights organization and its DC representative Arnoldo Torres was the community's most visible advocate inside the Beltway in 1981, MALDEF was without question the most respected Latino group in the country in that era. It was founded in 1968 after LULAC Texas state director Pete Tijerina, himself an accomplished civil rights lawyer, led a delegation of the organization's leaders to meet with the Ford Foundation to urge the establishment of a Mexican American counterpart to the NAACP Legal Defense Fund.[205] The Foundation agreed, later that year providing a massive $2.25 million grant, equivalent to over $15 million in 2017 dollars, to establish the organization, initially headquartered in San Antonio with a smaller office in Los Angeles.[206] As University of Texas professor Maggie Rivas-Rodriguez's research on MALDEF's founding has uncovered, the grant wasn't without its detractors, even among Latino activists. Labor economist and organizer Ernesto Galarza, a cofounder of the Southwest Council of La Raza, was negotiating with the Ford Foundation for his own grant and suggested that the proposed legal organization be housed within or established as a part of a broader organization (presumably the one he was trying start). But the combination of Tijerina's aggressive advocacy and the fact that the idea of an LDF counterpart to represent Mexican Americans made sense on its own merits encouraged the foundation to go ahead with the MALDEF grant.[207]

The organization was led briefly by Tijerina, followed by Mario Obledo, a former Texas state assistant attorney general, himself a future LULAC president. According to Obledo, his focus at the time was pushing the organization to "evolve from a legal organization of militants into a law firm for the Latino community."[208] He was only partially successful; one historian of the period observed that MALDEF initially was "something of an unofficial civil liberties bureau for militant Chicano students."[209] In its early years MALDEF, along with the Southwest Council of La Raza and their local allies the Mexican American Youth Organization (MAYO) and the Mexican American Unity Council, was a target of the wrath of Rep. Henry B. González. It didn't help that MAYO's José Ángel Gutiérrez, of the "kill the gringo" comment fame, had briefly been on MALDEF's payroll. Rep. González's attacks on MALDEF put enormous pressure on the Ford Foundation, which for years had been fighting off attempts by congressional conservatives to change the tax laws to prevent or eliminate funding for grassroots organizations that engaged in voter registration or lobbying. Following a formal "recommendation" by the foundation to relocate its national office, MALDEF moved its headquarters off González's turf to San Francisco, which fortuitously was the "finance capital" of the West Coast with many foundations of its own, while retaining a small presence in San Antonio.[210]

In 1973, former NAACP Legal Defense Fund lawyer Vilma Martínez was chosen to succeed Obledo, and the organization blossomed under her leadership. As she later recounted to a reporter, she'd been forced to fight to move forward at every stage of her education. Martínez didn't speak any English when she entered school in her native San Antonio, and only her father's persistence outweighed her eighth grade counselor's intention to assign her to a vocational rather than academic high school. There, her high school counselor had been "too busy" to help her fill out the admissions form to the University of Texas; upon graduation with "a straight-A average," her college adviser told her "Don't get your hopes up" about getting into law school.[211] After graduating from Columbia Law School, Martínez had worked with Tijerina on MALDEF's original funding proposal while on LDF's staff, and was thus intimately familiar with both organizations. Fortunately for her new employer, she'd been schooled in the legal strategies that made LDF the model for others in the field. She hired top-notch legal talent, a major challenge because unlike the LDF, which relied on a steady stream of law graduates produced by historically black colleges such as Howard University's highly regarded law school, well-trained Chicano civil rights lawyers were extremely scarce.[212] Martínez refocused MALDEF's resources away from "retail" cases and community organizing activity toward "impact litigation," which, as the term implies, involves lawsuits designed to effect broad, systemic change. It often requires the strategic pursuit of a series of carefully chosen test cases in lower courts that build toward the bigger, often Supreme Court–level case with the potential to produce large-scale impact.[213]

Martínez grew the organization's financial base, adding dozens of corporate donors to its growing list of foundation supporters. She also invested heavily in MALDEF's DC office, thinking an East Coast presence would not only help the organization to advance legislation and raise its national profile, it provided better access to the New York-based foundation funding sources relied on by many national civil rights groups.[214] In just a few years with Martínez at the helm, the "new" MALDEF increased its focus on police brutality, established a new department of public policy research, and, importantly, adopted a major focus on the media.[215] The focus on impact litigation, a diverse and growing funding base, and concentration on effectively telling its story positioned MALDEF at the vanguard of the mainstream Latino civil rights movement, in the court room, in the media, and in the halls of Congress and state legislatures.

Under Martínez's leadership, MALDEF lost little time making a difference in Texas and the broader Southwest, by 1975 winning lawsuits resulting in the desegregation or provision of bilingual education in ten Texas school districts, and a path-breaking case in Corpus Christi, Texas, which successfully argued that the *Brown v. Board of Education* decision outlawing "separate but equal" schools also should be applied to Mexican Americans.[216] The organization was active in political empowerment issues, winning landmark cases that created single member electoral districts to which Mexican Americans could be elected, and working closely with the Southwest Voter Registration Education Project (SVREP) to remove barriers to voter registration, eventually resulting in a 50 percent increase in registered Mexican American voters between 1976 and

1984.[217] The partnership between MALDEF and SVREP, augmented by Texas Rural Legal Aid, challenged exclusionary voting systems, almost always successfully, in some eighty-five jurisdictions in Texas in the 1970s and early 1980s.[218] One lawsuit overturned San Antonio's at-large election system that diluted the power of the Mexican American vote, paving the way for the election of Henry Cisneros to the city council several years later.[219]

The organization gained substantial national prominence through two sets of landmark cases, the first involving school finance issues. As the walls of de jure school segregation were crumbling across the country, albeit slowly in the face of deep resistance in many areas, the continued concentration of minority students in poor school districts—a consequence of housing segregation—resulted in persistent educational inequities: white students in affluent districts with greater resources were afforded better educations than their black and Latino counterparts in poor districts. Texas's property tax–based school finance system was a prime candidate for a court challenge, because historically high levels of residential segregation resulted in stark disparities in education spending between low-income and affluent school districts and because state budgets in the traditionally low-tax state did little to reduce these interdistrict disparities.

The three children of Demetrio Rodriguez, a civilian sheet metal worker at San Antonio's Kelly Air Force Base, were enrolled in the Edgewood Independent School District, one of thirteen segregated districts in the region (eight predominantly Anglo, five predominantly Mexican American). Rodriguez challenged the school finance system that required his children to attend class in a building "that had been condemned," with no air conditioning in the sweltering South Texas summers, cooled by "fans bought by the PTA."[220] A federal district court found in Rodriguez's favor, the state appealed, and the case eventually found its way to the nation's highest judicial body. While not the architect of the Rodriguez litigation, MALDEF supported and closely monitored the case at each stage of the federal court system. In its brief to the US Supreme Court in *San Antonio Independent School District v. Rodriguez*, MALDEF argued that the fact that "the poor receive one type of education by every measure, while the affluent are afforded a quite different and superior educational opportunity" was a violation of fundamental rights guaranteed by the equal protection clause of the Fourteenth Amendment to the US Constitution. The Supreme Court decided otherwise, ruling that education is not a "fundamental right" protected by the Fourteenth Amendment.[221]

Despite that setback, MALDEF had been building the foundation for future success by challenging public school finance systems on *state* constitutional grounds. It supported litigation leading up to a favorable California State Supreme Court ruling in *Serrano v. Priest* in the early 1970s. But the victory was short-lived, as school funding in that state dropped precipitously after a "tax-payer revolt" led to the passage of Proposition 13, a ballot measure that severely limited public funding, including support for schools.[222] MALDEF filed similar, ultimately more successful, litigation in Texas. While it took many years for the effort to come to fruition, in 1989 the organization scored a landmark victory in *Edgewood ISD v. State of Texas*, in which the Texas Supreme Court "unanimously found that the state's system of public finance of education was unconstitutional and ordered the legislature to alter it."[223] It was a huge win, forcing the notoriously conservative Texas legislature to adopt a Robin Hood school finance plan, taking revenues from affluent districts and giving them to poorer ones. But *Edgewood* was also a lesson that even precedent-setting court decisions aren't self-executing. Persistent monitoring, advocacy, and subsequent litigation were required to make it stick, as the Texas legislature tied itself up in knots trying to find ways to avoid full compliance. Even fifteen years later litigation was still taking place to enforce the *Edgewood* mandate against various school funding schemes that failed to sufficiently reduce disparities between rich and poor districts.[224]

It was an issue at the nexus of education and immigration that put MALDEF on the map in immigration policy circles. In 1975, the state of Texas enacted legislation permitting local school districts to charge tuition to undocumented immigrant children. While not all affected districts chose to implement the policy, many did, including the Houston Independent School District, the largest in the state, and a much smaller one in Tyler, just east of Dallas, both of which decided to charge undocumented students the prohibitively high annual tuition of $1,000—more than $4,500 in 2017 dollars. In 1977 MALDEF filed the lawsuit in the case that eventually became *Plyler v. Doe* against the Tyler ISD, arguing that the tuition unconstitutionally deprived undocumented residents of the district of the benefits of a public school education. MALDEF president and general counsel Vilma Martínez, national director for education litigation Peter Roos, and San Antonio office director Joaquín Avila together devised and implemented a complex, multilayered strategy to support the litigation. This was, to them, MALDEF's *Brown v. Board of Education*, a major precedent-setting case that would simultaneously break new ground crucial to the Latino community and build the organization's credibility, and the enormous resources they poured into the case—including the effort required to build widespread support from other interest groups, the press, and the Carter administration's Justice Department—reflected its importance.[225]

They benefited from both good fortune and smart tactics. When the Dallas INS office threatened to conduct immigration sweeps apparently designed to intimidate the undocumented plaintiffs to drop the lawsuit, Roos asked President Carter's INS commissioner Leonel Castillo to call off the raids, a request the former education advocate and MALDEF board member was more than happy to grant. MALDEF also chose the best possible forum to present the case: Tyler happened to be in the jurisdiction of federal District Court Judge William Wayne Justice, a rare left-leaning judge in the state, who liberal Texas columnist Molly Ivins later described as having "brought the U.S. Constitution to Texas" for his progressive rulings in school desegregation, prison reform, housing discrimination, and bilingual education.[226]

A parallel case, which came to be known as *In re: Alien Children* was filed against Houston ISD by local attorneys, including Isaias Torres representing the Houston Center for Immigrants, Joseph Vail of Gulfcoast Legal Services, and California-based lead counsel Peter Schey of the National Center for Immigrants' Rights.[227] Schey had been one of the attorneys involved with Rick Swartz and Ira Kurzban on the successful early Haitian litigation and had a reputation as an aggressive, take-no-prisoners-style litigator, sometimes viewed as being as tough on his allies as he was on his opponents.[228] Schey and Torres initially sought MALDEF's agreement to join the two cases, which Roos refused, probably for sound tactical reasons, although personal and institutional egos might well have been involved.[229] The relationship between Peter Schey and MALDEF's Peter Roos, as is often true when smart, ambitious litigators are forced to work together, was tense. "Conflicts over litigation strategy are common even among ideological allies," one eminent court watcher has observed. "Issues of timing, risk of adverse decisions, control of a case, and simple ego often lead to bitter feuds."[230]

After both prevailed in separate trials at the district court level, and *Plyler* at the Fifth Circuit Court of Appeals, the cases were consolidated for consideration by the Supreme Court, which agreed to hear the matter in May 1981. The consolidation of the cases required "the two Peters," Roos and Schey, to negotiate a "stiff and formal truce," with *Plyler* serving as the lead case and oral argument time "split down the middle."[231] They dodged a bullet, after the election of Ronald Reagan in 1980 threatened to turn the federal government from the ally it was under Carter to an opponent, just as the case reached the Supreme Court. Perhaps because of MALDEF's bipartisan spade work over the years, the brief ultimately submitted by Reagan's solicitor general Rex E. Lee "stopped short of urging the Supreme Court to reverse lower court decisions and uphold the Texas law."[232] As legal scholar Michael Olivas noted, the administration's ambivalent brief "likely worked to the advantage of the children's case."[233] But the administration's position, and the eventual outcome of the case, might have been different if one young Justice Department lawyer had had his way; future Supreme Court chief justice John Roberts coauthored a memorandum "chastising" the solicitor general for failing to side with the state of Texas.[234]

Regardless of the tensions between the plaintiffs' lawyers, they prevailed on the merits. On June 15, 1982, in a 5–4 decision, the court held for the first time "that the 14th Amendment's equal protection guarantee 'extends to anyone, citizen or stranger' within a state's boundaries, regardless of immigration status."[235] Foreshadowing an argument that weaved its way in and out of immigration debates for decades, writing for the court Justice Brennan acknowledged in his opinion that "persuasive arguments support the view that a State may withhold its beneficence from those whose very presence within the United States is unlawful," but concluded that "directing the onus of a parent's misconduct against his children does not comport with fundamental conceptions of justice."[236] Given the sometimes nonexistent federal enforcement of immigration laws, the court recognized the reality that "there is no assurance that a child subject to deportation will ever be deported." Indeed, about a decade later thirteen of the original plaintiffs were tracked down, and all had become lawful permanent residents of the US.[237]

Noting the bare majority, some eminent court-watchers hinted that the ruling might not prevail for long in a court that seemed to be trending conservative, while others observed, on technical grounds, that it might be a "doubtful precedent" for similar pro-immigrant rulings in other cases.[238] But *Plyler* has withstood the test of time, even as gains in other areas of civil rights and immigrants' rights law have been eroded by subsequent court actions. It has been called "epochal" in significance, and was, according to one prominent scholar, the "true high water mark of immigrant rights in the U.S."[239] At the time, it also marked one of the first truly unique national-level civil rights cases brought by Latinos that didn't build on or relate to ground broken previously by the NAACP Legal Defense Fund and or other African American litigators, focusing as it did not on race but on immigrant schoolchildren. While *Plyler* had not yet been accepted for review by the Supreme Court at the time of the National Immigration, Refugee and Citizenship Forum's "coming out" press conference, virtually every immigration advocate in the country knew it was headed there, and recognized MALDEF's signal role in the issue.

If MALDEF's organizational prestige was strengthened in legal circles by its appearances before the nation's highest courts, its stature inside the Beltway was enhanced by the talent and reputation of its Washington representative Antonia Hernández. Having headed MALDEF's DC office for just a year and barely into her thirties at the Forum's initial press event, Hernández already had established herself as a formidable presence in civil rights and immigration policy circles. After graduating from UCLA law school, she worked in legal aid agencies in Los Angeles, gaining considerable attention for a historic lawsuit challenging the sterilization of Mexican American women without their informed consent, and in some cases after considerable coercion, in the late 1960s and early 1970s.[240] The widespread practice had its roots in the eugenics movement that flourished in California in the 1920s; by the 1960s and 1970s, the rationale for sterilizations had shifted toward the seemingly less explicitly racist and more acceptable goals of reducing illegitimacy and alleged welfare abuse.[241] While she couldn't have known it at the time, the case pitted Hernández against eugenics advocates who went on to play a seminal role in the modern anti-immigrant movement.[242]

Then just twenty-six years old, Hernández was cocounsel on the case *Madrigal v. Quilligan*, which challenged the practice of involuntary sterilization on behalf of ten plaintiffs. Although the plaintiffs lost, the case led to significant reforms: bilingual consent forms and counselors and, according to one journalist, a "change in the medical profession's attitudes toward serving poor communities."[243] The litigation also earned the passionate, articulate, and telegenic young attorney considerable attention in both the civil rights and women's rights fields.[244] Soon thereafter, in late 1978, Hernández was recruited to join the staff of the Senate Judiciary Committee then chaired by Ted Kennedy. Hernández initially turned down Kennedy's job offer, preferring to stay close to her family in Los Angeles. However, her recruiter, senior committee staffer David Boies, who later became one of the most respected trial lawyers in the country, was extremely persistent.[245] Boies was uniquely qualified to appeal to Hernández; like her, he had overcome disadvantages to excel in a highly competitive field. As writer Malcolm Gladwell documented in his bestselling book *David and Goliath*, Boies has severe dyslexia, which makes reading very difficult. He has compensated by becoming "a superb listener," a skill that in turn made him extraordinarily effective in cross examination, with an unusual ability to discern and exploit weaknesses his opponents' cases.[246] Boies himself was extremely persuasive, but it didn't hurt that Hernández's husband, attorney Michael Stern, and her close friend Gloria Molina, then a Carter administration official and a future Los Angeles county supervisor, strongly encouraged her to take the job.[247] Eventually, she succumbed to the pressure.

Working under Jerry Tinker, staff director for Kennedy's subcommittee on immigration and refugee policy, she also covered judicial nominations and a broader portfolio of "Hispanic issues" for the senator. Because Kennedy was arguably the single most popular national political figure among Latinos in that era, the portfolio gave Hernández considerable personal power and prestige among Hispanic leaders. But when Republicans took over the Senate in the 1980 elections, the GOP took control of committee chairmanships and with them the vast majority of the staff appointments, and Hernández found herself out of work, albeit only briefly. The day after the elections, MALDEF president and general counsel Vilma Martínez called to ask Hernández to take over the organization's office in Washington, DC; despite a strong desire to return to her West Coast roots, in early 1981 she accepted the position.

While she may have sharpened her technical legal expertise on the subject during her two-year tenure on the Judiciary Committee staff, for Hernández immigration was always a deeply personal, visceral issue.[248] The eldest child of a US citizen father pushed out of the US during the "Decade of Betrayal," she returned from Mexico to Los Angeles with her family at age eight, speaking little English. She immediately felt the sting of discrimination at school. Although technically a US citizen, to her classmates, "I was the new immigrant kid. I was a wetback," she recalled later in a *Los Angeles Times Magazine* cover story; it was "like wearing a bull's eye that said 'direct all teasing here.' "[249] She overcame the stigma, but never forgot it.

If, inside the Beltway, her petite stature, impeccable fashion, and soft-spoken voice with just a trace of a Mexican accent might have led some to the ill-advised conclusion that she was a pushover or an empty suit, they soon learned otherwise. Profiles of Hernández after her ascension to the top job at MALDEF years later consistently described her through a series of contrasting adjectives: "Soft-spoken determination," wrote one reporter.[250] "Sweetness and fire," and "prag-matism and passion," noted another.[251] Her compatriots in immigration circles agreed; a close colleague once characterized getting into an argument with her as akin to being punched by "a steel fist in a velvet glove."[252] Before the congres-sional debate on the Immigration Reform and Control Act ended five years later, not just political opponents but erstwhile allies who in her judgment strayed from the path would feel the steel in Hernández's punches.

FAIR

On literally the opposite side of the issue from Hernández and her allies in the National Immigration, Refugee and Citizenship Forum, an equally talented and passionate advocate named Roger Conner and the organization he headed emerged as a force to be reckoned with. Conner was the executive director of the Federation for American Immigration Reform (FAIR), described by the *Wash-ington Post* as "the only national organization whose sole reason for existence is the promotion of stricter immigration controls."[253] If MALDEF and other Forum members found the Select Commission's report went too far in restrict-ing immigration, FAIR was at the other end of the spectrum, asserting it did not go nearly far enough. The group was founded by environmental activist John Tanton, an ophthalmologist from northern Michigan. A *National Journal* pro-file of the organization's founder noted Tanton: "as national president of Zero Population Growth (ZPG) in the mid-1970's, tried to steer it toward a largely-ignored element of population growth: immigration. When ZPG resisted, he persuaded some of its financial backers to help him set up FAIR in 1979."[254]

Tanton in later years gained considerable fame or, depending on the audience, infamy, but in the early 1980s Conner was the organization's public face, particularly on Capitol Hill. Then in his mid-thirties, the compact, boyishly handsome FAIR executive was described by one journalist as so intense that he seemed to be "struggling to resist grabbing his listeners by the lapels so as to be sure they'll hear all he has to say."[255] Conner was driven by deeply personal egalitarian instincts based on his own humble origins. According to a *Washington Post* profile: "The son of a short-order cook, Conner grew up as one of six children in Wichita Falls, Tex., in a family steeped in the Southern Baptist Church: no smoking, no drinking, no dancing. (He now indulges in the last two.) His mother named him for the religious libertarian and founder of Rhode Island, Roger Williams."[256]

Conner himself later described his upbringing more bluntly, saying that he was "born poor white trash" and only got to a top-tier university like Oberlin College through "an affirmative action program for poor Southern evangelicals."[257] After graduating from the University of Michigan Law School, Conner met Tanton while directing the West Michigan Environmental Action Council in Grand Rapids, and in 1979 turned down far more lucrative offers from law firms to go to Washington to help launch FAIR.[258] Tanton convinced Conner to join the cause of immigration restriction in part by introducing him to the work of historian Otis L. Graham, then at the University of North Carolina, who had developed a class-based economic case for the "liberal logic of [immigration] restriction." Consistent with organized labor's traditional neoclassical economic paradigm, Graham argued that large-scale immigration unduly expanded the labor supply and thereby undercut the interests of the domestic working class. Conner found the case convincing, given his roots in "a social class where I saw people ground up and spit out and hurt on a daily basis" by an economic and political system rigged against the little guy.[259]

One of FAIR's original objectives was to distinguish its own environmentally and economically based case for restriction from those who relied on explicitly nativist or xenophobic rhetoric. FAIR wanted to advocate for immigration control, in Conner's words, "without bringing the crazies out of the woodwork" and he disclaimed any desire to "tap into the racist, anti-immigrant feelings we all know exist in the country."[260] This stance initially enabled the organization to attract diverse sources of support, especially from large individual donors and family foundations with an interest in the environment. Among its largest early donors were the famed investor Warren Buffett, a political progressive then very interested in curbing population growth, and Cordelia Scaife May, a reclusive heiress to the Mellon fortune, then known mainly as an ardent supporter of arts, environmental, and population control programs.[261] FAIR sought to build ties with traditional civil rights groups; soon after arriving in DC, its leaders reached out to the NAACP to seek an alliance, but were rebuffed.[262] But FAIR's leadership did eventually recruit T. Willard Fair, head of the Urban League of Greater Miami, into its fold.[263]

Conner, a champion college debater, wasn't just zealous and highly skilled, but like his mentor Tanton, was a deep strategic thinker. Their experience in the environmental movement prompted FAIR to adopt a multifaceted advocacy strategy, augmenting lobbying with the production of policy materials that its research director boasted were designed to be "more numerate" than those produced by opponents, a heavy emphasis on shaping the news media narrative on immigration issues, and the creation of an individual membership structure.[264] The sophistication of FAIR's press work was noteworthy. Instead of just holding press conferences and sending out news releases, it prepared thick "pitch packets" of story ideas, polling data, policy analyses, and other materials and then distributed them widely to reporters and editorial boards.[265] While they wouldn't necessarily prompt stories about FAIR itself, the "pitching" was highly effective, saving reporters' time by pointing them to noteworthy stories such as the growing numbers of Latino construction workers, many presumed to be undocumented, and lining up national and local advocates willing to comment on the issue. FAIR wasn't only seeking publicity for itself, but was shaping a broader political climate more favorable to immigration restrictions.

Although the organization had only about five thousand dues-paying members in 1982, it was on a clear upward trajectory, claiming nearly ten times that number in just a few years; it invested heavily in then cutting-edge direct-mail programs designed to raise funds that were also developed with an eye to building a constituency of local activists concerned about growing immigration. Tanton didn't stop with FAIR; he later launched what one researcher called a "cluster" of nonprofit corporations linked by a "shared world view and philosophy, shared goals, and a pattern of relationships among their leaders transcending formal corporate boundaries."[266]

FAIR's unique leadership and structure offered both strengths and weaknesses. Its strengths were obvious. It made a powerful case for restriction based on a traditional view of the labor market and on environmental grounds, had a compelling, charismatic public leader in Roger Conner, built a well-funded infrastructure to pump out policy materials and shape the media narrative, and had the beginnings of a grassroots membership providing crucial "boots on the ground" in congressional districts. Eventually these core functions were augmented by a legal arm, a think tank, a publisher, a political action committee, "pro-English" groups, and others, providing Tanton and Conner with an unparalleled functional reach in the immigration advocacy field.[267]

Its weaknesses were not obvious until years in the future.

CHAPTER 3

The Battle Begins

SEEDS

With the release of the final report of the Select Commission on Immigration and Refugee Policy in early 1981, the principal commanders and forces were established, and the main battle lines drawn. Senator Alan Simpson and Representative Romano Mazzoli would turn the commission's recommendations into legislation. Organized labor, the NAACP, FAIR, and most of the nation's thought leaders supported the core employer sanctions provisions of the forthcoming legislation, although they differed on other parts of the commission's proposals. Working in concert with the new National Immigration, Refugee and Citizenship Forum, LULAC and MALDEF led the opposition.

While MALDEF's Antonia Hernández was focused like a laser beam on the voting rights legislation that ultimately passed in 1982, LULAC's Arnoldo Torres was seemingly everywhere in the run-up to the introduction of the long-awaited Simpson-Mazzoli bill. Right out of the starting gate of the new administration in early 1981 Torres blasted Reagan's proposed budget and tax bills, drawing a stern rebuke at the organization's annual convention later that summer, where Vice President George H. W. Bush, "took LULAC to task for failing to support the administration's economic program."[1] Coming from Bush, a former Texas congressman with close ties to many "LULACers," this was a serious reprimand. LULAC's attack on the Reagan tax and budget cuts confirmed the group's substantive leftward shift, since much of its traditional base of business owners and professionals might have been expected to be supportive of or at least open to the new administration's economic policies.

Torres led the charge against the nomination of William Bell, an African

American who was President Reagan's first choice to head the Equal Employment Opportunity Commission. At a time when some black civil rights groups seemed reticent to criticize one of their own, Torres's persistent broadsides questioning Bell's qualifications were noteworthy. A Detroit-based businessman who had purported to head an "employment agency" that had failed to place even a single client the previous year, Bell eventually withdrew.[2] In his stead, in February 1982, Reagan nominated another African American, Clarence Thomas, then assistant secretary for civil rights in the Department of Education and a future Supreme Court justice, to the EEOC post. Torres was unimpressed by this appointment as well, telling the *Washington Post* that he found Thomas to be "insensitive to Hispanic problems while in the education job."[3]

Within established immigration and refugee advocacy circles, Torres was thought of by many as something of a lone wolf, more inclined to go it alone than to work in coalition with others.[4] This reputation notwithstanding, in conjunction with the Forum's Rick Swartz, Torres was in fact at the time actively seeking allies. Swartz was simultaneously trying to shape the debate in Washington while "building a field of advocates" across the country. The Forum leader was in demand as a speaker all around the country and took advantage of each opportunity "in the field"—meaning outside of DC—to meet with organizations interested in becoming more involved in the immigration debate. One meeting led to another, and before long loose coalitions began to emerge. "Rick was like Johnny Appleseed," forum vice president Phyllis Eisen recalled, "planting seeds of 'little national forums' all over the country."[5]

Among Torres's earliest allies was Michael Myers of Church World Service, who began working closely with Torres just before the Simpson-Mazzoli bill was introduced, and was impressed by the LULAC leader. Myers thought Torres a "master of human psychology and the legislative chessboard who could predict how members would react to moves and countermoves."[6] Their engagement also shaped the views of Myers's constituency of mainstream Protestant church leaders. At first mainly concerned about refugees and legalization of unauthorized immigrants, Myers's "church people" eventually came to think that if Hispanic leaders said employer sanctions were going to cause discrimination, "then who are we to be second guessing that concern?"[7] Torres welcomed the imprimatur of the Church World Service's parent, the National Council of Churches, an old guard group seemingly open to new ideas; over time the two formed an especially close personal relationship.[8]

Other VOLAGs were uncomfortable with the sharp-edged advocacy Torres and Swartz espoused; their differences were stylistic, substantive, and political. Stylistically, the older white men leading the VOLAGs had relied on insider strategies, using their personal and institutional connections to quietly persuade policy makers to adopt their generally pro-immigrant positions. They were reluctant to criticize policy makers in the press, and then only after it was clear their behind-the-scenes approaches failed and they had no other choice.[9] In the period following the release of the Select Commission report, most were inclined to take a wait-and-see posture toward the yet-to-be-introduced immigration reform bill, in contrast to Torres's aggressive opposition and Swartz's public skepticism about the commission's product.

Substantively, the established groups were most concerned about protecting legal immigration and refugee flows, and legalization; many didn't take formal positions on employer sanctions. Relieved that the Select Commission supported modest increases in legal immigration and rejected calls to reduce refugee flows or crack down harshly on political asylum seekers, the VOLAGs were reticent to offend the architects of the upcoming legislation due to a simple calculus: when things seem to be going your way, you don't rock the boat. With the Select Commission reaffirming their core views most VOLAGs were disinclined to fully ally themselves with those, such as the Hispanic groups, who were agitating for more intense lobbying activity to shape the upcoming bill. Torres and Swartz were impatient with this perspective. They warned that the forthcoming immigration bill would not just target illegal immigrants but would spill over to adversely affect legal immigrants and refugees, and that the established groups needed to get ahead of changing demographics and make common cause with the growing cadre of Latino- and immigrant-led groups. While never exactly breaking from other VOLAGs, Church World Service's Myers allied himself with Swartz and Torres, if not always agreeing with their public statements or tactics.[10]

Especially around the more or less quarterly board meetings of the National Immigration, Refugee and Citizenship Forum, the DC-based groups were joined by a "New York contingent" including the AJC's Gary Rubin, Wells Klein of the ACNS, Michael Hooper of the National Coalition for Haitian Refugees (NCHR) and the ILGWU's Muzaffar Chishti, each of whom had slightly different priorities. The AJC, arguably the country's most powerful Jewish organization, was focused on protection for Jews seeking to emigrate from the Soviet Union but was also interested in building bridges between Latinos and Jews. Klein was self-interested in maintaining the flow of Indochinese refugees, but saw the need for a broader pro-immigrant movement for the next century and wanted his organization to be part of it.[11] Hooper spearheaded efforts for a legalization program for Haitian refugees, but perhaps based on his organizing background with the United Farm Workers of America, was determined to prevent the Haitian question from being used as a wedge issue between Hispanics and African Americans.

The garment workers' union's Chishti shared all of these concerns, but was uniquely focused on how employer sanctions could have the perverse effect of undermining labor protections for all workers. Because of the union's heavy immigrant membership—mainly Asian in New York but heavily Latino on the West Coast—the garment workers had powerful incentives to build connections to the Hispanic organizations. But Chishti's first contact with LULAC was inauspicious; he first sighted Torres in the Forum's offices, sitting in Swartz's chair, with his feet on the chief executive's desk, barking into the phone. "Who does this guy think he is?" Chishti thought to himself, although he soon discovered that in those early years of the debate, "all advocacy [on the immigration bill] in D.C. seemed to go through Arnold Torres."[12]

Forum board meetings, and the informal discussions that followed, were lengthy, sprawling affairs, combining elements of the standard nonprofit "business meeting"—status of the group's membership, finances, and fundraising—with sophisticated assessments of the political landscape, unveiling of new scholarly research, and heated disagreements over public policy and advocacy strategy. After the meetings, many continued their debates or plotted strategy over long, leisurely dinners. Junior staffers especially prized dinner invitations from Wells Klein, who had a seemingly unending trove of refugee "war stories," patronized finer restaurants, and *always* picked up the check. Some capped off the evening at Rick Swartz's Capitol Hill apartment with intense chats resembling the philosophical "rap sessions" that predominated on college campuses at the height of sixties-era activism that invariably drifted into heavy partying.[13] The opposition to the forthcoming immigration bill was coalescing in fits and starts, with tensions beneath the surface, as is inevitable when new relationships are forming and new ground is being plowed.

THE PROCESS

Mazzoli and Simpson spent most of the year following the release of the Select Commission report building the foundation for legislation, first through a series of hearings. There are several types of congressional hearings: *confirmation* hearings on judicial and executive branch nominees occur in the Senate to assist that body in fulfilling its constitutional "advise and consent" function. *Oversight* hearings typically are used to "review, monitor, and supervise" federal agencies, while *investigative* hearings "often involve allegations of wrongdoing by public officials."[14] Confirmation hearings on controversial nominees can produce fireworks and drama while some investigative hearings confer celebrity status on participants. By contrast, most *legislative* hearings, the kind Simpson and Mazzoli held, can be monotonous and uninteresting except to those directly affected. Monotonous or not, according to Mazzoli's counsel, the sponsors wanted extensive hearings to "educate and ultimately gain the support of their fellow subcommittee and full committee members" as well as "build a record for the House and Senate members" at large.[15] In this context "building a record" is only in part the scholarly exercise of putting the facts on the table. The process also serves the political purpose of convincing their colleagues that they'd gathered all of the data, heard all points of view, and carefully weighed all options before producing a bill for consideration by the full body. For Simpson and Mazzoli, new subcommittee chairs who had yet to prove their ability to move major legislation, demonstrating that they had done a thorough job of vetting an inevitably contentious issue such as immigration was especially important.

They began the process with almost unheard of joint House–Senate hearings. It is a cliché on Capitol Hill that oftentimes tensions between the upper and lower legislative bodies are as great, or even greater, than partisan or regional differences. Members of the Senate, which has embraced the description of itself as the "world's greatest deliberative body," have longer terms and represent more people than their House counterparts. Many senators see themselves as future presidential candidates, obviously superior to their colleagues in the "lower body." House members know and resent this, of course, asserting that because they stand for election more often, they're closer to their constituents than their uppity colleagues across the Capitol. They proudly refer to their body as "The People's House," a not-so-subtle suggestion that those in the "other body" answer less to "the people" than to Washington elites, special interests, or perhaps senators' own outsized egos. As Eric Redman wrote in *The Dance of Legislation*, a classic book on the legislative process: "Despite the condescending habit of Senators referring to the House as 'the lower body' . . . the House really considers itself the Senate's superior; superior in wisdom, superior in behavior, and (not least) in virtue. Congressmen and their staffs, in fact, cherish a fine disdain for the Senate and Senators."[16]

In this context, Simpson's and Mazzoli's desire to hold joint hearings was at least mildly audacious; a joint hearing was as likely to occur about as often as most people would be able to see "the other side of the moon," Simpson once joked.[17] The last joint Senate–House hearings had been held thirty years before, in 1951, coincidentally on what became the Immigration and Nationality Act, but in those days unlike in 1982, both houses were under Democratic control. It was no small feat that Mazzoli and Simpson overcame both intercameral and partisan tensions to hold three days of joint hearings in May 1981, with Select Commission chair Ted Hesburgh as the lead witness, together with other luminaries that supported the commission report, including Lane Kirkland, head of the AFL-CIO, former labor secretary Ray Marshall, and Althea Simmons of the NAACP, followed by dozens of witnesses from academia, business, the VOLAGs and other service organizations, and Hispanic groups.[18]

Unlike modern-day hearings that are carefully constructed to reinforce the majority's views while allowing the minority only a token witness or two, Simpson and Mazzoli made it a point to be highly inclusive of likely opponents of their upcoming bill. Their "old- fashioned" hearings were designed to educate the sponsors and members of their subcommittees on the issues, create a thorough record upon which they could base legislation they knew would be controversial, and by vetting the issues in detail, build a political consensus for the bill.[19] The hearings were also opportunities for legislators to take the measure of the witnesses, many of whom represented key constituencies affected by and thus likely to lobby on the legislation, and vice versa.

After pausing briefly to permit the still new Reagan administration to develop its own policy positions, the joint hearing process culminated in a session on July 30, 1981, featuring Attorney General William French Smith. Smith was a "lawyer's lawyer" who'd helped build the Los Angeles–based Gibson, Dunn & Crutcher law firm from obscurity into a global power, and had served on former governor Ronald Reagan's informal "kitchen cabinet" in California. With these credentials, Smith was a natural choice to be named attorney general in the new Reagan administration.[20] Smith later became known for playing a key role in advancing the nomination of Sandra Day O'Connor to be the first woman on the Supreme Court, but his lasting impact on the country's political landscape was mentoring a cadre of astonishingly talented attorneys in the Reagan Justice Department who would go on to bigger and better things: future New York City mayor Rudy Giuliani; Kenneth Starr, a future federal judge, solicitor general, and special prosecutor in the investigation that led to the attempt to impeach President Bill Clinton; and future chief justice of the Supreme Court John Roberts. Smith was from a Boston Brahmin family that went west, known for his unfailing courtesy and his "exquisitely skillful" ability to listen to others' views.[21] Perhaps because of these characteristics, it was his harder-edged, sharper-elbowed lieutenant, assistant attorney general for civil rights William Bradford Reynolds, who was viewed as the lightning rod in the administration responsible for trying to reverse the federal government's previous positions on a host of civil rights issues, and who thus drew most of the heat from the progressive advocacy community.[22]

Like its predecessors, the Reagan administration had set up an interagency task force to formulate recommendations on immigration policy. The administration's actual views were hotly contested. It officially supported employer sanctions, but many insiders, citing business opposition due to "undue regulation and government interference," seemed to prefer other options. It also clearly preferred a temporary worker program instead of the broad-scale legalization approach endorsed by its predecessors in the Carter administration, and was more overtly "political" in its deliberations, with some advisers concluding that a highly visible posture on immigration "may be more detrimental to domestic standing than living with the current situation."[23] The attorney general knew that his hurriedly produced proposals, coming on the heels of the Select Commission's report that was years in the making, would not be "considered an important vehicle" in Congress.[24] The real action would be on the Simpson-Mazzoli bill, and while Smith always carefully noted where the administration's official views differed from those in the bill, he became a reliable supporter of the legislation.[25]

THE SIMPSON-MAZZOLI BILL

Simpson and Mazzoli spent the remainder of 1981 and early 1982 drafting a bill and plotting legislative strategy, while continuing an exhausting hearing schedule. Simpson's subcommittee alone held fourteen days of hearings on legal immigration, mass asylum and adjudication issues, illegal immigration, and temporary worker programs, and Mazzoli almost kept pace with his Senate colleague, holding a dozen days of hearings himself. As Harris Miller, Mazzoli's chief immigration staffer accurately noted, "While many groups could complain that their ideas were not adopted, few could say they were not heard."[26]

Simpson and Mazzoli agreed to introduce the exact same bill in each chamber at the same time. Recognizing the conventional wisdom that controversial bills like immigration are difficult to move in election years, they originally hoped to introduce their bill in 1981, but soon learned it wouldn't be so easy. At one point Mazzoli, with excessive modesty, confessed to a reporter that, "My own personal feelings are pretty amorphous. I'm trying my best to halfway understand the subject matter."[27] Decisions about legislative details required each provision to be viewed through both a substantive and a political lens; the staffs worked in secret on neutral ground in the Capitol, exchanging drafts, calling in the principals when staff couldn't resolve an issue themselves. One of Mazzoli's staffers later proudly claimed, with only modest exaggeration, that "Not one line in this bill was slipped to us by a lobby group."[28] Ultimately, they decided to produce a relatively comprehensive bill generally adhering to the Select Commission's recommendations, but slightly pared down to the provisions the sponsors agreed were "essential" to their principal focus of reducing illegal immigration; their effort was not a wholesale rewrite of the Immigration and Nationality Act.[29]

While the Simpson-Mazzoli partnership was unusual in the time spent at the front end of the process to build support for the concept of immigration reform, they were following classic Capitol Hill strategy in withholding the details until they were ready to move, and move quickly. This is especially true in the modern Congress, where playing defense is easier than offense for myriad reasons. Consider the basic procedural steps required for major legislation to be enacted after its introduction. A bill must first overcome simple inertia. It must compete with thousands of other proposals for attention, and importantly, time on the schedule to be considered and advanced through a subcommittee, a full committee, and the full legislative body ("the floor"). Having completed this journey, it must then be reconciled with the counterpart proposal produced by the other body, usually through a joint House–Senate conference committee, and approved again by both houses, before it can be signed by the president.

Each stage of the legislative process is a hurdle that must be overcome; and even if the odds for advancement are high at each individual stage, cumulatively the chances of getting over the finish line of a presidential signature tend to be quite low. As one respected observer noted in paraphrasing the findings of the famous political scientist Aaron Wildavsky, who first applied the laws of probability to the public policy process: "even in a situation where the chances of success at any one of the steps required successfully to implement a new venture are 90%, it takes only a total of seven steps to bring the probability of final success below one-half."[30]

So any bill that goes through "regular order"—passage by a subcommittee, full committee, and floor action in both the House and Senate, a conference committee to resolve differences between the two bodies' bills, and votes in both houses to approve the conference report, eight steps even before it reaches the chief executive's desk—starts off with a mathematical probability of passage of well below 50 percent, *even when the likelihood of success at each individual stage is as high as 90 percent.*

Simple human nature compounds the mathematical problem: it is always easier to stir people up against a perceived threat to their interests than it is to mobilize support for an ephemeral future benefit. Reformers' heavy burden of proof has been known among scholars of statecraft for centuries; as Machiavelli, perhaps the seminal modern political theorist, wrote in *The Prince*:

> There is nothing more difficult than to take in hand, more perilous to conduct, or more uncertain in its success than to take the lead in the introduction of a new order of things, because the innovator has for enemies all of those who have done well under the old conditions, and lukewarm defenders in those who may do well under the new . . . [but] do not readily believe in new things until they have had long experience of them.[31]

No sponsor of a controversial proposal wants it exposed to criticism any longer than is absolutely necessary. Thus, proponents of measures to address large, seemingly intractable problems tend to favor quick action with the fewest procedural steps possible; they love "summits" or "grand bargains" to cut through the grinding of the legislative gears by moving a bill quickly with minimal scrutiny and debate. Opponents, by contrast, want maximum public exposure, and often respond to highly popular proposals by insisting that they be vetted through the process of regular order. When someone on Capitol Hill complains about "process," it's a good bet they're hoping to derail the expected outcome.[32] To paraphrase the legal cliché that lawyers can choose to argue the facts if they have a strong substantive case or the law if they don't, opponents of legislation can choose to concentrate their fight on the issues or the process, but a bill's proponents must succeed on both fronts.

Finally, on March 17, Saint Patrick's Day, a little over a year after the final report of the Select Commission on Immigration and Refugee Policy, Simpson and Mazzoli introduced their bill, the Immigration Reform and Control Act of 1982, at a joint press conference in the Russell Senate Office Building. Consistent with the Select Commission's three-legged stool, their bill included border enforcement, employer sanctions, and legalization. It also eliminated the so-called fifth preference in the legal immigration system that permitted entry of the siblings of US citizens. But reflecting Simpson's more restrictionist orientation, their bill differed from the commission's recommendations.[33] Contrary to the commission's recommendations, the bill:

- Did not modestly increase legal immigration but instead offered a hard cap, an overall ceiling that would effectively cut future levels of legal immigration significantly.
- Proposed significant changes to the existing H-2 temporary worker program, reflecting the section of the Immigration and Nationality Act in which such programs are codified, to ease entry of agricultural workers.
- Included tougher measures to crack down on asylum applicants, including limited opportunities to file claims and fewer appeals.[34]

On the tricky question of how employer sanctions would be enforced, the bill essentially threw the ball into the executive's court, requiring the president to "implement a secure verification system within three years."[35] While endorsing the bill overall, Select Commission executive director Lawrence Fuchs later wrote that he would have preferred a higher level of legal immigration, an explicit requirement for a counterfeit-resistant national identification card to enforce employer sanctions, and greater protections of the rights of asylum seekers and others in immigration proceedings.[36]

Reaction to the bill was overwhelmingly positive, and the quality of support was noteworthy, with many newspapers not just endorsing but championing the bill.[37] Mazzoli aide Harris Miller was not exaggerating when he observed that hundreds of newspaper "editorial boards from Maine to California adopted the central concepts of the immigration reform package as their own."[38] Simpson recognized that the legislative process would be "a tough, hard road. I harbor no illusions," he declared at the beginning of the process.[39] Still, the consensus of

Policy Primer: Temporary Workers

The H-2A temporary agricultural worker program was created in the Immigration Reform and Control Act as an expansion and "streamlining" of existing temporary worker programs authorized under then existing law [mainly in Sec. H(2) of the Immigration and Nationality Act]. Other new or expanded temporary worker programs, mainly for agriculture, were also debated during the IRCA era. Agricultural employers asserted that they would need access to lawful temporary workers from abroad once employer sanctions were enacted.

Under the new H-2A program:

- Employers were required to petition the Secretary of Labor, certifying that:
    o there were insufficient domestic workers available to perform the work, and that the employer had made good faith efforts to recruit such workers; and
    o entry of foreign workers would not adversely affect conditions of domestic workers.

- Employers were required to provide housing, transportation, and certain other benefits to the temporary workers, who were also eligible for federally funded legal services to enforce the terms of their contracts.

- A series of deadlines and tests were imposed on the secretary of labor to ensure timely review and approval of the petitions.

During the IRCA era, expansion and "streamlining" of the H-2A agricultural temporary worker program was:

- supported by agricultural employers, especially those with somewhat "predictable" harvest seasons

- viewed as insufficient by growers of certain "perishable crops" with unpredictable harvest seasons, who argued the certification process identified above could not guarantee sufficient numbers of workers on a timely basis

- opposed by organized labor, Latino groups, and advocates of immigration restriction such as the Federation for American Immigration Reform (FAIR), because of fear it would undermine domestic labor standards and promote unlawful immigration. Latino advocates also argued if foreign workers were needed they should enter as legal immigrants with full rights and labor protections, not as exploitable temporary workers.

important opinion leaders was optimistic; the *New York Times* editorial page hailed the Simpson-Mazzoli effort as "tough, fair and humane . . . a genuine political achievement" offering "a rare, fleeting moment to put the United States back in charge of its own borders."[40]

SIMPSON AND KENNEDY

The legislative environment in which this immigration bill was considered was vastly different than that which stymied previous reforms. The Republican takeover of the Senate in the 1980 elections was a big surprise; the Democrats' 53–47 margin had required the GOP to win a net 12 seats, including seven of nine elections decided by two percentage points or less.[41] But if many of the individual races were close, the more conservative direction of the Senate elected on Ronald Reagan's coattails was not. With Ted Kennedy still licking his wounds from his ill-fated 1980 primary challenge to Jimmy Carter, liberals were in retreat. The earlier ascension of West Virginia's Robert Byrd to be the Senate Democratic leader foreshadowed this trend. Byrd had moderated his once extremely conservative positions (he'd once been a member of the Ku Klux Klan) since defeating Kennedy for the Whip position in January 1971, when the junior senator from Massachusetts was under a cloud from the Chappaquiddick scandal.[42] But no one would have mistaken Byrd for a progressive on issues, like immigration, with racial overtones.

In many ways the election that took place two years earlier, in 1978, when Alan Simpson was elected as Wyoming's junior senator, was much more meaningful for the prospects of immigration reform, when longtime judiciary chairman James Eastland, the arch conservative who had almost single-handedly prevented Senate consideration of immigration reform legislation for two decades, declined to run for reelection. In what might have been the most crucial development of all for the prospects of major legislation like immigration reform, after being out of power for many years, according to the *Almanac of American Politics*, Republicans had "developed an impressive cohesion and solidarity" under the direction of centrist Majority Leader Howard Baker of Tennessee.[43] In this atmosphere of party solidarity new judiciary chairman Strom Thurmond, who many would have mistaken for Eastland's ideological twin on racial matters, surprised the skeptics and both deferred to and actively supported the junior senator from Wyoming in first crafting and then moving the immigration legislation. As *Congressional Quarterly*'s Nadine Cahodas later wrote, Thurmond was "willing and able to adjust to changing times," having supported the nominations of numerous black judicial nominees and voted for the 1982 extension of the Voting Rights Act.[44] While the "world's greatest deliberative body" could move as slowly as molasses, or sometimes not at all, in 1981 it was a far more congenial place for immigration reform than any time in recent memory. There were fewer liberals who might challenge immigration legislation from the left. On the right, a Republican conference that historically was hostile to measures that might adversely affect its key agricultural constituency seemed more open to some kind of bill. And Judiciary Committee chairman Eastland, who'd refused to even consider immigration reform, was replaced by Thurmond, who seemed eager to be a team player. Any GOP senator seeking to move centrist immigration reform legislation faced a far less hostile body than would've been the case just a few years earlier. And as he'd prove again and again, Alan Simpson wasn't just "any senator."

His father Milward had been elected both governor and senator in their home state of Wyoming, but the younger Simpson was more than qualified himself, having served fourteen years in the state legislature, earning both a leadership position and a reputation as a serious player. One profile of Simpson noted that former colleagues in the state legislature from both sides of the aisle thought of him as "an outstanding state legislator—the best they ever saw."[45] He was already a star after just two years in office; he was, according to the *Almanac of American Politics*, "a man other senators listen to when they are looking for good judgment and good sense."[46] The *Washington Post*'s David Broder, the nation's preeminent political writer, described Simpson as "relaxed, funny, direct, blunt, profane, and ingratiating."[47] The tallest senator at six feet, seven inches, he was thought to be the Senate's "funniest and earthiest" member, that rare public figure in the nation's capital who could count on little critical scrutiny and "reliably good press."[48] He had been appointed to the Select Commission in place of Thurmond who declined to serve; Simpson was "thrown into" the issue as subcommittee chair, he would later say half-jokingly, mainly because he was one of the more junior Republicans in the Senate eligible for a chairmanship, and nobody else wanted the role.[49]

His protestations to the contrary, his chairmanship of the subcommittee was the result of a conscious decision by his party's leadership. Almost immediately, Simpson confirmed his leaders' faith in his ability to handle the thorny issue. Hardly predisposed to shrink from controversy, he seemed to relish it, to thrive on it, to turn what would be a problem for other politicians into an advantage. Soon after assuming the chair Simpson said, "I'm fully aware I'm going to be called a Neanderthal, uncaring, an unloving slob, a racist, and just some old cob." But he took on the assignment because "there is one group of people in the world that is not being heard, and that's the people of the United States of America that are already here."[50]

There might've been some "show horse" in Simpson, who was always quotable when reporters were around, but he was a "work horse," too, proving to be an earnest, thoughtful student of the immigration issue. He almost never missed a Select Commission meeting, consulted often with the staff outside of the formal sessions, and was described as "engrossed" in the work of the commission from the very beginning. "This immigration," he once told executive director Lawrence Fuchs, "is an issue that can consume you."[51] Initially skeptical about the idea of legalization of undocumented immigrants, Simpson changed his mind after studying the alternatives, each of which he found unpalatable. More hawkish than the majority of his fellow commissioners on the question of legal immigration—he favored a hard cap on total admissions and reductions in certain family categories—and his bill reflected this proclivity, he was otherwise faithful to the commission's recommendations on illegal immigration.[52]

A key asset was staff director Richard Day, a longtime Simpson friend who reluctantly agreed to come to Washington shortly after Reagan's inauguration in 1981, just in time for the unveiling of the Select Commission's report. Dick Day was a successful lawyer who'd also been a college professor in their shared Cody, Wyoming, hometown. He was also the justice of the peace who had administered the oath of office to his friend Al Simpson at Christ Episcopal Church; the senator-elect had convinced his predecessor to resign early and the sitting Democratic governor to appoint him to the remainder of the term, giving Wyoming's new solon greater seniority than others elected that year.[53] An avid outdoorsman, Day was comfortable and happy in Cody, which is a scant fifty miles from the east entrance to the trout-fishing mecca of Yellowstone National Park; he wasn't the least bit anxious to engage in the messy politics inside the Beltway. Simpson used reverse psychology to entice Day to ramrod his staff, telling him:

> You may know nothing about the issue now, but you will learn quickly enough. Study the issue just as would the steady former college professor you were and the fine lawyer you are. Dick, I'm heading into an issue that will be fraught with bigotry, racism, and xenophobia. I'll be hit with full bucket-loads of bullshit. People will try and use emotion, fear, and guilt to hurt me. I need somebody who knows me and loves me and will help me cut through the crap. I need you.[54]

With that kind of pitch, it was no surprise that Day accepted the job. In a city full of climbers that view every new job assignment as a stepping-stone to the next one and have greater loyalty to their future careers than their current bosses, Simpson had what every public figure needs and few can claim: someone whose first priority was to watch his principal's back.

Simpson was reliably conservative on most questions, as anyone elected to statewide office in Wyoming had to be, but the racial overtones in immigration evoked his childhood memories of Japanese Americans interned during World War II at the Heart Mountain Relocation Center just outside his hometown of

Cody. Then a twelve-year-old boy scout, Simpson participated in joint activities with the Japanese American scout troop inside the barbed-wire enclosure, where he met fellow boy scout and future congressman Norman Mineta (D-CA), forming a lifelong friendship.[55] Simpson could also talk movingly about personally witnessing the exploitation that some Latino farm and ranch workers experienced under the bracero program in Wyoming.[56] Whatever sensitivity to questions of discrimination these experiences provided, Simpson's most powerful resource in navigating through the complicated politics at the intersection of immigration and race was the friendship and support, usually covert, of Senator Ted Kennedy.

When first elected to the Senate in 1962, Edward M. Kennedy's principal qualification was his ties to famous brothers John and Robert, then the president and the attorney general of the US, respectively. Just fifty years old in 1982, with nearly two decades of experience in the Senate, already Kennedy had experienced several lifetimes' worth of personal tragedy and professional setbacks: the assassinations of his brothers John in 1963 and Robert in 1968, a serious back injury suffered in a 1964 plane crash, the death of a female passenger in an auto accident at a bridge on Chappaquiddick island in 1969, followed by the death of his father, and his twelve-year-old son Teddy being diagnosed with a rare cancer requiring amputation of a leg in 1973. He received death threats regularly, roughly twice a week, more than any other government official save for the president and vice president. His marriage was on the rocks, and his wife, from whom he would soon be divorced, had a drinking problem.[57] His own colleagues had chosen West Virginia senator Robert Byrd to replace him as Whip a decade earlier, and he had launched a failed primary challenge against Jimmy Carter, a sitting president of his own party in 1980, and worse, had run what one expert journalist called an "inept" campaign.[58]

Despite the misfortunes, or perhaps because of his resilience in overcoming them, Ted Kennedy was an icon in liberal circles. His family's legacy was part of his aura, albeit not always inside the Senate, where his brother John had been derided by the Senate's "old bulls" including then majority leader Lyndon B. Johnson as a "show horse" able to make a nice speech and attract media attention but uninterested in getting things done.[59] When he was "on" there was no more compelling speaker in the Democratic Party; his address to the 1980 Democratic National Convention at the end of his unsuccessful campaign was the highlight of the gathering. When Kennedy shouted at the conclusion of his speech that, "For all those whose cares have been our concern, the work goes on, the cause endures, the hope still lives, and the dream shall never die," many in the crowd roared while others wept, and it wasn't lost on anyone that President Carter's nomination acceptance speech the following night paled in comparison.[60]

But this Kennedy was more than just a show horse capable of inspiring speeches, he was earning a reputation within the Senate as a work horse, and a highly successful one at that. He was often the left's point man on the major issues of the day, fighting against the Vietnam War and for nuclear disarmament abroad and championing the cause of a national health insurance program at home. Kennedy was also adept at winning incremental victories; if national health insurance wasn't doable, he created initiatives to address cancer research, mental health services, and child nutrition, and went back year after year to gain more funding for them. He won plaudits for bipartisan work in transportation deregulation, establishment of the Foreign Intelligence Surveillance Act, an overhaul of the federal criminal code, and management of dozens of other bills on an astonishingly broad spectrum of issues.[61]

Over time, his reputation as a playboy was superseded by his Senate performance, where he became known as "a very hard worker who masters details and outargues the opposition."[62] Every night he took home what staffers named "the bag," a bulging briefcase of memos and materials, and early the next morning the memos would be "full of notations and comments." He held policy forums in vacant rooms in the Senate or over dinner at his house, inviting experts to discuss the major issues of the day, often with a bipartisan cast of senators, resulting in deep, intellectually challenging conversations going late into the night.[63] His effectiveness owed much to his top-notch staff; in addition to the future trial lawyer extraordinaire David Boies who recruited Antonia Hernández, among his key staffers of the period were Stephen Breyer and Greg Craig, who would later become a Supreme Court justice and a White House counsel, respectively. Future Senate colleague John Kerry once observed that Kennedy, "was a magnet for brilliant, creative, progressive minds and hard-charging, hard-nosed operatives," who, said Kerry, "had an unparalleled loyalty to him because he was so unfailingly loyal to them."[64]

He was revered in the public interest world for calling in groups of advocates to discuss strategy, sometimes over takeout Chinese or pizza, for meetings that might last for hours and featured real, substantive, delightfully informal give and take, in comparison to the brief, stiff, pro forma exchanges typical of meetings with other senators. He enthusiastically took on the role of paterfamilias not just for his own kids but for the whole Kennedy clan, organizing rafting trips and outings to museums and concerts for the thirteen fatherless children of his slain brothers, teaching them to sail, and standing by them when they were in trouble.[65] All this led Washington insiders to note in 1981 that "he is more of a family man than many of those politicians who are always talking about family values," a statement that would have been laughable in the immediate wake of the Chappaquiddick scandal a dozen years earlier.[66]

But if the senior senator from Massachusetts was known for anything, it was his support for civil rights protections for minorities and women. "Civil rights had defined him as a senator and a leader," his biographers from the *Boston Globe* wrote, "and he was determined to be a firewall against President Reagan's efforts to roll back some of the hard-won victories" of the past.[67] On the related question of immigration policy, Kennedy had an equally distinguished record, having sponsored the landmark effort to end national origins quotas in in 1965, and during his stint as chair of the Judiciary Committee in 1979–1980, when he partnered with Simpson to codify the process for admitting refugees and judging the merits of political asylum claims in the Refugee Act of 1980.[68] Ironically, Kennedy's ability to play seminal roles in civil rights and immigration policy had been facilitated by none other than former Judiciary Committee chair James Eastland, the segregationist who'd declined to hold even a single hearing on immigration in the 1970s. As Kennedy related in his memoir, soon after he joined the Senate in 1963 he was summoned to meet with Eastland. After first ensuring that both were appropriately lubricated—scotch for Kennedy and bourbon for the chairman—Eastland told the new lawmaker:

> Now the Kennedys are always talking about immigration, and always talking about Eye-talians and this kind of thing. You drink that drink there and you're on the immigration committee. . . . [After Kennedy poured half the drink into a potted plant when the chairman was distracted and downed the remainder, Eastland filled the glass and continued.] You Kennedys always care about the Negras. Always hear you caring about those. You finish that [drink] off, and you're on the civil rights subcommittee. . . . [Again, Kennedy poured some and drank some of the scotch, and was given a re-fill.] Now I s'pose we have to fix you up with a third committee. Not a lot of people want a third committee, but I think you're always caring about the, you know, the Cons'tution. Kennedys always talk about the Cons'tution. You finish that, and I'll put you on the Cons'tution subcommittee.[69]

The nearly drunk but astounded Kennedy staggered away, a member of three subcommittees. He coauthored with Rep. Peter Rodino the 1978 legislation authorizing the Select Commission on Immigration and Refugee Policy and had served on the commission. Earlier, he'd introduced the Senate counterparts to Rodino's bills to establish employer sanctions for the hiring of unauthorized workers; his role in the effort was sufficiently prominent in that period that the legislation was commonly known on Capitol Hill as the "Kennedy-Rodino" bill.[70] But by 1981, his stance on the emerging Simpson-Mazzoli bill was ambiguous, even mysterious to those outside his inner circle. Kennedy had evolved from the chief Senate sponsor of employer sanctions legislation to an opponent, if perhaps a somewhat reluctant one; some attributed this change of heart to politics. According to Select Commission executive director Lawrence Fuchs: "Senator Kennedy, under increasing pressure from his national Mexican American constituency, was sympathetic to employer sanctions . . . but he was in no position as a potential candidate for the [1980] Democratic nomination for President to support employer sanctions, since opposition to it had become the civil rights litmus test of Mexican-American lobby groups."[71]

The real explanation for Kennedy's change of position on employer sanctions might've been more substantive; longtime aide Jerry Tinker noted that Kennedy's early advocacy for employer sanctions always had been "tentative" to begin with.[72] Hispanic organizations, indeed, were united in opposition to employer sanctions in the late 1970s, based on research studies and policy analyses outlining how this policy would lead to discrimination.[73] MALDEF's Antonia Hernández worked for Kennedy in 1979 and 1980, and wasn't shy about articulating her view that employer sanctions would lead to employment discrimination against Latinos.[74] And while backing off of support for employer sanctions may have solidified Kennedy's support with Latinos, it risked antagonizing organized labor, a much more powerful part of his base, suggesting that his evolving position was not a purely political calculation.

Whatever the reasons for his shifting, uncertain views on employer sanctions, as the debate began it was obvious that Kennedy would not be an obstructionist on immigration reform. He clearly liked and "always worked constructively with Simpson"; the senior senator from Massachusetts frequently praised the subcommittee chairman, even when he didn't agree with him, always emphasizing support for their shared goal of enacting immigration reform.[75] Until his dying day, Kennedy said that he "always knew he could count on" Simpson to keep his word, and that trust was reciprocated.[76] It was also widely known that Kennedy staffer Jerry Tinker and Simpson's point man Dick Day were close; they not only worked together but their families socialized outside the office.[77] Simpson would have preferred Kennedy's overt support on his bill, but he had the next best thing, which was his ranking member's cooperation, albeit often behind the scenes. Simpson later wrote of Kennedy, "He guided me around some pretty gargantuan boulders strewn along the path. No one knew the agendas of the various advocacy groups better than he."[78]

All of the stars seemed to be aligning in his favor as Simpson prepared to move his bill through the upper body. He was personally respected and popular, had the full backing of his party and committee leadership, and the political cover that only Ted Kennedy could provide. After the Cuban–Haitian boatlifts, at the height of a huge inflow of Indochinese refugees, and growing attention to the porous southern boundary, the issue seemed to be one "whose time had come." The view was much different in the lower body of Congress, however.

Policy Primer: Employer Sanctions and Employment Discrimination

In the IRCA era, it was argued that employer sanctions would increase or create several distinct types of employment discrimination against Latinos and others perceived as "foreign" by certain employers. Proponents of this view asserted that employer sanctions:

- would provide a pretext for employers inclined to discriminate anyway, and potentially a defense against charges of job bias.

- might encourage employers trying to comply with the law to:

  o screen out job applicants with speech accents, surnames, and certain physical characteristics associated with stereotypes of unauthorized immigrants

  o refuse to accept certain kinds of legitimate documents—for example, driver's licenses or birth certificates from US territories like Puerto Rico—from "foreign-looking" applicants

  o unlawfully limit new hires to US citizens, eliminating from consideration lawful permanent residents and others legally authorized to work

  o limit the proportions of their workforce that might be Hispanic in order to avoid charges they were violating employer sanctions

These advocates also argued that existing mechanisms to address employment discrimination from employer sanctions were inadequate because the jurisdiction or the federal Equal Employment Opportunity Commission, for example, was limited to employers of fifteen or more employees and could not address "citizens only" hiring policies, which would require adding "alienage" as a new ground of unlawful discrimination.

Proponents of this view included the Latino organizations, the ACLU and the American Bar Association, and most pro-immigrant advocates.

Opponents of this view included immigration restrictionists such as the Federation for American Immigration Reform (FAIR) and the NAACP.

THE LOWER BODY

The House of Representatives, which had twice passed major immigration bills in the previous decade, was becoming a far more difficult place to navigate. Although the 243–192 Democrat–Republican split appeared to give the majority party a decisive advantage, Democrats were on the defensive. Their party had lost the White House and the Senate, and the GOP had gained 33 House seats in the 1980 elections. Moreover, 46 Democrats, mainly back-benchers from the South and border states, belonged to the "Conservative Democratic Forum," meaning they were often ideologically closer to the Republicans than to their own leadership. Since Democrats could lose at most 25 votes and still command a majority in the 435 member House, these 46 "boll weevils" wielded disproportionate power.

For thirty years, from the mid-1940s through the mid-1970s, the House had operated as a body dominated by committees directed by chairmen—and they were *all* men—selected strictly on the basis of seniority. While not complete autocrats, chairs had almost unfettered authority to shape, move, or block legislation. Key decisions were made and negotiations invariably were held behind closed doors, usually by a small number of leaders. Even markups—formal meetings where bills are literally marked up as amendments are approved and inserted into the appropriate section of the legislation—were often closed, and committee votes were not routinely available to the public. As one informed observer noted, the pre-1980 Congress was "authoritarian, hierarchical, opaque."[79] The concentration of authority in the leadership and committee chairs made the House relatively efficient and highly productive on matters the leaders supported, but it was difficult, often impossible, for contrarian views to gain traction.

In part as a response to younger, more activist, and increasingly diverse members who chafed at the constraints of the seniority system, in 1973 the House had begun to adopt a series of reforms, including one requiring committee chairs and ranking members to be elected by secret ballot in certain circumstances. The Watergate class, elected in 1974, promptly rejected three sitting chairmen, demonstrating their willingness to flaunt previously cherished traditions. That year, a "Subcommittee Bill of Rights" eliminated committee chairs' authority to create subcommittees, appoint their chairs and members, and determine their jurisdictions. As one scholar understatedly observed, these actions "diminished considerably the authority of committee chairmen and in its place erected a system of semi-autonomous subcommittees."[80] Other reforms compelled that most markups be held in public, limited the use of proxy voting, and required recorded votes in committee upon request, all designed to promote greater transparency in the legislative process.[81] After the reforms, then-Speaker

Carl Albert noted that, "every chairman knew that power flowed not from personal longevity but from the entire Democratic membership."[82]

One last set of reforms, against the tide of dispersing power broadly, conferred near-complete authority to the Speaker to schedule bills, to refer bills to more than one committee, and to name all of the members of the Rules Committee, which determined the conditions under which a bill would be debated on the House floor.[83] As one legislative historian explains:

> The Rules Committee is the turnstile at the entry to the House of Representatives, the body that sets the terms and conditions—and exacts the price—for debating most every bill that reaches the House floor. Unlike the Senate, with its tradition of unlimited debate, the House is so large that legislative action would grind to a halt without limits on speaking time and procedures that its 435 members must follow. It is the Rules Committee that spells out those limits and procedures— those rules—and these can have major effects on a bill's ultimate fate.[84]

In 1979, the House also voted to allow its proceedings to be televised, after Speaker O'Neill, against his initial instincts, reluctantly bowed "to pressures from his young, more media savvy" Democratic Caucus members, giving birth to the cable channel C-SPAN, an acronym for Cable Satellite Public Affairs Network.[85] Together with increased media coverage of government due not just to C-SPAN but to the post-Watergate emphasis on investigative journalism and emergence of cable news channels—the reforms fostered greater independence among the rank-and-file, who were no longer completely dependent on the leadership for position and perks. Among the oldest sayings in Congress was that younger members should "go along to get along," and for decades, representatives abided by this rule, quietly doing their elders' bidding and waiting patiently for their turn in the spotlight. But as the seventies drew to a close increasingly the path to prominence lay outside traditional channels; one astute Congress watcher noted in 1978:

> What would have been defined as errant or maverick behavior in the past— challenging a committee's recommendation or expertise with amendments on the floor, criticizing the leadership or Congress itself, challenging the motives of other legislators—is no longer grounds for chastisement or even murmurs of disapproval. It may even bring two minutes of television exposure on the evening news, which would elicit widespread envy among colleagues.[86]

Nor were the momentous changes limited to the Democratic side of the aisle. In 1978, after twice losing by narrow margins to a moderate Democrat, Newton Leroy Gingrich, a history professor, was elected to represent a suburban

Atlanta congressional district. Gingrich was convinced that House Republicans had become too comfortable with their minority status, too accommodating of Democratic priorities, too willing to compromise. He organized like-minded "movement conservatives" including Representatives Vin Weber of Minnesota, Robert Walker of Pennsylvania, Dan Coats of Indiana, and Judd Gregg of New Hampshire to fight this complacency; calling themselves the Conservative Opportunity Society, their goal of a GOP takeover of the House of Representatives was viewed as extraordinarily audacious.

Newt Gingrich had grown up an army brat, was a student of military history, occasionally lectured at the War College, and thought of himself as a general in a war against the liberal welfare state and its supporters.[87] He deployed his lieutenants in military-like fashion to challenge the existing order at every turn, such that they became known as Gingrich's guerillas.[88] Rep. Robert Walker was stationed on the House floor, objecting to routine matters and exploiting every opening to portray the Democratic majority as corrupt and totalitarian. Much of any parliamentary body's business requires the unanimous consent of members to bypass what could otherwise be cumbersome procedural steps, such as reading the text of an entire bill or requiring votes on routine matters like approving the House journal. Objecting to, or even "reserving the right to object" to, "unanimous consent requests" gummed up the legislative works and slowed the usually efficient House to a crawl.[89] It was highly irritating to the House leadership and to many in the rank-and-file, but often made for great political theater.

More than most congressmen, Gingrich and his allies perfected the art of working with external groups to coordinate strategy, which helped grow an army of activists outside of Washington to support the Conservative Opportunity Society's agenda; this, in turn, strengthened Gingrich's hand inside the Beltway. Gingrich and his allies were said to have an "obsessive focus on messaging, cultivating a political vernacular aimed at exploiting and stoking mistrust of Washington."[90] On a typical day, they would start first thing in the morning with a series of "one-minute" speeches, that other members usually used to recognize constituents who'd won awards or passed away, discuss the significance of a holiday, or to address other routine, symbolic, nonthreatening items. Gingrich and his guerillas instead used their one minutes to jab at the Democratic leadership; the number of such one-minute speeches tripled from 1977 to 1981.[91] They applied their leader's dictum that repetition was the key element of messaging; as Rep. Guy Vander Jagt recalled, they "were all singing notes from the same set of music."[92]

The insurgents often played to the cameras on C-SPAN after hours, through a then rarely used technique called a special order, which allows speeches after the formal session ends. In the past, these were typically used by a few lawmakers to draw more attention to obscure issues; Gingrich's guerillas coordinated their special orders, lining up a series of speakers to attack the House leadership on a sustained basis. Although usually delivered before an otherwise empty chamber, the tactic gave the impression that the band of insurgents had far greater support than it did. An incensed Speaker O'Neill retaliated against what he called "phony-baloney theater" by ordering the C-SPAN cameras to pan the entire chamber instead of focusing only on those speaking in the well of the House, showing viewers that the speakers were speaking to phantom audiences. The first time this happened, Rep. Walker was passed a note that he'd been exposed as speaking to an empty House and needed to stop pretending that he was orating to a full gallery, a "gotcha" moment cherished by O'Neill and his staff.[93]

But Gingrich and his allies had the last laugh. They might've been the target of snickering among establishment figures inside the Beltway, but their principal audience was the five hundred thousand or so "C-SPAN junkies" outside of DC interested enough in public policy to write or call their congressman if they were upset about something. And they were given plenty of red meat to be upset about, as Gingrich and his colleagues spewed invective against Democrats that, observers noted, "shattered the era's boundaries of politically acceptable speech" to the devoted and growing cable channel's audience, which included among other emerging conservative activists a young radio talk show host named Rush Limbaugh.[94] While O'Neill's tactic temporarily embarrassed Walker among insiders, as Rep. Vin Weber noted years later, it "missed the point entirely," since Gingrich and his insurgents were building a constituency *outside* of the nation's capital, in part by demonizing the whole DC political establishment that O'Neill exemplified.[95]

Gingrich's hardball tactics also made for an uncomfortable, tense relationship with his own leadership. The House minority leader was Robert Michel of Peoria, Illinois, a city thought by market researchers and politicos to be a microcosm of the country; Peoria was often the site where companies would test the market potential of new products. Nixon White House aides were known to ask each other "Will it play in Peoria?" to assess the political viability of an idea with its core middle-American constituency, and Michel was an authentic product of his region. While Michel himself had ascended to his party's leadership in part because his predecessor was viewed as insufficiently aggressive, he was no firebrand. He was conservative on the issues but personally affable, a terrific vote counter, and a key player in forging coalitions with moderate and conservative Democrats.[96] Michel had served with distinction in Congress for more than two decades, he knew his business, and, as a veteran of the bloody Battle of the Bulge during World War II, made no secret of his discomfort when Gingrich, who had avoided service in Vietnam, sprinkled battlefield and warfare analogies into his speeches.[97]

In short, the House was in ferment, with significant shifts and trends often bubbling but hidden before they erupted at the surface. Democrats were troubled and uncertain as their once huge majority had eroded along with their loss of the presidency and the Senate, their ranks split across ideological, generational, racial, and geographical lines. Republicans were ascendant, but were themselves experiencing a growing divide between traditional "country club" Republicans and the new bomb-throwing movement conservatives. Having thrown out the old rules, written and unwritten, that had governed its work since the end of World War II, but without fully testing the new ones, the House was increasingly unpredictable. Legislative outcomes, experts wrote, were determined less by traditional measures of power and influence than by "skill and imagination—the legislative skill to take maximum advantage of every parliamentary device and the imagination to frame issues in terms most favorable to one's side."[98]

Into this highly uncertain arena, truly a minefield for a centrist Democrat, stepped Romano "Ron" Mazzoli, then serving his sixth term in Congress, the brand-new chairman of the Subcommittee on Immigration, Refugees and International Law. Mazzoli's third congressional district included Louisville, and had swung from Republican in the 1960s to Democratic in the 1970s, when Mazzoli, who'd represented the area as a state senator, was first elected in one of the closest congressional races in the country. He'd won reelection by healthy margins—except in 1976 after he courageously opposed a constitutional amendment to end school busing—but couldn't take his seat for granted; a Republican named Mitch McConnell was elected county judge in 1978, in the jurisdiction that included his Louisville district.[99]

The congressman's father, who laid concrete block and tile for a living, had come to the US through Ellis Island as a child and his grandmother, who spoke no English, lived with them; Mazzoli had lived the immigrant experience.[100] As he later acknowledged to an interviewer, although Mazzoli grew up in a Louisville that was southern enough to be highly segregated, he mainly accepted the reality of racial separation: "I really wish I could say that it affected me in a way that I was very conscious of it, that I was aghast at it, repelled by it, but I can't say that in truth. . . . I guess you'd say it was the norm, it was the way things were. I wish I could say that I wanted to change the way things were, but I didn't."[101]

In fairness, Mazzoli's indifferent acceptance of segregation echoed the behavior of the vast majority of white people who grew up in the 1940s and 1950s, including some now widely viewed as progressive on racial issues. When Jimmy Carter, who was often cited as a pioneer in race relations, said in his inaugural speech as Georgia's governor in 1971 that "quite frankly the time for racial discrimination is over," civil rights advocates and the national media cheered. But like Mazzoli, as he was growing up decades earlier Carter himself wrote that he largely "accepted" the reality of segregation "without really thinking about it."[102]

Mazzoli attended Catholic schools, where he was a successful athlete and an even more successful student, and proudly entered Notre Dame University, known in those days as "the Harvard for [Catholic] immigrants." Majoring in business, he graduated magna cum laude, and formed a lifelong friendship with Theodore Hesburgh, a priest who became the president of the university in 1952 in Mazzoli's sophomore year of college. These old-school ties proved enormously helpful later in the congressman's career. Hesburgh was a lifelong mentor and the "Notre Dame club" in Washington, in Mazzoli's words was "huge," offering both socializing and "a lot of professional networking," and his closest colleagues and most trusted staffers came from the ranks of the school's alumni.[103] Within weeks of graduation, he was drafted into the army, where he served as a court reporter, an experience that convinced him he should go to law school. He briefly practiced law, but inspired by the example of John F. Kennedy, the country's first Catholic president, he ran for the state Senate in 1967; Mazzoli first beat out the party-endorsed candidate in the primary and then won the general election by only 420 votes.[104] It wasn't his last close election; in his first congressional contest in 1970 he defeated his Republican opponent by all of 211 votes, a noteworthy enough race that President Richard Nixon immediately commented on it to Mazzoli in the receiving line at a black tie White House reception for newly elected lawmakers.[105]

Slightly shorter than medium height, slim and athletic, with an olive complexion that a century earlier might've been called swarthy, Mazzoli came to the issue with the freedom to do what he thought was right since, political analysts noted, immigration had not "been a pressing problem in Louisville since the Germans stopped coming over late in the 1800s."[106] Following the 1980 elections, two judiciary subcommittee chairmanships became available to Mazzoli: criminal justice, which had its attractions as the country was beginning what would become its "tough on crime era," and immigration. Mazzoli was keenly aware that the crime subcommittee offered numerous "political pluses" while there would be "no way to escape the downside" that would come with immigration.[107] The ability to follow his conscience and to advance his mentor Select Commission chairman Ted Hesburgh's product in a bipartisan fashion with fellow Notre Dame alum Rep. Dan Lungren, slated to be the panel's ranking Republican, all while carrying on in the tradition of fellow Italian American Peter Rodino, convinced Mazzoli to accept the chairmanship of the immigration subcommittee in 1981.[108] Not that the choice was completely selfless; Hesburgh privately advised Mazzoli that the immigration issue "had legs," meaning it would be prominent for years to come.[109]

Almost immediately thereafter, the Select Commission issued its report, and Mazzoli and his subcommittee aide Harris Miller were off and running, trying to learn a new, complex set of substantive issues while working with Simpson to craft legislation.[110] Mazzoli got a bit of a head start by attending several Select Commission meetings, and few who knew him well had any doubt about either his intellectual capacity to master the issues or his genuine desire to advance the national interest. By March 1982, when the Simpson-Mazzoli bill was introduced, it also appeared to most observers that, like his Senate counterpart, Ron Mazzoli had "the right stuff" to navigate the tricky crosscurrents buffeting "The People's House."

FIRST STEPS

Simpson and Mazzoli moved promptly to push their bills forward by scheduling formal subcommittee bill-drafting or markup sessions just two months after introduction. In one sense the committee and subcommittee consideration of proposed legislation are miniature versions of the full body's actions. A bill is scheduled on a committee or subcommittee calendar, and each session usually starts with opening statements by the chair, ranking member, and other members of the committee, in descending order of seniority (or, in some meetings based on order of attendance at that particular session), alternating between Republicans and Democrats. The bill is "read" by a clerk (a formality often dispensed with by simply reading the bill's title) and then is opened up for amendment, section by section. At the conclusion of the session, a vote is held on whether to "report" the bill onto the next step, either the full committee or "the floor" where the legislation is debated by the entire legislature. Every legislative body follows some form of this procedure, although often in truncated form.

Like other aspects of law making, markups have multiple dimensions. At the most fundamental level, they're an indispensable technical step: most bills cannot reach the floor without first being considered, written, rewritten, and reported out by a committee, and usually a subcommittee before that. They're also the places where a bill's political prospects can be assessed, and shaped. And since the process involves real people, markups illustrate the full range of human drama at a small enough scale that even casual observers can follow them. The body language or facial expressions that accompany a lawmaker's statements are often more illuminating than the actual words that are spoken. The degree of respect accorded to the chair and ranking member can be discerned, as can stature of key staff that the members frequently turn to for advice. The relative strengths and weaknesses of the members are on full display, as their colleagues, lobbyists, and journalists differentiate those that simply read what they're given by staff from the few that have a true command of the issues.

When committee membership has remained stable over several years, the pecking order and relationships among the members are well established. In 1982, both Simpson and Mazzoli were brand-new subcommittee chairs, and both panels had experienced substantial turnover. The markup sessions were often the first time that many of the panel's members saw each other in action; showing off and one-upmanship is inevitable in this circumstance. Particularly when few members of Congress could expect to garner national television coverage, future stars emerged at markups usually under the radar of all but those closely following the issues at hand. Sometimes this occurred through impressive speeches, as was the case with Rep. Barbara Jordan during the Nixon impeachment proceedings. Sometimes the speech that *isn't* made is even more impressive. When an amendment expected to be controversial sails through on a voice vote, it demonstrates that the provision's author and backers have done their homework, lined up their votes, and convinced the opposition that it's not even worth putting up a fight. The opposite is true as well: at many markups one can see eyes rolling in the audience and sometimes even on the dais where the members sit, when a blowhard goes too far, a dullard gets a point exactly backward, or a seemingly winnable issue goes down because of a sponsor's faux pas.

In a pattern that was repeated several times over the course of the legislative effort, Simpson moved first and with great dispatch, holding a subcommittee markup on May 6, proceeding to the full Judiciary Committee "amid intensive lobbying," according to the headline in *Congressional Quarterly*, then the "newsmagazine of record" on Capitol Hill.[111] The subcommittee approved the bill with only minor changes, producing "no startling results."[112] In an unsuccessful attempt to mollify the US Chamber of Commerce's concern that employer sanctions would place undue regulatory burdens on business, the bill was amended to apply criminal penalties—as opposed to civil penalties such as fines—only in the presumably rare circumstances where the offending employer had engaged in a "pattern or practice" of hiring unauthorized workers. Sen. Kennedy offered an amendment to require the president to certify after three years that employer sanctions had not resulted in employment discrimination, but it was defeated, which wouldn't stop him from offering variants of this proposal at subsequent stages of the process. Kennedy's proposal was a type of sunset provision; under the classic sunset rules, the provision in question would end—be sunsetted—after a certain period of time, requiring new legislation to continue the policy. Kennedy's version, known as a soft sunset, didn't result in employer sanctions being eliminated automatically. But opponents of employer sanctions believed at least it gave them a "second bite at the apple," a future opportunity to eliminate or modify this section of the bill.

More telling was the subcommittee's approval of a jurisdictional change in rule making for the existing, relatively small temporary worker program for agriculture. Under previous law, the worker-friendly Department of Labor had exclusive responsibility for determining whether a sufficient labor shortage existed before foreign workers were permitted to enter. The revised bill shifted major rule-making responsibility to the Department of Justice, and for the first time provided a formal role for the Department of Agriculture, which was inherently more favorable to growers, in writing program regulations. While not sufficient to satisfy growers, who told *Congressional Quarterly* that their "goal was to have the Agriculture Department be the final and number one decider on the matter," one Department of Labor official griped that "we were had." MALDEF's Antonia Hernández complained that under the new program, "the growers are guaranteed workers when they need them. They ship them back when they're not needed."[113]

In the context of a major bill, these small dustups could be brushed aside. Committee Chairman Thurmond obliged Simpson by scheduling a committee markup just two weeks later, where Kennedy succeeded in making the legalization program slightly more inclusive, but his amendment to sunset employer sanctions after three years failed again.[114] After four days of markup, the bill was favorably reported out to the full Senate on May 27. Although remarkably fast progress for a massive reform bill sponsored by a junior member, the extended markup did have a cost. Simpson had hoped to get his bill to the Senate floor by May 24, when Majority Leader Baker said there was a "window" in the crowded floor schedule sufficient to permit consideration of immigration reform. With the bill still stuck in committee, action by the full Senate had to await the next available "slot," which was not until August. And even then Baker was doing Simpson a favor. Since the earliest days of the republic, little Hill business was done in August, the hottest month of the capital's often sweltering summers, so members and staff plan family vacations to coincide with the traditional, month-long August recess. Scheduling a major bill in August was a clear statement that Simpson had the Senate leadership's full support. The timing was also tactically favorable in that few Senators would likely engage in obstructionist tactics that risked delaying their cherished summer break, an outcome that could bring upon them something they feared more than their leadership or even the voters: the wrath of their spouses and children.

Senate floor debate was preceded by a *New York Times* editorial on August 9, warning that the legislation was "adjusted as delicately as a clock," and unless amendments threatening that balance were defeated, "the opportunity of a generation would be lost." In particular, the *Times* urged defeat of an amendment by Sen. Jesse Helms (R-NC) to strike the legalization program, and one by Sen. Walter Huddleston (R-KY) to include refugees in the overall hard cap on legal immigration, reducing legal immigration by more than one hundred thousand admissions annually. Even with Congress winding down, the editorial optimistically predicted that if the Senate passed the bill intact, "the chances are . . . the House will act quickly."[115] If the *Times* editorial's optimism was to prove unfounded, its core thesis—that moving the bill in a more restrictionist direction could kill it—was not, especially when assessing its chances in the more liberal House of Representatives.

The next day's *Times* included a letter to the editor from none other than Senator Simpson, directly challenging the US Chamber of Commerce's opposition to employer sanctions, calling out the business group for its "selfish perception of employers' short-term, purely economic interest: profitability."[116] The Chamber's opposition, however irritating to Simpson, didn't threaten the bill's prospects, nor, as it turns out, were the *Times*'s other fears borne out. The Helms amendment to eliminate the legalization program was soundly rejected 82–17, although an amendment restricting the program, offered by Sen. Charles "Chuck" Grassley (R-IA), was adopted 84–16. Huddleston's amendment to cut legal immigration lost on a vote of 62–35.[117]

But if conservatives were unable to move the bill to the right, attempts to move the bill left also failed. Sen. Kennedy's amendment to sunset employer sanctions unless the president certified that employer sanctions did not result in discrimination was defeated on a 59–22 vote. A Kennedy amendment to strike the bill's expansion of the existing H-2 temporary worker program failed by a 62–28 vote, prompting MALDEF's Hernández to criticize what she called the bill's "underlying hypocrisy," observing, "undocumented aliens are being told to leave because they take jobs away from U.S. citizens, but . . . the growers still need cheap labor."[118]

It was no comfort to Hernández that California Republican Senator S. I. Hayakawa's proposal to create a new guestworker program that eventually could admit as many as one million temporary agricultural workers was defeated by a decisive 78–21 vote. Hayakawa had come to public attention as head of San Francisco State University when he cracked down on campus protests against the Vietnam War. He exploited this notoriety by upsetting incumbent Democrat John Tunney in the 1980 election, running an irreverent, self-deprecating campaign. Once in office, he was better known for falling asleep in hearings and meetings than for his legislative prowess.[119]

Simpson dismissed the amendment by noting that his bill already included provisions to assist growers and by arguing that after extensive hearings on the effectiveness of temporary worker programs across the globe, "we found nowhere in the developed countries of the world where the guestworker program was an attractive solution."[120] Hayakawa was a natural sponsor of an amendment advancing the agricultural interests in his state, but he proved no match against Simpson, a lesson western grower lobbyists took to heart in future battles.

Ultimately, the bill passed on August 17, 1982, by a vote of 80–19. Majority Leader Baker praised Simpson for the "extraordinary job" he had done in managing the complex bill through twenty hours of debate and thirty-one amendments.[121] Other plaudits followed. Sen. Paul Sarbanes (D-MD) applauded Simpson's "skillful handling" of the measure, while Sen. Chuck Grassley called his colleague's management of the bill "masterful." While noting his disagreement with parts of the bill, Kennedy characterized Simpson as being "absolutely open and willing to consider every point of view" on the issue. Even the bill's most ardent opponents were impressed; Sen. Gary Hart (D-CO) observed that the accolades reflected the Senate's sincere gratitude for the "highly responsible" way the junior senator from Wyoming had spearheaded the effort.[122] The debate was a triumph for Simpson in his debut on the national stage; his performance was a cornerstone of his reputation as "one of the Senate's most effective speakers, one of its hardest workers, and one of its most skillful legislators."[123] There was no reason to doubt Simpson's closing remarks: "I hope that my colleague Ron Mazzoli is ready as the ball comes down that end of the court. Rep. Rodino has been one of the most extraordinary persons involved in immigration reform for many years. I have every confidence that Congressman Rodino will process this measure and we will go to conference."[124] But in light of the events that followed, Simpson might well have chosen to reverse this framing. He should've been "confident" in Mazzoli's commitment to the bill; but was Rodino "ready"?

Mazzoli had convened his subcommittee for a markup on May 15. At first, Mazzoli's earnest, formal approach—in stark contrast to Simpson's colorful and occasionally very tough style—seemed to be just as effective as that of his Senate counterpart. The subcommittee approved the bill with only minor amendments on May 19, just two weeks after Simpson's bill had moved through the Judiciary Committee. Auspiciously, subcommittee staffer Harris Miller believed that "the fragile coalition [Mazzoli] had started to build during the subcommittee hearings was solidified during the mark-ups."[125] A crucial member of that "fragile coalition" was the ranking Republican on the subcommittee, Rep. Dan Lungren.

First elected to Congress in 1978, Daniel E. Lungren was a lawyer whose father was once Richard Nixon's personal physician. Early in his career, he was known as the "proud possessor of one of the House's most conservative voting records."[126] But as his career progressed, particularly on immigration and civil rights questions that were the bread and butter issues of the Judiciary Committee, he moved toward the center, perhaps reflecting the influence of Rep. Hamilton Fish, the epitome of the moderate Northeastern GOP establishment and Lungren's nominal superior as ranking minority member of the full Judiciary Committee. Others attributed Lungren's constructive approach to immigration reform to his close professional and personal relationship (as part of the Notre

Dame club) with Mazzoli and former Select Commission chair Ted Hesburgh; Lungren's father, in fact, had been Hesburgh's classmate at Notre Dame.[127] Lungren and Massachusetts Democrat Barney Frank, also a member of the subcommittee, were emerging leaders in the House's respective right and left wings, key players in the coalition Mazzoli was building.[128]

Mazzoli's hope to move his bill quickly was dashed when Rodino surprisingly announced he would not hold his own full committee markup until after Senate passage of its bill. This pushed Judiciary Committee consideration back until September, since the Senate wouldn't complete action until just before the August recess. The chairman's public explanation was that he was disinclined to have his committee "go through a protracted mark-up, as it had three times in the 1970s, only to have the Senate fail to act again."[129] Rodino's rationale was plausible given the history of his employer sanctions bills in the previous decade, but many wondered whether the chairman was truly backing Mazzoli's effort. Mazzoli rarely publicly questioned Rodino's role until years later, but his staff wrote that the full committee chairman "never gave his full support" to his subcommittee chair.[130] Many blamed the delay on Judiciary Committee staff director Jim Cline, who made no secret of his view that the comprehensive approach embodied in the Simpson-Mazzoli bill was "impossible" to achieve in the House.[131]

Others thought Rodino was growing disconcerted at the direction of the debate, that he feared the bill overall would become more restrictionist and less generous than he preferred.[132] And having tried and failed three times to pass his own immigration reform bills in the 1970s, some part of Rodino might've felt a pang of jealousy that the question had come to the forefront of public attention under the stewardship of two newcomers. With precious few weeks on the legislative calendar, and the House gone for the August recess, a disappointed Mazzoli publicly acknowledged that the prospects for immigration reform in 1982 had "lessened considerably" as a result of Rodino's announcement.[133]

THE GROUP

At the 1982 LULAC annual convention in July, the organization's keynote speaker was former senator and vice president Walter Mondale, front-runner for the 1984 Democratic presidential nomination. With more than a tiny bit of self-interest, Mondale urged LULAC to deepen its voter engagement efforts, a direction consistent with Torres's own aspirations.[134] Both Simpson and Mazzoli addressed the convention, attesting to LULAC's prominence on immigration policy, the issue that occupied most of Torres's time, and the bill sponsors' eagerness to court Hispanics, or at least neutralize their opposition to their bill. Over the ten hearings held by Senator Simpson's subcommittee from September

1981 through February 1982, Torres testified four times (and LULAC president Tony Bonilla testified on another occasion); in fact, LULAC testified at these hearings more frequently than any other nongovernmental witness.[135] It was hardly strong enough to fight off the bill alone, but wouldn't have to for long.

The core opposition group—National Immigration, Refugee and Citizenship Forum's Swartz and Eisen, Church World Service's Myers, and LULAC's Torres—was soon joined by Warren Leiden, executive director of the American Immigration Lawyers Association (AILA). Founded in 1946 as the Association of Immigration and Nationality Lawyers, the organization was undergoing enormous change. With just a few hundred members in the mid-1970s, AILA was at the beginning of a huge long-term growth spurt that saw its membership increase to some fourteen thousand by 2015.[136] AILA was in the early stages of professionalizing its organization to meet the growing demand for services typical of "specialty bar associations," such as resource texts, seminars and training sessions, meetings and conventions, and the expanding field of "government relations" that was especially important to legal practitioners, to both shape the imminent reforms and to update members on the ramifications of changes in the law.[137] For years driven by volunteers, in 1982 it established a permanent presence in the DC area by hiring Leiden, its first full-time Washington representative and executive director.

The tall, lanky Leiden grew up in a self-described conservative middle class household, and like many in his generation he was "radicalized" in college at Johns Hopkins University in the 1970s through the anti–Vietnam War movement and other activist causes.[138] After graduating from Boston University Law School, he joined the staff of the National Immigration Project of the National Lawyers Guild, known for the leftist political orientation of its members, many of whom also happened to be the leading immigration practitioners of the era. Inside the Beltway, Leiden quickly established a reputation as an exceptional technician, able to quickly translate policy goals of his members and coalition partners into legislative language and conversely to explain to reporters, congressional staff, and other laypersons the meaning of the often-convoluted passages of the Immigration and Nationality Act. This skill is more important than it might seem at first glance: immigration law is among the most complicated and difficult of any area of law to understand, much less navigate. As one practitioner observed, only half-jokingly, "if you read *Alice in Wonderland*, *Catch-22*, *Metamorphosis*, *The Trial*, and Machiavelli, you will know more about immigration law than most attorneys."[139]

In addition to professionalizing the association, Leiden wanted to improve the reputation of immigration lawyers, who "perhaps unfairly," according to one independent analyst, were ranked toward the bottom in prestige compared to other legal specialists.[140] The low professional status was compounded by

charges from some activists of incompetence and excessive fees charged by lawyers to their poor, vulnerable, often ill-educated clients with limited English
skills. Critics in government suspected high levels of fraud among applicants for
immigrant benefits, occasionally abetted or at least tolerated by immigration
attorneys; a *Time* magazine article once characterized the field of immigration
law as "A Booming but Tainted Specialty."[141] Leiden thus worked on many
fronts: building a "specialty bar association" essentially from scratch and
improving the shady image of immigration lawyers, all while serving as the
organization's chief lobbyist in DC.

Of his many roles, none was more important than shaping the direction of
upcoming legislative reforms. Soon after Leiden took the job, AILA's board of
directors voted overwhelmingly to oppose employer sanctions as part of its official position on immigration reform.[142] This was mildly surprising: most AILA
members' practices wouldn't be much affected by employer sanctions—expected
to be the province of employment lawyers—and the position was largely dic-
tated by principle and not financial interest. In effect, AILA was coming down
squarely on the side of Latinos in raising concerns about discrimination, and
was willing to risk the enmity of the bill's sponsors to do so. This pleased the
left-leaning side of Leiden but also required him to work on a broader front,
prompting him to look for allies. He soon found himself in frequent contact
with Swartz, Eisen, Myers, and Torres in meetings and symposia, connections
facilitated since AILA had been one of the Forum's original founding members,
and many of the attorneys that worked on Haitian issues were active in the association.[143]

The next key player to join the effort was Wade Henderson, legislative counsel of the American Civil Liberties Union. The tall, handsome Henderson was
unusual in policy circles: an African American representing the ACLU on immigration issues and the rare Washington insider who had grown up in the city.
The son of government workers, Henderson came of age in a city that was, in
the 1960s and early 1970s, still largely segregated, with the distinct cultural
norms and customs of the deep South. Job announcements routinely were listed
by race. Department stores refused to allow black shoppers to try on clothes,
and African American customers were routinely tailed by security when entering upscale establishments. When he was fifteen, over the objections of his parents who feared for his safety due to press coverage predicting widespread
violence, he joined the 1963 March on Washington, heard Rev. Martin Luther
King deliver his landmark "I Have a Dream" speech, and was inspired to pursue
a career in civil rights.[144] A graduate of Howard University and Rutgers Law
School, Henderson was hired in 1981 by John Shattuck, executive director of the
organization's Washington office, who was succeeded by Morton Halperin in
1983. One of the traditions embraced by the high-powered ACLU Washington

office staff was the expectation that their lobbyists "would be among the leading substantive experts in their fields," and while he'd had no formal immigration training Henderson was determined to meet this lofty standard.[145]

The ACLU's roots in advancing the rights of immigrants ran deep, beginning with its opposition to the Palmer Raids in late 1919 and early 1920. In the Red Scare era, Attorney General A. Wilson Palmer, assisted by a young aide named J. Edgar Hoover, executed a series of raids against largely immigrant socialist and communist groups.[146] Thousands were arrested, detained, and deported without formal charges filed.[147] The press generally applauded the effort, with the *Washington Post* editorializing that "there is no time to waste on hairsplitting over infringement of liberties."[148] The ACLU documented extensive violations of law, soon followed by a federal court decision declaring that "a mob is a mob, whether made up of government officials acting under instructions from the Department of Justice or of criminals," which ended the raids.[149] But while it had always been a potent litigator and state-level advocate, it wasn't until it opened a DC office in the early 1980s that the ACLU was a consistent player in national legislative debates.

Shattuck sensed that major immigration reform might be the next big thing and that reform legislation would be defined by the Select Commission on Immigration and Refugee Policy.[150] Concerned that a national identification system to enforce employer sanctions—anathema to civil libertarians—might be embraced by the Select Commission, Shattuck urged the ACLU's board of directors to elevate work on immigration. The board agreed, officially adopting formal policy to oppose employer sanctions because they would lead to employment discrimination and identification systems likely to violate privacy rights, and to protect the civil and due process rights of all persons, including undocumented aliens, in immigration and refugee policy.[151] Supported by Shattuck and later by successor Mort Halperin, Henderson wanted to be a player on every possible front of the multifaceted Simpson-Mazzoli debate within the bounds of the organization's official policy, albeit sometimes just barely.[152] Henderson had a long love affair with Haiti, admiring its status as the site of the only successful slave rebellion anywhere in the world, lamenting that ever since it "could never catch a break," weighed down by a colonial legacy, corrupt dictatorships, and natural disasters at the most inopportune times.[153] Already predisposed to Haitian issues, he represented the ACLU at board meetings of the National Coalition on Haitian Refugees, and later on the board of the National Immigration, Refugee and Citizenship Forum, where he was impressed by the "combination of substance and passion" of Hooper, Swartz, Myers, and Chishti; it was his gateway into the broader immigration field.[154]

Henderson's introduction to LULAC's Torres, however, was unpromising. At one meeting where the Latino advocate made his case for opposing the

Simpson-Mazzoli bill, Henderson was "horrified" to hear one of his older, more experienced ACLU colleagues lecturing Torres, telling him, "You Hispanics better get on board because this train [immigration reform] is leaving the station." Torres responded angrily and the meeting ended on a sour note. A chagrined Henderson immediately reached out and cleared the air over lunch with Torres; soon the two became close colleagues.[155] His colleague's faux pas was especially troubling to Henderson, who approached his job with an affinity for "underdog politics." He sympathetically viewed the current wave of Latino immigrants as akin to the Great Migration in the US—in which more than six million African Americans left the rural South for northern cities over the 1910–1975 time span—as less a matter of the sum of many individual choices than the consequence of massive economic and social forces that all but forced the movement of millions.[156] Here, he and Torres, who had studied international relations in school and thought that much of the immigration to the US from Latin America and the Caribbean was the inevitable impact of ill-considered US foreign policy, were kindred spirits.

Henderson instinctively agreed with the analysis that employer sanctions would lead to greater job bias against Latinos, and also felt that the issue of race was underlying much of the immigration debate, that many Americans were uncomfortable with the changing demographics of the country.[157] But he was also a political realist; Simpson's bill passed by a huge margin, so Henderson agreed with his new colleagues on a two-track strategy: oppose the bill but simultaneously seek improvements. This posture happened to be the most comfortable for the diverse members of the National Immigration, Refugee and Citizenship Forum, allowing some organizations to oppose the bill, some to support the bill provided improvements were made, and others to, in effect, try and have it both ways.

Frequently working with, but distinctly apart from, the coalition was MALDEF's Antonia Hernández. MALDEF had been a founding member and crucial early supporter of the National Immigration, Refugee and Citizenship Forum; she was familiar with and known to all of the key players in the field. She and other MALDEF staff shared intelligence freely at early Forum meetings—information sharing was vital before multiple media outlets, the internet, blogs, and email allowed one to sit at a desk and peruse news show transcripts or links, articles, and organizational postings—but rarely engaged deeply in the debates about strategy regarding the immigration bill. Partly this was a bandwidth issue: MALDEF's top priority, reauthorization of the Voting Rights Act, sucked up much of Hernández's attention in 1982.[158]

But even if she'd had more time, Hernández felt little inclination to debate strategy, because MALDEF's position was clear and unequivocal. While many Forum members considered a wide range of nuanced and subtle positions they might take on the Simpson-Mazzoli bill, MALDEF believed the bill's inherently discriminatory employer sanctions rendered it irredeemable, and the only acceptable position was straightforward, principled opposition. Hernández suspected that some, like LULAC's Torres, were a little "squishy," too willing to compromise, and she wanted no part of discussions that could lead in that direction.[159] For his part, Torres believed that simple opposition was a losing strategy, a belief he thought was confirmed by the huge margin Simpson mustered to support of the Senate bill. He believed MALDEF's position that it could simply state its opposition to employer sanctions, declare that the bill had to be defeated, and expect others to follow was unrealistic, even "arrogant."[160] Other coalition members worked hard to maintain cordial relations with MALDEF, working closely together on tactical issues like supporting or opposing specific amendments, but usually on separate, if generally parallel tracks.[161]

The emerging coalition of those opposed to or seeking major changes in the Simpson-Mazzoli bill was a chastened group after Senate passage. They'd crafted and worked hard to round up votes for amendments offered by Senator Kennedy and others, and had criticized the bill harshly in the press, but didn't have much to show for it. In truth, they had been taken aback by the speed with which Simpson had rammed his bill through the Senate in blitzkrieg fashion, his ability to crush amendments from both the left and the right seemingly at will, and his command of the Senate floor, resulting in the massive 80–19 vote for the bill he'd produced. They viewed the House, with its many factions bound to have serious parochial concerns with one feature or another of the bill, as more favorable terrain on which to prepare their defensive positions. By now cohesive enough to call themselves The Group, the advocates began by shoring up their base, beginning with the Congressional Hispanic Caucus.

ROYBAL

Working with the Congressional Hispanic Caucus on immigration meant, first and foremost, dealing with its founder, the estimable Rep. Edward R. Roybal (D-CA). Born in 1916 of a New Mexican *Hispano* family that traced its roots in the territory back hundreds of years, Roybal moved to East Los Angeles in 1922. He graduated from high school during the Depression, and enlisted in the Civilian Conservation Corps. He later studied business at UCLA and law at Southwestern University, served a stint in the army in World War II, and then joined the California Tuberculosis and Health Association, moving up the ranks to be its director of health education for Los Angeles County by 1949.[162] He was a cofounder, with famed community organizer Fred Ross, of the Community Service Organization (CSO), the seminal activist group that led voter registration, get-out-the-vote drives, and mobilized underrepresented communities first in

Los Angeles, and then statewide. Among CSO's alumni were farmworker leader César Chávez and Southwest Council of La Raza co-founder Herman Gallegos.

With CSO's help, Roybal was elected to the Los Angeles City Council in 1949, where he was a rare progressive voice, supporting subsidized housing, opposing McCarthy-era proposals to require "Communists and subversives" to register with the police, favoring establishment of a Fair Employment Practices Committee, criticizing police abuse against minorities, and fighting against the building of the Dodger's baseball stadium at Chavez Ravine, because it would displace thousands of low-income families. Over time, Roybal became known as the "spokesperson for minority groups," not just Latinos, on the council.[163] Roybal won a seat in Congress in 1962, becoming the first Hispanic from California elected to the House since 1879. He was a successful lawmaker, playing key roles in landmark legislation authorizing bilingual education programs and requiring the federal government to collect statistics on Hispanics. He was the founding member of the Congressional Hispanic Caucus in 1976, established five years after the Congressional Black Caucus, and later founded the National Association of Latino Elected and Appointed Officials. Not just an ethnocentric advocate, Roybal worked hard to support veterans, became a champion for the elderly and people with disabilities, and was a staunch supporter of antipoverty programs, all causes that contributed to and benefited from his appointment to a coveted position on the House Appropriations Committee in 1971.[164]

Even as he gained power inside the House, he maintained the activist edge that had propelled him into elected office; in 1971 he was a plaintiff, alongside LULAC and the American GI Forum, in a lawsuit charging federal agencies with "systematic [employment] discrimination against persons of Spanish-speaking descent." It wasn't a coincidence that the suit was filed on the eve of an Unidos conference, the first national convening of Mexican American, Puerto Rican, Cuban American, and other Latino groups seeking to build a unified agenda, a gathering he organized together with Rep. Herman Badillo (D-NY).[165] Roybal had latched onto a serious issue; chronic underrepresentation of Hispanics in the federal workforce continues to draw attention by Latino advocates to this day.[166] In 1981 he was elected chairman of the appropriations Subcommittee on Treasury, Postal Services, and General Government while maintaining a spot on the Subcommittee on Labor, Health and Human Services, Education, and Related Agencies. While the treasury subcommittee was perhaps not the sexiest jurisdiction to oversee, it made him one of the thirteen "cardinals" of the House, referring to those lucky enough to chair an appropriations subcommittee. Their life and death power on spending questions gave the cardinals, individually and collectively, disproportionate influence not just on appropriations but on other matters; any lawmaker needing funding for a pet project or cause—and virtually every member had such projects or favored programs whether they admitted it publicly or not—thought twice before crossing any of the appropriations sub-committee chairs, all of whom made it their business to take names and keep score. Roybal also chaired the House Permanent Select Committee on Aging, taking on issues such as Alzheimer's disease, well before its prevalence was widely known.

Few questioned Roybal's bona fides on the question of immigration; he had been an active participant in floor debates in the 1970s, opposing Rodino's employer sanctions legislation as discriminatory against Latinos and calling for increased visas and proactive trade strategies for Mexico and other western hemispheric countries as the best way to reduce illegal migration. When President Jimmy Carter announced immigration proposals that included employer sanctions and a limited legalization program, Roybal minced no words, saying employer sanctions would result in "a segregated, [national id] card-carrying portion of our population." Because Carter's legalization program reserved permanent resident status only to unauthorized aliens that had come to the US prior to 1970 and those who entered between 1970 and 1977 would receive an ambiguous "temporary legal alien status," Roybal charged that it amounted to permanently creating "a sub-class of people."[167]

Proud of his achievements, assured of his stature both in the House and as one of the few national Latino leaders, Edward Roybal at sixty-five was still in his prime by House standards, vigorous, and in good health. But for one problem he would have been at the zenith of his powers as debate on immigration reform began. That problem, a scandal known as Koreagate, originated with South Korean lobbyist Tongsun Park, who freely dispensed campaign contributions. Roybal was one of several members accused of accepting contributions from Park, in violation of the prohibition on members of Congress accepting gifts from a foreign government, and there was an allegation that Roybal wasn't fully forthcoming when questioned by the House Ethics Committee during its investigation in 1977–1978.[168]

The committee recommended a formal censure of Roybal, a humiliating penalty just short of expulsion, requiring a member to stand in the well of the House as the charges are read. After a bipartisan group of California members rallied to his defense, pointing out that Roybal had voted against every bill that could have benefitted Park, the House reduced the charge to a formal reprimand, a lighter penalty also meted out to others that accepted contributions from Park. Roybal viewed the House's action as something of a vindication, although any disciplinary action is unhelpful to a member's reputation.[169] Back home, he was only slightly damaged, analysts noted, as his "winning percentages dropped from 72% in 1976 to 68% in 1978 and 66% in 1980."[170] But in DC, his star that had once burned so brightly was clearly dimmed by the affair.

Tarnished or not, Roybal was the unquestioned leader of the opposition to the Simpson-Mazzoli bill in the House, and the advocates treated him with due deference. This was sometimes easier said than done; the "old man," a term used by friends as one of endearment and by foes in moments of frustration, was not easy to deal with, highly demanding of those around him. Once, as Roybal was leaving for a flight back to his Los Angeles district at the end of the week, his chief of staff Dan Maldonado mentioned that he had family coming into town that weekend and would be spending time with them. It didn't stop Roybal from calling Maldonado on Saturday, telling him of immigration reform developments that required immediate follow-up. "People's lives and liberties are at stake," Roybal said pointedly, "I expect you to be in the office whenever I'm not there!" Years later Maldonado recalled this and countless similar incidents ruefully, but with affection; "I was supposed to be in the office when Mr. Roybal was here, but also when he wasn't, sort of a catch-22."[171]

Roybal could be equally tough on the lobbyists, always making clear who was boss. He rarely made small talk or called the advocates by name. According to AILA's Warren Leiden, typically "Roybal would make pronouncements about strategy" he expected the advocates to pursue, followed by a series of assignments he expected them to execute.[172] He was very interested in knowing the views of key lawmakers, and would tick off a list of representatives the groups should communicate with. But he questioned any intelligence from the lobbyists that didn't come directly from the mouth of a member of Congress; on crucial questions like how a congressman was likely to vote on a controversial amendment or bill, "Staff don't count," Roybal would declare, as his own staff squirmed uncomfortably behind him, "only members matter!"[173]

Still, Roybal was as willing to take assignments as he was to give them and was diligent about following up. They'd often "tag team" important targets like the congressional leadership and key committee chairs, with Roybal personally grabbing a few minutes with the member on the floor or in the hallway, while the lobbyists went over the issues in detail with staff. Roybal and the young advocates developed an effective working relationship, built over meetings every few weeks with the congressman interspersed with frequent, sometimes even daily, check-ins with Maldonado or other aides. Roybal viewed the groups collectively as "his team" and he was intentional about deploying their resources as effectively as he could while giving them space to pursue their own ideas, provided those ideas were consistent with his.[174] And the groups definitely had ideas as they plunged into learning everything they could about how Congress really worked, and using every conceivable tactic to slow down the immigration reform bill.

THE CULTURE

After his first few months in Washington in the early 1990s, then secretary of housing and urban development Henry Cisneros was known to observe that going to Capitol Hill was like "visiting a foreign country. People up there have their own customs and culture, even their own language."[175] This was a telling comment coming from Cisneros, a smart, savvy, veteran politician who had two graduate degrees, was mayor of San Antonio for eight years and a city councilman before that, had served as president of the National League of Cities, and was on the shortlist for the vice presidential nomination in 1984. Over the course of his quarter century of public service before coming to Washington, he'd had hundreds of interactions with legislative bodies. Yet even Cisneros found much of the legislative process in Washington to be a mystery.

Capitol Hill culture was difficult for outsiders to navigate. Some of its "tribes," Republicans and Democrats, and those with natural affinities associated with state delegations and regional geographic groupings, race, gender, committee memberships, were familiar enough. Others required some insider knowledge. There were some seventy caucuses in 1982: industry categories such as the older Steel Caucus or newer Biofuels Caucus; groupings around specific diseases such as cancer or diabetes and general ones such as mental health, dental care, and vision; those organized to promote relations with other countries (Friends of Scotland Caucus), foreign policy positions (Members of Congress for Peace through Law, essentially the remnants of the anti–Vietnam War Caucus); and others. Other groupings formed around "classes" of members, especially those resulting from wave elections producing substantial turnover; the 1974 Watergate class of Democrats was prominent in the 1980s, as was the class of Republicans newly elected two decades later when, under the leadership of Newt Gingrich, the GOP took control of the House for the first time in forty years. Others were bound together based on living arrangements—members who didn't move their families to DC often shared housing—or common interests in sports, theater, or the opera, or past relationships established in state legislatures, colleges and fraternities, or previous membership in the same trade association.

Beyond tribal relationships, Congress had other unique cultural norms and values during this time. One such norm related to the unique expectations of workers on and off the Hill, closely mirroring the rhythms of the legislative process. It was simply assumed, for example, that congressional staff would work ridiculously long hours when their bosses were involved in a hearing, committee markup, or floor consideration of a bill that they had a vital interest in. In turn, it was not unusual for these staffers to contact a lobbyist or interest group at, say, 6:00 p.m., asking for statistics, legal precedents, or a summary of a complex issue by perhaps 8:00 a.m. the next morning, giving the aide time to digest the substance and brief their principal before a 10:00 a.m. hearing or markup. The operating assumptions on both sides were clear: if the lobbyist wanted to stay close to the aide, she or he was expected to produce the requested materials, even if it meant working virtually all night; if not, the staffer would go elsewhere. In turn, the lobbyist had an expectation that the favor would be returned: perhaps the member might make a reference to their organization in a hearing, at the markup, or on the floor, or invite the group to testify at the next hearing, all of which enabled the lobbyist's organization to demonstrate its clout to their members and other stakeholders. And conversely, after an especially grueling period like a markup or floor consideration of a major bill that might involve a week or two of twelve-hour-plus days, when Congress finally went out of session, it was expected that some staffers would "call-in well," taking a day or two of sick leave as compensation for the dozens of hours of unpaid overtime they'd racked up.[176] In turn, advocates used the hiatus to take a few days off, planning vacations around the congressional schedule.

Newcomers also tended to find that people on the Hill, like those of any distinctive, somewhat isolated culture, spoke their own special dialect that often bore only a vague resemblance to the English language. Portions of the dialect came from technical legislative terms and procedures. Budget and appropriations staffers referred to funding "baselines," "pay go" rules, "add ons," and "scores," all of which had specific, precise meanings in the context of funding bills. As a committee began consideration of a bill, one heard references to the "chairman's mark" or "base text," the version of the legislation that was formally considered by a subcommittee or committee, which often differed from the bill that was originally introduced. Staffers routinely used shorthand for the names of committees: "Labor-H" referred to the Subcommittee on Labor, Health and Human Services, Education, and Related Agencies of the Appropriations Committee. Only the unschooled would have confused that designation with the authorizing committee, known in 1982 as "Ed & Labor," for the Committee on Education and Labor (now Education and the Workforce). Throw in the alphabet soup of acronyms for hundreds of federal agencies, well-known interest groups, and nicknames of major laws and even subsections of laws and typical "Hill-speak" could be nearly unintelligible to outsiders.

So, for example, a lay bystander outside the Committee on Education and Labor's cavernous hearing room in September 1982 would have been completely baffled to overhear one staffer ask another, "Hey, the Judiciary mark references EEOC and Title VII so it'll get referred over to Ed and Labor, right?" Translated into English the question had real importance for the prospects of immigration reform. The questioner was noting that Chairman Rodino's mark, or the base text about to be considered by the Judiciary Committee, included a provision assigning a role for monitoring job bias claims resulting from employer sanctions to the Equal Employment Opportunity Commission, the enforcement agency created under Title VII of the Civil Rights Act of 1964. Because the EEOC fell under the jurisdiction of the Committee on Education and Labor, the question implied that this committee likely would ask for its own opportunity to consider and markup the bill—known as a sequential referral—after the Judiciary Committee completed its work. Furthermore, those fluent in Hill-speak would have inferred an answer, that the Speaker of the House would approve the sequential referral request from Ed and Labor. This could have disastrous consequences for the Simpson-Mazzoli bill, since so-called sequential referrals to other committees could delay full House consideration by weeks, even months, when Mazzoli must have already felt that he was running short of time.

THE GROUP WEIGHS IN

As Chairman Rodino, Rep. Mazzoli, and their staffs left town on their August break before preparing for Judiciary Committee markup of the immigration bill, The Group formulated its own plan. The first order of business was to gear up for the markup itself, trying to improve the bill by negotiating with Rodino's and Mazzoli's staffs, taking positions on amendments likely to be offered, and drafting and "shopping" their own proposals among committee members. Each amendment was time-consuming; the advocate started by analyzing the existing text, drafted alternatives, prepared position memoranda supporting the amendment (and opposing others), and then met with representatives or staff to encourage them to carry or vote for their amendment. Closely coordinated coalitions such as The Group prove their worth dividing up the work among many hands.

The coalition achieved a modest victory early on. Concerned about the charges that employer sanctions could lead to discrimination, Arthur "Skip" Endres, staff director of the immigration subcommittee met with LULAC's Torres and the ACLU's Henderson to address their concerns. Endres was a veteran of the immigration wars, having been originally hired by Rodino's chief Judiciary Committee aide Jim Cline in 1974, just before the impeachment of President Nixon. Endres recalled that he "hardly ever went home that entire summer" as the committee staff prepared and marked up the impeachment resolutions that led to Nixon's resignation.[177] Although hired by Cline, Endres technically reported to Mazzoli, the subcommittee chair. In many ways Endres served as a buffer between Rodino and Cline, someone known to have doubts about the trajectory of the immigration bill, and Mazzoli and Harris Miller, the aide the subcommittee chair had hired and thus controlled directly.[178]

Miller was by all accounts smart, skilled, a tough negotiator, and deeply loyal to his boss; he also later wrote a highly regarded and oft-quoted book chapter on the early debate on the Simpson-Mazzoli bill.[179] But he could be openly hostile to opponents, and as one member of The Group later said, "He made more enemies than friends, and this did not always serve Mazzoli well."[180] By contrast, Endres was always upbeat, and maintained good relations with both opponents and supporters of the legislation. At the request of LULAC's Torres and the ACLU's Henderson, Endres painstakingly redrafted the specific steps employers would be required to take to determine whether job applicants were eligible to work—so-called verification procedures under employer sanctions—to address the charge that the bill would encourage employers to simply screen out those suspected of being undocumented.[181] It didn't fully satisfy the advocates because they believed that sanctions would produce forms of job bias not covered by Endres's work, but they were pleased to get an improvement in the bill.[182]

The groups lobbied Rodino mainly through committee staff director Jim Cline, who was known to be unenthusiastic about the legislation. Cline was a large, burly man, impeccably dressed in expensive suits with a pocket square matching his flashy ties. The Group met frequently with Cline over that spring and summer, although these weren't typical lobbying visits.[183] A meeting with him resembled an audience with the oracle in ancient Greece, where supplicants would describe their venture and plead for a favorable omen. Cline usually responded to the lobbyists' questions opaquely, or even with questions of his own; Henderson said Rodino's confidant tended to "speak in riddles."[184] But Cline kept agreeing to meet, indicating to the advocates that the chairman's most-trusted staffer was, if not on their side, at least leaning in their direction.[185]

The Group's second strategy was to construct roadblocks to the bill's progress *after* Judiciary Committee action through appeals to various "Hill tribes." The ACLU's Henderson and the NCHR's Hooper, guided by Brenda Pillors of Rep. Chisholm's staff, shored up the Congressional Black Caucus. Caucus members chaired four full committees; just as important, nine subcommittees were chaired by African Americans. The Black Caucus had disproportionate symbolic importance; The Group needed the credibility of the caucus to add legitimacy to their charge that the bill would result in employment discrimination. Nearly half of the caucus members had Latino populations of at least 20 percent (only one district represented by a Latino—Bob García's seat in the South Bronx—had a substantial black constituency). This was a sore point for Hispanic advocates: in many urban areas, Latinos were spread across many districts, thus helping to elect African American candidates, but not one of their own.[186] But for advocacy on the immigration bill, this phenomenon encouraged African American lawmakers to be responsive to the Latino organizations; it helped that several members of the Black Caucus were certified "bomb throwers" willing to go to the mat to fight discrimination.

For example, Rep. Mickey Leland (D-TX), who'd succeeded Barbara Jordan in Houston's Fifth Ward (31 percent Hispanic population in the 1980 census) was described by the *Almanac of American Politics* as "less famous than his predecessor, . . . militant, inclined to protest, suspicious of the motives of whites in power."[187] It wasn't meant as a compliment, but the advocates needed militants on their side; Arnoldo Torres later said Leland was "extremely helpful" as he worked to derail the Simpson-Mazzoli bill.[188] Black Caucus members John Conyers (D-MI) and Ron Dellums (R-CA), both certified "bomb throwers," also cooperated with The Group in opposing the legislation. The Group worked key state delegations—California, Texas, New York, and others with large Hispanic populations—especially hard, finding many lawmakers who, if they didn't agree with the advocates' analysis entirely, were still anxious to avoid offending the organizations representing their fast-growing Latino constituents.

A third set of strategies, led by Torres, focused on procedural delays to impede movement of the bill after it left the Judiciary Committee. His colleagues admired Torres's uncanny ability to view the legislative environment like a Grand Master sees the chessboard, with the ability to think several moves ahead.[189] Torres knew the bill would likely pass the Judiciary Committee, and wanted to force it down a winding road complete with roadblocks instead of a straightaway leading directly to the floor. The most important roadblocks were sequential referrals to other committees with jurisdiction on the bill. Such referrals required a committee to request that it be allowed to consider the bill, and then for the Speaker to grant the request, often over objections of the committee of original jurisdiction, in this case the Judiciary Committee. The groups worked both parts of the equation; they asked Ed Cooke, a top aide to Rep. Augustus "Gus" Hawkins (D-CA), chairman of a subcommittee of the Committee on Education and Labor, to line up a sequential referral request. With Cooke's assistance, they also drafted an amendment designed to blunt the discriminatory effects of employer sanctions.[190] Hawkins's subcommittee had jurisdiction over the EEOC and related employment discrimination matters, but his real power, pundits noted, emanated from an impressive career as "the senior black legislator in the nation," observing that the slight, soft-spoken Hawkins combined a dignified demeanor devoid of "verbal militance" with a steady, consistent commitment to key causes.[191]

Others fanned out to try and set up sequential referral requests from almost every other committee in the House, with mixed success. MALDEF's Antonia Hernández was especially important in building a close relationship with Rep. Eligio "Kika" de la Garza (D-TX), chairman of the House Agricultural Committee, meeting with him several times and at length, to find common ground.[192] The chairman had served in Congress since 1964, when, political analysts wrote, "someone apparently decided it was time the 15th [congressional district, which was more than two-thirds Hispanic] had a Mexican American Congressman" to hold the seat.[193] The district was concentrated in the heavily agricultural Lower Rio Grande Valley in deep South Texas. By the time he retired in 1997, Kika de la Garza was legitimately described as "a strong supporter of civil rights" by his congressional biographers.[194] The description would have surprised Chicano militants decades earlier, when de la Garza joined fellow Texas Rep. Henry B. González in distancing himself from Chicano activists the lawmakers called "reverse racists."[195] The activists, in turn, thought of de la Garza as a lackey of the Anglo establishment that had ruled over "The Valley" in a manner that even neutral observers acknowledged was operated for decades "like something out of the feudal age."[196] Kika was close to the growers that held the money for campaign contributions but attracted the votes of those toiling in the fields as well, a testament to his political savvy.

Unlike the combative González, the amiable de la Garza didn't pick public fights with Chicano militants; as soon as their movement crested and many former radicals found respectable government and nonprofit positions, he worked with them, albeit carefully. Still, since it was viewed in the 1980s as one of the more militant among Texas Latino groups, a MALDEF representative might have been a strange choice to reach out to de la Garza. But Antonia Hernández simply charmed the chairman. They "agreed to disagree" on the guestworker issue that de la Garza would champion in the House over the strenuous objections of the Latino advocates, but decided to work closely together to oppose the bill.[197] A sequential referral to this committee was inevitable, but de la Garza's opposition gave opponents access to farm state representatives inclined to support the bill, but who'd think twice before crossing their chair.

The advocates paid special attention to the leadership, who would make the final decisions about sequential referrals and ultimately scheduling the bill for floor action. Torres and Rep. Roybal "double-teamed" the Speaker's office; Roybal took every possible opportunity to criticize the bill in his increasingly frequent conversations with the Speaker.[198] Torres carefully cultivated Tip O'Neill's chief legislative aide Ari Weiss, a young, whip-smart, "legislative whiz kid" who, one colleague recalled, "somehow had the knack of knowing what was happening in the House each morning within minutes of arriving at his desk."[199] Weiss was described by reporters as "a skilled operator in the politics of the House and also a brilliant analyst of the substance of legislation."[200] His conversations with Weiss deepened Torres's understanding of the paths the bill could take following committee action, and what was required to derail it.[201] The relationship also gave the bill's opponents a clear line of communication with the staffer to whom O'Neill routinely would turn and ask, "Where are we at on that, Ari?" whenever the status of a bill was brought up for discussion inside the Speaker's office.[202]

The advocates didn't stop there. They worked the House Rules Committee, with Henderson and Swartz partnering closely with Rep. Chisholm, then in her last term in Congress, and Torres targeting Martin Frost (D-TX), who represented sections of Dallas experiencing rapid Latino population growth.[203] Torres built a working relationship with majority leader and "Speaker-in-waiting" Jim Wright (D-TX), focusing on Wright's chief floor manager, John Mack. Wright, known as an outstanding floor orator, had moved unexpectedly into a leadership position in 1977, after a dramatic one-vote victory in a four-way race that was resolved only after three ballots in a tensely divided House Democratic Caucus.[204] He'd first been elected to represent Fort Worth in 1954, and for years had been considered the "most liberal member of the state's delegation."[205] He'd worked with LULAC, MALDEF, and NCLR closely for years, attending their conventions and supporting them when he could, and was known to be unsympathetic to the immigration bill. John Mack, who was to Jim Wright what Ari Weiss was to Tip O'Neill, and had risen from a file clerk to the majority leader's chief legislative aide, also agreed to consult with Torres and the opposition groups before making any major moves.[206]

The groups also sought to raise "awareness and controversy" outside Congress, with Swartz and Eisen working the constituencies represented on the National Immigration, Refugee and Citizenship Forum's board. Swartz encouraged state and local governments, which he called "state-locals," to demand more funding to support the potential costs of legalization, in part to ensure they wouldn't oppose legalization itself.[207] Eisen had regular "offline" communications with the AFL-CIO's chief lobbyist Jane O'Grady, a member of her women's lunch group, legendary in civil rights circles for the role she had played in enactment of the landmark civil rights legislation in the 1960s. During the House debate over the 1964 Civil Rights Act, she'd organized O'Grady's Raiders, the critical "whip operation" designed to make sure supporters showed up and voted:

> Jane O'Grady [was] the young, vivacious legislative representative for the Amalgamated Clothing Workers. Under her direction, about a dozen or so men and women were assigned to cover all floors of the two House office buildings. . . . As soon as an alert was phoned in from Capitol Hill that a vote on an amendment was coming up, the Raiders . . . dashed off to canvass the offices of all of the members presumed to be in favor of the bill.[208]

The ability to recruit, organize, and deploy dozens of people to serve as "vote herders" proved essential to defeating ninety-four amendments that would have weakened the bill.[209] Before voting records were routinely tracked and published online, lawmakers often ducked tough votes, or were easily distracted by other matters; her Raiders, O'Grady said, served as "the original beeper system" to ensure supporters actually showed up for votes, emulated by lobbyists for decades afterward until replaced by cell phones, emails, and texts.[210]

On immigration O'Grady worked with Janet Kohn, a sharp-eyed lawyer on the AFL's payroll assigned to the Leadership Conference on Civil Rights. Kohn never publicly contradicted the AFL-CIO's stated support for employer sanctions—or LCCR's studied neutrality—but the advocates suspected she was really on their side.[211] Seen together so often that they'd sometimes be referred to with a single name, "JaneandJanet" were an effective pairing; the legendary lobbyist O'Grady knew the Congress backward and forward, and Kohn was one of the few public interest lawyers with a detailed understanding of both civil rights and immigration law. While the AFL-CIO maintained its steadfast support for employer sanctions, Eisen reported that it was worried that provisions it could not accept, such as a large agricultural guestworker program, might be added to the bill, and labor's support for the bill was softening.[212] After being steamrolled in the Senate, The Group thought it was finally making progress.

HOUSE MARKUP

Mazzoli was anxious for the full Judiciary Committee to consider his legislation in early September 1982; four months had elapsed after his subcommittee had acted and time was running out. But even before the committee began consideration of his bill, Chairman Rodino blindsided Mazzoli with a letter to the editor in the *New York Times*, ominously declaring that while he did "not intend to stand in the way" of reform, neither the Senate bill nor Mazzoli's legislation "adequately protected" his priorities.[213] Rodino wanted to drop provisions related to legal immigration, a more generous legalization program, to eliminate asylum restrictions, and to cut back the bill's modest expansion of the existing H-2 temporary agricultural worker program. Rodino's statement that he did "not intend" to block movement of the bill, combined with a list of changes, could easily be read as a veiled threat that without improvements, the committee chair might well let it die. The fact that his chairman was laying down markers in the nation's newspaper of record instead of coming to a private understanding with Mazzoli energized the opposition advocates, who gleefully noted that except for Rodino's continued strong support for employer sanctions that he'd championed for more than a decade, his priorities were identical to theirs. The advocates' assiduous courting of Rodino aide Jim Cline seemed to be working.[214]

Then, Annelise Anderson, a Reagan budget official, said publicly that the identification system to enforce employer sanctions was "typical of totalitarian societies." The *New York Times* editorialized in response that this contradicted official spokesman Attorney General Smith, who had indicated that the administration was "open to the alternative" of a national identity card.[215] But Anderson wasn't forced to retract her remarks, revealing a split inside the administration and raising questions about how solid its support for the bill was. Years later, as a Hoover Institution scholar, Anderson wrote prolifically about immigration, often highlighting the danger to civil liberties from employer sanctions and an accompanying identification system.[216]

The long-awaited markup began on September 14, about three weeks before the October 8 target date for congressional adjournment. In his opening statement, chairman Rodino "appealed for support of employer sanctions, the heart of the bill" but also indicated an intention to address certain "reservations" through amendments.[217] Rodino praised Mazzoli for coauthoring the legislation, and often deferred to him in the markup, but kept a firm hand on the proceedings. Mazzoli had hoped for a quick markup leading to a vote on the House floor before the end of the month, but after just two days it was clear the process would drag on for another week. Things went his way at first when the committee rejected by voice vote an amendment to strike employer sanctions, the provisions Mazzoli called "the heart and soul of any effort" to reduce illegal immigration, but that same day majority leader Jim Wright released a letter to Speaker O'Neill urging that the bill be "given the extremely serious consideration that a matter of this magnitude deserves."[218] The letter placed Wright squarely in the opposition camp since in the context of the truncated congressional schedule "extremely serious consideration" was tantamount to pushing the bill into the next year, forcing the sponsors to start all over again.

As the markup began Rodino spoke strongly in support of an amendment by Rep. Barney Frank, supported by The Group to ensure court access for asylum applicants, removing a key element of the bill's "streamlining" of asylum procedures. Rodino declared that without judicial review of applicants' claims inappropriately rejected by the INS, "we become accomplices to the imprisonment, torture and murder that awaits them upon return to their home country."[219] The asylum "streamlining" provisions were removed from the Judiciary Committee bill; eventually they would return, be stricken again, and remain contentious for decades.[220] Rodino also succeeded in striking provisions on legal immigration, including those restricting the immigration of brothers and sisters of US citizens and the proposed overall cap on legal immigration.[221]

An amendment by Rep. Don Edwards (D-CA), one of the opposition advocates' closest allies, guaranteeing 100 percent reimbursement to the states for the costs of legalization passed initially, then was reversed after the Reagan administration declared "it was so costly it would, in effect, kill the bill," implying it would veto the measure if the amendment was retained. After state-local governments lobbied furiously, a compromise was worked out providing for 100 percent reimbursement but making funding "subject to appropriations."[222] The

Reagan administration had brought a radical emphasis on fiscal restraint. Conservative senator Russell Long (D-LA) complained that the whole session of Congress had degenerated into "cut this, cut that. Money, money, money, that's all we've been talking about," while former House minority leader John Rhodes (R-AZ) observed, "there's been a preoccupation on money matters I never thought possible."[223] With good reason, the "state-locals" feared the purported commitment could turn into an empty promise in later years.

Toward the end of the markup, Mazzoli's staff believed that while his bill had been altered, it emerged "with its core provisions intact, save for the removal of changes in the legal immigration admissions."[224] This characterization wouldn't have been made if Rep. Bill McCollum (R-FL) had had his way. McCollum, a lawyer then in his first term, represented the district centered in Orlando, home to the Walt Disney World theme park that had opened a decade earlier. It was relatively conservative but not decisively so; Democratic governor Bob Graham and senator Lawton Chiles both carried the district in 1982, albeit by smaller margins than their statewide totals.[225] Sharp, relentless, and articulate, it was during this markup that McCollum began to earn his reputation as perhaps the House's most effective opponent of legalization of undocumented immigrants. McCollum presaged arguments that remain potent to this day, suggesting that "amnesty" would be "a reward for lawbreakers," and would have "a magnet effect to draw millions of aliens across the border . . . without having to wait in line."[226] McCollum's amendment was defeated; while he remained a consistent supporter of immigration reform, he took every opportunity to push the bill toward greater restriction.

After five markup sessions spread out over nine days, on September 22, the bill was reported out of committee, technically passing "by voice vote, but only after a motion to send the legislation back to the subcommittee narrowly failed," Mazzoli aide Harris Miller recalled.[227] Prospects for the quick floor action seemed uncertain. Rodino claimed he was pushing the leadership for full House consideration of the bill, but Speaker O'Neill was quoted in the *New York Times* as saying that the legislation "had not been mentioned to me as a priority."[228] The Roybal-Torres double-team of O'Neill appeared to be having an effect, especially their political arguments that passage of the bill by a Democratic-controlled House might undercut Latino voter turnout and the rumor that Reagan might veto the bill to weaken Latinos' traditional Democratic leanings.[229] While later assessments suggested the veto rumor probably was groundless, the administration's publicly stated concerns about employer sanctions and the costs of legalization lent some credence to this theory. With Democrats anxious to maximize turnout of their base to exploit the historic tendency of the party holding the White House to lose congressional seats in midterm elections, at Roybal's urging the Speaker quietly agreed to delay scheduling of the bill for a floor vote at least until after the November election.[230] O'Neill also approved sequential referrals to four committees: Agriculture, Education and Labor, Energy and Commerce, which despite its name had jurisdiction over many health matters, and Ways and Means, the tax-writing committee of the House.[231] Mazzoli publicly complained that "a lot of people are feeding the Speaker erroneous information about the bill" but couldn't prevent the referrals.[232]

He went further in private. Mazzoli was clearly angry about the sequential referral process and the Speaker's refusal to schedule the bill for floor consideration. Upset about what he viewed as obstructionist tactics, on September 18, he called LULAC staffers into his office. Torres told the lawmaker that since the Senate bill included unacceptable agricultural guestworker provisions, unless Mazzoli could guarantee that the House version wouldn't include comparable language LULAC would "destroy" the bill.[233] According to LULAC's Joe Treviño, Mazzoli responded that, effective immediately, Torres was "persona non grata in my office and my home."[234]

A LAME DUCK

In a typical year, with Congress rushing toward adjournment in just a few weeks, the simple act of granting sequential referrals would have required Simpson and Mazzoli to start from scratch when the next Congress convened in 1983. But 1982 wasn't typical. Key parts of the massive tax and spending changes to implement the administration's economic plan had passed earlier, but fearing he'd lose his working majority in the House after the midterms, Reagan called for a lame-duck session after the election but before the new Congress was seated to ensure future appropriations were consistent with his budget targets. House leaders agreed, hoping to push through a major jobs program to stimulate the struggling economy. Lame-duck sessions weren't especially rare, having occurred in ten of the twenty-four congressional sessions between 1936 and 1982. But they face severe time pressures since they rarely begin until after Thanksgiving and always adjourn before Christmas Eve. The extra time was a boon to Mazzoli, who felt that the lame-duck session had given his bill "a reprieve" from otherwise certain death.[235] Two key decisions would determine the bill's fate—the date it would go to the floor, and how many amendments would be permitted by the House Rules Committee—both under the control of the Speaker.

When Congress reconvened after the elections, a *New York Times* editorial on December 3rd praised O'Neill for having promised to bring the bill to the floor.[236] But O'Neill had not indicated his views on the second key to the bill's fate: the "rule" that would govern the conditions under which the bill would be debated. As O'Neill later noted, the Speaker's authority lies first and foremost in his "power of scheduling" not just when but under what conditions legislation comes to the floor.[237] This power is exercised through the Rules Committee, whose status and history was summarized in the classic legislative case study, *Showdown at Gucci Gulch* as "the gatekeeper for the House floor, deciding which bills will or will not be voted on and how they can be altered."[238] The Speaker had granted the other committees until November 30 to consider the immigration bill—a lengthy but not outrageous amount of time—meaning the earliest the bill could be scheduled was soon after the lame-duck session began on November 29. Several of the committees conducted hearings and markups, producing their own packages of proposed amendments.

Almost every bill sponsor wants to limit amendments that could change the substantive direction of their legislation or affect the careful political balance worked out in subcommittee and full committee that, if altered, could doom a bill to failure. Mazzoli had another reason: time. Allowing too many amendments would permit opponents to "run out the clock." For him, the ideal outcome of Rules Committee consideration was a "closed rule" severely limiting the number of amendments permitted. Opponents wanted an "open rule" allowing unlimited amendments, to improve the bill or to plant "poison pills" that lead previous supporters to abandon the legislation. Although formal filibusters aren't allowed in the House, extensive debate on a long list of amendments while demanding recorded votes on each has the same impact, in effect a filibuster by amendment.

Here again the ongoing coordination of Roybal chief of staff Maldonado and The Group's work earlier that summer paid off. The Rules Committee's process is like a version of any other panel: it holds a hearing, followed by a markup, ending with a formal vote on a product, in this case a rule. On matters the leadership believes are vital, the whole process can be completed in hours, sometimes even minutes, but contentious rules can take days, even weeks, to produce, since mustering sufficient votes to approve a rule can be difficult if debate is overly stifled. The committee held two days of hearings to accommodate all of the representatives requesting to testify, many of whom were bill opponents encouraged to appear by Roybal or the advocacy groups. After a half-day markup, on Wednesday, December 8, the committee reported out a "modified" rule that seemed to split the difference between an open and closed rule: it placed no limitation on the number of amendments, but only amendments printed in the *Congressional Record* by the following day, Thursday, December 9, could be brought up for debate. This appeared to be a reasonable compromise; limiting the time to produce amendments to a single day seemed to give Mazzoli a fighting chance to get through the bill before adjournment. The Group's allies, Frost and Chisholm, lobbied for an open rule, and were the only two committee members that voted against sending the bill to the floor.[239] But the process consumed a precious three more days, and O'Neill finally placed the bill on the schedule for the following week on December 16, much later than Mazzoli would have preferred.

Roybal had been tipped off that the rule would allow many amendments, but with a tight deadline for filing them. Early in the post-election session he told his aide Dan Maldonado, "I want amendments, *lots* of amendments." In turn, Maldonado reached out to the opposition groups, parceling out assignments.[240] LULAC's Torres and AILA's Warren Leiden, their staffs, and many of their members were among the most prolific producers, working around the clock in marathon drafting sessions, often joined by ACLU staffers. Working in parallel, Hernández orchestrated the efforts of MALDEF attorneys around the country to draft dozens more amendments.[241] This wasn't mindless work—duplicative amendments, as well as those that weren't drafted well enough to be "germane" or relevant to the bill—could be thrown out. Some amendments were drafted on early, often crude word-processing programs, others on type-writers. The really old-fashioned lawyers wrote them out first in longhand, which had to be typed up by secretaries and returned to the lawyer for proof-reading before being finalized.

When the rule was announced, Roybal boldly predicted that the Hispanic Caucus alone would "offer 75 amendments and demand a roll-call vote on each one."[242] Most wrote it off as hyperbole, doubting that he could produce the amendments on such short notice. But sure enough when the deadline arrived, Hispanic Caucus members had filed two hundred amendments, more than one hundred on the employer sanctions provisions alone.[243] Overall, a total of almost three hundred amendments, including those produced by other committees during the sequential referral process, were timely filed and printed in the *Congressional Record* on December 9.[244] On the afternoon of December 16, the House agreed to the rule reported out by the Rules Committee, by a 257–137 vote, clearing the way for consideration on the House floor.[245] But first, the House took action on other bills, including the Futures Trading Act and legislation creating the Paddy Creek Wilderness and the Mark Twain National Forest in the Ozark Mountains in Missouri.[246]

On Thursday, December 16, at 10:25 p.m., debate started on the Immigration Reform and Control Act of 1982. Rodino began by reminding his colleagues that he'd tried to pass employer sanctions legislation a decade earlier, and that his warnings that illegal immigration would grow if they weren't enacted had come to pass.[247] Mazzoli noted that four administrations and the Select Commission had considered the issue, that three hundred witnesses had been heard over fourteen days of hearings, and that the bill "belongs to a whole generation of legal scholars, academicians, legislators, demographers, and others" who had worked on reform for decades. He expertly and succinctly summarized the bill's key provisions: employer sanctions, a slightly streamlined asylum adjudication system, a "limited and carefully circumscribed" agricultural worker program, and a "controlled" legalization program, and ended with a plea for members to "give the benefit of the doubt" to the committee when considering amendments.[248] Ranking Judiciary Committee member Hamilton Fish added his support, outlining protections against any potential discrimination resulting from employer sanctions; Fish was known as a champion of civil rights, giving weight to his reassurances.[249]

Rising in opposition, Roybal complained about the bill being taken up so late in the evening, as if dealing "with wilderness and frogs, with wild animals . . . took precedence over a bill that affects millions of individuals the moment it becomes law, and millions of individuals for generations to come."[250] Coming from someone who'd worked furiously to prevent the bill from being debated at all, this had to exasperate Mazzoli, who tried to respond, but the Hispanic congressman would not yield time to the subcommittee chairman. When Mazzoli was finally able to address the issue, he said that, "We have done almost everything from begging to shining shoes" to get the bill scheduled.[251] Roybal noted that no House minority members supported the bill, warned that employer sanctions would not work, would lead to discrimination, and eventually a national ID card. But he vented the most fury at the H-2 agricultural worker provisions that he called "a back-door *bracero* program."[252] Rep. Henry B. González reminded members that he had warned during the debates on the 1965 and 1976 bills that restrictive quotas on western hemispheric migration would make "legal immigration all but impossible for the typical Mexican or Bolivian or Central American—quotas that perforce create illegal immigration on a very large scale."[253]

There was a bit of excitement just before the House adjourned, well after midnight. Pointing out that no Hispanic groups supported the bill, Rep. Conyers asked rhetorically, "Don't they know anything about their own problems?" For the second time he called the bill "insulting"; Mazzoli had parried earlier remarks by walking through purported protections against discrimination in the bill, but this time he almost lost his cool. Staring at Conyers, but speaking of him in the third person to avoid breaking the House rule that prohibits direct personal attacks, Mazzoli shot back: "I certainly resent what the gentleman from Michigan has said. . . . If not this bill that is before the House, then what bill? And of course, there is no [other] bill pending. And if not now, this time of year, at this moment in the legislative session, then when?"[254]

As he left the chamber in the wee hours of the morning of December 17, Mazzoli could not have been optimistic; he faced a slew of amendments and Congress was expected to adjourn in a few days. When Majority Leader Wright had indicated earlier that day that debate on immigration reform would continue at least through a rare Saturday session, some members had indicated their displeasure by hissing audibly. The Speaker himself said, "I'm not enamored of the bill myself, to be perfectly truthful." Still, Mazzoli saw a tiny glimmer of hope in the fact that the Senate was still tied up in procedural debates over spending issues. "The only thing we have going for us is gridlock in the Senate," Mazzoli told the *New York Times*, expressing the hope that the bill could be finished after a few more days of debate.[255]

There was always the small chance that if the initial set of amendments could be disposed of quickly, then the mood of the House and the leadership might turn in the bill's favor, and that members otherwise inclined to be obstructionist might bow to the pressure and be persuaded to withdraw their amendments or accept time-saving voice votes. But right off the bat, at 10:40 p.m. the next evening, after unrelated matters had been considered and disposed of, Rep. Manuel Lujan (R-NM), the only Republican member of the Hispanic Caucus, demanded a "quorum call"—a classic delaying tactic—on a routine motion to bring up the immigration bill.[256]

Rep. de la Garza noted that his ancestors began as Spanish subjects living in "New Spain," later became Mexican, then Texans in the days of the Republic, and then Americans, even though the family had never moved. Long before it became a catchphrase, he foreshadowed the "we didn't cross the border, the border crossed us" rallying cry of Latino immigrants' rights activists of a subsequent generation.[257] Rep. Bob García (D-NY), a Puerto Rican from the South Bronx, revealed a personal connection, recalling an in-law who was undocumented for forty years and had "constantly looked over his shoulder making certain . . . that there was no INS close by. Let me just say that it is one hell of a way to live."[258] On the GOP side of the aisle, Rep. Sid Morrison (R-WA), a champion of western agriculture, supported temporary farmworker programs, Rep. John Erlenborn (R-IL), one of the body's more articulate restrictionists, called for a tougher bill, and Rep. Lungren concluded with a practical exhortation for Congress to finally deal with a problem that "would not go away."[259] It was nearly 1:00 a.m. when the body adjourned, and whatever tiny window that the bill might be able to slip through had closed; as Mazzoli's aide Harris Miller wrote, whatever debate remained was "anticlimactic."[260]

Just before noon on December 18, the final nail in the coffin was pounded in. A bill supporter asked whether the House might return to complete the immigration bill the next day, on Sunday, if other matters were delayed. Majority Leader Wright responded that "it is our plan that once the President signs the conference report for the appropriations to adjourn sine die," meaning until the next session of Congress in 1983. Passage of the conference report required to keep the government open before Christmas Eve was a virtual certainty, so in effect Wright was saying that they had a few hours to finish the bill, without a single amendment of the three hundred pending yet disposed of. Lest anyone doubt the leadership's intentions, the Speaker said that the immigration bill was being brought up simply "as a courtesy," meaning it wasn't a priority for the leadership.[261] It was an open invitation for opponents to continue stalling.

The first amendments considered were those from the committees to whom the bill had been sequentially referred. The Committee on Education and Labor proposed a package of amendments, many sponsored by Rep. Gus Hawkins, chairman of the subcommittee on employment opportunities. One Hawkins amendment, drafted by Hawkins's counsel Ed Cooke with LULAC's Arnoldo Torres and the ACLU's Wade Henderson earlier that summer, sought to ameliorate the discriminatory effect of employer sanctions by requiring employers to keep records of applicants rejected, as well as those hired, to permit a determination of whether discrimination against "foreign-looking" individuals had occurred. As Hawkins explained, "Under the bill as proposed, an individual seeking employment may offer documentation concerning that individual's legal status" that would have to be retained by the employer for three years as a protection against employer sanctions; his amendment extended this requirement to applicants, so if a question of discrimination arose at some later point, one would be able to identify the entire pool of applicants, and not just the person actually hired.[262]

The amendment was "reluctantly" opposed by Mazzoli, who said his bill already included adequate protections against discrimination, and by moderate Republican Hamilton Fish, who complained about the "almost impossible paperwork burden imposed on small employers for very little return." Rep. Rodino suggested that the amendment be accepted, and Hawkins's committee colleague George Miller (D-CA), also spoke in favor of the provision.[263] Nearly forty-five minutes had been consumed by the time Rep. Lungren made obvious what everyone was thinking, observing that "the length of the debate [on the Hawkins amendment] suggests that perhaps the bill will not be passed."[264] With debate on the first amendment continuing after more than an hour, Rep. Clay Shaw (R-FL), a supporter of the bill, rose to express his frustration: "The [opposition] Members have certainly proven one thing, that if they can take up 1½ hours of debate on one amendment without getting a vote they will have little trouble—little trouble in filling up 2 short hours with nothing but delaying tactics that will make it impossible for us to get a bill out this year."[265] Mazzoli, who almost certainly agreed with Shaw's observation, took the high road in responding, perhaps looking to avoid alienating those whose votes he would be courting in the future, saying, "I wish we could expedite the debate, but I think to do so would be to curtail a free and fair discussion of some very difficult concepts."[266]

At 4:50 p.m., nearly five hours after the beginning of the session, the Hawkins amendment was voted down by a 213–110 margin, with 109 members not voting, an indication that lawmakers had begun leaving town for the holidays. While disappointed to lose on the amendment, LULAC's Torres and the ACLU's Henderson were "happy, even ecstatic" that the provision they'd helped craft as part of their sequential referral strategy way back over the summer had borne fruit, consuming hours of precious floor time.[267] But they could count votes, and understood that they didn't have anything close to a majority for the procedural protections they believed were required to blunt the discriminatory effects of employer sanctions.

Soon, the discussion shifted to Mazzoli himself. First up with a tribute was Rep. Henry Hyde (R-IL), who was viewed as "a major legislative force . . . on the basis of strong convictions and political skill."[268] Hyde was at his bipartisan best, stating, "Nobody in America could have done as good a job as the gentleman from Kentucky [Mazzoli] nor the gentleman from New York [Fish]." Rep. Hal Daub (R-NE), a fierce opponent of legalization but a supporter of the bill, also praised Mazzoli for his work. They were joined by Rep. de la Garza, who despite his opposition to the legislation graciously noted that Mazzoli and Rodino's handling of the bill was "exemplary," while Rep. García added that Rodino and Mazzoli had "conducted themselves in a manner that truly reflects what this body is all about."[269]

Just before 5:30 p.m., as debate on the bill came to a close, Mazzoli received what his aide Harris Miller remembers as a spontaneous and heartfelt "standing ovation from his House colleagues—a rare occurrence for any member."[270] Ron Mazzoli had demonstrated a strong command of the issues, had been gracious to his opponents and respected their prerogatives when they were less respectful of his, earning the genuine admiration of his coworkers. Still, Robert Pear, the *New York Times* "reporter of record" on the bill, concluded that Mazzoli "failed to develop the necessary support for the bill at the top of his own party. . . . Ultimately, the bill failed because the opponents cared more deeply about it than the proponents."[271] Both Mazzoli and Simpson were philosophical, even conciliatory, at least in their public statements; the House sponsor said that "it was very much in the national interest to have long deliberation" on the measure, while his Senate counterpart professed to have "not a shred of bitterness or ill feeling" about the failure of the House to pass the bill.[272] The political smart money bet that the outcome would be different the next time around, when Mazzoli and Simpson could start afresh early in the year, with momentum and time seemingly in their favor.

As proved true time and time again when it came to the immigration bill, the conventional wisdom was wrong.

CHAPTER 4

New Blood, Shifting Strategies

THE SECOND TIME AROUND

With the beginning of the new Congress in 1983, the Simpson and Mazzoli duo were determined to try again, and why not? Simpson had emerged as a certified star. The *Almanac of American Politics* said he'd done "what even his critics must concede is a brilliant job" in managing immigration reform to passage with sixty votes to spare in a Senate "where opponents of any measure can choose from a dazzling array of procedural devices to kill it."[1] Mazzoli's industrious, diligent work had earned a standing ovation from his House colleagues at the end of the previous Congress, but bottom line, he hadn't delivered the final product. Simpson would never be anything but effusive in his praise of his House colleague, describing Mazzoli as "spirited," "cerebral," "intellectual," while also being "kind," "sweet," and "sensitive to others."[2] But a telling indicator of the relative power dynamic was that the senator from Wyoming had taken to calling Mazzoli his "sidekick."[3]

The two introduced legislation on the same day, February 21, 1983, but did not file identical bills as they'd done the year before. As Mazzoli aide Harris Miller explained, they "took up the legislation as it stood before adjournment of the 97th Congress" with Simpson introducing the Senate-passed bill and Mazzoli submitting the version that had been reported by the Judiciary Committee.[4] The *New York Times* story on the bills placed the latest immigration reform effort in a broader historical context, pointedly noting that: "Congress had been searching for ways to curtail illegal immigration for more than 15 years. The issue, however, has proved to be so complex and the affected interests so numerous that the lawmakers have been unable to complete action on a comprehensive bill within the two-year life of a Congress."[5]

Even as the *Times*'s news staff expressed caution about the bill's prospects, its editorial page accurately noted that for the bill to succeed "speed is essential."[6] Simpson and Mazzoli needed no outside prodding to move quickly. Both held hearings that, while hardly truncated, were less exhaustive than the year before. Given that his bill faced greater controversy in the House, Mazzoli again demonstrated a willingness to hear from all sides; his hearings heard from more than seventy witnesses over six days, with proceedings totaling 1,500-plus pages.[7] Opponents were undaunted. The *Washington Post* chronicled an exchange in which Latino groups were advised, " 'There will be no legislation without employer sanctions,' and urged compromise," but LULAC's Torres shot back, "then the alternatives we have are virtually nil except one: to work once again to defeat the legislation."[8] And the American Bar Association, the nation's principal organization of lawyers and a previous supporter of employer sanctions, reversed its position, stating that the policy "would be an unworkable, ineffective, expensive, and discriminatory procedure."[9] The ABA's reversal wasn't accidental. American Immigration Lawyers Association president Robert Juceam, a partner at the New York-based law firm Fried, Frank, Harris & Shriver, whose named partners included the Kennedy in-law and former vice presidential candidate Sargent Shriver, was influential in ABA circles, had served on MALDEF's board of directors, and worked closely with lawyers involved in Haitian issues.[10] Simpson was sufficiently concerned that he met with the ABA, and in his words, "laid it on them."[11] But the process still seemed fun to Simpson, who analogized management of the immigration bill to a childhood game: "where this peg pops up here and you smash that one, and then down the board another one pops up and then you smash that one, and the one in the middle pops up and you smash that one. That is what this game is in every sense, because you think you've solved one part of it or are headed toward a solution, then something pops up somewhere else."[12]

Despite having to play a constant game of "whack a mole," Simpson was well-positioned to move his bill quickly. Simpson supporter and Senate majority leader Howard Baker had a strengthened hand; pundits saw the 1982 midterm elections, when the president's party typically lost seats, as "something of a triumph" for Baker, who held onto his majority, while House Speaker Tip O'Neill's Democrats gained some twenty-six seats.[13]

Mazzoli faced a far more daunting landscape. Many members of the congressional class of 1983, including four new Hispanics—Solomon Ortiz from Corpus Christi, Texas; Bill Richardson from New Mexico; and Esteban Torres and Mathew "Marty" Martínez from greater Los Angeles—were likely opponents. The four freshmen nearly doubled the size of the Hispanic Caucus and were joined by non-Latinos elected from districts with growing Latino populations, including El Paso's Ron Coleman and the Los Angeles area trio of Howard Berman, Mel Levine, and Richard Lehman. Inasmuch as addition of these potential opponents might force Mazzoli to spend valuable time either ameliorating their concerns or overcoming their opposition, the Kentucky Democrat felt he had no time to waste. The feeling was well-founded since delay is often the most effective tactic for opponents of legislation. The key to its effectiveness is the congressional calendar; to oversimplify, the number of days available to move legislation is finite, while the list of bills that could be considered is nearly unlimited. If a bill's adversaries can postpone action on a measure long enough, any number of ensuing developments can cause a proposal's backers to run out of time and have to start from square one in the following Congress. Even partial delays at crucial phases of the legislative process can kill a bill as surely as a negative vote.

Simpson once again moved quickly, holding a perfunctory subcommittee markup on April 7 that lasted a total of forty-five minutes.[14] On April 19, the Judiciary Committee met to consider the bill, and as he had the year before, Simpson generally got his way. In pro forma fashion Kennedy proposed and the committee rejected a series of amendments to expand legalization, strengthen judicial review of asylum and other immigration proceedings, and "sunset" employer sanctions if a pattern of discrimination were documented. Kennedy won a small victory when he secured an amendment to narrow the bill's elimination of the so-called "fifth preference" immigration category covering brothers and sisters of US citizens. Simpson unenthusiastically agreed to Kennedy's formulation limiting the damage to married siblings, meaning that unmarried ones would remain eligible, although the Massachusetts senator was nearly reduced to begging to achieve that tiny concession.[15] MALDEF's Antonia Hernández asserted that the legislation "does not represent the interests of the Hispanic community, which is just as much a part of this society as business, labor and agricultural growers, whose concerns are reflected in the bill."[16]

Simpson had his own opinions about whose interests were represented in his legislation, remarking that he was fighting "a continuing, running gun battle with tunnel vision, short-term special interests" that in his view were attempting to undercut the nation's broader interests.[17] Majority Leader Baker scheduled the bill for Senate floor action just a few weeks later, where Simpson once again commanded the floor, and decided what would pass and what wouldn't, keeping his core bill intact. He also preempted the biggest threat. Attempts to include a broader agricultural temporary worker program failed the previous year when Sen. Hayakawa's amendment was rejected decisively. This time around, between the Judiciary markup and floor consideration, Arizona Democrat Dennis DeConcini, joined by Hayakawa's replacement Republican Pete Wilson of California, negotiated a deal with Simpson and Kennedy. Under their "transition program" agricultural growers, and only the growers, would be allowed three years to comply with employer sanctions: they could retain all of their unauthorized workers in year one; in year two, two-thirds of their workers could be undocumented, with the percentage falling to one-third in the third year. Only in the fourth year would growers be fully subject to employer sanctions. Simpson noted that only workers with a proven history of work with the affected employer could be considered "transitionals."[18] It seemed to some a throwback to the era when the INS permitted growers to retain their so-called "specials," undocumented workers who had exceptional training or skills, even in the midst of purported enforcement crackdowns.[19]

Wilson wanted to go further. He insisted that the bureaucratic nature of the existing H-2 system, even if streamlined, was unworkable for western growers of "perishable crops" given the unpredictable timing of harvests and the inherent fragility of their products. He proposed an extension of the transition period if the attorney general found that the H-2 program had an adverse impact on the "perishable commodities industry."[20] Simpson opposed the amendment, citing the unfairness of giving one industry an exception while expecting compliance from others, even though the transition program he had negotiated earlier provided precisely such a special exemption for agriculture. Kennedy cited traditional labor arguments predicting the provision would undercut domestic workers, inserting into the *Record* a detailed memorandum from the United Farm Workers union outlining the opposition case.[21] The Wilson amendment was crushed by a 72–20 vote.[22] Working in tandem, Simpson and Kennedy made quick work of arch-conservative North Carolina Republican Jesse Helms's amendments to strike the legalization program, to overturn the *Plyler v. Doe* decision that guaranteed undocumented children the right to public education, and to eliminate the "contiguous countries" section permitting higher legal immigration from Mexico; all went down by substantial margins.[23]

An apparently more serious challenge came from the Hart-Levin amendment, whose lead sponsor, Colorado's Gary Hart, was one of the highest profile Democrats in the Senate. He'd first come to attention as architect of George McGovern's surprising presidential nomination victory in a crowded field in 1972, was elected to the Senate by a wide margin in 1974, became something of a "New Democrat" even before the term had been invented, perhaps enabling him to survive, if just barely, the Reagan landslide in 1980. Tall, handsome, and smart, Hart was a serious contender for the 1984 Democratic presidential nomination but was seen as a "show horse" by some traditionalists. Few doubted that Hart had the brains and skills to be a serious legislator, but outside of environmental and defense issues where he had unquestioned expertise, Arnoldo Torres would later say he thought of Hart as "broad but shallow."[24]

The amendment's cosponsor was Carl Levin, a first-term Democrat from Michigan. Levin was often clad in rumpled suits and his eyeglasses kept sliding down his nose; he was no show horse. As president of the Detroit city council in a racially turbulent time, according to the *Almanac of American Politics*, he'd "earned the trust and votes of Detroiters of both races" and was seen as a "naturally creative legislator."[25] While Hart was an opponent of the bill, Levin vowed to support it; both were troubled by the charge that employer sanctions would cause discrimination. Much of their amendment prohibited bias against those not covered by existing laws, outlawed discrimination on the basis of "alienage"—qualified applicants could not be barred from jobs simply because they'd been born abroad—and was similar to the Hawkins amendment in the House but added a new "special counsel" within the Justice Department to enforce the provisions.[26] The enforcement section had originated with the ACLU's Mort Halperin, who'd discussed the problem with a friend, a judge with the National Labor Relations Board, who recommended using the NLRB statute as a model. As Halperin recalled: "So I Xeroxed a copy of the relevant section of the NLRB statute, and I hand-wrote a few changes on the Xerox copy. And that became the new [proposed anti-discrimination] unit in the Justice Department."[27]

Hart introduced his amendment by noting that the EEOC did not effectively protect Latinos from job discrimination, countering arguments that existing civil rights protections were adequate to address any new job bias that might be generated. He entered into the *Record* a letter from the commission's deputy general counsel, who wrote that, "To summarize the [EEOC's] administrative and litigation efforts on behalf of Hispanics as 'dismal' makes matters sound better than they actually are."[28] Hart also inserted into the *Record* a memorandum from the impartial Congressional Research Service supporting the view that without his amendment, lawfully present workers experiencing employment discrimination on the basis of alienage would lack remedies under existing law.[29]

Because prior concessions hadn't attenuated the intensity of the opposition, Simpson went into this debate thinking, "What's the use of compromising if they're not going to be satisfied with anything?"[30] Simpson had already agreed to accept the House's version of employer sanctions calling for "mandatory verification" of all new hires by employers, the provision that LULAC's Torres and the ACLU's Henderson had worked on with Mazzoli's staff the year before. It was for Simpson a significant concession, because it guaranteed continued opposition to the bill by the US Chamber of Commerce, which wanted a more relaxed procedure whereby verification wouldn't be required until after a first offense. Simpson had also agreed, if unenthusiastically, to Kennedy's soft sunset proposal for a General Accounting Office report on discrimination, and an amendment by Senator Mark Hatfield (R-OR) requiring congressional and executive branch review of proposals to create a "secure verification or employee identification system."[31] In other words, he felt he'd done more than enough for the civil rights–civil liberties crowd.

Simpson vigorously opposed Hart-Levin, making three basic points: the measure would not cause discrimination, it included a series of reports to uncover such discrimination if it did occur, and in any event existing law provided sufficient protections against job bias. He urged his colleagues to defeat the amendment, and they did, by a very large 59–29 vote.[32] Simpson actually lost a vote on an amendment by Idaho Republican James McClure, prohibiting INS from entering open fields without obtaining a search warrant; a "strange bedfellow" coalition of conservatives representing agricultural interests and civil libertarians produced 62 votes for this amendment.[33] One obstacle to the bill's momentum was removed when Kennedy and Simpson agreed to a compromise on asylum and related procedures, with the Massachusetts Democrat winning continued judicial review of all deportation, exclusion, and asylum cases in federal court.[34] The end of the Senate debate was anticlimactic; Simpson closed by concluding his bill was "not racist, not nativist, not mean." His colleagues agreed, passing the bill by an overwhelming 76–18 vote margin on May 18.[35]

Meanwhile, Mazzoli had also been moving forward with alacrity. After his hearings in March, he presided over a two-day subcommittee markup in April where pro-immigration advocates came away with some victories. Mazzoli authored an amendment to expand the legalization program by extending the eligibility cutoff date by a year, to January 1, 1981—allowing somewhat more undocumented immigrants to qualify—and turning it into a single-tier program, meaning that those legalized would immediately become permanent residents, eliminating the intermediate temporary status included in the Senate's two-tiered program. He sponsored another amendment to expand the range of organizations that could be designated by the government to assist legalization applicants. Rep. Lungren offered and won a version of the familiar "contiguous countries" amendment to provide more visas for Mexico and Canada. The Group's only major loss was adoption of an amendment by Rep. McCollum to severely limit judicial review of INS decisions, a particular concern of refugee advocates.[36]

Unlike the previous year, when Rodino declined to consider the bill until its counterpart had first cleared the Senate, the Judiciary Committee began its markup in early May. With aggressive support from the US Chamber of Commerce, Rep. Tom Kindness (R-OH) won an amendment that, in effect, postponed employers' responsibility to verify the immigration status of new hires until after a first offense. Rep. Don Edwards succeeded in winning 100 percent reimbursement to state-local governments for the costs of legalization. In perhaps the most contentious debate, Rep. Barney Frank's amendment to extend the legalization cutoff date by one additional year to January 1, 1982, prevailed by a 15–14 vote, and other attempts to limit legalization were soundly defeated. While characterized by "strong and at times heated debate," the outcome was generally in line with predictions of informed observers, meaning that the core elements of the legislation remained intact.[37] Auspiciously, it also seemed that Mazzoli had garnered Rodino's full support, after having failed to do so the year before.[38] In an unusually optimistic assessment, *New York Times* reporter Robert Pear identified many factors that seemed to augur well for the bill's prospects, including the sponsors' willingness to be "more conciliatory, more willing to negotiate and to cut deals" than in the previous session.[39] The bill's momentum was such that the INS revealed publicly that it had made "extensive plans," on legalization in conjunction with the US Catholic Conference and other groups. INS commissioner Alan Nelson said he was "trying to get a jump on the bill" by putting its plans in place before expected House passage in July.[40]

Amid the upbeat news was this warning from the National Immigration Forum's Rick Swartz: "The House . . . leadership may be more sensitive than the Senate to the concerns of blacks, Hispanics, and labor leaders who fear that employer sanctions will increase employment discrimination. The Reagan Administration's enthusiasm for this legislation may diminish if the full House insists on its legalization program, covering more people."[41] Swartz wasn't just speaking as an observer; he was working as hard as he could to turn this seemingly dispassionate analysis into a self-fulfilling prophecy.

AFFIRMATIVE DEFENSE

In predicting that the bill would face rougher waters in the House, Swartz and his colleagues in The Group weren't exactly bluffing, but they were hardly confident either. They'd killed the bill in 1982 through a flood of amendments on the House floor, but this was the type of audacious tactic that couldn't be repeated. Their argument that the issue needed to be considered more thoroughly had worked to some extent, but even as they achieved one delay, the weaker the argument for the next delay became. Simpson-Mazzoli had the aura of a "must-pass" bill; as the *New York Times* reported, rather than focusing on *whether* the legislation should be enacted, "lobbyists and lawmakers seem now to *assume* that the bill will pass [emphasis added]."[42]

The Group began moving from simple opposition toward what they would eventually call, in Swartz's terms, an "affirmative defense" strategy. As a litigator, Swartz knew that when representing what a judge or jury might view as a weak case, defense counsel would "go beyond answering or denying the plaintiff's charges" and instead go on the offensive.[43] The key term here was "affirmative," the idea that The Group would not simply oppose the bill, but proactively seek improvements and alternatives. This meant working simultaneously on four distinct "tracks." First, they would continue to strenuously oppose the legislation on its merits, particularly in public. Second, consistent with their previous opposition stance, they'd push for procedural delays using every device they could; Arnoldo Torres was particularly interested in exploiting the politics of the 1984 election cycle to obstruct movement of the bill.[44] Third, mainly in private, they would more consciously indicate flexibility, a willingness to negotiate. Rather than concentrating most of their energy on opposition while using amendments to underscore problems with the legislation, they in effect flipped their allocation of resources: focusing on advancing proposed fixes, while maintaining a façade of all-out opposition. This reflected in part the standard negotiating technique of having "fallback" positions to salvage whatever they could were a bill to pass. The more devious objective was to secure pro-immigrant "poison pill" provisions sufficiently noxious to other interests that they would turn against the bill; a key outcome of their "affirmative defense" posture, according to Swartz, was "getting a product agreeable enough to your position so that your opponents would oppose it."[45] Fourth, they would actively engage other interests dissatisfied with the direction of the legislation, like business, labor, and the growers, to try and build "strange bedfellow" alliances.

The Group opposed employer sanctions, and so did business; might they find common ground? As much as they disagreed with the growers' quest for a massive guestworker program, they'd seen Simpson suffer a rare defeat on Senator McClure's amendment requiring the INS to obtain search warrants before entering open agricultural fields. Members of The Group had long worked closely with labor; a rekindled relationship might spark some new understanding. The ancient proverb "the enemy of my enemy is my friend" had been followed by diplomats and politicians for centuries; but the practice could backfire as well. Despite the risks, The Group decided to test these waters anyway; without new tactics, it seemed, they were doomed.

But none of these approaches could work if the bill sped through the House, so delay remained a top priority. The Group needed other maneuvers to slow the bill's movement through the legislative labyrinth to buy time to put their new approach into motion. The process known as "sequential referral"—ensuring other committees with jurisdiction would take up the measure—was used successfully by opponents the previous year to defer House floor consideration after the Judiciary Committee completed action on September 22 until December 1, when the Agriculture, Education and Labor, Energy and Commerce, and Ways and Means committees were required to report out any amendments they proposed.[46] This two month-plus delay was crucial to ensuring that time would run out on the bill in 1982.

This time around, Mazzoli was determined to reduce the time allowed for

Raul Yzaguírre (NCLR), circa 1984. Courtesy of UnidosUS.

Emily Gantz McKay (NCLR), circa 1993. Courtesy of UnidosUS.

L-R: Doris Meissner (INS/Carnegie Endowment for International Peace), Muzaffar Chishti (ILGWU), and Wells Klein (ACNS), part of a US delegation that helped draft legislation on refugees for Russia after the collapse of the Soviet Union, 1992. Courtesy of Muzaffar Chishti.

Martha Escutia (NCLR) at NCLR Offices, circa 1985. Courtesy of Martha Escutia.

Foreground:
Gary Rubin (American
Jewish Committee),
1997. Courtesy of
Maurice Belanger.

L-R: Walter Mondale (former vice president, senator, and future presidential candidate), Tony Bonilla (LULAC president), and Arnoldo Torres (LULAC executive director) at 1982 LULAC National Convention. Courtesy of Arnoldo Torres.

Mike Hooper (NCHR), circa 1986. Courtesy of Jocelyn McCalla and Maggie Steber.

Seated L-R: Rep. Peter Rodino and Rep. Hamilton Fish. Standing in foreground L-R: Harris Miller (Mazzoli aide), Rep. Romano Mazzoli, Skip Endres (Rodino aide), Jim Cline (Rodino aide), Rep. Bob García, Peter Levinson (Fish aide) and Rep. Dan Lungren, Judiciary Committee markup, 1984. Courtesy of Bob García.

Mort Halperin (Center for National Security Studies/ACLU), 1985. Courtesy of Maurice Belanger.

Maurice Belanger (ACLU Political Asylum Project), with Kaypro computer, 1985. Courtesy of Maurice Belanger.

L-R: Michael Myers (CWS), Carol Wolchok (ACLU), and Wade Henderson (ACLU), testifying before Senate Judiciary Committee, 1985. Courtesy of Michael Myers.

Dianne Stewart (State of Texas) in halls of Congress, circa 1986. Courtesy of Dianne Stewart.

Speaker Tip O'Neill with President Ronald Reagan, St. Patrick's Day, 1983. Courtesy of the Library of Congress.

Foreground: President Reagan signing Immigration Reform and Control Act into law, 1986. Background L-R: Rep. Hamilton Fish, Rep. Dan Lungren, Rep. Peter Rodino, Sen. Alan Simpson, Vice President George H. W. Bush, Sen. Strom Thurmond, Rep. Romano Mazzoli, Rep. Carlos Moorhead, and Rep. Charles Schumer. Courtesy of Reagan Presidential Library.

Msgr. Nick DiMarzio (US Catholic Conference) and Vanna Slaughter (Dallas Catholic Charities), 1989. Courtesy of Maurice Belanger

Larry Kleinman (PCUN), second from the left, together with group of successful legalization applicants, 1987. Courtesy of Larry Kleinman.

Foreground L-R: President Reagan, Arcy Torres, Rep. Esteban Torres, 1988. Courtesy of Esteban Torres.

L-R: Wendy Young (NCLR), Warren Leiden (AILA), and Cecilia Muñoz (NCLR) at NCLR Offices, 1990. Courtesy of Carol Wolchok.

Muzaffar Chishti (ILGWU), Frank Sharry (National Immigration Forum), and Rick Swartz (National Immigration Forum), 1989. Courtesy of Maurice Belanger.

Rep. Howard Berman at National Immigration Forum's 25th Anniversary, 2007. Courtesy of Maurice Belanger.

Rep. Jim McGovern (former aide to Rep. Moakley) at National Immigration Forum's 25th Anniversary, 2007. Courtesy of Maurice Belanger.

Albert Jacquez (aide to Rep. Torres), Lynn Conway (aide to Rep. Mazzoli), and Cecilia Muñoz (NCLR) at NCLR offices, 1990. Courtesy of Carol Wolchok.

Mary McClymont (US Catholic Conference/Ford Foundation), Robert Bach (scholar), and Carol Wolchok (American Bar Association), 1989. Courtesy of Maurice Belanger.

L-R: Wade Henderson (ACLU/NAACP), Rick Swartz (National Immigration Forum), and Charles Kamasaki (NCLR), circa 1995. Courtesy of Carol Wolchok.

L-R (with IRCA-era identification): Sid Mohn (Heartland Alliance), Margie McHugh (New York Immigration Coalition), Lucas Guttentag (ACLU), Wade Henderson (ACLU), Cheryl Little (Haitian Refugee Center), Doris Meissner (INS/Carnegie Endowment for International Peace), Frank Sharry (National Immigration Forum), Steve Moore (Heritage Foundation), Demetrious Papademetriou (Center for Migration Studies), Mark Silverman (Immigrant Legal Resource Center), Vanna Slaughter (Dallas Catholic Charities), Patrick Young (CARECEN-New York), and Raul Yzaguírre (NCLR) at National Immigration Forum's 25th Anniversary, 2007. Courtesy of Maurice Belanger.

Sen. Charles Schumer at the Senate Judiciary Committee immigration reform markup, 2006. Courtesy of Shari Camerini and Michael Robertson.

Sen. Ted Kennedy, following remarks at a pro-immigration reform rally on the National Mall adjacent to the US Capitol, 2006. Courtesy of Shari Camerini and Michael Robertson.

other committees to act. If the other committees wanted to propose amendments, they should to do so in less than the ten weeks they'd taken the previous year, Mazzoli thought. Speaker O'Neill eventually determined that other committees would have six weeks, until June 28, to consider the bill and report out amendments. It seemed to be an artful compromise, in theory positioning the measure to get to the House floor just before or immediately after the August recess. With the Senate having passed its bill, and with some sixteen months left before the scheduled adjournment in October 1984, it appeared that enactment of immigration reform before the 1984 elections was a near-certainty. Events proved otherwise, in part because the ranks of the opposition coalition were about to be augmented by new players.

NEW BLOOD

In December 1982, NCLR legislative director Francisco Garza relocated to California to get married and switch careers. Garza had been NCLR's first full-time lobbyist, responsible for coordinating all of the organization's legislative work. He was also responsible for policy analysis and lobbying on job-training issues; he'd been a key player in protecting NCLR affiliates' interests in the Job Training Partnership Act enacted earlier that year, a bill sponsored by the unlikely pair of Senators Ted Kennedy and Dan Quayle (R-IN). The Kennedy-Quayle bill was a wholesale rewrite of federal workforce development programs, a major source of funding for NCLR affiliates, and replaced the Comprehensive Employment and Training Act, a remnant of Lyndon Johnson's Great Society. He'd also been covering immigration policy for NCLR for the previous two years. At his farewell event Garza's boss, Vice President Emily Gantz McKay, noted NCLR's good fortune in having attracted one of the first Latino graduates of the prestigious Lyndon Baines Johnson School of Public Affairs at the University of Texas, observing that Garza had always represented the organization "with grace and class."

Garza's departure accentuated serious, even existential problems the organization faced as a result of Reagan's budget cuts and block granting of antipoverty programs to the states. NCLR's budget and staff were devastated, with reductions in excess of 60 percent. Its affiliates, many heavily dependent on federal funds, were hit even harder; from a high of about 125 in 1980, about 50 had closed their doors by the end of 1981, and within a few years only 40 of the original 125 had survived.[47] The staff layoffs resulted in dozens of vacant desks at its downtown headquarters, giving it the feel of a ghost town, and NCLR soon moved to smaller space on F Street, next door to the Irish Times, a favorite Capitol Hill watering hole.

Charles Kamasaki had relocated to Washington from NCLR's office in the

Rio Grande Valley of South Texas to head the organization's Policy Analysis Center in 1982. His mother was a teacher and his father a researcher in the US Department of Agriculture who'd been transferred to Weslaco, Texas, at the beginning of the 1970s. Like many "Valley" towns, Weslaco was bisected by railroad tracks running roughly east-to-west; a 1921 ordinance "provided that the land north of the railroad tracks be designated for industry and Hispanic residences and businesses, while the area south of the tracks was reserved for Anglo residences and businesses."[48]

Kamasaki first encountered NCLR as an intern in a work-study program sponsored by Pan American University (now University of Texas-Pan American); he joined the staff as a community development specialist in the organization's small McAllen office in 1980, and moved to Washington two years later. After Garza's departure in December 1982, Kamasaki was assigned, largely by default, to cover immigration.[49] Knowing that the issue was complex and politically sensitive, his supervisors retained Rafael Magallán, head of the Hispanic Higher Education Coalition, which was housed at NCLR, to help with the transition. Magallán gently advised that NCLR wasn't perceived as an important player in the Latino opposition to the legislation, so it decided to get into the game by focusing on the organization's growing core competency: writing, research, and policy analysis; it would serve as the Latino community's "expert" voice on the issue.[50]

Soon afterward NCLR hired Martha Escutia, a Georgetown Law School graduate who'd worked briefly on the Hill, to fill its vacant legislative director position. The Los Angeles-born Escutia's maternal grandfather had been a bracero right after World War II, and she'd lived in Mexico briefly with her mother, who'd gone back to her home country to work in union organizing.[51] Her return to Los Angeles during her elementary school years echoed the discrimination faced by MALDEF's Antonia Hernández when her family had come back to the US. Escutia recalled that she "experienced all of the indignities immigrant kids faced, like being called a 'wetback,'" and when her schoolmates spied her unfashionable shoes, they would call out "TJ, TJ" meaning she must have just come across the river from Tijuana.[52] Having felt the sting of discrimination for being perceived as "foreign," she was passionate about defending the interests of immigrants; the issue "was our civil rights movement," Escutia believed. She was also personally motivated to help people, like her once-undocumented grandparents, achieve legal status.[53] Escutia had a large network of friends and professional acquaintances in DC; she was well-connected in Latino law student circles while at Georgetown, where she was active in a *Ballet Folklorico* group, and a regular at a weekend Capitol Hill Jazzercise class. She, like Kamasaki, was a neophyte on legislative strategy; "We were playing catch up," Escutia remembers, not only as newcomers to the issue, but because outside of a few issues important to its affiliate constituency, "NCLR did not have much of a presence on Capitol Hill."[54]

The third member of NCLR's team assigned to the bill was Dan Purtell, a Stanford graduate who had been snapped up by NCLR vice president Emily Gantz McKay, herself a product of the Palo Alto-based school, who wasn't the least bit self-conscious about her partiality toward graduates of her alma mater. Purtell was smart, tenacious, and hard-working, able to track down almost any statistic, document, or policy report, no matter how obscure, often gaining access to congressional staff, scholars, and activists through sheer persistence. It helped, given NCLR's financial constraints, that Purtell had signed on as an Immigration Policy Fellow, meaning he was paid next to nothing. That he was paid at all was due only to Yzaguírre's ability to capitalize on unfortunate remarks by Clare Boothe Luce, a *grande dame* of the "eastern establishment."

Before she even turned forty shortly after the end of World War II, according to one profile, the beautiful, ambitious, often witty, sharp-tongued Luce, "had written three Broadway hits, divorced a drunken golfing millionaire, master-minded *Vanity Fair*, married Henry Luce, head of the *Time* magazine empire, and covered both Europe and the Pacific as a war correspondent."[55] She was twice elected to Congress, where she once famously attacked Vice President Henry Wallace's foreign policy as "globaloney."[56] She served from 1952 to 1956 as US ambassador to Italy, and was appointed in 1959 as ambassador to Brazil, but was forced to resign after serving only four days, having characterized Senator Wayne Morse, who had opposed her nomination, as having "diminished mental capacity," and then suggesting in response to riots in Bolivia that the country be eliminated altogether by dividing it up among adjacent states.[57]

She was a prominent, albeit eccentric voice in conservative circles, appointed by Ronald Reagan in 1981 to the Foreign Intelligence Advisory Board, and named a "special advisor" on national security. In 1982, *GEO* magazine published an interview with Luce, who observed:

> In the 19th Century the U.S. absorbed something like 40 million immigrants . . . but they were all white, now they're black, brown, and yellow. Soon, there will probably be as many Mexicans in Texas, New Mexico, lower California and Arizona—and as many Cubans and Latin Americans in Florida—as there are natives. They are also pouring in from Haiti. . . . They're coming over the border, and they're coming with wives and sisters and nieces who get pregnant immediately so they can become American citizens and go on relief.[58]

Luce's observations might have gone unnoticed but for the *Washington Post*'s William Raspberry, whose column on Luce's "genteel bigotry" quoted Yzaguírre calling her remarks "a grave insult to all immigrants of color"; the column reported that NCLR had written a letter to Reagan demanding that she be removed from her government posts.[59] The matter might have ended there—Reagan never acted on the demand—but Yzaguírre would not let the issue rest, mentioning it frequently in speeches as emblematic of biases facing minorities, even among supposed pillars of high society. One day Yzaguírre got a call from an official with the Henry Luce Foundation, the charity established in 1936 by Luce's late husband, suggesting that they might find a way to address the unfortunate incident. After some face-saving discussions where both sides made it clear that neither would retract any remarks, the foundation awarded NCLR a grant to support resident fellowships for those interested in studying Hispanic issues.[60] Thus was born NCLR's fellowship program, providing a future assistant secretary of agriculture, chief executive of the National Association of Latino Elected and Appointed Officials, and a dozen other young future stars with their first exposure to the policy process in the nation's capital.

SEQUENTIAL REFERRALS

The legislative gears ground on, as the committees that had obtained sequential referrals began to hold hearings and subsequently to propose amendments. First up was Rep. Gus Hawkins's Subcommittee on Employment Opportunities; on May 19, 1983, Hawkins held a hearing on "Employment Discrimination and Immigration Reform"; those testifying included Laurence Gold of the AFL-CIO, ACLU counsel Richard Larson accompanied by Wade Henderson, LULAC's Arnoldo Torres, and a representative of the American Bar Association. The event was a love-fest: most of the witnesses agreed with Hawkins that employer sanctions could lead to increased job bias, and all, including the AFL-CIO, recommended the inclusion of additional protections. No one from the Reagan administration testified, while the US Chamber of Commerce was content to submit a statement for the record.[61] Three other subcommittees of the Education and Labor Committee also held hearings, mainly making the point that temporary worker programs should be accompanied by stronger worker protections.

The Agriculture Committee's agenda was to make the opposite case on temporary worker issues. Chairman Kika de la Garza presided over a marathon session of the full agriculture body, with thirty members, an unusually large number, present for opening statements. Of the twenty-four witnesses that testified, six opposed guestworker programs. MALDEF's Hernández and LULAC's Torres predictably railed against both the bill and the prospect of adding yet another guestworker program on top of the agriculture provisions already in the legislation. Legal services attorneys representing farmworkers listed a host of alleged grower abuses of the existing H-2 program; United Farm Workers' legislative representative Stephanie Bowers argued that if foreign workers were, in fact, required, they should be "legalized" as lawful permanent residents.[62] No one present, probably including Bowers herself, thought this anything other than a rhetorical point; years later the fate of immigration reform hung in the balance as Congress considered whether previously undocumented farmworkers should receive green cards instead of being relegated to a temporary worker program.

By contrast, the third hearing, of Chairman Henry Waxman's Subcommittee on Health and the Environment of the Committee on Energy and Commerce, focused exclusively on the health costs that might result from the legislation; the esoteric topic alone suggested the session's relative unimportance, underscored when the chairman himself was late to his own hearing.[63] But because the projected health costs were dependent on the size of the legalization program—while the newly legalized were ineligible for most benefits, as they acquired citizenship they would over time access services unauthorized aliens would never qualify for—the small audience heard a rare substantive discussion on how many people amnesty might cover. Health and Human Services deputy assistant secretary Anthony J. Pellechio, representing the administration, estimated the total size of the unauthorized population at 6.3 million, with 60 percent, or about 3.8 million, successfully completing legalization. He projected four-year costs of up to $6 billion, and argued forcefully that federal costs should be capped at no more than $1.1 billion. The nonpartisan Congressional Budget Office's Charles Seagrave projected a much lower $2.4 billion in total costs over four years, based on the assumption that the undocumented population was 4.5 million, of which only 50 percent, or 2.25 million, would be legalized.[64]

The TransCentury Foundation's David North, coauthor of a seminal research study of undocumented workers with the Labor Department's Marion Houstoun, had studied legalization programs in other countries, and scoffed at the government estimates. Citing the experiences of other countries that had implemented simpler and more generous programs than IRCA's with far lower-than-expected results, North testified he would "be very surprised if more than one and one-half million people come forward for a legalization program."[65] Those in The Group that had studied the issue, such as Church World Service's Michael Myers and AILA's Warren Leiden, had come to the same conclusion, and thus placed a high priority on changing the bill's program details—what they called the legalization program's "substructure"—in ways that would make amnesty a far more generous exercise.[66]

The Ways and Means Committee "discharged" the bill without taking any action; its sequential referral request was symbolic, to clarify it would assert jurisdiction on any bill that could change the tax code. Thus, the first consequential legislative action was by de la Garza's Agriculture Committee on

June 21. To no one's surprise, its amendments were designed to ease entry of workers under the existing H-2 program, and it adopted a hugely consequential new amendment sponsored by Reps. Leon Panetta (D-CA) and Sid Morrison (R-WA). In contrast to existing programs, Panetta-Morrison didn't have an "advance notification" period during which petitioning employers must recruit US workers, nor was there a limit on the total number of workers allowed to enter the US. Testimony before the committee suggested that "between 300,000 and 500,000 temporary foreign workers" would be admitted annually, dwarfing the 20,000–40,000 agricultural workers under the existing H-2 program, and doubling the number expected under the bill's "streamlined" H-2 program.[67] It seemed at first glance an overreach from growers, whose guestworker proposal was defeated decisively the previous year in the Senate, a body known to be more favorably disposed to the farm lobby than the House.

Energy and Commerce slightly expanded the eligibility of newly legalized immigrants for health programs under the committee's jurisdiction. In preparing for the "Ed & Labor" markup on June 23, one scholar wrote that committee staff, "anxious to devise a way to mend election year fences between its liberal labor and Hispanic factions," strengthened the previous year's version of the Hawkins amendment.[68] This version—based on the Hart-Levin proposal defeated in the Senate—expanded the universe of employers covered by antibias protections, made job bias on the basis of "alienage" unlawful, and created a new office in the Justice Department to enforce the provisions. The unfortunately named "alienage" coverage was required since under current law, businesses fearing employer sanctions could refuse to hire anyone, including a legal immigrant, who was not an American citizen. A greater concern was that ill-willed employers would use the new sanctions as a pretext for discrimination. A greater concern was that ill-willed employers would use the new sanctions as a pretext for discrimination, providing a defense to employers already inclined to discriminate, a huge new loophole in the rights enforcement system.[69] Hawkins's package also tightened up employer verification and expanded record-keeping requirements.[70] The committee also proposed a series of amendments by California Democrat George Miller to strengthen protections in the H-2 temporary worker program, presaging a showdown with the Agriculture Committee that sought to pull the bill in the opposite direction.

As the sequential referral process wound down and with a presidential election on the horizon, Mazzoli wanted his bill on the House floor before the end of 1983; his aide Harris Miller noted that, "Mazzoli and Rodino, with the backing of the [Reagan] administration and the Republican Party leadership, pressed the House leadership for quick floor action."[71] Mazzoli also lobbied the Rules Committee to limit the number of amendments that could be considered on the floor.[72] The leadership was unmoved, and the bill was stuck in limbo. Mazzoli wasn't the only player focused on presidential politics. On June 30, LULAC's 54th annual convention program featured the major Democratic candidates: Sen. Gary Hart, the Rev. Jesse Jackson of the civil rights group Operation Push, and presumed front-runner and former vice president Walter Mondale.[73] LULAC president Tony Bonilla, who had succeeded his brother Ruben in 1982, had his own distinct identity. Tony shared his sibling's left-leaning politics, but while the svelte Ruben's personality leaned toward the dignified, the stockier, gregarious Tony often added colorful rhetorical flourishes to his speeches; commenting about the Reagan regime he said, "If we had to describe this administration in civil rights, we could describe it as a cockroach administration, because everything they've touched, they've messed up."[74]

Reagan was not by any means conceding Hispanics to the Democrats. Reporters wrote he'd won about 30 percent of Latino voters in 1980, "more than any other Republican candidate in memory," and had "made a point of attending a Cinco de Mayo celebration in San Antonio" earlier that spring.[75] He'd followed up with many appearances before Latino business groups, receiving a standing ovation as he told one gathering in Los Angeles, "Let's make one thing clear. Our goal isn't welfare or handouts, it's jobs and opportunity."[76] LULAC's Torres was unimpressed, declaring that "Mr. Reagan's idea of a statement to the Hispanic community is to point out he served enchiladas to the Queen of England."[77] Nor did Torres give Democrats a pass; unlike Sen. Gary Hart or the Rev. Jesse Jackson who both regularly attacked Simpson-Mazzoli, front-runner Mondale tried to stay above the fray. Torres thought that, "This was about empowering our community, not getting Mondale elected. If Mondale had to go down as a way to kill the bill, so be it."[78] He soon had his chance to make good on the thought.

100 VISITS

In May 1983, Richard P. Fajardo came to DC as a new MALDEF staff attorney and joined many of The Group's discussions. The grandson of a farmworker family, Fajardo graduated from UCLA law school and clerked for a federal judge in Tucson, Arizona, before coming to work for Antonia Hernández, just as his boss was in the midst of a difficult pregnancy. He'd barely started familiarizing himself with his job when Hernández's pregnancy unexpectedly turned into a premature birth, thrusting Fajardo, in his own words then "just a rookie," into representing MALDEF on immigration, its highest legislative priority. As a result of his student activism and stint in federal court on the Arizona border, Fajardo was familiar with immigration issues; he was also supported by colleagues at MALDEF, including the Los Angeles-based immigration project director Linda Wong, a leading expert in the field.[79]

Like his fellow newcomers at NCLR, MALDEF's Fajardo faced challenges in gaining acceptance into the tightly knit opposition group. The Group had begun its complex, multilevel "affirmative defense" strategy, and had already begun, if obliquely, and only in private, exploring conditions under which they might acquiesce to, or conceivably even support, an immigration reform bill.[80] Before her maternity leave, Fajardo's boss Antonia Hernández made it clear that she was dubious, even contemptuous of this approach, believing that nothing less than an outright opposition posture was acceptable.[81] Facing the bill's likely rapid movement in the House, she worried that measures that softened the adverse impact of employer sanctions might give "political cover" to those induced to vote for the bill.[82]

Just as the newcomer Fajardo began building his own relationships with the opponents' coalition, Hernández's maternity leave pushed him into the middle of a tense controversy over tactics and strategy on the Hawkins antidiscrimination amendment about to be considered by the Education and Labor Committee. The ACLU's Wade Henderson, the major advocate for the amendment, demanded Fajardo's aggressive support. The younger MALDEF staffer felt boxed in, unwilling to contradict his boss's skepticism with The Group's "affirmative defense" strategy while also aware that Henderson, who'd given deference to the more established Hernández, wouldn't do the same to a self-described "rookie." Fajardo declined to support the Hawkins amendment, beginning what eventually turned into a major break from The Group.[83]

The newcomers—MALDEF's Fajardo and NCLR's Kamasaki, Purtell, and Escutia—thought it obvious that their full acceptance into the coalition could be a "force multiplier," but were disappointed for much of 1983, as LULAC's Torres only occasionally and grudgingly invited them into the coalition's deliberations. And even when they were included Torres was often quick to brush off their occasional suggestions with sarcastic comments about their relative inexperience.[84] But the rookies were not easily brushed aside. In a reversal of the old "if you can't beat 'em, join 'em" adage, if not initially permitted to fully "join 'em," the three newcomers were determined to beat the more experienced advocates at their own game. If the big guys wouldn't let them in, they'd "push their way in," Escutia thought.[85] Fajardo proposed that they do a series of their own visits to Capitol Hill offices, and NCLR eagerly agreed.

It was a huge undertaking for the young advocates. Appointments had to be made with busy staffers through landline phone calls screened by receptionists. Initial calls rarely were returned, requiring multiple requests and going through third parties to secure an appointment. Most staffers had never heard of either MALDEF or NCLR, while those working for conservatives of either party who had were disinclined to meet. In the days before email and cell phones, when appointments had to be rescheduled because staffers were called away to another matter—a frequent occurrence—the advocates found out only after showing up for the meeting. It was difficult to convert downtime between meetings to productive use without laptop computers, smartphones, or tablets, and traveling up to Capitol Hill for a single meeting or returning to their offices in between meetings was a rare luxury, especially from MALDEF's offices just off Dupont Circle. NCLR's new F Street headquarters was closer to Capitol Hill, still a brisk fifteen-minute walk to the House office buildings, with taxis limited to extreme emergencies.

Escutia's wide network of friends served them well at this point. From law school circles she knew Jose Luis Sanchez, aide to Rep. Ron Coleman, who represented El Paso, Texas, and chaired a new "Congressional Border Caucus" created at Coleman's instigation. Escutia was friendly with numerous Hill staffers, including Michele Lord, who worked for the Congressional Caucus on Women's Issues chaired by Colorado Rep. Pat Schroeder; Thelma Elizalde, staffer to Dallas Rep. John Bryant; Diana Padilla, aide to California Senator Alan Cranston; and many others. Escutia was especially close to Congressional Hispanic Caucus executive director Susan Herrera, who was herself well-connected on the Hill.[86] Using her relationships with these offices and through the Border, Women's, and Hispanic Caucuses, Escutia arranged dozens of meetings. Fajardo was equally resourceful, getting help from progressive lawmakers familiar with MALDEF's work and unlikely sources, such as South Texas Rep. Kika de la Garza, who helped the civil rights groups gain access to many rural, conservative members of his committee not otherwise inclined to give them a hearing.[87]

Over the course of that summer the rookies made more than one hundred lobbying visits to Capitol Hill offices, many of whom previously had not been approached on the immigration issue, or any issue for that matter, by a Latino organization.[88] They often crammed three or four meetings into a day. Adding in time to travel to and from the Hill, walking between the six different congressional office buildings, plus waiting time—even junior Hill staff seem obliged to keep the lower-level nonprofit lobbyists waiting for a few minutes just to show 'em who's boss—the total investment in a single visit might be two hours. Forced to keep the middle of the work day open for congressional visits, they tended to perform their "other" duties before or after normal office hours, often going late into the night and coming in most weekends.[89]

If somewhat by happenstance, their timing was perfect. The civil rights groups' opposition to Simpson-Mazzoli was getting attention, albeit often negative, in policy circles, but there was genuine curiosity among lawmakers and staff not directly involved with the bill or with few Latinos in their districts—at that time the vast majority of the Congress—wondering what the fuss was all about. As one chronicler of the bill observed, the convergence of imminent action on immigration reform and the growing contest over the Latino vote provided "the public-interest groups fighting the immigration bill a certain amount of lever-age; and the Hispanic lobbyists—generally young, single, and with time to spare—made the greatest possible use of it."[90]

In the larger strategic picture the visits added to the sense of controversy about the bill. Even representatives and staffers who didn't fully agree with the rationale for the groups' opposition usually acknowledged that they made some good points; the young advocates did not come off as the wild-eyed radicals the bill's supporters portrayed them to be.[91] Questions they received forced them to address issues on which others in The Group had not developed expertise. Fajardo worked with MALDEF regional counsel Ray Romero, who'd filed litiga-tion challenging the Systematic Alien Verification for Entitlements (SAVE) pro-gram, an INS pilot project, to address questions he was receiving about alleged immigrant abuse of welfare programs.[92] NCLR's Purtell also delved deeply into that issue, which had importance beyond the question of access to benefit pro-grams because the INS intended to use the SAVE database to potentially verify the eligibility of people to work once employer sanctions were instituted. Escu-tia used her expertise on employment issues to explore the relationship of labor law enforcement to the issue of undocumented immigration, coauthoring a policy analysis on the subject the following year.[93] Kamasaki was asked so often about the costs of legalization that he coauthored an analysis rebutting conven-tional wisdom that legalization would be a fiscal drain on public coffers.[94]

The rookies benefitted enormously from the mentorship of Brenda Pillors, legislative director for Rep. Edolphus Towns (D-NY), who'd previously worked closely with Swartz and others in The Group when she'd been on the staff of Rep. Shirley Chisholm. She schooled them on lobbying tactics and facilitated their access to congressional offices with African American staffers, all of whom it seemed she knew well. "Child," she would address MALDEF's Fajardo or NCLR's Kamasaki although they were all about the same age, "Lemme 'splain somethin' to you," she'd say in the vernacular, giving them the skinny on a pro-cedural rule or congressional feud or friendship that could be exploited to the Simpson-Mazzoli opponents' advantage.[95] On a particularly sensitive matter she'd tell the receptionist she was taking a break and take them outside to the hallway or downstairs to the Rayburn cafeteria to set them straight.

Unlike Pillors's former boss Chisholm, outside of issues that directly affected his district, Rep. Towns was not especially active in the immigration policy debate. But he gave Pillors broad latitude to deploy the powers of his office to assist the Simpson-Mazzoli bill's opponents. The Group often used the office as a hub, sometimes they all but took over the office. But when the line was crossed and the lobbyists' presence interfered with her colleagues' ability to get their work done, Pillors would announce, "OK, last call, everybody out!" The advocates would meekly duck out as quickly as possible, and might avoid coming back for a week or two. But they always came back.

FAIR TAKES THE GLOVES OFF

The 100 visits eased the newcomers' entré into the inner circle of advocates, as The Group appreciated the intelligence the rookies gathered, respected their developing issue expertise, and especially valued their willingness to work hard.[96] Still, through that summer a definite hierarchy remained within The Group, with Torres, Henderson, Leiden, Myers, and Forum cofounders Phyllis Eisen and Rick Swartz serving as principals occupying an inner circle. The next circle included LULAC deputy director Joe Treviño and Church World Service staffer Joy Olson, "extended family members" such as the garment workers' Muzaffar Chishti, Michael Hooper from the Haitian coalition, and the American Jewish Committee's Gary Rubin, followed by "the rookies" like MALDEF's Fajardo and NCLR's Escutia, Kamasaki, and Purtell.[97] The coalition's growing ranks proved essential as their main interest group opponent unleashed a major attack on their main asset: their credibility as spokespeople for their constituency.

FAIR's Roger Conner was increasingly frustrated with the pace of the debate, as one roadblock after another was thrown in front of the Simpson Mazzoli bill. This was, in one sense, completely natural; as the chief nonprofit advocate for immigration restriction, he shared the bill sponsors' irritation at the various impediments The Group was placing in the bill's path toward what they felt was certain passage. But part of his frustration seemed to stem from Conner's own intense competitiveness; one media profile characterized the FAIR executive director as "driven by an overwhelming urge to win. 'I'm a winner' he told one associate."[98] Another staff member said of his boss, "Winning is mother's milk to Roger."[99] Conner's intensity and frustration was manifested in his increasingly aggressive and personal advocacy; a FAIR fundraising letter singled out LULAC's Arnoldo Torres as "the self-appointed leader of the anti-immigration forces" who did not truly represent his community's views or interests.[100] While hardly unheard of—having a "bogey man" is always helpful in the world of direct-mail fundraising—in the era before "political correctness" was widely derided, such personal attacks were unusual, especially between organizations that both claimed to be fighting for the "little guy."

Another sign that Conner was "taking the gloves off" was illustrated by a far more effective direct shot at the Latino groups and their African American congressional allies: a poll released during the summer congressional recess in 1983. This was not just any poll claiming to show broad public support for one's position, a common interest group tactic, if one generally limited to those that have the resources to pay for expensive opinion surveys. Instead, it was designed specifically to show that the Hispanics and blacks were supportive of greater immigration restrictions in general and FAIR's positions in particular. Produced by respected pollsters Republican Lance Tarrance and Democrat Peter Hart, the FAIR-sponsored poll found majorities of both blacks and Hispanics supported lower levels of legal immigration and employer sanctions, and opposed providing welfare benefits to "illegal aliens."[101]

For interest groups such as LULAC, MALDEF, and NCLR, and their supporters in the Congressional Hispanic and Black Caucuses, there are few more potent charges than the argument that they're misrepresenting those they purport to speak for. And Conner maximized the impact of the poll; starting by telling FAIR members, "We can now discredit their effort of bullying the American people and many of our congressmen" to oppose immigration reform.[102] FAIR made sure that prominent black voices weighed in; a columnist who'd been a reliable supporter of the bill reveled in the "surprising, almost startling, agreement" among blacks and Hispanics for Simpson-Mazzoli's key provisions, and called for swift passage of the bill.[103] The poll received widespread press coverage, with the *New York Times* editorializing as Congress returned from its break, "Though leaders of Hispanic organizations oppose the bill, a national survey last summer showed that a substantial majority of Hispanics favor its two themes."[104]

The Hispanic groups reacted angrily. LULAC's Arnoldo Torres noted that other civil rights groups, including those representing Jews or African Americans, rarely were attacked by the mainstream press for taking positions that might've differed from those of their constituents. NCLR's Kamasaki thought the editorial judgments "paternalistic and condescending," later telling reporter Ellis Cose, "Who in the hell were they to tell us what our interests were?"[105] The advocates' righteous indignation notwithstanding, their impassioned response was a sure sign that the FAIR poll had drawn blood.

Like any opinion poll, the FAIR survey relied on a small sample of a larger universe and was hardly perfect: a subsequent analysis by the nonpartisan and presumably impartial Congressional Research Service at the request of the Congressional Hispanic Caucus revealed a number of material methodological flaws.[106] As any survey researcher knows, poll questions can be crafted in a way that almost guarantees the sponsor's preferred answers. For example, with questions that were worded slightly differently—such as using the term "workers without papers" instead of "illegal aliens"—a contemporaneous *Los Angeles Times* poll in California produced far different results, with only a third of Latinos favoring employer sanctions and three-quarters supporting amnesty, aligning exactly with the Hispanic groups' policy priorities.[107]

Still and all, the poll was a major tactical coup for FAIR, hitting the Latino advocates right where it hurt the most: their credibility. The poll reinforced the view among the bill's backers that they, and not the Hispanic opposition, truly represented the "public interest."[108] It also demonstrated that FAIR had the resources to commission a major poll, and the press contacts to ensure widespread coverage. It had only marginal impact on the actual course of the legislation, but by attacking the motives of its opponents so directly, FAIR almost invited return fire from pro-immigrant forces, a battle that wouldn't always inure to its benefit.

THE SPEAKER

The 100 visits that the newcomers Fajardo, Escutia, and Kamasaki conducted conveniently reinforced Arnoldo Torres's strategy to get House Speaker Tip O'Neill's help in killing the bill by exploiting electoral politics. Although a rapidly improving economy and Ronald Reagan's skills as "The Great Communicator" made the incumbent president a prohibitive favorite in the 1984 elections, in politics hope springs eternal. A few analysts thought that if the election were close, even the small Hispanic vote could prove decisive in the then-battleground states of California, Texas, and Florida, where most of the nation's Latinos were concentrated. More importantly to O'Neill, even if Democrats lost the presidential contest, as seemed likely, enthusiastic turnout by Hispanics could help prevent losses in the House. O'Neill had just master-minded an off-year Democratic pickup of twenty-six House seats in the 1982 elections and wasn't anxious to give the GOP any advantages in the upcoming campaign. O'Neill had famously coined the phrase that "all politics is local"; as Speaker his main "local" constituency group was the House Democratic Caucus, and he was acutely aware that both Hispanic and Black Caucus members were unhappy with the Simpson-Mazzoli bill. He'd experienced massive defections of conservative boll weevil Democrats in showdown votes over Reagan's tax and budget proposals in the previous Congress, and he wasn't anxious to start turning off some of his core supporters. It didn't help Mazzoli's case that the Kentucky Democrat had a strong independent streak.[109]

Meanwhile, internal disagreements about the Reagan administration's true position on immigration issues kept resurfacing. Office of Management and Budget official Annelise Anderson had long complained that employer sanctions would lead to a national identification system, which she opposed.[110] Her husband, Martin Anderson, Reagan's domestic policy adviser, aggressively advanced this view with the president himself. As often recounted, at an early Cabinet meeting, Attorney General William French Smith explained to the president that a national identification card might be required to enforce employer sanctions.

Martin Anderson essentially killed the idea by offering an alternative, with tongue firmly planted in cheek: "I would like to suggest another way that I think is a lot better. It's a lot cheaper. It can't be counterfeited. It's very light-weight and impossible to lose. It's even waterproof. All we have to do is tattoo an identification number on the inside of everybody's arm."[111]

Anderson cleverly unleashed the civil libertarian instincts of the small government conservatives who dominated Reagan's Cabinet, isolating Attorney General Smith. As the story was retold, as in the childhood game of telephone, inevitably the details were embellished. In some retellings, the Cabinet had seriously discussed tattooing Latinos to prove their eligibility to work or making Hispanics wear tags like Jews in Nazi Germany, distortions that made the rounds of the rumor mills and eventually made their way to Rep. Edward Roybal.

Other Office of Management and Budget officials had made it known that they objected to the House bill's legalization provisions, and they weren't contradicted by anyone speaking for the president either.[112] Then, in mid-August, a letter from Agriculture Secretary John R. Block to Labor Secretary Raymond J. Donovan outlining "sharp disagreements" on wages paid to H-2 agricultural workers was leaked. It was hardly a secret that departments representing grower and worker constituencies with conflicting interests disagreed, but it was unusual for Cabinet heads to be duking it out openly in letters leaked to the newspapers.[113] Despite Attorney General Smith's public support for the immigration reform, administration officials were now on record questioning each of the three major provisions of the House bill, and Smith himself wasn't fully candid about his purported consistent support for the bill, which, in fact, was highly conditional. In a July letter to Rodino, Smith listed strong reservations with the scope and cost of the House legalization program and the likely inclusion of protections against discrimination resulting from employer sanctions, concluding that without changes to these and other provisions of the bill the "administration cannot support it."[114] Not quite a veto threat, perhaps, but pretty close.

The smart money still predicted in August that "it remains likely that Simpson-Mazzoli will be enacted before the end of the year."[115] But with the administration's position highly uncertain, and with still no word from the House leadership about scheduling his bill, Mazzoli and other reform supporters wondered "whether the bill would ever go to the House floor."[116] The *Christian Science Monitor*, a strong advocate for tougher border controls, raised the alarm by asking, "Are reports true that top Democratic leaders in the U.S. House of Representatives are deliberately attempting to bury the Simpson-Mazzoli immigration reform bill this year?"[117]

Even with the election a year away, Reagan was already courting the Latino vote, "darting around the country addressing a host of Latino organizations."[118] In a single one-week span in mid-September, the president spoke before a huge gathering of Latino donors, unveiled a wing at the Pentagon dedicated to Hispanic soldiers, appointed Latina Katherine D. Ortega as treasurer of the US, and unveiled his Latino outreach campaign, named "Viva '84."[119] Rumors that Reagan would veto the bill in order to gain Hispanic voter support began to circulate, which Roybal happily passed along to Speaker O'Neill.[120] Concerned that White House aides had been "taking shots" at the bill "for months without being firmly contradicted," Simpson received assurances of support from the president, Budget Director David Stockman, Chief of Staff James Baker, Counselor Ed Meese, and Attorney General Smith at a meeting on September 19.[121]

Simpson tried to pass the assurances from the White House along to O'Neill, but LULAC's Torres and Rep. Roybal had the inside track to the Speaker's ear. Torres had been regularly meeting with O'Neill's top staffer Ari Weiss for over a year, and Roybal had served with the Speaker for decades and spoke with him often. Amid rumors of a politically motivated Reagan double-cross, the conflicting amendments produced by the sequential referral process, and the concerns he heard from offices The Group's rookies visited, the Speaker had plenty of reasons to slow-walk the legislation. As of mid-September, the Speaker had yet to decide when, or even whether, to schedule the bill. Rep. Roybal knew that the earthy, old-school O'Neill ultimately would be most easily persuaded by what he could personally see, hear, and feel, so he pressed the Speaker to attend the Congressional Hispanic Caucus annual dinner.

By the mid-1980s, the dinner wasn't just any stop on DC's "rubber chicken" circuit, it was becoming *the* DC event of the year for Latinos with any interest in politics. Ever since he had cofounded the Caucus, Roybal and the tiny Hispanic Caucus staff worked tirelessly to build up the event as an indicator of the growing power and prestige of the Hispanic community. The event was well-funded, with sponsorships from corporations, advocacy groups, and lobbyists, and Roybal personally lined up attendance from the House leadership and appropriations subcommittee chairs.[122] Latino groups scheduled other events to attract constituents to come to town in mid-September, so hundreds of Hispanic elected officials, corporate executives, and community leaders from all over the US were attracted to DC for what came to be known as "Hispanic Hysteria Week," where they would don their tuxedos and cocktail dresses to rub shoulders with politicians, corporate moguls, and their counterparts from other states.

At the festive gala dinner, O'Neill took note when Roybal attacked the Simpson-Mazzoli bill and drew a sustained, loud, "emotional ovation" from the packed house of Latino leaders.[123] The sight of a thousand Hispanics from every corner of the country standing in unison and wildly applauding Roybal's call to defeat the bill was something that O'Neill, indeed any politician, could easily understand. Just as Roybal hoped, it crystallized for the Speaker that among Latino leaders nationwide, opposition to the bill was deep, genuine, and widespread. The *New York Times* was sufficiently worried that it editorialized on September 25 that denying the bill a floor vote would be "a tragedy."[124] On October 4, O'Neill announced that he would not bring a bill to the floor that year; citing the fear of a Reagan double-cross, he said to the *Washington Post*, "Do I think the president is political enough to veto a bill to gain votes for his party? The answer is yes. He's the most political man I've ever seen over there."[125]

O'Neill was known to say that while he could not find a constituency for the bill, there were plenty of constituencies that were against it. He told the *New York Times* that one group he did care about—Hispanic members of Congress—had informed him that the bill would "be the most devastating thing that could happen to them."[126] He declared that the "legislation would not reach the floor in 1983, and perhaps not even in 1984, unless it could be rendered acceptable to Hispanic members of Congress."[127]

Predictably, the opposition couldn't help but gloat. LULAC's Arnoldo Torres pronounced himself "extremely pleased" with the result, and MALDEF's Joaquín Avila, "praised the Speaker for blocking action on a 'flawed and discriminatory' bill."[128] Rep. Bob García (D-NY) said the death of the bill "was a major victory for the Hispanic Caucus," which García then chaired.[129] One person in particular was especially pleased to hear O'Neill say about the bill, "Hitler did this to the Jews, you know. He made them wear a dog tag."[130] In his conversations with O'Neill, Roybal, who had been using this exact analogy, emphasizing the impact a national ID card would have on the country, was gratified that his arguments were sticking politically.[131] When paired with the rumors about tattoos emanating from the earlier Reagan Cabinet meeting, the analogy didn't seem all that farfetched at that moment.

The administration pushed back, in part to deflect blame for killing immigration reform. White House spokesman Larry Speakes tried taking the high road, noting that immigration was neither a partisan nor a political matter, but one that "concerns all Americans, and it is in the best interests of all Americans to have the nation regain control of its borders."[132] The *New York Times* editorial board lambasted the House leader as acting solely "for coarse political gain."[133] Hundreds of newspapers published editorials and columns in response to the Speaker's announcement, almost all of them highly critical of O'Neill. It wasn't the number of editorials but the tone of the commentary that was telling; as Mazzoli aide Harris Miller observed, the nation's intelligentsia: "launched a personal attack on the Speaker, the likes of which he had rarely suffered. From one end of the country to the other, editorials and ostensible news stories questioned his judgment. Few believed the President intended to veto the bill. Most saw the Speaker putting short-term partisanship above the national interest on a bipartisan issue."[134]

Even his hometown paper, the *Boston Globe*, trashed O'Neill's decision and ridiculed the Latino groups' concerns about the bill, asserting that they'd "inflated the bill into an ogre of Halloween proportions."[135] Simpson and Mazzoli generally kept a low profile in the immediate aftermath of the Speaker's decision, happily permitting the editorial writers and commentators to vent on their behalf.[136] Instead, they worked to revive the legislation, mainly behind the scenes. As Simpson staffer Carl Hampe later recounted to researcher Rosanna Perotti:

> Simpson called O'Neill's office and said, who is your guy (on immigration)? And they said, Ari Weiss. So Simpson said to Weiss, I'd like to come visit you at your office. Weiss said, no, that's not necessary, I'll come see you at your office. But Simpson wouldn't hear of it; he visited him (Weiss) alone, no staffers or anything. He tried to explain why Reagan would not veto it . . . , told Weiss he'd take the Conference version to Reagan and if Reagan didn't like it, Simpson would kill the bill on the Senate floor. . . . He worked and worked on O'Neill, called him several times, tried to reassure him. Simpson would just say, "Look, I'm a man of my word."[137]

In a rare personal public comment on the issue, on October 18, President Reagan himself told a national television audience that, "This country has lost control of its borders. No country can sustain that kind of position."[138] The president tried to assure the House leadership that he wanted to sign an immigration bill "as soon as possible," albeit hedging somewhat by referring specifically to the Senate version, which was not lost on O'Neill, who remained unconvinced.[139] A group of twenty-one leaders led by Select Commission chair Ted Hesburgh, including former presidents Gerald Ford and Jimmy Carter, sent a telegram to O'Neill urging action on reform.[140]

Other dynamics put considerable pressure on O'Neill, already under fire from Newt Gingrich, who accused him of being "ruthlessly partisan"; Gingrich charged that the House had been "corrupted" under his rule, in part through procedural gimmicks that thwarted debate.[141] Not scheduling a bipartisan bill duly reported out of committee fit right into Gingrich's portrait of the Democratic leadership as tyrannical and autocratic. O'Neill was also fully aware that in the age of television he was at a distinct disadvantage in a public conflict with President Reagan, who even after surviving an assassination attempt remained handsome, vigorous, and fit. As political columnist David Broder once wrote, the overweight, often-rumpled Speaker was "easily caricatured as a bumbling relic of the political past, a ward heeler who threatens harm to the Queen's English every time he puts down his cigar and opens his mouth."[142]

Simpson, occasionally accompanied by Mazzoli but often acting alone and in secret, kept up the pressure, meeting with Judiciary chairman Rodino, Rep.

Claude Pepper (D-FL), chairman of the powerful House Rules Committee, and others.[143] On October 25, Simpson finally got his private, one-on-one meeting with O'Neill, with no staff present. "You don't even know me," Simpson began, "Why the hell are you sticking it to me?"[144] In response to the possibility of a Reagan double-cross, the Senator reiterated the commitment he'd made to O'Neill's aide Ari Weiss that if Reagan would not sign the final bill, Simpson himself would kill it, eliminating the potential for an election-year veto. Simpson also emphasized something likely to resonate with the Speaker: the unfairness of refusing a vote on the bill "to all of those who had worked so hard on the measure."[145] He was referring not just to himself or Mazzoli but to Rodino, who'd toiled on the issue for more than a decade. Simpson later said O'Neill pledged to bring the bill up "before Congress adjourned in 1984," but swore the senator to secrecy.[146]

In late November, O'Neill finally relented publicly. Word first began leaking out through his staff that he'd promised Simpson and Mazzoli a vote on their bill, with Ari Weiss telling the *New York Times* that his boss was "satisfied that the political risks have been diminished."[147] The Speaker himself went even further, telling the *Boston Globe* that the bill "will come to the floor. It will pass."[148] The *New York Times* responded to O'Neill's about-face with wary, half-hearted praise in an editorial just before the holidays, grumbling that, "The Speaker can change his mind but he cannot roll back the clock. The bill can no longer be acted on before the Presidential campaign."[149] As always, the *Times*'s legislative analysis was right on target; the bill may have been revived, but after months of delays its survival was by no means assured.

THE ROYBAL BILL

The Group never had any illusions that O'Neill's October decision not to schedule the bill was cast in stone. By the time O'Neill recanted, they'd been at work for months on their boldest, riskiest move to date: drafting an alternative bill of their own. Proposing an alternative bill was the ultimate expression of their "affirmative defense" strategy, using a seeming willingness to compromise as a stealthier way to kill the Simpson-Mazzoli bill. But it was extraordinarily dangerous, clearly shifting the debate from *whether* there should be a bill to *what form* it should take. The Group met at least once a week and frequently more often, usually in NCLR's basement conference room, carrying on a classic DC tradition of coalition politics: the weekly meeting. As former Leadership Conference on Civil Rights executive director Marvin Caplan described, during the push for the historic civil rights bills of the 1960s: "Once a week, representatives of the participating organizations [in the Leadership Conference] would crowd into the conference room to be briefed on the latest developments . . . , compare notes, and take assignments. [NAACP Washington representative] Clarence Mitchell presided at these sessions, with [Leadership Conference General Counsel] Joe Rauh at this side."[150]

A major difference between The Group's meetings and those of their civil rights forebears was that the latter almost invariably met during normal working hours. Typically, The Group's bill-drafting meetings would begin at 5:00 or 6:00 p.m., when most of the participants had completed their routine day jobs, and would last for two or three hours. Most would head home immediately after the meeting, but others often walked around the corner to the Sheraton hotel on New Jersey Avenue, where the "She Crab soup," a benefit of DC's proximity to fresh seafood from the Chesapeake Bay, was a favorite of Wade Henderson's. Arnoldo Torres preferred the Hunan Dynasty on Capitol Hill, where he'd order prodigious quantities of food, including its "Poo Poo Tray" of appetizers and the "Crispy Prawns with Walnuts" house specialty. The restaurant, frequented by congressmen and staff, was the destination of choice when The Group was coming from meetings near the Capitol.

The drafting meetings followed a fairly regular process, going title by title, section by section. For each major subject, the advocates went over in general terms what their bill should try and accomplish. Then they'd move on to address, and sometimes debate, the legislative details. They discussed the politics— whether a proposal was achievable and one they would actually pursue—and the "optics," how to best sell their ideas. Torres was the de facto chairman, presiding over the discussions. Swartz was the "idea guy" capable of throwing out more concepts than The Group could process adequately. Leiden and Myers were the technicians, refining and modifying broad ideas into legislative proposals, with the AILA lawyer determining the appropriate legal construction and the Church World Service advocate leading the discussion on how the provision might actually play out in the real world. Torres and Henderson generally had the last word on political judgment calls and strategy. Eisen contributed the latest political intelligence and was also attentive to and helped soothe the inevitable tensions that would arise, nipping imminent clashes of egos in the bud and smoothing over hurt feelings.[151] New Yorkers Muzaffar Chishti from the garment workers' union, Gary Rubin from the American Jewish Committee, and Michael Hooper from the National Coalition for Haitian Refugees, invariably found their way into the meetings when in DC. The others—LULAC's Treviño; occasionally MALDEF's Fajardo; NCLR's Kamasaki, Purtell, and Escutia; Joy Olson from Church World Service; and other junior staffers—were the "worker bees."

Each drafting session was like a mini-tutorial in the law. Appropriately, Leiden of the AILA was first among equals when it came to the actual drafting. When difficult technical questions arose, Leiden consulted with AILA members, many of whom were the most accomplished immigration specialists in the country, and having expert practitioners involved was invaluable. Most lawyers can translate policy into practice: read the law as written and interpret it for clients. But "reverse engineering"—crafting legislative language that will produce a specific, desired outcome in the real world—is a highly refined skill that was precisely in Warren Leiden's "wheelhouse."[152] The weekly law "seminars" helped the nonlawyers immensely, but everyone benefited. MALDEF's Fajardo, by then only an occasional participant, said years later, "Much of the legal analysis I did, in fact that most of us did, really relied on [Leiden's] work."[153]

Much of the discussion centered on judgment calls; all wanted their bill to produce the most inclusive legalization program possible. But there were two paths toward achieving this goal: the simplest approach was to provide a more recent legalization cutoff date prior to which unauthorized residents had to have entered the US. The more complex option was to tinker with the details—what Leiden and Myers called the legalization program substructure—so that more of the undocumented would qualify. They decided on the latter course, believing that advancing the program's cutoff date too far would attract inordinate opposition, but technical, substantive changes were subtle enough to fly "under the radar" of amnesty opponents.[154]

Arnoldo Torres was adamant that the bill include provisions addressing "push factors" in sending countries. Everyone agreed but none had professional expertise in designing international development programs. Swartz and Chishti were friendly with several people who worked in international development, and passed on what they'd heard, including numerous complexities and ambiguities in the field.[155] After several aborted attempts to craft specific provisions, The Group decided in essence to punt, and their bill ultimately proposed a "National Commission on Immigration" to study the problem.[156]

Every couple of weeks, one or more of The Group accompanied Rep. Roybal's legislative aide Elaine Sierra to meetings with Ed Grossman of the House's Office of Legislative Counsel, which is charged with assisting House members " 'in the achievement of a clear, faithful, and coherent expression of legislative policies' and is prohibited from advocating any position."[157] Lobbyists cannot access these services directly, although representatives' staff can bring others along to their meetings. Grossman was just in his mid-thirties, having spent his career following graduation from Yale Law School in the "Leg Counsel" offices in the bowels of the House Rayburn building.[158] Even at a young age, he displayed the traits that would lead others to call him "a brilliant, meticulous, and tireless technician who finds enormous pleasure in the mastery of legislative details."[159] Even in the Hill's workaholic culture, he was unusually diligent; Simpson approvingly said of him, "Ed works like a dog."[160]

He was also a "policy artist." A staffer who worked with Grossman a decade later to draft the complex Clinton health proposal described a drafting session with him as akin to "going to someone with preliminary renderings of a cathedral and having this artisan turn it into Notre Dame."[161] When meeting with The Group, Grossman peppered Sierra and the lobbyists with questions about why they approached an issue in a particular way, offering more elegant alternatives to achieve their policy objectives. Arnoldo Torres formed a close relationship with Grossman, who often began sessions with good-natured barbs aimed at the LULAC official along the lines of "Well, have you guys finally figured out what you want?"[162]

Some issues generated bitter disagreement. The most heated debate within The Group happened toward the end of the months-long process, as they considered whether to include some form of employer sanctions in their alternative. Rick Swartz, in particular, aggressively and incessantly pushed for what he called "targeted sanctions." In his formulation, the Texas Proviso would be repealed, making it unlawful to employ an undocumented worker. But unlike the Simpson-Mazzoli bill, Swartz proposed a limited regime under which only those employers found to have engaged in a "pattern or practice" of hiring unauthorized workers would be required to verify future hires. Swartz asserted the concept was correct on the merits, focusing enforcement resources on the few "bad actors" that hired most of the undocumented, and thus reduced incentives for other employers to engage in employment discrimination. He believed "targeted sanctions" offered political advantages: without more enforcement measures, Swartz said, the Roybal bill couldn't meet the "laugh test," it wouldn't be taken seriously by the pundits and the press. He also argued that the US Chamber of Commerce might appreciate the lessened burdens on business, while his proposal offered the AFL-CIO a serious opportunity to compromise with Hispanic and civil liberties groups.[163]

While not disputing the policy arguments, Henderson and Torres pushed back harshly. They thought the "optics" were wrong, arguing it was simply not possible to demonize employer sanctions as inherently discriminatory and unworkable while simultaneously proffering their own, slightly modified version of the scheme. Swartz's idea seemingly was killed early on, but he kept bringing it back up, even after a consensus decided to move on. Torres sometimes would allow a brief discussion, declare the matter resolved, and proceed to the next item. Henderson tried to push the issue aside with humor by saying somewhat mockingly, "I know what Rick wants to talk about. Targeted sanctions, targeted sanctions, targeted sanctions!" But as they wrapped up their deliberations and Swartz raised it again, an angry and exasperated Henderson exploded, "We're done, Rick. We're not going to talk about this anymore. Now cut the shit!"[164]

The final bill was as notable for what it did not include as for what it did. It did not include any form of employer sanctions, did not address legal immigration except by giving more visas to Mexico and Canada, and left existing law on asylum essentially untouched. It proposed more funding for border enforcement and tougher labor law enforcement as its alternative to employer sanctions, but sharply limited INS enforcement activities and those by state-local governments. It eased naturalization requirements slightly and outlined a legalization program superficially similar to Mazzoli's bill, but actually far more generous. And it created a commission to recommend proposals to reduce incentives for migration from source countries.

Earlier that fall, NCLR had begun working on a brief paper on immigration to advance three of Yzaguírre's priorities: producing a fact-based analysis; chastising the mainstream media for failing to accurately cover Hispanic issues; and positioning NCLR as an expert, reasonable, moderate voice on Latino issues.[165] The paper's completion happened to coincide with a meeting between Yzaguírre and Donald Graham, publisher of the *Washington Post*. Along with many Latino organizations and scholars NCLR had been critical of media coverage of Hispanics, and as one of the country's "newspapers of record" the *Post* was a common target. One evening, with a reporter's notebook in hand, Graham himself came to NCLR's offices to meet with Yzaguírre to discuss the newspaper's coverage, an outcome of which was the publisher's commitment to hire more Latino reporters, along with an invitation to submit an op-ed for consideration. Yzaguírre submitted the immigration piece, eventually published by the *Post* later that month. The editorial, "What's Wrong with the Immigration Bill?," earned accolades from many of Yzaguírre's nonprofit peers, some of whom had been mystified about why Latinos were so vociferously opposing what seemed to be commonsense legislation. It also caught Simpson staffer Dick Day's attention, prompting a sharp exchange of letters.[166]

The piece's visibility strengthened NCLR's standing in The Group; some who'd been skeptical that NCLR should be fully included in the coalition now felt that, in Lyndon B. Johnson's immortal phrase, it was safer to have it "inside the tent pissing out" instead of "outside the tent pissing in." It helped that NCLR was "all-in" with the alternative bill strategy, the moderate posture that the organization's CEO Raul Yzaguírre had hoped to be in from the very beginning of the debate.[167] But MALDEF and The Group were uncomfortable with each other's strategy, and MALDEF's participation in The Group grew sporadic. Ironically, MALDEF's Richard Fajardo had earlier gone out of his way to vouch for NCLR's bona fides with the other advocates, easing their entry into the coalition, but their roles now had reversed. As Fajardo ruefully observed to Kamasaki later, "I brought you in. Then they kicked me out."[168]

As The Group finished up the details of their legislation, they received a personal commitment from Rep. Roybal to introduce "their" bill, and left for the holidays cautiously optimistic. They thought the existence of an alternative would serve as the basis for "further consideration," in other words, more delay, of Mazzoli's bill. Torres hoped the Roybal bill would spark a new conversation on the need to take into account the "push factors" that drive people to migrate in the first place in formulating a truly effective, sustainable policy.[169] At worst, they knew the time invested in drafting the Roybal alternative could be put to use by breaking the legislation up into amendments, especially provisions to improve the effectiveness of the Simpson-Mazzoli legalization program. In truth, their bill had less immediate impact that they'd hoped, but other steps they'd taken earlier that year bore fruit.

FEET PEOPLE

As the year came to a close, a new phrase entered the lexicon as President Reagan warned of an influx of "feet people" from Central America, including El Salvador and Nicaragua.[170] The region had been within the American sphere of influence since the issuance in 1823 of what became known as the Monroe Doctrine: that interference in the Western Hemisphere by European powers would be viewed by the US as an act of aggression. The doctrine reflected an increasingly self-confident, emerging New World power telling "the powers of the Old World that the American continents were no longer open to European colonization."[171] Over the next 150 years the US itself felt few qualms about intervening in its own hemisphere, especially in neighboring Central America; in 1901, President Teddy Roosevelt added his own "corollary" to the Monroe Doctrine, reserving the US's right to exert "international police power" when faced with "flagrant . . . wrongdoing or impotence."[172] The power was only rarely exercised overtly. According to historian Walter LeFeber, the US informally controlled its neighbors through what he called "the system": support for American business interests exploiting the region's natural resources through alliances with local military dictatorships, backed by US aid and, if necessary, military intervention, usually of a covert nature.[173] As military historian Andrew Bacevich wrote, while maintaining stability in the hemisphere, "the system" of supporting local elites "prioritized order over democracy, social justice, and the rule of law."[174] The resulting poverty and injustice strengthened pressures for future northward migration.

Compared to most of its Central American neighbors, El Salvador was an outlier in the early 1970s. Unlike Honduras or Guatemala, its main export was coffee, not bananas or other perishable fruit, and it had thus not been a major target of American corporate capital. Nor had the country experienced US military intervention. What it did have was an interlocked ruling class known as *Los Catorce* (The Fourteen), after the oligarchy of fourteen families that controlled most of the land and the economy.[175] Most Salvadorans were desperately poor;

the country's per capita gross domestic product in 1980 was $1,219, less than one-tenth that of the US.[176] It had experienced just one peasant rebellion in the twentieth century, in 1932, put down after some thirty thousand rebels and civilians, mainly of the indigenous Pipil people, were slaughtered in a single month; one commentator noted that "for the next forty years, the poor remembered this lesson."[177] One of those executed in the insurrection was Agustín Farabundo Martí, leader of the country's tiny Communist Party, who was aiding the peasants.[178] The poor's quiescence changed in the late 1960s and early 1970s, wrote LeFeber, when the Catholic Church, "whose main mission in Central America for centuries had been to comfort the rich, bless the military, and Christianize (but not disturb) the peasantry" turned into an "engine for revolution" through what later became known as "liberation theology."[179] Indirectly supported by the institutional church, the guerilla movements grew, sparking increased "government and paramilitary repression," which in turn strengthened the insurgents, wrote one scholar of irregular warfare.[180] The guerillas eventually merged to form the Farabundo Martí Liberation Front (whose Spanish acronym was FMLN).

In the late 1960s, José Napoleón Duarte, a moderate Notre Dame–educated engineer and mayor of the capital San Salvador, emerged as the country's most popular political leader. He ran for president in 1972, and was defeated by the oligarchy's candidate, a military leader, in a race marred by massive fraud. After the election, Duarte was arrested, beaten, and deported, barely escaping assassination.[181] A subsequent centrist junta re-installed Duarte as president in 1980, although he was something of a figurehead; as he later wrote of this era: "No one seemed to be in control, either the Junta, the security forces, nor the leftists. The Army officers were fighting among themselves. . . They had staged a coup, but they could not control the Army or the government. Nor did the government control them. There was a power vacuum."[182]

That power vacuum was filled by the Organización Democrática Nacionalista, or ORDEN (which means "order"), a quasi-official, part-vigilante group responsible for thousands of murders and disappearances; by the mid-1970s, ORDEN had become "a dreaded, uncontrollable power."[183] Among those standing up against the violence was Archbishop Óscar Romero. He was not a "liberation theologist," but as assassinations and disappearances grew, he began "calling on soldiers to disobey orders to kill civilians."[184] On March 24, 1980, Romero was shot and killed while celebrating mass; it was said that his last words were, "May God have mercy on the assassins."[185] The Organization of American States' Human Rights Commission later found that General José Alberto Medrano, founder of ORDEN, and former army major Roberto D'Aubisson, founder of the White Warriors, a notorious death squad, were responsible for Romero's murder.[186] Soon after, four American Catholic religious workers were kidnapped, raped, and killed.[187] By the end of the year, according to the Catholic Church, there had been nearly ten thousand political murders in El Salvador, "the overwhelming majority committed by the government or right-wing vigilante groups."[188]

After the 1980 assassination of Archbishop Romero and the rape and murder of four American Catholic churchwomen, Reagan advisor and future United Nations ambassador Jeanne Kirkpatrick blithely observed that those who "lived by the sword would die by the sword," and falsely charged that the murdered churchwomen "weren't just nuns" but in reality leftist activists.[189] Almost immediately after taking office, the administration issued a "white paper" alleging that the Soviet Union and Cuba were largely responsible for violence in El Salvador, claims that according to historian Walter LeFeber were "shredded" by independent journalists and analysts from across the political spectrum.[190] Tens of thousands of Salvadorans began fleeing the country each year, almost all headed north.

Before the conflict ended in 1992, some seventy-five thousand civilians caught between the government, the death squads, and the guerillas were dead or "disappeared" and more than a million displaced, roughly equivalent to nearly four million dead and fifty million displaced had these events occurred in the US.[191] Over the coming decades, many of those displaced found their way to the US, beginning as a trickle, then growing into a flood; as one scholar wrote: "The U.S. Census counted 94,000 Salvadoran-born inhabitants in the entire country in 1980. That figure skyrocketed to 701,000 ten years later—an eightfold increase—and [in 2010] more than 1.2 million Salvadorans reside here, nearly 20% of their homeland's population."[192]

Once Salvadorans entered the US, the administration said they were "no different than [other] undocumented aliens and should be afforded no special treatment."[193] Its actions were fully consistent with its rhetoric: over a two-year period in its first term, only 0.026 percent, or one-quarter of 1 percent, of the rapidly growing number of Salvadoran asylum applications were approved by the INS; over 99.7 percent were denied.[194] In 1984, the INS approved 328 Salvadoran asylum claims, rejecting 13,045, while applicants from Nicaragua, where US-backed contra rebels sought to overthrow a leftist government, had what one writer characterized with only slight exaggeration, a "reverse ratio" of asylum approval rates.[195] Refugee advocates said that the administration's asylum decisions were tainted by its need to downplay human rights abuses to justify continuing support to the country's ruling junta.

Senator Simpson vigorously supported the administration's policy. While acknowledging that, "the political murder of 200–400 persons a month is considered an improvement in human rights," a 1983 report written by Simpson's aides concluded that "compared to 1979–1980, progress has been achieved in El

Salvador." The report directly challenged refugee advocates, asserting that despite "exhaustive efforts . . . no evidence had been found to document" that Salvadorans returned to the country were harmed.[196] Attorney General Smith warned that if Salvadorans were allowed to stay, the US could expect a "flood-tide of illegal immigration."[197] The messy conflict limited the ability of many Salvadorans to demonstrate a "well-founded fear of persecution," the standard required for designation as a refugee or asylee.[198] But those that couldn't meet the refugee standard, advocates said, deserved Extended Voluntary Departure status. According to the ACLU, the awkwardly named EVD status:

> has been used in the past to allow citizens of countries which are experiencing dangerous conditions to remain in the U.S. temporarily and to obtain permission to work. Granted at the discretion of the Attorney General, upon recommendation of the Secretary of State . . . EVD is currently enjoyed by Ethiopians, Poles, Lebanese, Ugandans, and Afghanis. In the past, it has been enjoyed by groups as diverse as Chileans escaping both the Allende and Pinochet regimes, and Cubans escaping the Castro regime. Persons who today fear returning to El Salvador have at least as much to fear as these groups [emphasis in the original].[199]

The unlikely champion for Salvadoran EVD status was Joe Moakley (D-MA), the representative of Massachusetts's ninth congressional district. Elected in 1972, he was described in the *Almanac of American Politics* as "a solid party man . . . fully responsive to Speaker Tip O'Neill."[200] There was little in Moakley's record to suggest he might emerge as a champion for Salvadorans in the US, but several factors led him to take up the cause in 1983. One was Moakley's hiring of Jim McGovern, a twenty-three-year-old Boston-area native who'd briefly been on the Hill while earning a master's degree from American University. The second factor was a routine meeting in late 1982 with a delegation of local activists pushing a "peace agenda" calling for an end to US military aid to Central America; their agenda also included EVD status for Salvadorans. Listening to the activists, Moakley was offended by the murders of priests and nuns in El Salvador, by death squads operating with impunity, and the implied backing of the US government. As his biographer Mark Schneider noted, during the meeting "something started to click for Moakley. He didn't like bullies." To the activists' surprise, after first checking with McGovern who enthusiastically encouraged support, the congressman "volunteered to defend the Salvadoran immigrants."[201] The chance meeting proved to have enormous consequences for the fate of some one million Salvadoran "feet people."

MUDDIED WATERS

No sooner had O'Neill's concession to schedule a vote on immigration reform in 1984 sunk in when other problems arose. The *New York Times*'s Robert Pear broke a story that Reagan budget director David Stockman had circulated a memo to the Cabinet that the cost of legalization was "unacceptable," and that Agriculture Department officials were lobbying hard for a major guestworker program that everyone knew would be opposed by the AFL-CIO.[202] In one article, the administration had both threatened a potential veto and offered support for an amendment that, because it would undermine organized labor's support for the bill, might be a "poison pill." The president's public assurances of support for immigration reform were undermined once again by his staff, a development that Arnoldo Torres brought to the attention of O'Neill aide Ari Weiss. If Reagan could play both sides, his boss could as well, Torres suggested: the Speaker had committed only to bringing the bill up in 1984; he had not said *when* in 1984 he would do so, especially since more time might be needed to consider an alternative.[203]

That alternative was introduced by Rep. Edward Roybal, along with thirty-six cosponsors, on February 22, 1984. The effort invested by The Group to produce the Roybal alternative turned out to be far less rewarding than they'd hoped when they'd first begun working on the measure the previous fall. Relations between The Group and the congressman were increasingly difficult, even painful; while at one level both needed each other, neither was completely comfortable being joined so closely at the hip. The advocates obviously needed a sponsor to introduce "their" bill, and just as importantly needed certain services that only a congressional office could provide, such as access to the Office of Legislative Counsel.

Roybal needed The Group as well. Although he was a veteran lawmaker and had a long record of legislative achievement, like all senior appropriators he'd organized his staff operation around that crucial budget function. His stature as an Appropriations Committee "cardinal" meant that Roybal was asked to carry funding requests from across California, the most populous state in the country. He was also the only Latino on the powerful body and thus had a national constituency of Hispanic interests asking for his help on money matters. Roybal took these responsibilities seriously, but it meant that there was a clear need to work closely with advocates to address the complex political and substantive issues associated with immigration reform. He wanted The Group to "staff" him on immigration policy, thinking himself "the general" in charge of the campaign, with the advocates as "his troops."[204]

The Group saw it somewhat differently. Like any set of major lobbying interests, they thought the sponsor of the bill they'd spent months drafting should be working *through them*, not the other way around. The advocates believed that *they* represented national organizations with constituents all across the country while, notwithstanding his considerable achievements, Mr. Roybal represented a single congressional district. In fact almost every interest group prefers to have a lawmaker act as its "front man," while the lobbyists, like puppet masters, control strategy from behind the scenes. The Group knew that the proud, distinguished Edward Roybal was nobody's front man or puppet, but hoped for a co-equal relationship. Disputes about the bill's contents grew frequent as they rushed to ready the legislation for introduction, and some advocates grew disillusioned with the partnership. Although he introduced the bill, Roybal was a less-than-enthusiastic sponsor; some in The Group thought that he issued frequent commands to them but apparently was unable or unwilling to perform as basic a function as recruiting cosponsors for his own bill.[205]

In part as a result, virtually all of the Roybal bill's short list of cosponsors included the "usual suspects": progressive, hard-core opponents of the bill, with whom the advocates already had developed strong relationships. As described in chapter 1, The Group tried to interest reform supporters like Democrat Barney Frank to cosponsor the bill, failing, they believed, because Roybal was not fully invested in his own legislation. New Mexico's Manuel Lujan, a reliable Simpson-Mazzoli opponent and perhaps the most visible Hispanic Republican elected official in the country, also declined to cosponsor the alternative.[206] Nevertheless, the bill served a major procedural purpose, which was to buy time. Roybal and the Hispanic Caucus demanded that even if the immigration subcommittee wouldn't act on their bill, at a minimum Mazzoli should grant them a hearing. Borrowing from the guerilla warfare tactics popularized by Gingrich's Conservative Opportunity Society, the advocates equipped cosponsors and other supporters with one-minute speeches, delivered day after day in late February and March, calling on Rodino, Mazzoli, and the House leadership to give them the "minimum courtesy" of a hearing.[207]

Mazzoli refused to take the Roybal bill seriously and never granted it a hearing, giving Arnoldo Torres another argument to encourage O'Neill to stall more. Swartz rang alarm bells about the lobbying campaign by western growers seeking a major new agricultural guestworker program to Judiciary Committee staff director Jim Cline, who seemed sympathetic to the argument that if the growers prevailed, producing a bill acceptable to Rodino wasn't possible.[208] It was therefore not surprising when the normally all-but-anonymous staffer was featured in a *New York Times* story in early April, where Simpson damned the heavyset Cline's influence with the faintest of praise, calling him: "a real heavyweight. He's an old pro. He has seen lots of Simpsons and lots of Mazzolis come and go. He's an awesome part of the process, a whale in a pond. His lack of enthusiasm for the bill is contagious in the House."[209]

Each gyration—the administration's waffling, introduction of the Roybal bill, and the lack of enthusiasm of Rodino's closest confidant—individually was a minor drag on the bill, but collectively they seemed to be working as February passed, then most of March, without any action by the Speaker to move the bill forward. O'Neill finally instructed the Rules Committee to begin consideration of Mazzoli's bill in early April. More than forty-five representatives—a number the *New York Times* noted was "unusually large"—asked to testify at the hearing, in part the result of The Group's efforts to encourage as many opponents as possible to testify, but also because House leadership was encouraging witnesses to find compromise among themselves.[210]

Meanwhile, at the insistence of Arnoldo Torres, early in 1984 The Group began a series of meetings with Democratic front-runner Walter Mondale's deputy campaign manager George Dalley, who supervised the candidate's relationships with constituency groups. Not everyone in The Group was enthusiastic about schlepping over to the Mondale campaign's headquarters on upper Wisconsin Avenue, a lengthy and expensive twenty- to twenty-five-minute cab ride from their Capitol Hill offices, but Torres was adamant. The African American Dalley had worked on Capitol Hill and in the Carter administration before coming onto the Mondale campaign.[211] He was a "fixer" charged with nipping problems in the bud when he could and smoothing over damaged egos when tough decisions had to be made. His major problem at the time was maintaining ties with African Americans flocking to the insurgent campaign of the Rev. Jesse Jackson. When Mondale was on stage accepting the coveted endorsement of the AFL-CIO in October 1983—the first time in history that it had endorsed a presidential primary candidate—Dalley was in the back room meeting privately with black trade unionists, trying to head off an open rebellion from those who wanted labor to stay neutral, which would've helped Jackson.[212]

Fully enmeshed in a series of presidential primary battles, the harried Dalley met The Group in shirtsleeves, constantly checking his watch as he was frequently interrupted to take or make urgent phone calls. At their first meeting, The Group demanded that Mondale help them kill the Simpson-Mazzoli bill by opposing it aggressively and publicly asking O'Neill not to schedule the bill for floor consideration. At a minimum, Torres urged, Mondale should send the Speaker a letter asking that Simpson-Mazzoli not be scheduled until the House had "given full consideration" to the Roybal bill.[213] Initially, the Mondale aide ducked and dodged, but the advocates kept pushing him, and he had to pay attention. Mondale was already on thin ice with Hispanics: due to a "misunderstanding," he'd failed to attend or send a representative to a meeting of the National Hispanic Leadership Conference, a convening of the national Latino groups during presidential election years. NCLR's Yzaguírre, who chaired the conference that year, criticized Mondale's absence in an interview with the

Washington Post, pointedly noting that the groups were busily registering hundreds of thousands of new Latino voters for the upcoming primaries in Texas and California, slated for May 5 and June 7, respectively.[214]

In later meetings Torres told Dalley that Mondale's failure to disavow the legislation would damage the candidate if, in the middle of these primaries, the purported standard bearer for the party was silent as the Democratic-controlled House was passing a bill Latinos considered anathema. Although the Mondale staffer never articulated a personal view on the Simpson-Mazzoli bill, the advocates believed him sympathetic to their cause, perhaps because of his own immigrant, even quasi-Latino roots: Dalley was born in Cuba of Jamaican heritage.[215] Dalley also had to have been keenly aware that there were no senior Hispanics on the front-runner's campaign, and it fell to him to represent their interests to the candidate and his inner circle.

In late April, nearly a month after its hearings on the legislation, the Rules Committee had yet to issue a rule to govern floor debate, a clear indication of the Speaker's lack of enthusiasm. Rules Committee chairman Claude Pepper took the unusual step of writing House members to advise them that "it is likely a large number of amendments would be offered," and circulated a list of eighty possible amendments, many drafted by The Group.[216] Mazzoli professed confidence in his ability to fight off damaging changes, saying, "I'll go toe-to-toe with anybody out there and we will win because we start with more than 100 votes in our favor on any issue."[217] But the sheer number of amendments—the two dozen or so produced through the sequential referral process were accorded a privileged status and could not easily be excluded—also made the bill difficult to schedule, since debate required a week or more of floor time.

On April 27, the *New York Times* editorialized that "Hispanic groups have mobilized against the Simpson-Mazzoli immigration reform bill and the Democratic Presidential candidates have rushed thirstily to their side."[218] Rep. Roybal pressed O'Neill to delay consideration of the bill, citing likely negative political fallout from Latino voters offended by the party asking for their votes at the same time they were passing legislation that many opposed. He organized almost the entire California Democratic delegation to join him in asking the Speaker to put off the vote.[219] O'Neill made it official on May 2, announcing that he was postponing floor action on the bill at the request of California House Democrats. The newspapers the following day also revealed that Mondale had "asked the Speaker, in a telephone call today, to postpone action on the bill."[220]

Roybal was quick to claim credit for the delay, and he certainly deserved much of it; the postponements in scheduling the bill he'd helped win were, wrote one scholar, "a high point . . . in the demonstration of the [Hispanic Caucus's] veto power."[221] Yet, O'Neill's statement the year before that he'd refuse to move a bill "unless it could be rendered acceptable" to the Hispanic Caucus contained an implicit qualifier: the Speaker expected Roybal and his Latino colleagues to be willing to compromise at some future point. Although the introduction of his own bill implied flexibility, neither the bill's sponsors nor Roybal himself ever evidenced interest in sitting down and working out a deal. At the height of his prominence in the debate, having successfully thrown another roadblock in the way of the Simpson-Mazzoli bill, Edward Roybal's actual influence inside the Capitol was beginning to wane. No one was more pleased than Arnoldo Torres, whose influence was if anything still very much on the rise, that Mondale had made his crucial phone call to O'Neill urging another delay. But if pushed to choose sides between Latino organizations and the AFL-CIO, which still supported Simpson-Mazzoli, The Group knew that Mondale would support labor. As Dalley later acknowledged, "Bottom line, Mondale . . . did not want to risk what he had seen as a cornerstone of his strategy"—the voter registration, canvassing, telephone banks, and other support only the unions could provide.[222]

Knowing this, some in The Group explored an option that didn't require Mondale to pick sides. They asked the candidate to convince organized labor to support an alternative compromise, especially since it appeared likely that the growers, with the tacit approval of the Reagan White House, would win a large guestworker program, anathema to the unions, on the House floor. Knowing that the AFL-CIO's support for the bill was growing tepid, they hoped that pressure from Mondale could help bring about agreement on an alternative more left-leaning formulation, with the Roybal bill as its centerpiece. Swartz, the ILGWU's Muzaffar Chishti, and NCLR's Kamasaki held a series of back-channel discussions with sympathizers within the AFL-CIO, exploring a compromise built on the "pattern and practice" or "targeted" version of employer sanctions. The talks eventually led an AFL lobbyist to send a memorandum to labor's leadership suggesting that The Group "would support employer sanctions when hiring of undocumented aliens involved a pattern of practice [sic]," in return for the unions' support for the other elements in the Roybal bill.[223] It's unclear that the AFL leadership itself ever seriously contemplated alternative legislation centered on the "targeted sanctions" concept. While Mondale's intervention *might* have been enough to jumpstart this potentially potent coalition, the candidate demurred, which meant the Simpson-Mazzoli bill would likely hit the House floor in mid-June, right after the California primary.

THE PRIMARIES

All eyes in Washington were looking toward the June California primary, but a bigger problem for Simpson-Mazzoli was emerging in the Texas contest, held two days after Mondale's phone call led O'Neill to announce the latest and, the Speaker claimed, last delay in scheduling a vote on the bill. The hot race in the

Lone Star State was for the US Senate seat being vacated by Republican John Tower, who had made a surprise announcement the previous August that he would not be seeking reelection in 1984.[224] The unexpected opening led to a wild scramble for the prized seat occupied by Tower since Lyndon Johnson had given it up to run for the vice presidency in 1960. The GOP contest was plenty interesting. Rep. Phil Gramm, who'd led the Democratic boll weevils' alliance with President Reagan in 1981 and 1982 that beat Tip O'Neill on key budget and tax bills, was the acknowledged front-runner, having recently switched parties. Gramm, who had been stripped by the Speaker of his seat on the budget committee, deftly fought off charges he wasn't a real Republican, telling his constituents, "I had to choose between Tip O'Neill and y'all, and I decided to stand with y'all."[225] Rob Mosbacher Jr., whose father later became George H. W. Bush's secretary of commerce and who'd served previously as an aide to Senate majority leader Howard Baker, was the well-financed center-right moderate. The third candidate was a then almost unknown young congressman named Ron Paul, described as "politically eclectic" by the *New York Times*.[226] Gramm won easily.

The real fun was in the Democratic primary. The early favorite was former congressman Bob Krueger, who'd lost to Tower by a tiny 2,000 vote margin out of more than 2.3 million total ballots cast in the previous election in 1978. Moderate on the issues, Krueger had learned from the 1968 gubernatorial race, when liberal Sissy Farenthold's Democratic primary bid had been upended in part by the unexpectedly strong showing by La Raza Unida candidate Ramsey Muñiz; he'd worked hard to cultivate the support of Mexican Americans. His liberal opponent was Lloyd Doggett, studious, serious, and unfailingly progressive. Doggett was called "tough, angular, intense" by one reporter, and even his own staff joked, "We use cue cards to tell him when to laugh."[227] Doggett's lack of humor was more than made up for by his top campaign aide, a wise-cracking young consultant from Louisiana named James Carville, who gained widespread recognition a decade later as an adviser to candidate Bill Clinton.[228]

The dark horse was Rep. Kent Hance from Lubbock, in the West Texas panhandle. Like Gramm, he had supported Reagan's tax cut bill, but unlike his fellow boll weevil he hadn't made enemies in the process. According to Majority Leader Jim Wright, Gramm had conspired secretly with Reagan's aides against his own leadership after earlier winning a budget committee post by promising to be a "team player."[229] By contrast, Hance had been open about his intention to work with Reagan all along. Hance had garnered notoriety by beating George W. Bush in what was the first congressional race for both in 1978. He'd gained an initial advantage by attacking his opponent's TV ad that showed the young Bush jogging, to which the Hance campaign responded that if a man was running in West Texas, it meant "somebody is after him." Hance's ads that year portrayed his opponent as the privileged outsider, contrasting his own in-state education at Texas Tech and the University of Texas Law School with Bush's degrees from Yale and Harvard Business School.[230] But "Dub-ya" was a tough out. After starting from behind he steadily gained ground; a week before election day *Congressional Quarterly* moved the race from "Leaning Democratic" to "No Clear Favorite."[231] Hance ultimately put Bush away with a cheap shot, a letter to voters addressed "Dear Fellow Christians" that attacked his adversary for allegedly promising free beer at a rally; Hance won by a 53–47 percent margin.[232] The letter was especially hypocritical since Hance himself had business interests in the liquor industry.[233]

Hance demonstrated the same "whatever it takes" attitude in the 1984 primary. Starting from near-zero name recognition statewide, he entered the race with a barrage of TV ads pledging to oppose "amnesty for illegal aliens," stimulating a rapid rise in the polls.[234] With Doggett hounding him from the left and Hance from the right, Krueger went from the safe, centrist choice to the blandest of three alternatives. The three candidates split the vote almost evenly, with Hance slightly ahead of Doggett, who edged Krueger by less than 1,500 votes to earn a place in a June runoff. Even with Krueger's endorsement, Hance lost to Doggett in the June 2 runoff by the razor-thin margin of a little over 1,000 votes, after it appeared for much of election night that he was ahead of his progressive rival.[235] Doggett went on to lose to Gramm decisively.

Having emerged from the primary proving that opposition to amnesty was a potent political issue, and with a considerably higher profile, Hance himself immediately tried to mend fences with Latinos, guided by an astute young adviser named Tom O'Donnell who later ascended to become House Majority Leader Richard Gephardt's chief of staff and afterward was named a "star consultant" by the *Washington Post*.[236] Hance and O'Donnell starting reaching out to Hispanics as soon as the primary campaign ended, pointing out that candidate Hance opposed employer sanctions because they "would make it harder for all Hispanics to get jobs."[237] Owing to a good-natured, aw-shucks personality, and the fact that he still harbored legitimate statewide ambitions—Hance later won a statewide race for railroad commissioner and lost close contests for attorney general and governor—he came to a quick rapprochement with LULAC, appearing at the group's 1984 convention, and with NCLR.[238] Still, the concept of legalization was severely, perhaps fatally damaged; no one could overlook the grassroots appeal that amnesty opponents like Hance had mustered.

In this atmosphere, LULAC's Arnoldo Torres and Joe Treviño, and NCLR's Kamasaki were summoned to meet with Majority Leader Jim Wright and top aide John Mack to discuss an idea Wright said could "save legalization." Opposition to legalization was based on perceptions that Hispanic immigrants didn't want to learn English, the majority leader said, so he wanted to offer an amendment to make legalization contingent on applicants passing an English test.

After Wright accepted the advocates' perfecting language to allow those enrolled in a course, and not just those who passed an English test to legalize, and committed to support funding for the required courses, the advocates agreed to quietly cooperate.[239]

It was the kind of private understanding routine in the legislative process, except it was caught on videotape. Wright had agreed to be filmed that day for a documentary by KERA-TV, the Dallas PBS station, on his likely ascendancy to the speakership after the expected retirement of Tip O'Neill.[240] The camera-savvy veterans Torres and Wright seemed completely unaffected by the filming, going about their business as if they were having a truly private conversation. But the cameras, TV lights, boom microphones, and questions from the documentary's striking associate producer Sylva Komatsu made Treviño and Kamasaki nervous: they didn't want to be "tagged" later as having made the legalization process more difficult. They were mildly comforted when assured that most of the footage was "B-roll" likely to end up on the cutting room floor, and that the documentary wouldn't be aired for years. "The Speaker From Texas" eventually was shown four years later, with the deal-cutting scene mercifully omitted.[241]

In contrast with the Texas contest the June 5 California primary went as scripted; Mondale won enough delegates to all but lock up the nomination. O'Neill promptly instructed the Rules Committee to clear the bill forthwith, earning rare, if not entirely unconditional praise from the *New York Times* editorial board, which wrote, "despite past wobbles, Mr. O'Neill now looks to be as good as his word."[242] On June 7, the Democrats held a party caucus behind closed doors to discuss the bill; press reports noted that Mazzoli "was said to have been one of the few [speakers] who strongly defended the proposal," after which O'Neill pointedly observed that, "I'm cool to the bill, to be perfectly truthful."[243] Rep. Ed Roybal's opposition was still white hot. Some of his colleagues apparently thought this inconsistent with the implied understanding that he would work toward compromise in return for the Speaker's frequent delays; *New York Times* political reporter Steven Roberts's story on the caucus meeting cited many of them, albeit anonymously, since one never knew when a favor from an appropriator might be needed:

> To many of his colleagues, Mr. Roybal throughout the debate has seemed like a man with something to prove. In 1978, he was reprimanded by the House for failing to report a $1,000 campaign contribution from a Korean businessman and then lying to the House Ethics Committee. Victory on the immigration bill, said one aide to the House leadership, would be something of a vindication for the lawmaker. Moreover, added a Democratic Representative, Mr. Roybal has always wanted to be a "major actor" on the Washington scene, but has never really

achieved top billing. . . . [T]he immigration issue enables Mr. Roybal "to claim national leadership of the Hispanic community."[244]

While most lawmakers had left town soon after the contentious caucus session, the Rules Committee stayed behind to finalize the procedures that would proscribe debate on the bill. The rule reported out on Friday, June 8, was an artful balancing of competing interests. In contrast to the "open rule" in 1982 that had allowed unlimited amendments, the committee issued a "modified closed rule." In deference to opponents and those who wanted changes in the bill, it allowed sixty-nine amendments, with no time limits for debate on each amendment. But in a nod to the legislation's supporters, the committee also warned that if the bill became "bogged down by dilatory tactics" it was prepared to "reconvene, if necessary, and report a subsequent rule" that presumably would not be so favorable to opponents. It also permitted the bill's managers to call for time limits at any time, although this required either unanimous consent or a majority vote of the House. Because conflicting amendments to the same sections had been made in order, the rule provided that the last amendment passed would prevail, a procedure informally known as "King of the Hill," after the children's game.[245] As Mazzoli's aide Harris Miller explained: "For instance, on legalization, members were given a chance to vote either for any or all of three amendments to limit the generous Judiciary Committee legalization program, or for an amendment that would strike legalization altogether."[246]

Debate on the rule began on Monday, June 11, at 3:50 p.m., on a typically hot Washington summer day, with the temperature in the mid-nineties and humidity approaching 80 percent.[247] But the debate inside the House chamber was, perhaps surprisingly, cool and dispassionate. Reps. Rodino, Mazzoli, Fish, and Lungren, who held the top posts in the Judiciary Committee from whence the legislation emanated, predictably opened with strong, forthright presentations in favor of the rule. The bill's opponents lined up in opposition. Reps. Roybal and García were joined by Rep. Don Edwards (D-CA), chairman of the Judiciary Committee's Subcommittee on Civil and Constitutional Rights, who offered a masterful presentation of the bill's shortcomings from a progressive perspective. Edwards was among the most respected members of the Democratic Caucus, both for his substantive and lawyerly advocacy for often unpopular liberal positions as well as his willingness to shield colleagues from tough votes. When constitutional amendments were proposed to restore school prayer, ban school busing, or balance the budget—which most Democrats privately thought were a bad idea but were scared to death to vote against—they relied on Edwards to kill them in committee. He did so unrepentantly, making erudite legal arguments against the proposals, simultaneously taking the heat for and giving political cover to his less courageous colleagues.[248]

Rep. Pat Schroeder perhaps best summarized the case for the opponents: the politically painful bill was, at the end of the day, at best a shot in the dark. Quoting a former Speaker of the House, Thomas Reed, she noted that like many proposals seeking the mantle of reform, the Simpson-Mazzoli bill was "an undefinable something to be done, in a way nobody knows how, at a time nobody knows when, that will accomplish no one knows what."[249] The House passed the rule anyway on June 11, by an overwhelming 291–111 margin. Votes on a rule are not always predictors of a bill's fate, since even opponents may support moving forward with the debate, believing that the bill "deserved a hearing" or "out of loyalty to the leadership."[250] But the margin could only be interpreted as a promising sign for the bill's supporters.

THE WAR ROOM

Just before House floor consideration The Group girded itself for battle. Church World Service's Michael Myers, AILA's Warren Leiden, and their colleagues took the lead on preparing for debate on amendments, often working out of Henderson's ACLU offices across the street from the Capitol. Earlier, Leiden and Myers had begun the process of breaking up the Roybal bill's legalization provisions into separate amendments, with Leiden doing most of the technical work and Myers "shopping" the various provisions around to prospective sponsors. Now they assisted the sponsors to draft floor speeches and rebuttals to potential objections while garnering supporters through visits and phone calls to congressional offices.[251] Henderson managed work around antidiscrimination measures and other employer sanctions-related issues. All three, joined by the American Jewish Committee's Gary Rubin, ACNS's Wells Klein, and others who came down from New York for the much of the debate, worked together to build support for a series of amendments to strike, or at least water down, the bill's harsh asylum restrictions. Rubin, Leiden, and Myers were also heavily focused on collecting the votes to defeat an amendment to restore an overall ceiling or cap on legal immigration that had been stricken in committee. Michael Hooper, from the National Coalition for Haitian Refugees, was on point to strengthen the bill's Cuban–Haitian legalization program. For technical reasons, aspects of the program would be weakened if certain amendments aimed at legalization were adopted, making approval of a Rodino amendment at the end of the process crucial for Haitians, since it would be the "King of the Hill" that prevailed in the final version of the bill.

Hooper was joined for a few days by the ILGWU's Muzaffar Chishti, who enlisted the union's legendary lobbyist, Evelyn Dubrow, to augment The Group's meager forces. Evy Dubrow was among labor's most prominent advocates according to the *New York Times*:

Just 4 feet 11 inches tall and famed for working 15-hour days, Ms. Dubrow was one of the most colorful and respected lobbyists in Washington, and one of the first powerful women among them. One fellow lobbyist called her the "little engine that could." Sometimes she visited 30 senators in a day. She said she trudged so many miles around Capitol Hill that she wore out 24 pairs of her size 4 shoes each year. . . . She was so well-liked and such a fixture on Capitol Hill that House Speaker Thomas P. O'Neill assigned her a chair among the Congressional doorkeepers' chairs outside the House of Representatives so she would not have to stand all day while waiting to buttonhole arriving or departing House members. She was the only lobbyist to have such a seat.[252]

By 1984, Dubrow was well into her sixties, heavyset, and her days of making multiple daily congressional visits were over. But her constant presence outside the House chamber, calling on hundreds of House members by name to lobby them as they went onto the floor to cast votes, signaled that one important part of the labor movement did not support the bill.[253] The obvious affection and respect that House members had for her also showed some of the harder-edged advocates in The Group that there was more than one way to skin a cat; in comparison to their typical intense, "take no prisoners" approach to lobbying, she relied on what she called her "BAT" principles: "I don't beg. I don't assume I know all the answers, and I don't threaten."[254]

Swartz and Eisen, who weren't supposed to be lobbying at all, worked the phones from their offices, connecting disparate parts of the pro-immigration coalition, including state-local governments and the VOLAGs. Swartz was in close touch with advocates in the field, including many of the Forum-like local coalitions he'd helped start. Eisen, in effect, was the hub of a back-channel communications system that mainly involved her broad network of friends on Capitol Hill, in the Immigration and Naturalization Service, and other federal agencies.

NCLR opened its basement conference center as kind of a war room, where the DC-based Fajardo and several of his interns and law students were joined by MALDEF's immigration project director, Los Angeles-based Linda Wong, and Chicago-based associate counsel Ray Romero, who had flown into town to lobby against the bill, along with Bill Tamayo, a young lawyer with the San Francisco-based Asian Law Caucus. There they worked with NCLR staffers, often augmented by various LULAC staff, interns, and volunteers, to write, copy, and collate packets of materials the lobbyists would use in the visits to Capitol Hill. In the inevitable ebb and flow associated with lobbying campaigns—hours of frantic intensity while cases are researched, materials drafted, pulled together, reproduced, and then delivered to congressional offices, often followed by lulls in between meetings or while the next set of materials was finalized—there was a fair amount of downtime when the three Asians got to know each other a bit.

Hired in 1981, Wong had built the organization's immigration program essentially "from scratch."[255] Like NCLR's Kamasaki, Wong was an anomaly, an Asian working for a Latino organization. Unlike the NCLR staffer, however, she already was a high-profile veteran on the issue, having earned accolades as MALDEF's acknowledged "national spokesperson" on immigrants' rights.[256] Wong later went on to successively higher-ranking positions in a wide range of fields, but her *métier* was immigration policy. Known as a smart, tough, give-no-quarter advocate, she and Kamasaki found common ground in their shared experience that the Latino organizations and their constituents were welcoming of the Asians in their midst.

Tamayo, whose forebears were from the Philippines, had much broader ambitions, not so much for himself but for the emerging "immigrants' rights" movement. In between good-natured jabs at "Kamasaki-san" for Japanese war crimes in the Philippines during World War II, Tamayo talked often about building a network of immigrant-led organizations to advance a more progressive immigrants' rights agenda. He was frustrated that the broad-based civil rights organizations' multi-issue agendas made them too deferential to moderate voices inside the Beltway, too cautious about taking the lead on immigration issues. "Wouldn't it be great," Tamayo would muse, "to have an umbrella for immigrant-led grassroots organizations totally devoted to protecting the rights of immigrants?"

He wasn't only musing; he was already hard at work trying to turn this vision into reality. Tamayo was then chair of an informal, California-based network of local activist groups that eventually became a national organization devoted solely to protecting the rights of immigrants, especially those from "third world" countries. He would later note that the venerated Statue of Liberty had "its back on Asia and South America," a stark demonstration that immigrants from countries east and south of US borders "were never welcomed here."[257] Tamayo's own career eventually took a more conventional turn as he became a highly respected senior attorney with the EEOC and a law school professor. But he made a lasting contribution to the field by helping to found and support the National Network for Immigrant and Refugee Rights (NNIRR), for many years an often lonely, unapologetic, aggressive advocate for the rights of the foreign-born.[258] Decades later, when Simpson-Mazzoli was but a fading memory in the minds of most policy makers and activists, NNIRR was a prominent catalyst in the immigrant rights' movement's heightened role in the seemingly never-ending debate on immigration.

CHAPTER 5

Climax, Postponed

THE FLOOR

Consideration of the bill began on June 12, 1984, presided over by Kentucky Democrat William H. Natcher, a moderate thought of as the "ideal presiding officer: courteous, scrupulously fair, but determined to move the proceedings along."[1] Natcher looked the part: tall, standing ramrod straight, and always dressed in a freshly pressed three-piece suit.[2] He also was the "politically correct" choice: as third-ranking member of the Appropriations Committee he was a fellow "cardinal" with opposition leader Ed Roybal, but Mazzoli had confidence there'd be "no mischief" taking place on the floor with his fellow Kentuckian in the chair.[3] Natcher had the air of a Southern gentleman and a bit of a border-state drawl. When calling on the bill's chief sponsor, as he often did over the next few days, he'd pronounce "Mazzoli" like "Muh-zo-la," the way some say "Muh-zoo-rah" when referring to the state of Missouri.

The first significant action was on the Hawkins amendment seeking to address the potential discriminatory effects of employer sanctions, which had two parts. One part banned discrimination attributable to employer sanctions and created a new entity with the Justice Department to enforce the ban. The second mandated that employers maintain records—so-called "paperwork" requirements—not only for those hired but for unsuccessful applicants, to help bias victims and investigators uncover patterns of discrimination. After Rep. Hawkins's able but understated presentation on the need for and provisions of his amendment, Mazzoli opposed it. As presaged by the defeat of a slightly different version of the proposal in the waning hours of the 97th Congress, Hawkins's amendment was defeated by a significant 253–166 vote margin.[4]

Then, Rep. Barney Frank pulled a bit of a surprise. The progressive supporter of the legislation was called "a leader of younger members of Congress" who could bring other votes with him.[5] But Frank worried about discrimination and thought the Hawkins amendment's prospects were not good. Almost completely under the radar, according to scholar Rosanna Perotti, a few weeks earlier Frank had "quietly asked Education and Labor staff people to draft an amendment with only the antidiscrimination provision in it [and omitting the 'paperwork' requirements of the Hawkins amendment]. He then proceeded to line up the support of the AFL-CIO and Judiciary Committee members for the antidiscrimination-only amendment."[6]

The Group had not anticipated this development.[7] It would have been highly unusual for Hawkins's Education and Labor Committee staff to help prepare an amendment that arguably undercut their boss's more comprehensive provision, but unusual or not, Frank seemingly found the perfect sweet spot, taking firm measures against discrimination while eliminating paperwork provisions that business vehemently opposed. The Group embraced the amendment, with a condition that they wouldn't be victimized by the common bait-and-switch tactic of including the amendment in one chamber's version of the legislation only to see it dropped when the two bodies' bills were reconciled. Hispanic Caucus chairman Bob García posed exactly this question, which Rodino answered by stating, "Insofar as this person is concerned, and I expect to be sitting on the conference [committee] . . . I can assure the gentleman that there will be no equivocation, there will be no possible effort by me or anyone else that will be on this [Democratic] side, to diminish the amendment's effectiveness."[8]

If not an ironclad commitment, Rodino's assurance seemed to satisfy García (and thus the advocacy groups). Rep. John Erlenborn, a reliably conservative Republican from Illinois rose in opposition, but was challenged immediately by fellow GOPer Steve Bartlett from Texas. Elected in 1982 while in his mid-thirties, the Dallas-based congressman was already earning a reputation as an unusually effective legislator.[9] While proud of his 100 percent rating by the US Chamber of Commerce, along with classmate John McCain (R-AZ) he'd worked hard to reach out to Hispanic groups. Bartlett offered strong support for the Frank amendment, and then yielded time to McCain, who followed suit; the amendment passed by a near-unanimous 404–9 margin.[10]

At 6:30 p.m., Rep. Sam Hall, a conservative Texas Democrat, offered his amendment to exempt employers of three or fewer employees from employer sanctions coverage.[11] Hall supported the bill, but wanted to give employers of "casual labor"—maids, cooks, yard workers, and the like—an exemption from employer sanctions. After a sprawling debate lasting the better part of an hour, Hall's small-employer exemption passed by voice vote.[12] He then offered an amendment to create a telephone verification system to allow employers to check the validity of job applicants' Social Security numbers based on the system then used for credit card transactions. After more than an hour of debate, Hall's amendment passed by a 242–155 vote margin.[13] While largely forgotten as a contributor to immigration policy, the spiritual descendant of the telephone verification system Hall advocated, an online employer verification program known as E-Verify, has become a cornerstone of later immigration reform proposals.

Rep. Roybal entered the fray with an amendment to eliminate a section of the bill authorizing the president to establish "a secure system to establish employment eligibility." Despite language in it that prohibited issuance of a national identification card, Roybal insisted that the section would allow some form of objectionable ID system. The wide-ranging, sometimes technical, and often emotional discussion consumed nearly two hours. Just before 10:30 p.m., Roybal's amendment prevailed. It had taken nearly ten hours to consider the first nine amendments, with as many as sixty more to go. With the political convention season less than a month away, Mazzoli's hope to complete House consideration, a conference committee with the Senate, and final passage of a conference report before the end of the summer was fading fast.

When the House reconvened a little after 10:00 a.m. the next day, after first praising his colleagues and urging that debate continue "with restraint and calm and dignity," Rep. Mazzoli indicated he'd be taking a tougher line against certain amendments.[14] Ranking subcommittee member Dan Lungren, alluding to the extensive debate required to dispose of amendments the day before, added his own warning against delaying tactics.[15] The anti-employer sanctions crowd got another win after El Paso Democrat Ron Coleman won an amendment to remove criminal penalties for violations of employer sanctions.

The day's main event was Colorado Rep. Pat Schroeder's proposal to sunset employer sanctions after three years, requiring a future Congress to affirmatively vote to continue the policy. Crisply outlining the questions raised by scholars and advocates on discrimination, costs, and ineffectiveness of sanctions, Schroeder summarized her proposal as "keeping employer sanctions as an experiment before we institute it as a policy."[16] Mazzoli responded unusually harshly and personally, saying that Schroeder had, "fought me tooth and nail every step of the way, refused to support our bill and refuses to support it now. Hers is a killer amendment."[17] The Group lined up more than a dozen supporters to speak in favor of Schroeder's amendment to no avail; after a lengthy debate Mazzoli prevailed by a crushing 304–120 vote.[18] Tempers heated up, as the bill's antagonists seemingly rallied to Schroeder's defense, by asking questions, raising obscure procedural points, and engaging in other stalling tactics. Just before 2:30 p.m., Rep. Roybal offered an amendment to strike employer sanctions and substitute labor law enforcement provisions from his bill as an alternative means of enforcement, another proposal that Mazzoli called a "killer amendment." The subcommittee chair then made a series of unanimous consent requests to limit debate on the amendment, each of which was objected to.[19] Roybal's amendment lost overwhelmingly, but ominously for Mazzoli, it consumed more than another hour of debate.[20]

The House next considered amendments to deal with due process protections in asylum and other immigration proceedings. The Reagan administration claimed that the country's asylum procedures, with determinations made by trained administrative judges whose decisions were subject to full judicial review, were inadequate to cover large "mass asylum" situations like the Cuban–Haitian boatlifts or those fleeing civil war in Central America. Both the Senate and House bills included a new "expedited exclusion" or "summary exclusion" process whereby INS officers, not administrative judges, could make determinations about the legitimacy of asylum claims, although the House bill included a layer of administrative review.[21] The first amendment, by Rep. Richard Ottinger (D-NY), sought to restore the right of those ordered excluded to challenge INS decisions via class action lawsuits, an opportunity that had been foreclosed by a recent appeals court decision. Ottinger's amendment initially passed by voice vote.[22] But it was a temporary victory, since this section of the bill was governed by the "King of the Hill" procedure under which the last amendment adopted would prevail.

The next amendment offered by Rep. McCollum called for a "restoration" of the House provisions back to their original form, eliminating protections added in committee. His key argument, that the current system allowed too many frivolous asylum applications followed by excessive administrative and judicial reviews, rang true in the wake of the Cuban–Haitian refugee crisis.[23] Although vociferously opposed by Representatives Ottinger, Rodino, Fish, and others, McCollum skillfully parried their arguments, and prevailed by a close 208–192 vote.[24]

Amendments by Rep. Gary Ackerman (D-NY) and Texas's Ron Coleman that restored modest protections for immigrants and refugees in detention, both drafted by the AILA's Warren Leiden and "placed" with supportive congressmen by Church World Service's Michael Myers, were considered next. Mazzoli and Lungren expressed concerns, but with an eye on the clock, accepted them. A surprised Coleman praised the bill's managers effusively, prompting Lungren to interject that his acceptance was contingent on "no more compliments" that would consume time. Ottinger's final, emotional attempt to restore all asylum provisions back to current law was defeated by voice vote after a sharp exchange with Mazzoli.[25]

The next two amendments, offered by Rep. Roybal and reflecting provisions from his bill, proposed greater limits on immigration enforcement, addressing concerns of Hispanic advocates that application of the law inherently led to civil rights violations. Roybal withdrew the first, more complex amendment detailing the specific powers and authorities of federal immigration officers after Mazzoli promised to give the proposal a hearing. The second amendment, eliminating the ability of state-local law enforcement officials to make traffic stops based on suspicion of immigration violations, was defeated on voice vote.

The next major amendment, proposed by Rep. García and also reflecting a section from the Roybal bill, was a variation of the old "contiguous countries" proposal that had been in and out of immigration legislation going back to the Rodino bills in the 1970s. Mazzoli's bill already proposed increased visas for Canada and Mexico; García's amendment clarified that unused visas from one country (Canada) could be used by the other (Mexico). The additional visas remedied the cuts in legal immigration from Mexico resulting from Rep. Eilberg's 1976 bill that President Ford had promised to fix, but was unable to after his electoral defeat. After Mazzoli accepted the amendment, Lungren followed suit, saying, "We are overturning a bad mistake we made . . . when we cut in half the admissions from our closest neighbor Mexico."[26]

The next amendment was a big one, a proposal by Rep. Carlos Moorhead (R-CA) to establish a "hard cap" on legal immigration, effectively reducing lawful entries. At issue was the simple fact that, as entries of immediate family members of US citizens—unlimited under current law—increased, under the proposed cap they would crowd out all other categories including relatives of lawful permanent residents and siblings of American citizens. The provision was defeated in committee, but since Simpson strongly supported the hard cap in his version of the bill, The Group worried it couldn't be deleted if it passed in the House. Barney Frank opposed the amendment, saying that Moorhead's provision would "undercut the kind of coalition we need" to pass the bill, and to prove the point, Peter Rodino followed by inserting into the *Record* letters and memoranda of opposition from dozens of diverse groups, including an op-ed from the American Jewish Committee's Gary Rubin that made an impassioned defense of family-based legal immigration. Perhaps the most important opponent was Attorney General William French Smith, who urged that "consideration of changes in the legal immigration system be deferred for another day"; the administration's opposition contributed to the defeat of Moorhead's amendment by an unexpectedly comfortable 231–168 margin.[27]

The victory represented a conscious choice by pro-immigration advocates to build coalitions across ideological sectors. Swartz in particular believed that the legal immigration system retained strong political support and was vulnerable only if mixed with the illegal immigration issue. He had long been in discussions with pro-immigration business and conservative advocates, including Heritage Foundation policy analyst Steven Moore, who later gained fame as a member of the *Wall Street Journal* editorial board supportive of legal immigration and temporary worker programs as pro-growth, pro-business measures.[28] Opposition from the left, along with a nudge from the pro-immigration right, convinced the Reagan administration to back off of proposals to cut legal immigration; a huge win for The Group and its allies.

The House called it a day well after 10:00 p.m., having yet to complete even half of the sixty-nine amendments made in order under the rule. At 10:20 the next morning, Rep. Daub introduced his amendment to eliminate the "fifth preference," the provision allowing US citizens to petition for their siblings. Backlogs in this category were extensive; unlike immediate relatives of US citizens whose entry was permitted without regard for numerical limits, brothers and sisters were subject to both overall and per-country ceilings. Another, largely unspoken concern: brothers and sisters weren't part of the traditional American "nuclear" family and should receive no immigration preference at all. The fifth preference was especially valued by Asian American groups, whose constituents relied on it heavily. After debate consuming nearly an hour, likely in recognition that the fate of his provision would mirror that of Moorhead's sixty-vote loss from the night before, Daub withdrew his amendment. The issue has bedeviled immigration reformers since, as backlogs have continued to grow, and subsequent bills and blue ribbon commissions have almost unanimously called for the elimination of the category, vigorously—and to date successfully—opposed primarily by Asian American groups.[29]

Roybal won another victory when his amendment to relax slightly the requirements for "suspension of deportation," a procedure to adjust the status of long-term undocumented residents of the US on a limited case-by-case basis, prevailed on a 411–4 vote after receiving endorsements by Rodino and Lungren. The body then went on to consider amendments to the temporary worker sections of the bill. There was some initial sparring on a series of minor amendments to tweak the compromise H-2 agricultural worker provisions in the legislation; Rep. Sid Morrison (R-WA) won an amendment to transfer certain regulatory authority over the program from the worker-friendly Department of Labor to the purportedly "neutral" Department of Justice, within which the Immigration and Naturalization Service resided.[30] Dueling amendments by Illinois Republican John Erlenborn and California Democrat George Miller to toughen H-2 program requirements were defeated after ninety minutes of debate.[31]

THE PANETTA AMENDMENT

But these were preliminaries to the day's main event, the Agriculture Committee amendment that proposed a massive new guestworker program. Hispanic advocates' enmity for temporary worker programs stemmed from the still-fresh memories of abuses in the bracero program in the 1950s and 1960s; they believed that if foreign workers were needed for dangerous, low-wage jobs like farm work, they should be allowed to enter as legal immigrants, with the full labor law protections, not as exploitable temporary workers with limited rights. There was also a tactical issue in play: agricultural interests had always been a key opponent of immigration restriction; if they were satisfied by a guestworker program, it might decisively improve the prospects for the bill's enactment.[32]

The guestworker amendment was sponsored by Leon Panetta, a former official in the Nixon administration who left over a difference in principle and was elected to Congress as a Democrat in 1976, viewed as "one of the most influential and powerful members of the House," according to the *Almanac of American Politics*.[33] He was a rare Democrat, both fiscally conservative and progressive on social issues, befitting his northern California district ranging from the wealthy Monterrey peninsula down through the fertile Salinas Valley to the south. When growers began "looking for a member who was reasonable, respected and also had an agricultural constituency, Panetta's name stood out as a star," one agricultural lobbyist observed.[34] Such was his still-growing prominence that he later served as chair of the Budget Committee, and in the administrations of both Bill Clinton and Barack Obama, as budget director and chief of staff for the former and director of the CIA and secretary of defense for the latter.[35]

Panetta was in almost every way the perfect sponsor of an amendment to expand temporary worker programs: clearly an ally of growers in his heavily agricultural district, he was also sufficiently progressive that the standard ad hominem attacks on growers and their allies—that lawmakers from agricultural districts were in the pocket of unscrupulous farmers that exploited and mistreated their workers—simply would not stick to him. But this choice came with a price, as he was "constantly questioning the merits of the proposal" growers offered and insisting on changes to address problems identified by farmworker advocates; "Panetta was no dupe," noted a prominent grower lobbyist.[36] Washington's Sid Morrison, the lead GOP face of the proposal, was another inspired choice, with a reputation as a serious legislator with a relatively moderate record, voting with labor, consumer, and environmental interests almost one-third of the time.[37]

Panetta made a straightforward presentation for his amendment, based on what he called "some basic realities." One such reality was that the harvest times for perishable crops—citrus fruit, vegetables, grapes, and berries among others—grown in his state were unpredictable and needed to be picked within a brief period after ripening. Another reality, he said, was that harvesting such crops was extremely labor intensive, requiring "tough" manual labor. He said the "50 to 80 percent" of the labor force performing this work that was undocumented was another "reality we have to deal with." Panetta concluded with an explanation of the H-2 program's inadequacies in addressing these realities, since under that program employers needed to apply for workers far in advance, and then promptly put them to work, requirements unsuited for the unpredictable harvest times faced by perishable crop growers.[38] Morrison emphasized the proposal's worker protections, especially the ability to move from employer to employer (but only among growers of covered perishable crops), so-called portability of temporary legal status, which many labor-oriented advocates and scholars had long called for in guestworker programs.[39] Left unsaid by Panetta was the scope of his proposal; according to expert observers and unexpectedly candid testimony from a few grower representatives, were his amendment adopted and added to the bill's "streamlined" H-2 program, the number of foreign agricultural workers legally entering the US would jump from "about 40,000 under current law to 500,000 or more annually."[40]

Opponents attacked the amendment on multiple fronts. Rep. Frank got to the heart of the matter, noting that the Panetta provision would come on top of the bill's existing transition program allowing growers three years to wean themselves from undocumented workers, the substantial "streamlining" of the existing H-2 program that itself could grow to several hundred thousand workers annually, search warrant protections, and other special benefits that amounted to "a virtual total exemption for agriculture from the immigration laws of this country."[41] Opponents rebutted the effectiveness of the program's purported worker protections, with Henry B. González calling the amendment, in a memorable and oft-quoted phrase, a "rent-a-slave" program.[42] Esteban Torres personalized the life hardships suffered by farmworkers in recalling, "I worked in those vineyards with *braceros* working side by side. I saw the squalor and the unsanitary conditions. I saw the intimidation. I saw the exploitation."[43]

But Panetta matched the opponents blow for blow; he lined up support from conservatives representing rural districts and from first-term California Democrat Richard Lehman, thought to be a typical "welfare state-environmental protection" liberal, and Pennsylvania moderate Republican Bill Goodling, a profoundly principled and decent man known to cross party lines to support education programs "slated for extinction or severe cuts by the Reagan administration."[44] It wasn't until the very end of the debate when Mazzoli addressed the guestworker provision, starting off by saying, "The amendment of the gentleman from California (Mr. Panetta) is not a mean spirited offering. However, it is an offering I oppose." But in the same breath he almost seemed to take his opposition back by concluding, "Whatever the vote is the committee will live with it. . . . [T]he gentlemen and gentlewomen who support or oppose this amendment are in each and every way trying to do the best thing. Whatever happens, we can deal with."[45]

It was a far cry from the label of "killer amendment" Mazzoli had given to other proposals, like those modifying employer sanctions, that would make major changes to his bill. It wasn't clear whether the subcommittee chairman was all but conceding passage because he could count the votes, or whether there was something else going on. In any event, Panetta's amendment prevailed by a much larger-than-expected 228–172 margin.[46] The House was just two-thirds of the way through the sixty-nine amendments to be considered by the time they concluded the session just before 7:30 p.m., unusually late for a Thursday evening when many representatives are rushing to catch planes back to their districts for the weekend.

ROYBAL AMENDMENTS

The overwhelming passage of the Panetta amendment was a devastating defeat for organized labor, farmworker advocates, and The Group. But the latter had gained tactical leverage for another set of priorities, for coming up next for amendment were the bill's legalization sections, including many program substructure changes emanating from the Roybal bill. By pushing the debate into Friday, when all but die-hards would be out of town campaigning for reelection, Mazzoli and Lungren, who desperately needed to finish the bill early the following week, came under greater pressure to accept The Group's proposals simply to save time. When the House returned June 15, the process followed The Group's script. First up was Rep. Major Owens (D-NY), a Roybal bill cosponsor who proposed an amendment to extend the planning period to prepare for legalization from three months in the Judiciary bill to six, and the application period from twelve months to eighteen, which passed by voice vote.[47]

Next to offer an amendment was California Rep. George Brown from the eastern Los Angeles suburbs of Monterey Park, Riverside, and San Bernadino, described by the *Almanac of American Politics* as a "peacenik—a scientist with a Quaker upbringing."[48] Brown's amendment, also emanating from the Roybal bill, was designed to address a technical but critically important issue, the so-called public charge exclusion. Denying entry to those who might become burdens to the taxpayers has a long history in the immigration laws, dating back to the first restrictions enacted in the late 1800s. Scholars wrote that the provision had been implemented in a way that disproportionately affected unpopular racial groups, such as Mexicans.[49] Because many of the undocumented legalization applicants earned low wages and some of their children had received public benefits, The Group feared INS would disqualify them from legalization as "public charges." CWS's Michael Myers had persuaded Brown to carry the amendment, which stated that those "with a history of employment evidencing self-support without reliance on public assistance" could not be excluded from legalization.[50] After Rep. Hamilton Fish supported Brown's proposal, it was agreed to by voice vote.[51]

Henry Waxman offered another provision from the Roybal bill for a more flexible approach to interpreting the requirement that legalization applicants had to have maintained continuous residence in the US since prior to the program's cutoff date, generally thought of as an antifraud measure to prevent ineligible immigrants from being drawn into the US after passage of a legalization program. After Mazzoli promised to pursue in the final conference language that "would suit the gentleman's purposes," Waxman withdrew his amendment.[52]

Parren Mitchell (D-MD) followed with yet another technical provision with origins in the Roybal bill. Elected to Congress in 1970, the younger brother of the NAACP's legendary Clarence Mitchell had many brethren in prominent state offices.[53] His amendment sought to protect undocumented persons eligible for legalization that might be arrested or detained before the program began from deportation. Mazzoli accepted the amendment, and another from Rep. Dante Fascell (D-FL) that expanded those entities eligible to assist legalization applicants, one of the few in this series that did not originate with Roybal's bill.[54]

Michigan Democrat William D. Ford, third highest ranking member of the Education and Labor Committee, offered his amendment to ensure that the newly legalized would be eligible for school lunch and child nutrition, Head Start, job training, and higher education assistance programs. Ford was an influential patron of migrant farmworkers; he'd sponsored the Migrant Education Program providing federal funds and systems to follow farmworker children as their parents moved along the migrant stream.[55] His longtime chief aide Patricia Rissler authored the Farm Labor Contractor Registration Act, and defended from constant attack two tiny education programs giving migrant students the opportunity to finish high school and go to college.[56] Ford's amendment went further than Lungren was comfortable with, but Mazzoli accepted it and it was approved by voice vote.[57] Henry Waxman followed with a similar amendment from the Energy and Commerce Committee expanding legalization recipients' access to federal health programs, which was also quickly accepted and adopted.[58]

But all of this was a prelude to a broader point Mazzoli wanted to make after passage of the Panetta amendment, which he knew could force labor to turn against the bill and energize Hispanics and other opponents.[59] After reviewing provisions in the legislation that should attract progressives, he asked them to hold their fire: "I would tell my friends not to say that you are going to vote against the bill simply because of one amendment that passed. The amendments, all of them that we have accepted or rejected, will be dealt with in conference which the gentleman from Kentucky hopes to be a member of, under the leadership of the gentleman from New Jersey (Rodino)."[60]

Unfortunately for Mazzoli, the gentleman from New Jersey didn't necessarily agree; Rodino was quoted in the following day's *New York Times* saying he "had very, very serious questions" about whether he could support the bill if it authorized a major guestworker program.[61] The Panetta proposal, which over time could allow the entry into the US of as many as half a million foreign guestworkers each year, certainly qualified as "major" by any standard.

The House returned to the bill for two final days of debate just after 3:00 p.m. on Tuesday, June 19. The upcoming amendment to strike legalization from the bill was the big imminent vote most Congress watchers focused on but The Group was more concerned about others that would limit those eligible for legalization, especially since the bill's January 1, 1982, legalization cutoff date had prevailed in committee by a single vote.[62] They also worried that adoption of certain amendments could, in a single swoop, wipe out many of the individually minor but collectively important program substructure changes they'd won in preceding days.[63]

California's Dan Lungren offered the amendment to establish a more restrictive two-tier legalization program, tracking the Senate bill. Under his amendment, only those undocumented people that had entered the US prior to January 1, 1977, would be eligible to apply for permanent status; those entering between 1977 and January 1, 1980, would receive three-year temporary status, after which they could apply for permanent status.[64] Lungren's approach was strongly encouraged by the Reagan administration.[65] Among those supporting Lungren were not just usual legalization opponents, but also border state conservative Eldon Rudd (R-AZ) and the moderate Tom Lewis (R-FL), who'd been known as an outspoken GOP opponent of Social Security cuts.[66] For its part The Group produced more than a dozen opponents to speak against the proposal, including Connecticut Republican moderate Stewart McKinney and Democrat John Seiberling of Ohio, a progressive close to the churches, neither of whom had previously weighed in on the immigration debate. In the end, it was stalwart bill supporter Barney Frank who stuck a dagger through Lungren's proposal, stating, "The guts of this bill will be lying all over the floor if this amendment passes. I am afraid I will not be able to support it."[67] Lungren's amendment was handily defeated by a 245–181 margin after nearly two hours of consideration; Florida Republican Clay Shaw's proposal to adopt the more restrictive 1980 cutoff date for legalization also failed by a similar 246–177 vote after a perfunctory debate.[68]

It was nearly 6:00 p.m. when Majority Leader Jim Wright of Texas introduced his amendment to require legalization applicants to pass an English test, or be enrolled in a certified course, before receiving permanent resident status. Like the Lungren amendment and the Senate bill, it created a two-tier program, a concept that The Group publicly opposed. But when Rep. Kent Hance's senatorial campaign seemed to put amnesty in mortal danger, LULAC and NCLR had privately agreed not to oppose Wright's proposal in return for his support for legalization and increased funding for English classes. Kamasaki was thus relieved that NCLR wasn't mentioned in the majority leader's remarks, but Joe Treviño was dismayed when Wright seemed to indicate during the floor debate that he'd consulted with LULAC in fashioning his proposal.[69] The amendment passed 247–170.[70] It was nearly 8:00 p.m. when Mazzoli rose to indicate that consideration of the last amendments and the vote on final passage would take place the following day.[71]

After two weeks straight of working twelve-plus-hour days, the advocates were burning out, sleepwalking through their last tasks. With the end of the debate in sight, the coalition war room in the NCLR building's basement wound down. The out-of-towners went home, and those who remained steeled themselves for what appeared to be the inevitable passage of the legislation. As the debate ended on June 19, a phone call from Swartz caught Kamasaki at his desk near the end of the evening; Swartz asked about NCLR's plans for the next day. The exhausted lobbyist replied that they would head to the House to watch the last hours of the debate, since the bill probably would pass anyway. "You're wrong," Swartz declared. "It's really close. If I were you I'd keep making phone calls and firm up your floor operation," the National Immigration Forum executive "advised," since he wasn't supposed to lobby. Re-energized, NCLR's Kamasaki and Purtell began calling undecided offices, urging opposition, and Escutia activated her network of friendly congressional staffers to augment the tiny opposition "whip" organization run by Jorge Lambrinos, who'd succeeded Dan Maldonado as Rep. Roybal's chief of staff.[72]

The term *whip* has its origins in the British House of Commons in the eighteenth century, and comes from the "whipper in," the individual responsible for managing the dogs that flush the game in English fox hunts.[73] Each party's whip operation performs three key functions, starting with head counts of their members' support or opposition to legislation or major amendments. On votes deemed "party issues," the whip team will coax undecided or ambivalent lawmakers to support the party line, with varying degrees of persuasion employed depending on the political importance of the issue. The third, often overlooked, task for whip teams is simply making sure their members show up for key votes, or not, as the case may be; opponents of the party line are often quietly encouraged to "take a walk" and miss the vote. Since the immigration legislation cut across party lines, neither party's whip team was officially engaged. Instead, the lead sponsors of the bill led by Mazzoli and Lungren, supported by his ranking member Hamilton Fish, and the opponents led by Rep. Roybal, were forced to develop their own informal whip operations. Roybal's staff, augmented by Escutia's network, was soon blanketing undecided congressional offices with multiple phone calls urging a "no" vote on the bill, while tracking down opponents to ensure they would record their votes the next day.[74]

SQUEAKING THROUGH

The final day of floor debate on the bill began at 10:30 a.m. on June 20. Rep. Norm Mineta (D-CA), Al Simpson's childhood friend, offered an amendment to strengthen the appeals procedure for those denied legalization. Mazzoli and Lungren agreed to accept the amendment, yet another provision from the Roybal bill that had been adopted.[75] Two minor amendments were disposed of before Rep. McCollum offered his widely anticipated amendment number 61, to strike the legalization program altogether. McCollum put forth arguments against amnesty still heard today. He argued that the nation should secure its borders before any other measures were considered, anticipating by three decades the standard rallying cry of many GOP opponents of legalization.[76] He noted that legalizing unauthorized people already here would be unfair to those "waiting in line" to enter legally. He echoed administration estimates of the expenses the bill would rack up, and also asserted the program was politically unpopular. And finally, the "magnet of legalization," he suggested, would draw "probably millions across our borders in the hopes that they can somehow fake their way to amnesty," or "in the false belief that we will grant amnesty again, as many other countries have done."[77]

Rodino rose in opposition by recounting his own long history on the issue, which Rep. Esteban Torres personalized by emotionally recalling his own father's deportation in the 1930s and reciting into the *Record* a full stanza and the refrain from folksinger Woody Guthrie's Depression-era classic song "Deportee."[78] But the outcome was already foretold, and a good part of the discussion then devolved into platitudes unrelated to the question at hand. For example, Rep. Jack Kemp (R-NY) praised fellow New Yorker Bob García's fortitude in participating in all seven days of the debate, calling it his "finest hour."[79] Ultimately, McCollum's amendment was defeated by a surprisingly comfortable 233–195 vote.[80]

It was 2:40 p.m. when Rep. Rodino offered his own Cuban–Haitian Adjustment Act as an amendment. Rodino's bill, largely drafted by Mike Hooper of the National Coalition for Haitian Refugees with input from Cuban American organizations, was broader and more comprehensive than either the Senate or pending House bills. Unlike the underlying bill's amnesty provisions, Mariel boatlift Cubans and Haitian entrants, whose entry into the US had jump-started consideration of immigration reform four years earlier, would be eligible immediately for permanent resident status and federal benefits. Unlike the Simpson-Mazzoli bill, Rodino's provision retained the Cuban Adjustment Act at the insistence of Cuban American leaders such as Manuel Diaz of the Spanish American League Against Discrimination and Guarione Diaz of the Cuban American National Council, advocates that Swartz had long courted.[81] Their support was crucial since Cubans expected favorable treatment from the Reagan administration whether Rodino's provision passed or not; it was the Haitians that needed the legislative boost.

The amendment was a long time coming. Although he'd always been favorably disposed toward the Haitians, throughout 1983 and early 1984, Rodino was undecided about whether to introduce his own bill or instead to accept Mazzoli's weaker provisions. Led by Hooper, advocates descended on Rodino's staff, urging him to introduce the stand-alone legislation and, later, to attach it to Simpson-Mazzoli. But when their lobbying failed to convince the chairman to get off the dime, the Haitian advocates decided to escalate.

They prevailed on the aging but still iconic civil rights leader Bayard Rustin, a cofounder of the National Coalition for Haitian Refugees, to deliver a speech in Rodino's district demanding justice for the Haitians.[82] They followed up with a discreet request to Donald Payne, a Newark city councilman and the first black president of the YMCA, which was closely associated with the National Council of Churches, to give the chairman a nudge. African Americans had long been a majority in the chairman's district, and while Rodino had easily defeated black primary challengers for more than a decade, he had to be sensitive to requests from Payne, who challenged Rodino in 1980 and eventually won the seat after Rodino retired. Coming on top of pressure from Rustin, Payne's "request" to accommodate Haitians was fully intended as a veiled threat that he might challenge Rodino again if the Haitian issue wasn't resolved satisfactorily. It's very tricky for advocates to mess with a congressman's election, especially with a key ally, but they decided to play this card, with Myers ultimately making the call since Payne was his contact. In February, Rodino introduced H.R. 4853, the Cuban–Haitian Adjustment Act of 1984, and Payne testified in its favor.[83]

Many factors drew so many to the cause of Haitian refugees. Some were compelled by the sheer brutality of Francois "Papa Doc" and Jean-Claude "Baby Doc" Duvalier, the father-son "Presidents-for-Life" who ruled the island nation for generations and ordered the execution of thirty thousand people in their twenty-nine-year reign, according to Human Rights Watch.[84] Good government types were offended not just by its poverty—90 percent of the population had an annual income of $150, or less than $500 in 2017 dollars—but because the Duvaliers raked millions off the top of aid from abroad.[85] One estimate in the 1980s put Baby Doc's take from embezzlement at $300 million, not counting what his father, extended family members, and friends and cronies might have stolen.[86] Haiti's revolution, scholars wrote, was the "first and only successful slave revolt in the history of the world," in which former slaves on the island defeated in succession France, Great Britain, and then Spain to win independence in 1804.[87] Many academics believe that the independence from Spain of Venezuela, Colombia, Bolivia, Ecuador, and Peru might not have happened without the material and inspirational support from newly independent Haiti. "The Liberator" Simon Bolivar received backing for his cause from an initially reluctant Haitian president Petion only after committing to "take immediate steps to abolish slavery" in Latin America.[88] Perhaps it was poetic justice that LULAC and NCLR supported the bill, even though some of their Cuban constituents only grudgingly agreed to link their fortunes with those of the politically weaker Haitians.

Other legalization amendments that were drafted in a way that could restrict the number of Cubans and Haitians that could adjust to permanent resident status provided a convenient excuse for the advocates to urge Rodino to attach his bill to Simpson-Mazzoli, and eventually the chairman agreed.[89] The amendment was adopted, but Rep. Henry B. González, while nominally supporting Haitians, made the point that with Mexican immigrants, "justice has yet to be done with respect to that bronze skin, the one who came over, built the highways, plucked the cotton balls, erected the skyscrapers of Dallas and Houston and San Antonio and is so forgotten. In time of war, illegal or not, he fought bravely and died valiantly in great numbers for our country."[90]

It was a classic move by "Henry B," highlighting what even supporters viewed as a highly inconvenient truth—virtually all of the Haitians and Cubans that had entered unlawfully would be legalized but many undocumented Mexicans wouldn't—illustrating an evolution by the crusty congressman who'd earlier railed against Chicano militants for their race-based agenda but now seemed comfortable making ethnocentric appeals of his own.

Several technical or minor amendments were disposed of before Rep. Roybal rose to offer amendment number 68 to create a national commission on immigration, another provision from his bill, to conduct research and make recommendations to Congress on "the push and pull factors affecting unauthorized migration" and "the development, in partnership with Latin American countries, of reciprocal trade and economic development programs."[91] Few agreed with Roybal that this was "the most important amendment" considered by the House, but Mazzoli quickly accepted it, as did a somewhat reluctant Lungren.[92]

At 4:50 p.m., on the seventh day of debate, the question occurred on final passage. On bills of this magnitude, the typical bill's sponsor could expect the party's whip operation to help count votes, keep wavering supporters in line, and persuade shaky opponents to cross over. Even on measures that neither party's leadership operation can formally support, oftentimes ad hoc groups of committee chairs or other elders are formed to informally whip the bill. And on some truly divisive bills, key interest group supporters will organize their own whip operation, as legendary labor lobbyist Jane O'Grady famously had done on behalf of the Leadership Conference on Civil Rights to defeat killer amendments and push the Civil Rights Act of 1964 over the top two decades earlier.

Mazzoli had none of these institutional mechanisms to back him. The House Democratic leadership was indifferent, "cool" to the bill in O'Neill's words. His own chairman, Peter Rodino, was openly lukewarm about the legislation. Passage of the Panetta amendment had forced the AFL-CIO to formally retract its previous support for the bill, meaning there'd be no outside group "whip system" from labor either. So as the vote on final passage began, Democrat Mazzoli and Republican Lungren, the two Notre Dame alums, found themselves almost alone except for committee ranking member Hamilton Fish, as they frantically tried to rally support for the bill. With his wife Helen looking on from the House Gallery, Mazzoli vividly recalled the blinking lights—red for "no" votes, green for "yes" votes—on the giant electronic scoreboard.[93] Dozens of "no" votes were recorded immediately, while the "yes" votes trickled in slowly, indicating that opponents were more enthusiastic about recording their position than the bill's backers, and that fence-sitters were waiting to see which way the wind was blowing.

Mazzoli checked the vote tally and thought to himself, "Son of a gun, we were down."[94] Mazzoli and Lungren redoubled their efforts, working furiously to buttonhole undecided colleagues and nail down the critical swing votes. With the fifteen-minute roll call nearing its end and still a few votes short, the Kentuckian approached New York Democrats Tom Downey and Robert Mrazek. "These guys were friends of mine," Mazzoli noted later, but they had problems with the legislation. He asked them to at least give him a chance to get his bill to conference, promising he'd do his best to resolve their concerns.[95] Mazzoli later recalled his last-ditch effort: "I begged those guys. I said, 'For God's sake, don't let us come up empty-handed.' "[96] Lungren and Fish worked the Republican side of the chamber equally hard. As described by researcher Rosanna Perotti, the final vote on the bill played out "like a suspense novel, as its fate teetered back-and-forth during the 15-minute roll call. 'No' votes outnumbered the 'yes' until just a few seconds before the end, when the tally tied at 210 and Congressional arm-twisters on the floor obtained the few more votes that led to victory."[97]

The bill squeaked through by a shockingly close 216–211 vote. Mazzoli later told a writer that "nothing in my life, including the birth of our children . . . left such an indelible mark in my brain as that few minutes on the floor going to final passage."[98] The razor-thin margin of victory, in many ways, underscored the

Kentuckian's achievement. With no help from his party's leadership, formidable interest group opposition, and tepid support at best from his committee chairman, he and Simpson had managed to do what no other legislators had done since 1965: get a major immigration reform bill through both houses of Congress in the same session. Mazzoli had done everything humanly possible to get the bill this far; the normally spry and vigorous congressman had deep, dark bags under his eyes and looked haggard, having lost eleven pounds off an already slender frame.[99]

For the bill's sponsors, the road to victory was, finally, clearly in sight. It was still June, and even accounting for extra-long recesses for members to attend the political conventions, Congress was expected to be in session for ten to twelve more weeks, presumably ample time to complete action on the legislation. Understandably, Mazzoli and Simpson were happy to take a couple of victory laps in the media and the think tank circuit. "For a while Al and I were the lions of the scene around here," Mazzoli recalled in a rare outright admission of pride at the adulation he and Simpson received from the pundits and press in the wake of House passage.[100] Ron Mazzoli could not have known that this would be the high-water mark of his personal identification with this bill. The fates were unkind, even cruel, to him at every subsequent stage of the process from this point until its conclusion years later.

CONVENTIONS

Some in The Group thought it strange that they saw little of Arnoldo Torres over the nearly two weeks the bill was on the floor. They knew that LULAC's national convention was coming up, which would naturally occupy the executive director, and Torres had confided to some that he was having trouble adjusting to new LULAC president Mario Obledo. Obledo was an institution in the Mexican American community, a cofounder and first president and general counsel of MALDEF in his native San Antonio in the late 1960s. After moving to California, he was appointed secretary of health and welfare by Governor Jerry Brown, serving from 1975–1982.[101] While Obledo shared Ruben and Tony Bonilla's left-leaning politics, unlike his predecessors, Obledo didn't give his subordinate Arnoldo Torres much freedom to implement strategy. Even before his installation became official, the incoming LULAC president was, in Torres's view, micromanaging his executive director, much to the latter's consternation.[102]

Obledo and Torres did agree that the Simpson-Mazzoli bill at this stage could only be defeated by making it politically radioactive for Democrats. And the way to do that, they believed, was by publicly threatening Mondale's candidacy at the upcoming Democratic National Convention. Torres attempted to make this case several times to others in The Group, but most declined to actively participate in a direct assault on Mondale's candidacy at the Democratic Convention.[103] They were, after all, employed by nonprofits explicitly prohibited by IRS rules from participating in partisan politics (LULAC had a different designation under the tax code, allowing greater political engagement). Only Swartz, who almost always seemed willing to bend the rules, joined LULAC at the conventions.[104]

Sandwiched in between the congressional recess and the beginning of the political conventions was a development that proved highly significant for the future trajectory of those purporting to speak for Latinos: the first Hispanic Conference on Immigration Reform held on July 15–16 in Los Angeles. Funded by the Spanish International Network (SIN), forerunner to the Univision television empire, participants included former MALDEF head Vilma Martínez , former INS commissioner Leonel Castillo, San Antonio mayor Henry Cisneros, Republican National Hispanic Assembly chair and businessman Fernando Oaxaca, Emilio Nicolas, owner of SIN's original flagship station in San Antonio, and Los Angeles-based KMEX TV president Daniel Villanueva, who'd gained fame as an NFL kicker for the Los Angeles Rams and the Dallas Cowboys. The elite group of the few Latinos with a claim to national name recognition was joined by about a dozen others with prominent regional followings, including Colorado state senator Polly Baca, a member of the Democratic National Committee and an early NCLR staffer, and Denver mayor Federico Peña, the first Hispanic to be elected to that position who later held two Cabinet posts in the Clinton administration. LULAC, MALDEF, and NCLR were also represented, and one of the few non-Latinos invited was Rick Swartz, who impressed the Latino leadership group with his knowledge of the issue.[105]

National, cross-sector gatherings of Latinos were quite rare in those days, but SIN had considerable convening power; almost every Hispanic politician and advocate understood the potential reach of the network through which they could "narrow cast" a message to "the base." It was also immensely profitable, meaning that the network, almost alone among national Hispanic institutions, had the resources to completely underwrite events like these. SIN itself was under something of a cloud. Critics alleged that it was secretly controlled by Mexican media mogul Emilio Azcárraga in violation of Federal Communications Commission rules prohibiting foreign ownership of broadcast stations, circumvented only via the "time-honored business stratagem known, in Spanish, as the '*presta nombre*,' which translates literally into 'lending a name,' or in colloquial English, a 'front',," where the stations were technically owned by US citizens with close, often familial ties to Azcárraga.[106] Others, mainly from within the Latino community, argued that the network's programming, virtually all of which was produced abroad by Azcárraga's Mexico-based company Televisa, didn't provide sufficient public affairs and news content.[107] There was also considerable angst in many circles about whether a Spanish-language television network should even exist. These and other issues eventually forced an auction won by Hallmark in 1987, which purchased the network rebranded under the Univision name, the first of several future major ownership changes.

Charges from Latino activists that the network was insufficiently engaged in public affairs pushed many of the local stations to be "at the cutting edge with advocacy type of journalism," according to Villanueva.[108] This development was of considerable help to the advocates, presaging the roles that Fox News and MSNBC later played for activists on the right and left, respectively: their own television network to inform and mobilize the base. The SIN immigration conference event advanced The Group's cause, beginning with the official conference press statement characterizing Simpson-Mazzoli as a "sham and an attack on our community."[109] That a high-profile bipartisan group would take a tough stand against the bill validated the activists' opposition to immigration reform in Latino establishment circles. Equally crucial was the widespread coverage that SIN subsequently provided to the Simpson-Mazzoli bill in key markets like Los Angeles, San Antonio, New York, Miami, Chicago, Dallas, Houston, and Phoenix, giving the advocates the ability to sidestep what they saw as inadequate mainstream media coverage of their issues by taking their case directly to their community.

Within days of House passage of the bill, LULAC held its 55th annual convention in El Paso, where its president Mario Obledo, standing next to Jesse Jackson, threatened to organize Hispanic delegates pledged to presumptive nominee Walter Mondale to engage in a "first-ballot boycott" to protest his failure to stop the immigration legislation. Former LULAC president Ruben Bonilla noted the immigration bill was the "overriding political issue" at the convention, and because Democrats "were responsible for the bill's passage" LULAC was obligated to "send a message" to Mondale, the titular head of the party.[110] While some press coverage focused on Mondale's failure to attend the LULAC event as a purported reason for the group's ire, in truth the maneuver had been in the works for weeks, starting with a letter sent to all Democratic Hispanic delegates from LULAC's political arm urging a first-ballot boycott if the House passed the Simpson-Mazzoli bill.[111]

The threat to Mondale wasn't existential—there weren't enough Hispanic delegates to prevent his nomination even if all boycotted the first ballot—but was symbolically potent. Democrats were counting on an unprecedented turnout of the base to have a fighting chance at beating Reagan, a popular president starting to reap the benefits of an emerging economic recovery.[112] Mondale's primary victory in a three-way race with Sen. Hart and the Rev. Jesse Jackson had exposed deep fissures within a party aptly criticized by David Broder, the dean of the nation's political reporters, as "zigzagging in search of an iden-tity."[113] Polarizing debate between unions inclined to favor the immigration bill and Hispanics that opposed it was the last thing party leaders wanted at a time when above all else political parties seek unity for the fall campaign.[114]

They got the unwanted debate anyway. Briefed in advance by LULAC presi-dent Obledo and executive director Arnoldo Torres, most Latino delegates entered their caucus meeting on July 17 prepared to support a motion by Cali-fornia delegate Carlos Alcalá "recommending abstention on the first ballot to protest" the party's support for the immigration bill.[115] With "crisis in the air," Mondale himself met with many of the delegates and issued a statement oppos-ing the legislation, after first being urged to do so privately by San Antonio mayor Henry Cisneros.[116] Vice presidential nominee Rep. Geraldine Ferraro, who had voted against the bill in the House, spoke to the delegates, calling the bill "wrong, wrong, wrong."[117] Cisneros, along with Reps. Bob García and Edward R. Roybal, both of whom had strong credentials as Simpson-Mazzoli opponents, lobbied the delegates to accept Mondale's statement and end the boycott threat. After a "stormy debate" the boycott motion failed on a tie vote among Hispanic delegates, although some die-hards booed the elected officials and pledged to keep at it.[118]

Jackson kept up the pressure, stating in his convention address that evening, "The Rainbow Coalition is making room for Hispanic Americans who this very night are living under the threat of the Simpson-Mazzoli bill."[119] Getting even that fleeting reference into Jackson's speech turned out to be an adventure in itself. Joe Treviño had been tasked with drafting the language on Simpson-Mazzoli for Jackson's speech, but he'd also been in charge of an earlier demon-stration against the bill. Rushing to get his paragraph of suggested language to the candidate's hotel room on the afternoon of Jackson's speech, and unfamiliar with Secret Service protocol to lock down the entire hotel floor occupied by candidates, Treviño was puzzled when he couldn't get the elevator to stop on the proper floor. Unwilling to give up, he took the stairs and managed to find an unlocked door into the hotel room corridor. He soon found himself with his hands up, staring down the barrels of several guns pointed at him by Secret Ser-vice agents, until he was rescued by a Jackson staffer and allowed to deliver his precious paragraph.[120]

A smattering of Latino delegates did indeed withhold their votes for Mon-dale two nights later, during the formal nomination roll call on July 19. Cisneros put the best possible spin on the controversy, telling the *Washington Post*, "It has been a great week. I don't think we could have written a better script."[121] The boycott forced the top of the Democratic Party's ticket to publicly and repeat-edly denounce the immigration reform bill. It also led the AFL-CIO's Lane Kirk-land to promise Hispanic delegates that labor would actively oppose the House bill that now included the massive Panetta-Morrison guestworker program. The commitment was highly conditional since it was expected that the troublesome provision would be eliminated in the upcoming conference committee. If The Group was using an "affirmative defense" strategy to kill the legislation, Kirkland showed he could play that game, taking a nominal opposition posture in public while working hard to get a bill he could support: "defensive affirmation," if you will.

Torres took his campaign to the Republican Convention in Dallas a few weeks later, where he met with outgoing Texas senator John Tower. Tower had previously opposed the bill, and presumably was a reliable vote against the product of the House–Senate conference committee. But Torres came away with what he believed was a more important commitment from Tower to filibuster the legislation if the conference committee was able to reconcile differences between the two chambers' bills.[122] The first-ballot boycott controversy, labor's public wobbling, and the filibuster threat were deep, cutting wounds to legislation that even Simpson characterized as entering the political convention season "hanging by a thread."[123]

Arnoldo Torres returned to DC exhilarated by the effort, later calling it, perhaps with some hyperbole, "the most exciting time in the history of our [Latinos'] presence" in the policy-political arena.[124] Cisneros, for his part, thought that much of what Torres did in San Francisco amounted to unnecessary grandstanding, since he felt he had the issue well under control. The San Antonio mayor had been one of five vice presidential prospects interviewed by Mondale before the selection of New York congresswoman Geraldine Ferraro. Having established a close working relationship with Mondale through this process, Cisneros believed his own intervention was the decisive factor in securing the ticket's visible, public opposition to passage of immigration reform, and that the boycott threat wasn't needed.[125] Indeed, just prior to issuing his formal opposition statement, Mondale had met with Cisneros and other Latino elected officials and advocates, but had "pointedly excluded LULAC's leadership."[126] Regardless of whether LULAC's outside pressure, the San Antonio mayor's inside negotiation, or some combination of both proved decisive in securing Mondale's public opposition, Cisneros came out of the struggle smelling like a rose. He managed to simultaneously stand up in public for his base while helping his party's candidate to resolve the controversy, displaying the deft political skills that led to a Cabinet position in the Clinton administration a decade later.

The convention gyrations reverberated immediately inside the Beltway. House leaders seemed to be slow-walking appointment of conferees, an essential step before proceeding to a conference committee required to reconcile the two bodies' bills. Simpson and Mazzoli met to discuss their strategy on July 24. The next day, Simpson told the *New York Times* that he and Mazzoli were shocked by the "pandering and posturing" at the Democratic event, concluding that the "raging partisan hysteria, hoopla, and hype against this legislation . . . may have seriously damaged the chance that the House could accept any bill."[127] After six weeks of waiting for the House leaders to name conferees, Simpson finally decided to call their bluff.[128] On July 25, Mazzoli joined Simpson in floating the idea that perhaps the Senate would accept the House bill, avoiding a conference committee altogether.[129] This was in all likelihood a tactical ploy by Simpson, but it became moot the next day when the White House, which had publicly tried to give the impression that the president would sign whatever bill Congress produced, pronounced the House bill "unacceptable," a veto threat that forced Simpson in his own words to start "tumbling around" to figure out how to rescue the bill.[130] Having no other choice, Simpson and Mazzoli had to go to conference, with Simpson warning that if the bill failed, "No politician is going to stick his tootsies in the fire on this baby for another 10 or 20 years."[131]

House leaders really had no way of avoiding a conference committee either. Speaker O'Neill was surely not interested in exposing himself to yet another wave of criticism for killing the immigration bill. And while he and Majority Leader Wright were hardly fans of the legislation, they were "men of the House," committed to the traditions of the institution, which meant that any bill that passed the lower chamber, which Mazzoli's bill had, if only by the tightest of margins, deserved a chance to get over the finish line. As Washington shut down for its much-prized August recess, it was clear that the fate of immigration reform would be determined in September, when a conference committee would convene to hammer out differences between the two bills. But other developments sharply affected the future trajectory of the legislation, and the organizations trying to shape it.

DISPARATE DEVELOPMENTS

The first such development was framed by a long-form article in the *New York Times* in late July, not by beat reporter Robert Pear but by Bill Keller, an editor in the Washington Bureau who later secured the paper's top job. The Group first learned of the article when the ACLU's Wade Henderson pulled it out of what came to be called his "magic bag." Since the world, and thus the lobbyists, were entirely paper-based in the 1980s, getting quick access to the most recent documents affecting one's issues—a newspaper or magazine article, a "Dear Colleague" letter through which lawmakers outlined their views or circulated materials to all members of their body, a key report, or the most recent draft of a bill or amendment—was a critical part of the tradecraft. It was not uncommon for lobbyists to make special trips to Capitol Hill to pick up a document— corporate and other well-heeled interests could send interns, pay for messenger services, or even use the newfangled telefacsimile (fax) machines that some had in their offices by the early 1980s—but for most nonprofits the only other alternative was the US mail.

The Group's own special alternative to the mail was the enormous, bulging briefcase Henderson carried; not a briefcase really, it was more like a very large leather pouch that once may have had a clasp and handles, but if so, they'd long since fallen off. For the otherwise fashion-conscious Henderson, the extremely large bag he carried awkwardly under his arm seemed incongruous; as he made his rounds on the Hill he stopped in and chatted with staffers, often coming away with a hot-off-the-copy-machine document. He was even known for his ability to persuade reporters to send him confidential or embargoed materials. Years later Henderson acknowledged that while the bag might not have been especially trendy, "Isn't it amazing that it always had exactly what we needed?"[132]

Such was the case when Henderson's magic bag produced an advance copy of Keller's lengthy *New York Times* piece, headlined "Obscure Western Farm Groups Won Foreign Worker Program." It was in part a classic insider lobbying story, detailing how western growers, dissatisfied with the bill's existing agriculture programs, methodically went about winning passage of the Panetta guest-worker program on the House floor. The article began:

> They are not names widely known in Washington, much less held in awe: the California Grape and Tree Fruit League, the Raisin Bargaining Association, the Northwest Horticultural Council, the Nisei Farmers League. Yet, this summer these and similarly obscure groups of Western fruit farmers taught Washington an advanced lesson in the art of persuasion. Banded together as the Farm Labor Alliance, the groups won House approval of a bitterly disputed new program that would permit foreign workers to cross the border and harvest American crops.[133]

These agricultural employers had tangled often with César Chávez's United Farm Workers union in the previous decade and had learned a thing or two about the importance of messaging as a tool in shaping public policy. After fiercely resisting Chávez's attempts to organize vineyard workers, many had been forced to accept union contracts by the UFW's brilliantly conceived and executed international grape boycott. When, in 1976, the UFW went all-out to pass a ballot initiative to strengthen California's labor laws, the growers fought back. Among their unlikely leaders was Harry Kubo, a short, wiry thin, Japanese American grower who had been working on farms in northern California since the age of eight; just before World War II his father had managed to start a small farm on leased property the family was unable to purchase because of "Alien Land laws."[134] Like other Japanese Americans, he and his family were interned during the war. Seared in his memory was the experience of how "vultures" purchased the family's appliances and other possessions at fire sale prices as the Kubos left for relocation centers with only what they could carry. "It took a lifetime to buy those things, and they were offering my parents for the refrigerator and washing machine two dollars, a dollar and a half, five dollars," Kubo recalled bitterly.[135]

Following the war, after sharecropping for several years, Kubo's family was finally able to buy a small farm of its own near Fresno. Along with several other Japanese American growers, Kubo's operation was targeted for organizing activity in the early 1970s by the UFW, not so much on ethnic grounds, scholars wrote, but because "they were vulnerable to union efforts . . . small in size, unable to cope with sustained losses, and focused on crops that depended on migrant labor."[136] Kubo responded by forming the Nisei Farmers League, whose initial 100 members eventually grew to 1,500 participants, only 40 percent of whom were of Japanese descent.[137] Kubo became the face of a statewide committee of growers organized to fight the ballot initiative backed by César Chávez and strongly supported by Gov. Jerry Brown. It hardly seemed a fair fight, pitting two of the most charismatic leaders in the country against the farmer coalition headed by Kubo, who even supporters said was "not polished and not professional."[138] He was nevertheless effective. He had a powerful personal story and ran a well-funded campaign backed by corporate agribusiness resources and with self-imposed fees from the Nisei Farmers League and dozens of other grower organizations; the pro-farmworker proposition was crushed by a nearly two-to-one margin.[139] Many of César Chávez's closest associates believed this defeat began what became a severe downward spiral for both the union and its iconic leader.[140]

Keller's meticulous reporting described how alliance members taxed themselves to raise and spend more than $1 million, mainly on well-connected Washington lobbyists, to push the amendment through. One of their firms included the brother tandem of James and Monte Lake; the elder James Lake had been a high-level staffer on three of Ronald Reagan's political campaigns and a longtime agribusiness lobbyist who would soon move over to the 1984 Reagan reelection committee. The younger Monte Lake was a legal technician as well as a lobbyist, inclined to work quietly behind the scenes. Their initial task was to keep the Reagan administration formally neutral, helped along by "receptive Californians" presidential counselor Edwin Meese and deputy agriculture secretary Richard E. Lyng. This purported neutrality—cutting Attorney General Smith, who sided with Simpson in opposing a major new agricultural worker program, out of the action—allowed the growers to win the support of the House Republican leadership and much of the rank-and-file. The result, according to Keller's reporting, was that "House Republicans supported the amendment 138–15, more than enough to offset Democrats, who voted 157–90 against the measure."[141] Some thought Keller overestimated the power of the grower lobby's funding and political muscle. According to Monte Lake, the secret to their success was "old-fashioned retail lobbying": bringing growers to DC to make their case directly to lawmakers. Said Lake, it was the cumulative effect of "real people, real relationships, with real businesses at stake" that truly made the difference.[142]

While GOP support for the growers wasn't surprising, the degree to which key Democrats had helped the growers was. Rep. Panetta's sponsorship of the amendment was understandable, even forgivable, given the heavy agricultural presence in his district. But Hispanic advocates were appalled by how the supposedly "progressive" Democratic Party establishment, led by the venerable firm of Akin Gump Strauss Hauer & Feld, had helped the growers. Its founding and best-known partner was Robert S. Strauss. As chairman of the Democratic National Committee, Strauss was widely credited with uniting Democrats behind Jimmy Carter's winning presidential campaign in 1976; in the early 1980s he was one of the Capitol's "wise men," highly respected on both sides of the political aisle.[143] Keller's revelation that the grower's chief Democratic lobbyist was Ruth Harkin, a lawyer at Strauss's firm and the wife of Rep. Tom Harkin (D-IA), then in a tight race for a Senate seat, enraged the Latino lobbyists, confirming that when push came to shove, their "liberal" supporters would abandon them.

Harkin represented a farm state, but most Iowa growers did not have a deep interest in the immigration issue. They either grew highly mechanized grain crops like corn, wheat, or sorghum that used few if any immigrant workers, or to the extent they did, their generally predictable harvest seasons already were accommodated by the streamlined H-2 program in the bill. The Group also suspected that organized labor's supposed deep opposition to the Panetta-Morrison guestworker program had been trumped by its stronger support for employer sanctions; Harkin was known to be close to labor and few thought he'd "go off the reservation" unless given a bit of a pass by the AFL-CIO, especially when facing a close election.

The most telling part of Keller's article was Mazzoli's acquiescence to the Panetta amendment, explaining why his nominal opposition had a noticeable lack of conviction. Keller quoted Thomas Hale, head of the Farm Labor Alliance, as saying, "if Mazzoli had stood up and really opposed this thing, I know we would have lost it."[144] The revelation damaged Mazzoli's personal image as a technocratic, earnest, substance-driven reformer, showing that as much as anyone else, he was willing to cut unsavory deals with powerful special interests to get what he wanted.

There wasn't much The Group could do to punish Mazzoli—they'd pursued similar *realpolitik*-driven tactics throughout the debate, including obstructing his bill in myriad ways—but they could, they thought, make Rep. Harkin pay for his support of the growers. LULAC had an unusually strong Iowa chapter and, according to the organization's national leadership, a "stone cold great" state director, Miguel Teran, capable of mobilizing the community and attracting press coverage.[145] Arnoldo Torres dispatched his deputy Joe Treviño to hold Harkin accountable; although only 1 percent of the state electorate, Hispanics could plausibly make the difference in the race that was at the time too close to call. Once in Iowa, Treviño spoke at a series of rallies and community education events that also included other grassroots and religious leaders invited by members of The Group, culminating in a press conference where he attacked Harkin as one of the leaders in the effort to "import and exploit cheap labor" from Mexico. By the time Treviño returned to DC, the telephone switchboard and fax machines in the LULAC offices were "working overtime" with complaints from Harkin and his allies.[146]

One of those complaints reached Rep. Bob García, chairman of the Congressional Hispanic Caucus. "There's this Hispanic guy running around Iowa giving me a hard time," Harkin told García, asking for his help to call off the dogs.[147] As a result, the chairman summoned LULAC staff to meet in his office. García had a habit of giving his own nicknames to friends and colleagues, and often addressed Arnoldo Torres as "Arnie," which in the congressman's "New-Yorican" accent sounded more like "Ahh-Knee." "Arnie, Arnie, Arnie," García pleaded with Torres, accompanied by his deputy Treviño, "Tom Harkin's a good guy." Noting his election could be the difference in getting the Senate back to Democratic control, García asked the LULAC leaders, "Could you please give him a break?" They demurred but were taken aback when Harkin himself suddenly appeared to personally plead his case. In the end, they agreed to disagree, but it was clear that LULAC's willingness to inflict potential electoral damage on Democrats was beginning to draw blood.[148]

The potency of LULAC's foray into Iowa was confirmed when, in anticipation of the upcoming conference committee, NCLR, LULAC, and MALDEF met with Sen. Kennedy to discuss strategy for retaining the major gains in the legalization program they'd managed to win in the House. Knowing of Kennedy's close ties to Simpson—the major obstacle to improving legalization—NCLR wanted the Massachusetts senator to make the House's more generous legalization one of his "bottom lines."[149] But Arnoldo Torres and Sen. Kennedy quickly got into a shouting match. As retold by researcher Rosanna Perotti, in a clear reference to LULAC's attack on the Harkin campaign, the senator asked the groups to "ease up on their election year attacks" on liberals, but "Torres refused to go along. Kennedy, impatient with Torres' brashness, left the room. . . . Nevertheless, Torres was unrepentant. 'I felt honored he would do that,' Torres later said in an interview. 'I didn't give two [hoots] what he felt. They were not going to tell me what I had to do for my country, my people.' "[150]

NCLR's Martha Escutia was upset that an opportunity to potentially improve the legalization program in conference committee "had been hijacked by Arnold's ego."[151] Most lobbyists would be concerned at having angered any senator, much less one of Kennedy's stature; normal protocol would require expressions of contrition, sincere or not. But Torres was, if anything, buoyed by Harkin's and Kennedy's reactions, convinced that LULAC's work at the political conventions and in Iowa had begun to shift the very landscape not just for immigration reform, but for Hispanic advocacy in general. "I never saw a politician walk out of a meeting in his own office before, but it shows we were on a completely different level," Torres said later. "If politicians don't fear you, they don't respect you. Now they had to fear us."[152]

On the opposite side of Capitol Hill, a quieter meeting was taking place that had a more significant impact on the outcome of immigration reform. It was no secret that Peter Rodino had serious reservations about the Panetta amendment.[153] He likely was even more disturbed by the *New York Times*'s revelation that Mazzoli may have all but acquiesced to its passage. Rodino didn't just raise concerns in the press, he swung into action, discreetly calling in California Democrat Howard Berman for a private meeting.

Berman was just completing his first term in Congress, but he was far from a rookie legislator. He'd been majority leader of the California Assembly in just his third term and seemed destined for the top job until losing out to eventual Speaker Willie Brown. He was a kingmaker in Democratic politics in Southern California, partnering with Henry Waxman to draw electoral districts, and then recruiting and backing favored candidates. He also had impeccable credentials as an advocate for the interests of farmworkers, having authored and pushed through the nation's most progressive farm labor law while in the State Assembly.[154] In that sense, he seemed a perfect candidate to serve as a stalking horse for Rodino's deep concerns with the guestworker provisions the bill was now saddled with.

But he was in many other ways an unlikely representative of the chairman, who had been working to enact employer sanctions legislation for two decades. Berman nominally opposed employer sanctions, had voted against Simpson-Mazzoli on the floor, and few thought of him as a major player on the bill; although a member of the Judiciary Committee, he was not on the immigration subcommittee. But Berman was at heart a legislator not inclined to join the hard-core opposition except as a tactical step to gain leverage for a better bill in the future; his first instinct in any confrontation was to try and work out an acceptable outcome. Sensing this, Rodino asked Berman to explore whether it might be possible to craft a compromise to both satisfy the growers' concerns and protect the interests of farmworkers. He deputized Berman to represent Rodino on the guestworker issue during the remaining debate, giving him the latitude to do what he thought was necessary to build the leverage required to reach an acceptable agreement. Berman was both surprised and grateful that Rodino would empower him, "a first-termer who wasn't even on the subcommittee," with this responsibility.[155]

With conference committee rapidly approaching, the congressman's judiciary aide was moving on to another job. Faced with the new responsibility of serving as the chairman's point man on farmworker issues, Berman recruited Mark Schacht, executive director of the Farmworker Justice Fund, to join his staff on a temporary basis. Schacht first had been exposed to the plight of undocumented Mexicans while playing on a semipro baseball team, where he learned how his teammates were ruthlessly exploited by employers at their day jobs. Schacht was also a leading expert in the field, having previously worked at MALDEF and the Migrant Legal Action Program (MLAP), the Legal Services Corporation-funded "back-up center" specializing in farmworker issues, before becoming the first executive director of the Farmworker Justice Fund, created in part to carry out aggressive litigation and lobbying activity that federally funded legal services organizations like MLAP were prohibited from pursuing.[156] Schacht, who'd worked closely with Berman to oppose the Panetta amendment, was in the congressman's office when the measure was debated. After it passed by an unexpectedly large margin, the normally cool and composed Schacht was so distraught that he slipped into Berman's private restroom and wept uncontrollably.[157] Given a rare second chance to address that defeat, Berman and Schacht were eager to engage in battle again.

Even among insiders, few knew of the Rodino-Berman understanding. By choosing Howard Berman as his lieutenant on the guestworker issue, the Judiciary Committee chairman had in effect delegated to an opponent of the bill, if a somewhat reluctant one, greater authority over the troubling guestworker issue than to Mazzoli, his own subcommittee chair. This development, hidden to virtually all of the other major players, eventually had a greater impact on immigration reform than anything else mentioned in the bill's growing press coverage.

ACTS OF GENEROSITY

NCLR had received a rare bit of that press coverage just before the August recess when Alma Guillermoprieto, then a young *Washington Post* staff writer who later gained extensive critical acclaim for her writing on Latin American affairs, covered the group's annual conference in Washington. The event's heavily attended immigration workshop featured AILA's Warren Leiden, CWS's Michael Myers, and Arnoldo Torres from LULAC; in true Washington fashion, members of The Group invited each other to present at their events, giving their friends some visibility while earning a future invitation to their colleagues' events in return. Kamasaki was annoyed and a little envious that the *Post*'s article on the workshop included both a prominent picture of and quote from LULAC's Torres.[158]

The disparity in the two groups' press coverage, even of an NCLR-hosted event, stung because for advocates in Washington, press visibility is invaluable. It establishes the advocate's personal credibility as someone to whom the media turns. It provides an opportunity to present the views of the advocate's organization to a larger audience. It becomes part of a broader narrative that the advocate can help shape to advance his/her policy goals. But the press also has more nuanced uses. Trial balloons can be floated, to gauge public reaction before deciding whether to advance a position officially or not. Clever advocates can attack an opponent while seemingly staying above the fray by saying, "Well, some might conclude that so-and-so is a raving lunatic, even though I know better." There are few vehicles better than the media for rallying the base: hyperbolic statements that the "other side" is poised to destroy everything "our side" holds dear is an essential prerequisite to mobilizing the grassroots. For the skilled advocate, the media are not so much a passive recorder of events or a simple reflection of legislative developments, but a tool to be deployed to actively advance one's interests.

While within The Group LULAC's Torres had the largest personal public profile, few in Washington were more skilled at engaging the press than the ACLU's Wade Henderson, an avid, voracious consumer of not just the *Washington Post* and *New York Times*, but rare among progressives, the conservative *Washington Times*. "Gotta know what the other side is thinking," he'd say. He talked to press secretaries at supportive Hill offices, learning what messages they were putting out, and what they were hearing. He was judicious in his personal press visibility; "The most important thing is to shape the story," he'd say, and if he wasn't quoted he was fine with that. He was unusually proactive in his press work; Henderson wouldn't just send out a press release hoping to be quoted, he reached out to reporters directly without waiting for them to call. Most advocates in DC guard their press contacts carefully. By contrast, Henderson shared his contacts widely, making him an unusually good source for reporters he trusted, because he was willing to help them connect with other sources. All this gave Henderson a finely tuned instinct for what reporters were thinking, what they wanted, and how to get them to do what *he wanted*.

Kamasaki learned firsthand how this worked in early September 1984, just as the advocates were preparing for the upcoming conference committee. Earlier that summer the Reagan administration had issued proposed new rules sharply reducing the number of jurisdictions required to provide language assistance, including bilingual ballots, under the Voting Rights Act, the "language assistance" provisions that were included in the 1975 amendments to the original 1965 Act as the result of advocacy led by MALDEF and NCLR. Extension of these provisions had been MALDEF's Antonia Hernández's top priority in 1982, when the act was reauthorized. But an amendment to the 1982 extension had asked the administration to come up with a more precise method of determining those needing language assistance. Reagan proposed cutting the number of covered jurisdictions in half, from 384 counties to 197, even as the population of Hispanics and other language minorities was growing rapidly, justifying the decision by citing an otherwise obscure Census Bureau language survey.

Kamasaki and NCLR education policy analyst Lori S. Orum, an expert on language issues, prepared an analysis opposing Reagan's interpretation of the census study, published as a memorandum, signed onto by LULAC, ACLU, MALDEF, and other civil rights groups. The memo argued that the Census Bureau had used an inappropriate methodology to make its calculations, and if a more accurate method were used, the number of jurisdictions required to provide language assistance would have been higher. But the memo attracted little interest. After the Labor Day break, as immigration was returning to the front burner, Kamasaki had all but forgotten about it until on the evening of September 9, his phone rang; Wade Henderson was on the line, and barked, "Quick! Fax your language assistance memo over to Robert Pear at the *New York Times*. Give it five minutes to go through, and then call him on his direct line. He's on deadline doing a story on bilingual ballots. Do it, right now!"

Kamasaki did as he was told: dug up a clean copy of the memo from one of the piles of paper in his office, then walked upstairs to the organization's single fax machine to feed the memo, page by page, into the machine, and waited until he'd received confirmation that the communication had gone through. He then called the number Henderson had given him and was greeted by a famously quiet and raspy voice, "This is Robert Pear." As the beat reporter on immigration for the nation's most respected newspaper, Pear was an important journalist. His ability to convey technical issues was widely recognized; he was the "reporter of record" on Simpson-Mazzoli, as he would later become in the 1990s during debate over the Clinton health care proposal, and even later, Obama's Affordable Care Act.[159]

Kamasaki explained who he was, and then started outlining the technical policy issues involved, as fast as he could. Pear cut him off, saying something like, "Look, I'm on deadline and need to finish the story in the next few minutes. Is it okay if I just quote from the memo and attribute it to you?" Kamasaki quickly agreed, relieved that he didn't have to come up with a soundbite on the spot. The following day, the front page of the *New York Times* ran a story under Robert Pear's byline, "Federal Regulations Pare Requirements for Bilingual Ballots," and both Henderson and Kamasaki were quoted.[160] The piece appeared just as the conference committee on Simpson-Mazzoli was beginning, requiring the NCLR team to join The Group for yet another round of congressional visits, this time concentrating on the offices of the twenty-nine House conferees.

Between visits, NCLR staff often used the office of Rep. Esteban Torres as a "hub," sometimes to use the phone, other times to use the copiers or fax machines, but often to chat with legislative assistant Albert Jacquez. NCLR's relationship with Mr. Torres's office was unusually close. The congressman and NCLR's president had been friends since Torres's time as chief of protocol and the highest-ranking Hispanic in the Carter White House early in Yzaguirre's tenure at NCLR. Farther back, Torres headed The East Los Angeles Community Union, one of the seven original affiliates of NCLR's predecessor, the Southwest Council of La Raza. Yzaguirre viewed Esteban Torres as a trusted elder in the "NCLR *familia*." The ties were even closer at the staff level. Escutia had worked side by side for months with Jacquez on the campaign team that elected Torres and his fellow Southern Californian Marty Martínez in 1982. They'd been mentored by Fernando Torres-Gil, a UCLA professor active in Latino political circles and a highly regarded member of NCLR's board of directors. Escutia and Jacquez were extremely close, such that she often jokingly called him her "son."[161] Another Torres legislative assistant, Mauro Morales, had interned at NCLR before joining Torres's staff. And Kamasaki and Jacquez frequently worked together on housing and financial services issues, which both were assigned to cover.

NCLR staffers, and eventually The Group, took full advantage of the relationship, showing up at the office without notice and peppering the Torres staff for favors that only a congressional office could deliver quickly: copies of hearings, reports from the General Accounting Office and Congressional Research Service, the latest "Dear Colleague" letters lawmakers use to stake out positions, and passages from the *Congressional Record*. Torres staffers routinely agreed to these requests, and the advocates needed the support as they worked feverishly to kill the bill if possible, but also improve it, just in case it passed, especially since as the bill progressed, it increasingly intertwined with matters of life and death.

SAFE HAVEN

Having been convinced by constituents in a chance meeting after his 1982 reelection to champion temporary safe haven status for Salvadorans in the US, Rep. Joe Moakley and his aide Jim McGovern immediately got to work. In 1983,

Moakley passed a nonbinding House resolution declaring a "Sense of Congress" that Salvadorans in the US "should be granted extended voluntary departure until the situation . . . changed sufficiently to permit their safely residing in that country."[162] He wrote to the attorney general and the secretary of state, urging the granting of EVD status to Salvadorans, and organized other representatives to do the same, requests that were quickly rebuffed.[163] Once it became clear the administration would not act, together with Arizona senator Dennis DeConcini, a moderate Democrat, Moakley introduced the first of a series of what became known as the Moakley-DeConcini bills, whose core provision was *requiring* the executive branch to temporarily suspend deportation of Salvadorans until a government study demonstrated it was safe for them to return.

The bill was widely acknowledged to be the handiwork of Mort Halperin, then transitioning to overseeing the ACLU's entire Washington office, in the process replacing John Shattuck as Wade Henderson's boss.[164] Just in his mid-forties, Halperin was already an institution in Washington circles. After earning his BA at Columbia College, he'd received a PhD in international relations from Yale, then joined the Harvard faculty.[165] He served in the Defense Department in the 1960s under Secretary Robert McNamara, part of a group of so-called whiz kids, a label first applied to McNamara's young staffers credited with reviving the Ford Motor Company, later expanded to his staff at Defense, all of whom were steeped in the application of statistics, the social sciences, and game theory to business and government.[166] After Nixon won the 1968 election, Halperin stayed on, working under Henry Kissinger, with whom he'd taught at Harvard. When Nixon and Kissinger suspected their holdover staffer of leaking information about the expansion of the US Vietnam War effort into Cambodia, which Halperin opposed, he became the subject of a FBI wiretap, which was later successfully challenged in court.[167]

By the time Nixon was impeached in 1974, Halperin had authored several books, and was founding the Center for National Security Studies, a project of the ACLU that worked at the intersection of civil liberties and national security policy.[168] At the request of the organization's DC affiliate, which had established a political asylum project to represent the growing number of Salvadorans in the region, in 1983 Halperin agreed to support the refugee protection effort. At an early meeting of refugee advocates discussing Reagan's opposition to extended voluntary departure status, Halperin recalled, "People were going around and around about whether the administration really did have the authority not to deport entire classes of people. I said, 'Whether they do or not, why don't we give them the authority?' So I turned around in my swivel chair and banged out on a typewriter the language giving them the authority."[169]

The ACLU's Washington office and local affiliate collaborated in other ways.

Under the direction of Amit Pandya, the ACLU's political asylum project coordinated the work of lawyers providing pro bono representation to the growing number of Salvadorans in DC and around the country. In January 1984, Pandya hired Carol Wolchok, an attorney who'd worked with Michael Maggio, a nationally recognized immigration lawyer who'd brought one of the first successful Salvadoran political asylum cases in the country.[170] She'd personally witnessed the grim human rights situation in Central America as part of a women's delegation to the region that included former New York congresswoman Bella Abzug and Jacqueline Jackson, the wife of the Rev. Jesse Jackson.[171] Pandya's legal strategy focused on "shaping the jurisprudence" across the entire field, mirroring the "impact litigation" approach of groups like MALDEF and the NAACP Legal Defense Fund. Halperin augmented that legal strategy with an aggressive press effort, directing Wolchok to send newspaper editorial boards in key districts extensive materials on the Moakley-DeConcini bill, eventually producing over one hundred supportive editorials.[172]

The national and local ACLU collaborated to conduct research to rebut the administration's claim that returnees to El Salvador had not been harmed; the ACLU was a rare group outside of a university setting capable of performing such research in-house, in part due to Halperin's interest in gadgets. He told an interviewer that he'd "always been fascinated by computers" since his first exposure to them, finding them "magical."[173] The ACLU's Washington office was thus an early adopter of a Kaypro, among the most capable of the new breed of desktop personal computers. With this capacity in hand, as Wolchok remembers: "A lot of lawyers around the country doing asylum cases were showing that the Salvadoran military was killing people in certain villages. . . . Mort [Halperin] had the idea of going to the human rights documents listing [death squad] victims and their towns, getting lists of deportees from the [US] government through the Freedom of Information Act, and then doing a [computer] match."[174]

The Kaypro was operated by Maurice Belanger, a skilled "techie" before the term had been invented. Working with María del Carmen Boza, a native Spanish speaker and coordinator of the DC affiliate's documentation center, Belanger set up a database program to match names of returnees with publicly available information about victims of human rights violations.[175] They soon were able to solidly document the deaths or disappearances of deportees to El Salvador; an initial fourteen cases were included in an April 1984 report published by the national ACLU.[176] In June, the administration published its own study based on postcards mailed from the US embassy in San Salvador to returnees that purportedly identified only one deportee that had been killed, supposedly by leftist insurgents, and another returned postcard marked "deceased"; the State Department concluded that "not a single one [of the respondents] recounted a story of persecution."[177] In September, the ACLU's DC affiliate issued another report questioning the validity of the government survey and documenting an additional 112 likely cases of harm to returnees, many confirmed by independent human rights groups; attached was a twelve-page printout of the matches produced by the ACLU's Kaypro computer.[178]

Many others in The Group were active on the issue. Rick Swartz had first introduced Rep. Moakley and his aide Jim McGovern to Salvadoran asylee Leonel Gómez. Called a "mysterious exile" by the congressman's biographer, Gómez served as Moakley and McGovern's "guide through the Salvadoran thicket" of complex, often confusing political factions.[179] CWS's Michael Myers and his deputy Joy Olson delivered much of the lobbying power behind the bill, inside and outside of DC. A key source of grassroots energy behind the bill was the Sanctuary movement, which began when Rev. John Fife of Southside Presbyterian Church in Tucson, Arizona, declared in 1981 that he would defy the INS and provide sanctuary for Central Americans; in just a few years, the movement grew to over 150 congregations.[180]

Soon a number of mainstream Protestant denominations—most members of the National Council of Churches, CWS's parent organization—adopted resolutions supporting sanctuary.[181] The Moakley-DeConcini bill naturally became one of CWS's top legislative priorities. Joy Olson, who'd worked in Honduras for two years before earning a master's degree in Mexico, conducted dozens of congressional office visits, and more importantly coordinated the DC lobbying for the Moakley-DeConcini bill by churches and human rights groups.[182] CWS's signal role on the issue was reflected at one of the National Immigration, Refugee and Citizenship Forum's first events. The 1983 "Working Conference on International Refugee Protection and Care" featured government officials, United Nations and Red Cross dignitaries, congressional staff, and among nonprofit advocates, the ACLU's Mort Halperin, Salvadoran asylee Leonel Gómez, and Michael Myers.[183] The Moakley-DeConcini bill went nowhere in the 98th Congress; Mazzoli declined to give it a hearing, much less move it out of his subcommittee, but Moakley vowed to keep pushing.[184] He couldn't have envisioned just how long it would take for his efforts to bear fruit.

TRICKS

Even after being buffeted by hostile crosscurrents—the Reagan administration's near-veto-threat over the cost of the House legalization program, organized labor's formal opposition based on the House adoption of the Panetta-Morrison guestworker program, the tumult of the political conventions, and contretemps over appointment of conferees—in early August the bill's future appeared brighter. On August 7, the Senate named its seven conferees, a move it would not have made without indications that the House would reciprocate. Speaker

O'Neill indicated that very day his intention to appoint his body's conferees soon.[185] Even the calendar gave Simpson and Mazzoli a rare break; Labor Day fell early in 1984, on September 3, allowing more than a month for differences between the bills to be resolved and passed by both houses before the expected early- to mid-October adjournment date.

But it seemed with this legislation every piece of good news had to be accompanied by some bad. Earlier that summer at the NCLR annual conference, Vice President Bush had promised a cheering crowd that, "The President will not sign any legislation that would permit employers to discriminate against Hispanics or anyone else."[186] This wasn't a real threat: the administration's formal position was that employer sanctions would not cause discrimination, so the president could sign Simpson-Mazzoli without violating Bush's pledge. But the administration's opposition to Rep. Frank's antidiscrimination amendment was a real problem. The week the Senate appointed conferees, Attorney General Smith privately told Simpson that the administration objected to the amendment because of its protections against discrimination based on alienage, prohibiting employers from refusing to hire those lawfully present based on immigration status. William Bradford Reynolds, the assistant attorney general for civil rights, told the press that "it is understandable that some private employers might prefer to provide employment for United States citizens rather than citizens of other countries," although whether Frank's amendment actually would have prohibited this conduct was disputed.[187] White House chief of staff James Baker was said to be alarmed about the amendment.[188] Arguing that his provision was a "thoughtful and very practical scheme to protect potential victims of discrimination" Rep. Frank, supported by Rodino, gave no indication of backing off.[189]

Another obstacle was the administration's long-standing concern about the cost of the House bill's legalization program. Because Mazzoli's bill had a more generous 1982 cutoff date than the Senate counterpart's 1980 date, the size of the newly legalizing population, and thus the costs associated with it, would be higher. The House bill provided 100 percent reimbursement to the states for their costs; the Senate bill merely provided for block grants in amounts to be specified later. Initially, most observers agreed with Mazzoli that "a bill like this is not going to go down over money."[190] But when presidential spokesperson Larry Speakes said that the president found the House bill "too expensive" and "unacceptable," Simpson felt compelled to ask for yet another meeting with Reagan and top White House officials. At the meeting, which included Attorney General William French Smith, counselor Ed Meese, budget director David Stockman, Chief of Staff James Baker, and Treasury Secretary Donald Regan, the president assured Simpson "he would sign a bill if the Frank amendment could be modified and if the conference reported a statutory cap of $1 billion a year for four years" on legalization costs.[191] With this private deal in his back pocket affording him negotiating room, and more than a month before adjournment, Simpson began feeling more optimistic about the bill's prospects.

On September 6, O'Neill appointed twenty-nine House conferees from all four committees—Judiciary, Agriculture, Education and Labor, and Energy and Commerce—that had conducted markups on the bill, plus Ed Roybal, nominally from Appropriations but in truth representing the Hispanic Caucus, since the bill had never been referred to Roybal's committee.[192] Technically only Judiciary Committee conferees had jurisdiction over the entire bill. The rest were limited to speaking and voting only on sections of the bill their committees had jurisdiction on. The unusually large group of conferees did Mazzoli no favors since almost by definition the larger the body charged with completing a task, the longer it will take for that group to act. The conference committee, chaired by Peter Rodino, was slated to begin on September 13, just three weeks before the October 4 target date for adjournment, although most believed the session likely would go at least a week longer to address other business. The inclusion of freshman Howard Berman—Rodino's secret lieutenant on farmworker issues—in the House delegation drew little attention but had significant consequences.

The Group still had a couple of tricks up their collective sleeves. Just as Congress reconvened, Wade Henderson invited several of his colleagues to a "big meeting" at the US Chamber of Commerce.[193] Dealing with the Chamber was dicey for civil rights advocates; they both opposed employer sanctions, but for opposite reasons. The Chamber thought that employer sanctions were an example of excessive government regulation, and the way for business to thrive under the new sanctions regime was by the amendment won by Thomas Kindness (R-OH) exempting most employers from verifying employees until after an initial offense. The civil rights organizations thought that sanctions would cause discrimination; their remedy was the Frank amendment to expand job bias protections. It was also known that one Chamber lobbyist was actively trying to cut a deal with the bill's sponsors to obtain a "voluntary verification" system, in effect the Kindness amendment on steroids, in return for business support.[194] From a civil rights perspective, this would've been the worst of all worlds: the threat of employer sanctions that might induce some employers to engage in discrimination, without records available for job applicants experiencing unlawful bias to prove their case, and a free pass to unscrupulous employers to keep hiring undocumented workers. Many in The Group were hesitant to attend the discussion, nervous about what to expect.

When they arrived at the Chamber's offices on H Street, a block from the White House, they were surprised, not by the room full of business lobbyists but by how warmly they were greeted by Virginia "Ginny" Lamp, a young labor relations specialist at the Chamber with a reputation as a conservative hard-liner. Lamp later married future Supreme Court Justice Clarence Thomas, headed the Heritage Foundation's government relations unit, and started a consulting business associated with the Tea Party.[195] Even as junior staffer, it was clear Lamp, who exuded both a winning charm and the tough assuredness of an ideologue, was going places; later feature stories described her as a "compelling and persuasive figure."[196] Lamp began the meeting by stating that the bill needed to be defeated because employer sanctions were an unwarranted governmental intrusion into the rights of business owners; others at the Chamber might've wanted to cut a deal with the bill's sponsors, but she wasn't one of them.

It was clear that Henderson and Lamp had worked together before as they orchestrated the participants to work toward the shared goal of defeating the bill. When potential compromises were raised, Lamp turned to Henderson. As if on cue, he said if a bill passed, it was certain to include the Frank amendment, exposing employers to lawsuits that ACLU chapters would be happy to file. The business lobbyists almost physically shuddered every time the words *ACLU* and *litigation* were uttered, and Henderson, joined by Lamp, repeated the point often. The result, wrote one scholar, was an "unprecedented telegram to all members of Congress urging defeat of the bill," signed by the ACLU, Latino civil rights groups, the US Chamber of Commerce and numerous business associations, and even the construction workers union.[197] Since telegrams were expensive, it indicated that a well-heeled interest such as the US Chamber of Commerce cared enough to spend a considerable amount of money to get Congress's attention.

The advocates' second "trick" came courtesy of the Spanish International Network. On September 10–11, it sponsored another meeting on immigration at the posh Wye River Conference Center on Maryland's eastern shore. Most of The Group attended, and while they appreciated the opportunity to rub shoulders with the assembled Latino power elite, they especially enjoyed the plush facilities and gourmet food, a rare treat. After a day and a half of strategizing, the participants made their way back over the Chesapeake Bay Bridge to a news conference in DC, where, speaking on behalf of the conference attendees Henry Cisneros called on presidential candidate Mondale and Democratic party leaders to kill the Simpson-Mazzoli bill. "The promises they made [at the Democratic National Convention] in San Francisco are now due," the San Antonio mayor declared, adding that he had "no doubt whatsoever" that Mondale would follow through.[198] To reinforce the point, the Latino groups followed up by sending an NCLR-drafted "Action Alert" to virtually every Hispanic elected official and community leader in the country—signed not just by LULAC, MALDEF, and NCLR but also by Harry Pachon of the National Association of Latino

Elected and Appointed Officials (NALEO) and Democratic National Committee vice chair Polly Baca—calling on Congress to defeat the bill.[199] The signatures of Baca, a sitting Democratic National Committee member, and NALEO's Pachon, whose organization rarely worked outside of its core voting rights and citizenship issues, signaled a matter of unusual importance. It also allowed the Alert to be disseminated far beyond the networks of activists on the LULAC/MALDEF/NCLR mailing lists, to Latino state legislators, local city officials, school board members, and the Hispanic delegates to the summer's political conventions. The extensive Spanish-language press coverage of the SIN event combined with the massive action alert mailing produced a considerable buzz among Hispanic elite and grassroots leaders alike against the pending legislation.

RUNNING OUT THE CLOCK

The Simpson-Mazzoli bill that was brought before the joint committee of the two chambers that would decide its fate was, if battered, still very much alive. The core elements—employer sanctions, legalization, and a streamlined H-2 agricultural worker program—were a given. Only three issues posed real threats. As Lawrence Fuchs recalled, the antidiscrimination provisions sponsored by Rep. Barney Frank "created tremendous problems" for Simpson, as did the question of reimbursement to the states for the costs of legalization.[200] The Panetta guestworker amendment was also a major problem for the bill's supporters: its inclusion was a bottom line for growers while its elimination was organized labor's top priority. A major vulnerability was the ticking clock, although since conference committees rarely exceeded a couple of weeks, the bill's prospects appeared to be auspicious.

To many observers, a conference committee is a mere formality before a bill lands on the president's desk. But they have their own unique dynamics, as veteran Hill-watchers have noted: "Many of the nation's laws are ultimately written in one of the most unusual, most difficult, and least understood institutions of American government: the conference committee. . . . The inter-play of personality—always an important element in the workings on Capitol Hill—takes on magnified significance in conference. Conference meetings are like labor-management bargaining sessions, and the skill and stamina of the lead negotiators can be critical."[201]

On Thursday, September 13, the conference committee on the Immigration Reform and Control Act of 1984 convened in the immense Judiciary Committee hearing room on the second floor of the Rayburn House Office Building. Conferees were seated around a huge square table; the seven representatives of the Senate heavily outnumbered by their twenty-nine House counterparts, many of whom appeared briefly to give a speech, offer an amendment or vote on specific aspects of the bill they were charged with negotiating, then promptly left to attend to other, presumably more important business. Rep. Roybal's jurisdiction technically was restricted only to matters involving his Appropriations Committee, but he rarely left the sessions, often asking for and receiving permission from Rodino to speak to issues outside of his formal charge. But after he engaged in what appeared to be delaying tactics, a frustrated Rodino began refusing to recognize Roybal to speak, something the staff had never seen their chairman do before.[202] Rep. Bob García, chair of the Hispanic Caucus but not a conferee, prowled the hallways outside, asking advocates for updates and buttonholing lawmakers for last-minute lobbying.

The lobbyists and the press loved the setting, which gave them an up-close and personal insight into the proceedings, as well as nearly unfettered access to the conferees. For reporters the physical setting added to the sense that this was a monumental occasion. Not only was an important issue to be decided, but the unscripted debates and deal-cutting took place in the open. The unforgettable cast of characters arrayed before the media included both historic figures like Rodino, Kennedy, and Fish and bill sponsors Mazzoli and Simpson, plus rising stars Berman, Frank, Schumer, and Lungren, all of whom clearly had big futures. One veteran immigration beat reporter remembers being "struck by the intelligence, and the ambition, in the room."[203] Simpson hated dealing with the large, unruly group of House conferees who came and left frequently, leading the senator to complain to journalist Ellis Cose, who wrote: " 'I came here to work and these guys came to screw around. I haven't even seen these bastards [previously].' Simpson believed many had showed up just because the television cameras were rolling, and he resented that as much as he did their uninformed comments and contributions."[204]

Rodino had his own challenges managing the mammoth House delegation. "We had a bunch of personalities to deal with on our side while Simpson was on the other side by himself, with all of the [Senate conferees'] proxies in his pocket," Rodino aide Skip Endres recalled.[205] Still, the conferees moved quickly at the beginning, beginning with Title I of the bill covering employer sanctions. They rapidly agreed to a compromise on the US Chamber of Commerce-backed Kindness amendment House language shielding employers from verification requirements until after their first offense, allowing what amounted to a two-and-a-half year transition period before most businesses would face actual penalties for hiring undocumented workers. The conference also agreed to split the difference between the two bills' slightly different range of penalties for offending employers, eventually settling on civil fines of up to $1,000 per unauthorized employee for a first offense and $2,000 for a second offense.[206]

Texas Rep. Sam Hall then began speaking in favor of his provision to exempt employers of three or fewer employees from employer sanctions, what critics called the "nanny loophole" but he preferred to label a "small business exemption." As recalled by *Houston Post* reporter Kathy Kiely, Simpson interrupted him, leaned back in his chair, fixed the Texan with one squinting eye, and said, "I know what you're doing. You're offering the '*Jua-ni-ta* amendment,'" drawing out the Spanish name for emphasis. After pausing for a moment, with more than a few in the audience wondering about the apparent non sequitur, the senator resumed with a snarl:

> You know what I hate about this job? What I really hate about this job is going to a Georgetown cocktail party and people ask what you do, and you say you're working on immigration. And they say to you, *sloshing their martini over your shoes*, 'What you're doing isn't going to affect Juanita is it? Because she's just like one of the family.' But then you look over at Juanita serving the *canapes* and she looks like she's been on the Bataan death march [emphasis in original].[207]

Hall was a large barrel-chested man who normally was not easily intimidated, but he wilted under Simpson's glare. The *New York Times* headline the following day, "Conferees Agree on Sanctions in Immigration Bill," was hardly news since both bills included similar provisions.[208] The real news was how the junior senator from Wyoming was exerting his will over the rest of the conferees, while providing ongoing entertainment for reporters, lobbyists, and other observers. "Thank you, Al Simpson," Kiely whispered under her breath to another reporter as they recorded the Wyoming senator's "Juanita" quote in their notebooks.[209] Kiely didn't know it at the time, but she was one of a baker's dozen out of the hundreds of reporters who covered immigration, that Simpson would later praise in his book *Right in the Old Gazoo*, which otherwise was an exuberant critique of the journalism profession.[210]

Reconvening after the weekend on Monday, September 17, the conferees promptly resolved the thorny question of amnesty. They split the difference between the two bills with a 1981 legalization cutoff date, retained the Wright amendment restricting permanent residence to those who could demonstrate a command of English or enrollment in an approved course of study, and limited unsuccessful applicants to a single level of administrative review. Only about half of The Group's legalization substructure improvements were retained; Kamasaki told the press the resulting legalization program was "a sham," while LULAC's Treviño said "a sizable population" of undocumented would remain even after the program was implemented.[211]

Although conferees were moving quickly, the bill's fate was still very much in doubt, a point underscored by a September 18 telegram to Congress from former presidents Gerald Ford and Jimmy Carter on behalf of a broad bipartisan coalition of influential Americans, which warned that the bill's failure would "arouse deep cynicism about the ability of Congress to face difficult issues."[212] The very next day, on Wednesday, September 19, the pace slowed as conferees were unable to make progress on the controversial Frank amendment. The Massachusetts Democrat, backed by Rodino, strongly defended his amendment, declaring that, "people in the United States legally ought to be able to compete for jobs on equal terms," while Simpson, backed by Lungren, responded that punishing employers for allegedly preferring a citizen over a legal immigrant wouldn't sell "anywhere" in the US.[213] Notwithstanding their apparently antithetical public positions, Mazzoli, Frank, Simpson, and Lungren and their staffs already were privately exchanging drafts of various compromise proposals.

With the Frank amendment still unresolved, on Thursday the conferees moved on to the conditions under which foreign workers could enter the US for agricultural jobs. The Senate bill included two measures for growers dependent on unauthorized labor: a "streamlined" H-2 temporary worker program and a so-called "transition" program that gave agricultural employers four years to completely wean themselves from foreign workers before being fully subject to the bill's employer penalties. The House added a third agricultural worker program for growers of perishable crops: the Panetta-Morrison amendment. Simpson had twice beaten the western growers on the Senate floor and saw no reason to concede now. Rodino also opposed guestworker programs, while Mazzoli had been thought to be soft in his purported opposition to the amendment; under enormous pressure not to be responsible for killing immigration reform, Panetta accepted a compromise that one grower lobbyist called "a significant improvement over existing law" but that fell "far short of meeting the needs of Western agriculture."[214]

After recessing for the weekend, the conferees returned on Monday, September 24. They had accepted a streamlined H-2 program in principle the previous week but had to dispose of amendments from Howard Berman before completing this part of the bill. Berman first offered an amendment to strike the entire section, which predictably was rejected overwhelmingly. He then proceeded to offer more than a dozen others, addressing each proposed change in the H-2 program. Crafted largely by his aide Mark Schacht, with help from West Virginia-based Gary Geffert, another attorney with the Farmworker Justice Fund, one by one Berman offered amendments to keep each of the H-2 program's current labor protections, which the new streamlined version would eliminate or weaken, explaining the historical and substantive rationale behind each labor protection. Having been included in every version of the Simpson-Mazzoli bill, most thought of the bill's H-2 changes as a "done deal"; but Berman and Schacht weren't trying to win votes as much as they were seeking to "educate the conferees, the staff, and the press" on how seemingly technical changes would adversely affect farmworkers.[215]

Berman not only received the requisite five minutes to explain each proposal, but other members, including Berman's fellow Californian George Miller and even Rodino himself, often spoke in support of the proposals. Initially, Simpson, Lungren, Fish, and Mazzoli each joined Agriculture Committee conferees to speak in opposition, but it soon became clear how much time the debate on the amendments, each clearly doomed to failure, was consuming. The bill's sponsors then attempted procedural maneuvers to cut the debate short, requesting that the amendments be considered as a group, or *en bloc* in legislative parlance, urging the chairman to limit the total number of amendments to this section, or limit the time that each amendment could be debated, but Rodino firmly rejected each attempt, permitting Berman to proceed.[216]

It's rare for a lawmaker to continue down an obviously losing path—and indeed each of Berman's amendments was soundly defeated; typical protocol was for lawmakers to offer one, or perhaps two amendments, making it clear to constituents that they'd given it the "good old college try" before deferring to their colleagues' impatience and withdrawing the rest. But supported by Rodino, Berman persisted, gamely going through each provision, offering lengthy, detailed answers to every question posed, while Schacht distributed articles and citations to key court cases, all the while earning severe stare-downs from Simpson and frequent expressions of exasperation from Mazzoli and Lungren.

Berman later admitted that part of his strategy was "running out the clock" to consume time, convinced that the bill's agricultural worker provisions were fatally flawed and the legislation needed to be killed.[217] After taking two days to dispose of Berman's dozen amendments and a few others, the conferees affirmed that they would retain the "transition" program for agricultural employers, the last remaining farmworker provision to be voted on. Notwithstanding the bill's significant concessions to agriculture, the American Farm Bureau Federation announced on September 24 that it would oppose the legislation for its failure to include the complete Panetta-Morrison amendment, while Berman vowed to keep fighting to retain protections for farmworkers.[218] Still, because Panetta himself had accepted the compromise, the Farm Bureau's opposition didn't seem to be a fatal blow. Jane O'Grady, speaking for the AFL-CIO, told the *New York Times* that "organized labor could not support the bill as it now stands" inasmuch as even the compromise in the bill "did not provide enough protection for domestic workers."[219] On the other side, Rep. Sid Morrison, cosponsor of Panetta's guestworker program that had been watered down by the conferees, indicated his probable intention to vote against the bill. Still and all, labor's "not support" position could be interpreted as acquiescence and Morrison's "probable" no vote suggested he still might be swayed.

The Frank amendment, apparently the last stumbling block to a conference agreement, wasn't resolved easily. Early on, Simpson proffered several suggested changes, which Frank, supported by Rodino, rejected. Mazzoli then offered another proposal, adopted by a narrow 13–10 margin of House conferees, which Simpson, supported by the Reagan administration, promptly rejected. Mazzoli tried again on September 26, offering another compromise, winning 14–9 support from House conferees, but it failed to gain Simpson's agreement. New York congressman Hamilton Fish, widely viewed as a strong supporter of civil rights but in this case sticking with his party, voted against his friend Mazzoli's compromise, saying the Frank amendment was "the most overblown issue" being considered. Rodino sharply disagreed, stating, "This is a core issue. It goes to the heart of employer sanctions. How inconsistent would it be to legalize these illegal aliens, but then tell them they could not work in this country? In addition, we have 500,000 legal immigrants come into the country each year. What are their rights?"[220]

The conferees were deadlocked. Simpson ruefully said the next day that negotiations were "at the end of the line. We have reached a standoff, a true sticking point."[221] On September 28, the *New York Times* editorial board weighed in with a vengeance: "There's a molehill growing on Capitol Hill. It's called 'alienage,' and it's growing so fast that unless somebody does something today, it will crush the bipartisan Simpson-Mazzoli immigration reform bill. If so, the country will lose the chance of a generation to end the lawlessness on its borders."[222]

With the parties at an impasse, Rodino recessed the conference committee subject to "the call of the chair," an indication that he saw little reason to continue discussing the bill while leaving the door open for the conferees to reconvene if a compromise could be worked out. Luckily for the bill's proponents, other must-pass bills were stalled, and Congress wouldn't adjourn until October 10 or 11, giving them at least two extra weeks to find a way to break the deadlock.

Not for the last time, New York Democrat Charles Schumer stepped forward to try and rescue the bill. Chuck Schumer, a second-term representative from Brooklyn, was described by the *Almanac of American Politics* as "young, liberal, and serious."[223] So he was, although he quickly displayed other qualities: energy, persistence, and deal-making skills that later made him a major player on a wide range of issues for decades. Schumer started a round of "shuttle diplomacy" with Simpson, Mazzoli, and Frank, working nonstop to find common ground.[224] After several days of frantic, round-robin talks, the outlines of Schumer's proposal emerged. To satisfy objections to creation of "alienage" as a new basis for discrimination, Schumer proposed to limit protections for those "declaring their intention to become citizens."[225] In another concession to opponents, Schumer's proposal required a "knowing and intentional discriminatory act or a pattern or practice of discriminatory activity" for "alienage" claims, a much higher level of proof than the "effects standard" used under other civil rights laws.[226] Schumer met several times with Henderson, Kamasaki, and other members of The Group to sell his ideas, but the advocates believed that Schumer's proposals amounted to little more than a fig leaf permitting the bill's supporters to claim they'd done something about discrimination while in reality adopting an ineffective, unworkable system.

As conferees grappled with Rep. Schumer's proposal, The Group convened in Rep. Esteban Torres's office, gravitating toward unused phones to call conferees' offices to check on their positions on the unresolved antidiscrimination and state reimbursement provisions, and shore up wavering supporters. Surprisingly, Rick Swartz managed to get Rep. Frank himself on the phone. From hearing Swartz's end of the conversation it was clear that the Massachusetts representative seemed to be saying he would accept Schumer's changes, a disaster from The Group's perspective; once the amendment's sponsor gave in, others would surely follow. Rather than getting the best of both worlds by getting the other side to either kill the bill or accept tough new civil rights protections, they were on the verge of getting the worst: both a bill and the weakest of antidiscrimination provisions. Others in the room ended their own conversations to listen in as Swartz offered to bring The Group down to Rep. Frank's office to personally make their case, loudly informing the Massachusetts lawmaker that "we're all here in Esteban Torres's office" just a few minutes away, since both congressmen were located in the Rayburn office building. Swartz kept pushing, and his voice kept rising, but Frank declined to meet. "Well, then *fuck you* Barney!" Swartz shouted, angrily slamming down the receiver.

Swartz then looked up and realized that everyone, staffers and advocates alike, was staring at him, most of them slack-jawed. It wasn't every day that one heard a nonprofit staffer, and one that wasn't even supposed to be lobbying at that, drop the F-bomb directly on a congressman. A sheepish Swartz explained that Rep. Frank had started it by "F-ing" him first. But Torres's aide Albert Jacquez was not amused; the cursing didn't bother him, but he didn't appreciate Swartz bringing his boss into it. Esteban Torres had a good relationship with Frank—both were active proponents of affordable housing and consumer protections on the Banking Committee that they sat on together—and Jacquez didn't want that relationship jeopardized by Swartz's outburst.[227]

The next day, Friday, October 5, with perhaps a week left before adjournment, Schumer announced he had brokered a compromise among the parties. Rodino promptly called the conference back into session, and on Tuesday, October 9, the House conferees, including Rep. Frank himself but, interestingly, not Rodino—who was perhaps keeping the commitment he'd made on the House floor to Rep. García to support the provision—voted 15–8 to accept the Schumer compromise. Simpson might've been doing a little posturing himself when he accepted the proposal only with the "gravest reservations."[228] One last question remained for the conferees: How much would they provide to cover costs of legalization for state-local governments?

STATE-LOCALS STEP IN

The issue had been contentious since the inception of the debate. State-local governments, supported by most Democrats and some Republicans, demanded that they should be "held harmless" from any federal action that imposed greater costs on them—legal status would make beneficiaries eligible immediately for some state programs denied to the undocumented and eventually the full array of safety net programs, many requiring a state match—the view reflected in the House bill's "100% reimbursement" provisions. The fiscally conservative Reagan administration, backed by most in the GOP and some moderate Democrats, insisted that federal costs must be controlled. The issue appeared to have been resolved earlier in the conference on September 21, when the House conferees had voted 19–7 to accept in principle a four-year, $1-billion-per-year cap on payments to the states, which Simpson gladly accepted, knowing that Reagan had privately agreed to that level.[229]

But as happened with regularity on this legislation, appearances were deeply deceiving. Soon after the initial straw vote, the National Association of Counties, typically the most conservative of the government interest groups, announced its public opposition to the bill based on its failure to fully reimburse state-local governments for legalization costs.[230] Few noticed, but they should have. Taken by many as just a pro forma expression of concern from often quiescent counties on an issue that wouldn't affect the final outcome of the bill, it was actually an existential threat to the legislation. Patricia Craig, NACo's director of legislative affairs, had served on the National Immigration Forum's board since its founding press conference, even serving as interim board chair on occasion. That Craig was able to bring her right-leaning constituency along to oppose the legislation for failing to spend enough federal money to help previously illegal immigrants—when it would've been more expedient politically for county officials to support stricter limitations on legalization and thus lower costs—was a testament to her skill in methodically locking her governing body into positions that forced the association to oppose the compromise. It also reflected Swartz's vision in bringing state-local governments into leadership positions in his Forum early on, when few viewed them as important players.[231]

It also helped The Group's cause that the often cautious, narrowly focused state-local lobby received a considerable boost with the addition of an energetic young Texan to their ranks. Earlier that year Dianne Stewart, who represented the state's centrist Democratic Governor Mark White, began attending The

Group's meetings occasionally, then more frequently, encouraged by fellow Texan Kamasaki.[232] Stewart started her career while in graduate school working as an intern with the state women's commission, where she made connections with some of the most powerful and influential women in Texas politics, including Helen Farabee, the wife of a state senator and the founder of the state mental health system.[233] Another commission member was Liz Carpenter, who had staffed both Lady Bird and Lyndon Johnson, perhaps best known as the aide who "effortlessly drafted the 58 difficult but perfect words spoken by President Johnson after the assassination of President Kennedy."[234] Stewart's boss at the commission was Sarah Weddington, who at age twenty-eight argued *Roe v. Wade* before the US Supreme Court and went on to head the Texas Office of Federal-State Relations under Governor White. This was heady company for Stewart, rubbing shoulders with the most influential women in state government, and she made the most of it, earning an invite to Washington to work under Weddington in late 1983, where she was immediately assigned to cover the immigration bill.[235]

In historically low-tax Texas, the first instinct of both Democrats and Republicans was toward fiscal conservatism. The easiest position for state officials to take would have been to simply oppose legalization, which was not especially popular. Indeed, aspirants for retiring Senator John Tower's seat, including Reps. Phil Gramm and Kent Hance, were both boll weevils who had worked closely with the Reagan administration and had indicated their strong opposition to amnesty. However, with a growing Mexican American electorate and the memory of the La Raza Unida party's ability to serve as a spoiler in state politics a decade earlier still fresh, most Democratic public officials were not anxious to raise the hackles of Latino organizations by openly opposing legalization, the groups' top priority.

If legalization was enacted, Texas would join other states to insist that the federal government pay for the costs for education, health care, and other services to the previously undocumented immigrants, especially since the legislation made the newly legalized ineligible for most federal programs.[236] That part was clear enough. But until Stewart's arrival, Democratic state officials were reticent to speak too forcefully on one side or another regarding the merits of legalization, since doing so would offend either the party's traditional centrist base or its growing Mexican American constituency, both essential to statewide electoral success at a time when much of the South was trending Republican. Most representatives of state-local governments in Washington faced similar dilemmas and tended to take a "minimalist" approach toward immigration issues: monitoring the progress of legislation while articulating their government's or trade association's positions very cautiously and carefully, and only when asked.

Stewart did the opposite, pushing the envelope to its maximum limit, noting "nobody ever stopped me."[237] She dutifully reported to Weddington and others in the chain of command in the governor's office, but didn't hesitate to develop close ties to other centers of power. One key relationship she developed was with Lieutenant Governor William Hobby's office. Bill Hobby, who held the office from 1973 to 1991, was not an especially well-known figure outside the Lone Star State, nor was it widely understood that political scientists had long regarded the lieutenant governor as the most powerful position in state government: the office presides over the state senate and awards committee chairmanships and, most importantly, controls the flow of legislation in the upper body. But in Texas political and business circles, everyone respected the office and the man who held it, described by an astute observer as "the embodiment of the state's business establishment; Hobby's father had been governor, and his family [had] owned the *Houston Post*, the city's longtime morning newspaper, and a TV station."[238]

Having a line into Hobby's office was the equivalent of political gold in Texas, and Stewart nurtured and guarded the relationship carefully. She also built ties to the state's growing number of Republicans, such as Rob Mosbacher Jr., son of a future secretary of commerce under George H. W. Bush, a centrist Republican who despite losing several political races was one of the state's most respected figures.[239] Seeing the bright, gutsy, and progressive Stewart as willing to push the envelope in favor of a generous legalization, Swartz and Kamasaki encouraged her activism on a broader immigration agenda beyond the narrow question of cost.[240] She became the advocates' link to the centrist "Tory Democrats" such as Governor White and Lt. Governor Hobby who, in turn, had significant influence with their brethren in Congress. For Stewart, joining the immigration advocates' circle was "a life-changing experience"; she loved working with the "brilliant, dogged, intense advocates" in The Group, who were if nothing else more interesting than the typically staid, cautious state-local lobbyist. To The Group, her major accomplishment was helping them to "do the right thing," producing pro-legalization statements from key figures in the state's political establishment, which conveniently empowered her to fight that much harder for full reimbursement as the most fiscally responsible position.[241]

After the conferees had seemingly approved the cap on legalization costs in principle, the NACo's Pat Craig, Stewart, and other state-local analysts began dissecting the purported compromise. At first glance, the $4 billion ceiling seemed a fair middle ground between the Reagan administration's $1.1–$1.8 billion limit and the unknown but undoubtedly higher House bill's cost, but while it placed a ceiling on costs, it didn't set a floor; whether they would receive even a penny of funding was dependent on future Congresses passing, and the president signing, annual appropriations. At a time when the administration's opposition to federal spending generally carried the day, the prospect of getting not only less than "100% reimbursement" but "zero reimbursement" in a given year seemed eminently plausible. And it wasn't clear from the language that unspent funds from one year could be carried over into future years. Stewart, Craig, and other state-local lobbyists mobilized their networks to oppose the proposed $4 billion cap. While reporters' attention was riveted on negotiations over the Frank amendment, state-local governments were hammering the conferees, demanding changes.

WHO KILLED THE IMMIGRATION BILL?

Even close Congress watchers assumed that once the Frank amendment was disposed of on October 9, the conferees would formally reaffirm their previous support for the $4 billion/four-year cap on legalization costs, clearing the way for both chambers to enact the compromise bill. But no sooner had the Schumer compromise on the Frank amendment passed when the question of a statutory cap on federal payments for legalization came up for final consideration. To open the discussion, Simpson emphasized that the president would veto the bill without the ceiling on legalization costs; what had been a veiled threat was now an open one.[242]

The provision's fate would be decided by House conferees, since Simpson had the Senate side locked up. As debate began, Mazzoli nervously noted "sub-rosa signals" that some supporters of the bill "were killing it with kindness [by getting] caught up in some detail," such as specific programs the states would be responsible for.[243] This wasn't exactly a "detail" from the state-locals' perspective; they were on the hook for covering costs the feds would not, and part of the proposed compromise trimmed federal responsibility for program expenses that the Energy and Commerce and Education and Labor Committees included during the sequential referral process. The state-locals thought it a raw deal: more responsibility and less funding, a classic "unfunded mandate." The roll call was unpredictable, since this was one of the few issues that almost all House conferees had jurisdiction to vote on.

In a shocking development, House conferees, including Rodino, voted 15–13 against the funding cap, immediately after which the chairman calmly stated, "We are in complete disagreement" as he promptly adjourned the conference session.[244] A stunned silence prevailed as the assembled lawmakers, staff, reporters, and lobbyists tried to come to grips with exactly what had just transpired. Instead of the expected routine vote to reaffirm their previous agreement, after which the conference report could be hustled through both chambers, the bill had just been killed. For several minutes supporters and opponents alike were numb, unable to fully process that they had just witnessed the death of the Simpson-Mazzoli bill for the 98th Congress.

As Rodino gaveled the committee session to a close, Schumer jumped up and rushed over to the chairman to plead for more time. After listening for a few moments, Rodino wordlessly gathered his papers, turned, and walked away. Simpson didn't even bother to make an attempt to keep the conference going, writing that he "would never forget the stunned look on the faces of those in the hearing room."[245] He later told Ellis Cose: "I had been accommodating, continually, and then guys would wander into the room from other [non-Judiciary] committees' who didn't really have any sense of what the hell was going on. . . . I just thought, 'This old cowboy doesn't have to take that. I'm doing one here which doesn't give me one nickel of any kind of political power, fame and fortune, what in the hell. I just decided, I don't have to sit here any longer.' "[246]

The bill was dead, but the finger-pointing had just begun; the first of no fewer than three separate *New York Times* postmortems on the death of the bill noted that the parties simply "blamed one another. Republicans said the Democratic House leadership had delayed the bill so it would perish in the maelstrom at the session's end. Democrats said the Reagan Administration had helped kill the measure by balking at its cost."[247]

But did it really? Years later, some, including Simpson, fingered western agricultural interests as the key culprit in killing the bill because they'd failed to get the full Panetta-Morrison guestworker provision. Simpson said that "the growers in their district got to" previous House Democratic supporters and persuaded them to use the funding issue to "kill the bill."[248] While also placing principal responsibility on the agricultural lobby, Rick Swartz noted that the growers' ties with White House counselor Ed Meese and others in Reagan's inner circle almost certainly stiffened the administration's posture, when a greater willingness to compromise on guestworker and money issues might've produced a bill.[249] These interpretations were confirmed a year later when *Congressional Quarterly*'s Nadine Cahodas reported that during the conference committee deliberations, growers had lobbied conferees "to vote against any final compromise because they were unhappy with losing their guestworker program."[250]

Arnoldo Torres was convinced that even if the conference committee had completed its work, the threat of a filibuster by Texas senator John Tower doomed the legislation anyway.[251] He believed this contributed to Simpson's decision to walk away from the table without making additional efforts to negotiate compromises on agricultural workers or legalization funding. Others focused on Rodino's role. Mazzoli's aide Harris Miller complained that the committee chairman's staff actively engaged in "undermining the bill," the

ACLU's Henderson observed that Rodino "helped to kill the bill by not helping to pass it," while Kamasaki's take was "It was weird. . . . It almost seemed like Rodino had it wired to kill the bill."[252] Still others blamed partisan politics; a GOP aide recalled being told by a Democratic staffer that "Mondale was the candidate, he was against the bill, and [killing the bill now] would save everyone the trouble" of the conference report dying on the House floor.[253]

The Group marked the occasion, hastily convening in NCLR's conference room over cheap champagne purchased at the tiny liquor store/carryout located next door. The mood wasn't especially celebratory. While proud of winning so many amendments with origins in the Roybal bill, their positive feelings were balanced by deep anxiety, knowing they'd be back on the firing line in the next Congress. Arnoldo Torres presided over the brief event. After offering lavish, extended compliments while toasting Swartz, Eisen, Henderson, Leiden, Myers, and his own deputy Joe Treviño, he turned to Kamasaki, uncharacteristically struggling to find the right words to say. "You . . . , you . . . , you always asked good questions," Torres finally blurted out. Kamasaki waited in vain for more than this tiny bit of faint praise, slowly realizing that even after their apparent acceptance by the rest of The Group, he and his NCLR colleagues, at least in Arnoldo Torres's mind, still seemed outside the inner circle.

Torres received a comeuppance of his own when just before the end of the year Simpson called him into his office for a meeting. He expected a substantive discussion, an attempt to narrow their differences. What he got was far different; as Torres recalled years later:

> Because he was so tall, Simpson's desk was raised up high on cinderblocks, making him even more intimidating. He peered at me over the top of his glasses, like he often did, and then cursed me out. He said I just wanted to be a celebrity, talked about groupies, told me I had gotten carried away with myself. I was shocked that he spoke to me like a naïve kid. I told him, "You know, Senator, I thought you understood me, that I was willing to do everything I could to stop bad public policy. Now you're making it personal."[254]

Torres was shaken by the exchange, suspecting that Simpson would get back at him, somehow. Only later did he learn how bitter, and personal, that retribution could be.

CHAPTER 6

It's Over

A BITTER CUP INDEED

Soon after the shocking demise of the bill, lawmakers quickly left town to campaign. With a rapidly improving economy and his classic "Morning in America" campaign ads, Ronald Reagan was a prohibitive favorite for reelection, except for a brief period when the incumbent appeared confused during his first debate with Democratic opponent Walter Mondale, raising doubts about the effects of the seventy-three-year-old president's age. Reagan rebounded with a strong performance in the next debate, declaring with a wry smile that, "I will not make age an issue in this campaign. I am not going to exploit, for political purposes, my opponent's youth and inexperience."[1] Even Mondale knew the race was over, and Reagan won reelection in an historic, forty-nine-state Electoral College landslide, along with nearly 59 percent of the popular vote. Despite his huge victory, Reagan had short coattails: Republicans picked up a scant fifteen House seats, leaving the GOP with ten fewer House members than in 1981, while Democrats gained a net two seats in the Senate.[2]

The Group, ever-obsessed with immigration reform, continued meeting on a near-weekly basis. Although most worked on many issues, they typically referred to the immigration legislation as "The Bill"; LULAC's Arnoldo Torres could get so emphatic that coming out of his mouth the word *bill* sometimes sounded like "BEE-ILL," as if it had two syllables, not one.[3] Earlier that year, facing imminent movement of the bill, several of them read *The Art of War* by Sun Tzu, the ancient Chinese general, then being reincarnated (pun intended) as a business strategy best seller, searching for lessons—some might say grasping for straws—they could apply to their predicament. "My God, here it was even when the bill was moving we were down in the [NCLR office] basement reading *The Art of War*!" Escutia recalled.[4] Several read other books on war and strategy like Prussian general Carl Von Clausewitz's *On War* and *The Book of Five Rings* by legendary samurai Miyamoto Musashi.

Even movies they saw were interpreted through an immigration reform lens. In late 1984 Arnoldo Torres started their evening meeting with a lengthy monologue on the movie, *Repo Man*. A cult classic about a car "repossession agent" starring Harry Dean Stanton and his protégé, played by Emilio Estevez, the film is set in Los Angeles, with a zany plot including "ruthless government agents, hired thugs, a lobotomized nuclear scientist, and the infamous Rodríguez Brothers," Stanton's rival repossession company.[5] *Repo Man* featured heavy drug use, massive amounts of profanity, and a New Wave soundtrack, including a theme song by punk rocker Iggy Pop, and some in The Group were delighted that the notoriously straightlaced and often solemn Torres enjoyed such an edgy movie so much. Over the next several meetings, The Group engaged in rambling, semiserious technical discussions about whether the extraterrestrial aliens alluded to but never actually shown in the film were "undocumented." They almost certainly were, The Group eventually decided, but should be afforded full due process before a final determination was made that they could be deported.

Swartz and Torres also thought The Group needed a formal "retreat" to plot strategy, which was arranged by Forum senior adviser Norman Lourie. Norman Victor Lourie, then seventy-two years old, slight in stature, with unruly silver hair that flew in every direction, looked a bit like an Albert Einstein with thick glasses, but he'd long been a giant in several human services fields. Lourie began his career working with settlement houses in New York City in the 1930s, before serving as the first director of the US Army's Psychiatric Social Work section during World War II. He was either secretary or deputy secretary of Pennsylvania's Department of Human Services over a quarter century from 1955–1980, all while teaching at the Wharton School, Penn State, the University of Pittsburgh, and consulting with various federal, state, and private agencies.[6] Lourie had been president of the National Association of Social Workers, and the *Harrisburg Evening News* called him "the senior welfare officer in Pennsylvania history."[7]

After retiring from government in the late 1970s the crusty, outspoken Lourie became an advisor and something of a father figure to Swartz.[8] Lourie also was a member of the Cosmos Club, the toney association located in DC's upscale Dupont Circle neighborhood; at Swartz's request, he procured free meeting space for The Group to hold a "strategy retreat" that Torres had long pushed for. According to *Washingtonian* magazine, the club's "Beaux-Arts style mansion" was where Walter Lippman wrote the "memo urging President Woodrow Wilson to enter World War I" and where Herman Wouk drafted parts of his epic novel of World War II, *War and Remembrance*.[9] Meeting under the gaze of the portraits and plaques honoring club members, including famous government officials and Nobel Prize winners, all of whom were white men, it wasn't lost on the predominantly minority retreat participants that most of them wouldn't have been welcome at the club in times past; it wasn't until four years later, in 1988, that the Cosmos Club deigned to accept women members.[10]

If some in The Group lamented the lack of time to devote to immigration strategy, their families thought "the boys" already spent far too much time working. They counter-offered that a social event—with families included—would be a healthier way to spend time together. After the bill's death, The Group bowed to familial pressures and scheduled a picnic at Great Falls National Park in Virginia, just upstream from Washington, where the placid Potomac River narrows into a series of falls and fast water. The idea was for spouses, family members, and "significant others" to attend, and almost all did. But soon it became painfully obvious that the advocates had little in common other than work. On their picnic outing on a beautiful, unseasonably warm Indian summer day with family present the unwritten rule was that they couldn't talk business; after a few hours most couldn't wait to get home. They never held a similar outing again. The Group didn't identify any startlingly new strategies at their Cosmos Club retreat, nor did much come from their social outing at Great Falls. As they speculated at the end of 1984 about the outcome of the next battle over immigration, none could have predicted what actually took place over the next few years, even in their wildest dreams.

As the New Year of 1985 dawned and lawmakers, their staffs, and lobbyists trickled back from vacation, there was considerable uncertainty about how immigration would be handled, and by whom. Alan Simpson was elected to the majority whip position along with new Majority Leader Bob Dole of Kansas, but it wasn't clear whether his new leadership responsibilities would detract from the Wyoming senator's ability to concentrate on the immigration issue or add even greater weight to his already powerful persona. In the House, Speaker Tip O'Neill, as expected, announced that this would be his last Congress, automatically elevating the stature of Majority Leader Jim Wright, his presumptive successor. But the mysterious circumstances of the bill's demise in the previous Congress—and the increasingly obvious tension between bill sponsor and subcommittee chairman Ron Mazzoli and his full committee chairman, Peter Rodino—left even veteran prognosticators hedging their bets about the future path of immigration reform.

Simpson was riding high. His run for majority whip was accomplished with considerable panache, winning the post without even having to campaign since no opponent was willing to challenge him; analysts wrote that "it was clear long in advance that he had the votes sewed up."[11] The Dole-Simpson pairing earned accolades across the board, with political reporters writing that the "Republicans now have a leadership team as wise and witty, as humane and as humorous, as the Senate has ever seen," while the *Washington Post* editorial board praised them as "tough, realistic men."[12] His leadership post enhanced the already large press corps that gathered whenever he was speaking, all eagerly seeking another colorful Simpson zinger. And he often obliged, once saying of certain of his colleagues, "about 15% of the people are screwballs, lightweights and boobs, and you would not want those people unrepresented in Congress."[13] Balancing criticism with self-deprecation, he said he ran for the leadership post only after consulting "friends, colleagues, family . . . and my own expanding ego."[14]

Those who wondered whether the senator's new leadership responsibilities would distract him from moving immigration legislation soon got their answer. In mid-April, Robert Pear of the *New York Times* reported that Simpson was planning to introduce an immigration reform bill, but with some important changes. The new bill would retain employer sanctions, but would make "verification and paperwork" optional, a major concession to business. He also planned to include the conference committee version of the agricultural guest-worker program that had been far more generous to growers than his original bill, if not nearly enough to gain agriculture's support. But the most consequential change would "make amnesty contingent upon a showing of improved enforcement of the immigration laws."[15] It wasn't lost on The Group that although Simpson seemed willing to compromise with business and agricultural interests that had opposed his bill in the past, his proposal for a "triggered legalization" program singled out legalization, Latinos' top priority, for a sharp cutback. On May 23 Simpson introduced a bill numbered S.1200, whose major feature "would delay the granting of legal status to illegal aliens until after the United States had better control of its borders."[16]

Simpson professed to maintain opposition to mass deportation and thus a continued support for legalization. But to The Group, his formula posed a "heads I win tails you lose" proposition. If enforcement worked, then there would be few left to legalize once the actual program began. An unspoken assumption was that this was precisely the point: effective enforcement would result in unauthorized workers leaving of their own accord, avoiding expensive, messy, and complicated legal proceedings and removal efforts. It was this formula that FAIR and other restrictionists soon called "attrition," and that almost three decades later, presidential candidate Mitt Romney infamously called "self-deportation."[17] The political significance of what The Group called "triggered legalization" has been long-lasting; the then novel position that regularization of the status of unauthorized immigrants already in the country could not begin until the border was sealed is now almost de rigueur among GOP politicians.[18]

But if enforcement wasn't effective, in Simpson's formula there'd be no legalization at all; as MALDEF's Richard Fajardo told the *New York Times*, since employer sanctions wouldn't work, the bill was designed to assure that legalization would never occur.[19] Lost in the debate over Simpson's triggered legalization proposal was the notion that legalization was an integral part of any sustainable enforcement strategy, perhaps best captured by the familiar "needle in the haystack" metaphor: when looking for needles, the smaller the haystack, the better, and amnesty would reduce the size of the haystack. In its original rationale for the concept of legalization, the Select Commission on Immigration and Refugee Policy found that regularizing the status of long-term unauthorized residents "would enable the INS to target its enforcement resources on new flows of undocumented/illegal aliens."[20]

But the message Simpson delivered to The Group was clear: the longer they obstructed his bill, the worse he would make it for them. They'd certainly been given fair warning: in earlier meetings the senator had told them, in effect, "If you choose not to drink from this well now, it may be poisoned the next time you're passing through." As LULAC's Treviño later testified before Simpson: "I am reminded of your comment to me after LULAC returned from the [1984] Democratic National Convention in San Francisco. You said LULAC may have poisoned the well forever. It is a bitter cup indeed in S.1200 ['s legalization program]."[21] Simpson aide Carl Hampe later acknowledged, "Well, we certainly weren't going to *reward* opponents of the legislation for having delayed movement of the bill in the past."[22]

THE BLOODY EIGHTH

The reliably supportive *New York Times* editorial board promptly approved of the "rough justice" in Simpson's "triggered" legalization program. But noting the absence of a counterpart bill in the lower body the *Times* pointedly asked, "Where are the House Democrats?"[23] Unlike the previous two sessions, Simpson and Mazzoli didn't introduce bills simultaneously. Mazzoli had not attended the press conference at which Simpson introduced his bill and despite repeated requests for comment from reporters, was "silent on his intentions."[24] Speculating that Mazzoli was now less eager to engage the immigration issue after having been foiled in his previous two tries, one House colleague suggested that, "The fight's gone out of the dog."[25] The full story was a bit more complicated, with roots in Southern Indiana of all places.

One might have been forgiven for thinking of Indiana's 8th congressional district as unlikely to alter the future direction of immigration reform. Tucked into the southwest corner of the traditionally Republican state, it was known among pols as the "Bloody Eighth" for the frequency of its tight elections, a classic "swing district," carried successively by senatorial candidates of opposite parties, Democrat Birch Bayh in 1980 and Republican Richard Lugar in 1982. Democratic Bloomington mayor Frank McCloskey had narrowly won the seat in 1982, but only after his opponent was charged with drunk driving shortly before the election.[26]

Matched against Richard McIntyre, a young, attractive GOP state legislator, McCloskey's 1984 reelection bid was a nail-biter. After nearly a week of counting, McCloskey led by a 72-vote margin out of over 230,000 ballots cast; a partial recount put McIntyre up slightly, hurriedly certified by the Republican secretary of state, but the Democratic-controlled House refused to seat either candidate without another recount.[27] The House-supervised recount that consumed several months put McCloskey ahead by 4 votes, and on May 1, the Democratic leadership moved to seat him, having earlier rejected the GOP's call for a special election by a 229–200 margin on a near party-line vote; 19 Democrats joined a "united Republican bloc" in supporting a do-over election.[28] The incident turbocharged the "Gingrich wing" of the GOP. The Georgia congressman—still a back-bencher if a rapidly rising and highly visible one—called it "blatant thuggery" by the Democratic leadership. Analysts later pointed to the "ill will arising from this exercise in partisanship on both sides as a contributing factor in the unyielding party-line system in Congress" that became the norm by the mid-2000s.[29]

The incident had an immediate impact on the course of immigration reform, because Ron Mazzoli was one of the nineteen Democrats who joined Republicans in calling for a special election. Coming from an otherwise consistent party loyalist, Mazzoli's vote for the special election might have been tolerated in the Democratic Caucus. But Mazzoli wasn't a loyalist. He was fully aware that he was viewed by some in his party as "a heretic, an apostate, off the reservation," but insisted on charting an independent course.[30] And to party leaders Mazzoli had not only voted incorrectly on the McCloskey-McIntyre affair, he'd done so much too enthusiastically: he was the only Democrat to speak on the House floor on behalf of the recall, and was prominently featured in media coverage of the controversy.[31]

Mazzoli had also begun to blame his own committee chairman Peter Rodino, a figure of near-iconic stature in the House, and not Republicans or the Reagan White House, for past failures of immigration reform. Of his frustration with Rodino, Mazzoli later told a reporter that, "I could easily have [succeeded] if Mr. Rodino would ever have said, 'Okay, it's yours, and it's not mine.'"[32] Possibly, but it seemed naïve to assume that Rodino would ever cede full control to Mazzoli; he'd been deeply and personally engaged in immigration reform for decades, and by then was the fourth highest member of the House in seniority.[33] Some Democrats let it be known that they were uncomfortable with Mazzoli's continued leadership of so high-profile and delicate an issue as immigration reform; as described by reporter Ellis Cose: "The message, sent by myriad sources and in countless ways was sometimes subtle, sometimes direct, but always jarringly clear. Mazzoli had to go—or his bill would not survive. Too many factions had been offended; too many calls had been ignored; and too many egos—including Judiciary committee chairman Peter Rodino's—had been inadequately massaged."[34]

Among those most perturbed by Mazzoli's actions in the McCloskey-McIntyre matter was Speaker-in-waiting Jim Wright who, according to one aide, told insiders that immigration reform "would never see the light of day" as long as the Kentuckian was in charge.[35] But it was Al Simpson who delivered the most telling blow, telling his "side-kick," "Ron, you're going to have to bring Rodino into this." The Kentuckian didn't protest, responding simply, "I know."[36] Mazzoli then went to Rodino and asked him to be the lead sponsor of immigration reform in the 99th Congress.[37] After pouring his heart and soul into the effort for nearly five years, Mazzoli was accepting that he would no longer be the captain of the ship, but Rodino's subordinate; a high-ranking one to be sure, but a subordinate nonetheless. His concession, just the first of many to come, would be critical to the future viability of the Simpson-Rodino legislation that apparently would no longer bear his name.[38]

Still, a month passed, then two, after Simpson announced his intention to introduce his bill, and Rodino remained nearly Sphinx-like regarding his own thinking. He finally told the press that he would not act until the Senate did first, returning to a common theme he'd expressed since his first two immigration bills had passed the House before languishing in the upper body a dozen years earlier. Rodino also made a direct challenge to the administration, pointedly observing that President Reagan's purported previous support for the legislation had in the end "turned out to be half-hearted."[39] But even with Rodino's and Reagan's full attention, the bill's fate in an increasingly polarized Congress was uncertain at best; one respected journalist noted that coming out of the McCloskey-McIntyre battle, "the only sure result of the current rancor and guerilla warfare in the House is that it's almost impossible to get anything done."[40]

CHANGES

The shift in the chief House sponsorship of immigration reform wasn't the only important change in the offing. By late spring 1985, LULAC's Arnoldo Torres was besieged by internal organizational battles. Even as they recognized the benefits of their director's high profile, one academic wrote, several LULAC board members had begun to resent "the flamboyant executive director's obstructionist stands" on immigration and other issues.[41] Some divisions were ideological. The organization's persistent, often strident opposition to the Reagan domestic agenda under Torres and the Bonillas, wrote one activist Chicano scholar, "fostered internal schisms within LULAC's rather conservative membership."[42] Some thought that San Antonio businessman Oscar Morán, "known for his support of Ronald Reagan and conservative Texas governor William Clements," and the front-runner in the upcoming 1985 LULAC presidential elections, exploited the divisions to push the organization in a more moderate direction.[43]

Equally consequential was tension between Torres and his boss, LULAC president Mario Obledo. They'd managed to work effectively through the 1984 political conventions, but never seemed to work out a mutual understanding of their respective roles. The National Immigration Forum's Rick Swartz later observed that while previous presidents Ruben and Tony Bonilla were happy to share the limelight with their executive director, "Obledo wanted to be the center of attention" on LULAC matters.[44] Obledo was used to doing business by dictating memos and firing off missives to subordinates, and Torres bristled at what he viewed as excessive micromanagement.[45] By early 1985 the relationship had reached a breaking point.

The organization's long-standing financial problems exacerbated the discord. Prior to the ascendancy of the Bonillas in 1979, the organization had run up significant deficits, avoiding bankruptcy only by taking on considerable debt.[46] In 1983, again LULAC came close to declaring bankruptcy, saved in part by furloughing some staff for part of the year.[47] Its shaky fiscal status had been obscured for a time by the Bonillas' willingness to use their own personal financial resources to cover their travel expenses, reducing the group's costs. But no financial model reliant on the personal beneficence of elected volunteer leaders who served a maximum of two one-year terms is sustainable. Periodic fiscal pressures are nearly universal among nonprofits, and there tends to be a recurring "chicken and egg" quality to internal debates about closing financial deficits. Boards of directors inevitably instruct staff to cut costs and raise more money, while the staff invariably responds that excessive cuts would be counterproductive by undermining fundraising efforts. Torres argued against staff cuts in the Washington office, believing that a visible presence in policy debates, and therefore in media coverage, was essential for fundraising.[48] LULAC board member and presidential candidate Oscar Morán disagreed, asserting that improved relationships with corporations, a less confrontational style, and fewer attacks on the Reagan administration would better position the organization to raise funds.[49]

These tensions came to a head at LULAC's spring board meeting, held in advance of its upcoming national convention later that summer that would, as always, feature an election for LULAC president. Before he left for the meeting, Torres says he received a confidential phone call that likely incoming president

Oscar Morán was bragging that he would "clip Arnold's wings" in the upcoming board session.[50] The meeting played out like a soap opera episode. On the first day of the two-day affair, the board narrowly passed a motion to lay off most of Torres's DC-based staff. Torres says he undertook a vigorous lobbying campaign that night, and the following day the motion was rescinded after bitter debate. With acrimony still in the air, Torres was called on to deliver his executive director's report, a routine part of the meeting agenda. Relishing his reversal of the attempt to clip his wings, he laced his talk with thinly veiled jabs at his critics. Obledo attempted several times to cut short the presentation, but Torres, already convinced his days were numbered, refused to yield the floor. Obledo became so enraged at his staff's insubordination that the normally dignified LULAC president had to be restrained from coming after Torres physically.[51] In the uproar that followed, recollections differ as to whether the executive director ultimately resigned or was dismissed, but clearly he was out.[52]

Torres was succeeded by his chief deputy, Joe Treviño, who'd been on the LULAC national office staff since early in Torres's tenure, and who had an unusual background for a Washington lobbyist. After graduating from high school in San Antonio, as he described it, he briefly "joked around" in community college before enlisting in the army. While many of his contemporaries were protesting against the Vietnam War or evading the draft, Treviño wanted to "go over there and get it over with." After his tour in Indochina, he was posted for a time in Germany, and when he returned to the states he got married and worked for seminal Latino community organizer Bert Corona in Los Angeles while attending college. He and his wife decided to go to law school; Antioch School of Law in Washington, DC, accepted them both, so they headed east. Treviño started at LULAC in 1980 as an intern working for $300 per month; he and his wife lived in the basement apartment of a small office building, which they cleaned daily in lieu of rent.[53]

Antioch law school was heavily subsidized, with tuition covering only a third of the institution's budget; the rest was raised by Edward S. Cahn and his wife Jean, the school's founders, who'd also played a major role in designing what later became the Legal Services Corporation.[54] Even with the low tuition, the cash-strapped Treviño sought greater responsibility—and the higher wages that came with it—and quickly moved up to the position of deputy executive director. When asked by Obledo to accept the executive director position, Treviño felt obligated to take the job, believing that continuity was critical for an organization challenged on so many fronts. The transition was not smooth. Treviño knew how much the job meant to Torres, who had kept taped to his desk a slip of paper from a fortune cookie that read "Happy is a man who has found his life's work." Although Treviño says he "loved Arnold like a brother," he had to execute the "awkward and painful" task of managing his former boss's physical departure from the office, overseeing the collection of Torres's personal belongings and cutting his final paycheck.[55]

Almost everyone in or around The Group was shocked and saddened at the news, except for NCLR's legislative director Martha Escutia. In her view, Torres had never fully valued NCLR's or her own individual role in the lobbying effort, and the two had never clicked on a personal level. Escutia had her own contacts in LULAC leadership circles, and immediately after the fateful board meeting she started spreading the news of Torres's separation among her wide network of friends and contacts, perhaps a bit too gleefully in the former LULAC executive's view.[56] While acknowledging Torres's considerable contributions to the debate, for her part, Escutia made no bones of her belief that what had happened was a case of "chickens coming home to roost."[57] Ironically, Torres's appreciation for MALDEF and NCLR had come around by this time, as he told a reporter that compared to groups representing similar interests like African Americans and women, "nobody can lobby like LULAC, litigate like MALDEF, or research like La Raza"; one scholar cited the statement as evidence that the three Hispanic groups had, by then, "developed an effective division of labor within the Beltway."[58]

A few months later Torres granted an interview to *Nuestro*, one of the first national, English-language, Hispanic-focused periodicals, a magazine that was closely followed by Latino elites, where he said, "Republicans on the [LULAC] board are concerned more with placating the White House than in really advocating for the community. I wanted a program of aggressive advocacy . . . , a lean, mean fighting machine. Just look at what it's done recently: nothing. The letters to the Hill have not gone out. The lobbying hasn't taken place. The strong advocacy has not been there. That speaks for itself."[59] There was both truth and hyperbole in Torres's observations; upon taking the job, Treviño was confronted with addressing a debt that was much larger than he'd expected.[60] One consequence of the organization's outmoded fiscal system was its failure to accurately assess and promptly remit various payroll deductions to the appropriate federal and state agencies. Because LULAC could not quickly resolve the issues, according to Treviño, for a brief period early in his tenure "the IRS came in and padlocked the doors to the LULAC office. But what they didn't know was that we were connected to [the separately incorporated but related] LULAC National Educational Service Centers office. So I just went through LNESC to get to my office to work every day."[61]

The new executive director's top priority for the next year or so was to get the organization's financial house in order, although he remained a valued member of The Group throughout; as Rick Swartz put it, "We missed Arnold, but we also tried to rally around Joe [Treviño]."[62] Still, as a result of the challenges of fixing the organization's financial and management issues with reduced staff, according to one academic, after Torres's departure LULAC "necessarily took a backseat to some of the other players."[63]

With the help of past LULAC president Tony Bonilla, Torres seemed to have arranged a "soft landing" for himself. Bonilla had formed a new organization, the National Hispanic Leadership Conference, which confusingly bore the same name as the coalition of national groups that came together in presidential election years to influence the candidates' platforms, and asked Torres to represent him. It appeared at best an interim stop while Torres considered his options, including formation of his own advocacy organization.[64]

On June 17, Torres represented the National Hispanic Leadership Conference and the Arizona Farmworkers Union, a splinter group that had broken away from the better-known United Farm Workers, at a hearing chaired by his old nemesis Al Simpson, testifying on a panel with NCLR's Raul Yzaguírre, LULAC's Joe Treviño, and MALDEF's Richard Fajardo. For Simpson more than most senators, holding a hearing was very much a contact sport, a chance to have some fun. Simpson once wrote that before a hearing he'd ask his chief counsel Dick Day to find "the orneriest rascal in the country" who had views opposed to theirs, and "he would name a person or two . . . and we would invite them to testify. These people would say their piece, and often would take a few shots at us. We would then fire a few shots in return. And I think both sides enjoyed themselves."[65]

Simpson thrived in the give and take of the hearing process, although it's highly questionable that witnesses he targeted for "a few shots" truly "enjoyed themselves." Lawmakers, especially committee chairs, hold all the cards during a hearing. They demand *yes* or *no* replies to complex questions, ask "When did you stop beating your wife?"-type queries, cut off witnesses who refuse to follow the script, make damning statements without giving witnesses a fair chance to respond, and otherwise engage in all manner of prosecutorial theatrics. Some wondered why Simpson would've given Torres a platform when he no longer had LULAC's imprimatur. They soon got their answer. As soon as the panel of Hispanic witnesses completed their oral statements, the senator lit into Torres, sticking him right where it hurt the most:

> I do try to listen to what you say . . . and I have done that for all the years that I have been dealing with the issue. I must say I do not handle that well at all times because the injection of racism has never come from me, it comes from you, Arnoldo, it comes continually from you, the issue of racism, and that is offensive to me. And it does not come from any other source but you, and *perhaps that is why you have been discredited in the process.* I wanted to say that. It is painful and hard and tough, but it is in my craw, and I have said it [emphasis added].[66]

In fact, Torres's testimony that day had made only a brief, passing reference to racism, but Simpson declined to give Torres a chance to answer, leaving much of the audience in stunned silence for a minute, before he moved on to question other witnesses. When finally given an opportunity to respond later in the hearing, Torres gamely tried to maintain his composure and engage in a substantive dialogue with the senator.[67] But all of the metaphorical oxygen had been sucked out of the room by Simpson's devastating, deeply personal, cutting put-down, and the senator evinced little interest in a dialogue; he'd made his point, and he wanted it to stick.

Later, the senator took some delight in telling a related story. After he'd addressed a local LULAC chapter and told them of his battles with Torres, according to Simpson their leaders responded, "You think *you* had trouble? *We* had worse trouble with him than you did—and if he were here right now, he'd tell you the same thing [emphasis in the original]."[68] Still, the incident perhaps revealed more about Simpson than Torres. It was moments like this—when the second-ranking leader of the "world's greatest deliberative body" would so publicly kick a civil rights leader who was already down—that would lead one journalist years later to ask why so gifted, popular, and acclaimed a senator as Al Simpson could on occasion "be so abusive in his dealings with reasonable people whose only offense seems to be that they disagree with him."[69] Torres later opened a highly successful government affairs shop in his hometown of Sacramento, but his singular role in the immigration reform debate of the 1980s was over.

MORE CHANGES

Even before Simpson's hearings the Reagan administration made clear that it preferred the new Senate bill to those previously considered; Attorney General Meese and INS commissioner Alan Nelson said that the bill's "deferred legalization" provision "represents a better balance with enforcement and avoids some of the serious cost issues in a time of needed deficit reduction."[70] With Reagan's support in hand, Simpson decided to skip subcommittee markup and went straight to the full Judiciary Committee. Simpson mainly had his way during the markup but was clearly frustrated with the increasing clout of the western growers, saying of them: "Their greed really knows no bounds in the perishable food industry. . . . I don't know what the hell to do with them. I don't know how I can accommodate them. I'll never be right [in their eyes]. They're the toughest guys to deal with."[71]

At the end of July the bill was reported out of the Judiciary Committee with just one major change: a proposal by Senator Kennedy to guarantee implementation of legalization within three years (whether or not the conditions required to meet the "trigger" in the original bill) was adopted with Simpson's grudging concurrence.[72] Although a guarantee that legalization actually would occur was better than nothing, it wasn't lost on The Group that they'd had to fight hard just to obtain a legalization program that was just a shadow of the measure they'd achieved in the last House bill following adoption of virtually all of their amendments from the Roybal legislation. The bill also retained the proposal to make employer verification of new hires optional, which was supported by the US Chamber of Commerce, but NCLR argued, "Some members of the business community argue that the [mandatory] verification process will impose severe recordkeeping burdens on business, but the history of our civil rights laws shows that such records are essential to identify patterns of discrimination. . . . [W]e believe that recordkeeping is a small price to pay to further this nation's commitment to equal opportunity."[73]

While Simpson's "lean bill" had thankfully taken off the table two major concerns of The Group—a reduction in legal immigration and cutbacks in asylum protections—they seemed to be losing ground on their other priorities: maximizing legalization, minimizing discrimination resulting from employer sanctions, and limiting expansion of guestworker programs, which even Simpson seemed to think was inevitable.

By this time, The Group was meeting frequently with Skip Endres, soon to succeed Jim Cline, who was retiring as staff director of the Judiciary Committee, and Lynn Conway, who a year earlier had replaced Harris Miller as assistant counsel to Mazzoli's immigration subcommittee. The veteran Endres was a well-known quantity in the field, having served as a Judiciary Committee staffer since the early 1970s. While his substantive expertise in immigration law was widely respected, as was his knowledge of the legislative process, perhaps his greatest assets were his "soft skills": a genial, winning personality and a well-earned reputation as a straight shooter. Everyone he came into contact with—lawmakers, staff, and lobbyists—felt that he'd both understand their concerns and treat them fairly.[74]

Lynnette R. Conway was like a breath of fresh air to The Group; like many of Ron Mazzoli's closest aides and allies, Conway had a Notre Dame connection, having graduated from its law school in 1983, and had joined the subcommittee staff just before floor debate on the bill in 1984. She'd first met Mazzoli while in law school when she clerked for a congressional group in DC, and connected again when he spoke to her graduating class, urging them to "forsake the lucrative law careers in . . . corporate law firms and instead come to Washington to work on public policy." She had little coursework in immigration, but her father, himself a British immigrant, was a university dean with substantial contact with foreign students, some who'd had visa problems. This gave her, she thought, some small degree of understanding of what the system looked like from an immigrant's perspective.[75]

Her predecessor Harris Miller once told an interviewer that his job was to be Mazzoli's "spear catcher," a role some thought he embraced much too enthusiastically.[76] To some in The Group, conversations with the hard-nosed Miller could seem pointless, since he appeared to have his mind made up on virtually every issue of concern to them.[77] By contrast, Conway listened intently and asked probing questions; her openness to different perspectives was genuine—she later said she'd had to learn immigration law "from scratch" when staffing Mazzoli during the bill's floor consideration the previous year.[78] And unlike Miller, who battled constantly with Rodino's aides, Conway appeared to work seamlessly with Endres. While Conway took her work seriously, the bright, upbeat young lawyer also never evidenced excessive self-importance; visitors to the crowded, bustling space she shared with other Judiciary Committee staffers were greeted with a sign on her desk reading "I'd Rather Be Eating Chocolate."[79]

With the new pecking order—Rodino in command, Mazzoli as chief subordinate—firmly established, and key staffers Endres and Conway in place, on July 19 the Judiciary Committee chairman told the press that he and Mazzoli would jointly sponsor the House bill, making clear that with his leadership he expected the bill to have "fewer obstacles" than previously.[80] No institution celebrated this indication of progress on immigration reform more than the *New York Times* editorial board, whose lead editorial on July 21 was entitled "Peter Rodino Rides to the Rescue."[81] This was just the latest in a long series of *Times* editorials unabashedly supporting immigration reform written by deputy editorial page editor Jack Rosenthal, who had won a coveted Pulitzer Prize in 1982.[82] And little wonder.

Rosenthal was a student of the immigration issue and sought out discussions with experts, albeit generally those with a somewhat restrictionist bent such as Michael Teitelbaum, a respected analyst associated with the Alfred P. Sloan Foundation, a combination think tank and funding source, who'd authored a highly influential article in *Foreign Affairs* on immigration.[83] He had an insider's knowledge of the political process, having reported on events in the nation's capital for nearly two decades. He later climbed the executive ladder at the newspaper, retiring in 2000 as editor of the prestigious *New York Times Magazine*. He had exquisitely well-developed sources, none more important than his friend Al Simpson, who said of Rosenthal, "He knew more about immigration than perhaps anyone else in the media. He knew lawmaking; Jack had been a congressional staffer. He knew the Hill, he knew the players, and knew their games. . . . He was always supportive [of immigration reform]."[84]

Rosenthal also cultivated advocacy contacts, consulting "frequently, sometimes on a daily basis," with FAIR's Roger Conner during the reform debate.[85] Rosenthal's enthusiasm for the bill's apparently improving prospects was thus expected, and Rodino didn't disappoint. On July 25, he and Mazzoli introduced their version of immigration reform legislation. Like Simpson's bill, the House legislation excluded major changes to the legal immigration and asylum adjudication rules, and contained only a modest expansion of the H-2 agricultural temporary worker program. But unlike the Senate version, the Rodino-Mazzoli bill included the Frank amendment's antidiscrimination protections, what writers called a "far more generous" legalization program with a 1982 eligibility cutoff date and most of the substructure improvements from the original Roybal bill, and 100 percent reimbursement to the states for costs associated with that program.[86]

Although Rosenthal's support for Rodino's decision to move immigration reform was expected, it was also lauded by previous critics of the legislation, including columnist Frank del Olmo of the *Los Angeles Times*. Del Olmo, himself a Pulitzer Prize winner, was viewed as the *LA Times*'s "Latino conscience," an important persona for the largest daily newspaper in the country's largest Hispanic market.[87] Del Olmo wrote that "rather than opposing the new Rodino bill [Latino advocates] should work to influence passage in the House of a version that would leaven Simpson's [less generous] proposal, which is likely to emerge from the Senate unchanged."[88]

That del Olmo had come out so openly for compromise reflected growing questions among Latino leaders across the country on whether obstruction was still the best way to deal with immigration reform. Even perennial hardliner Ed Roybal, who had led the opposition to employer sanctions legislation no less than four times—twice in the 1970s and twice in the 1980s—briefly embraced the idea that it might be time to compromise as a way to kickstart a different kind of discussion on reform. Without consulting outside groups or colleagues within the Hispanic Caucus, Roybal earlier that year introduced legislation that included a softer "modified form of employer sanctions."[89] Simpson and Mazzoli immediately praised their longtime adversary, with the latter calling Roybal a "profile in courage" for having embraced the concept of employer sanctions.[90] But according to a Roybal aide, neither of the bill's sponsors made an effort to reach out to him, so Roybal withdrew the bill, acknowledging "a fierce, negative response" from MALDEF and other advocates.[91] Roybal subsequently introduced legislation similar to that he'd offered the previous year, downplaying the bill that had included a form of employer sanctions as a "trial balloon."[92]

The Group could hardly complain since they also had explored an alternative bill without intending for Roybal to serve as chief sponsor. They'd hoped to pull together a larger coalition including business and labor around a modified version of their bill, but like Roybal's brief flirtation with employer sanctions, this new bill-drafting effort was soon abandoned.[93] Nevertheless, there was clearly within The Group and, more importantly, among some Young Turks in the Hispanic Caucus led by Rep. Esteban Torres a sense that the time was ripe to more actively negotiate with the bill's proponents.

Esteban Edward "Ed" Torres had a distinguished resume. He was born in Arizona but grew up in Southern California. After returning from a tour of duty in Korea, he was an assembly-line worker in a Chrysler plant, became chief steward for United Auto Workers Local 230, and steadily moved up the UAW hierarchy all while earning a college degree. He was the first CEO of The East Los Angeles Community Union (TELACU), one of the original flagship affiliates of the Southwest Council of La Raza, which under his leadership became one of the most successful organizations of its kind in the country. Torres was one of the highest-ranking Latinos in the Carter White House and later was ambassador to UNESCO. In 1982, he was elected to Congress from Southern California in a congressional district redrawn in part to reflect the state's rapidly growing Latino population documented in the 1980 Census.[94]

But his professional biography, impressive as it was, didn't do justice to his stature in a Hispanic community that had precious few national leaders: he was a native-born American citizen, the son of a bracero worker who'd been "repatriated" to Mexico in the 1930s. While a young man he'd worked in the fields and seen with his own eyes the exploitation and abuse of agricultural guest-workers; there was an "everyman" side to his character reflecting his humble upbringing. He had solid roots in the labor movement, but tight connections to NCLR and other activist Latino groups that opposed labor's immigration restrictionism. He kept close ties with Hispanic advocates while serving in a Carter administration that had a mixed relationship with the Latino community, but was sufficiently crafty that he engineered a public, if somewhat reluctant, endorsement of Carter by then LULAC president Ruben Bonilla in 1980.[95] It was a huge coup for Esteban Torres, since Carter faced a primary challenge from Ted Kennedy, the most popular national politician in the Latino community.

In his second term in Congress, the understated Rep. Torres was slated to succeed his flashier classmate, New Mexico Rep. Bill Richardson, as chairman of the Congressional Hispanic Caucus for the 1985–1986 term. Richardson, who'd succeeded Rep. Bob García as caucus chair, had himself earlier explored compromise with Mazzoli and Simpson, although researchers noted he ultimately "cast his lot with the Hispanic lobbying groups" opposing the bill in 1984.[96] Richardson made no secret of his future ambitions—he would later serve in two Cabinet positions in the Clinton administration and be elected governor of New Mexico—but had made little headway in bringing others along with him when he'd previously flirted with the idea of compromising on immigration reform. By contrast, Esteban Torres, who rarely evinced interest in higher office, was seen as a steadier, more trustworthy point man in negotiations that everyone recognized could become very risky for all parties involved; Ron Mazzoli thought of the Californian as someone who could bring other votes with him.[97] NCLR President Raul Yzaguírre later called Rep. Torres "exactly the right man, in the right place, at the right time" to lead the effort to seek a compromise with Rodino and Mazzoli.[98]

Early in 1985, encouraged by NCLR and other members of The Group, Rep. Torres began sounding out other Hispanic Caucus members to assess whether they might join him in a more flexible posture on the immigration bill.[99] While it took place completely under the radar of all but the closest insiders, as researcher Rosanna Perotti aptly noted, by the spring the "Hispanic Caucus had split" on the strategy to address immigration reform, with congressman Torres leading a moderate faction that included Representatives Tony Coehlo, a Californian, New Mexico's Bill Richardson, and Solomon Ortiz and Albert Bustamante of Texas.[100] Part of the rationale for the moderate faction's posture was fear of enforcement-only legislation with no legalization program at all. They'd received signals that the House leadership was "tired of screwing around with this," as Rep. Torres's staffer Albert Jacquez noted, and feared that a restriction-oriented bill would "be passed over our heads."[101]

There was a significant measure of hope as well, embodied in the personage of Peter Rodino. Outside of his commitment to employer sanctions, the Judiciary Committee chairman was more sympathetic to their core priorities and had proven his willingness to let legislation die rather than accede to an unacceptable bill. As The Group's Michael Myers noted, the ascension of Rodino as lead sponsor of the bill meant that "the good elements" of the legislation would be preserved; NCLR's leaders also thought of the committee chairman as "someone on point whom they could trust."[102] They were also aware that Rodino wouldn't be around forever; already reporters were writing stories about the "post-Rodino era."[103] Advocates were thus tantalized by the potential "window of opportunity" but feared it might soon close.

The Group and the Hispanic Caucus moderates saw real opportunities to improve the bill. They hoped to include provisions to sunset employer sanctions, the amendment previously sponsored by Pat Schroeder claimed this go-round by Rep. Bob García. The ACLU's Henderson and Church World Service's Myers wanted to attach the Moakley-DeConcini bill to protect Salvadoran and other Central American refugees onto the bigger legislation. And they were working with a safety net of sorts: each improvement they achieved would make the bill less attractive to business, the Reagan administration, and other current supporters. They could seek the best bill possible, and if that forced some other faction to kill it, so much the better; at least their own fingerprints would not be on the bill's corpse.

This shift toward compromise heightened NCLR's role, both because it had always been predisposed in this direction and also because of close personal relationships between the principals, CEO Raul Yzaguírre and Rep. Esteban Torres, and their staffs. NCLR's reputation also was buoyed that year by a formal, independent evaluation of its policy center commissioned by its main funder, the Rockefeller Foundation, which found:

> Among elected officials, both Hispanic and non-Hispanic, NCLR may be the most respected of the three principal organizations that represent Hispanic interests in Washington. . . . In sum, La Raza's policy analysis efforts fill a critically important need, the organization has excellent leadership, the staff has gained a reputation for informed judgment among potential allies in Washington, and the group is at least as effective as—and perhaps more effective than—any other Hispanic organization in Washington.[104]

The evaluation boosted NCLR's standing just as it was playing an increasingly important role in the immigration policy debate, while Arnoldo Torres's departure and the institution's fiscal constraints reduced LULAC's. MALDEF's role was limited by its estrangement from The Group and exclusion from key meetings on Capitol Hill as the focus of the debate shifted. MALDEF's Antonia Hernández later told a reporter that she heard from Hill insiders that her organization "was regarded as an unpredictable kamikaze—likely to sabotage negotiations it was no longer asked to join."[105] Simpson's aide Carl Hampe agreed; while negotiations with MALDEF were impossible, he said, "we always felt we could talk to [NCLR]."[106] Aware of the dangers of proceeding without first protecting his flanks, Yzaguírre instructed his staff to discreetly sound out NCLR board members and other Latino "influentials" about a formal shift toward compromise. The staff touched base with more than forty leaders during what it later called "an extraordinary consultation process" in the spring and summer of 1985.[107] After receiving substantial, if not universal, agreement that pursuit of a compromise made sense, NCLR aggressively supported Rep. Torres's efforts to negotiate an acceptable bill.

Still, for NCLR, The Group, and the moderate faction of the Hispanic Caucus, the shift involved a tricky balancing act, what one writer called a "delicate minuet."[108] They retained their official position against employer sanctions—both on principle and to retain leverage—but went beyond signaling a willingness to bargain and engaged in real negotiations. While a logical extension of their previous affirmative defense strategy, with NCLR playing an increasingly important role, The Group was clearly taking a big step toward "affirmative" and away from "defense."

TOUGHER POSITIONS

Just as Arnoldo Torres left Washington, Monsignor Nicholas DiMarzio entered the scene, succeeding Don Hohl, who had served capably as associate director of Migration and Refugee Services of the US Catholic Conference for many years before a brief tenure in the top job. A relatively small department of the American Catholic Church's sprawling conglomerate of operating divisions and subsidiaries, the Migration and Refugee Services division, known among insiders as "MRS" for short, had a huge footprint in the immigration and refugee field, in no small part because the Catholic Church had always been an "immigrant church."[109] It was by far the largest of the VOLAGs, the nonprofit voluntary agencies that, according to Hohl's predecessor John McCarthy, had successfully resettled some two million refugees in the US between the end of World War II and 1980, even before the flow of Indochinese entrants had peaked.[110] But while appreciated and well-liked in the broader immigration and refugee fields, inside the church hierarchy—and few institutions are as hierarchical as the Roman Catholic Church—Hohl had a problem: he was a layman, not an ordained priest. Even very talented, high-ranking lay people in the church bureaucracy face inherent limitations; lower-ranking staff that happen to be priests have a certain degree of access and privilege unavailable to the "hired help." Thus, during Hohl's tenure the church took the safest position possible on immigration reform: supporting the Simpson-Mazzoli bill "with some reservations."[111]

Hohl's successor Nick DiMarzio had all of the right credentials for the job: a trained social worker with a master's degree, he later took courses in immigration law, and graduated from the doctoral program in social policy at Rutgers, where his PhD dissertation focused on the use of social services by undocumented immigrants in New York City.[112] That research later became the basis for a book, coauthored with a prominent immigration scholar named Demetrios Papademetriou.[113] The two had met during the early stages of DiMarzio's research, when the young priest sought assistance from the Center for Migration Studies, a Catholic-linked think tank where Papademetriou was research director.[114] DiMarzio was a seasoned practitioner as well, having served for nine years as the Archdiocese's refugee resettlement director, all while also an associate pastor, pastor, or chaplain at six churches in Newark and surrounding areas.

But his greatest assets were institutional, and personal. He wore "the collar," the white band around the neck that signals a priest's identity and dedication to the church. The grandson of Italian immigrants, DiMarzio was born, raised, and later ordained in the Archdiocese of Newark, squarely centered in Peter Rodino's congressional district, giving him an easy familiarity with and access to the Judiciary Committee chairman that few others in Washington could claim. And at a time when partisan politics were becoming more polarized, the church maintained close ties to both Republicans and Democrats, and their allied interest groups. Conservatives liked the Catholic bishops' leadership in the "pro-life" movement. At the same time, the US Catholic Conference had long been a mainstay in liberal coalitions supporting civil rights and antipoverty programs. These relationships positioned the Catholic Church as one of a decreasing number of American institutions that worked effectively and consistently across party and ideological lines.

The new executive director of the church's immigration arm wasn't the least bit reticent about taking advantage of the Catholics' potent political positioning. DiMarzio was a big, burly man with a personality and presence to match; in private, he could be loud, earthy, and aggressive, although in public settings writers described his persona more simply, as "articulate and plain spoken."[115] Through his friend, coauthor, and later part-time consultant Papademetriou, he connected with the American Jewish Committee's Gary Rubin, who closely followed the academic literature. DiMarzio soon linked up with the National Immigration Forum's Rick Swartz, whose board of directors he immediately joined and would later chair. Papademetriou and Rubin then helped DiMarzio to arrange a series of "get to know you" meetings with members of The Group. Church World Service's Michael Myers was impressed, saying that "Nick was cool, a fun guy to be around and work with."[116] The ACLU's Henderson thought DiMarzio had a "powerful presence."[117] NCLR's Yzaguírre, a deeply religious man with connections to the church via his close friend Pablo Sedillo, who headed the Bishop's Secretariat for Hispanic Affairs, wasn't sure what to think of DiMarzio at first. After what he laughingly called their "audience" during which DiMarzio did almost all of the talking, Yzaguírre told the openly agnostic Kamasaki, "Your Monsignor is a pretty opinionated guy."

The new MRS director quickly translated his opinions into church policy. It wasn't coincidental that less than six months after DiMarzio's arrival, the Catholic bishops adopted a new resolution stating that until such time as "legalization is treated as the centerpiece of immigration reform . . . we shall oppose employer sanctions."[118] If Simpson wanted to condition legalization on enforcement, the Catholics did the reverse: condition acceptance of employer sanctions on an effective legalization program. More than his predecessors, DiMarzio engaged The Group, not in the day-to-day minutiae of lobbying, but through his willingness to weigh in when most needed with the full moral and political force of the Catholic bishops.[119]

The bishops weren't the only group toughening up their message. The Federation for American Immigration Reform, arguably the most important organization promoting immigration restriction, began as a traditional public interest group, advocating its positions through policy research, lobbying, savvy use of the media, and using direct-mail techniques to build a grassroots membership. In the previous Congress, it sharpened attacks against advocacy opponents, especially LULAC, arguing that the venerable civil rights group was not truly representing the interests of its constituency, upping the ante through a poll that tried to show that Hispanic advocates were out of step with their own constituency. If its rhetoric was occasionally harsher than average, it was well within the mainstream in the first two rounds of the debate.

The failure of Simpson-Mazzoli at the end of the 98th Congress marked a transformation in the organization's persona and ethos. Executive director Roger Conner considered himself a "liberal," thinking that through "sheer force of will" he could overcome critics who equated immigration restrictionism with racism, but complained that the "rights-based groups" constantly tried to "delegitimize" FAIR and its allies.[120] During the third round of immigration reform, his organization fought back by pushing the envelope of traditional nonprofit discourse. Its fundraising letters began targeting lawmakers by name in unusually harsh and personal terms. Soon after the bill died in conference committee, an appeal on founder John Tanton's letterhead attacked Rep. Barney Frank's antidiscrimination amendment, claiming that although FAIR "pulled out all stops and eventually forced him to change his position," the contretemps over the provision "stalled the bill just long enough so that time ran out."[121] An angry Frank called Conner to "ask him to give me specifics about how he had forced me to change my position," noting that he was "unable to do so." Frank then wrote to Tanton, asserting that the FAIR letter was "a form of consumer fraud," concluding it was "now clear to me that trying to work with you was a mistake and I will avoid it in the future."[122] Another FAIR fundraising letter accused Arizona senator Dennis DeConcini of "working for . . . illegal aliens and their bosses"; at a later hearing, the senator demanded that Conner provide evidence to support the charges. The FAIR executive was forced to promise DeConcini that he would "write a letter to every person who received the first [letter] and correct the misimpression."[123]

FAIR's direct-mail constituency-building efforts also shifted the tone and substance of its core arguments. Direct-mail fundraising was as much science as art: test different messages with different groups, then target the winning messages to the audiences most willing to write checks. Given FAIR's origins, the first mailing lists it targeted its appeals to were liberals that had donated to environmental causes, but it also tried other lists, a customary practice in the field. It also tested a wide variety of messages. Over and over again, the lists that produced the highest returns were of conservative activists, and the most effective anti-immigration messages emphasized cultural if not necessarily explicitly racial concerns about immigration. Conner later said that, much to his own consternation, as a result of these "dynamics of direct mail," FAIR's membership base over time increasingly "became more culturally conservative."[124]

But if executive director Conner was uncomfortable with this direction, FAIR founder John Tanton was not. In 1983, Tanton had established a new organization, US English, "dedicated to preserving the unifying role of the English language in the United States."[125] With its unabashed opposition to bilingual ballots and bilingual education, the group grew rapidly, and soon boasted more than two hundred thousand dues-paying members.[126] Its first major foray into public policy was in California, which was feeling what one *New York Times* story speculated might be a "re-birth of anti-immigrant politics that appears in turbulent cycles in American history."[127] In 1985, US English began organizing in support of a public referendum offering the seemingly innocuous proposition that English should become the state's "official language." MALDEF led the unsuccessful opposition to what later became known as Proposition 63, arguing that the measure was confusing and overly broad, affecting not just increasingly unpopular bilingual education and bilingual ballot policies, but generally accepted ones, like court interpreters and 911 emergency operators. It argued that unnecessary litigation would ensue and that increased access to English classes would be a more constructive alternative.[128] The ACLU and others also asserted the measure was "a mask to hide anti-immigrant character."[129] But it was the normally more moderate NCLR that explicitly used the "R" word, calling the English-only measures "fundamentally racist."[130] Whether they were or not, all parties in the increasingly contentious debate taking place outside the halls of Congress soon faced a reckoning on issues at the intersection of immigration and race.

EMOTION, FEAR, GUILT, AND RACISM

It was a hot, sticky August afternoon in Washington when The Group split up for congressional visits before meeting on the "Capitol steps," the outside stairways leading up to the House and Senate chambers, to compare notes. The area was a great vantage point for networking and people-watching; one could catch a lawmaker or staffer headed to or from the Senate or House floor for a quick chat, all the while checking out the dozens of lobbyists, aides, tourists, or other visitors streaming by. Many on the Hill that day were thinking of reform, not of the Immigration and Nationality Act but of the Internal Revenue Code. Negotiations on a massive tax reform bill had begun in earnest, and the House Ways and Means Committee was about to begin marking up its version of the legislation when legislators returned to the capital in September. It was a bonanza for DC's "government relations" firms: tax reform's prospective winners and potential losers both employed armies of lobbyists to protect their interests. The corporate lobbyists were easily distinguished by their high-end attire, such that the hallways outside the tax-writing committees were referred to as "Gucci Gulch" after the "expensive suits and shiny Italian shoes" favored by the influence peddlers.[131]

The ACLU's Henderson and NCLR's Kamasaki and Purtell got to the Capitol steps first that day, sweating heavily in the summer heat. Almost every corporate lobbyist walking by with a lawmaker or staffer was dressed in the Capitol Hill "summer uniform" of baby blue pinstriped, lightweight poplin or linen suits, preferably with designer labels, that most efficiently vented body heat. As Henderson surveyed the impeccably dressed assemblage streaming by, he complained to his colleagues, "Look at 'em, all perfectly cool, while we're here sweating like pigs, in our . . . *wool*," which that sweltering day sounded like a harsh expletive. "And polyester," Kamasaki chimed in under his breath, thinking of his own "365 weight" dress clothes that invariably seemed too cold in winter but too hot in summer. Neither mentioned that the even more poorly paid Purtell's sole business ensemble was a pair of khakis and a single blue blazer.

Wardrobe limitations notwithstanding, The Group was gearing up for Senate consideration of Simpson's bill, which began on Tuesday, September 10. The majority whip observed that he knew that debate on immigration reform wasn't just substantively complex but also evoked a combination of "racism, fear, guilt, emotion."[132] Simpson later latched onto variants of the phrase—mostly expressed alphabetically as "emotion, fear, guilt, and racism"—to characterize almost every difficult subject, including deficit reduction. After retiring from the Senate a decade later, Simpson attributed his defeat on a subsequent immigration proposal to advocacy groups whose "lobbying was filled with emotion, fear, guilt, and racism. They go right for the emotional gut. The violins and the choruses start, and shit, that's it."[133] Even twenty years later, he repeatedly said, "Emotion, fear, guilt and racism control" debate on immigration policy.[134] However the phrase was deployed in future years, it was oft-quoted because it illustrated the complex web of passion that various interests brought to the debate. It was Simpson at his finest: coining a witty, memorable phrase to express understanding of and sympathy for his colleagues as he forced them to take tough votes that often generated harsh political and personal attacks.

Consistent with the previous two times his bill had been considered, the majority whip generally had his way over the eight days the Senate debated his bill, with one critical difference: whether there would be a major new temporary worker program for western agricultural growers. The growers lined up behind an amendment sponsored by California senator Pete Wilson similar to the temporary worker program won by Reps. Leon Panetta and Sid Morrison in the House in the previous Congress. Wilson and his staff had seen how the issue had fared in the 1984 conference committee, and claimed to have made a series of changes to address opponents' concerns.[135] But those opponents asserted the changes were mainly cosmetic, and by a razor-thin two-vote margin, Simpson, with strong support from Senator Kennedy, beat back the Californian's first attempt to enact a proposal that some estimated would allow the importation of half a million or more foreign agricultural workers annually.[136]

Wilson refused to give up, demonstrating the political savvy that propelled him to the governorship of California less than a decade later. He called an aide at 11:30 at night after losing the first time, and said "I want you to redraft the amendment and try one more time." His staff then modified the amendment to cap the number of workers at 350,000, while Wilson worked the phones to ask senators who'd previously voted against the measure to reconsider.[137] Wilson then offered his revised amendment, insisting that western agriculture's "financial survival" depended on it; Simpson bitingly responded that the proposal represented "not survival but greed." Having managed to convince five senators to switch votes as a result of his cap, Wilson prevailed by a 51–44 vote.[138] It was, according to Lawrence Fuchs, "the first time [Simpson] had been beaten on a really big issue" on the Senate floor.[139]

Simpson did accept a soft sunset amendment on employer sanctions from Senator Kennedy, whose provision required the General Accounting Office, the official congressional watchdog agency, to conduct three annual studies to determine whether employer sanctions caused "a widespread pattern" of employment discrimination. The Senate also approved another Wilson amendment capping reimbursement to the states for legalization costs at $3 billion over six years.[140] The amount was higher than in Simpson's previous bills but below the $4 billion the Reagan administration had tacitly agreed to accept the previous year. Otherwise, Simpson's core provisions—employer sanctions without the Frank amendment's antidiscrimination unit and the "triggered legalization" that even when implemented retained a 1980 cutoff date, less generous than the 1982 date in the House bill—remained intact. The majority whip faced one final hurdle when Senator John Heinz (R-PA) offered a nongermane amendment on Social Security; as Simpson's biographer noted, "Al took Heinz aside and lowered the boom [telling Heinz], '. . . either you get that damn thing off the bill or I am going to *stick it up your ass!*'"[141]

While the bill, sans Heinz's amendment, passed by a healthy 69–30 vote, support was trending down from the 80 and 76 senators that voted for the bill in 1982 and 1983, respectively. Simpson admitted that he "could not help but notice that we were getting fewer votes each time out."[142] The trend worried the sponsor, since opponents were inching closer to the 41 votes required to uphold a filibuster.[143] Simpson's influence over the body, it seemed, might be slipping.

Passage of the Wilson guestworker amendment was a bitter defeat for farmworker advocates. MALDEF's Richard Fajardo said the Senate had made clear that Mexicans were "welcome as our field hands, but not as our next-door neighbors in the community."[144] Since the similar Panetta amendment had won by a decisive margin in the House the past year, inclusion of the provision in final legislation now seemed all but certain. Wilson's amendment also provoked tough criticism from the *New York Times*, with editorial writer Jack Rosenthal turning a particularly elegant phrase, telling readers that "the Senate finally passed immigration reform, but only after nearly giving away the farm." Rosenthal's piece pointedly called out Attorney General Edwin Meese's ties to growers, noting that while he "professes strong administration support for the legislation . . . the bill has been attacked by White House guerillas before."[145]

House Judiciary chairman Peter Rodino put down his own marker, proclaiming he was "adamantly opposed to any massive importation of foreign agricultural labor" that would "seriously jeopardize the job opportunities as well as the wages and working conditions of American farmworkers."[146] New York Rep. Chuck Schumer was playing the role of a broker between the farmworkers Berman represented and the growers backing Rep. Leon Panetta, and already had begun moderating discussions between the two factions. Schumer responded to the challenge posed by the passage of the Wilson amendment by accurately noting that the outcome of the agricultural worker issue would "make or break" the bill's prospects in the lower body.[147]

Noticeable by their absence in most of the press coverage of Senate passage of the bill and its implications for final legislation were the core members of The Group, who weren't convinced that the Wilson amendment was harmful to their "affirmative defense" strategy. If the bill died now, the press and pundits were primed to blame the "greedy growers" and not, for once, The Group, as the major villains of the piece. And Simpson's "leaner" measure, now without the harmful legal immigration or asylum provisions included in his previous legislation, opened up space for The Group to add proposals they favored, like the Moakley-DeConcini bill.

MOAKLEY-DECONCINI

As he had vowed at the end of the previous Congress, Rep. Joe Moakley's "first order of business" in 1985 was to reintroduce his bill to suspend the deportation of Salvadorans, and Senator DeConcini followed suit in the Senate. Moakley staffer Jim McGovern and the advocates tweaked their legislative formula a bit: the new bill still required temporary protection against deportation for Salvadorans, but left it to the independent congressional watchdog, the General Accounting Office, to determine when it would be safe for them to return.[148] The situation on the ground in El Salvador was mixed: centrist José Napoleón Duarte had been elected president, and the number of death squad killings had come down. Advocates continued to condemn the country's human rights record, and the ACLU noted that the estimate of forty thousand to fifty thousand civilians killed from 1979 to 1984 "can only be appreciated if one recalls that the total population of El Salvador numbers fewer than 5 million."[149] Holly Burkhalter of America's Watch, now known as Human Rights Watch, found that the reduced deaths reflected a more grisly reality, observing that "death squad killings were down only because the urban populist leaders had all been killed."[150]

The Moakley-DeConcini bill was gaining momentum in Congress; just a few weeks after introduction it attracted 154 cosponsors in the House and 24 in the Senate.[151] In April, Simpson held a hearing on the bill, likely reflecting a calculus that although the event might give the issue more attention, it was also an opportunity to kill the effort before it gained more traction. Testifying on behalf of the ACLU, Henderson argued that "documentation of the severity of the human rights situation is thorough, credible, and extensive," and characterized the 112 likely cases of persecution of returnees identified by the group's research as "just the tip of the iceberg."[152] Church World Service's Myers called the bill "a reasonable, modest proposal, well-grounded in the humanitarian customs and practices" of the United States.[153]

Opponents pushed back hard. Assistant Secretary of State Elliott Abrams contended the bill was unnecessary, since the conditions in El Salvador were getting "better and better." Commissioner Alan Nelson of INS made the more potent argument, warning of "an invasion of 'feet people'" if the Moakley-DeConcini bill was adopted.[154] FAIR's Roger Conner added that violence against civilians was a global problem and the bill was unfair to selectively admit victims from one place while excluding others.[155] Coining a phrase he also employed to oppose guestworker programs, Simpson scoffed at advocates' claims that the bill only afforded temporary status. "There's nothing more permanent than a temporary" immigrant, Simpson would say. "They come here, they have a child and that child is an American citizen, and then when you do try and deport them . . . it's impossible."[156] Privately, some advocates acknowledged that while the "temporary" part might be squishy, the need for "protection" was real; as the ACLU's Mort Halperin put it, "We didn't necessarily think all of them would go back. But we had to do the right thing by saving people from a civil war. So even if it was temporary, the next time around, we would do the right thing again and find a way for them to stay."[157]

NCLR had only recently endorsed the bill. When the question of NCLR, at the time a rare "pan-Hispanic" organization, taking a position on the bill first came up in 1983, Raul Yzaguírre demurred. His reticence was linked to the bill's foreign policy overtones; the NCLR CEO feared that taking a position on the legislation could set a precedent that might force to the fore other matters—normalization of relations with Cuba, the status of Puerto Rico, military aid to Central America—that would divide his bipartisan, multiethnic board of directors. He also noted the decidedly mixed views that Chicano activists had of the leaders of the burgeoning Sanctuary movement. Refugee advocates saw them as heroes, but some Chicano activists were irritated by, and likely envious of, the attention given to Central Americans by the same purported progressives that had ignored lynchings, repatriations, segregated schools, and other deprivations experienced by Mexican Americans and Mexican immigrants for a century.

Now in a staff position, Dan Purtell kept pushing NCLR to endorse the bill; he'd taken the lead on researching the subject and it had become "his" issue. Executive vice president Emily Gantz McKay was also supportive, having befriended and mentored Salvadoran leaders in DC, many of whom lived or worked in her Mount Pleasant neighborhood.[158] But Yzaguirre kept putting them off. Then late one night in early 1985, as one of The Group's meetings was breaking up, the ACLU's Henderson happened to run into the Yzaguirre. As they were chatting, Henderson handed Yzaguirre a copy of the ACLU report *Salvadorans in the U.S.: The Case for Extended Voluntary Departure*.[159] Yzaguirre politely flipped through the report, in a manner suggesting he intended to put it aside as soon as the ACLU lobbyist left. But Kamasaki later found his boss sitting on the dilapidated old couch in the NCLR "policy shop," reading the report's appendix, which documented, sometimes in graphic detail complete with photos and affidavits, beheadings and other confirmed killings of some deportees to El Salvador. The NCLR president was shaking his head, visibly moved as he read the affidavits from relatives of deportees who'd been killed and Salvadoran newspaper stories on the murders. "Ok," Yzaguirre said to Kamasaki, "Let's take this to the board." At its next meeting, NCLR's board voted overwhelmingly to "support legislation to suspend deportation of Salvadoran and other Central American refugees until conditions in their home countries permitted their safe return."[160] Purtell's coauthorship of NCLR's position paper on the bill recognized the signal role he'd played in the outcome.[161]

But as a practical matter the Moakley-DeConcini legislation had no future as a stand-alone bill. One issue was Mazzoli's opposition, which greatly displeased the bill's sponsor. "*Roman*, why aren't you helping me?" the frustrated Moakley was known to say, deliberately mispronouncing Mazzoli's given name of "Romano," and declining to use "Ron," the subcommittee chair's preferred nickname.[162] One could conceive that it might pass the House, but not the Senate, where Simpson opposed it vigorously. If somehow it managed to pass Congress it faced a certain Reagan veto. It needed what legislators and lobbyists call "a vehicle"; a must-pass bill to carry it past the opposition, and the most obvious was immigration reform. But this seemed at best an unlikely marriage: most of the Moakley-DeConcini bill's supporters opposed the immigration bill, and vice versa. But you never know in the legislative process. As 1985 came to an end, NCLR's Purtell and Kamasaki, along with a group of other advocates, met with a staffer whose boss opposed the immigration bill and supported Moakley-DeConcini. Asked whether the legislator might support adding protections for Central Americans to the broader immigration reform package, the staffer responded sharply, shaking her head and speaking loudly so all in the room could hear: "I hope you're not suggesting that we support adding something we like to a bill we oppose!" Once she made sure that the congressman's official position was known, the aide slyly turned to the NCLR staff, who were known to be exploring compromise . . . and winked. "Wow! Did you see that?" Purtell asked Kamasaki as they left the office. Maybe, they mused, a Moakley-DeConcini amendment strategy might work after all.

NEGOTIATIONS

At the beginning of 1986, the major roadblock preventing movement of the Simpson-Rodino-Mazzoli bill was the unresolved question of temporary workers, and the single mechanism authorized by Chairman Rodino to address it was a private, backroom, three-way negotiation. The key players: Representatives Howard Berman, described by *Congressional Quarterly* reporter Nadine Cahodas as a "master strategist," representing farmworker interests, and Leon Panetta, a political "natural" representing agricultural employers, with Chuck Schumer, known for his "energy and zest," playing the role of mediator.[163] Although the principals and their allies largely kept the details of the negotiations to themselves, there was plenty of very public advocacy involved, as the various actors all played to their respective constituencies.

And this meant Dolores Huerta, vice president of the United Farm Workers union, was at center stage, serving as Howard Berman's political alter ego during the high-stakes negotiations. Dolores Clara Fernández Huerta had deep union bloodlines: her father was a coal miner and a member of the United Mine Workers, while her mother was a cannery worker who belonged to the United Cannery, Agricultural, Packing and Allied Workers of America.[164] She helped César Chávez start the Agricultural Workers Association, and then the National Farm Workers Association, the precursor to the United Farm Workers union that would bring both considerable fame.[165] The comely, diminutive, and fiery Huerta also had a powerful record of achievement in her own right: she had directed the brilliantly conceived international boycott that immeasurably expanded the union's reach and visibility, and eventually led to a landmark collective bargaining agreement with the California grape industry in 1970. She'd played a major role in the passage of the California Agricultural Labor Relations Act in 1975 that was sponsored by then assemblyman Howard Berman, and later became something of an icon in Latina and feminist circles, racking up numbers of awards almost too numerous to list.[166]

The prestige of the United Farm Workers had fallen since its halcyon days in the 1960s and early 1970s; César Chávez was in declining health and no longer active or visible on the national political stage. Huerta, increasingly the public face of the UFW, had some liabilities: according to one scholar, for a variety of reasons her "esteem within the union had diminished since the early 1970s."[167] Her pro-immigration credentials were also open to question given the union's mixed record on the issue. She once disrupted a hearing on temporary workers by loudly accusing growers who were testifying of labor law violations, which precluded publication of the transcript for fear of reproducing what some saw as libelous charges.[168] She often admonished staffers and lobbyists against any compromise, arguing that "worse is better" because only truly terrible conditions motivated the masses to embrace revolutionary change. This was anathema to DC types who lived on compromises.[169] And to some, this "incendiary revolutionary" pose seemed somewhat affected, given her longtime role as a Democratic party insider, although Huerta herself seemed completely unbothered by the apparent contradiction.[170]

Still, Huerta had a lot of other things going for her, not the least of which was her powerful personal connection to Berman, who in turn had the confidence of Peter Rodino. Although the two had "a complicated relationship," the mutual loyalty she had with César Chávez was also unquestioned.[171] But one thing was clear: on immigration reform Dolores Huerta, perhaps alone among farmworker advocates, could speak with absolute authority on behalf of Chávez and the UFW. She also brought to the debate an "out of the box," audacious proposal: instead of fighting with the growers over the scope of protections afforded to the temporary guestworkers, she asked, "Why not legalize them instead?"[172] Legalized agricultural workers automatically would have the same labor rights as others in the industry, rendering moot the excruciatingly complex and contentious bargaining over the specific rights and protections afforded to the guestworkers, and the concomitant obligations of their employers.

It wasn't a completely new concept. The UFW's own legislative representative had testified in 1983 that legalization of undocumented farmworkers would be preferable to the creation of new guestworker programs.[173] Various grower groups had also discussed versions of the proposal, but they thought it "too good to be true," and unlikely to pass political muster.[174] Lawrence Fuchs recalled that a variation of the concept had been raised in deliberations of the Select Commission but was thought to be "politically unrealistic."[175] The idea had even come up during The Group's drafting of the Roybal bill, but like their predecessors they agreed that one legalization program seemed controversial enough; adding another, and one benefitting a single industry at that, seemed well beyond the pale. But with Huerta's and Howard Berman's prodding, the idea of a special, farmworker-only legalization gained traction in the negotiations early in 1986. As Panetta aide Chris Womack later told researcher Rosanna Perotti, at the "third or fourth meeting" around late February 1986, "We said, what are we fighting over? . . . The green card is clearly the key vehicle. So why not develop a system to expedite the green card protections for people who work in agriculture?"[176]

Based on Schumer's assurances that negotiators were close to a deal, in March Rodino said that he'd soon take up the bill in his Judiciary Committee.[177] But it turned out that going from an agreement in principle on the basic concept of a farmworker legalization program to a final deal required working through a host of details. The negotiators would tentatively agree on a compromise, check-in with their constituents, and then be forced to backtrack, reopening the issues all over again. Huerta was a frequent presence in DC during negotiations, and former Berman aide Mark Schacht, now at California Rural Legal Assistance, a legal aid group, made a few appearances as well. But when they weren't in town, Berman interrupted the talks so often by saying "I have to call California"—meaning Huerta and/or Schacht—that it became something of a running joke among the negotiators.[178]

Two months later, with no agreement in sight, Rodino postponed a scheduled May committee markup, this time until June. Rep. Lungren charged that the delay put the bill in mortal jeopardy, telling the *Los Angeles Times* that, "The body isn't in the morgue yet, but this is giving it the last rites," while a FAIR spokesman called Rodino's "go-slow" approach "a death of a thousand cuts."[179] The *New York Times*'s Robert Pear had a slightly different take. Acknowledging that some viewed the attempt to broker a deal between farmworkers and growers as an "impossible dream," the savvy reporter noted that Schumer "is not naïve; indeed, he has a knack for legislative maneuvering honed in the New York State Assembly." The story also reported that Rodino was a "shrewd tactician" who, "after 30 years in Congress, has begun to think of his place in history" and would not take lightly the failure to pass an immigration bill.[180]

Negotiations between Rep. Esteban Torres and subcommittee chairman Mazzoli also intensified as the markup approached. In addition to frequent staff-level meetings between Rep. Torres's aide Albert Jacquez and Mazzoli staffer Lynn Conway, the two principals engaged in a series of private, one-to-one negotiation sessions.[181] Rep. Torres's agenda, shaped in close consultation with The Group, included a strengthened legalization program, retention of the Frank antidiscrimination protections, a sunset on employer sanctions, an absolute assurance that no major guestworker program would be included, and other improvements.[182] The Group also began meeting on a near-weekly basis with

Schumer. The check-ins usually were fairly cursory, with the congressman giving the groups his view on the status of the all-important farmworker negotiations while they updated him on the Torres-Mazzoli discussions.[183]

LIGHT 'EM UP!

After a visit home for Christmas, Kamasaki returned to DC in 1986 with clothing that his father, who'd be bedridden until his death a year later, no longer needed; fortuitously, father and son were almost exactly the same size. The initially bittersweet act of wearing his dying father's hounds-tooth jacket and sixties-era skinny ties was soon overtaken by the discovery that they were old enough to be "vintage cool." The NCLR staffer wasn't the only member of The Group facing tragedy. In May 1986, Michael Myers's brother was killed in an automobile accident. As one of their meetings ended on a chilly late spring evening soon after Myers's return from the funeral, Kamasaki noticed that the Church World Service advocate had a beautiful topcoat that was considerably dressier than his typically understated style. Thinking he understood what had happened, he sidled up to his colleague and said quietly, "Hey Michael, nice coat." Myers replied with a knowing, wan smile, "Yeah, it's my brother's."[184] But neither could dwell on their wardrobes or their family troubles, because Bert Corona was coming to town.

That spring, as it did at least once a year, The Group coordinated a major "lobby day" activity with Bert Corona and his deputy Natívo Lopez, of the Hermandad Mexicana Nacional (Mexican National Brotherhood). Bert Corona was, according to Latino scholars, a leader "of historical significance . . . , one of the most important *Mexicano* political leaders in the United States."[185] He began his career as a labor organizer with the Longshoreman's Union in California in the late 1930s, through which he built close ties to the Congress of Industrial Organizations. Although Corona himself never joined the Communist Party, his circle of friends and colleagues in the CIO and the then-nascent Mexican American civil rights movement on the West Coast did include some party members.[186] One might note, however, that no lesser an authority than President Lyndon B. Johnson once said that no one who had come of age in the Depression era "who wasn't a communist or a dropout was worth a damn."[187]

By any standard, Bert Corona was worth a damn. He founded the Mexican American Political Association that in the 1960s was, wrote one journalist, "at least in California, the dominant Mexican-American political organization."[188] He'd also worked with the Community Services Organization, the organizing network closely linked with Edward Roybal and César Chávez in the 1960s, although he'd broken with Chávez on the immigration issue. According to Corona:

I did have an important difference with Cesar. This involved his and his union's position on the need to apprehend and deport undocumented Mexican immigrants who were being used as scabs by the growers. We differed. The Hermandad believed that organizing undocumented farmworkers was auxiliary to the union's efforts to organize the fields. We supported an open immigration policy, as far as Mexico was concerned, that did not victimize *mexicanos* because they did not have documents. We did not support deportation of people.[189]

Sixty-seven years old in 1986, the still spry Corona was personally soft-spoken, polite, even genteel in his dealings with others. Although some were wary of being too closely associated with the socialist Corona and kept him at arms-length, the Hermandad had a real constituency of thousands of undocumented workers and their families, and wasn't dismissed easily. Corona and his sharper-edged deputy, Natívo Lopez, also had their "good cop-bad cop" routine down to an art form. The elderly, dignified Corona spoke slowly and soothingly, even as he was advocating positions that by contemporary standards were fairly extreme. His younger associate was stylistically Corona's opposite, a fiery speaker who didn't hesitate to threaten opponents and allies alike with dire consequences if they failed to toe the line. Even his friends and colleagues privately, but gleefully, often referred to him as "Negativo" Lopez.

Corona's *métier* was neither the one-on-one "lobbying visit" nor the mass rally; his self-described most effective tactic by far was one he'd been using regularly since first coming to DC to fight against the Kennedy-Rodino employer sanctions legislation in the 1970s. As he explained in his biography, he regularly led groups of undocumented workers to DC: "We would take as many as forty to fifty people on a lobbying trip. We sponsored fundraisers to pay for the travel costs, or got individuals to donate certain amounts. The undocumented themselves turned out to be the best spokespersons for their cause."[190]

They met with lawmakers to tell their stories—the circumstances of their entry to the US, how most could not readily obtain legal visas, and why they wanted to stay. Some legislators who'd demonized the population as a group unexpectedly found themselves sympathizing with individual unauthorized immigrants as human beings; exactly the response Corona sought. His approach revealed a core truth about lobbying: it was far easier for lawmakers to dismiss certain positions in the abstract than it was to tell real, live people that they wouldn't help them.

Though they often disagreed on policy positions and strategy, Corona worked closely with The Group, made easier because LULAC's Joe Treviño had once worked as an organizer for Corona, and they still maintained a close personal relationship.[191] NCLR's Yzaguírre also had a soft spot for Corona. Still, the DC-based lobbyists in The Group and Corona's grassroots organizers had a more-or-less permanent, barely concealed, love–hate relationship with one another.

To oversimplify (but only slightly), as a general rule, DC lobbyists tend to view activists from the field as either "hicks" who need to be schooled in the ways of Washington, or extremists who don't accurately represent the "real" rank and file. And to some extent these stereotypes are true. Conversely, with only modest exaggeration, grassroots groups are convinced that DC-based lobbyists are at worst sellouts willing to sacrifice substantive interests in return for keeping cozy relationships with the powers that be, or at best, eager to settle, to compromise with opponents for too little gain.[192] However suspicious of each other's motives they were, the two groups desperately needed each other. The national groups required grassroots advocates to pressure lawmakers in their states and districts, and Corona knew that he needed the national organizations' help to schedule meetings and provide inside information. The Group welcomed Corona's and other organizers' forays into DC, fully understanding that some of activists' passion occasionally would turn into "friendly fire" directed at the lobbyists themselves. "We always helped Bert because it was very important for the members [of Congress] to hear from immigrants directly," one lobbyist said, while acknowledging, "But it was also important for us to know we would be held accountable by the community."[193]

The in-person lobby days were accompanied by telephone call-in days orchestrated by the DC groups to mobilize those unable to personally come to Washington. It took a few thousand phone calls at one time to shut down the Capitol Hill switchboard, but even a few dozen calls to a particular office on an issue was noticed, especially at a time when long-distance calls were expensive, running as high as a dollar per minute for peak daytime calls. The call-ins were organized weeks in advance through alerts sent via snail mail, augmented by telephone trees where local activists mobilized their colleagues, families, or neighbors who, in turn, were asked to call Congress. When they did manage to pull it off, their success could be highly visible.

Capitol Hill offices in the 1980s had telephones capable of handling a half dozen separate phone lines. The receiver had a band of push-button lights at the base of the instrument, each light representing a separate telephone line, and a master button used to transfer or place calls on hold. A fully lit button reflected a line that was being used; flashing lights signaled callers placed on hold. The ACLU's Wade Henderson reveled in checking in with a series of offices and seeing a full row of blinking lights on the phones, as receptionists fought losing battles to distribute calls to harried staffers or to mollify angry constituents, many of whom had been kept on hold for lengthy periods at long distance rates. We're "lighting 'em up," he'd chortle to The Group at their evening meetings. Henderson's metaphor only partially referred to the rows of lights on lawmakers' phones; he also thought that the one-two punch of meeting with real people while being subjected to nonstop calls from constituents was unusually effective in turning up the temperature on Congress. Eventually, The Group used the phrase "light 'em up" as both a rallying cry and a catch-all term for any activity that generated "heat" on lawmakers.

DEALS

Even as the halls of the House office buildings were being "lit up" by grassroots advocates from the Hermandad or via telephone in the Spring of 1986, insiders knew that events largely hidden from view, like the farm labor talks, would decide the bill's fate. By early June, with frequent assurances from Schumer and the negotiating team that they were close to a deal but with no final bargain actually in hand, Rodino finally seemed to lose patience, or more likely consciously imposed on the negotiators a hard deadline, and scheduled his committee markup for June 17, which continued into the following day. Amendments to weaken or eliminate the legalization program were handily defeated. Attacks on the bill's antidiscrimination provisions were beaten, although a proposal from Lungren that The Group believed would weaken the protection barely lost. The Group also managed to win an amendment by Barney Frank to add procedural protections to the Systematic Alien Verification for Entitlements or SAVE program, a high-priority system for the INS, designed to prevent undocumented people from accessing federal benefits.[194] It was a particularly sweet victory for NCLR's Dan Purtell, who had worked closely with Tina Poplawski, an expert on federal benefits from the Farmworker Justice Fund, to craft the language included in the amendment sponsored by Frank to protect lawful residents from being denied benefits due to inaccuracies in the INS databases.[195]

Another amendment by Rep. Schumer, designed to strengthen the bill's verification provisions to minimize the possibility of employment discrimination under employer sanctions, also prevailed at the end of the long first day of markup. Drafted by NCLR and sponsored somewhat reluctantly by Schumer, it succeeded only because of support from Republican Hamilton Fish. The Ranking Republican on the Judiciary Committee, Hamilton Fish IV of New York, was the scion of one of the most distinguished political dynasties in US history. Elected to his Hudson Valley district in 1968, his lineage dated back to 1842, when his great-grandfather, the first Hamilton Fish, was elected to Congress. The latest Fish's father had led an African American regiment known as Harlem's Hellfighters in World War I, and after election to Congress, sponsored the bill establishing the Tomb of the Unknown Soldier in Arlington National Cemetery. A staunch opponent of Franklin Delano Roosevelt's New Deal and a virulent anti-Communist, Rep. Fish also fought unsuccessfully in Congress for measures to help Jews fleeing Nazi Germany.[196] His father, the second Hamilton Fish, served in Congress in the early 1900s after years as Speaker of the New York State Assembly. But the first Hamilton Fish was the most accomplished, having been a New York State governor and US senator, as well as a US representative; he was also secretary of state under President Ulysses S. Grant, and named one of the "Ten Best" ever to have held that post by *American Heritage* magazine.[197]

Consistent with family tradition Rep. Hamilton Fish IV held "conservative views on economic issues" but tended "to be somewhat liberal on cultural issues," according to the *Almanac of American Politics*.[198] He'd served with distinction on the Select Commission, where he was known as "one of its hardest-working" members.[199] He also happened to be a close family friend of Wells Klein of the American Council for Nationalities Service; the upstate New York Fishes had been friendly with the Vermont Campbells from Klein's mother's family for generations.[200] Just before the markup, as a coalition meeting was ending, NCLR's Kamasaki asked Klein to help set up a meeting with Fish to seek his support for Schumer's highly technical amendment to strengthen the employment verification system, explaining that with Schumer preoccupied with guestworkers, they needed another heavy hitter to support the provision. The ACNS head promptly picked up the phone, called Fish's office to request the meeting, and after a brief pause, asked the younger advocate, "Can you head up to the Hill right now?"

Since the meeting had been arranged so quickly, Fish's immigration staffer Peter Levinson wasn't available, but Rep. Dan Lungren's staffer, Kevin Holsclaw, happened to be in Fish's office when the two nonprofit advocates arrived. As Kamasaki handed a copy of the amendment to Fish, Holsclaw walked over and asked whether he could help; the congressman waved the staffer away, instead pulling out his own dog-eared copy of the bill and studying how the amendment would work. Klein interjected at that point, imploring his friend "Ham" to support the provision, and after studying the language Fish agreed. Kamasaki's worry that Holsclaw and his boss Lungren might be a problem—it wasn't a secret that Fish was distrusted by some movement conservatives, a group Lungren was closely associated with—proved groundless as Lungren joined Fish in speaking for the amendment.[201]

But the farmworker negotiators still could not close the deal. The parties had agreed to the core solution of a special legalization program for farmworkers months earlier, but the program's details were proving difficult to resolve. Schumer's role grew from that of a simple mediator to more like an orchestra conductor: he and his chief immigration aide, Alan Greenberg, took care of all of the logistics, set up the meetings in neutral locations, drafted agendas, and developed draft proposals to resolve disagreements.[202] As of the first day of Judiciary Committee markup, the deal's prospects didn't seem promising; both Simpson and Lungren raised concerns about details that had leaked out, but Rodino gave the negotiators one last week to resolve their differences.[203] It all came down to a single final negotiating session that began on June 24, just a day before the deadline set by Rodino. As researcher Rosanna Perotti described the scene:

> Schumer's staff arranged a meeting in which legislators and the major interest group representatives would negotiate—at times together and at times separately—the final details of the agreement. It was the only meeting in which interest group advocates from both sides were present along with legislators and aides. The location was neutral. It was Schumer's turf—the Banking Committee hearing room. To ensure that the agreement would be in final form when the negotiators left the room, Schumer's staff invited an attorney from the Office of Legislative Counsel to work with the group representatives to get acceptable wording for the provisions.[204]

They worked "all day, all night, and into the next morning," according to one lobbyist; Schumer was chief mediator and cheerleader, but more than that. He and his staff ordered pizzas and beverages, with the congressman himself frequently serving food and pouring drinks for everyone, so no one had an excuse to leave the table.[205] As Schumer's staffer later recounted, after a marathon negotiating session, they had a deal, or so it seemed, but Berman kept asking for additional details and assurances. "We went through hours of negotiations, six pizzas, and finally at five a.m. it was all done," Greenberg recalled, "and Berman's still going at it."[206]

Assured that the deal had been struck, Rodino called the Judiciary Committee to order at 2:00 p.m. on June 25, although it wasn't until a couple of hours later that legislative language was publicly available.[207] The Schumer-Berman-Panetta proposal was breathtaking in scope; under its key provision, the Special Agricultural Worker (SAW) program, undocumented "farmworkers who worked 60 man-days in U.S. agriculture between May 1985 and May 1986 would be able to apply for permanent residency."[208] Unlike participants in the "regular legalization" program, SAW workers would be eligible immediately for most federal assistance programs. In a major concession to Berman, SAWs would be able to leave agriculture once they obtained green cards. And to protect growers, so-called Replenishment Agricultural Workers (RAWs) would be permitted to enter if a commission certified the existence of agricultural labor shortages.[209] Ron Mazzoli and Dan Lungren, who had been cut out of the negotiations, both voted against the proposal; the subcommittee chair called it "unparalleled, unprecedented, and unacceptable."[210] Ranking subcommittee member Lungren said that the negotiators were supposed to draw "a racehorse" but instead came up "with a camel."[211]

After a contentious seven-hour final day of markup, at 9:15 p.m., the bill was reported out of committee by a 25–10 vote; the hotly disputed SAW proposal squeaked by with a 19–16 margin.[212] The last major obstacle to immigration reform, it seemed, had been overcome, leading the typically insightful *New York Times* reporter Robert Pear to write about immigration reform, "In the past, various groups fought to a standoff. . . . But things may be different this year."[213]

The bill's sponsors were once again racing the legislative clock. The next step was the sequential referral process, giving committees other than Judiciary that had jurisdiction over a portion of the bill an opportunity to offer their own amendments. Four years earlier, the ten-week delay for the sequential referrals had proven decisive, pushing House floor consideration almost to Christmas Eve, giving opponents the opportunity to engage in the "filibuster by amendment" that killed the bill. In 1983, the six-week sequential referral period after the bill left the Judiciary Committee had moved floor consideration into 1984, where election year politics contributed to its demise. This time, the leadership initially determined that other committees would have a deadline of July 28, or a month after the end of Judiciary's markup, to complete action.

Although committed to a deal-making posture, The Group still instinctively sought more delay; here they were in sync with Rep. Berman, who judged that getting the bill considered at the last possible moment would maximize his leverage. Even though he'd generally prevailed in the negotiations producing the SAW program, Berman noted that at this point "taking time was in my interest. I had internal incentives. I saw a bill passing and wanted it either passed my way or for [the SAW program] to bust up the bill. As we got closer to the end, there were more chances of getting it my way."[214]

The Group added a couple of twists. A few weeks before, as it appeared that the bill would soon be headed out of the Judiciary Committee, Rep. Towns's aide Brenda Pillors arranged a meeting with the House Parliamentarian's office to assess their options. The House Parliamentarian is a nonpartisan, technical support division of Congress, charged with giving members unbiased information and advice; its head is appointed by the Speaker without regard for political affiliation, aided by professional career (nonpolitical) staff.[215] The Parliamentarian's staff members don't generally meet with lobbyists, but they do meet with members of Congress and staff, who occasionally might bring a few lobbyists along. Henderson and a few others accompanied Pillors to meet, perhaps by coincidence, with one of the few African Americans on the Parliamentarian's staff. The staffer was noticeably uncomfortable in the presence of the lobbyists she'd not met previously, but already knew Henderson; clearly, he had done this before.[216]

After learning of other maneuvers that could be used to slow the bill down,

The Group decided to expand the number of committees that would request referrals beyond the four that had done so previously. They also decided to explore whether the one-month period allotted to the sequential referral process might be stretched out. It would be unusual for such an extension to be either requested or granted, since this was the third opportunity that the committees had to review the legislation. The timing was also inconvenient. The committee staffers wondered why they should delay their August recess vacation plans to work on the same, tired old issues; this was precisely what The Group heard when they met in mid-July with staff from several of the affected committees, who indicated that their intention was to dispense with the hearings held in previous years and proceed quickly with markups in order to meet the July 28 deadline.

Henderson wasn't happy to hear of the staffers' hurry to leave town, not from friends and allies that previously could be counted on to go along with the advocacy groups' requests. Informed of their intention to move the bill quickly through their committees, he strenuously objected. Rising up to his full six-foot-two-inch height and pounding his fist on the table, he shouted at them, "That's not acceptable! *We* have amendments!"[217] Whether or not he intended to be intimidating, the sight of the normally erudite, smooth-talking Henderson in full "angry black man" mode had an almost physical effect on the mostly white, politically progressive committee staff, several of whom shrank back in their chairs as if they were about to be assaulted. Immediately the discussion turned to how much additional time the committees should ask for.

The audacity of Henderson's demand was astonishing. To start with the obvious, amendments can only be proposed by those actually elected to legislate, that is, senators and representatives, not advocacy groups. It's true that the ideas, language, and supporting arguments for laws and amendments often originate with lobbyists, who usually are extremely careful to preserve the impression that the lawmakers are in charge, and the advocacy groups are merely assisting them.[218] Typically, advocates will use solicitous language—"Here's what I suggest to advance *your* amendment," or "Would it be helpful for me to draft some *proposed* language to achieve *your* goal?"—to perpetuate the illusion. It was also true that this was the third time around for the same bill, and the staffers might logically have been skeptical that the groups truly had any new amendments to recommend. Henderson's outburst violated all of the unwritten rules, but the committee staffs—all of them—dutifully asked for and then received extensions until August 5, buying an additional week of delay, with a couple receiving even longer extensions.[219]

Meanwhile, Kamasaki had another duty to attend to: preparing for NCLR's annual conference, held each July, which he thought consumed too much of the group's scarce time and resources. As a practical matter, his view was irrelevant—NCLR CEO Raul Yzaguírre loved the conference and it wasn't going away. But after a meeting where the NCLR policy director sharply criticized conference staffers about some purported shortcoming, Yzaguírre asked Kamasaki to remain behind as the gathering ended. The advocate knew he'd probably stepped over the line and steeled himself to be rebuked. Instead, the NCLR CEO pulled out a legal pad and asked his staffer, "Where do you think the money to cover your lobbying budget comes from?" Explaining that under IRS rules, nonprofits needed "unrestricted revenue" to cover expenses for legislative advocacy, Yzaguírre gave his subordinate a quick lesson in the NCLR "budget model." Event sponsorships were "unrestricted," and thus could be deployed to cover lobbying expenses. Noting that Kamasaki had often pushed for larger lobbying budgets, the NCLR CEO said, "A bigger conference means more sponsorships and more unrestricted revenue. If you want a bigger lobbying budget, help me grow the conference. Get it?" Years later, scholars studying Hispanic groups would write that despite constrained budgets, NCLR's management "made the decision to continue with the organization's annual conference despite the cost. This paid off by strengthening La Raza's relationship with its affiliates and by helping to intensify a sense of identity and family [among organizations and leaders] within the Latino community. The organization's strategic approach helped it navigate a difficult time."[220]

Soon afterward Yzaguírre had another unwelcome assignment for his subordinate, personally insisting that Kamasaki meet with a recent Kansas Law School graduate in town looking for a job. With immigration reform about to hit the House floor and with no available staff vacancies in his policy shop, the NCLR staffer thought the last thing he needed was an unessential meeting, and his demeanor during the "informational interview" reflected the attitude that he had far more important things to do. As it turned out, the law graduate didn't need his help, as she quickly found a job on Capitol Hill. But Kamasaki might've been more courteous had he known that a decade later she'd be covering immigration issues for the Clinton White House, and two decades later she'd become his boss. The young law school graduate was Janet Murguía, who succeeded Yzaguírre as NCLR's president and CEO in 2005.[221]

BACK FROM THE DEAD

Following the August recess, all eyes were on the Rules Committee, which would decide the terms under which the bill would be debated on the House floor. Furious at having been excluded from the crucial farmworker negotiations and unhappy with the final product, immigration subcommittee chair Mazzoli and ranking Republican Lungren lobbied heavily for a rule that would allow them to substitute a more traditional guestworker program for the Special Agricultural

Worker program produced by the Schumer-Berman-Panetta negotiations. With Rodino's support, the farm labor negotiators successfully protected their fragile compromise from being amended on the House floor.[222] The Group worked furiously to add the Moakley-DeConcini bill suspending deportation of Salvadorans to the immigration bill. Since bill sponsor Joe Moakley was now the rules panel's second ranking Democrat and heir-apparent to the chairmanship, they had a chance, albeit an uncertain one. Human rights violations in El Salvador were still rampant. During one of his many fact-finding trips to the region Moakley aide Jim McGovern had met with María Teresa de Canales, a leader of the Mothers of the Disappeared who had lost both a son and her husband to the death squads. Soon afterward, Canales herself, who had won a Robert F. Kennedy prize for her human rights work but was denied a visa to enter the US and accept the honor by Reagan's State Department, was abducted, tortured, and imprisoned by the Salvadoran government.[223] Mazzoli still declined to markup the legislation, so Moakley moved the bill through his own subcommittee, an unusual maneuver since that panel rarely acts on substantive bills. The action positioned Moakley's bill to be attached to the larger immigration measure, since legislation reported out of a subcommittee is often favored as a potential amendment to another vehicle.

The administration's opposition became more entrenched. After its earlier 1983 mail survey had been unpersuasive—postcards from people that the US embassy claimed didn't feel persecuted couldn't explain the real, often headless bodies turning up in San Salvador's streets with alarming regularity—the State Department commissioned the International Committee for Migration (ICM, now the International Organization for Migration) to conduct an "independent" study of the fate of returnees to the country. ICM sent surveys to some 3,800 returnees, finding only 35 that complained of persecution. ICM itself cautioned that its study shouldn't "be considered as a scientific data base upon which to construct definitive analyses of situations of returnees."[224] But this didn't prevent Reagan officials from claiming that the study "shatters the sanctuary movement's claim to legitimacy."[225] The ACLU responded with its own earlier computer match findings, and argued ICM's report had been "misused and mischaracterized."[226]

Moakley-DeConcini supporters had deeper suspicions. ICM was a respected international group associated with, but not formally a part of the United Nations, that worked with governments to solve specific migration problems.[227] Such an organization typically would be reluctant to insert itself into domestic political debates of its member countries, but the ACLU's Henderson thought he knew why it did so in this case: the chief of ICM's Washington office was one Gretchen Bolton, née Gretchen Brainerd, who happened to be married to John Bolton, then a high-ranking Reagan Justice Department official who'd previously worked at State.[228] Henderson conjectured it wasn't coincidental that ICM's State Department-funded study seemed designed to support the administration. Ironically, prior to her marriage to Bolton, the former Gretchen Brainerd had served on the board of the American Immigration and Citizenship Conference, which had later merged with Rick Swartz's National Immigration, Refugee and Citizenship Forum.[229]

CWS's Michael Myers and Henderson didn't just want to include Moakley-DeConcini into the broader immigration bill, they demanded that, like the SAW compromise, it be "walled off" from amendments. They prevailed after Rules Committee Chairman Claude Pepper (D-FL) added Nicaraguans to those protected against deportation.[230] The eighty-six-year-old South Florida congressman had made his national reputation as an outspoken advocate for Social Security, a highly popular position in a district where nearly a third of the population was age sixty-five or over. His district was also home to many Nicaraguans who'd fled the Sandinista regime, a group closely allied with the Cuban American community that by this time constituted nearly half of Pepper's constituents.[231] With the right-leaning Nicaraguans and the left-leaning Salvadorans both covered, Myers and Henderson thought they might prevail.

On September 24, the Rules Committee reported a "modified closed" rule that did not allow amendments to either the SAW or Central American provisions. The rule was brought up the next day, but the combination of the agricultural workers compromise and the last-minute addition of the Central American program, with no chance of amendment, proved to be a "bridge too far" for previous GOP supporters of the legislation. Backed by the Reagan administration, which opposed both of the major new additions to the bill, Lungren lobbied furiously against the rule. He called the SAW provision "an abomination," and heatedly "denounced" the temporary protections for Central Americans.[232] Schumer, Berman, and Panetta responded mainly with political arguments, indicating that their proposal was "the only compromise that united growers and labor and that without their support, the bill would die."[233] But with a nearly unanimous Republican conference augmented by some of the bill's traditional Democratic opponents, Lungren won the day, as the rule was defeated by a 202–180 vote; Republicans opposed the rule by a 145–13 margin, while Democrats supported it by a 167–57 vote.[234]

It appeared the bill was dead. For several days, as Lawrence Fuchs put it, "everyone rushed to play the game, 'Who Murdered the Immigration Bill?,'" but the "blame game" was soon put aside as Schumer led another round of negotiations to resurrect the legislation.[235] The New Yorker was going well above and beyond the call of duty: his wife was nine months pregnant, forcing Schumer to commute daily to and from the capital instead of the typical schedule of staying three or four nights in DC and heading home for weekends. "I'm just dying here," he confided to a fellow negotiator at one meeting, "I don't know how I'm going to make it."[236] But he persevered, flying to DC early every morning, working long days to seek compromises that would permit a reconsideration of the bill, and then taking the last flight home at night.

On September 29, the *New York Times* urged all sides, especially President Reagan, to try and resurrect the bill, observing that there was still enough time to pass the measure "if there's enough will."[237] Literally that day, as one scholar documented, "Mazzoli was accommodated" by Schumer, Berman, and Panetta, who agreed to a series of modest changes to the farmworker compromise. The House "Ag trio" then reached out on September 30 to Simpson, knowing his support was key to obtaining the Reagan administration's acquiescence, but the Senate majority whip was a harder nut to crack, demanding and receiving commitments for more changes.[238] With Mazzoli and Simpson on board, Rodino, who was said to be "ready to wash his hands of the negotiation" then re-engaged.[239] Republican holdout Lungren finally provided his grudging acceptance on October 7.[240]

An unrelated issue gave them a few more precious days. Congress had been scheduled to adjourn as early as October 10, and members involved in close races had begun to miss floor votes to maximize their time on the campaign trail.[241] But the administration asked Congress to stay in session until mid-October, just in case the summit meeting between President Reagan and Soviet leader Mikhail Gorbachev, held October 11–12 in Reykjavik, Iceland, produced a nuclear weapons treaty requiring Senate ratification. Although the talks later stalled and failed to produce an agreement, they came tantalizingly close to a deal.[242]

The immigration bill negotiators needed every bit of this extra time. On October 8, a group of House members met again with Simpson and Sen. Pete Wilson to pre-conference the agricultural provisions.[243] The Senators eventually signed off, but not before Howard Berman raised one more issue. As Simpson aide Carl Hampe recalled:

> During the pre-conference meeting with the members, the final item was the issue of getting Legal Services Corp. representation for agricultural workers. Berman brought it up after everything was done, and said, "I want to raise something but I don't want to be an asshole when we're this close together" [bringing his thumb and index finger within an inch of each other]. And Simpson, moving his arms apart, blurted out, "But you were an asshole when we were this far apart!" Everyone lost it—Schumer was doubling over. There had just been so much tension, and it was a release.[244]

Berman eventually prevailed on this issue as well, but at first glance, it looked like the House negotiators had given up a lot during the often-heated week or so of discussions. Instead of most farmworkers needing to have worked for *sixty* days in agriculture in either of two previous years to qualify for the SAW program, they now were required to have worked at least *ninety* days in each of the past three years. They wouldn't immediately receive green cards, but be temporary residents for a year before becoming permanent residents. But critically for Berman, he'd retained the concept of labor mobility—the SAW workers would not be bound to a single employer as they were under the H-2 program, and would be able to leave agriculture once they obtained temporary status.[245] Mazzoli's aide Lynn Conway thought at the time that although they appeared significant, the changes were more of the face-saving variety, unlikely to limit the actual scope or size of the program, a judgment proven correct by subsequent events.[246]

Still, they had a deal that was supported not only by the Schumer-Berman-Panetta trio, and thus by Rodino, but however reluctantly by key subcommittee leaders Mazzoli and Lungren, and Senators Simpson and Wilson as well. And, finally, at long last, the bill was supported by the House leadership. As the negotiations were wrapping up, House Majority Leader Jim Wright walked into his office and asked his chief aide, John Mack, "What's up?" After briefly covering a couple of other issues, Mack told his boss that "it looks like the immigration bill is all wired"; Wright, who had been at best a tepid supporter of the legislation previously, responded simply, "Maybe that's best. 'Bout time we did something."[247]

But it wasn't quite wired yet; Schumer had another problem; he'd been forced to make one additional concession to obtain Republicans Fish and Lungren's support: the new rule allowed a motion to strike the Moakley-DeConcini protections from the bill. As Schumer ticked off the changes to The Group in their weekly check-in before the bill went back to the floor, the advocates strenuously objected. Since the rule would expose the Moakley-DeConcini bill, one of their core priorities to possible defeat, they argued, they needed one more "sweetener," and demanded addition of the sunset amendment, sponsored by Rep. Robert García, to end employer sanctions after a certain period. Schumer was exasperated. "You guys are good negotiators," he began with a bit of faint praise; but then sternly lectured them, "Every time you get something, you want more. You can't keep moving the goalposts."

Schumer refused to carry their water on the sunset issue, but Rep. Esteban Torres did; he had previously pushed for inclusion of the García sunset proposal as one of key priorities through his back-channel negotiations with Ron Mazzoli, and now renewed his demand.[248] As a result, much to García aide Lisa Navarrete's surprise, she soon received an unexpected phone call: "It was weird after four years of doing this [unsuccessfully attempting to win the 'sunset' provision] to have the immigration subcommittee call you up and say we want your amendment, and we want to get it through the rules committee. We didn't want to believe it. We were so happy."[249]

Debate on the revised rule began on Thursday, October 9, again with Rep. William Natcher in the chair. Rep. Roybal complained about the process used to revive the bill, while Rep. González called the Rules Committee a "Star Chamber." Notwithstanding inclusion of his sunset amendment, García maintained his opposition, complaining that the immigration bill was "like Rasputin, it refuses to die." From the right, Wisconsin's James Sensenbrenner and previous supporter Rep. Hal Daub concentrated their fire on the "triple amnesty" of the regular legalization program, the SAW provisions, and the Moakley-DeConcini protections for Salvadorans. But a parade of supporters, including some reluctant ones like Mazzoli and Florida's Bill McCollum, a very enthusiastic Bill Richardson, a member of the Hispanic Caucus's moderate faction whose amendment to create a border revitalization zone had also been included in the bill via the proposed rule, and heavyweights Minority Whip Trent Lott and ranking member Fish all weighed in, joining with Rodino to ask the core question, "If not now, when?" The rule was adopted by an overwhelming 278–129 vote.[250]

The rule as passed permitted only fourteen amendments, and the outcomes of most of those were all but decided even before debate began; there was little interest in further debating details of a bill whose passage seemed a foregone conclusion. Amendments from the Education and Labor Committee to permit state employment agencies to avoid verification requirements and to provide a twenty-four-hour grace period before employers were required to verify the immigration status of new hires lost. Rep. Steve Bartlett's amendment to strike criminal penalties from employer sanctions, which had passed the House previously, was beaten decisively.[251] Next up was a provision from Rep. Lungren to modify the Frank amendment to allow an employer to hire an American citizen over a legal immigrant if both were "equally qualified." The Group opposed the innocuous-sounding provision because they feared Lungren's proposal would create an automatic defense against any bias charge from legal residents who weren't yet citizens. But once the amendment was permitted—a concession to Lungren for acceding to the agricultural workers compromise—they knew defeating it would be virtually impossible. Barney Frank admitted as much when he said, "I do not like this amendment, but I do not like it less than I do not like some others." With that, the Lungren amendment was agreed to by voice vote.[252] Rep. Sensenbrenner's amendment to strike the entire Frank amendment was handily beaten by a 260–140 vote after Rodino, Fish, and Mazzoli all spoke against it.[253]

At 8:40 p.m., Rep. Bill McCollum again tried to strike the legalization program. The amendment had been handily defeated by a 233–195 vote in the previous Congress, with only five absent members. But advocates in The Group were worried, because already many of their supporters were campaigning: 41 members had been absent from the earlier vote on the Frank amendment. McCollum's amendment to kill legalization was defeated by an uncomfortably close 199–192 margin, with 41 members not voting.[254] Some later argued that the narrow margin reflected growing public opposition to amnesty, but analysis of the actual vote count revealed that those voting against legalization had actually gone down, from 195 in 1984 to 192 two years later; it was the failure of many supporters to cast votes because they were on the campaign trail or out fundraising that produced the tight margin.

At 10:15 p.m., the final amendment to the bill, a motion to strike the Moakley-DeConcini provision, was barely defeated by a 199–197 vote, with 37 members absent.[255] House Speaker Tip O'Neill then paid a special tribute to Rep. William Natcher, who he had called on again to preside over the debate on the immigration bill, expressing his "profound thanks" for the "exemplary job" that had been done.[256] O'Neill's gesture prompted a spontaneous standing ovation from the House; acknowledging the applause, the dignified Natcher first "bowed to his colleagues, then turned and bowed to O'Neill."[257]

The House passed the bill by a resounding 230–166 vote.[258] Nadine Cahodas of *Congressional Quarterly* reported it was a "stunning reversal" that the House had "approved an overhaul of the nation's immigration laws less than two weeks after the controversial legislation was pronounced dead."[259] The *New York Times* confirmed the notable shift in the bill's politics: "The 64-vote margin by which the House passed the bill . . . was a major departure from the 5-vote margin of approval in 1984. In 1984, House Democrats opposed the bill 138–125, and Republicans supported it 91–73. But this week House Republicans opposed the bill 106–62, and Democrats supported it 168–61.[260]

Led by Rep. Torres, five of the eleven-member Congressional Hispanic Caucus voted for the bill, a stark contrast to the group's unanimous opposition to the previous two iterations of the legislation.[261] Beyond the substantive improvements in the bill attractive to Democrats, the approval of Rep. Torres's moderate Hispanic Caucus faction gave other members who were wary of offending Latinos "permission" to support the bill; as Rodino aide Skip Endres later noted, "We always knew there were a lot of votes there."[262] The overwhelming vote for the bill also vindicated the quiet back-room discussions that Mazzoli and his aide Lynn Conway had been having with Rep. Torres and his staffer Albert Jacquez for nearly a year; both sides had proven they could deliver when it counted. The legislation, now tilting decidedly left-of-center, entered the home stretch, bruised but still standing.

BEHIND CLOSED DOORS

Rep. García's amendment to sunset employer sanctions, which had never garnered anything remotely resembling majority support in committee or on the floor in either body, had been incorporated into the bill, by fiat, in the Rules Committee. The Group knew that the only conceivable chance they had to retain the provision was for García to agree to vote for the final bill if the amendment was kept by the conference committee. The ACLU's Henderson and NCLR's Kamasaki, accompanied by the National Forum's Rick Swartz, went to see Rep. García and his aide Lisa Navarrete to make their case. García had always appreciated the advocates' contributions, saying to one of the lobbyists years later, "Ed Roybal and I may have been the members, the ones voting, but we were taking all of our cues from you guys."[263] In turn, the lobbyists were deeply grateful to García, a Puerto Rican who wasn't obligated to carry their water on what was perceived as a "Mexican" issue.[264] He never "mailed it in"; he'd personally attended markups, stationed himself on the House floor during lengthy debates, and even pushed his way into conference committee deliberations by buttonholing conferees as they came and left the sessions. The *New York Times* noted, "García brought a flair . . . to the role he played in political fights over immigration," a role that the lobbyists in The Group uniformly praised.[265]

The advocates appreciated his diligence, accessibility, straight talk, and good humor, but also got a kick out of the congressman's foibles. García often referred to his provision to sunset employer sanctions as "my sunshine amendment"—confusing his amendment's nickname with so-called sunshine laws promoting transparency in government. At their pre-conference meeting, the advocates discussed the rare leverage the congressman had due to the precarious state of the bill, the substantive benefits of having the proverbial "second bite at the apple" to repeal employer sanctions if the sunset provision was retained, and concluded that supporting the bill was the only chance to retain the provision in conference. García was intrigued at the prospect of actually winning his "sunshine amendment," but after opposing the bill for nearly five years, he just couldn't bring himself to reverse course; his aide Navarrete later said of the meeting, "they convinced me, but not him."[266]

Conferees were appointed and began deliberations on October 10, with the *New York Times*'s Robert Pear understatedly observing that lawmakers were "moving with unusual speed."[267] The conferees met in open session for several hours that Friday, a day *Congressional Quarterly* noted, was "traditionally not one of Congress' most productive times except when adjournment is near."[268] They made little progress at first, so when they gathered again in open session the next day, Simpson surprised them by announcing there would be no votes that day, saying, "We are here because we are going to do all the 'root canal' work and get every issue laid out on the table—and get the maximum of shrieking and gnashing of teeth out of the way right now. Next Tuesday, since Monday is Columbus Day, the bill will be ready for consideration."[269]

After several hours in open session with little progress made, according to Simpson: "Peter Rodino called me aside for a word. He said, 'Meet me in my office. Let's see if you and I alone can't hammer something out. If so, we'll take the rest of them along with us. . . .' So on a bright and sunny morning before the next (and possibly last) conference committee meeting, the two of us sat down."[270] Simpson often belittled "what conference committees do in their infinitely grotesque wisdom. You haven't lived until you've seen a conference committee."[271] It pleased him greatly that this time he and Rodino would conduct their negotiation mainly behind closed doors. The back-room negotiation frustrated the US Chamber of Commerce's Virginia Lamp, who complained at being held at arm's length from the process.[272] But if Lamp felt excluded, The Group was engaged in the negotiations, albeit one step removed, via ongoing communications with the conferees. As Swartz said later, "We may not have been in the room physically, but we *were* in the room, so to speak."[273] As Rodino and Simpson privately, in the senator's words, "thrusted and parried . . . shoved and jousted . . . pushed and pulled," then resolved most of the major issues, the Senate majority whip and his House counterpart felt a little like "Dr. Frankenstein . . . attaching an electrode to a grayish looking toe and shooting a charge in there—and then watching that big lug get up off the table and stagger out into the marshes."[274]

At first, the bill looked like a Frankenstein monster to The Group. As predicted, because he'd vowed to continue to oppose the bill regardless of the outcome of the conference negotiations, "García's sunset provision was the first to go," one scholar documented.[275] Rep. Moakley reluctantly agreed to gut his provisions to protect Central American refugees after Attorney General Meese told Rodino that if the language stayed the "whole bill is dead."[276] Then, in the back-and-forth between the negotiators Simpson agreed to give up his "triggered legalization" formula but in return insisted on a 1981 legalization cutoff date; Rep. Esteban Torres thought this violated the understandings he had reached with Mazzoli and Rodino to retain the House program's more generous 1982 date, and crucially, most of the House bill's legalization substructure that had originated with the Roybal legislation. As Ellis Cose recounted, "Word leaked out that the bill would have a 1981 legalization eligibility date instead of the House date of 1982. Dismayed, Esteban Torres—who was not a member of the negotiating team—confronted conferees and snapped, 'You may still get a bill, but you will lose us (Hispanics) forever.' Subsequently Rodino fought for the later House date, which Simpson accepted."[277]

Having worked through the major elements of an agreement over the long holiday weekend, Rodino and Simpson privately orchestrated one final maneuver. When the conference committee formally reconvened on Tuesday, October 14, as Simpson recalled, "Peter Rodino . . . said, 'Let's go back into the large room just outside of this hearing room. Just us members. No staff. . . . Three hours later we all walked out of that room—with a bill!"[278]

When all was said and done, the Senate had acceded to the House position on forty-three issues, while the House had conceded on forty-six.[279] One final detail of the deal required some bending of Congress's usual budget procedures. The distinction between authorizing legislation, which sets policy, and appropriations bills, which actually allow agencies to spend money, is enforced both by rule and tradition. Most legislative bodies allow points of order against appropriations for programs that aren't already authorized.[280] Until recently, the rule was routinely violated to allocate funding to favored projects whether or not they were authorized, provisions derided as "earmarks." The reverse, directly spending money in authorizing legislation like the immigration bill, is exceedingly rare since the powerful appropriations committees jealously guard their turf.

Unable to get an increase on the amount of reimbursement to states for legalization above the $4 billion agreed to, state-local lobbyists, led by Texas's lobbyist Dianne Stewart, demanded a guarantee that they'd receive every penny of the $4 billion everyone had signed off on, protecting it from future annual appropriations debates.[281] With a nudge from Majority Leader Wright, who'd promised LULAC and NCLR funding in return for accepting his amendment requiring legalization applicants to pass English tests or courses, first Rodino, then Simpson, and finally the White House agreed to the unorthodox move. Rodino aide Skip Endres then got a call from his boss, who said, "Skip, we gotta appropriate the money in the bill itself." The deal required a redraft of the bill's "State Legalization Impact Assistance Grants" section to both authorize and appropriate the funding, creating what Rodino's staffer called a "$4 billion reverse earmark." Endres then got Rules Committee staff to waive budget-related points of order to the bill, and a little after midnight called his counterpart on the Appropriations Committee, so he could at least claim to have given him a "heads up" on what was coming.[282]

On October 15, the House passed the "Simpson-Rodino" conference report by a vote of 238–173, with about two dozen members absent. Still deeply invested in the bill that no longer bore his name, Ron Mazzoli summed up the feelings of the majority, saying, "This is historic legislation, watershed legislation. It is not a perfect bill, but it is the least imperfect bill we will ever have before us."[283]

Simpson had hoped to bring the conference report up before the Senate the next day, October 16, but ran into another snag. Unlike the House, where the all-powerful Rules Committee, with the quick stroke of a pen, can dispense with technical matters like a violation of budget procedures, in the Senate virtually everything is debatable, and Texas Sen. Phil Gramm insisted on having his say. Together with fellow budget hawks Warren Rudman (R-NH) and Ernest "Fritz" Hollings (D-SC), the Texan had coauthored a landmark bill of his own, the "Gramm-Rudman-Hollings Deficit Reduction Act of 1985," requiring automatic spending cuts—known as sequestration—if budget targets weren't met.[284] Never a fan of the bill, Gramm was unhappy with the procedure used to fund the states, which circumvented the budget rules his previous legislation had set in place. He spoke at length against the bill on October 16, making a point of order against the violation of budget procedure, forcing a vote on a motion to waive the rules, which passed 75–21.[285] Gramm did not formally initiate a filibuster, but Simpson was taking no chances, and the next day successfully invoked cloture, the procedure to shut-off any potential filibuster, which passed 69–21.[286] The last barrier in the way of immigration reform had been removed.

THE BEST LEGISLATION POSSIBLE

With passage assured, interest groups focused on articulating their formal positions on the bill. FAIR had long prepared itself to swallow amnesty in return for employer sanctions, but the SAW program initially tipped the organization's board of directors against the bill. Simpson himself intervened, noting the considerable Hispanic Caucus support for the compromise despite the inclusion of employer sanctions, telling FAIR executive director Roger Conner, "You're not giving in as much as the Hispanics are."[287] Conner himself ultimately came to a judgment that achieving a foot in the door on employer sanctions was worth the cost, and convinced his skeptical board to go along.[288] But FAIR's deep misgivings were obvious when its spokesperson said, "We wanted a Cadillac, we were promised a Chevy, and we got a wreck."[289]

Of the major interests engaged in the debate, the decision was perhaps easiest for the AFL-CIO. Although in the words of one academic, "Labor did not go all out" for the immigration bill, it had laid out clear markers required for its support, insisting on inclusion of employer sanctions, and the absence of a major guestworker program. With the Schumer-Berman-Panetta deal having resolved their last major concern, organized labor enthusiastically supported the legislation.[290] MALDEF had long before decided that it would, as one scholar noted, push a no-compromise position; since IRCA included the hated employer sanctions provisions, it opposed the bill in the strongest possible terms.[291] One might have expected the ACLU to do the same. Like MALDEF and other litigating organizations, the group historically was "more worried about the downside than the upside" of proposed legislation, according to Mort Halperin, director of its Washington office, but he and his colleague Wade Henderson thought: "We needed to have an affirmative, as well as negative position; you get to the point where you have to say 'yes.' The bill was as good as it's gonna get, [so] we quietly helped it pass, even if we couldn't formally or publicly support it. Because if [legislators] knew that you would denounce them no matter what they do, then what's their incentive to talk to you?"[292]

Ultimately, the rest of The Group ended up in a similar stance as the ACLU: nominal opposition or a neutral posture on the legislation, but with a heavy "forward lean," in Capitol Hill parlance.

There were powerful countervailing pressures at work for NCLR, which had actively encouraged previous opponents, especially Rep. Esteban Torres, to take significant risks by engaging in negotiations to improve the bill. On the eve of the House vote on the conference report, NCLR CEO Raul Yzaguírre had a difficult, uncomfortable, sometimes even heated conversation with his friend Esteban Torres. There was an unwritten rule in Congress that if the authors accede to another legislator's request for major changes, then the beneficiary is obligated to support the final product. The corollary is that the interest groups that encourage elected officials to seek such improvements are expected to publicly support those lawmakers, to provide them with "political cover," in the vernacular. After the bulk of his requests to Mazzoli and Rodino, most instigated by NCLR and The Group, had been included in the bill, Rep. Torres felt obligated to support the legislation. He expected NCLR to do the same.[293] Congressman Torres contacted Yzaguírre to call in his chit, characterizing NCLR's intention to praise parts of the bill while nominally opposing the whole package "cowardly," and warning that he wouldn't forget their failure to support him "the next time you ask me to do something with you."[294]

Yzaguírre was conflicted. On the one hand, the final product—no cutbacks in legal immigration or asylum, a far more generous legalization than in the original legislation, an agricultural labor program providing legal status and full labor protections, and a guarantee that the discriminatory effects of employer sanctions would be monitored and partially mitigated—would have easily earned NCLR's support at the beginning of the debate. And Esteban Torres was a friend; the NCLR president did not take lightly displeasure of a lawmaker he expected to work with closely for many years into the future. On the other hand, over time Yzaguírre's opposition to employer sanctions had hardened, had "toughened up" in his staff's view.[295] And while Yzaguírre was loyal to Torres, he was more intensely loyal to his staff, which insisted that as a civil rights organization NCLR could not, on principle, formally endorse a policy like employer sanctions that it believed actually promoted new forms of discrimination.

Others, including Reps. Bill Richardson and Albert Bustamante who also called Yzaguírre to urge NCLR's public support for the bill, were more easily finessed. "Bill [Richardson] was laughing, saying 'we're playing in the big leagues now so you gotta go along with the leadership,' and Bustamante was calm and understanding," Yzaguírre told his staff. But the difficult call with Rep. Torres troubled him. Although he rarely involved himself in details like the wording of press releases, the NCLR CEO insisted that their statement on the bill not use the word *oppose* and ought to emphasize the positive aspects of the bill. He further indicated in no uncertain terms that he expected NCLR to "get some ink" (newspaper coverage) on this nuanced posture to give his friend Esteban Torres as much political cover as he possibly could.

So two nights later, on October 17, as the Senate was debating final passage, Kamasaki found himself with an oversized envelope stuffed with news releases, heading to the Capitol press gallery intent on hand-delivering NCLR's statement to reporters as they finished their stories. Initially denied entry by a security guard who offered to distribute the releases—the gallery technically was open only to credentialed press and congressional aides—he eventually snuck in with the help of a friendly staffer; given his boss's instruction to "get some ink" he wasn't about to trust some anonymous guard with this task. Kamasaki viewed himself as a serious analyst, not some "flack." But there he was, shoving his organization's statement in front of reporters as they typed their stories. As uncomfortable as it made his subordinate, the late evening jaunt produced exactly what Yzaguírre intended; the next morning's *New York Times* story included this passage: "Raul Yzaguírre, President of the National Council of La Raza, a Hispanic organization, said he could not endorse the bill, but he described it as 'probably the best immigration legislation possible under current political conditions.' "[296]

The Senate passed the conference report that night by a 63–24 vote. The legislative debate on the Immigration Reform and Control Act was, at long last, finally over.

CHAPTER 7

Aftermath

CELEBRATIONS AND GATHERINGS

O n November 6, President Ronald Reagan signed the Immigration Reform and Control Act of 1986, inevitably called "IRCA" by insiders, in what the *New York Times* called, "a brief ceremony in the Roosevelt Room of the White House, surrounded by Administration officials and members of Congress who were instrumental in passing the legislation."[1] Some present at the bill signing blew off some steam at a different kind of celebration when *Congressional Quarterly*'s Nadine Cahodas hosted an "IRCA Survivors" party; as Simpson recalls:

> Several weeks later, many of us involved in immigration reform—legislators, staff, supporters and detractors, reporters—got together to celebrate the end of our work. The party was held in the D.C. apartment of one of the reporters who covered the issue through the years. The invitation described the event as "survivor's party." The place was festooned with banners, signs, sketches, slogans, and graffiti, all of them commenting on our long journey together.[2]

The party featured group sing-alongs to popular tunes with immigration-themed lyrics by Cahodas and other reporters: "The Yellow Rose of Texas, they used to call Marie, she used to be illegal, but she got amnesty."[3] Other titles included "Somewhere Over the Rio," and an "Immigration Rag" to the tune of "Vatican Rag," a satirical ditty by Tom Lehrer, a piano-playing singer-songwriter popular in the 1960s.[4] A portion of the rag's rewritten lyrics:

First you get down on your knees,
Crawl through sewers hide in trees,
Get a job, establish ties and
Legalize, legalize, legalize[5]

The only members of The Group invited to the party were the National Immigration Forum's Rick Swartz and the ACLU's Wade Henderson, evidence of their stature as perceived by Cahodas. But Swartz, accompanied by girlfriend and future wife Jeannette Noltenius, an exile from El Salvador, was "disgusted" by the sing-along, thinking some of the new lyrics revealed "latent racist sentiments" too common in the immigration debate, and left early.[6]

On the day the bill was signed, Reps. Esteban Torres and Edward Roybal "announced the formation of a national ad hoc coalition on implementation of the Immigration Reform and Control Act" to promote "successful implementation of the new law's legalization program and prevention of discrimination under the new law's employer sanctions provisions." Listed at the top of the press release were the American Immigration Lawyers Association, National Council of La Raza, Mexican American Legal Defense and Educational Fund, National Council of Churches, American Civil Liberties Union, US Catholic Conference, National Immigration, Refugee and Citizenship Forum, and the National Association of Latino Elected and Appointed Officials.[7] Rep. Torres had supported the bill while Rep. Roybal had opposed it; the joint release reflected a *rapprochement* between them, as well as a similar closing of ranks among the groups on the pro-immigrant side of the spectrum. They might've differed on legislative tactics, but faced with the reality of the new law, they were compelled to work together.

Implementation—turning often aspirational or abstract concepts in legislation into actual programs in the real world—is not so much a single act but an ongoing process. Bill drafters and deal cutters in the proverbial smoke-filled rooms might imagine how their prized provisions should work but complex laws are not self-executing; they often require armies of federal civil servants, state-local government officials, and private sector players to execute a coordinated series of actions. Scholars of the art of implementation have learned that enacting "policy is often entirely distinct from implementing it—or for that matter, having it work."[8] Experts agree that high-quality implementation requires a *process* that should: be "evidence-based" or "evidence-informed"; include "dedicated resources and dedicated [staff] time"; have an "ecological perspective," that is, account for the individual, institutional, and interpersonal factors that can affect how the policy will actually be carried out; and include "monitoring, measurement, and continuous learning."[9] Ideally, all of this takes place in a planned sequence, choreographed if you will, with all of the relevant stakeholders at the table and working in sync.

Measured against this ideal, the new law's implementers were heavily handicapped. IRCA's major features—such as a large-scale legalization—had never been tried before in the US. Entering almost completely uncharted territory in an American context, those engaged in the new law's implementation had little previous data to rely on.[10] Nor would the major players easily cooperate; as Bill Ong Hing, a law professor and former head of the Immigrant Legal Resource Center wrote, "Congress left implementation of legalization in the hands of two key "players"—the INS and CBOs [nonprofit community-based organizations]," which were longtime adversaries.[11] Even when major actors cooperate, as one expert summarizes, too often "there is simply too much spontaneity, chaos, and irrationality in [human] nature" for ideals envisioned by legislators or bureaucrats "to be a reliable predictor of the most salient current events."[12]

The INS faced two implementation challenges. INS needed to draft, issue for public comment, and finalize formal regulations—regs—interpreting the legislation. And it was required to stand up an infrastructure—staffing, offices, furniture and equipment, etc.—to handle applications for legalization. The regulation drafting process itself is extraordinarily complex and resource-intensive; according to one description, "A single federal rule can take years to develop and put in place, consuming significant resources and political capital along the way.[13] But INS didn't have years to draft program rules; IRCA required the legalization and SAWs programs to begin within six months of the bill's passage.[14] Perhaps serendipitously, the timeline put the programs' start dates on the Cinco de Mayo Mexican holiday. Nonprofits' challenges mirrored those facing INS. Shaping regulations to ensure a generous legalization program—an "advocacy" function—was a priority. They, too, needed to build an infrastructure to assist potentially millions of applicants to navigate the amnesty process, a "service" function. They also envisioned aligning the nonprofits into a coherent field, an activity requiring vision, tact, and diplomacy. Like INS, the nonprofits were drawing up their legalization blueprints while constructing the building; they needed a plan to harmonize their sector's disparate interests.

PLANS AND SHIFTS

Rick Swartz was a man with the plan. He'd always had a vision of building a broad, diverse field of pro-immigrant organizations, and IRCA's passage offered an opportunity to bring that vision to fruition. Knowing implementation would require an even larger coordinated effort than the legislative phase, with funding from the San Francisco-based Rosenberg Foundation, in 1983 the Forum had organized a series of meetings, attended by some thirty organizations, to begin planning for legalization. Another series of planning meetings occurred in summer 1984, when it appeared virtually certain that the bill would pass.[15] What emerged was both a strategy and a division of labor. The strategy combined aggressive "outsider" advocacy with careful "insider" negotiations to produce the most generous legalization permissible.

The advocates would advance their own vision of how legalization should be implemented, and attack the government's efforts as inadequate; this constituted one part of their "outside" game. Legal groups—led by the National Center for Immigrants' Rights, the San Francisco Lawyers Committee for Civil Rights, AILA, ACLU, and the Immigrant Legal Resource Center—would sue the government when it fell short. They also needed "insider" negotiations with INS. The US Catholic Conference and other VOLAGS, with a long history of partnership with the government in refugee resettlement, would lead the inside game. Groups with constituencies that included advocates and service providers would play multiple roles.

Swartz had a typically ambitious vision for the Forum's role in implementation: he hoped to organize his members to shape the regulations, create a clearinghouse to provide information to local organizations counseling legalization applicants, monitor employer sanctions to identify discrimination, and raise funding—for the Forum itself and for its members—to accomplish all of this. In his vision, the Forum would lead the national effort to shape how the law played out while building stronger state-local cooperation, a vision he'd first articulated in 1985.[16]

Not everyone agreed with Swartz's vision that gave his National Immigration Forum *the* central role in the process. Some Forum members believed that Swartz's organization instead should "staff" but not necessarily "lead" the effort. Others, such as the Forum board chair Wells Klein of ACNS, thought that by pursuing this expansive agenda Swartz was neglecting his institution's crucial, if pedestrian, administrative duties.[17] A third set of players, small immigrants' rights groups increasingly led by immigrants themselves, thought they were closer to the immigrants most likely to be affected by the law than the DC-based players, and were demanding a greater say in the positions that pro-immigrants groups would advocate for and who should receive philanthropic funding. Despite the tensions, most agreed on the need for a coalition effort to support implementation of the law, and that the National Immigration Forum would play a critical, if not necessarily commanding, role.[18]

Within a week of IRCA's passage a meeting was held to organize the "Ad Hoc Coalition."[19] Two main task forces were created: one on regulations chaired by the AILA's Warren Leiden, itself divided into sub-task forces on various issues, and another on outreach and public education, cochaired by the garment workers' Muzaffar Chishti and NCLR's Charles Kamasaki, although the latter's irregular attendance left the chair duties largely to the former.[20] Weekly task force meetings were held in November, mainly to plan for a major national conference in Washington on December 15.[21] The December conference had two goals: organize the pro-immigrant sector to shape the regulations and other policies that would govern implementation (an advocacy function) and help national and local groups prepare for implementation (a service function). Although less than two weeks elapsed from the time invitations were sent and the meeting date, and despite proximity to the holidays, the gathering was enormous, attended by some three hundred lawyers, advocates, and service providers from around the country, not just from traditional immigrant gateway communities but even from fly-over states.[22]

The Ad Hoc Coalition's conference was chaired by ACNS's Wells Klein, who presided over the plenary sessions from the raised dais normally occupied by members of Congress in the huge Caucus Room in the House Cannon building on Capitol Hill, and he enjoyed the experience immensely.[23] Swartz might've preferred a more prominent role for the National Immigration Forum itself. But Klein and other VOLAGs resisted what they saw as Swartz's attempt to control what had always been their turf—provision of immigration and related services to newcomers. Eventually a compromise was worked out whereby the Ad Hoc Coalition maintained a separate identity, but the coalition's letterhead acknowledged that it was "a task force of the National Immigration, Refugee and Citizenship Forum."[24] Regardless of the underlying tensions, the coalition emerged from the meetings "organized and energized," Swartz recalls, with "stronger relationships between advocates in Washington and in the field."[25]

Well before the conference, coalition members had already begun shaping the forthcoming regulations. Believing that INS might more likely be swayed by a major law firm than by advocacy groups, Swartz persuaded his former employer Hogan and Hartson, the prestigious DC-based law firm, to develop draft regulations on legalization both to inform coalition members' positions and for submission directly to the agency. He also hoped the INS might see the firm's engagement as a potential threat, that if the firm had agreed to provide pro bono legal analysis to the groups, it might follow up with litigation if the advice wasn't followed.[26] AILA's Warren Leiden also obtained the assistance of several law firms to support the coalition's regulations work, as did other organizations, both in DC and in the field.[27] With materials drafted by AILA and a dozen other groups, initial draft regulations on behalf of the Ad Hoc Coalition's legalization task force were submitted to the INS on the final day of 1986.[28]

This pre-regulation level of activity was almost unprecedented. Most stakeholders await draft regulations before drafting and submitting formal comments. Others engage in advocacy activity through the press to try and shape upcoming regulatory decisions. A few bold groups, especially those who fear they might be on the losing end of agency actions, might be brave enough to threaten litigation. Those with strong grassroots constituents may orchestrate their field networks to submit joint comments as well. And stakeholders with connections in Congress encourage legislators to weigh in. The Ad Hoc Coalition did all of this, and more. Part of the motivation for the furious activity was fear: the advocates didn't believe that the Reagan administration's INS was invested in an inclusive legalization program. The intense advocacy during the normally quiet holiday period was also driven by a strategy; as Swartz recalled, "We wanted to set a high standard for what was considered acceptable, not through rhetoric but through rigorous analysis. We also made sure INS knew it was being watched carefully."[29]

There were technical considerations as well. AILA's Warren Leiden and CWS's Michael Myers had written many of the features of the legalization program that originated in the Roybal bill and added to IRCA as amendments; they were able to offer highly authoritative interpretations of what Congress intended. There was also a more subtle aspect of the campaign aimed at agency worker bees responsible for actual drafting of the rules. While some envisage that government lawyers have limitless resources at their disposal to draft regulations, reality is far different. Most federal departments actually are understaffed, and an agency's political appointees learn over time that some of their career legal staff are incompetent, others hold views antithetical to those of agency heads and thus resist rather than help implement administration policy, and a few actively undermine it by leaking unflattering information to the press or to political opponents. Agency heads soon learn not to trust these career staff with delicate assignments.

INS and its parent agency the Justice Department might have had, say, a dozen lawyers that theoretically could draft the IRCA regulations, but as a practical matter the largest burdens fell on perhaps half that number. Knowing they would be heavily overworked in trying to draft thousands of pages of regulations in the midst of the holiday season, the advocates believed that submitting rational, well-argued draft proposals backed by reputable law firms' legal analyses might not only be persuasive on the merits, but would be seized on by overburdened agency lawyers looking to save time. The strategy worked even more effectively than the advocates had hoped; Chishti remembers that as the year ended it was becoming clear that while they weren't winning every battle, they "were clearly setting the agenda."[30]

As is common at the end of major legislative campaigns, there was considerable turnover on and off Capitol Hill. Phyllis Eisen had moved on from the National Immigration Forum, and after a period of consulting accepted a senior position at the National Association of Manufacturers.[31] Michael Myers joined Sen. Kennedy's staff at the end of 1986, and State of Texas lobbyist Dianne

Stewart moved to a new position with the American Public Welfare Association; among her duties were monitoring IRCA implementation for the trade association of human service program administrators.[32] Mazzoli aide Lynn Conway left Congress to practice law with Monte Lake, one of the architects of the SAW program. The ACLU's Carol Wolchok, a key player in advancing the Moakley-DeConcini bill, accepted a position with the American Bar Association, heading up a new center on immigration policy.[33] Dan Purtell had left NCLR earlier that year to attend law school, replaced by a new immigration policy fellow, Rose Briceño, who focused on preparing NCLR affiliates to assist legalization applicants.[34] She played a major role that winter as her supervisor Charles Kamasaki's father died in December after a lengthy illness.

The changes went beyond personnel. AILA created a nonprofit arm, the American Immigration Law Foundation, in part as a vehicle to raise grants from foundations. It promptly attracted a grant from the Ford Foundation to create a brief bank—sample briefs for practitioners to appeal decisions by INS to deny legalization applications. It also served as a back-up center for litigators challenging INS rules themselves.[35] Now known as the American Immigration Council, it expanded its mission, and today serves as AILA's research and policy arm and operates several discrete programs.[36] The National Immigration Forum started an "IRCA clearinghouse" to collect and disseminate information on the law's implementation to its members. INS and the VOLAGs believed that at least half of the applicants for legalization would apply through their agencies and other nonprofits dubbed Qualified Designated Entities, or QDEs, in IRCA.[37] All of the VOLAGs, including ACNS, Lutheran Immigration and Refugee Services, Church World Service, and World Relief—the immigration and refugee arm of the National Association of Evangelicals—expanded to prepare for amnesty.

Of the VOLAGs, the US Catholic Conference would play the dominant role: it had the program capacity and the majority of legalization applicants were expected to be predominantly Catholic Latinos. Nick DiMarzio hired Mary McClymont, a former Justice Department and ACLU Prison Project attorney, to direct the church's legalization program. The Prison Project was one of the ACLU's most successful initiatives, winning a series of cases that forced both federal and state prison officials to meet basic standards for the inmates under their care.[38] Few of McClymont's cases actually went to trial; most were resolved through consent decrees, agreements between the parties overseen by judges. In negotiating these agreements, McClymont says she learned "how to engage in step-by-step consultations, in good faith, to achieve a fair resolution" for both sides. Without experience in immigration law but with deep interest in international and refugee issues, after IRCA passed and the Catholic Conference position opened up, McClymont jumped at the chance, signing up in December

1986. She was joined by Luis Torres, a specialist in farmworker issues, and Peggy Gleason, who developed special expertise on family law issues.[39] The team worked in basement space around the corner from the Catholic Conference's main offices, then located between Scott and Thomas Circles on Massachusetts Avenue in downtown DC.

McClymont's team provided back-office support for over one hundred local legalization programs, many run by local arms of Catholic Charities USA, a separate legal entity with "bureaus" in each of the 145 Catholic dioceses in the country. CCUSA personnel were heavily credentialed, reflecting a priority of group's famed executive secretary Monsignor John O'Grady, who headed the group for over four decades beginning in 1920.[40] Other dioceses ran their own projects; larger dioceses hired lawyers to assist amnesty applicants while smaller programs relied mainly on volunteers. McClymont and her team had no formal authority to dictate how local church units should operate; as scholars of the program pointed out, "Bishops have absolute administrative authority in their diocese."[41] Still, the national headquarters staff was enormously influential; Vanna Slaughter, who headed the respected Dallas Catholic Charities program, noted decades later, "The [immigration legal services] field still owes Mary McClymont for the review and quality control process she developed" for legalization, versions of which are still used by providers today.[42]

DiMarzio led negotiations defining terms under which QDEs like the US Catholic Conference would receive government funding. The administration had decided legalization would be "self-financing": applicants' fees would have to cover all program costs, including contracts with QDEs. This put immigrant assistance organizations in a bind. They were concerned about the deterrent effect and financial hardship that high fees could place on amnesty applicants, especially families with more than one applicant. But they didn't want to lose money either, and as the largest service provider, the Catholic Church had the most to lose if government funds didn't cover its costs. The US Catholic Conference thus urged a congressional appropriation that would allow both lower applicant fees and more generous support to the QDEs.[43]

Toward that end, in early 1987 DiMarzio led a delegation of AILA's Warren Leiden, ACLU's Wade Henderson, and NCLR's Charles Kamasaki to meet with Rep. Mazzoli to seek support for a special appropriation for legalization. Mazzoli was clearly still smarting from The Group's longtime opposition to his bill. It didn't help that Henderson and Kamasaki were giggling like schoolkids as the meeting began. Lawmakers adorn their outer public offices, which double as waiting rooms, with home-state-themed art and other memorabilia; Mazzoli had hung a huge painting of a pastoral Kentucky horse farm scene, complete with African American stable workers, just outside the entrance to his private inner office. The African American Henderson glanced at the painting, did a quick double-take, and then whispered to Kamasaki, "He's got a painting of 'darkies' in his office!," referring to the offensive term for black field hands once included in Stephen Foster's song "My Old Kentucky Home."[44] Both began laughing, only partially suppressed, as Mazzoli opened the door and beckoned them to enter his inner office.

The meeting began auspiciously; the advocates knew that Mazzoli agreed with their view that IRCA did not require legalization to be self-financed.[45] DiMarzio thanked Mazzoli for supporting generous regulations, which the chairman acknowledged, then laid out the case for more funding: the large number of low-income applicants in the eligible population, the potential deterrent effect of high application fees, and the unnecessary financial hardships that would be placed on recipients. Mazzoli listened politely, nodding in agreement at several points. But when DiMarzio turned to the US Catholic Conference's challenge of trying to staff up to prepare for legalization in the face of uncertainty regarding the funding it would receive from the government, Mazzoli's mood soured in a flash. "I'm Catholic. I *know* the church has money," he said. Losing his normally studied formality as he slammed his hand on his desk, he declared in a raised voice, "You need to pony up some jack!"[46] The meeting ended quickly.

DiMarzio seemed stunned by the outburst, but others in The Group were used to harsh reactions from the subcommittee chair; Warren Leiden thought it was "quintessential Mazzoli."[47] An appropriation was impossible without Mazzoli's backing, so legalization was to be entirely self-financed from fees paid by applicants.[48] The resulting fiscal squeeze forced radical reductions in the size and scope of the nonprofits' legalization programs. It also cemented the precedent, still followed today, that the cost of virtually all services to immigrants, including visa and naturalization applications, are borne by the immigrants themselves.[49] But they left with one consolation: a colorful new addition to their lexicon. When faced with splitting a dinner check or sharing costs for an event, they'd race to tell each other to "Pony up some jack!"

OLD DOGS, NEW TRICKS

As 1987 began, the INS seemed determined to prove that it was possible for an old dog to learn new tricks. Many doubted its ability to implement legalization; indeed, in writing an explicit role for nonprofit QDEs in the bill, Congress assumed that the agency could not, on its own, make the program work.[50] INS surprised its former nonprofit adversaries in planning for amnesty; citing interviews with INS staff, Bill Hing wrote that it wanted to make " 'the maximum' effort to refine IRCA implementation plans and regulations in 'the most open manner.' "[51] On January 20, 1987, INS commissioner Alan Nelson took what he called the "unprecedented step" of releasing "informal preliminary draft regulations" for public review and comment. INS requested that comments on the informal draft regulations be submitted to INS by February 5, which would then be analyzed by the agency before publication of proposed regulations in the *Federal Register*. Following the requisite thirty-day review and comment period, INS planned for final rules to be issued well before the beginning of the legalization and SAW programs in early May.[52]

Having submitted its own draft regulations earlier, the coalition was ready to meet this challenge despite the two-week turnaround time. On February 5, the coalition submitted detailed comments on the legalization program, prepared largely by AILA and the US Catholic Conference and endorsed by some twenty-five national organizations. The advocates' comments highlighted several dozen changes the groups thought were required to "permit the vast majority of those who are statutorily eligible to be legalized in an efficient and economical manner."[53] Also included in the package was a memo CWS's Michael Myers drafted just before he'd left to join Kennedy's staff, outlining how INS should interpret the program's "special rule for determination of public charge" to permit the many low-income people in the undocumented population to adjust their status if they hadn't relied on public assistance.[54] The Hogan and Hartson law firm submitted its fifty-five-page set of formal comments to the INS, largely mirroring those submitted by the coalition.[55] Rep. Rodino weighed in as well, indicating in a February 13 letter to Attorney General Meese that he was "deeply disturbed" that the direction of the INS draft regulations on legalization would result in an insufficiently generous program.[56]

March 1987 was a critical month for those engaged in implementation, as they worked on multiple tracks to prepare for opening of the legalization program on May 5. One track focused on program regulations; another was funding. INS was scheduled to finalize contracts for and start accepting bids from QDEs in March. The process was fraught with conflict. Over years of informal negotiations, both INS and major groups expected that QDE contracts would be based on a "cost-plus reimbursement" model—combining a *per-applicant* cost and an amount for overhead—used for refugee resettlement, a model that covered most, if not always all, of the nonprofits' expenses. But in March, the agency announced it would reimburse QDEs only $15 per *completed application*, plus an additional dollar for overhead. INS argued that it wanted to control costs to applicants, but nonprofits responded that the funding wouldn't cover assistance to those that sought their help but either didn't apply or that applied directly to INS instead of through QDEs. As a result, only six hundred nonprofits initially applied to become QDEs—far fewer than expected—and those that did were forced to seek outside resources to supplement government funding.[57] Even before legalization started, many nonprofits—eventually estimated to reach 20 percent—began dropping out of the program.[58]

INS worked feverishly to open and furnish 107 "legalization offices" and fill two thousand positions to process applications, purchase new computer equipment and software to support application processing, and print millions of new forms.[59] It made some canny decisions, like separating its new legalization offices from existing district offices that many thought were too closely identified with enforcement. It also re-hired recently retired federal employees who needed only minimal training to serve as senior executives; at the agency's request IRCA allowed these retirees to return to federal service without losing their pensions by waiving rules against "double-dipping."[60] The nonprofits faced similar logistical challenges, with a difference: they needed to hire and train staff, buy supplies and equipment, and often rent new space knowing that government revenues wouldn't cover their costs.[61]

The advocates and the INS were soon engaged in a host of other disputes. Once the draft regulations hit the streets, the coalition and its allies provided most of the public comments, and won more than they lost. On one key issue—defining what absences would be permitted in determining "continuous residence" in the US since the January 1, 1982, legalization eligibility cutoff date—the draft INS rules limited single absences to 30 days at a time with no more than 150 days in the aggregate. As David North and Anna Mary Portz noted in their detailed, authoritative post-legalization report to the Ford Foundation: "The commenters ganged up on the INS on this issue; all 130 of them who responded in writing on this point said that INS was being too rigid . . . . INS [eventually] agreed, in the proposed regulations, to [allow] up to four 45-day absences with a total length of 180 days. The final regulations maintained this position."[62]

The next round of the rules issued in mid-March, published as "proposed regulations" in the *Federal Register*, reflected dozens of similar wins for the coalition. But controversies remained; the fee for legalization applicants was hotly contested. Rep. Torres and the coalition argued for a fee of no more than $30–$50, while the INS eventually decided on a $185 fee for adults, $50 for children under eighteen, and a "family package deal" capped at $420, not including a variety of other fees for a medical exam, fingerprints, and photos.[63] A half-dozen other major eligibility issues remained in dispute, but none brought forth more emotion than the question of "family unity." Many undocumented families contained people—often the male breadwinner—who'd arrived in the US before the eligibility cutoff date of January 1, 1982, but had spouses and children who arrived afterward and thus weren't eligible. Advocates demanded that INS adopt a uniform national policy that ineligible family members would receive protection from deportation, to both maintain family unity and encourage program participation; the government insisted on flexibility to address the issue on a case-by-case basis.

If anything, the advocates were losing ground on the "public charge" issue, a provision in immigration law since the nineteenth century designed to exclude prospective immigrants that were likely to become a burden to taxpayers. Legalization advocates believed that applicants' previous undocumented status had forced many to work in the underground economy at below-poverty-level wages. "Mixed-status" families with both undocumented and lawful members added a complication, since citizen children might have received benefits—to which they were perfectly entitled—but past receipt of public assistance was often used as a basis to invoke the exclusion. The law did not permit a waiver for applicants for permanent residence; however, IRCA's two-step process—where legalization recipients first received temporary residence followed eighteen months later by an application for permanent status—did permit a waiver at the first step. The advocates wanted the initial waiver to give applicants the chance to earn above-poverty-level wages once they were able to legally work, but the first-step waiver included in the first round of the draft regulations mysteriously disappeared in the final rules.[64]

Nevertheless, when final regulations were published in the *Federal Register* on May 1, less than a week before legalization's scheduled start date, the *New York Times* characterized them as more generous than expected.[65] Muzaffar Chishti agreed, noting years later with perhaps a little hyperbole, "My God, they accepted 75% of our recommendations in the regulations!"[66] The advocates had indeed won more battles than they'd lost, perhaps more than they had any right to expect, but they wanted to put maximum pressure on the INS to keep ceding ground.

I'M FROM WASHINGTON AND I'M HERE TO HELP

A few LULAC chapters were involved in implementation, but there was no national effort to coordinate their work.[67] Joe Treviño, who had succeeded Arnoldo Torres in 1985, left LULAC in September 1987 to enter the private sector.[68] It wasn't until the tenure of Belen Robles (1994–1998) that LULAC increased presidential terms from a single year to two years, effectively doubling presidents' tenures, assuring greater stability of the organization. LULAC also substantially strengthened its administrative and fundraising systems in this period.[69] But at the height of IRCA implementation, LULAC was without the leaders and staff who'd played formative roles in the organization's immigration policy strategy. MALDEF's role in legalization was also modest in comparison with its previous high profile on immigration policy, due in part to an internal schism. In January 1987, a faction of the MALDEF board of directors sought to replace president and general counsel Antonia Hernández with former New Mexico governor Toney Anaya. She sued and won a temporary restraining order against the action, and in March the full board voted to retain Hernández, giving her a minimum two-year term in order to "dispel any misinterpretation by the public that this will continue—we have put that behind us."[70] Hernández, in fact, led MALDEF with distinction for nearly two more decades.

By contrast, NCLR ramped up for legalization. Its CEO Raul Yzaguírre always insisted that his group play a dual role as an advocate for the community at large and an umbrella for a network of local service groups, believing this kept NCLR "relevant at every stage of the process."[71] When program opportunities arose, it often held "consultations" with affiliates to jointly develop program strategies, as it did in mid-February 1987.[72] NCLR informed the three dozen affiliates in attendance that it had decided not to apply for QDE status. Instead, Wells Klein was on the agenda and offered to include NCLR affiliates as part of ACNS's QDE application.[73] ACNS became a major resource to NCLR's network, allowing the less experienced Latino groups contemplating a new immigration service to learn quickly about service delivery models, program costs, and the fees groups might charge.[74] ACNS also provided each of its network organizations, including NCLR affiliates, with the Immigrant Legal Resource Center's legalization manual, whose price was prohibitive for many smaller groups. Released within days of the final INS regulations, the manual became "The Bible" for legalization practitioners. ACNS's assistance was especially valuable for NCLR's Rose Briceño, whose portfolio covered training and technical support to the group's affiliates.[75]

Given NCLR's resource challenges, it also helped that Rick Swartz, a key contact point for foundation funders in the field, steered funding for implementation to his members; NCLR soon received grants from the Rosenberg and Joyce Foundations for its immigration work. NCLR was also increasingly visible in the media, telling the *Washington Post* that if INS's draft regulations were adopted, "there would be few persons left to legalize," claiming that "most people in the United States [even US citizens] couldn't meet" the documentation standards the agency was requiring to prove continuous residence in the US.[76] NCLR closely monitored the State Legalization Impact Assistance Grants program—SLIAG, the funding to states and localities to help offset costs of legalization—that had twice nearly brought the bill down. Many of its affiliates offered English-language courses and health services that were eligible for funding, and the principal outside group engaged in SLIAG monitoring was the American Public Welfare Association through a project initiated by former Texas state lobbyist Dianne Stewart, who'd long worked closely with NCLR.[77] NCLR also produced well-regarded policy memoranda on "ancillary" but key issues, including the tax liability of legalization applicants and the proposed addition of controversial AIDS testing to the medical examination required of all immigrants to the US, including legalization applicants.[78]

Its work earned it an invitation to testify at the Senate immigration subcommittee's first oversight hearing on IRCA implementation in early April, with a sympathetic Ted Kennedy in the chair, as Democrats had regained control of the Senate in the November 1986 elections. Kennedy, now staffed by former CWS staffer Michael Myers, reversed the normal practice of beginning with witnesses from the administration followed by scholars and interest groups. Instead, the first panel of witnesses consisted of advocates to whom the administration would have to respond. NCLR's Kamasaki joined the Catholics' Monsignor Nick DiMarzio in addressing legalization, the ACLU's Wade Henderson and a US Chamber of Commerce representative provided their perspectives on employer sanctions, and the United Farm Workers' Dolores Huerta testified on the SAW program. DiMarzio and Kamasaki made similar points, asserting that INS's proposed regulations were too restrictive, the nonprofit legalization infrastructure was insufficient in large part because of inadequate funding, and the lack of effective public education by the agency was leading to widespread confusion in the applicant population.[79] It wasn't surprising that DiMarzio or high-profile groups like the ACLU, US Chamber of Commerce, and the United Farm Workers were on the hearing's coveted opening panel, which typically received the most attention. The invitation to NCLR likely did raise a few eyebrows; Kamasaki himself always assumed he was the beneficiary of residual favoritism from his former colleague in The Group, but Myers later insisted that the invitation was legitimate. "I always liked the way NCLR approached the issues," Myers said, noting the organization's "careful, thorough" work.[80]

Another test of NCLR's stature came when, just before amnesty began, its Kansas City, Missouri-based affiliate, Guadalupe Center, Inc., cohosted a conference on legalization. After the first day of the two-day session, Guadalupe Center director Cris Medina pulled Kamasaki aside to ask for a favor. A rival group reportedly was telling local funders it was the only ACNS network member in the city authorized to conduct legalization assistance, and that the Guadalupe Center would soon be excluded from the network. The threat was significant: as a newcomer to the field, the Guadalupe Center needed ACNS's technical support and imprimatur to raise funding to support its legalization work. In a meeting later that afternoon, the rival group claimed to have "an in" with ACNS and demanded that Guadalupe Center back off. Medina refused to be pushed around on an issue vital to his community. Kamasaki broke the deadlock by suggesting they call ACNS executive director Wells Klein. The rival group backed down, and its relationship with ACNS might've been weaker than claimed.[81] Medina thought "it was huge" that NCLR used its clout to stand up for its local group, and it confirmed the benefits of the center's affiliation with the national organization.[82]

The visit also gave Kamasaki an unexpected education. Ronald Reagan once famously quipped, "The nine most terrifying words in the English language are: 'I'm from the government and I'm here to help.' "[83] The potency of the line wasn't only based in Reagan's "small government" ideology, or his flawless ability to deliver a zinger with a smile.[84] Rather, the phrase's power lay in a fundamental truth: people from Washington, inside and outside of government, inevitably adopt an elitist attitude toward those in the hinterlands. Buttressed by his Senate testimony and his ability to deliver for his affiliate in a local turf battle, Kamasaki possessed more than his share of this arrogance. After the workshop session he asked to observe the group's legalization intake procedure. He soon was literally looking over the shoulder of a middle-aged female clerk, one of the center's lowest-paid staffers, tasked with interviewing prospective amnesty recipients in the organization's bustling waiting room.

Kamasaki was quick to offer unsolicited advice, showing off his "superior" knowledge. But the unassuming clerk with few formal credentials showed her own skills, what experts today call "cultural competence." One applicant acknowledged receiving support from the government but couldn't identify the specific type, an issue that could affect her eligibility under the "public charge" provisions of the law. Kamasaki "helped" by interjecting the acronyms of benefit programs—AFDC? SSI?—producing only uncomprehending stares from the applicant. The clerk looked back over her shoulder, all but rolled her eyes at the "help," turned back to the applicant and asked simpler, easily answered questions: What day of the month did the check arrive? What color is the check? She quickly confirmed that the benefits were not disqualifying and scheduled an appointment with a professional staffer to complete the application. The next applicant was having trouble getting records from a local utility needed to document his eligibility for legalization; the clerk promptly called her contact at the company—they already were on a first-name basis the NCLR staffer noted—and arranged for the documents to be picked up.

Another applicant who'd filled out the intake form had checked "no" in response to the question about receipt of government assistance. The clerk examined the form and then respectfully, but forcefully, probed until the applicant admitted she in fact had received benefits, protesting, "it's for my kids, not for me." The clerk explained that these kinds of benefits complicated her application and that the agency didn't handle complex cases. She then reviewed a list posted next to her desk, picked up the phone and scheduled an appointment with an attorney, part of a group of local AILA lawyers that had agreed to provide back-up support to nonprofits. After the applicant had left, the clerk turned to Kamasaki and said, "I know this family, they're all on welfare." Over dinner that night—center director Cris Medina's family owned the best Mexican restaurant in town—the NCLR staffer was asked what he thought of the intake procedure. As the chastened Washington lobbyist relayed what he'd learned that day, Guadalupe Center staffers couldn't conceal their delight. "Hah! We took Charles to school!" deputy director Bernardo Ramírez crowed. Having begun his visit with an attitude exemplified by the dreaded phrase, "I'm from Washington and I'm here to help," the NCLR staffer left town suitably humbled.

The Guadalupe Center, a large, well-established agency, eventually assisted some five hundred families to successfully apply for legalization.[85] This was a very respectable number for a city in a state that INS estimated had a total of about 6,500 legalization-eligible immigrants.[86] NCLR affiliates El Centro and Harvest America operated similar programs in Kansas.[87] In Florida, the Homestead-based Coalition of Florida Farmworker Organizations, or COFFO, was a tiny group with just four staff when IRCA passed, but its executive director Artúro Lopez had a keen understanding of immigration issues, having successfully challenged INS racial profiling practices in his previous job at the Illinois Migrant Council. Working under the umbrella of the South Dade Immigration Association, with just two attorneys and a single paralegal augmented by volunteers, COFFO assisted 2,300 amnesty applicants in a community that then had a permanent population of just 36,000 people, mainly farmworkers and their families.[88]

Some forty NCLR affiliates, most with no previous immigration background, ran IRCA legalization programs. Perhaps because these newcomers had strong case management systems and extensive cultural competence, subsequent assessments found they, and a few for-profit start-ups, handled higher volumes of applications than traditional legal service providers using law firm–style, one-to-one consultations and several layers of legal review.[89]

IMPLEMENTATION IN THE REAL WORLD

As amnesty officially began on May 5, it was described by the *New York Times*'s Robert Pear as "one of the great experiments in American history."[90] It did not have an auspicious beginning. In the run-up to the program, nonprofit service providers complained that insufficient funding provided by INS stymied their preparations. "We're not ready," declared the North Texas Immigration Coalition's Joe Murray on the front page of the *Dallas Times-Herald*.[91] Advocates also asserted that the program's rules, not issued until the very week the program began, were too restrictive. They griped that the agency's public education campaign to inform potential applicants of the opportunity to legalize, had barely gotten off the ground as the INS's spanking new legalization offices opened their doors. Much of the initial news coverage of legalization was similar to the *Washington Post*'s headline on the eve of the program's start: "Critics Predicting Chaos in Alien Amnesty Effort."[92] The *New York Times* described the program's beginning as "surrounded by confusion and uncertainty."[93]

INS publicly projected that a minimum of 2 million and up to 4 million undocumented immigrants were eligible for the regular or "general" legalization program (not counting those eligible for the SAW program), even though an internal memo produced by its respected Statistical Analysis Branch actually estimated that between 1.3 and 2.7 million people might be eligible (with a midpoint of 2 million).[94] The Carnegie Endowment for International Peace projected that between 1.8 and 2.6 million people might be eligible for legalization.[95] But few ventured to predict what percentage of the eligible population might actually apply. Pessimists pointed to other countries where less than half of those eligible actually applied, while the Congressional Budget Office projected that 1.4 million, about 60 percent of those it estimated were eligible, would come forward.[96] INS needed to average about 140,000 applications per month to meet even these fairly modest CBO projections; monthly application rates of 167,000 were required to meet the agency's own minimum public projection of 2 million applicants.

By that standard, the program got off to a decent start. Only about 50,000 people applied in May, but over the next four months application rates hovered around 150,000.[97] Advocates relentlessly pushed INS to be more generous, warning that absent changes, the program would fail. A lawyer brought up a legalization applicant in Texas who had been denied legalization due to a conviction on a misdemeanor charge that the INS had redefined as a felony.[98] Advocates produced other stories demonstrating wild inconsistencies in INS standards, including one set of school-aged children with a documentation gap that had been approved quickly while another with a similar gap was denied, even though the latter's mother named her kids' teachers.[99]

By July, with INS claiming that it was on target to meet its minimum projection of two million legalization applicants, frequent critic Rep. Charles Schumer praised the agency's performance noting that the INS is, "not necessarily seen as a friend, but given all the perils involved, I'm not disappointed by the progress thus far."[100] But there were clear warning signs: World Relief, one of the major QDE networks, began shuttering some of its legalization offices in August for lack of sufficient numbers of applicants and revenue.[101] And Rick Swartz warned, "The earliest cases are going to be the easiest ones, the ones with the fewest legal problems. When the toughest cases come along is when the need for help will be the greatest, and it might not be there."[102]

At issue were differing assumptions about the shape of the application curve. While the INS anticipated some month-to-month fluctuation, its posture was that early problems had been resolved and the program was gaining momentum; in other words, it projected a steadily rising rate of applications. Experts in the Ad Hoc Coalition anticipated something of a U-shaped curve, with applicants who were most ready and had the easiest cases applying first, while those with complicated cases or money issues would hold back. They'd hoped to have a major public education campaign combined with a strong nonprofit infrastructure in place to tackle the tougher cases after the initial surge died down, but feared it was already crumbling. The advocates called on private philanthropy to help fill the gap; the Ford Foundation stepped in with a $2.1 million "special appropriation" for legalization implementation in 1987.[103] The Chicago-based Joyce Foundation, the San Francisco-based Rosenberg Foundation, and many local community foundations also chipped in. But it was the immigrant-serving groups that shouldered the greatest burdens; the Catholic Bishops ended up investing some $25 million in their legalization program, and other national QDE networks added an estimated $5 million.[104] Groups like NCLR affiliate Guadalupe Center also lost significant amounts of money on the program, but felt obligated to invest heavily in the one-time opportunity for amnesty.[105]

It wasn't enough. As summer ended, application rates fell from a peak of some 170,000 in August to about 140,000 in September, to below 100,000 in October.[106] Inevitably, the INS and the nonprofits pointed fingers at each other. The advocates argued that failure to clarify INS's position on family unity—whether ineligible family members of legalization applicants would be subject to deportation—excessive documentation requirements, and restrictive or inconsistent eligibility interpretations were holding applicants back. INS blamed the nonprofits for taking their advocacy battles public, claiming the groups' complaints about those who weren't eligible overshadowed the message that those who were should apply.[107] But even the government acknowledged that efforts to publicize the program had gotten off to a slow start.[108] It was also widely understood that for many applicants, saving money to pay fees and collect documents required time. And many undocumented took a "wait and see" approach, holding back from applying until they saw proof positive that the program worked.[109]

These and other issues were formally discussed with the INS on a biweekly basis by Muzaffar Chishti and Mary McClymont, who cochaired a group of nonprofits in biweekly meetings with the INS legalization team headed by Associate Commissioner Richard Norton to discuss the details of implementation. The nonprofits—a group officially known as the National Coordinating Agencies (NCAs) with multistate networks of QDEs—represented about two-thirds of the groups designated by INS to assist applicants and accept applications.[110] The group of six or seven NCAs, chaired by McClymont, typically met formally with Norton, Assistant Commissioner William Slattery, and his deputy Terrence O'Reilly at INS for a couple of hours. But for some nonprofit staffers, several of whom like Chishti took early morning trains or flights to DC from their New York headquarters, these came to be known as marathon "three meeting days." The groups would first convene for a pre-meeting at NCLR—conveniently located just a few blocks from INS headquarters—to identify the issues and problems they wanted to raise, and then walk over to meet with the agency staff. After the parley with INS, they returned to NCLR to hold a formal meeting of the Ad Hoc Coalition's public education task force, chaired by Chishti, to report on and discuss the implications of new developments. The New Yorkers then rushed to Union Station or National Airport to return home.[111]

The results justified the NCAs' time investment. Guided by her experience as a litigator, McClymont viewed the process as "one ongoing negotiation"; she saw her role as raising and documenting each issue, making her case, and returning to it again and again until it was favorably resolved.[112] The meetings became the key forum to negotiate changes in the program, and to distribute new information and decisions learned from the INS meetings to the broader field of QDEs, lawyers, and others assisting legalization applicants. It was so effective that local nonprofits often were able to produce key cables and guidance from INS headquarters—for example, demonstrating that a previously borderline applicant was now clearly eligible—to the agency's own field staff before they'd received it through official channels.[113] In lieu of simple minutes, a few days after each meeting McClymont sent Norton a lengthy letter cosigned by the other NCAs, written in lawyerly, matter-of-fact prose, listing each item discussed, the nonprofits' requests, the agency's response, and agreed-upon follow-up.[114] Inevitably, the NCAs played good cop to the bad cop advocates and litigators showering the agency with criticism in the press and in the courts. Chishti recalls that McClymont never violated a confidence, but "held [INS's] feet to fire, but in an unassuming way, and just wore them down."[115] According to one definitive account of the program, "significant regulatory policy shifts resulted from the NCA-INS meetings," virtually all in favor of making the program more generous.[116]

The advocacy-versus-service tension played out at the local level, too. Dallas Catholic Charities' Vanna Slaughter had come to the issue in the 1970s when she interned at INS under Commissioner Leonel Castillo, whom three decades later she still called the "most influential supervisor of my career." Castillo took the intern under his wing; he once told her, "You're not angry enough Slaughter," and assigned her to join agents on an INS raid to witness apprehensions of undocumented workers slated for deportation. After stints in Latin America with Catholic Relief Services, she returned to Dallas and applied for a position at Catholic Charities to run its immigration program. Told by the priest in charge of the program that she "didn't have what it takes" for the job, she signed up as a volunteer, a position she held for nine months before being hired in 1985; she then cofounded a local advocacy coalition and joined the board of the National Immigration Forum.[117] Even before the program began Slaughter was an active critic of the INS, claiming that high fees and "little-publicized restrictions" could prevent many from legalizing.[118] A month into the program she slammed the agency for inaccurately telling some eligible legalization applicants they didn't qualify.[119]

Despite her advocacy profile, Slaughter's forte was program operations. Dallas Catholic Charities trained dozens of volunteers and recruited private attorneys to assist its ten professional staff, and held three group orientation/intake sessions, each with several dozen prospective applicants, every day.[120] Even as she bashed their bosses in the papers, Slaughter built close working relationships with local INS staff, and arranged a regularly scheduled day each week devoted exclusively to processing her group's cases. Every Wednesday at 5:30 a.m., about two hundred Catholic Charities clients assembled at the district's legalization office in a strip mall in the Dallas suburb of Arlington, accompanied by staff carrying client case files. In the soft glow of flashlights and portable lanterns carried by Catholic Charities staff, applicants were met by INS officials, twins named Delia and Dalia, who shouted instructions to the group using bullhorns.[121] After a few weeks, to the surprise of experts, legalization applications in Dallas were higher than those from Houston and San Antonio, cities with bigger immigrant enclaves, and reporters noted that applications from Texas "outpaced those in California and the West."[122]

These cooperative relationships were replicated across the country; most independent analyses concluded that as a general rule INS staff were welcoming and supportive.[123] But it wasn't all sweetness and light. While Catholic Charities was known to file well-documented applications—"clean cases" in the vernacular—when a problem arose, applicants would be directed to an area behind the front desk for intensive questioning. Applicants "taken to the back" were fearful, knowing this meant there was a problem with their paperwork or apparent inconsistencies in their applications, and Slaughter felt some INS staff asked inappropriate questions unrelated to the applicants' eligibility, recalling one adjudicator who demanded of an applicant, "Well, you already have seven children. Are you gonna have any more?" Catholic Charities filed a complaint, and eventually the adjudicator was reassigned.[124]

Slaughter and her counterparts elsewhere enjoyed sympathetic press coverage. Not only did many applicants have compelling personal stories, the theme of "little guys" fighting an uncaring government bureaucracy fit reporters' natural inclinations.[125] It didn't hurt that the feisty *Dallas Times-Herald*, then engaged in a fierce, eventually losing battle to the death with the more-established *Dallas Morning News*, devoted extensive coverage to immigration, and Slaughter was often quoted in its pages. The *Times-Herald* produced a twenty-eight-page, bilingual special section in late March, complete with basic legalization program rules, key dates, frequently asked questions, and profiles of potential applicants, a section on employer sanctions provisions, and two dozen other articles.[126] Lisa Hoffman, the *Times-Herald*'s Washington Bureau immigration reporter, arrived at the paper just after IRCA's passage and soon built close relationships with The Group; in turn, they connected the paper's state reporters with their own local contacts.[127] The synergy made the small, spunky paper something of the nation's newspaper of record on legalization implementation, vaulting Slaughter and her Catholic Charities program to national prominence. Not that it wasn't deserving of the coverage: Slaughter and her colleagues filed 4,200 applications, making it one of the largest and most productive QDEs in the country.[128]

As the program unfolded, the advocates' story line that the INS was not implementing the program effectively took hold. Both by design and happenstance, the Ad Hoc Coalition members built a highly cohesive network of advocates, service providers, and litigators, all of whom were pounding on the message that the program was failing to achieve its potential.[129] Carol Wolchok, director of the American Bar Association's Center on Immigration Policy, remembers being "constantly amazed" at how "a tiny group of nonprofit staffers working in DC on legalization implementation seemed like a huge 'machine' in every article, every day, on every [implementation] issue, getting the message out" that the INS was endangering the success of the program because of its ungenerous rules and policies.[130]

Slowly, often grudgingly, in many cases only after losing litigation, INS acceded to the advocates' push for a more generous program. In June, it accepted the advocates' contention that a single DWI conviction—a misdemeanor under Texas law—should not alone be disqualifying. In two separate revisions in September and November, it clarified standards the agency would use to determine those likely to become a "public charge," largely ending up where the advocates had urged back in February. In all, between June and November, INS issued a dozen revised rules or interpretations, all moving the program in a more inclusive, generous direction.[131] The advocates kept up the pressure. They warned that new requirements for HIV/AIDS tests for legalization applicants announced in August would impose significant costs to applicants and could be counterproductive from a public health perspective.[132] They complained that INS raids, which diminished in the first few months of legalization, had returned with a vengeance, intimidating applicants from coming forward.[133] They even documented cases of people eligible for amnesty who'd been picked up and deported without an opportunity to apply.[134] And all along, they chided the agency for failing to adequately publicize the program in general, and the rules changes in particular, observing that the INS's own surveys confirmed that many eligible applicants were confused about the program, unable to collect enough documents to prove their eligibility, or were deterred from applying by high fees.[135]

But it was the failure of the INS to deal generously with the "family unity" question—reassuring applicants that ineligible family members wouldn't face deportation—that drew the greatest fire. Advocates produced cases of undocumented people who themselves qualified for legalization but were reluctant to apply, fearing that spouses or children who'd joined them after the cutoff date would be deported. Researchers noted that the numbers affected were "substantial," and legislators introduced bills requiring the agency to defer deportation of the ineligible immediate relatives of legalization recipients.[136] The agency responded with what the advocates viewed as half-measures. In October, INS unveiled a "Family Fairness" program whereby minor children *might* be allowed to stay if *both* parents qualified for legalization; it listed "special humanitarian factors" under which agency officials *might* defer deportations, but refused to issue a uniform national policy.[137] NCLR labeled the policy "ridiculous and irrational," and soon after, a "visibly angry" INS commissioner Alan Nelson had a heated exchange with Rep. Mazzoli at a hearing when the subcommittee chairman, ever the centrist, urged the agency to allow ineligible minor children [but not spouses] to stay in the US if *either* parent qualified for legalization.[138] INS didn't budge, even after former commissioner Doris Meissner, in a November *Los Angeles Times* piece, praised INS's work on amnesty but concluded that the agency's position on the family unity was "an early reminder that the spirit of Ebenezer Scrooge is alive and well."[139]

By then, at its midpoint in November 1987, the program was in deep trouble, and the news kept getting worse. Application trends continued downward, from about 160,000 per month over the summer to less than half that in November, and fell further in December and January, although a "holiday lull" when Mexican immigrants went home for the holidays had been expected.[140] INS publicly expressed confidence that it was on track to receive at least two million applications by the end of the program on May 4, 1988.[141] But after eight months, total applications remained well under a million.[142] It didn't require a math whiz to figure that if this rate continued over the program's remaining four months, the agency would fall far short of its two million goal.

EXTEND AND EXPAND

There was near unanimity among advocates as the year ended that, absent major changes, the program would fail to legalize even close to two million people; the question was what to do next. They agreed to push for extension of the application period; practitioners had long believed a longer application period included in the Roybal bill but dropped in conference committee was required for a successful legalization.[143] They also agreed that the INS's public education campaign, contracted out to a firm called the Justice Group, had failed to meet expectations. The Justice Group was headed by former Nixon and Reagan budget official and entrepreneur Fernando Oaxaca, who as chair of the National

Republican Hispanic Assembly had been allied with The Group in opposing IRCA. His partner was Tom Castro, a former Democratic Hill staffer who ran several media businesses. After IRCA passed, they built a miniconglomerate— creative types, ad buyers, publicists—that won the INS contract over upscale Madison Avenue competitors. A major issue plaguing the campaign was size: INS had originally planned on a $25 million effort but the contract was reduced to $10.7 million, split between publicity for legalization programs, including SAWs, and employer sanctions.[144] Castro later recalled, "There just wasn't enough money to educate either employers or the undocumented, but we were asked to do both."[145] A related problem was timing; originally planned to begin well before the May 5 legalization start date, the campaign didn't begin in earnest until June.[146]

The campaign was also hindered by the frequent changes in INS's eligibility and documentation rules, and by the agency's own red tape. "It was a nightmare," Castro remembered years later, "We'd produce ads, get them cleared, buy ad space, then do it all over again" when the agency's regulations, priorities, or procedures changed. He also complained about repeated delays in getting INS to pay its bills, recalling in some cases it required former Reagan official Oaxaca to go around the INS bureaucracy through connections to former colleagues at the Office of Management and Budget, just to get paid.[147] In part as a result, as one chronicler of the legalization program understatedly observed, "The actual course of action embarked upon by the Justice Group bore little resemblance to its [more ambitious] original contract proposal."[148] To shape the latter stages of the campaign the Justice Group commissioned two surveys— one in the summer and another that fall—which found that confusion about how to apply, financial barriers, uncertainty about eligibility, fear of INS, and concerns about family separation were the top five reasons for not applying; a Ford Foundation-sponsored study and a survey by the *Dallas Times-Herald* came to similar conclusions.[149] Based on the data, the Justice Group was poised to launch a revised "Phase III" campaign in January, but given considerable skepticism of the effectiveness of the national campaign, it was augmented by many ad hoc local efforts, including some by local INS officials acting on their own and others by QDEs and other nonprofits conducting grassroots outreach, often with support from private philanthropy.[150]

The strategic question of what other steps to take split the advocates into two factions. The national groups believed that winning an extension of the application period was a "heavy lift" in Beltway vernacular, but agreed that the debate itself would pressure INS to invest more funding in public education and apply more generous standards for the rest of the program. The second camp, mainly activists outside of DC, sought nothing less than a major expansion of legalization, arguing that too many undocumented people, including growing numbers of Central American refugees, were left out of the program by the 1982 cutoff date. They feared that even if they won all of the pending litigation against the INS—which arguably could make several hundred thousand people initially deemed by INS not to qualify eligible for the program—legal technicalities would make it impossible for many of them to legalize.[151] Proponents felt that even if they failed to expand amnesty, the debate would seed the ground for future broader reforms. With both camps represented in his constituency, the National Immigration Forum's Rick Swartz tried to bring the two factions together by proposing an inclusive "extend and expand" advocacy campaign to push legislation on both fronts: extend the application period and expand the numbers of those eligible.[152] Beyond the narrow questions of family unity for legalization recipients and ongoing advocacy for safe haven for Central American refugees, the "expand" campaign never really got off the ground. By contrast, the DC groups jumped in with both feet on extension legislation, convincing Rep. Charles Schumer and Sen. Ted Kennedy to introduce bills to extend the application period for a full year, just before Congress left for the holidays.[153]

INS commissioner Alan Nelson opened 1988 with a press conference outlining his agency's progress in implementing IRCA. Nelson, a former corporate lawyer, had been part of the "Alameda County Mafia," a group of administration officials who'd worked previously in law enforcement with Attorney General Edwin Meese.[154] The genial Nelson offered a predictably upbeat assessment of his agency's work, reporting that by the end of 1987:

> INS had received 1,148,057 million legalization applications, of which 909,277 were under the general legalization program and 238,780 were SAW applications. . . . Though the application rate has been declining somewhat in recent weeks, that was anticipated around the holidays. We have no reason to believe we will fall short of the two million projected applicants. We stand by such previous projections and believe that the application rate will increase dramatically as the deadline for filing approaches.[155]

There was truth in Nelson's statement—applications were indeed expected to fall during the holidays and most experts did expect a spike in applications at the end of the program—but it also contained a considerable sleight-of-hand. The agency's estimate of two million legalization applicants, earlier articulated as a "minimum" number, now was referred to as something akin to a "middle case" projection.[156] More importantly, previous estimates of those eligible for legalization had excluded SAW (Special Agricultural Worker) applicants; in fact, INS had separately "for planning purposes, figured there would be 800,000 [SAW] applicants" *in addition* to those for the general legalization program.[157]

Under pressure from the advocates of "extend and expand," Nelson gussied up the numbers by adding together applicants for both the general legalization and SAW programs. A true "apples to apples" comparison would have compared the combined legalization and SAW total of 1,148,057 applicants against a "middle case" benchmark of 2.8 million, not 2 million. Even with a huge late surge, a combined legalization and SAW application total of nearly 3 million seemed unachievable.

Nelson's maneuver was standard Washington fare; all agencies put their work in the best possible light. But with legalization applications falling short of projections—and even IRCA supporters like Rep. Schumer and GOP cosponsor Hamilton Fish pushing legislation to extend the application period—the agency floated trial balloons of administrative steps it would take to give applicants who "could not meet the deadline for reasons beyond their control" extra time to collect documents; Schumer took credit for the agency's newfound flexibility, telling the *New York Times* that "I think our bill pressured them to do something."[158] Soon, INS announced an administrative extension of sorts, saying it would allow applicants two months to complete the paperwork if they filed what became known as a skeletal application by the May 4 deadline; Schumer called the extension "virtually meaningless."[159] The advocates weren't accepting what they saw as half-measures either, and in early February they helped Schumer draft and circulate a "Dear Colleague" letter with the headline: "THE DEADLINE IS IMMINENT/ EXTEND AMNESTY NOW," accompanied by a *New York Times* editorial supporting extension.[160] Hispanic Caucus members who'd voted for IRCA at considerable political risk then wrote to Peter Rodino urging him to move the legislation.[161] NCLR and other DC groups followed up by issuing "action alerts" to their networks urging support for the Schumer-Kennedy bill.[162]

But the advocates' exertions were less influential in the debate on extension—or the larger question of whether the legalization program was fulfilling its potential—than the publication of a think tank report in February. Then, as now, dozens of "major" policy reports were issued on a daily basis by government agencies, think tanks, trade associations, and advocacy groups. All purport to influence the policy debate; in reality, few are read by anyone outside a small circle of specialists, and even fewer have any actual policy impact. The rare report that does break through the policy clutter almost always includes some combination of credible authorship, strong content, and good timing. *The Legalization Countdown*, coauthored by former INS acting commissioner Doris Meissner and immigration scholar Demetrios Papademetriou, exploded onto the scene in February 1988, just as Congress was beginning to consider the extension question, but its impact reverberated for decades.

The report had all the ingredients for success, beginning with its coauthors' credibility. Meissner had come to Washington as a prestigious White House Fellow in 1973, and after several positions at the Department of Justice, she was named acting commissioner of the INS, presiding over the transition from the Carter to the Reagan administration. When Commissioner Alan Nelson was confirmed in late 1981, Meissner was asked to stay on as executive associate commissioner, the third-highest ranking position in the agency.[163] As the IRCA debate was ending, she left INS to start an immigration policy program at the Carnegie Endowment for International Peace, one of the city's oldest and most respected scholarly institutions."[164] Meissner was that rare Washington figure universally respected by all sides. Her opinions had unusual weight, not only because she was smart and well-spoken—the city is filled with bright and articulate people who have little influence—but because her pronouncements carried that rare, indefinable but unmistakable quality known as gravitas. Coauthor Papademetriou was a well-known immigration scholar. He'd written many books and articles on immigration and refugee policy, taught political science at Duke, the University of Maryland, and the New School for Social Research, and had served as executive editor of *International Migration Review*, the preeminent scholarly journal in the field.[165] He was progressive in political orientation but sufficiently acceptable to conservatives that he would later serve as director for immigration policy and research at the US Department of Labor in the Bush administration.[166] Crucially for the report he and Meissner coauthored, Papademetriou had collaborated closely with the US Catholic Conference's Nick DiMarzio over the years, first as a mentor, later as coauthor, and as a consultant as the church's immigration program was reorganized during the IRCA debate. More than the typical academic, he had easy access to leaders of major legalization programs.

Given their bona fides, the two easily could have sat at their desks, reviewed public data and press stories, and cranked out a report. Instead, they requested and received unprecedented access to records and staff of both the INS and the US Catholic Conference, and mined these sources deeply. They supplemented this inside access by interviewing another one hundred people from the government, nonprofits, foundations, and others in a dozen cities. The resulting report, issued with exquisite timing in February, was remarkably even-handed, concluding with some three dozen findings and recommendations. It declined to endorse a legislative extension of the application period, but its core conclusion generally supported the advocates' narrative that the program was in trouble: "[Even with a late surge] between 1.3 and 1.4 million applications are likely to be filed by May 4. This is a shortfall of 300,000 to 400,000 from our most conservative estimate of the eligible population. . . . We believe that the legalization program is in danger. Unless there is thoughtful, strong policy intervention, a unique opportunity to bring better order to this nation's complex immigration structure will be squandered."[167]

Both the Ad Hoc Coalition and the INS found plenty to complain about in the report. Advocates were disappointed it declined to endorse their extension legislation, convinced that it all but ended prospects for passage of the Schumer-Kennedy bill, but were heartened that it validated their critique of INS's implementation efforts. INS staff disagreed with much of the report, but after its release appeared more open to adopting the recommendations that the Ad Hoc Coalition advocated, seemingly softened up by the fact that they were endorsed by Meissner, one of their most respected former colleagues. The collaboration bore fruit in another way. With refugee and development expert Kathleen Newland, in 2001 Papademetriou founded the Migration Policy Institute, soon joined by Meissner, and built what many believe is the preeminent think tank on migration issues in the world.[168]

In early March, members of the Ad Hoc Coalition sent a letter to Congress urging support for the extension bill on US Catholic Conference letterhead cosigned by sixteen national groups.[169] The same organizations, with an additional sixty signatories and supporters, sent another letter to the Senate in April.[170] Their efforts proved only partially successful. At the end of March, the House Judiciary Committee approved the bill by a 22–12 vote, opposed by traditional amnesty opponents but aided by a federal court decision that overturned an INS regulation that previously precluded an estimated fifty thousand people from applying.[171] On April 11, the *Christian Science Monitor* published an unusual side-by-side pair of editorials supporting extension of the amnesty deadline. One, by Doris Meissner, supported extension "despite the good job that INS has done" while the other, coauthored by Joe W. Pitts of the Dallas Bar Association and Dallas Catholic Charities' Vanna Slaughter advocated a longer application period "because of the poor job INS has done."[172] But then the General Accounting Office, the congressional watchdog, punted, writing "We have no basis to challenge or support extending the [amnesty] deadline."[173]

On April 20, with little debate, with subcommittee chair Romano Mazzoli a somewhat reluctant lead sponsor, the House passed the bill, by a narrow 213–201 margin.[174] Like most authors of major bills, Mazzoli was unenthusiastic about making major changes to the law so soon after passage. When Schumer first introduced his extension bill, few of the DC advocates expected Mazzoli's support. But he came around at the urging of Rep. Esteban Torres, who had supported IRCA because of the promise of a generous legalization; with that objective endangered, he asked the subcommittee chairman to return the favor.[175] But Mazzoli's support did not sway his colleague in the upper body. No longer the subcommittee chair but still highly influential, Al Simpson was well aware that some advocates wanted to "expand" as well as "extend" legalization and was having none of it. His aide Dick Day told the press that Simpson "feels an extension is the first step in broadening the program or going on to a second one. He feels very strongly that when

Congress asked the general public to go along with [amnesty], it was as once-only legislation, and that's what he's trying to keep it."[176]

A little over a week after House passage, the bill died on a procedural vote in the Senate.[177] The extension debate was over. Faced with a firm deadline, both the government and the nonprofits redoubled their efforts. Even as the extension debate heated up, applications had begun to surge: from a low of 50,000 in January to over 100,000 in February and hitting the 221,000 mark in March.[178] Some of the surge resulted from the sum of numerous small program improvements, such as the final phase of the Justice Group's public education campaign, which the INS finally augmented with additional funds.[179] The INS began accepting skeletal applications—a signed form and application fee—giving late-filers two months to finalize applications.[180] Several local advocates convinced the INS to adopt procedural improvements, like establishing "problem windows" to help resolve difficult cases, and even to open a brand-new office in an Asian neighborhood in Los Angeles to address disappointing low take-up rates in that population.[181]

But larger macro developments likely outweighed these micro improvements. One factor was the growing number of those the INS deemed eligible, reflecting the dozen or so regulatory changes adopted by or forced on the agency. Another was the simple fact that INS and the QDEs got better at doing their jobs as time went on: both at the national and local levels, the two sides slowly came to a shared understanding of what constituted an approvable application, sharply reducing the number of instances when QDEs were advising applicants that they were eligible while INS was declaring they weren't. Perhaps the most significant factor was the success of earlier applicants who'd received their temporary resident cards; as North and Portz observed, "Applications filed in the first few months were largely those of persons who were quit[e] confident of their eligibility and their ability to manage the system. Their somewhat less confident neighbors watched to see what happened to those first applicants; when the TRA [Temporary Resident Alien] cards began arriving for the early applicants, more of the eligible began to apply."[182] These "walking advertisements" for the effectiveness of legalization also increased as INS's processing times and backlogs of unprocessed applications were cut by more than half.[183] And any procrastinators in the undocumented population seemed to finally be prodded to apply by the existence of a hard deadline.

Both the QDEs and the agency were short-staffed during the last-minute surge, the result of "belt-tightening" forced by lower-than-expected fee revenue in the preceding months.[184] But both intensified their efforts within their resource constraints; one provider remembered "getting the call from the [National Immigration] Forum that extension was dead" and thinking for her QDE, "it was crunch time, big time."[185] In the final weeks of the program those assisting legalization applicants worked frantically, putting in eighteen-hour-plus days to accommodate the last-minute rush. Long lines were common at INS legalization offices, as many civil servants voluntarily worked often uncompensated overtime to address the late surge.[186] INS legalization offices allowed those in the queue as of midnight on May 4 to apply; one of the last was Carlos Suarez at the INS legalization office in Arlington, Texas, a Dallas suburb, around 1:30 a.m.; according to the *Times-Herald*, in line at 11:30 that night, Suarez realized

> he had forgotten the $185 money order for the filing fee, and phoned his wife in Fort Worth to bring it. She left in the family pickup, but the truck soon broke down. Undaunted, she hailed a cab but couldn't communicate with the cab driver, who didn't speak Spanish. Eventually she managed to get him to return her to her home, after failing to explain where the amnesty center was. At about 1:00 a.m., Suarez told Arlington Police officer Mario Gomez, who was working as an off-duty security guard at the center, about his dilemma, and the officer advised him to [go home and] pick up the check and take his chances on getting the application accepted when he returned. Suarez did as instructed, and officials accepted the form 30 minutes later. 'This man gave us a big chance that for our entire lives we'll be grateful for,' Suarez said of the police officer.[187]

Some 323,000 applications were filed in the final month before the May 4 deadline. An additional 75,000 late applications, many from people given litigation-related extensions or from QDEs that had thirty days to file applications, were accepted in May and June. In all, 1,767,000 applications were filed under the general legalization program.[188] More than 90 percent, or about 1.6 million, eventually were approved to become lawful permanent residents of the US.[189]

WHAT'S FAIR?

At the beginning of IRCA's implementation the Federation for American Immigration Reform pledged to be an active advocate for aggressive employer sanctions enforcement and a limited legalization program. It created a litigation arm, the Immigration Reform Law Institute, pledging to fight lawsuits by the ACLU, MALDEF, and the National Council of Churches; longtime FAIR staffer Dan Stein told the *Washington Post* that, "The battle has just begun."[190] Notwithstanding Stein's declaration, subsequent accounts of the bill's implementation concluded that "while advocates of the restrictionist position were extremely active during the debate about IRCA, they played a much smaller role in the implementation of the legalization . . . ; thus virtually all of the external pressures on the INS during the implementation of legalization came from the pro-immigrant side of the table."[191]

One reason for the discrepancy might have been a new flurry of problems for FAIR, rooted in publications, discussions, and decisions that had taken place even before IRCA's passage. FAIR founder John Tanton had come to the subject of immigration as an offshoot of his interest in limiting population growth. Other advocates of reducing population size, most prominently Paul Erlich, author of the 1968 bestseller *The Population Bomb*, had predicted starvation of "hundreds of millions" and shortage-induced massive commodity price spikes in the 1970s and the 1980s due to overpopulation; but reality stubbornly refused to conform to their prediction of a Malthusian catastrophe.[192] FAIR's first director, Roger Conner, believed that the restrictionist case was best made on "liberal economic" grounds, reflecting his own humble origins, but also to avoid the taint of racism that had plagued previous advocates of immigration restriction.[193]

FAIR board member and historian Otis Graham both influenced and agreed with Conner, noting that in immigration debates a century earlier, "intellectuals concerned with racial purity" had "given nativism a bad name."[194] So seriously did FAIR try to disassociate itself from racism that early in Conner's tenure it was averse to even retaining members that overtly expressed nativist views; according to the *New York Times*, "When a member wrote that Hispanic immigrants should be shot—because they 'multiply like a bunch of rats'—a staff member offered to refund his dues."[195] Although responses to FAIR's direct-mail appeals showed that cultural and racial arguments were effective in building donors and members, according to one writer, early on when Tanton "tried to steer the group in that direction, its board of directors resisted."[196] But up through the summer of 1986, immigration reform had yet to pass.

Tanton grew increasingly frustrated with the stalemate on immigration reform and with Conner and Graham resistant to explicitly racial or cultural appeals, FAIR's founder had created US English, to promote what it called "official English" and its opponents labeled "English-Only" laws, a think tank called the Center for Immigration Studies, the aforementioned Immigration Reform Law Institute, and smaller groups Population-Environment Balance, Californians for Population Stabilization, and Americans for Border Control.[197] US English openly advanced cultural and racial, if not openly racist, arguments—suggesting that Hispanic immigrants resisted assimilation and raising the specter of separatist movements—and these appeals attracted both funds and members: it was called "the cash cow" of Tanton's conglomerate of organizations, with an annual budget as high as $8 million in the mid-1980s to push a "pro-English" agenda.[198] By comparison, the *combined* yearly budgets of LULAC, MALDEF, and NCLR to cover much broader portfolios of issues likely never approached $8 million at the time.

US English's parent, US, Inc., funded and assisted a wide network of groups, political action committees, and activists to promote official English-ballot propositions and legislation in California, Florida, Arizona, and other states. According to James Crawford, a reporter for *Education Week* who later became something of a pro-bilingual education activist, US English and FAIR "went to great lengths to conceal" the connections between Tanton's many organizations, in part to avoid the appearance of ethnic intolerance.[199] As the Center for New Community reported, Tanton wrote to a donor in 1985 regarding another of his start-ups that, "For credibility, this will need to be independent of FAIR, though the Center for Immigration Studies, as we're calling it, is starting off as a project of FAIR."[200] The National Immigration Forum's Rick Swartz said that Tanton tried to "camouflage the links between these organizations, their true origins, so they appear to have arisen spontaneously."[201]

In October 1986, Tanton sent a memo to attendees of "WITAN IV," named after the *witenagemot*, an Old English term for a "council of wise men to advise the king" that he described as "a whimsical name" for retreats of leaders in his network to discuss "problems of language and assimilation and population."[202] Tanton's WITAN memo asked attendees to consider whether "Latin Americans will bring with them the tradition of the *mordida* (bribe)," mused about "unmeltable ethnics" that could never assimilate, questioned the "educability" of Latinos, and regarding faster population growth rates of Hispanics and Asians compared to whites, a worry that "those with their pants up are going to get caught by those with their pants down."[203] For nearly two years after IRCA, the memo stayed out of the public domain.

In October 1988, in the midst of a heated battle over a US English–backed ballot proposition to require Arizona state employees to speak only English on the job, the *Arizona Republic* first published excerpts of Tanton's WITAN memo.[204] Author-activist James Crawford pounced on the story, uncovering one damning revelation after another. He reported that Mellon heiress Cordelia Scaife May had financed Tanton's distribution of an apocalyptic novel, *Camp of the Saints*, called "racist, xenophobic, and paranoid," while also giving $5.8 million to FAIR, US English, the Center for Immigration Studies, and related groups in the 1980s.[205] It was later revealed that May had also funded a columnist who decried "all efforts to mix the races of mankind" and bequeathed half her fortune—more than $400 million—to a foundation solely dedicated to immigration control, which itself distributed a good chunk of its funding to FAIR and other groups in Tanton's network.[206] Crawford also discovered that FAIR had received grants from the Pioneer Fund, a group created in 1937 to support "applied genetics" in Nazi Germany and "eugenics research" purporting to prove that blacks had lower IQs than whites.[207]

The ballot proposition passed, although just barely, and was later ruled unconstitutional by the Arizona Supreme Court.[208] The revelations emanating from the Tanton WITAN memo and Crawford's subsequent research had a lasting impact. US English executive director Linda Chavez—a Latina who'd previously served as staff director of the US Commission on Civil Rights under President Reagan, a prize catch for an organization seeking to avoid charges of racism—called Tanton's memo "repugnant" and "anti-Hispanic," and resigned. Newscaster Walter Cronkite "severed his ties to the US English advisory board."[209] Investor-philanthropist Warren Buffet ceased his support for FAIR.[210] Tanton himself left the US English board of directors (but stayed on at FAIR's), but disclaimed knowledge of what the Southern Poverty Law Center later called the Pioneer Fund's "unsavory history." FAIR continued to accept grants totaling over $1.2 million from the Pioneer Fund until 1994, six years after the Fund's support for eugenics first came to light.[211] Other departures from US English followed, including the firing of its research director who'd come to the opinion that Tanton "is a racist," and its public relations director who left after concluding that some in the FAIR founder's network "see people—cultural, racial, and immigrant groups—as a negative factor in the environment."[212]

Tanton publicly acknowledged that his WITAN memo "said some things badly and awkwardly" but decried the "guilt by association" by those who charged that he, US English, or FAIR supported racism or eugenics, asserting that being labeled as a racist "is a nearly fatal accusation."[213] But privately, according to a later *New York Times* profile, "Dr. Tanton grew more emboldened . . . to make his case against immigration in racial terms."[214]

By then, Roger Conner had had enough; FAIR's founding executive director left the organization at the end of 1988, deeply troubled that the case for immigration restriction had been diverted from his original "liberal economic" and environmentally focused vision to one dominated by race.[215] He went on to postings at the Brookings Institution, an organization called the American Alliance for Rights and Responsibilities, and Vanderbilt University Law School.[216] He later expressed regret for choosing not to confront Tanton for asserting racial arguments on immigration.[217] Conner's last act at FAIR was recommending that longtime FAIR staffer and then head of the Immigration Reform Law Institute, Dan Stein, succeed him as executive director of the organization. He came to regret this choice as well.[218]

RODINOS

Unlike the general legalization program, the Special Agricultural Worker (SAW) application deadline was December 1988; its more generous eighteen-month application period was the product of the SAW compromise, whose last-minute addition had catalyzed IRCA's passage. Two-thirds through the SAW program, just under 600,000 SAW applications had been filed with INS, but even experts had no clue whether this was higher or lower than should be expected. One internal government estimate projected that 250,000 people might apply to become SAWs.[219] The US Department of Agriculture had estimated that 300,000–500,000 undocumented workers were employed in agriculture, while one lawmaker had suggested perhaps 800,000 might apply, but experts accepted that there was little basis to "make even the most basic assumptions about the accuracy" about the size of SAW-eligible population.[220]

Projecting the number of SAW program applicants was a speculative exercise. Applicants needed evidence of employment in farm labor, an industry notorious for incomplete records. Many farmworkers traveled along the migrant stream with a dozen or more separate "employers" in a season, were hired by intermediaries like labor contractors, and often were paid in cash, or a combination of in-kind benefits like housing and cash.[221]

Some of these factors actually ended up working in favor of SAW applicants; the provision's drafters recognized the realities of farmwork, so applicants for the SAW program faced a lower burden of proof than those for the general legalization program. Furthermore, growers exercised the same political clout in the implementation process that they'd brought to bear on Congress, and fearing the eventual enforcement of employer sanctions, they wanted to secure a reliable labor force; they pressured the INS to treat SAW applicants leniently. For these reasons alone, close observers had always expected substantial fraud in the SAW program.[222] Those eligible for both programs had incentives to choose the agricultural program route over general legalization, since SAW recipients weren't required to pass an English and civics test and were eligible for most federal benefits. And some unknown number of those that missed the general legalization deadline likely took their last remaining shot and applied for the SAW program whether or not they were eligible.[223] Even though the highest pre-implementation estimate of SAW program participation was 800,000, by the end of the eighteen-month application window in December 1988 over 1.3 million applications were received by INS.[224]

Although experts almost unanimously agreed that few general legalization applications were tainted by fraud, it was widely accepted that many SAW applications were fraudulent.[225] Some was petty or nonmaterial fraud, resulting from the inability of legitimate farmworkers who'd worked the requisite ninety days in agriculture to procure records to prove it; many purchased fake documents from a cottage industry that inevitably developed.[226] But blatant SAW fraud was also rampant; one INS official complained about "an Indian doctor who worked at a hospital claiming that he had worked for three months picking watermelons."[227] Informed guesstimates ranged from a low of 20 percent to a high of 50 percent of applications that might've been from individuals that had little or no actual background in agricultural work.[228]

One factor driving SAW applications was INS's bureaucratic incentive to rack up fee revenue. Fees from applicants for the general legalization program were automatically applied to the costs of that infrastructure for both programs, meaning SAW fee revenues far exceeded expenses. Seizing the opportunity to score surplus funds, INS cut a deal with its overseers in the administration and Congress. It allocated a portion of surplus fees, about $50 million, to the US Treasury, but a larger amount—estimated at $57 million—was kept by INS for "enhancement of its examination program," which expert analysts wryly observed was "broad enough to allow INS a certain leeway in its internal budgeting."[229] Publicly, the agency claimed that the surplus funds were used to "take INS from the 19th to the 21st Century" by upgrading its computer systems to adjudicate applications for legalization and the SAW program.[230] But as North and Portz noted, by 1989 it was common knowledge inside the agency that funds were "being used for a variety of purposes that may seem distant from determining the validity of farm workers' claim to legal status, such as the funding of 21 positions in INS' overseas offices."[231] This gave INS a powerful incentive to push applications for the agricultural legalization effort despite the fraud, a development hidden from all but the most expert analysts. Had the $107 million surplus been applied instead to the legalization and SAW programs, applicant fees could have been cut or funding for QDEs could have been increased considerably. Notwithstanding the widespread publicity about fraud, ultimately some 84 percent of the SAW applicants, about 1.1 million, were approved for lawful permanent resident status.[232]

In sum, more than 2.8 million previously unauthorized people obtained lawful permanent resident status through IRCA's four legalization programs: 1.6 million through general legalization and 1.1 million SAWs, plus almost 38,000 Cuban–Haitian entrants [some number of Haitians likely received SAW status] and some 50,000 "registry" recipients.[233] As predicted by its proponents and subsequently documented by a robust series of government evaluations and academic studies, the ability of legalization recipients to "come out of the shadows" resulted in substantial improvements in their lives; as one analysis summarized: "Legalization had profound, positive economic effects for its beneficiaries. Wages of those legalized increased by as much as 15 percent within five years and 20 percent over the long run, while educational attainment, occupational status, and homeownership markedly increased, and poverty rates declined."[234]

They weren't the only ones who benefited. Those that assisted legalization applicants, like Dallas Catholic Charities' Vanna Slaughter recalled the program as, "Exhausting . . . but more than that, exhilarating."[235] Even people a step removed, such as those who'd lobbied on IRCA but didn't play a direct role in implementation, lived the experience vicariously as they followed news coverage of legalization. Except for raising her children, NCLR's Martha Escutia thought that shaping legalization was her "greatest achievement."[236] Former LULAC official Joe Treviño, who went into the private sector after leaving the Hispanic nonprofit, thought that seeing undocumented people legalized as the result of his legislative labors "was life-changing."[237]

The emotional impact of viewing millions of immigrants "coming out of the shadows" softened and even changed perceptions of the law's toughest critics. MALDEF, in particular, wasn't shy about expressing the view that NCLR and The Group had made a grave mistake by "making it easier to pass" an immigration bill.[238] But such was the impact of witnessing the legalization of millions of undocumented immigrants; afterward some well-informed people, including a former board member, couldn't recall, indeed at first refused to believe, that MALDEF had actually opposed the final legislation.[239]

Members of Congress who'd helped craft IRCA, like California's Howard Berman, were often honored by immigrant assistance organizations. Thinking back to the ceremonies where he was surrounded by grateful beneficiaries of legalization, Berman—who shaped dozens of bills over four decades in public service—would say, almost wistfully, that meeting those the bill legalized was "one of the most rewarding experiences of my professional life."[240] A decade after IRCA, Al Simpson professed "no qualms about three million people from 93 countries coming forward," for legalization, writing, "I still see those people on the street and it pleases me greatly."[241] Judiciary Committee chair Peter Rodino received perhaps the highest compliment, bestowed on him by the program's recipients themselves; a *New York Times* reporter covering the SAW program noticed a new term had worked its way into Latino immigrants' vocabulary: "In Mexican slang, there is now even a special term used to describe [SAW applicants]. They are known as "los rodinos" because the bill that created this category of immigrant was co-sponsored by Rep. Peter W. Rodino, Jr., Democrat of New Jersey."[242]

At first the nickname Rodinos was limited to farmworkers legalized under the SAW program; it was soon applied, especially in California, to everyone legalized by IRCA.[243] Many thought this an apt term for SAW workers; their status was traceable directly to Rodino, whose consistent opposition to guest-worker programs and deputizing of Howard Berman produced the SAW program. But it might've been fairer for beneficiaries of the general legalization program, which had been designed and twice shepherded through the House by a certain gentleman from Kentucky, to have been called Mazzolis.

But perhaps the most lasting legacy of legalization was the modern immigrant rights movement; according to some movement pioneers, it was during IRCA implementation that, "for the first time, 'immigrant rights' entered the lexicon."[244] As with any diverse social justice field, the movement's "tree" has many roots and branches. The "legal arm" of the movement has deep roots in

IRCA. The ACLU expanded its litigation footprint right after IRCA, spurred by the establishment of an Immigrants' Rights Project under the leadership of Lucas Guttentag.[245] The Oakland-based Immigrant Legal Resource Center, whose manual was the single indispensable resource for practitioners during legalization, also grew substantially in the immediate post-IRCA era.[246] The American Immigration Council, AILA's nonprofit arm created initially to support IRCA implementation, broadened its policy and litigation role considerably afterward. The National Immigration Law Center also emerged in the IRCA era. And an entirely new legal institution sprang directly from legalization. As the first stage of amnesty ended, the Catholic Conference's Mary McClymont moved on to a position at the Ford Foundation, soon followed by Nick DiMarzio, who later was named bishop of the church's Camden and Brooklyn dioceses. The infrastructure they left behind became the Catholic Legal Immigration Network, or CLINIC, a national nonprofit independent of the church's migration and refugee services division. CLINIC established an affiliate relationship with church-related entities that had run legalization programs and later expanded to cover a broad range of immigration legal service providers; from an initial core group of 17 affiliated programs in 1988 it grew to some 245 by 2013.[247]

Other groups—often led by immigrants themselves—formed the vanguard of the modern immigrant rights movement. Remnants and offshoots of Bert Corona's Hermandad Mexicana Nacional, prior to IRCA the largest and best-known of the membership organizations explicitly organizing the undocumented, remain. Another distinct network, many but not all with the name "Central American Refugee Center" (CARECEN), grew in San Francisco, Los Angeles, Boston, Houston, New York, Chicago, and the Washington, DC, area. While the bulk of the Central American population had arrived in the US after 1982 and was foreclosed from IRCA's legalization, those that were eligible, often aided by a local CARECEN group, participated in high numbers.[248] The CARECENs initially were led by white lawyers; most soon intentionally transitioned to immigrant leadership, many of whom were focused on community organizing, a natural development since some previously had been active members of the antigovernment resistance fighting death squads and human rights violations in their home countries.[249]

Now at the Ford Foundation, Mary McClymont wanted to build on IRCA's momentum to institutionalize an infrastructure of organizations combining policy advocacy and direct services in key immigrant gateway communities. Among her first cohort of grantees: the New York Immigration Coalition (NYIC), the Massachusetts Immigrant and Refugee Advocacy Coalition (MIRA), the Chicago Committee on Immigrant Protection (CCIP), the Coalition for Humane Immigrant Rights of Los Angeles (CHIRLA), and the Northern California Coalition for Immigrant and Refugee Rights.[250] Many of these coalitions, some "seeded" by Rick Swartz and colleagues at the National Immigration Forum, served as both advocacy voices and service coordinating hubs during legalization. Some, like NYIC, began solely as service coordinators, and wouldn't hire full-time staff or operate their own programs until later.[251] But most were active advocates from the beginning.

MIRA, led by Muriel Heiberger, a respected member of the National Immigration Forum's board, served as a leanly staffed "policy shop" advocating for its member organizations working on amnesty implementation.[252] Among its early policy victories was the establishment of an immigrant rights unit in Boston city government in 1987.[253] CCIP, cochaired by Sid Mohn of Travelers and Immigrants Aid of Chicago, an ACNS affiliate and board member, and MALDEF's Artúro Jáuregui, began IRCA implementation by calling together the city's major QDEs—Travelers and Immigrants Aid, the Catholic Diocese, Lutheran Immigration and Refugee Services, World Relief, and others—and "divided up the territory." Soon after amnesty ended, it broadened its reach, rebranded as the Illinois Coalition for Immigrant and Refugee Rights.[254] CHIRLA was formed in 1986 under the leadership of MALDEF, the Central American Refugee Center, and the Asian Pacific American Legal Center, with the United Way serving as its initial fiscal agent.[255] In addition to coordinating services among its members, CHIRLA sponsored a radio public service announcement (PSA) campaign to promote legalization. One PSA caught the attention of Angelica Salas, then assisting extended family members to apply for legalization; she soon became the group's executive director.[256]

One of the most successful groups combining service delivery, advocacy, and community organizing was Pineros y Campesinos Unidos del Noroeste (United Tree Workers and Farmworkers of the Northwest, known by its Spanish acronym "PCUN") in Woodburn, Oregon. The term *pineros* began as the Latino label for workers engaged in cultivating and harvesting pine and fir trees ubiquitous in Americans' homes at Christmas, and eventually expanded to cover all tree workers in the heavily-forested northwest.[257] The group emerged in the context of several other Latino-focused efforts, including Colegio César Chávez, for nearly a decade the country's only Chicano-focused, fully accredited institution of higher education.[258] PCUN began as a farmworker union with informal ties to the United Farm Workers; it later expanded to lead boycotts of nonunion growers, build low-income housing, start a radio station, and lobby both state and federal lawmakers. The group was just two years old when amnesty began.[259]

Despite its relative youth, PCUN was unusually well-prepared for the legalization program. The group's cofounders—Colegio César Chávez alums Cipriano Ferrel and Ramon Ramírez and immigration specialist Larry Kleinman—were all activists. A scholar of the region noted that both Ferrel and Ramírez had "cut their teeth as student organizers at Colegio César Chávez" and that PCUN's leadership successfully built on widespread immigrant rights activism in the area.[260] Kleinman, the son of an appellate lawyer, had "grown up with the law," had worked as a paralegal in a public defender's office, and had been one of the first nonprofit staffers in the state to be accredited by the Board of Immigration Appeals of the Justice Department to represent clients in immigration proceedings. He'd also helped start one of PCUN's predecessor groups—the Willamete Valley Immigration Project—through which he established close relationships with attorneys from the National Lawyers Guild's National Immigration Project and the emerging National Network for Immigrant and Refugee Rights.[261]

More than many groups that viewed legalization as a service program and only later organized the program's beneficiaries for advocacy purposes, PCUN's leadership saw the program's potential for mutually reinforcing service and organizing functions almost immediately, and jumped into implementation with both feet.[262] By the end of the program PCUN had filed 1,300 legalization and SAW applications, with a 98 percent approval rate by the INS.[263] Perhaps more importantly from a movement-building perspective, according to Kleinman amnesty "came at the perfect time" for PCUN, which used the program as both a recruitment and organizing vehicle. "We went from 120 members to 2,000, or 10 years' worth of growth in one year," Kleinman later recalled.[264] While unique in many ways, PCUN was a forerunner of a new kind of community organization synergistically linking service provision with community organizing and advocacy that was replicated many times over in decades to come.

Combining program services with aggressive community organizing or advocacy on a sustained basis was then and remains highly unusual in the nonprofit sector. In the mid-2000s, researchers at OMB Watch, Tufts University, and the Center for Lobbying in the Public Interest conducted a landmark study of over 1,700 nonprofits. The study found that about 70 percent, "never" or "rarely" engaged in public policy activity, prompting the researchers to conclude that "the frequency of policy participation by nonprofits is inconsistent and generally low."[265] In other words, only a small minority of nonprofits pulled off what the new immigrant rights groups were able to do, beginning with IRCA implementation. The ability of the field-based organizations and networks emerging from IRCA to successfully combine service and advocacy proved critical as they formed the vanguard of a movement representing the Rodinos, those left out of the program, and generations of immigrants to follow.

CAPSTONE

As legalization wound down, Rick Swartz and his National Immigration Forum faced a reckoning on issues that had festered for years. Before IRCA's passage,

Swartz had long pushed his board of directors to pursue several shifts in direction; the most controversial was to change its bylaws to allow the group to take formal positions on public policy issues. He found the bylaws "too constraining," but some Forum members were leery of giving him carte blanche to speak on their behalf.[266] The organization's field-based membership wanted a greater say in shaping national advocacy strategy, and some saw the Forum founder and the largely male DC-based advocates as operating an already too-exclusive, insider boys' club.[267] The Forum's principal funder, the Ford Foundation, thought that adopting formal policy positions might undermine the group's mission of fostering dialogue and hurt the ability to forge consensus, and warned against a "fundamental change" that could "be looked on unfavorably" by its foundation supporters.[268] It was a grantor-grantee standoff. Ford was disinclined to renew its grant funding unless the Forum agreed not to become an advocacy group, but Swartz wouldn't budge, and felt so strongly that for a time he declined to be paid while the grant was pending, devoting much of his time off to advising the presidential campaign of Democrat Mike Dukakis. The Forum's future was on hold in the fall of 1988 as Swartz entertained thoughts of entering a Democratic administration when Dukakis led in early polling. But after Vice President George H. W. Bush won the November election, the Forum's board leadership quietly worked out a compromise with the Ford Foundation that satisfied no one, least of all Swartz, who a little over a year later left the organization he'd founded.[269] He started a successful government relations practice specializing in left-right coalitions to advance public policy on immigration and other issues. An equally profound change was happening across town, when in September 1988 NCLR hired Cecilia Muñoz as a senior immigration policy analyst.

Unlike many of her colleagues who learned immigration after being assigned to the subject, Muñoz came to the issue with experience. She'd worked on immigration cases as a volunteer for a Catholic immigration program while in graduate school at the University of California-Berkeley in 1984, where one of her trainers was the Asian Law Caucus's Bill Tamayo, who'd spent much of that year lobbying against Simpson-Mazzoli. In September 1986 she relocated to Chicago, working as an organizer in the Catholic Charities' Parish Community Services office. Latinos were about half of Chicago's Catholics, and Cardinal Joseph Bernadin made it clear he wanted to "go big" on legalization. Muñoz got on the radar of Catholic Charities' officials charged with setting up the dioceses' legalization program via a constant barrage of questions: "What about this? "Have you thought of that?" she remembers pestering them. Just three months before amnesty's beginning, a senior Catholic Charities official appointed Muñoz to head the program, telling her that he'd had a dream in which, " 'The Lord told me you should run the legalization program.' I was 24 years old. It was crazy," she later recalled.[270]

Muñoz's awakening to the centrality of immigration and civil rights issues to her core identity had come just a few years earlier in high school. Born in the US of Bolivian immigrant parents who'd settled in the Detroit suburbs; according to one profile, she knew

> about the civil rights struggle which her parents told her was also their struggle. But she didn't feel a part of it until one day in high school when her boyfriend was over at the house listening to her father express his horror at the Central American wars, including the role of the United States. "Well you know Cecilia," her boyfriend said, "if we do end up in a war it seems like your parents should be interned. I couldn't know where their loyalties lay." Muñoz was astonished that anyone could think her family was anything other than fully American.[271]

Muñoz ditched the boyfriend and dedicated herself to a career in civil rights. Cardinal Bernadin's urge "go big" was translated to the young legalization director by her immediate superiors as "spend what you need to spend," so she did. The operation grew to twelve offices staffed with attorneys and paralegals—virtually all older and more experienced than their supervisor—trained by Mary McClymont's national office. Muñoz was active in the CCIP, which coordinated service delivery and pressured INS to interpret amnesty rules generously, holding community hearings as a way of "generating press coverage and elevating the visibility of the issues" the coalition had with INS. A young, obscure, highly articulate alderman named Luis Gutiérrez emerged as a key witness at one of these community hearings.[272] Elected to Congress in 1992, Gutiérrez later became perhaps the immigrant community's strongest advocate on Capitol Hill. It was her advocacy role that earned Muñoz a national reputation, which convinced NCLR in September 1988 to cobble together the funding to create a position for her when she expressed interest in relocating to DC.[273] Among NCLR's priorities was to address IRCA's "unfinished business": liberalizing procedures for the "second stage" of legalization that required amnesty recipients to pass an English and civics test or be enrolled in an approved course. NCLR called on Congress to extend the second-stage application period and to restore funding for SLIAG, which legislators had "borrowed" from the previous year, to finance the needed English and civics courses.[274] To support their networks, NCLR and the American Council for Nationalities Service produced a handbook on structuring the required English and civics courses and an "advocacy packet" outlining how to monitor and shape distribution of state SLIAG funds.[275]

But no issue generated more intensity at NCLR than the "family unity" question. After INS adopted in October 1987 its much-criticized "family fairness" policy, Rep. Roybal sponsored a provision preventing deportations of spouses and children of legalization recipients if either spouse qualified for amnesty; opposed by Rep. Mazzoli as overly broad, it passed the House but died in conference committee by a single vote.[276] A similar attempt by Senator John Chafee (R-RI), among the last of a dying breed of liberal Northeastern Republicans, also failed.[277] Soon the press was filled with stories of the children of legalization recipients, some as young as three years old, placed in deportation proceedings.[278] Expressing considerable exasperation at INS's "stonewalling," NCLR urged the enactment of generous family unity legislation.[279] This and other IRCA-related recommendations were included in a report Muñoz soon authored, titled *Unfinished Business: The Immigration Reform and Control Act of 1986.*[280]

Alan Simpson had some unfinished business of his own; at the top of his list was legal immigration reform. Under the nation's highly complex legal immigration system, in the late 1980s about 500,000 permanent residents were allowed into the US annually (not counting refugees), about three-quarters of whom had family ties; fewer than 10 percent were employment-based. Two distinct questions drove legal immigration reformers: one was qualitative: a trade-off between skills- and family-based immigration. Citing think tank reports that the economy needed more "high-skill" immigrants to fill projected labor shortages over the next dozen years, the business-oriented *Fortune* heavily favored increased visas for such workers.[281] Proponents of increased high-skill immigration such as Al Simpson favored a new "independent" stream of visas allocated through a point system rewarding educational attainment and other skills. But future job growth wouldn't be limited to high-skill occupations; in late 1985, the Department of Labor projected substantial growth in the next decade in the restaurant and hospitality industry, janitorial and cleaning services, and other sectors dependent on low-skill immigrants, many who could enter only as family-based immigrants.[282]

The second question was quantitative: How many legal immigrants should the country permit to enter? Simpson had proposed inclusion of a hard cap on legal immigration in IRCA, dropped the proposal in the face of staunch opposition from Peter Rodino, but vowed to return to the issue. The nominal 450,000 ceiling on legal immigration in existing law was routinely exceeded since it didn't apply to citizens' immediate relatives. Simpson argued that over time, legal immigration inevitably would rise as those legalized by IRCA naturalized and petitioned for relatives abroad, even though an analysis by the General Accounting Office suggested this concern about "chain migration" was somewhat exaggerated.[283] Immigration subcommittee chairman Ted Kennedy favored family immigrants, but was also under pressure from Irish constituents to provide visas to those without established family ties to the US. Irish immigration had fallen sharply following Europe's rapid economic recovery after World War

II, so few would-be Irish emigres had American family connections, while channels for "independent" immigrants with no family ties in the US had been further limited by the 1965 reforms.[284] As Ireland's economy stalled in the 1980s, growing numbers of undocumented Irish immigrants clamored for a "diversity" program to allow easier entry for themselves and their brethren.[285]

Alan Simpson no longer chaired the subcommittee in 1988 but, as one seasoned observer said, "He's so much become the key figure on immigration that he's almost got veto power over any bill."[286] Subcommittee chairman Kennedy and Simpson thus collaborated on a compromise: the legal immigration ceiling would be raised from 450,000 to 590,000 annually, mainly to accommodate so-called independent high-skill immigrants petitioned for by employers and diversity immigrants from places like Ireland, but immediate relatives of US citizens would, for the first time, be brought under a hard cap, with no more than 480,000 visas allocated to all family categories. The American Jewish Committee worried:

> If [visas for] immediate relatives of American citizens expanded even slightly, family immigrants would bump up against the cap. That would mean that other types of family sponsored immigrants, such as brothers and sisters of citizens or spouses and children of permanent resident aliens . . . would have to drop out of the system to make way for immediate relatives of citizens. . . . At current rates of immediate family entry, this offset process could happen as early as 1992.[287]

Concerns of family immigration proponents notwithstanding, with Kennedy and Simpson ramrodding the effort, the compromise passed the Senate by an 88–4 margin in May.[288] As usual, the lower body moved more slowly; it wasn't until July 28 that Rodino and Mazzoli introduced their own House counterpart that attempted to satisfy both sides of the "skills versus family" debate. Their bill maintained the existing family reunification system, provided an additional 150,000 high-skill worker visas, modestly increased temporary workers, and offered 800,000 more visas for close family members of newly legalized immigrants. At its core, Rodino's bill was based on his conviction that "the principle of family unity must remain the primary basis of our immigration policy"; it pointedly did *not* include an overall hard cap on legal immigration.[289]

While pleased with the direction of Rodino's bill, pro-immigrant groups' true preferences lay with legislation introduced in September 1988 by Rep. Howard Berman, which would have added even more family visas than the Rodino-Mazzoli bill by allowing the entry of immediate family members of lawful permanent residents without limitation, a privilege previously allowed only to relatives of US citizens.[290] Berman's bill had been drafted with help from the "Family Immigration Coalition" which was considerably larger than its predecessor, The Group, since the subject of legal immigration touched all of the field's core constituencies. In addition to the VOLAGs, the American Jewish Committee, represented by Director of National Affairs Gary Rubin and Legislative Director Judy Golub, was a major player. Asian groups, led by the Organization of Chinese Americans' Melinda Yee, were also very active, anxious to protect the immigration category allowing entry of brothers and sisters of US citizens, which was heavily backlogged and in danger of elimination. The AFL-CIO's Jane O'Grady and Janet Kohn were mainstays, reflecting labor's inherent suspicion of efforts to expand business-related visas. Muzaffar Chishti played a major role, in part because the legal immigration bill was the obvious vehicle for fixing IRCA's remaining loose ends. Rick Swartz remained engaged on the issue as a consultant. Aided by policy fellow Wendy Young, NCLR's Cecilia Muñoz was the most prominent voice for Latinos.

The coalition was nominally "chaired" by AILA's Warren Leiden, in the immediate post-IRCA era the unquestioned leader of the pro-immigrant forces in DC. For Leiden, "legal immigration reform was a 'meat and potatoes' issue, directly affecting the livelihoods" of his membership.[291] He was also one of the few players who truly understood the legal immigration system in all of its complexity; as Muñoz says, "Warren had the most expertise, he trained us all up, and led the [Family Immigration Coalition] meetings."[292] Leiden also was a key player in a business-oriented coalition hosted by the US Chamber of Commerce, whose main goal was securing increases in business-friendly temporary worker programs. As one scholar recounted, "the two coalitions met formally only once or twice, but they had a tacit agreement not to oppose each other's demands. Furthermore, the American Immigration Lawyers Association, a member of both coalitions, informally coordinated the flow of information about legislative goals and strategies between the two groups."[293] Despite the potential conflict in a contest between family and business visas Leiden had a clear strategy: "We realized that if each side (those favoring family vs. business visa supporters) thought of immigration reform as a zero-sum game in which visas for one group were seen as a loss for the other, there would be an ugly fight and someone would lose. The solution was to work together and make the pie bigger."[294]

Family immigrant advocates preferred the Rodino-Mazzoli version over its counterpart but feared that the less generous Senate bill would prevail in conference committee. To forestall that possibility, Cecilia Muñoz's first assignment at NCLR was to draft a letter "to stop the [Rodino-Mazzoli] legal immigration bill from going through the House."[295] However, that letter didn't come from NCLR but instead from eight members of Congress—three Hispanics, two Asians, and three African Americans, a precursor of the grouping that would later become formalized as the House "Tri-Caucus" representing the country's largest ethnic minorities—to Peter Rodino urging him to "commit yourself to opposing enactment of any legislation" that cuts family immigration.[296] The uniform opposition to movement of the House legal immigration bill by the Tri-Caucus effectively froze the Rodino-Mazzoli bill.[297] It seemed as if any bill to reform immigration had to die at least once in the House before being seriously considered.

Peter Rodino left Congress at the end of 1988; his successor was Texan Jack Brooks, who was a protégé of both House Speaker Sam Rayburn and President Lyndon Johnson, and was described by the *New York Times* as "pro-labor, pro-gun, fiercely partisan."[298] Reporters wrote that Brooks tried hard to cultivate an "irascible, cigar-chomping" persona that was distinctly Texan.[299] From the moment Brooks took over the committee in 1989, he was one of the strongest defenders of fellow Texan, embattled House Speaker Jim Wright, who'd assumed the speakership in 1987 but soon found himself embroiled in an ethics scandal, charged by Newt Gingrich with evading House rules limiting outside income.[300] The *New York Times* observed that Brooks offered an "outraged, not-give-an-inch defense" of Wright; by contrast, Ron Mazzoli, who personally attended some House Ethics Committee proceedings, told the press, "It is going to be very difficult for anyone to believe this was a partisan effort out to get the Speaker.[301] *Congressional Quarterly* noted that Brooks's "take-charge personality" bore "scant resemblance" to that of the more careful, cautious Rodino.[302] Mazzoli, who'd had his share of disagreements with Rodino, didn't see Brooks's ascension to the chairmanship as ominous, at least not at first. The immigration subcommittee chairman knew Brooks was "a tough cookie, and very, very partisan" but his biggest concern, given the direction of the committee room's air conditioning system, was that Mazzoli's seat on the committee dais was "downwind" of the chair's "smelly cigar."[303]

The gentleman from Kentucky soon had greater cause for complaint. In early 1989, Mazzoli was the victim of what writer Ellis Cose called "a brutal and humiliating coup" when his colleagues on the Judiciary Committee voted to remove him as chair of the immigration subcommittee, in part they said, because of his failure to support extension of the legalization application period aggressively enough. Mazzoli knew that his bipartisan approach to immigration, his earlier support for a do-over in the contested McCloskey-McIntyre election, and his open-minded posture on the ethics charges against Speaker Jim Wright ruffled Democrats' partisan feathers. Still, the move to strip him of his chairmanship caught him by surprise. Mazzoli later admitted, "I didn't see it coming until the night before, which is to say I didn't see it coming at all."[304] He was replaced by Connecticut's Bruce Morrison, then entering his fourth term in Congress. Unlike Mazzoli's, Morrison's liberal credentials were unquestioned: he'd headed New Haven Legal Services, which represented the poor and the elderly, before entering Congress.[305]

Despite the sea change in the lower body, some things seemed to stay the same in 1989. Again the Senate moved quickly, with Simpson and Kennedy introducing a compromise legal immigration reform bill, numbered S.358, in February. The bill added new business visas and raised the existing law's annual ceiling on legal immigration from 450,000 to 600,000, but included the hard cap on legal immigration opposed by the Family Immigration Coalition.[306] In March, the Judiciary Committee invited NCLR's Raul Yzaguírre to testify at a hearing but he wasn't available and designated the twenty-seven-year-old Muñoz to represent NCLR. Given her inexperience Kennedy's aide Michael Myers "politely requested" that she ask Yzaguírre to reconsider; instead, the NCLR CEO told his young staffer to "rise to the occasion."[307] Tracking the consensus positions of the Family Immigration Coalition, her testimony recommended removal of the hard cap and protections for family reunification, a legislative fix to the "family unity" problem for relatives of those newly legalized, and additional visas for family members of green card holders who'd yet to become citizens.[308] After the hearing, the AFL-CIO's Jane O'Grady and Janet Kohn called NCLR's leadership to assure them Muñoz had done well; as the younger NCLR staffer gratefully noted years later, "Without me even knowing it," the highly respected veterans O'Grady and Kohn, "were looking out for the younger women."[309]

However well Muñoz had done, Kennedy and Simpson had a deal. Kennedy would get a higher overall ceiling and the new "diversity" category of immigrants to placate the Irish; Simpson got increased visas for "high-skill" immigrants plus the hard cap.[310] The overall ceiling would go up, but visas for family members other than those of US citizens would drop. The bill passed Judiciary Committee in June. Demonstrating a flair for turning complex issues into soundbites, Muñoz told the *Los Angeles Times* that, "It looks like we're getting more when we're getting less. This legislation would completely undermine family immigration." Simpson shot back that his bill would bring in more "'classic immigrants'—those with something valuable to offer the nation," which advocates took to mean those from places other than Latin America and Asia.[311]

A CHANGING SCRIPT

Had the Senate followed the typical script, it would have swiftly approved the bill with minimal amendments. But under Leiden's tutelage, the Family Immigration Coalition worked the bill hard, armed with a GAO study suggested by NCLR and quietly requested by Kennedy that, according to Muñoz, showed that Simpson's hard cap would "decimate family immigration."[312] When floor debate on the bill began on July 11, the coalition gathered at the ACLU offices to work the phones and watch the action on C-SPAN. AILA staffer John Ohmer "narrated" the proceedings with an uncanny impersonation of John McGlaughlin, the pioneering host of *The McGlaughlin Group*, one of the first media "talking heads" television shows. The host introduced each segment of his show with his trademark phrase "Issue One!," offering his take before turning to a panel of pundits and concluded each program by demanding "Predictions!" of his guests on the outcome of a pending issue.[313]

On July 12, Ohmer announced, "Issue One: Family Unity!" as Sen. Chafee offered his amendment to stay deportations of the relatives of the newly legalized. The Family Immigration Coalition had lobbied the amendment heavily, recruiting allies like Rep. Howard Berman to weigh in with key senators. Simpson opposed the amendment, but perhaps sensing that the tide was running against him, expressed interest in negotiating with Chafee, who agreed to explore a compromise, a reasonable position since his minority whip had beaten him before on the issue. Watching the exchange on C-SPAN, an alarmed Muñoz raced to the Capitol and caught Chafee on the shuttle that ferries members between their offices and the floor. She told him that with Berman's help the coalition had nailed down the votes and urged him not to negotiate; Chafee agreed to hold firm.[314] Before the vote on Chafee's amendment, Ohmer called for "Predictions!" from the assembled lobbyists. Most thought they'd win a majority but perhaps fall short of the sixty votes required if Simpson chose to filibuster the provision; Ohmer and Muñoz predicted an outright win. Sure enough, Chafee's amendment prevailed by a filibuster-proof 61–38 margin.[315]

Next up—"Issue Two" in McGlaughlin parlance—was an amendment cosponsored by conservative Utah Republican Orrin Hatch and moderate Arizona Democrat Dennis DeConcini, setting a "floor" below which family visas could not fall, "piercing" Simpson's hard cap to maintain a minimum number of family visas equal to current law.[316] Again the coalition prevailed, by a healthy 62–36 vote.[317] "Issue Three" was a provision, opposed by Asian and Latino groups, to ease entry for independent immigrants that were proficient in English. It had been included in the original bill, but was knocked out in committee after Kennedy backed away from it, "much to Simpson's annoyance."[318] Simpson tried to restore the provision on the floor, but lost again, this time by a 43–56 vote margin.[319] The next day, on July 13, moderate Republican Arlen Specter scored a win for the business coalition, winning thirty thousand additional business visas on a 78–21 vote, with both Kennedy and Simpson voting "no."[320]

It would've been surprising for Simpson to lose any major immigration vote, much less four big ones, which Muñoz attributed to the Family Immigration Coalition's hard work, broad diversity, and depth: "We visited every single Senate office, most several times. Even though our 'field' was mostly smoke and mirrors we had some unusual assets. . . It made a difference when OCA [the Organization of Chinese Americans] brought in major [campaign] donors to lobby Republican offices."[321] Leiden was a bit more matter-of-fact, later saying, "The conventional wisdom was that Simpson couldn't be beaten in the Senate. But we had a job to do, we took it seriously, and we did our job."[322] Ohmer had a simpler take: "Simpson rolled by Family Immigration Coalition!" he "announced" at the conclusion of the debate.

As amended, the Senate bill increased the overall "pierceable" immigration ceiling to 630,000 visas annually.[323] The bill passed the Senate on the evening of July 13, 1989, by a 81–17 vote, and both Kennedy and Simpson were "optimistic" that the House would also act that year.[324] But the lower body took no action on legal immigration reform in 1989. New subcommittee chair Bruce Morrison had not yet articulated his own priorities, although major bills had been introduced earlier that year by Howard Berman and the Judiciary Committee's ranking member Hamilton Fish. Berman's bill outlined the Family Immigration Coalition's wish list, while Fish's more centrist legislation was his indication of how far he thought he could go before losing the Bush administration. As NCLR noted at a hearing that fall, both Berman and Fish proposed significant increases in family immigration, and neither proposed a hard cap on immigration overall.[325] Morrison did introduce an important bill of his own, best characterized as IRCA "cleanup" legislation, that among other measures prohibited the INS from deporting immediate family members of newly legalized immigrants.[326]

INS commissioner Nelson had been replaced by Eugene McNary, county executive of St. Louis, whose sole qualification seemed to be that he'd headed the region's Bush campaign. NCLR opposed McNary's nomination due to his limited immigration background, but he was quickly confirmed and sworn into office in October.[327] The canny McNary quickly requested a meeting with NCLR. Echoing candidate Bush's call at the Republican National Convention for a "kinder and gentler" America, McNary emphasized his desire to improve the agency's image. Muñoz shot back that exposing newly legalized immigrants' families to deportation was "neither kind nor gentle." McNary promised to resolve the long-simmering issue as soon as he could. At a House hearing in November, much of the attention focused on Morrison's proposal to prohibit the INS from deporting immediate relatives of those legalized. Opponents like former INS commissioner Nelson testified that "the potential number is obviously enormous," while the Center for Immigration Studies estimated that Morrison's bill "would grant *de facto* residence status to some 1.5 million" people.[328]

The advocates fought back with compelling human interest stories. In December, some two dozen service providers met with McNary. Dallas Catholic Charities' Vanna Slaughter raised what she called the "outrageous" case of "a 35-year-old hotel employee, who was handcuffed and removed from his home near Dallas on September 20 and deported to El Salvador," leaving behind his newly legalized wife, a maid, to support their six-week-old child and three other US citizen children alone.[329] McNary got the message. On February 2, 1990, the INS revised its previous "Family Fairness" policy to provide all spouses and children under eighteen of legalized immigrants, with protection from deportation and work authorization.[330] The *Washington Post* editorialized that the new policy was "sensible, humane, and fair."[331] NCLR's Muñoz said she was "very pleased with a policy that keeps families together."[332]

Subcommittee chair Bruce Morrison also drew attention at the beginning of 1990, by announcing his candidacy for governor, unusual because the representative was challenging an incumbent of his own party.[333] And on March 19, Morrison introduced the "Family Unity and Employment Opportunities Immigration Act of 1990"; it was breathtakingly generous, proposing an increased overall visa ceiling of 800,000 from the nominal 450,000 limit in current law.[334] It incorporated the provision of Berman's bill that allowed immediate relatives of permanent residents to enter without limitation, and included 95,000 new employment-based admissions, several IRCA "cleanup" measures including "family unity" protections, and in a nod to organized labor, a 65,000 limit on high-skilled temporary workers, with slightly relaxed entry requirements to placate business.[335] Said one observer, it was a "something-for-everybody strategy" perhaps motivated in part by Morrison's gubernatorial candidacy.[336]

With multiple demands on its chairman's time, subcommittee markup took nearly a month, beginning on March 20, but not ending until April 18.[337] There was also a considerable delay before the full Judiciary Committee took up the bill, due in part to Morrison's campaign schedule as he moved from longshot to front-runner status in his gubernatorial bid.[338] In the interim, various parties raised concerns. Labor was uneasy with higher visa numbers for employment-based immigrants, while business thought they weren't high enough. Bush administration officials weighed in against the expansion of uncapped admissions to immediate relatives of permanent residents and limits on temporary workers, indicating they would recommend a veto if left unchanged.[339] Judiciary Chairman Brooks laid down his own markers, expressing his interest in limits far closer to the Senate bill than those preferred by Morrison and Berman, prompting Michael Hill, the US Catholic Conference's chief lobbyist, to send an urgent memo to the Family Immigration Coalition in July titled "Saving the Legal Immigration Bill."[340] As Morrison was campaigning, California Rep. Howard Berman served as the de facto lead sponsor of the bill. Coming off of the pivotal role he'd played in the negotiations that had produced the SAW program in IRCA and helping win the Chafee family unity amendment, Berman was a known quantity, trusted by key players on immigration policy; according to NCLR's Muñoz, "Howard [Berman] really took the lead behind the scenes in orchestrating" various interests to support the bill.[341] Swartz agreed, writing to

Moakley aide Jim McGovern that Berman had, "done much more member work than Morrison. He is also close to relevant Democratic groups and key Republicans on this issue."[342]

Full Judiciary Committee markup of the bill was completed in a single day, just before the traditional August recess.[343] Despite the Family Immigration Coalition's concerns that it might move in a more restrictionist direction, Morrison's bill passed largely intact by a 27–12 vote.[344] Back on the campaign trail, Morrison won the Democratic gubernatorial primary, putting him in a three-way race in November against a Republican and former liberal GOP Senator Lowell Weicker, running as an independent.[345] Meanwhile, Swartz organized pro-immigrant business interests, as well as allies inside the Bush administration, such as senior domestic policy staffer Charles Kolb, to support the bill.[346] Archbishop Bernard Cardinal Law, chair of the Catholic Bishops' Committee on Migration, wrote to White House Chief of Staff John Sununu emphasizing the legislation's "pro family" provisions and urging support.[347] The payoff: Bush's official "Statement of Administration Policy" on the bill, while raising a few concerns, replaced its previous veto threat with more favorable language: "The Administration supports legal immigration reform that would enhance skill-based immigration while facilitating unification of families. It also supports an increase in immigration levels above those in current law."[348]

The House began floor action on the bill on October 2. An outspoken opponent was Rep. Lamar Smith (R-TX), in just his second term in Congress but already ranking minority member of the immigration subcommittee, succeeding Dan Lungren, who'd left Congress in 1989 for a post in California state government and a successful run to become the state attorney general in 1990.[349] Unlike Lungren, who'd worked closely with his Democratic counterpart, Smith was an anti-immigration, partisan hardliner; he framed the choice posed by Morrison's bill simply: whether the country should have more or less immigration. "Every poll taken in the last decade has shown that the majority of Americans do not want an increase in legal immigration," Smith said.[350] He offered an amendment to "recommit" the bill to the committee—essentially killing it—which failed by 72 votes.[351] Just after noon the next day the House passed the measure by a comfortable if hardly overwhelming 231–192 vote; Democrats supported the bill by a 186–65 margin, while Republicans broke against the legislation 127–45.[352]

Despite Smith's best efforts, the bill that passed the House was undeniably generous, increasing the overall immigration ceiling to 775,000 annually, although the unlimited entry of immediate relatives of permanent residents initially included was replaced by a modest increase in that visa category.[353] The bill also included the "family unity" protections for ineligible family members of newly legalized immigrants and an additional 55,000 visas for three years to speed their adjustment to permanent status, as well as an extension of the "second stage" legalization application period.[354] Concerned with the direction of the House bill and with evidence of growing undocumented immigration, Senator Simpson said in September that the legal immigration reform should be linked to a more secure Mexican border, widely interpreted as a threat "to scuttle a bill he no longer liked." After passage of the House bill, for a time the Senate minority leader resisted going to conference with his counterparts in the lower body to reconcile the two bills.[355] But it was no longer his call to make. Some twenty-four House conferees were appointed on October 17, the large number required to accommodate members from other committees with partial jurisdiction over the bill; the now Democratically controlled Senate followed by appointing its five conferees on October 23.[356]

The target congressional adjournment date, already postponed several times, was Friday, October 26, so once again the sponsors of immigration reform were racing the clock. Informal talks began even before conferees were appointed, and the big issues were settled relatively quickly. Simpson conceded that there would be no hard cap on overall legal immigration; in return the total "pierceable" ceiling would be 700,000 for the first three years and 675,000—slightly less than the midpoint between the Senate's 630,000 and the House's 775,000—thereafter.[357] Of the 675,000 total, 480,000 (71 percent) were allocated to family visas; 140,000 (21 percent) to independent immigrants and skilled workers; and 55,000 (8 percent) to the new "diversity" category.[358] Over the weekend before the conferees were to convene formally, Morrison predicted "smooth sailing." But pushed by the Family Immigration Coalition, conferee Howard Berman said the compromise was less generous than he'd hoped on family immigration, while Rick Swartz declared "the process is far from over."[359] The conferees met on October 24 and 25, and rapidly confirmed the major elements of the pre-conference deal-making.

The last loose end was the Moakley-DeConcini bill to protect Salvadorans from deportation. Conditions had continued to deteriorate in El Salvador since 1986, when it was excised from IRCA. In November 1989, six Jesuit priests, their housekeeper, and her daughter were murdered by a death squad; Speaker Wright appointed Joe Moakley to head a task force to investigate the murders. Two decades later, declassified documents analyzed by the Institute for Policy Studies revealed that the Salvadoran military planned the murders, and that US officials had "foreknowledge" of the plan.[360] Moakley couldn't know that at the time, but still smelled a rat; his task force's April 1990 report found that the Salvadoran government's own investigation was "at a standstill" and implicated the US-backed military in the murder and cover-up.[361] A year earlier, Moakley had succeeded Claude Pepper as chairman of the Rules Committee, making it possible for him to orchestrate House passage of his bill providing protection

Policy Primer: Legal Immigration

Around the time of IRCA's passage, operating under the legal immigration system largely established by the Immigration Act of 1965, about 500,000 immigrants entered the US annually, distributed among seven categories, called preferences in the Immigration and Nationality Act [with 1987–1991 average annual entries in brackets]:

- "Exempt" immigrants—spouses, unmarried minor children, and parents of US citizens—allowed to enter without limitation [224,842 annually].

- First Preference—unmarried adult children of US citizens [13,599 annually].

- Second Preference—Spouses and unmarried children of lawful permanent residents [108,824 annually].

- Third Preference—Professionals, especially gifted scientists and artists [26,939 annually].

- Fourth Preference—Married children of US citizens [24,697 annually].

- Fifth Preference—Adult brothers and sisters of US citizens [64,943 annually].

- Sixth Preference—Skilled and unskilled workers filling labor shortage needs [26,844 annually].

(Note: this listing excludes refugees and certain other limited programs.) Except for those in the exempt category—immediate family members of US citizens, refugees, and a few other exceptions—entry of immigrants was also limited by "per-country ceilings" of 20,000 per country (although Canada and Mexico gained higher ceilings in IRCA).

In that era, while somewhat difficult to generalize:

- Advocates of immigration restriction, including the Federation for American Immigration Reform, favored a hard cap on immigration such that increases in the exempt category would be offset by reductions in other categories.
- In general, business interests supported while organized labor opposed increases in the skills-related categories (Third and Sixth Preferences).
- Latino, other ethnic, and religious organizations opposed the hard cap and supported increases in family categories.

against deportation and work authorization for Salvadorans and Nicaraguans, but Simpson had blocked action in the Senate. Advocates for Moakley-DeConcini saw the legal immigration bill as the perfect "vehicle" for it to be attached to, as they'd come so close to achieving with IRCA.[362]

With conference committee winding to a close, advocates, including the ACLU's Wade Henderson, Rick Swartz, now a private consultant, Swartz's successor Frank Sharry, CWS's Joy Olson, and the ABA's Carol Wolchok, gathered to attend the waning minutes of the conference committee. Simpson clearly felt he'd already conceded too much: in what he called an "anguishing" compromise, he'd lost his hard cap on legal immigration and thus failed to cut family visas.[363] He'd also been forced to swallow the legalization "family unity" provisions that had passed both houses, and he was worried about rising apprehensions at the border.

As Sharry recalls, Moakley made a powerful plea for his bill, and Simpson asserted that the "temporary" Salvadoran migrants wouldn't return home. Simpson then nudged fellow conferee Kennedy, who reiterated his support for Moakley-DeConcini but said perhaps it shouldn't be attached to this bill; the two Senators had agreed to support each other's "bottom lines" and this wasn't on either's list.[364] Moakley blew by his home state senator's half-hearted opposition; he spoke directly to Simpson, and countered that while he would never force people back into a war zone, he *was* prepared to put *"real teeth"* into the bill to ensure that Central Americans returned once conditions in their home countries allowed. "What do you need, Senator Simpson? Just tell me, what do you need?" Moakley demanded. Simpson hesitated before responding, providing an opening for House Judiciary Committee chairman Jack Brooks, with his trademark cigar in hand and consciously deploying his Texas drawl for emphasis, to intervene:

> Now, *Mistuh* Simpson, uh, *Senatuh* Simpson, you know I have great respect for you. I would like to remind you *suh*, over here in the House *Mistuh* Moakley is chairman of the *Ruuuuuules* Committee. And that makes *Mistuh* Moakley a very important person when we want to pass bills and move projects and so forth. And I just want to ask you, *suh*, as a personal courtesy, that we find some way to accommodate *Mistuh* Moakley.[365]

All eyes shifted to Simpson. Moakley remained quiet, knowing when not to break the weighty silence. The Senate minority whip slowly raised his head, looked across the table at the Massachusetts congressman, and asked, "Are you really serious about putting teeth into this thing? Because if you are, we can have our staffs work out the language." There was an audible sigh from advocates who'd worked for nearly a decade for safe haven as they rushed out of the room to help Moakley staffer Jim McGovern to craft the "teeth" Simpson wanted.[366]

The result was a new "Temporary Protected Status" allowing the executive to defer deportations of those "from countries experiencing war, natural disaster, or other extraordinary conditions" for renewable eighteen-month periods (half of the bill's original time period).[367] The law specifically named nationals from El Salvador as beneficiaries of the new status, benefitting an estimated half-million Salvadoran nationals then in the US, although in a way that didn't codify the designation in the Immigration and Nationality Act itself.[368] Providing the "teeth" that Simpson demanded, the bill denied recipients a path to permanent residence, and required "any legislation that would provide such a route" to obtain approval of three-fifths (60 votes) in the Senate.[369] Senate sponsor Dennis DeConcini later recognized many longtime advocates of the legislation, including congressional staffers Michael Myers and Jim McGovern; Wade Henderson, Morton Halperin, Amit Pandya and [executive assistant] Susan Hansen of the ACLU; the American Bar Association's Carol Wolchok; Church World Service's Joy Olson, Frank Sharry, Rick Swartz and others for their help in passing the legislation while taking his "victory lap" during final floor debate on the Immigration Act of 1990.[370]

Still, it wasn't certain the consensus would hold. Several lobbyists in the Family Immigration Coalition felt they'd been short-changed by the conference agreement; a heated discussion on whether to support the final compromise ended only when Muñoz announced that NCLR's board of directors had voted unanimously to support the bill.[371] The main House architects were sufficiently concerned they held a press conference to extol the bill's virtues just before it went to the floor. Lead sponsor Bruce Morrison noted the bill promoted "the fundamental values and goals of immigration policy," like family unity, economic competitiveness, and diversity. Hamilton Fish called the bill "masterful" in the way it balanced the various interests, noting that the Bush administration did not oppose the bill's higher levels of immigration. Howard Berman pointedly observed that the House measure rejected the premise of the original Senate bill to "increase skilled worker visas at the expense of family reunification."[372]

Almost lost in the last-minute conference deliberations was Simpson's price for accepting the Moakley-DeConcini provisions: tougher enforcement measures against illegal immigration, including a new pilot program to test a "more secure form of identification" for job applicants to prove their eligibility to work.[373] The provision was so obscure that the typically thorough *New York Times* story on the conference bill failed to mention it.[374] But Rep. Edward Roybal thought it tantamount to a national ID card, and led the fight against it on the evening of October 26 by opposing the rule providing for consideration of the conference agreement. Roybal had been the face of the opposition to IRCA, but seemingly had lost influence when Rep. Esteban Torres and other moderates in the Hispanic Caucus had broken away to negotiate a more palatable bill. But on this issue Torres backed his senior colleague.[375] The rule was defeated as the Hispanic, Black, and Asian Caucuses joined with GOP opponents of the higher immigration levels allowed by the bill to vote against the rule by a 235–186 margin.[376]

With just two weeks left before the midterm election on November 6, it appeared the bill was dead. Howard Berman, who had done as much as anyone to shape the measure, lamented that, "I don't know when we'll ever get a bill this good for the Hispanic and Asian communities."[377] It seemed IRCA's "follow on" bill was destined to die twice before it could be passed; many were resigned that, as with its predecessor, the third time would have to be the charm. But unlike IRCA in 1984, the legislation was revived in record time. That evening, Simpson agreed to remove the offending provision in what were literally "11th hour negotiations."[378] The revised bill flew through the Senate floor, Moakley pushed a rule through his committee at 1:49 a.m., and hours later, on October 27, the bill passed the House by a 264–118 vote in a rare Saturday session, hours before the end of the 101st Congress.[379] President Bush hailed the bill as "the most comprehensive reform of our immigration laws in 66 years."[380] Bruce Morrison had helped produce a major reform, but narrowly lost his gubernatorial race.[381]

According to Warren Leiden, the Immigration Act of 1990 was "sweeping reform" that provided a "modest but important increase in family-based immigration," and more employment visas.[382] The New York Times cited estimates that the bill "would increase legal permanent immigration to the United States by more than 35 percent."[383] Others predicted larger increases in legal entries "far above the 700,000" ceiling, due to the growth in uncapped visas for immediate relatives of US citizens.[384] Academic Carolyn Wong understatedly observed that the bill was "unexpectedly expansive," and fellow scholar Rita Simon found it "amazing" that the "most liberal immigration act" in history "actually passed."[385] Taking a deserved victory lap, the American Jewish Committee said, "For advocates of a generous, family-oriented and pluralistic immigration policy, the 1990 legislation must be regarded as a considerable triumph."[386]

NCLR claimed credit for helping to preserve family immigration, procure IRCA family unity protections, an additional year for legalization's "second stage" applications, and a separate bill that facilitated correction of legalization applicants' Social Security earnings records, predicting a "new era" reflecting "an overwhelming consensus that immigrants are good for the United States."[387] Even activist-academic critics known to criticize it for insufficient militancy took note, writing: "Through the NCLR's monitoring of legislation, research on issues, lobbying, and public pronouncements . . . [it] replaced LULAC as the leading Hispanic organization."[388] Warren Leiden thought that IRCA had been "the last time that Congress would give the Latino community the back of the hand and get away with it," and the 1990 Act seemed to portend a brighter future for pro-immigration and Hispanic advocates.[389] But 1990 arguably was the high point for influence of Latino and immigrant communities that later experienced spectacular population growth, but without a concomitant increase in political clout.[390]

A BIG TENT

After the release of the explosive WITAN memo and the disclosure of grants from the eugenics advocate Pioneer Fund to groups in FAIR founder John Tanton's network provoked a firestorm of criticism, he seemed defensive as he decried allegations of racism, writing to supporters, "No, I am not a racist."[391] But if Tanton publicly distanced himself from the darkest interpretations of the WITAN memo and Pioneer Fund grants, Dan Stein, who'd succeeded Roger Conner as FAIR's executive director, eagerly embraced them, telling a reporter, "I stand by our taking grants from the Pioneer Fund."[392] He charged that immigrants were engaged in "competitive breeding," asking, "Should we be subsidizing people with low IQs to have as many children as possible, and not subsidizing those with high ones?" adding that, "Certainly we would encourage people in other countries to have small families. Otherwise, they'll all be coming here, because there's no room at the Vatican."[393] Rather than fleeing from the implications in Tanton's WITAN memo, Stein explicitly connected the dots: white Americans (with high IQs and small families) were losing a "breeding competition" with ineducable, unmeltable, low IQ, Catholic, Latin American immigrants.

Tanton's own "contrition period" was brief. In 1990, he founded and still serves as publisher of the Social Contract Press, which issues a quarterly journal often featuring white nationalists.[394] US Inc., Tanton's "holding company," funded a group called American Patrol/Voice of Citizens Together in 1992, and the next year supported the California Coalition for Immigration Reform. Others followed, including a political action committee first called FAIR PAC and later renamed US Immigration Reform PAC and NumbersUSA.[395] Publicly, Tanton claimed no knowledge of some of his network's unseemly ties, a posture one critic derided as "willful ignorance."[396] Privately, Tanton corresponded with white nationalists and developed his own eugenics theories. He wrote one donor that, "One of my prime concerns is about the decline of folks who look like you and me" and told a friend, "for European-American society and culture to exist requires a European-American majority, and a clear one at that."[397] He started his own eugenics group, but to deflect controversy, wrote that it would do its work "under the term genetics rather than eugenics."[398]

The coarsening of the public rhetoric emanating from groups in Tanton's growing network was almost immediately noticeable. FAIR director Stein told the *Village Voice* that if immigration was not curtailed, "a bloody battle . . . would be settled in the street."[399] Barbara Coe, of the Tanton-funded California Coalition for Immigration Reform, repeatedly and publicly referred to Mexicans as "savages"; American Patrol posted a cartoon on its website picturing a Latino winner of the Presidential Medal of Freedom being urinated on, although the post was later deleted.[400] According to the Center for New Community, Rick Oltman, FAIR's western regional director in the 1990s, was a member of the Council of Conservative Citizens, whose statement of principles states in part:

> We . . . oppose the massive immigration of non-European and non-Western peoples into the United States that threatens to transform our nation into a non-European majority in our lifetime. We believe that illegal immigration must be stopped, if necessary by military force and placing troops on our national borders; that illegal aliens must be returned to their own countries; and that legal immigration must be severely restricted or halted through appropriate changes in our laws and policies. We also oppose all efforts to mix the races of mankind.[401]

Local chapters of the Council of Conservative Citizens went on to hold some thirty rallies or demonstrations in the 1997–2003 period protesting the entry of "brown-skinned immigrants."[402] Tanton quietly promoted the work of Jared Taylor, the publisher of *American Renaissance*, where he wrote, "When blacks are left to their own devices, Western civilization—any kind of civilization— disappears." Taylor and Glenn Spencer of American Patrol together concocted and promoted a new theory: the "Reconquista," that, in various iterations, the Mexican government, Mexican Americans, Mexican immigrants, or Latino activist organizations planned to reconquer the southwestern US and return it to Mexico. Spencer confidently predicted that as a result of the conspiracy, "a second Mexican-American War would erupt in 2003."[403] Lack of any actual evidence to support the existence of the "Reconquista" plot or the forecasted race war between the US and Mexico hasn't stemmed its frequent propagation. In form and content, the theory bears remarkable resemblance to Anglo fears in the early 1900s of a border "race war," used to justify the violence against and repatriations of Mexican-origin residents that followed.

In 1998 Tanton set his sights on forcing the Sierra Club to step into the immigration debate on the side of the restrictionists. The club was prize target, with more than 550,000 members, a brand strong enough to be a household name, and what one reporter called "a score of legislative triumphs." Its democratic structure—board members and initiatives could qualify to be voted on by the membership with just a few hundred signatures—made it vulnerable to campaigns by a motivated subset of members.[404] Tanton friend Alan Kuper led the campaign for "Alternative A," a proposition to require the club to support reduced immigration, by recruiting support from "environmental heavy-weights."[405] The Sierra Club leadership, which earlier voted to take no position on immigration policy, warned the initiative "would drive away minority groups, especially Asian and Hispanic people in the club's traditional stronghold of California."[406] Club executive director Carl Pope charged that some Alternative A proponents were "extremists acting from racial prejudice," and Zero Population Growth's policy director called FAIR "just reprehensible."[407] The initiative failed by a 60 percent to 40 percent margin in an election with an unusually high number of ballots cast. According to the *New York Times*, club officials "reacted with relief that bordered on glee" at what Pope called "a landslide."[408] The relief might've been tempered had they known that this was just the first such effort.

FAIR and its allies found a more receptive audience among conservative intellectuals. In the late 1990s, a *Wall Street Journal* column warned that *National Review*, the magazine that for decades was the standard-bearer for conservative intellectual thought, was "making common cause" with FAIR and "touted FAIR positions in its editorials." The column also observed that FAIR had partnered with conservative icon Paul Weyrich to produce fifty hour-long programs for his National Empowerment Television network.[409] *National Review* and Weyrich were big "catches" for FAIR. Known for espousing the free-market, limited-government principles bedrock among conservatives, in 1962 the *National Review*'s longtime chief William F. Buckley Jr. had gained plaudits for purging the extremist John Birch Society from the "respectable right."[410] Now driven by the belief that everyone in the US must assimilate to "the WASP norm," as eminent immigration historian Aristide Zolberg wrote, the *National Review* became "in effect an outlet for the Federation for American Immigration Reform."[411]

FAIR's other new ally Weyrich was a founder of the Heritage Foundation, and had coined the term "moral majority" before it was adopted by the Rev. Jerry Falwell for his own evangelical-political group. When it came to racial and cultural issues, Weyrich once wrote of the "unbreakable and causal relationship between traditional Western, Judeo-Christian values, definitions of right and wrong, ways of thinking and ways of living—the parameters of Western culture—and the secular successes of Western societies."[412]

National Immigration Forum founder Rick Swartz grew alarmed by FAIR's growing power in conservative circles. He'd developed strong relationships with pro-immigrant conservatives linked to former New York congressman, Bush cabinet secretary, and later vice presidential candidate Jack Kemp. Kemp was a pro football star turned congressman who many credit with convincing candidate Ronald Reagan to make "supply side economics" the core of his administration's economic program, and a "big-tent" Republican so committed to reducing poverty among minorities that he was called a "bleeding heart conservative" by his biographers.[413] Kemp was passionately pro-immigrant and had a large circle of protégés; many worked with Swartz to push back against FAIR.[414]

In 2000, FAIR took another step in its evolution, running negative "issue advertisements" against incumbent GOP Michigan senator Spencer Abraham, then in a tight race against centrist Democratic challenger Debbie Stabenow. Then chair of the Senate Immigration Subcommittee, Abraham worked closely with the pro-immigrant left to support family visas and with businesses seeking workers to fill technology-related jobs in Silicon Valley, and FAIR wanted him out of the Senate. It was rare for any nonprofit group to engage directly in an election; ads had to be carefully constructed and timed to comply with election and tax laws. When nonprofits did engage in elections, they often did so through front groups, but FAIR proudly "branded" its ads, which proved controversial. One issued in both TV ad and brochure formats, was headlined "Why is a U.S. Senator trying to make it easier for terrorists like Osama bin Laden to export their war of terror to any city street in America?"[415] Below the headline were pictures of Abraham, who is of Lebanese heritage, next to that of bin Laden, prompting a critic to write, "The despicable implication was clear: Abraham, an Arab-American, wanted to repeal the provision [capping numbers of high-tech guestworkers allowed to enter the US] in order to protect his terrorist kinfolk."[416] The *Detroit News* editorialized that "FAIR's established sympathy for virulent causes and organizations does not entitle it to be taken seriously."[417] The city's Jewish Community Council compared the ads to "the ugly rhetoric that stimulated ethnic cleansing in Bosnia and Kosovo, and was used by the Nazis throughout Europe."[418] Alan Simpson, who'd joined FAIR's national advisory board after his retirement from the Senate, resigned in protest.[419] The ads were pulled, but Stabenow beat Abraham by a little over one percentage point. Although their impact on the outcome was unclear, virtually all election recaps mentioned FAIR's ad campaign.[420]

At the close of the twentieth century, FAIR's evolution toward the right both reflected and drove the movement of grassroots conservatives toward immigration restriction. It may also have been inevitable: FAIR's first direct-mail fundraising and recruitment efforts three decades earlier had revealed a membership ready for harder-edged racial-cultural messages, much to the chagrin of then-executive director Roger Conner, who would have preferred a constituency of old-fashioned labor liberals. John Tanton's other major creation, US English, had also begun by promoting itself as a centrist, even progressive organization, but according to journalist and critic James Crawford, a survey of US English's membership in the late 1980s—two-thirds or more were elderly, white, male, and Republican, the majority college-educated and many quite affluent—showed a strikingly "candid admission of ethnic intolerance": "When asked what had prompted them to support the organization, 42% endorsed the statement: 'I wanted America to stand strong and not cave in to Hispanics who shouldn't be here.' "[421]

Apparently without even trying to, US English had attracted a large dues-paying constituency, a significant plurality of which was driven by a desire to "not cave in to" Latinos, while FAIR's losses seemed more than offset by new recruits: white nationalists, intellectual elites committed to preservation of a dominant white, European majority in the US, and ordinary people worried about the rapid pace of demographic change. Tanton, it seems, had created a new "big tent" for anti-immigrant restrictionism.

CHAPTER 8

Ripples

SANCTIONS

A year after IRCA passed, then-INS commissioner Alan Nelson touted declining border apprehensions as evidence that IRCA was "working effectively," concluding, "The evidence is strong that employer sanctions is [sic] having a major impact on discouraging people from illegal entry into the United States."[1] Private scholars moved quickly to test Nelson's claims. Two think tanks, the left-leaning Urban Institute and the center-right Rand Corporation, jointly launched an ambitious, multimillion-dollar round of research studies on IRCA.[2] Their first assessment, in 1989, came to no conclusions about employer sanctions' effectiveness in deterring unauthorized migration.[3] One study in the series speculated that employer sanctions might have reduced illegal entries, although even its authors doubted the impact was permanent.[4] But most Urban and Rand researchers found little if any reduction in unlawful migration due to employer sanctions.[5]

Others confirmed that the law was ineffective. One survey of recent immigrants by US and Mexican scholars in June 1988 found, "no sign the legislation has had any impact on flows [of immigrants from Mexico]."[6] Another reported that it "found no evidence that the 1986 law has shut off the flow of undocumented migrants."[7] By 1991, even the government conceded the law wouldn't work; a Labor Department study said sanctions would not "significantly deter illegal immigration" or "curb the growth in the underground economy."[8] Before long, as Roberto Suro of the *New York Times* wrote, Nelson was "almost alone in asserting that sanctions have substantially cut the flow of illegal immigrants."[9]

The most commonly cited reason for the failure of employer sanctions was the widespread availability of fraudulent documents. IRCA required employers to verify the eligibility of new hires by checking a list of approved documents, but given the wide variation of different types of papers issued by federal and state agencies, it couldn't force employers to make judgments about their authenticity. Under the law, said Kitty Calavita from the University of California-Irvine, "Because of the ready availability of fraudulent documents, employers can comply and still employ the same [undocumented] people they always have."[10] But when INS cracked down on the growing cottage industry that produced false documents, the counterfeiters—often with the cooperation of employers, tacit and otherwise—found other ways to evade the law.[11] Defenders of the law said a "secure identifier," what opponents labeled a "national ID card," would solve the problem. But that proposal had been rejected by the Select Commission and in IRCA in part because "polls revealed sharply negative [public] reactions to a national identity card."[12] Expansion of the "telephone verification" pilot program, the high-tech alternative to an ID card proposed in the 1990 Act, wrote Roberto Suro, "encountered fierce resistance" that almost killed the bill before it was removed.[13] The pilot program soon morphed into an online system now known as E-Verify, but it was also fraught with problems, as later analyses showed.[14]

Rep. Chuck Schumer blamed continued unauthorized migration on the Reagan and Bush administrations' failure to fund border enforcement.[15] This was true enough; sustained increases in funding for enforcement didn't begin until a decade after IRCA, in the second term of the Clinton administration.[16] Others attributed the reticence of successive administrations to invest heavily in enforcement of employer sanctions or border controls to lack of political will.[17] For example, a prominent immigration lawyer found that when representing legalization applicants, INS was "very adversarial," but when it came to employers, the Service became "very easy going and cooperative."[18] And post-IRCA, it was common for lawmakers to exert pressure on INS to back off of enforcement efforts when they interfered with constituent business interests.[19] Independent analysts began to doubt that there was ever any intent to enforce the law; the Urban Institute's Michael Fix concluded that sanctions weren't designed in a way to reduce unlawful migration, but to "create a symbol and perception" of control.[20]

Or, it might've been that the employer sanctions weren't enforceable at all. INS relied heavily on the idea that employer sanctions would "work, like tax laws, if the majority of employers comply voluntarily."[21] This may have been true for mainstream employers that only rarely and inadvertently employed unauthorized workers, but the fact that most employers complied with the law was essentially irrelevant if most undocumented workers were hired by a few firms at the margins of the economy; as *Fortune* reported, "Employers who rely on undocumented workers are not in the mainstream of American business."[22] These firms, typically in tough, low-margin, ruthlessly competitive businesses like agriculture, garments, textiles, construction, and other manual labor, soon found multiple ways to avoid enforcement. Some actively assisted workers in procuring false documents or faked the paperwork, providing the appearance of compliance while retaining their unauthorized workers, a practice still widespread today.[23]

Others kept the workers without actually hiring them. The practice of outsourcing the responsibilities of employment wasn't new, but employer sanctions offered an additional incentive for growers and other immigrant-heavy businesses to avoid formal hiring of employees, instead misclassifying them as contractors. Until stopped by a 1989 California State Supreme Court decision, some growers in that state had relied on the legal fiction that some twenty thousand farmworkers were purported "sharecroppers," and thus not employees, as a way of avoiding wage and hour, occupational safety, child labor, and workers compensation rules.[24] But even after this decision, variants of the practice continued, even expanded.[25] While agriculture may have pioneered the practice of outsourcing legal liability for hiring unauthorized workers, it spread rapidly and remains prevalent in the modern era.[26]

Starting with Reagan, each successive administration promised tougher employer sanctions enforcement.[27] Still, after 1990, the unauthorized population stubbornly kept growing by about 350,000 annually, and even more rapidly later on.[28] As one analysis later concluded, even if toughened up with better document verification systems, employer sanctions could never be effective against the "small number of employers that knowingly hire unauthorized workers precisely *because* they are cheaper and more exploitable than those with legal status."[29]

Beyond the policy's ineffectiveness, more critical to The Group was its conviction that employer sanctions would cause job discrimination against Latinos and others perceived to be "foreign-looking."[30] During the IRCA debate few "influentials" had agreed and many mocked the advocates' predictions of discrimination, but after the law's enactment, the evidence mounted. An ACLU-MALDEF report documented hundreds of cases of job bias caused by IRCA. One Latina, Sandra Garcia Johnson, a US citizen, had no issues with her job search until she separated from her husband and reverted to her maiden name; interviewers then began asking her for a "green card" and accused her of fraud when she asserted her American citizenship. Another US citizen, Richard Trujillo, was denied a job because he couldn't produce an INS number or work visa.[31] A half-dozen other reports issued by local immigrant coalitions, state or local agencies, and the US Commission on Civil Rights all found that employer sanctions led to increased job bias against authorized Latino and other "foreign-looking" workers.[32] Subsequent survey research confirmed the largely anecdotal early studies: scholars comparing pre- and post-IRCA earnings of various groups found that after controlling for relevant variables, sanctions produced "substantial" declines in Latinos' wages, compared to those of whites, which rose during the period studied.[33]

But the study that really mattered was issued in the spring of 1990, by the General Accounting Office, or GAO. Under Senator Kennedy's soft sunset amendment, GAO was required to conduct a series of studies to determine whether employer sanctions caused "a widespread pattern" of discrimination; an affirmative finding would trigger an automatic joint resolution forcing Congress to consider sanctions repeal.[34] (The hard sunset version sponsored by Rep. Garcia that was dropped in conference committee would have automatically terminated employer sanctions after six years, requiring an affirmative vote by Congress to reinstate them.) GAO's first report, in 1988, had estimated that over a half-million employers had adopted unlawful discriminatory practices after IRCA, but speculated that INS's employer education efforts would reduce job bias.[35]

But in March 1990 GAO published its long-awaited report; according to the *New York Times*, GAO "estimated that as a result of the law, 461,000 employers, representing 10% of the total in the United States, adopted practices that discriminate on the basis of national origin. In addition, the agency said, 430,000 employers, 9% of the total, had decided that because of the law they would hire only United States citizens and would exclude legal aliens who are authorized to work in this country."[36] The *Washington Post* reported that GAO supplemented its employer survey with 360 "paired tests" where the agency "sent a pair of testers—one of which was Hispanic-looking, the other Anglo-looking—to 360 randomly selected employers. Hispanic testers were three times as likely to encounter unfavorable treatment when applying for jobs, and Anglo testers received 52% more job offers."[37]

Whether the job bias caused was a "molehill" as employer sanctions proponents charged, or a "mountain" as its opponents had predicted, was in the eye of the beholder. Senator Simpson criticized the GAO report, citing an internal memo that questioned how much of the discrimination found could be attributed solely to employer sanctions. GAO head Charles Bowsher stood by the finding, saying that "all points made" in the memo were taken into consideration, and that the memo's author had signed off on the final draft.[38] In introducing the repeal resolution triggered by the report, Senator Kennedy admitted that "congressional sentiment at this time is not to vote on repealing employer sanctions but to try and reform them first before any repeal is found necessary."[39]

Kennedy was right, but employer sanctions opponents hoped to use the report to force a vote in the short term and to strengthen the longer-term case for repeal. Their only chance was for the repeal campaign to be viewed as a civil rights question, and that required the Leadership Conference on Civil Rights—the civil rights community's preeminent voice—to join the effort. The Group long believed that the LCCR's reticence to speak to the issue had undercut their claim that sanctions would cause discrimination but now hoped that the third GAO report would convince skeptics that sanctions-induced job bias was real, forcing the coalition to revisit the issue. In late March, NCLR's Raul Yzaguirre sent a hand-delivered letter to the Leadership Conference's executive director Ralph Neas—copied to the coalition's executive committee—to "formally request" an opportunity to discuss "the enormous and growing problem of employment discrimination resulting from" employer sanctions. Citing the reports documenting discrimination and the coalition's previous refusal to take a stand, the letter concluded that those who continued to support employer sanctions, "whatever their motives, will be responsible for denying hundreds of thousands of Hispanic Americans and others the right to seek and hold a job."[40] He upped the ante with an op-ed in the *Washington Post* demanding repeal of employer sanctions, calling it "the classic definition of a bankrupt policy—all costs, no benefits."[41]

Despite the pressure, the NAACP and the AFL-CIO twice blocked the Leadership Conference from endorsing employer sanctions repeal.[42] The frustrated Latino groups then decided to quit the coalition. MALDEF and NCLR agreed to announce their resignations on the day of the Leadership Conference's fortieth annual gala dinner in May, and also planned a demonstration outside the event followed by a walkout. In a news release issued that day, Yzaguirre said, "We can no longer belong to a coalition which neither respects nor supports the civil rights of the Hispanic community."[43] The walkout threat—which would have been the first public resignations from the coalition since 1967—led to a hastily called meeting at the Hyatt Regency on Capitol Hill, the site of the dinner, just hours before the gala was slated to begin.[44] Among those called to LCCR chairman Ben Hooks's suite were executive director Ralph Neas, Wade Henderson of the ACLU, Elaine Jones of the NAACP Legal Defense Fund, the AFL-CIO's Kenny Young, LCCR vice chair Judith Lichtman of the Women's Legal Defense Fund, MALDEF's Antonia Hernández, and NCLR's Yzaguirre and Kamasaki.

Hooks, then in his thirteenth year heading the NAACP, had considerable "standing" to resolve the issue. By tradition the NAACP's CEO chaired the LCCR's governing body and Hooks was personally liked and respected by the parties.[45] African Americans Jones and Henderson urged cross-racial solidarity, and Neas, Hooks, and Lichtman asked the Hispanics to "keep the coalition together" while they resolved the dispute. Hernández later told the press, "Some of our closest friends and allies were asking us not to resign. They were asking for time." The Latino groups agreed to stay, at least for the moment.[46] They came to an uneasy deal: Hooks would try to reverse the NAACP's position on employer sanctions at the association's upcoming convention. They'd look for ways for LCCR to support the Latino groups' call to repeal employer sanctions within the coalition's rule that required a consensus of the executive committee to take a formal policy position. But it was too late to call off the demonstration; some one hundred protestors greeted the arriving attendees dressed in tuxedos and party dresses.[47] That night, indirectly referencing discrimination against Latinos that he believed the Leadership Conference had long been reticent to acknowledge, Yzaguírre told the dinner's attendees:

> We have experienced the pain of being an afterthought. We have watched as our issues were ignored; and we have witnessed a process that says we do not count as much as other groups. . . . Once more we are asked to be statesmen, to be concerned about the larger issues and the long-term consequences. And once more we have reached deep into our reservoir of good will. . . . But know that our hope is not unlimited, that our patience cannot be taken for granted, and that our faith is not fathomless.[48]

Tears were shed during his remarks, and as Hernández spoke, but especially when Hooks, in his beautiful baritone voice, led the participants, each clasping their neighbors' hands, in the movement's traditional closing hymn, "We Shall Overcome." True to his word, Hooks led a tough floor fight at the NAACP convention in July, where the venerable association voted to call for employer sanctions repeal despite, a reporter observed, "opposition from a vocal minority who briefly disrupted" the event.[49] But the AFL-CIO resisted allowing the coalition to endorse sanctions repeal while footnoting labor's disagreement, a typical resolution of divisive issues, until Mort Halperin of the ACLU, which by tradition did not take positions on federal judicial nominations but had never blocked the Leadership Conference from doing so, warned the AFL-CIO's general counsel Laurence Gold: "'If the AFL-CIO continues to block consensus, then . . . going forward, the ACLU will prevent the LCCR from ever taking a position on [nominations of federal] judges.' He came back a week later, and said, 'We'll take the footnote.'"[50]

Notwithstanding the Leadership Conference's footnoted support, Kennedy's employer sanctions repeal legislation and a similar repeal effort the next year sponsored by Rep. Edward Roybal and Sen. Orrin Hatch died quiet deaths.[51] But the Hyatt Regency meeting did produce a side benefit for one participant: it put Wade Henderson squarely on Ben Hooks's radar screen. After the NAACP's Washington representative Althea Simmons passed away a few months later, Hooks tapped Henderson for the prestigious, highly visible job.[52]

IN THE INTERIM

Pro-immigrant reformers soon suffered three bitter defeats on immigration policy. The first was passage of California Proposition 187 in 1994. The proposition known as Save Our State sought to eliminate undocumented immigrants' access to almost all public services. It was drafted in part by former INS commissioner Alan Nelson, now a FAIR consultant, and was supported by the Tanton-funded California Coalition for Immigration Reform. Former senator Pete Wilson made it the centerpiece of his gubernatorial campaign, launching his successful candidacy with an infamous television ad that "showed grainy footage of Mexican migrants racing across the border as a narrator intoned, 'They keep coming. . . . Enough is enough.'"[53]

Recognizing the threat posed by an anti-immigrant initiative in the nation's most populous state, Frank Sharry went on leave from the National Immigration Forum to work with the opposition group, Taxpayers Against 187.[54] Its campaign focused heavily on the threats to the general well-being of the public if Proposition 187 was adopted, and was criticized by activists for putting "middle class concerns front and center" and failing to adequately defend immigrants.[55] For his part, Sharry noted that activists' opposition rallies featuring Latino protestors waving Mexican flags predictably fueled support for the ballot proposition.[56] The initiative passed with 62 percent support from a deeply divided electorate: 75 percent of Latinos voted against Proposition 187, 75 percent of white voters supported it, and African Americans were evenly split.[57] Ultimately, the initiative was found unconstitutional by the courts.[58] But within pro-immigration advocacy circles, the stinging defeat deepened a growing divide between DC-based advocates and field-based organizers. Echoing past debates and presaging future ones, the Beltway groups were viewed as excessively cautious by the activists, while the national organizations thought the field-based community organizers naïve and unrealistic.

In truth, Proposition 187 was propelled by forces outside the control of either camp: highly racialized white resistance to the state's growing Latino population. Conventional wisdom attributed the proposition's passage to fiscal policy concerns exacerbated by the state's sluggish economy, but researchers that actually interviewed the initiative's backers found something else:

> While supporters would first offer seemingly colorblind defenses of the initiative—concerns with law or with the state budget—they almost all soon shifted to racial defenses that made clear the "our" in Save Our State meant that the state was, ultimately, the property of white and native-born Californians. As one supporter put it, "When you look at this country, you see it's kind of an island of English-speaking people surrounded by Latinos. Lots of Mexicans. . . . You know you're an island here and eventually that island's going to be swamped."[59]

The Republican takeover of Congress was equally consequential. Led by Speaker-to-be Newt Gingrich, the GOP won a net of 54 House seats, and a majority in the Senate, and thus control of the levers of power—committee chairmanships and the scheduling of bills—in both legislative bodies.[60] Anti-immigrant hard-liner Lamar Smith became chair of the lower body's immigration subcommittee and Alan Simpson resumed his leadership of its Senate counterpart, although he suffered a personal defeat when he was replaced as minority whip by Trent Lott, viewed by many as a tougher, more conservative alternative. It was a sign of the GOP's harder-line orientation, leading M. Stanton Evans, longtime chairman of the American Conservative Union, to wonder how once-iconic figures were now seen as "having strayed from the right's own version of political correctness."[61]

The shifting political winds had direct impact on immigration policy. After passage of Proposition 187 and huge Democratic losses in midterm elections, President Bill Clinton disappointed pro-immigrant advocates by appointing former Rep. Barbara Jordan, a civil rights icon but a longtime immigration hawk, to chair the Commission on Immigration Reform, a body created by the Immigration Act of 1990. As part of a larger package of reforms, Jordan's commission called for creation of a national ID card to enforce employer sanctions, cutbacks in protections for asylum seekers, and reduction of legal immigration by a third.[62] Clinton promptly endorsed the proposals. Building on the report, as usual Simpson moved quickly, introducing in early 1995 a series of bills that proposed stronger enforcement against illegal immigration, cutbacks in legal immigration—including the so-called hard cap he had failed to procure in the 1990 legislation—and tougher restrictions on asylum.[63]

New House subcommittee chair Lamar Smith, expertly staffed by Cordia Strom, who'd once worked for FAIR's litigation arm, quickly made his mark. He introduced breathtakingly comprehensive legislation to cut legal immigration by one-third, impose significant new enforcement measures to stop illegal immigration, sharply restrict entry of refugees and cut back on due process protections for asylum-seekers: it was virtually the entirety of FAIR's "wish list." Smith held a single hearing within days of introduction, then marked up the bill in subcommittee just two weeks later. By the August recess, the legislation was poised to hit both the House and Senate floors.[64]

Faced with a three-front battle—legal immigration, illegal immigration, and refugees were addressed in Smith's bill—the Beltway groups, including the National Immigration Forum and NCLR, decided to try and remove the legal immigration provisions from consideration. Forum founder Rick Swartz played a significant role in building his trademark "left-right" coalition to support the effort. Among the DC advocates' most important allies was Rep. Sam Brownback (R-KS), staffed by a bright young intellectual named Paul Ryan.[65] The DC advocates, joined by high-tech companies, pro-immigrant conservatives, and quietly and reluctantly by the Clinton administration, ultimately succeeded in "splitting the bill" to preserve legal immigration.[66] But the strategy also split the pro-immigrant advocacy community. As head of the National Immigration Forum, Frank Sharry bore the brunt of the ire of activists outside the Beltway; they believed he was abandoning the undocumented, while he countered that the advocates' limited resources could best be deployed to preserve legal immigration.[67]

The bill's attacks on refugees and asylum protections were partially mitigated only after heroic lobbying by pro-immigration and human rights advocates.[68] A grave threat to the bill arose when California Rep. Elton Gallegly won, by a huge 257–163 margin, a floor amendment that echoed the harshest aspect of Proposition 187, to bar undocumented children from public schools.[69] The amendment's backers weren't the least bit deterred by the fact that it violated the Supreme Court ruling in *Plyler v. Doe*; with the courts moving in a more conservative direction they welcomed the chance to revisit *Plyler*.[70] Urged on by political advisor Rahm Emmanuel, President Clinton, who was up for reelection that year, was inclined to support whatever Congress passed.[71] But Gallegly's amendment was too much for Clinton, who threatened a veto if the provision was included.[72] It was duly removed in conference committee, clearing the way for enactment of the Illegal Immigration Reform and Immigrant Responsibility Act (IIRIRA, often referred to by its acronym pronounced "ira-ira" by insiders).[73]

The enforcement provisions that remained were still extraordinary. In particular, the bill established what are now known as the 3/10 year bars. As one expert analyst explained, the 3/10 year bars state that any immigrant that enters the US unlawfully

> and stays in the U.S. illegally for more than six months but less than one year may not leave, re-enter, or apply for a green card for three years [3-year bar]. Any immigrant who illegally stays for more than a year may not leave, re-enter, or apply for a green card for 10 years [10-year bar]. Any immigrant who violates it triggers a twenty-year ban from re-entering the United States *for any reason*. That's a problem because almost all applicants for a green card or visa have to visit a U.S. embassy or consulate abroad to apply . . . thus triggering the bars. The 3/10 year bars prevent any unauthorized immigrant from using the legal immigration system [emphasis in the original].[74]

Intended to reduce the undocumented population by providing a strong deterrent against entering illegally, the law had exactly the opposite effect. For decades prior to IIRIRA, substantial numbers of people already in the US, including those who had entered unlawfully, had been able to adjust to permanent residence status or engage in what scholars call "circular migration," coming to work temporarily and then returning home. Since employer sanctions had failed to reduce unlawful employment and border controls were just ramping up, large numbers of undocumented people continued to enter the US. IIRIRA both prevented them from adjusting to lawful status and discouraged them from leaving, a phenomenon firmly established in a series of studies by Princeton University professor Douglas Massey and his colleagues.[75] As a result, the unauthorized immigrant population more than doubled from about 5 million in the mid-1990s to a peak of 12 million over the next decade. An estimated 5.5 million of these were people who otherwise would have been able to adjust to legal status if not for IIRIRA's 3/10 year bars.[76]

Another IIRIRA provision, known as 287(g) after its designated section in the Immigration and Nationality Act, exposed the growing unauthorized population to exponentially greater risk of deportation.[77] The 287(g) program authorized formal agreements between the INS and state-local police, allowing the latter to perform the duties of federal immigration agents, serving as a "force multiplier." Operating under various names and its scope ebbing and flowing with the political winds, eventually the program became a key lynchpin of the strategy of attrition to force undocumented immigrants to self-deport by increasing their likelihood of apprehension. Proponents framed it as a bulwark against crime committed by unauthorized immigrants.[78] But independent studies later found that the program was not effectively targeting serious offenders.[79] Critics also charged that it facilitated racial profiling and decreased public safety by discouraging immigrants from reporting crime.[80] But all of that came later.

Legal immigrants were hardly unscathed in 1996. President Clinton had distinguished himself from "tax and spend" liberals by famously pledging to "end welfare as we know it." After negotiations between Clinton and House Speaker Gingrich, a compromise welfare reform bill, the Personal Responsibility and Work Opportunity Reconciliation Act, opposed by virtually every progressive group, passed and was signed by the president. The law did reduce welfare rolls, but it also gutted the social safety net.[81] A key question in the negotiations was how to pay for job training and other supports to help people move from welfare to work. In the final bill about $23 billion—nearly half of the total financing—came from eliminating *legal* immigrants' eligibility for most federal benefits: not just welfare or Aid to Families with Dependent Children, but Supplemental Security Income (SSI), food stamps, Medicaid, and others; it also authorized states to deny other benefits to legal immigrants.[82] Recognizing the cuts were targeted at predominantly Hispanic immigrants, NCLR's Sonia Pérez, head of NCLR's Economic Mobility Project, called the move "a conscious decision to cynically exploit anti-immigrant sentiment."[83]

Stunned by the double-whammy of IIRIRA and welfare reform, the immigrant advocates regrouped into two overlapping coalitions. One, the Rights Working Group chaired by Karen Narasaki of the National Asian Pacific American Legal Consortium (now Asian Americans Advancing Justice), included legal-oriented organizations, refugee advocates, and the National Immigration Forum. They sought to restore the due process protections for immigrants, refugees, and asylees lost in IIRIRA under the banner Fix '96.[84] A second group, an expanded version of the Family Immigration Coalition that had shaped the Immigration Act of 1990, focused on restoring the benefits to legal immigrants lost in welfare reform. Key players included the National Immigration Law Center, the National Asian Pacific American Legal Consortium, the Council of Jewish Federations, and antipoverty advocates, all coordinated by the National Immigration Forum and NCLR, which hosted its weekly meetings.[85]

By 1996, the National Immigration Forum had become a very different organization. Soon after Swartz's departure in 1989, it became a straightforward, pro-immigrant advocacy group. Through the mid-1990s the immigrant rights coalitions catalyzed by IRCA implementation remained represented on its board, along with DC-based unions, business, and civil rights groups. Along with streamlining its name, it gradually shed its founder's goal of serving as an "organization of organizations" for the pro-immigrant field in favor of concentrating on its core competencies of communications and lobbying. Executive Director Frank Sharry had developed considerable skill and expertise in communications strategy and built a prominent press profile. Longtime Deputy Director Angie Kelly, of a Bolivian immigrant family, ran the Forum's legislative operation coordinating pro-immigrant lobbying by national advocacy organizations and state-based activists; inside the Beltway, the Forum generally was viewed as the "voice" of the pro-immigrant field in the nation's capital.[86]

The advocates knew that reopening just-passed, popular legislation like welfare reform would be a huge challenge, but they were aided by other factors. President Clinton expressed regret about the immigrant benefit cuts and promised to help reverse them.[87] Immigrant billionaire George Soros, outraged by the cuts in benefits to noncitizens, created the $50 million Emma Lazarus Fund to support programs to help immigrants naturalize, setting aside 10 percent for advocacy to restore the lost benefits.[88] Soros's funding underwrote a major expansion of local advocacy as well as citizenship programs, much-needed since, as NCLR's Cecilia Muñoz recalls, the immigration grassroots field capacity was extremely limited.[89] Until Soros's investment, pro-immigrant advocates couldn't mobilize large protests or rallies; that soon began to change.

Another factor was a sophisticated communications strategy; DC advocates realized they needed to augment research, policy analysis, and lobbying with new, potentially game-changing strategies to reshape the environment in which the legislation would be considered.[90] Frank Sharry thought that "strategic communications" was that game-changer. In his work against Proposition 187, Sharry had learned how political campaigns used "public opinion research"—polling, focus groups, and message testing—to shape communications strategies.[91] Just before IIRIRA and welfare reform passed, he asked Mary McClymont of the Ford Foundation for help to build the pro-immigrant advocacy field's strategic communications capacity. She arranged for the Communication Consortium Media Center to conduct the research and assist in developing more effective messaging.[92] Armed with the research, the advocates, led by Sharry and Muñoz, launched a two-pronged strategic communications campaign. One targeted the general public, but required advocates to shift from their traditional "civil rights-oriented" messaging to "simple, human, emotional appeals to fairness and compassion" and to emphasize that diversity was good for the US. The second focused on immigrants and their families, mainly via the ethnic press, and "included a sharp-edged appeal to these communities to stand up for their rights, naturalize, and vote."[93]

The campaign required both "message discipline" and diplomacy. For ethnic advocates, it meant backing off of their traditional civil rights rhetoric toward messaging designed not to offend a public increasingly uncomfortable with demographic change. Managing dynamics within NCLR also required Muñoz to convince her group's management, as a colleague later wrote, "to *hold press conferences where we would not speak and generate articles and news stories in which we would almost never be quoted* [emphasis in original]."[94] The National Immigration Forum increasingly served as the pro-immigrant field's communications hub, providing media training in using the new messaging to advocates across the country.[95] Combining the sophisticated messaging, cooperation between local and national groups, and lobbying, the benefits restoration campaign, Sharry noted, was "a completely new approach to the [immigration advocacy] field."[96] It was also stunningly successful.

In 1997, working closely with Clinton White House legislative aide Janet Murguía, the coalition tackled the restoration of health programs and SSI benefits for the blind, elderly, and disabled, highlighting stories of diverse groups whose benefits were threatened. They brought forth an eighty-five-year-old Russian Jew who'd lost an eye fighting the Nazis who was facing loss of his $484 monthly SSI check, and a sixty-eight-year-old Laotian refugee who had worked with the CIA to rescue downed American fighter pilots in Vietnam who was being cut off from his only source of income.[97] One advocate warned of a forthcoming "spate of suicides" among the disabled or elderly losing SSI benefits.[98] Many scoffed at the warnings until seventy-five-year-old Ignacio Muñoz fatally shot himself two weeks after receiving notice that his $440 in monthly disability benefits were being terminated.[99] Congress soon agreed to restore SSI and many health benefits for all legal immigrants in the US as of the date of enactment of welfare reform.[100] The 1997 bill restored nearly 50 percent of the benefits lost just a year earlier.[101]

In 1998, again working closely with Janet Murguía and the Clinton administration, the coalition succeeded in restoring food stamp benefits for about 175,000 low-income, legal immigrant children. Backed by the National Immigration Law Center, local coalitions joined with antipoverty advocates to enact legislation in dozens of states and large cities to help offset some of the lost federal assistance.[102] In Texas, NCLR's Clarissa Martínez De Castro collaborated with the Center for Public Policy Priorities, headed by former state lobbyist Dianne Stewart, to pass unexpectedly generous benefits restorations.[103] By 2000, the benefits restoration campaign was widely applauded, and Cecilia Muñoz's role in it was recognized via a prestigious MacArthur Fellowship, the so-called genius grant. When Muñoz went to her boss Raul Yzaguírre to inform him of the honor, a staffer recalls, she "could not get the words out. She burst into tears because she felt he [Yzaguírre] should have gotten the award."[104] In 2002, this time working with George W. Bush's administration, the coalition restored food stamp benefits to an additional 363,000 legal immigrants who'd resided in the US for at least five years.[105]

Trendier NCLR staffers were more impressed when in 2002 "La Raza" was mentioned in an episode of the television series, *The West Wing*.[106] They thought this was a *real* sign of the group's prominence. Even before that, polls of Latino "influentials" found that NCLR had emerged "by all accounts" as the community's leading advocate.[107] And years later, it was one of a dozen groups recognized by scholars in the book *Forces for Good*, the nonprofit equivalent of the bestseller *Good to Great*, which analyzed key ingredients of corporate success.[108] Quoting Yzaguírre, *Forces for Good* cited the combination of policy advocacy and field programs as one of the six essential practices of high-impact nonprofits.[109]

NCLR's ascendance took place against a backdrop of unique challenges facing its two major competitor-allies. LULAC was hit by the indictment and then conviction of a past president, Jose Velez, on ten counts of immigration fraud.[110] Velez had been elected president at the group's 1990 convention in a hotly disputed election.[111] A self-described entrepreneur, Velez had operated a highly lucrative immigration consulting business to assist IRCA legalization applicants in Las Vegas. According to INS officials, he charged his eight hundred clients a total of $300,000; but submitted only seventeen completed applications, "leaving the rest to collect dust."[112] After his conviction in 1995, Velez essentially became a nonperson in LULAC's public communications; evidence of his tenure was even removed from the organization's website.[113] The group understandably reduced its profile on immigration policy for a time, and focused on addressing its long-standing structural and financial issues.[114]

MALDEF faced a different problem: an increasingly hostile federal judiciary. More than any president before him, Ronald Reagan consciously changed the direction of the judiciary by appointing numerous "movement conservatives" to the federal courts.[115] Many predicted that Reagan judges would limit the effectiveness of litigation-focused organizations like MALDEF.[116] Reagan's strategy worked, as federal courts began to reverse course from that set by their more liberal predecessors.[117] The trend also constrained MALDEF's resources: fewer lawsuits meant reduced revenue from legal fees awarded to lawyers on the winning side, and with fewer major cases filed, many foundation funders that supported racial justice strategies began to look elsewhere. And in part as a result of its financial constraints, MALDEF experienced substantial turnover in its DC office, especially compared to the high degree of "continuity of NCLR's staff."[118]

NCLR had just emerged from its own fiscal problems. In the late 1980s, its media center had become "a major [financial] drain on the organization, and the group had trouble keeping up with its bills." Phoenix-based housing director Mark Van Brunt recalled that, "my paycheck bounced at one point and I got on the phone to find out what happened, and the phone was dead!"[119] The group's 1988 audit said NCLR had "a net capital deficiency that raises substantial doubt about its ability to continue as a going concern."[120] In plain English: it was insolvent and probably wouldn't make it. In response, NCLR CEO Yzaguírre reduced his salary and deferred several paychecks and Executive Vice President Emily Gantz McKay took out a second mortgage to lend cash to her employer, which was also forced to ask an affiliate for a loan.[121] NCLR somehow raised enough unrestricted revenue—particularly from its growing annual conference that Kamasaki had complained so much about earlier—to generate regular operating surpluses, and pulled out of the red by 1993.[122]

As the new millennium approached, pro-immigrant advocates were confident. They'd won a round of major legislative battles to largely restore benefits to legal immigrants. Naturalization rates increased "for the first time in decades," spurred by funding from Soros's Emma Lazarus Fund.[123] The new citizens promptly turned out to vote in record numbers, especially in California. Before 1996, GOP presidential candidates had won the state's electoral votes for two decades straight; except for the flukish election of quasi-Republican Arnold Schwarzenegger, generally pro-immigrant Democrats have dominated statewide elections ever since, with supermajorities in the legislature. Although it's a more complex story, the conventional narrative, as professor Nicole Hemmer wrote, was that "Republican nativism helped turn California blue."[124] Both demography and political momentum seemed to be on the side of Latino and immigrant rights advocates. But FAIR founder John Tanton had other ideas.

UN-FAIR

Even after failing in 1998 to force the Sierra Club to adopt formal policy calling for reduced immigration to the US, FAIR founder John Tanton kept trying. In 2004, he and his allies lost another election in a result one former Sierra Club president called a "stunning rejection of the anti-immigration forces."[125] But Tanton kept coming back.[126]

Tanton had more success cementing ties with white supremacists. A FAIR-produced TV program, *Borderline*, featured Samuel Francis, editor of the Council of Conservative Citizens newsletter, and the political action committee run by Tanton's wife Mary Lou, US Immigration Reform PAC, hired a staffer with white nationalist connections.[127] In response, in 2008 the Southern Poverty Law Center added FAIR and other Tanton groups to its official list of "hate groups."[128] The typically careful and reticent Anti-Defamation League followed suit, referring to the group as "extreme" and to Tanton as "racist," concluding one exposé by writing, "FAIR claims that it is mainstream. Its record says otherwise."[129]

FAIR also made inroads with conservative media. By the mid-2000s, FAIR executive director Dan Stein was a frequent guest on *Lou Dobbs Tonight*, the CNN program that focused on immigration in a tone that media watchdogs called "consistently alarmist."[130] Dobbs even once broadcast his radio program from a FAIR event.[131] But it was FAIR's synergistic relationship with conservative talk radio that was a true breakthrough. Rapid growth of talk radio programming began in 1987 when the Federal Communications Commission ended the so-called fairness doctrine that previously required broadcasters to present diverse opinions. It accelerated rapidly as technological advances—MP3 players like the iPod, music streaming over the internet, and satellite radio—made it difficult for radio stations to retain young music lovers.[132] The remaining demographic—smaller, older, and whiter than before—wanted other programming; the most popular format was what became known as talk radio.

FAIR courted the talk radio "shock jocks" at its annual Hold Their Feet to the Fire event that hosted fifty or more hosts at the Phoenix Park Hotel on Capitol Hill.[133] The event soon had its own acronym, F2F, short for "feet to the fire," where lawmakers, law enforcement officials, and celebrities were interviewed by popular radio talk show hosts who used inflammatory language. One host at F2F 2016, Jeff Katz, suggested that "drivers who run over illegal immigrants at the border should win food from Taco Bell." Another, Steve Gill, mused about sending armed forces to the border to shoot people. Others at the event were "obsessed with exposing 'Radical Islam,'" stated that the Congressional Black Caucus was "racist," called President Obama an "affirmative action hire," and, of course, questioned the authenticity of his birth certificate.[134]

The inroads Tanton-sponsored groups were making in the "respectable right" alarmed Linda Chavez, a darling of movement conservatives. After a controversial stint as a Reagan-appointed director of the Civil Rights Commission, in 1992 she wrote *Out of the Barrio*, which forcefully attacked bilingual education, called on Latino immigrants to assimilate, and often blamed government programs and left-leaning civil rights groups for disadvantages experienced by Hispanics.[135] Widely admired on the right, she was "vilified" by the left, a frequent target of demonstrations when invited to speak at college campuses, and was once even punched by a protester.[136] She had briefly worked for US English before resigning in protest after release of Tanton's WITAN memo, and went on to head the Center for Equal Opportunity, a respected conservative think tank dedicated to promoting "a colorblind society."[137]

The smart, well-spoken, and attractive Chavez often chided civil rights groups for being overly sensitive to perceived racial slights with articles like "Lighten Up on Political Correctness."[138] In the mid-2000s, she grew concerned that coverage of immigration on conservative media, influenced by FAIR and the Center for Immigration Studies, had infected the GOP mainstream.[139] By 2007, she'd had enough of thinly veiled racial rhetoric from some Republican reform opponents, and wrote an article entitled "Latino Fear and Loathing" for the conservative website *Townhall.com*, where she observed:

> Some people just don't like Mexicans—or anyone else from south of the border. They think Latinos are just freeloaders and welfare cheats who are too lazy to learn English. They think Latinos have too many babies, and that Latino kids will dumb down our schools. They think Latinos are dirty, diseased, indolent, and more prone to criminal behavior. . . . Unfortunately, among this group is a fair number of Republican members of Congress, almost all influential radio talk show hosts, some cable news anchors—most prominently, Lou Dobbs— and a handful of public policy "experts" at organizations such as the Center for Immigration Studies, the Federation for American Immigration Reform, NumbersUSA, in addition to fringe groups like the Minutemen.[140]

Her article produced a torrent of exactly the kind of loathing referred to in her piece: some three hundred responses in *TownHall*'s comments section called Mexicans or Latinos: pigs, human locusts, baby factories, inferior, retards, lazy, disease infested freeloading moochers, lazy good for nothing drunks, and so on. Chavez wryly commented in a second installment that, "It seems I've touched a raw nerve among my fellow conservatives."[141] The conversation resumed on *National Review Online*, where she went after the Center for Immigration Studies' Mark Krikorian, a contributor to *National Review*, for calling Latino immigrants "illiterates from south of the border." Writing that she'd made a career of "attacking the Left when it veered into anti-Americanism or promoting racial divisions," she concluded, "I expected more from my fellow conservatives."[142] But by then they were listening to different messengers.

A month after Chavez's *National Review* article, in July 2007, a comprehensive immigration reform bill collapsed on the Senate floor under a deluge of more than a million faxes, largely generated by NumbersUSA, another one of John Tanton's creations. Most attributed the bill's failure to opponents' ability to generate enormous resistance to amnesty for undocumented immigrants. NumbersUSA's Roy Beck credited his "grassroots army" of nearly a half-million members with the bill's defeat.[143] According to Beck, in 2013 his email list included two million "ordinary Americans," and a video of his original 1996 traveling roadshow and an updated version cumulatively had more than 7.5 million online views.[144] Equally important was the growing influence of Tanton's progeny in the burgeoning Tea Party movement.

Arising after the election of President Barack Obama at the height of a massive recession and what many viewed as unjustified government bank bailouts, the Tea Party was an interconnected but not always cohesive set of local and national groups said to be united by anger about the economy and distrust of the "establishment." It was an authentic grassroots movement, researchers wrote, "almost uniformly white, disproportionately older than the general public, more likely to have a college or advanced degree, and . . . fairly or very well off."[145] It had a collective membership of three hundred thousand, another three million had attended at least one rally or given money to a Tea Party group, and as many as sixty-three million Americans, or 27 percent of US adults, "strongly approved" of the movement.[146] Tea Partiers opposed federal debt, although "the great majority" of them also strongly supported Social Security and Medicare—by far the two largest sources of federal budget outlays.[147]

Tea Party supporters were also inclined toward immigration restriction. Many Tea Party members were drawn to immigration based on what they saw as an overlap between their twin goals of reducing immigration and shrinking government budgets. According to a study by Harvard's Theda Skocpol and Vanessa Williamson, "Tea Partiers regularly invoke illegal immigrants as prime examples of freeloaders who are draining public coffers."[148] Some Tea Party groups waded into immigration heartily, and not coincidentally, since NumbersUSA's Roy Beck and other restrictionists were key players in the Tea Party movement. A 2010 report by the Institute for Research and Education on Human Rights named Beck as a leader in Tea Party Nation, a former FAIR staffer as a leader in Resist.net, and said that leaders of the 1776 Tea Party, "were imported directly from the anti-immigrant vigilante organization, the Minuteman Project."[149] Others found that Tea Partiers were driven in part by racial resentment and support for immigration restriction, noting that two other Tea Party groups, Voice of the People USA and Tea Party Patriots Live, were supported by ALI-PAC, and another had ties to FAIR.[150] It wasn't surprising then, that Tea Party Nation jumped in with both feet into immigration issues, such as the 2010 debate over Arizona's SB 1070, also known as the "papers please law."[151]

Tea Party Patriots, with its claimed 2,200 local affiliates, insisted that it would not get involved in immigration policy. But some Patriots' affiliates violated their leadership's desire to stay out of immigration, in part because of close personal ties to FAIR and NumbersUSA. When a leader in the Patriots' Philadelphia affiliate was approached for help in the Arizona debate, she felt like "she could not say no," and went on to work actively with the immigration restrictionists.[152] Fear of changing demographics reinforced many Tea Partiers' hard-line attitudes. One scholar of the movement found that its members were unwilling to compromise on immigration reform because they passionately believed large-scale immigration put the country's very identity at risk.[153] This passion even overcame their core belief in limited government. Researchers found that on immigration "Tea Partiers endorse a heavy-handed government response," including "checking the immigration status of everyone" encountered by police, and large federal expenditures to secure the border.[154] For many in the Tea Party, race trumped ideology. And even as the formal Tea Party movement faded its supporters constituted 40 percent of GOP primary voters.[155] It was a constituency primed for leaders to make direct, explicit appeals to the cultural and racial resentments they held toward immigrants. It was ready, in other words, for Donald Trump.

DREAMERS

The ranks of immigrant rights activists also grew in the 1990s, in part because of a growing constituency of undocumented immigrants. Conceived at a time of economic stagnation, IRCA's three-legged stool of border enforcement, legalization, and employer sanctions had not expanded "future flows" of workers; later analysts called this the legislation's "fatal flaw."[156] The Immigration Act of 1990 did expand legal immigration, but only modestly, and mainly for highly skilled workers. The late 1990s economic boom highlighted the need for legal channels for low-skilled immigrant workers to enter the US; absent these legal channels, workers came anyway, albeit unlawfully. Even in the midst of an unprecedented ramp up in border enforcement and enactment of IIRIRA in 1996, entries of people without documents continued apace.[157]

As researchers observed soon after its passage, because IIRIRA's 3/10 year bars all but eliminated decades-old circular migration patterns and prevented those already here from achieving legal status, an increasingly large portion of unauthorized migrants that did cross the border hunkered down in the US. The result was that the more-or-less-permanent undocumented population grew much faster than ever before. According to data from the Pew Research Center, just prior to IIRIRA the unauthorized population had an annual net increase of about 400,000–500,000; in the four years after IIRIRA it doubled, reflecting net growth of about 850,000 per year.[158] In short, IIRIRA's harsh enforcement provisions, augmented by growing border enforcement, actually increased the size of the unauthorized population.

At the turn of the century, capitalizing on its expertise in research-based messaging, the National Immigration Forum's Frank Sharry and his colleagues honed a new mantra that acknowledged the need to "control" the borders, permit increased legal immigration, and allow long-term unauthorized immigrants to "earn legalization by coming forward, paying a fine, passing a background check, working, and paying taxes"; the goal was to make the immigration system "safe, orderly, predictable and fair."[159] The 2000 election campaign seemed to validate the hope that positive reforms were possible, especially when every presidential candidate in both parties—including winner George W. Bush— repeated some variation of the Forum's talking points.[160] Experts agreed: a US–Mexico binational panel organized by Doris Meissner and her colleagues at the Carnegie Endowment for International Peace endorsed a package of policies, including stronger enforcement, increased legal immigration, and a legalization program for long-term undocumented immigrants, all under the banner of "comprehensive immigration reform."[161] Sharry gratefully noted, "A comprehensive approach was finally on the table."[162]

Negotiations between Mexican president Vicente Fox and the new Bush administration in early 2001 offered hopeful signs: Secretary of State Colin Powell seemed supportive of Fox's request for some form of legalization even if at first the president himself leaned toward a guestworker program offering the undocumented temporary work permits but without a path to permanent status and eventual citizenship. Faced with the mixed signals, NCLR's Cecilia Muñoz told the press that a Bush endorsement of legalization of undocumented immigrants would "electrify the Latino community."[163] President Fox came to Washington for a state visit, and appealed to Congress to consider granting permanent residence to the estimated three million undocumented Mexicans in the US. After a private meeting on September 6, President Bush seemed amenable to the idea, saying, "One of the things I have told President Fox is that I am willing to consider ways for a guest worker to earn green card status."[164]

The next day, on September 7, on a panel of witnesses that included the heads of the AFL-CIO and the Chamber of Commerce, NCLR's Yzaguírre testified to the Senate that in addition to enforcement, increased legal immigration, and limited temporary worker programs, "legalization must be the central element of any policy change."[165] His fellow witnesses and most of the senators agreed, and immigration reform appeared imminent. Then came the terrorist attacks four days later on September 11. The environment reversed, and "comprehensive immigration reform" was dead for the foreseeable future.[166] The 9/11 attacks also all but ended the Fix '96 campaign that sought to restore due process protections in the immigration system that had been lost in IIRIRA.[167] Ever-tougher enforcement measures became the default position in a political debate that many analysts already believed had an inherent pro-enforcement bias.[168]

Outside of Washington, however, pro-immigrant activism was growing. The original flagship immigration coalitions in Los Angeles, Illinois, New York, and Boston catalyzed by IRCA's legalization program flourished, strengthened by the successful benefits restoration campaigns. And it seemed as if similar coalitions were springing up everywhere—Florida, Pennsylvania, Colorado, Nevada, Washington State, New Jersey, Kentucky, Idaho, and even Hawaii. Several states and some large cities had more than one coalition, as groups like the Northern Manhattan Coalition Immigrants' Rights were established.[169] Viable coalitions even sprang up in smaller suburban cities such as Long Beach and Santa Clara.[170] And the expanding activism on immigrant rights wasn't limited to the post-IRCA immigration coalitions.

For example, CASA de Maryland (now called CASA as it expands to other states), founded in 1985 as the Central American Solidarity Association of Maryland, was highlighted by experts as an unusually effective organization that "combines services and advocacy in a way that builds the political power of its base."[171] From its headquarters in the capital's suburbs, CASA earned substantial press coverage in the DC and the Baltimore media markets, garnering many awards in the process.[172] It recruited thousands of immigrant members and pushed them into the spotlight in both local and national policy debates where, according to its executive director, Gustavo Torres, "We can bring the perspective and experiences that happened two days ago, as opposed to something that's in a report."[173] Other groups, such as Make the Road New York, pursued a similar mix of services, advocacy, and community organizing. Often consciously and sometimes by accident, many of the new coalitions and membership organizations like PCUN in Oregon, CASA, and Make the Road New York increasingly were integrating "community organizing" techniques into their advocacy strategies.

The literature on American community organizing is very rich, although even attempts to define the term can generate controversy; in this context it might be characterized as the process that: (1) enables relatively powerless people (such as immigrants) (2) to have a collective voice (3) through institutions that (4) generate political power over the long term.[174] Although theorists insist that not all organizing relies on direct action—rallies, marches, demonstrations, pickets, and protests—and conversely, that not all direct action reflects true organizing, the two terms are closely identified.[175] The new immigrant rights organizers were entering a well-developed if somewhat balkanized field. Students of community organizing trace its modern roots to the famed Saul Alinsky and the national network he built, known today as the Industrial Areas Foundation.[176] By the 1970s, there were at least seven "national" community organizing networks; five—IAF (Industrial Areas Foundation), PICO (People Improving Communities through Organizing) National Network (now called Faith in Action), DART (Direct Action & Research Training Center), and the Gamaliel Foundation—were faith-based, while Citizen Action, ACORN (Association of Community Organizations for Reform Now), and National People's Action weren't sectarian.[177]

Despite successes, the field had its limitations. Some insiders asserted the movement was insufficiently attentive to racial inequity.[178] Others found that national networks had difficulty in replicating local successes in other places.[179] And many recognized that although organizers could claim many local victories, they had generally failed to achieve systemic national changes; one veteran wrote that organizers won "many battles" while "losing the war" for greater economic or social justice.[180] These limitations were complicated by the inability of turf-conscious organizing networks to coordinate their work at the national or local levels. As longtime ACORN organizer and scholar Gary Delgado once said, "Somewhere along the line, many of us got stuck in our own brand of organizing. Instead of believing that all of our organizations might have a shot at building a movement, we began to believe that our network was the movement and that everybody else should join, die, or get out of the way."[181]

One DC-based group, the Center for Community Change, or CCC, had shown at least occasional success in coordinating work across organizing networks. Established in 1968 as the first project of the Robert F. Kennedy Memorial Foundation, CCC was a national "intermediary" providing training, technical assistance, and other support to local organizations representing low-income communities; it combined support for programming and organizing with a policy presence in DC.[182] In the late 1990s, the center was in the early stage of a major transition, as longtime head Pablo Eisenberg was succeeded by his veteran deputy Andrew Mott in 1998. Mott led the group until 2002, when he was succeeded by the CCC's policy director Deepak Bhargava.[183] CCC and NCLR had a close relationship—chief executives Eisenberg and Yzaguirre were friends, as were their longtime seconds-in-command, Mott and Emily Gantz McKay—often jointly sponsoring and nurturing various coalition efforts.

In part as a response to the 1996 welfare reforms, in 2000 Bhargava conceived and led CCC's National Campaign for Jobs and Income Support, a coordinated effort of several organizing networks to repair the social safety net and create a major federally funded public jobs program.[184] The campaign was groundbreaking, not least in its aspiration to coordinate national-level advocacy among the notoriously independent community organizing networks. Organizers that had been engaged in state-local efforts to restore benefits to legal immigrants, led by Angelica Salas of the Coalition for Humane Immigrant Rights of Los Angeles (CHIRLA), formed an Immigrant Organizing Committee and asked the campaign to endorse comprehensive immigration reform. Salas had unusual standing among both antipoverty and immigrant rights advocates; CHIRLA was extraordinarily effective in seamlessly integrating service programs, community organizing, and policy advocacy.[185]

Bhargava had an insider's view of the legislative process and instinctively wanted to back Salas but felt his board wasn't steeped in the issue's policy or politics. He asked NCLR's Kamasaki, with whom he'd often worked on housing issues, to arrange "an audience" with Muñoz to seek her support for CCC to build a national immigration-focused network of local community organizing groups. Long concerned about the absence of a powerful field capable of matching FAIR's and NumbersUSA's growing ranks, Muñoz "blessed" CCC's move into immigration, and she addressed the center's board of directors to support Bhargava's initiative.[186] Angelica Salas's Immigrant Organizing Committee soon became the Fair Immigration Reform Movement, a consortium of immigrant coalitions and organizing groups working toward comprehensive immigration reform housed at the Center for Community Change.[187] Muñoz joined, and would eventually chair, the center's board of directors.[188]

The advocates' attention turned to a highly sympathetic and increasingly vocal set of young people: undocumented immigrants brought to the US as children. The decades-long circular migration pattern previously had allowed undocumented immigrants, especially from Mexico and Central America, to return home regularly to see their children. But as border enforcement increased—making it more difficult for the undocumented to reenter—and with IIRIRA's draconian penalties for those who were caught, immigrants increasingly brought their kids with them, or sent for them soon after arriving. By the early 2000s, many were graduating from high school and ready to enter college; by one account their number was then a million.[189] Most had "played by all the rules" by staying out of trouble and completing high school, and in the words of Rep. Luis Gutiérrez, they were fully "American in everything but a piece of paper."[190] IIRIRA required states to enact legislation before offering "higher education benefits," including in-state tuition rates, to the undocumented.[191] With out-of-state tuition prohibitively expensive and denied access to other government financial aid by their undocumented status, the young people organized, initially around in-state tuition legislation. Reasoning that a college degree without a legal right to work wasn't enough, a consensus emerged that legalization should be pursued for these young people, who, after all, were minors, even toddlers, when they'd crossed the border.

In 2001, Representatives Berman, Chris Cannon (R-UT), and Lucille Roybal-Allard (D-CA)—the daughter of Rep. Edward Roybal, who'd established her own bona fides as an advocate for children—introduced the Student Adjustment Act, largely drafted by MALDEF staffer Angelo Amador and Josh Bernstein, the National Immigration Law Center's director of federal policy. The bill offered in-state tuition rates and adjustment to permanent resident status for some undocumented students brought to the US as minors; Sens. Richard Durbin (D-IL) and Orrin Hatch soon followed suit.[192] The next year Durbin and Hatch filed a new bill, the Development, Relief, and Education for Alien Minors (DREAM) Act, with refinements drafted by Bernstein and NCLR staffers Raul González and Melissa Lazarín.[193] Focused mainly on comprehensive reform, NCLR's leaders thought DREAM a "fallback" to pursue if broader reforms stalled.[194] The young people affected, increasingly called DREAMers after the bill introduced on their behalf, didn't agree; nor did Bernstein and Lazarín who, together with the Center for Community Change's José Quiñonez, led the early advocacy campaign seeking immediate enactment of the bill.[195]

Part of the DC advocates' strategy was "the recruitment of a handful of exemplary undocumented students with the most compelling stories to give a face" to the campaign's core message that the bill offered fairness to youth who "had done everything right."[196] Many were honor graduates, most spoke in unaccented English, virtually all were extraordinarily articulate. Even in the post-9/11 landscape, the bill seemed to have "legs": in June 2002, Hatch and Durbin moved the bill through the Senate Judiciary Committee.[197] To keep up the momentum, the next year, CCC and an informal network of local DREAMer organizations collaborated on a mock "graduation ceremony" for undocumented high school students on the mall adjacent to the Capitol grounds to highlight the fact that they had "played by the rules."[198]

Not everyone agreed with the tactic of presenting an unthreatening face to the public. The DREAMer movement was building just as the campaign for marriage equality was beginning to crest, and many young immigrant activists consciously adopted many of the LGBT advocates' tactics. As Frank Sharry wrote years later, LGBT activists "created a monumental shift in American culture . . . by being brave and loud, out and proud."[199] Just as LGBT advocates found coming out of the proverbial closet an empowering act, the equivalent for many DREAMers became the slogan "Undocumented and Unafraid."[200] After the bill again passed the committee but went no further, some DREAM advocates felt they were being relegated to a "kids table" as the "adults," seeking nothing less than comprehensive reform, declined to pursue "piecemeal" bills like the DREAM Act.[201] By 2005, disparate DREAMer groups united to form a national umbrella organization, United We Dream.[202] "Direct actions," such as sit-ins at congressional offices, increased, reflecting frustration with the lack of progress. As their rhetoric grew more strident, gadfly columnist Ruben Navarrette chastised them, writing, "Some in the DREAMer movement now insist they're entitled to more than run-of–the-mill illegal immigrants," including people like their parents who "fed them, clothed them and sheltered them."[203]

COMPREHENSIVE IMMIGRATION REFORM

Tension between comprehensive and piecemeal reform was set aside for a moment, after George W. Bush was reelected with substantial Latino support in the 2004 elections.[204] The momentum for comprehensive immigration reform was unmistakable, and it was certain to include the DREAM Act. Under the auspices of the Migration Policy Institute and two other think tanks, a bipartisan, star-studded task force that echoed characteristics of the Select Commission began deliberations. Cochaired by former GOP senator Spencer Abraham and former Democratic Rep. Lee Hamilton, the task force membership included Senators Kennedy and John McCain (R-AZ), Representatives Jeff Flake (R-AZ) and Howard Berman, heads of the US Chamber of Commerce and the labor union UNITE HERE, and others, including the National Forum's Frank Sharry and NCLR's new CEO, Janet Murguía. The task force advocated a wholesale redesign of the immigration system: both tougher and "smarter" border and interior enforcement, including a secure Social Security card to combat fraud; more worker visas through temporary, provisional, and permanent streams; modest reductions in family visas along with a standing commission to recommend future adjustments; and an "earned legalization" program. All but one task force member endorsed the report, although several expressed reservations.[205]

Bipartisan, bicameral comprehensive immigration reform legislation consistent with the task force recommendations sponsored by Senators Kennedy and McCain and Representatives Luis Gutiérrez, Jim Kolbe (R-AZ), and Jeff Flake had been in the works for some time. Their bill combined tough enforcement with a generous legalization program, modest cuts to family-based legal immigration, and expanded skills-based visas, including for temporary workers. Although the AFL-CIO opposed the temporary worker programs seen as vital by business, Kennedy decided to move ahead.[206] But to the dismay of reform advocates, Bush, already engaged in an unpopular war in Iraq, chose as his chief domestic priority the privatization of Social Security, which failed badly.[207] It also stalled action in the Senate. Responding to pressure from its anti-immigrant base, at the end of 2005 the GOP-controlled House enacted enforcement-only legislation sponsored by Rep. James Sensenbrenner (R-WI). The bill criminalized the heretofore civil offense of undocumented status, and exposed those like clergy who provided humanitarian assistance to unauthorized immigrants to criminal prosecution.[208]

Immigrant activists were outraged, promptly planned a series of protests, and recruited popular Spanish radio deejays to fan the flames. By mid-February 2006, huge anti-Sensenbrenner rallies sprang up around the country. Before they crested on May Day, according to one summary, "an estimated 4 million immigrants and their supporters took to the streets in 120 cities in a series of pro-immigrant marches never before seen in the United States." It was, activists thought, "a fully-fledged movement that would have been unimaginable . . . a quarter of a century earlier."[209] An elder statesman of the pro-immigrant movement, Eliseo Medina, vice president of the Service Employees International Union, was elated by the marches. SEIU was one of the first major unions to break from the AFL-CIO's philosophy of immigration restriction in the 1990s; since then, the "quietly charismatic" Medina had helped orchestrate labor's endorsement of immigration reform.[210] Medina saw in the demonstrations "a whole new surge of activism" representing a broadening of the pro-reform movement.[211]

Building on the energy from the marches, in 2006 the Atlantic Philanthropies, a new funder in the field, made a huge investment in the Coalition for Comprehensive Immigration Reform, in essence a joint venture between the DC-based groups and field-based organizers. Veteran NCLR staffer Clarissa Martínez De Castro was drafted as the CCIR's campaign manager, tasked with coordinating input from an unwieldy "35–40 person Strategy Council." Over time, through CCIR and its successors, Atlantic Philanthropies injected tens of millions of dollars mainly into immigrant coalitions and organizing networks.[212] But if Eliseo Medina welcomed the increased focus on direct action, former ACLU lobbyist Wade Henderson, who'd moved from the NAACP to head a Leadership Conference on Civil Rights that was now unabashedly pro-reform, wasn't so sure. In Philadelphia for a speaking gig at the height of the 2006 marches, with time to kill he ducked into a bar and watched the local protests on TV. As Henderson listened to the almost uniformly negative comments about the protestors from a racially diverse group of bar patrons, he recognized that the demonstrations "were a double-edged sword"; the marchers, he thought, "were rubbing America's nose in the inevitable reality of massive demographic change."[213]

The Senate Judiciary Committee was spurred to action by the demonstrations; now chaired by moderate Arlen Specter (R-PA), it began marking up immigration legislation on May 8. The first four days were devoted to adoption of a series of tough enforcement provisions and increases in worker visas, but prospects for priorities of pro-immigrant advocates were uncertain. Majority Leader Bill Frist (R-TN) threatened to bring up his own enforcement-only legislation if the committee failed to act quickly, which backfired, pushing Specter, who'd been seeking to build a broader consensus within his panel, toward Kennedy and McCain's approach. On the final day of the markup, all of the measures pro-immigrant advocates sought were on the table. The DREAM Act prevailed, as did an agricultural worker program called AGJOBS, the "spiritual descendant" of IRCA's SAW program. The big showdown came over what to do about the rest of the undocumented already in the US: a legalization program sponsored by McCain ally Lindsey Graham (R-SC) or a temporary worker program favored by Sens. John Cornyn (R-TX) and Jon Kyl (R-AZ). Responding to charges that legalization was a "get out of jail free card" amounting to "amnesty," Graham parroted the National Immigration Forum's talking points while adding his own flourishes: "You have to pay a $1,000 fine, get a background check, work for six years, learn English, and pay back taxes . . . and that probably excludes half of my family. It's not getting out of jail free. . . . Lots of people on talk radio morning, noon, and night talking about [amnesty] while these folks are out there working."[214]

On a 12–5 vote, the legalization program was included in the bill. It covered perhaps 10 million of the undocumented population then estimated at between 11.5 to 12 million.[215] Just before the Memorial Day recess, the Senate passed the bill by a 62–36 vote, with 23 Republicans joining 1 Independent and 38 Democrats in support of the legislation. The bill's House cosponsor Jeff Flake estimated the odds of getting a final bill at fifty-fifty; most DC-based groups supported the legislation, but with "real reservations" regarding what a final product would look like if merged with the Sensenbrenner bill.[216] Presaging future developments, legalization was increasingly seen as a divisive wedge issue, and became a popular target in congressional town hall meetings that summer.[217] Still, pro-immigrant advocates were confident. With President Bush presiding over an increasingly unpopular occupation of Iraq, even cautious commentators were discussing a potential "wave election" in 2006 producing a presumably more immigrant-friendly Democratic Congress.[218] Buoyed by the mass demonstrations, few in the burgeoning network of activists felt much pressure to risk a conference committee with the hated Sensenbrenner legislation.

Ted Kennedy's instincts told him otherwise. Over his half-century in the Senate, he'd come to believe that "there is a kind of rhythm, even a chemistry" to the legislative process.[219] He now thought the chemistry was right for a compromise. Kennedy quietly called the Forum's Sharry and NCLR's Muñoz. They'd have to accept some harsh enforcement provisions in the House bill, the senator warned, but they would get a broad legalization program in return, albeit perhaps without a path to citizenship. Kennedy said he wouldn't go ahead without their approval but urged their support. Many field-based organizers, Sharry and Muñoz knew, believed that even the moderate Senate bill already went too far on enforcement.[220] Understanding they'd face severe blowback from their left wing if they supported Kennedy, they declined the senator's offer. Even a decade later Muñoz said that this decision "still haunts me."[221]

In the 110th Congress in 2007, Democrats held a slim 51–49 majority in the upper body, and newly installed House Speaker Nancy Pelosi, who'd broken the "marble ceiling" to become the first female leader of the lower body, held a 229–201 majority over her GOP counterparts.[222] The Senate again moved first in 2007, but under far different circumstances. Analysts wrote that past GOP bill supporters McCain, Graham, Brownback, Chuck Hagel, and Mel Martínez all "tacked to the right while considering presidential runs . . . or re-election."[223] Kennedy's negotiating partner this time was Jon Kyl, one of the 2006 bill's strongest opponents. Backed by the Bush administration, Kyl pushed for a series of changes to the formula that passed the prior year; Kennedy reluctantly agreed, thinking it could be improved in the Democratic House. The resulting "grand bargain," analysts later wrote, was "superficially similar to the previous McCain-Kennedy legislation" but "included additional enforcement measures, a far more restrictive legalization program, a new legal immigration 'point system' favoring high-skilled immigrants while reducing family-based visas, and a larger, business-friendly temporary worker program, reflecting Kyl's long-held views."[224]

Floor debate began in May and thirty amendments were quickly addressed, but procedural disputes delayed action.[225] Debate reopened in June, but provisions noxious to both progressives and business were adopted, "fracturing the fragile coalition backing the effort," analysts wrote.[226] The pro-immigrant field was divided on whether the bill was worth saving; it was, said one, "about as right-leaning a comprehensive bill as conceivable." As lobbyists gathered in the hallway after meeting with Sen. Kennedy, Wade Henderson advised support, noting that if the bill failed, "It's open season on Hispanics. . . . You're gonna get a big dose of enforcement." Jeanne Butterfield, who had succeeded Warren Leiden as executive director of the American Immigration Lawyers Association, agreed, saying, "It's this bill or 'enforcement only.' "[227]

"Enforcement only" was exactly what opponents demanded. NumbersUSA's activists flooded senators' email inboxes with messages opposing the bill.[228] Radio talk show hosts spewed invective against the bill and the Capitol Hill switchboard crashed under the volume of calls, mainly opposing the measure.[229] Most immigrant advocates in DC decided to "hold their nose" and support the effort, but since the measure had moved right, much of organized labor and most field-based activists mobilized against the bill. One last procedural move to force an up or down vote was made at the end of June. It was the kind of vote, Sharry said, "You win by one or lose by a dozen."[230] Officially, they ended up 15 votes short of the 60 votes required, with only 12 of 49 Republicans joining 33 Democrats voting for consideration of the bill.[231] Advocates believed they actually were at most only 2 or 3 votes short of the 60 required, but "lacking the decisive margin, a number of the bill's supporters changed their votes," and opposed the measure.[232] Senator Kyl had pushed the bill to the right, but with a weakened president and despite enthusiastic business lobbying, facing energized opposition to amnesty, the legislation's GOP Senate support was halved from the 23 that had supported the more centrist 2006 effort. It was, analysts observed, yet more evidence of a growing hyper partisanship in American politics.[233]

The collapse of the grand bargain was, Frank Sharry later said, "like a death in the family, only worse."[234] Severe recriminations followed. Advocates and funders held post-mortems to pick over the corpse of the 2006–2007 effort: the near-consensus conclusion: "the anti-immigration communications machine" had beaten their own smaller-scale media operations, and that "inside-the-Beltway" lobbyists had failed. CCIR was disbanded. Frank Sharry left the National Immigration Forum to start America's Voice, a pro-immigrant communications group, and his longtime deputy Angie Kelley briefly joined the American Immigration Council before starting an immigration policy project at the Center for American Progress. Ali Noorani, director of the Massachusetts Immigrant and Refugee Advocacy Coalition, was chosen to head a restructured Forum that, together with the Center for Community Change, spearheaded a field-centric, direct action–oriented, Reform Immigration for America (RIFA) campaign, succeeded by the Alliance for Citizenship (A4C) in 2012, to mobilize the "boots on the ground" to beat back the growing anti-immigrant tide, and to coordinate field organizing with DC lobbying.[235]

The assumption was that replicating the massive anti-Sensenbrenner protests was the "game-changer" the pro-reform advocates needed, a sentiment not limited to pro-immigration reformers, or even to progressives, as the growth of the Tea Party at the same time amply demonstrated.[236] And in the social media age, organizing protests and demonstrations became easier than ever before; it seemed a natural extension of the direction of progressive activism generally.[237] There is a rich literature on the effectiveness of social protest in catalyzing policy change. Some of it questions direct action altogether, labeling it as "folk politics" incapable of "transforming society."[238] Others cite specific factors—organization, messaging, and nonviolence—as key ingredients underlying successful demonstrations.[239] Much scholarship suggests that what comes after the direct action—such as effective messaging and lobbying—seems to shape policy more than the demonstrations themselves.[240] Still, after the grand bargain died, there was an unmistakable shift of resources and power from DC to the community organizing groups that could produce more "boots on the ground" across the country.[241]

Those "boots" increasingly were concentrated in Democratic districts. Journalist Bill Bishop has written about Americans' growing tendency to live among people who have similar lifestyles, beliefs, and political orientations. In his book, *The Big Sort*, Bishop showed that this clustering was both long-standing and accelerating, writing, "Americans have been sorting themselves for the past three decades into homogeneous communities—not at the regional level, or the red state/blue state level, but at the micro level of city and neighborhood."[242]

A key question for all advocates, but perhaps particularly for organizers, is whether their "message resonates for more people than just the core supporters."[243] Some polls, for example, have found that if not "on message," protests can be counterproductive because they harden existing predispositions.[244] Since many organizers had long been self-critical about the movement's insufficient diversity, RIFA's and A4C's leadership consciously empowered immigrants to serve as spokespeople, what some have called "the rise of immigrant-led advocacy."[245] But events later proved that direct actions led by immigrants, mainly of color, speaking to white voters in red states or districts didn't necessarily attract the needed GOP support; the field-centric strategy itself proved insufficient to produce reform legislation.

The 2008 election of Barack Obama, a candidate who unequivocally supported comprehensive reform, brought new hope to pro-immigrant advocates, buttressed by his appointment of NCLR's Cecilia Muñoz to a top White House job.[246] But there were impediments to rapid movement of immigration reform, the first being the imperative to enact a "stimulus" to rescue an economy on the verge of a depression.[247] Health care reform followed, resulting in the Affordable Care Act in 2010.[248] Neither body of Congress considered comprehensive reform, although the DREAM Act passed the House in 2010, only to die in the Senate.[249] After the GOP won back the House in 2010, Republicans sympathetic to reform told the White House that legislative action wasn't possible until Obama first demonstrated his enforcement bona fides, a view privately shared by many DC advocates. A sharp increase in deportations that had begun under Bush accelerated under Obama.[250] With deportations rising to record levels, DREAMers and other advocates demanded that Obama take unilateral executive action to reduce the suffering in immigrant communities; he repeatedly responded he lacked such power, and Muñoz won no applause from her former allies when she explained, "Even broken laws have to be enforced."[251] DREAMERs pushed back hard, directly at the president of the United States. As detailed by political scientists Matt Barreto and Gary Segura, at the 2011 NCLR Annual Conference: "When the president took the podium, DREAMers rose in the audience wearing T-shirts that said 'OBAMA DEPORTS DREAMers.' When the president said again that he was powerless to act, the crowd rose to their feet and began chanting, 'Yes you can,' a bitter recycling of the president's campaign slogan."[252]

Frank Sharry recalls watching the event and "thinking that the president's explanations were falling flat and he would have to make big changes. If not, he risked a very depressed Latino turnout in 2012."[253] United We Dream held demonstrations in two dozen cities in early 2012, and that year Gaby Pacheco, a savvy young Florida-based DREAMer activist, encouraged Senator Marco Rubio (R-FL), a Tea Party favorite and likely 2016 presidential candidate, to threaten legislation to protect DREAMers and thus pressure Obama to take executive action.[254] Activists then recruited some ninety immigration law professors to send the president a letter "specifying the legal precedents" for executive action to protect DREAMers from deportation.[255] The result was Obama's Deferred Action for Childhood Arrivals (DACA) program, announced in June 2012, which provided temporary protection from deportation and work permits to some DREAMers, renewable every two years.[256] Aided by a record turnout of Hispanic voters, Obama defeated GOP candidate Mitt Romney and his "self-deportation" immigration strategy. The Republican National Committee's "autopsy" of Romney's defeat observed, "If Hispanic Americans perceive that a GOP nominee or candidate does not want them in the United States (i.e. self-deportation), they will not pay attention to our next sentence," and concluded, "[W]e must embrace and champion comprehensive immigration reform."[257]

In June 2013, a bipartisan "Gang of Eight" pushed a comprehensive immigration reform bill through the Senate on a 68–32 vote.[258] Activists took to the streets, in Washington and in 150 cities and towns, to demand that the lower body take up immigration reform.[259] But the GOP-controlled House leadership was unconvinced and announced in March 2014 that it would not act. With deportations continuing at unprecedented levels, NCLR's Janet Murguía called on the House to move the legislation, but also warned Obama that if he failed to take executive action to reduce deportations, his legacy would forever be known as the "Deporter-in-Chief."[260] Obama responded to the field activism, the GOP's inaction, NCLR's biting criticism, and his own staff's encouragement by announcing a series of actions in November 2014: an expansion of DACA and a new Deferred Action for Parents of Americans and Lawful Permanent Residents (DAPA) program, potentially covering as many as 5.5 million undocumented immigrants.[261] But in June 2016, the US Supreme Court let stand a lower court ruling that enjoined DAPA, which was never implemented.[262] It seems former constitutional law professor Barack Obama's assessment of limits on his own legal authority might've been right after all.

As the GOP became steadily more restrictionist on immigration, Democrats moved rapidly in the opposite direction, exemplified by Socialist senator Bernie Sanders. He'd voted against the 2007 Kyl-Kennedy bill, in part based on the opposition from the AFL-CIO, saying that "the last thing we need is to bring . . . millions of people into this country." But by 2015, Democratic presidential candidate Sanders was an unabashed supporter of comprehensive reform, prompting one reporter to write that being pro-immigrant was now "a litmus test for Democrats."[263] Sanders's evolution reflected the common tendency toward groupthink in DC, as one Hill veteran noted, "politicians, journalists, analysts, and lobbyists spend a great deal of time talking to one another."[264] Conventional wisdom that Democrats support immigration reform was enforced by powerful peer pressures; as some on the left have said, "There's an orthodoxy you're supposed to conform to, and if you don't, you become a bad, evil person."[265]

Some who'd previously acknowledged the need for enforcement to balance legalization now said, "The pro-immigrant movement is not interested in a 'balanced approach' " that combines enforcement for Republicans and legalization for Democrats. To those who suggested otherwise, a United We Dream spokesperson warned, "The community is ready to stand up against them if Democrats think that that old way is the way forward."[266] It was thus a major coup for immigrant rights advocates when, in 2015, Democratic front-runner Hillary Clinton spoke at the field's flagship event, the National Immigrant Integration Conference, held by the National Partnership for New Americans, a group allied with the Fair Immigration Reform Movement.[267] Clinton's presence in a solid "blue" state usually avoided by campaigns that maximize events in swing states, was noteworthy, as was the endorsement of Clinton's candidacy by the New York Immigration Action Fund, the 501(c)(4) arm of the New York Immigration Coalition.[268]

Clinton, whose husband had signed IIRIRA and welfare reform twenty years earlier, now was openly pro-immigrant; as one analyst noted, "eight of the nine positions articulated on her website were pro immigration, and the ninth only peripherally refers to enforcement."[269] It was a natural evolution for a Democrat appealing to "the base," but some thought it curious that immigrant rights activists were now fully engaged in Democratic partisan politics. One of seminal organizer Saul Alinsky's "rules" for activists was to have "no permanent friends, no permanent enemies, only permanent interests."[270] Immigrant activists had adopted many of the trappings of Alinsky's community organizing philosophy but were now perilously close to becoming a "permanent friend," even an "arm," of the Democratic Party. Their "permanent enemies" had been moving in the opposite direction for some time.

TRUMPED

When John Tanton and Roger Conner founded FAIR in 1979, its center of gravity leaned left; by the 2000s, their successors were grounded in the rising "populist wing" of the GOP, no one more than the Center for Immigration Studies' Mark Krikorian. Krikorian was a contributor to *National Review*, arguably still the most influential conservative publication, adopting the posture of a GOP partisan, albeit of the Tea Party variety. He cosigned a letter from Tea Party leaders to senators in May 2013 opposing the "Gang of Eight" immigration bill, writing, "Hispanic voters are Democrats, so the idea of importing more of them . . . is kind of silly."[271] A CIS colleague urged Republicans to abandon immigration reform along with any attempts to woo minorities into the GOP and focus instead on turning out more white voters.[272]

This advice echoed what paleoconservative Pat Buchanan, in an earlier column for *WorldNetDaily*, called "A New Southern Strategy," urging the GOP to concentrate on appeals to white voters by explicitly playing on racial resentment to demand "sealing of America's borders against any and all intruders."[273] White Nationalists fought to claim the idea as their own, demanding they be credited for having advocated the concept for more than a decade.[274] The strategy conflated the terms *Hispanic* with *immigrant*, and *immigrant* with *illegal alien*, a cynical approach that resonated with much of the body politic, even though over three-quarters of Latinos in the US are American citizens, and two-thirds are native-born.[275]

Increasingly at issue in contemporary debates was less a matter of policy details than the core question of American identity, which restrictionists said was threatened by demographic change. As political scientist Lee Drutman wrote, the GOP had "spent the last half-century winning over socially conservative, non-college-educated whites on issues of race and identity to the point that these voters became the dominant faction within the Party."[276] And when it came to race, as political scientists Marisa Abrajano and Zoltan Hajnal observed in their 2015 book *White Backlash*, during the late 2000s, the identity-based partisan "sorting" that was long associated with the Nixon "Southern Strategy"— concerns about civil rights laws, affirmative action, and school integration—was now based on highly racialized concerns about Hispanic immigrants.[277] Pew Research Center data supported the same conclusion, observing that while anti-black sentiment was the main predictor of Democrats-turned-Republicans prior to 2000, since then such party switchers seemed mostly motivated by animus against Latinos.[278]

By 2015, white supremacist views were openly circulated on the internet, often through what become known as the Alternative Right. A combination of news websites like *Breitbart.com*, Tea Party offshoots and splinter factions, and white nationalist groups coalesced in the "alt-right," a loose, largely online community billing itself as the alternative to GOP establishment orthodoxy. The *Washington Post*'s primer on the alt-right begins with Jean Raspail's 1973 novel, *Camp of the Saints*, the book John Tanton had rescued from obscurity in the 1980s, an apocalyptic vision of a Europe invaded and overwhelmed by third world immigrants.[279] Its core message: nonwhite immigrants and refugees pose an existential threat to Western society, a view that prominent mainstream conservatives called "racist, xenophobic and paranoid."[280] Others in Tanton's network were among the alt-right's leading figures. Jared Taylor, of *American Renaissance*, and Peter Brimelow, author of the anti-immigrant screed *Alien*

Nation and founder of the *VDare* website, were key players in the movement.[281] Taylor was known as a "close friend" of Tanton's; Brimelow and Tanton organized meetings with the eugenics-promoting Pioneer Fund.[282] The alt-right's opposition to immigration was race-based, making little distinction between legal and unlawful migration. As a writer for the mainstream conservative *Weekly Standard* noted, "What makes the alt right so radical is that it categorically disagrees with even supposedly 'extreme' positions of conservatives. Being against illegal immigration and for deportation isn't enough; the alt right wants to cut back on *legal* immigration as well [emphasis in the original]."[283]

The connections came together around the presidential candidacy of Donald J. Trump, who opened his campaign in June 2015 by calling for "a wall" along the southern border, paid for by Mexico because, "They're bringing drugs. They're bringing crime. They're rapists." As a *New Yorker* profile chronicled, the longshot candidate's favorability rating, "among Republicans leaped from sixteen percent to fifty-seven percent, a greater spike than any other candidate's debut. Immigration became the centerpiece of his campaign."[284] Trump's immigration plan also included a ban on admissions from nations with large Muslim populations, severe cuts in family-based legal immigration, and dramatically heightened enforcement targeting unauthorized immigrants.

Some initial analyses attributed Trump's appeal to downscaling whites' anxiety about economic issues, but an Ipsos poll found nativism was the greatest driver of his adherents.[285] Analysts of the National Republican Voter Survey also found that nativism was the single most powerful predictor of Trump's support.[286] A Pew Research Center poll reported in *Vox*, the "explainer journalism" website, showed that, "The top reason for supporting Trump: agreeing that a growing number of newcomers from other countries threatens US values."[287] Matthew Yglesias and Dara Lind, also writing in *Vox*, found that what attracted many to Trump was "that Americans are less worried about American jobs than they are about American culture."[288] Former Bush official Peter Wehner lamented during the primaries that "with every racist statement or nativist appeal, every cruel insult, every new conspiracy theory . . . [Trump] grew stronger rather than weaker."[289] And veteran GOP operative Avik Roy admitted that "conservative intellectuals and conservative politicians have been in kind of a bubble. . . . We've had this view that the voters were with us on conservatism—philosophical, economic conservatism. In reality, the gravitational center of the Republican Party is white nationalism."[290]

In the wake of Trump's primary victory, a few Republicans left the party and others either declined to endorse their candidate or openly held their noses while doing so. But most went along because, some said, the campaign had revealed "how much of the GOP coalition responds to a racially barbed message of defensive nationalism."[291] Others disavowed the candidate while embracing his message. CIS's Mark Krikorian called Trump "something of a circus clown" but lauded his harsh immigration enforcement plan as "sound" and "well thought-through"; NumbersUSA and FAIR similarly praised Trump's plans.[292] That anti-immigration extremists applauded Trump's plan was no surprise. What was surprising, wrote *The New Republic*'s Jeet Heer, was that "conventional conservatives" endorsed Trump's "extreme positions on immigration." Centrist Republican David Frum praised Trump's "commonsense" immigration policy and Rich Lowry, who edited an edition of *National Review* wholly dedicated to opposing Trump's candidacy, called the nominee's positions "rock solid on policy."[293] Trump, they might've said, was an imperfect messenger, but they loved his message.

After Trump's inauguration as the nation's 45th president, the corpse of comprehensive immigration reform, thrice nearly jolted back to life in the 2000s, was dormant once again.

CHAPTER 9

Reflections

AN INCONCLUSIVE CONCLUSION

What's next? Readers should be advised of the inherent limitations of any scholarly work as a predictive or prescriptive tool. Even with thirty years of hindsight, precisely how and why IRCA was the last comprehensive immigration reform bill to be enacted remains something of a mystery, at least to this author. Such an inconclusive conclusion to an inquiry about the origins of important events is hardly unique.

For example, the one hundredth anniversary of the start of World War I in 2014 saw the release of many books explaining the massive conflagration. Even prior to the centenary of this epochal event, it had been well-studied by historians, producing by one estimate "more than 25,000 volumes and [scholarly] articles."[1] One, the 1960s bestseller *The Guns of August*, by amateur historian Barbara Tuchman, laid major responsibility for the war on Germany; it was the conventional narrative about the origins of the war for decades thereafter.[2] The *Guns of August* was so influential that in the Cuban Missile Crisis, President Kennedy cited it to explain his refusal to "tumble into war" with the Soviet Union based on "stupidity, individual idiosyncrasies, misunderstandings, and personal complexes of inferiority and grandeur."[3]

Several meticulously researched books that followed challenged the apparently settled wisdom that Germany was the principal villain. One pointed the finger squarely at Russia as the major culprit for "accelerating the rush to war."[4] Another cited entangling alliances of the major European powers as leading to the "slow motion train wreck few wanted but none could avoid."[5] A third major work traced the conflict to the "micro-politics" of "the Balkans," a region that Tuchman all but ignored.[6] Another book, praised as "the last word on the subject" in the *New York Times Book Review*, in an ironic twist, affirmed "the thesis of German guilt" for starting the conflict.[7] After digesting these alternative narratives, another informed observer eventually returned to *The Guns of August* as the "peerless chronicle" of the war.[8] A century after one of history's most-studied events about which millions of pages have been written, even the discerning reader is left with contradictory narratives, hardly the basis for assuming that any single scholarly work can identify definitive lessons to guide future action.

The saga of the Simpson-Mazzoli bill and events since its passing show that the existence of famed political scientist John Kingdon's three key preconditions for legislative action—a widely recognized *problem*, a set of widely accepted *policy* proposals, and existence of *political will*—were hardly sufficient for legislative success. Each of the preconditions seemed in place in both the 97th and the 98th Congress, but IRCA failed to pass until the waning days of the 99th Congress, and only after literally rising from the dead. IRCA's follow-on bill, the Immigration Act of 1990, also passed the Senate in 1988 then died when the House failed to act. After passing the Senate in 1989, it died again in 1990 on the House floor before being resuscitated at literally the eleventh hour. Similar preconditions seemed to exist in 2006–2007 and again in 2013–2014, when the Senate passed but the House failed to consider comprehensive immigration reform bills. These events led some analysts to write that on immigration reform, "the difference between victory and defeat is often a matter of personalities, chance, and timing."[9] But this prognostication equivalent of "flipping a coin" seems too facile. Even accepting the uncertainties inherent in the legislative process, this author believes there are lessons from the IRCA debate that if adopted could materially improve the chances for success of the next round of reforms.

A major prerequisite for future legislative success is a clear understanding of the nature of the process itself. It's common to picture the legislative process as "linear": think of a train moving from one station to another on a fixed track. Advocates using this model—one might call them determinists for assuming the process has a linear path—attempt to minimize the chance that anything will stop their legislative train. They develop elaborate game plans, equivalent to pre-positioned equipment to repair broken tracks, to respond to potential scenarios. They rely on time-tested aphorisms, like one recounting the downfall of the English King Richard III in the mid-1400s, memorialized by Shakespeare in the famous phrase, "A horse, a horse! My kingdom for a horse," after Richard is thrown from his dying mount. A proverb from the Middle Ages blamed the loss of the kingdom on a single missing nail on a horseshoe:

For want of a nail, the shoe was lost;

For want of a shoe, the horse was lost;

For want of a horse, the rider was lost;

For want of a rider, the battle was lost;

For want of a battle, the kingdom was lost![10]

The lesson for determinists is that the smallest details matter, but they forget that it's only *after the fact* that the importance of the single missing nail was identified. No plan developed *beforehand* can account for every detail that might be the difference between success or failure.

The tendency, as has been said of generals, to "fight the last war," is thinking that "fixing" the problem that foiled previous campaigns will assure success the next time around. But this has proven unsuccessful in the immigration context, with respect to both policy and strategy. On policy, presaged by Simpson's 1985 "triggered legalization" proposal, reform skeptics have long demanded an undefined degree of "border security" as a prerequisite to legalization. By 2012 the nation was spending 24 percent more to enforce the immigration laws than on all other federal law enforcement *combined*.[11] On top of what's been called this "formidable machinery" for immigration enforcement, in 2013, Senate-passed legislation proposed a massive surge to increase border security by almost 700 percent.[12] Even if this contributed to Senate passage of reform, it wasn't sufficient to even produce a vote on the bill in the House. Nor was Obama's unprecedented level of deportations enough to convince House GOP leaders to act.

Regarding strategy, after reform's failure in 2007, many immigrant advocates and foundation supporters agreed they'd lost mainly due to insufficient "boots on the ground." In response, they made a huge investment in building local advocacy and organizing capacity; over a decade, the Atlantic Philanthropies alone invested some $70 million, mainly in field-based coalitions and organizing networks.[13] Whatever else one might say about this strategy, it failed in 2013–2014 in the same way as in 2006—in both cases the Senate passed a bill, but the House failed to act. And while pro-reform advocates have galvanized support for immigration reform among Democrats, some argue that their message and tactics risk losing an equal amount of support from centrists and moderates and may even be pushing many white voters out of the party altogether.[14]

The most recent generation of pro-reform advocates and lawmakers may have failed in part because they naturally approached the challenge of enacting immigration reform as a puzzle, looking for policy tweaks or new tactics based on the policy landscape—but *in retrospect*. As science writer Malcolm Gladwell has noted, social science research tends to cast doubt on the accuracy of predictive formulas of any kind. They're inevitably affected by what scientists call "'creeping determinism'—the sense that grows on us, in retrospect, that what has happened is actually inevitable . . . that turns unexpected events into expected events."[15] Because determinists are locked into what Gladwell calls a puzzle paradigm, real solutions evade them. Puzzles, like train accidents, are inherently amenable to solution: work hard enough, long enough, with enough attention to detail, and eventually you'll find the last piece to complete the puzzle, the bent rail on the train track, the "missing nail" that doomed King Richard. But the policy process simply isn't linear. Congress—and forces that bear on it—are constantly in transition. Even with twenty-twenty hindsight, just fixing what went wrong the last time—fighting the last war—is unlikely to produce results when not just the playing field but the very rules of the game are ever-changing. Nor is the legislative process a standard input–output model where the best-resourced interests, the largest constituencies, or those advocating positions most favored by public opinion polls always win.[16]

The legislative process is actually a complex system, like the weather, in which a seemingly innocuous or routine action at one stage of the proceedings can have enormous consequences later, like the metaphorical butterfly drying its wings in one part of the world that leads to a major storm elsewhere.[17] In the mid-1970s, as Rep. Rodino was moving his first employer sanctions bills, economists, biologists, ecologists, astronomers, and researchers from a wide array of fields were developing an entirely new kind of science to find "order in chaos." That new science, "chaos theory," brought together experts from across disciplines to study "the global nature of systems," to address questions that previously were unanswerable, like predicting the weather, the timing of earthquakes, the paths of hurricanes, or outcomes from any other nonlinear system.[18] In assessing prospects for future immigration reform, one might reflect on IRCA's successful path through Capitol Hill's complex, chaotic system.

In 1982, Simpson and Mazzoli introduced their bill following a decade of congressional failure on immigration reform. They first relied on tried and true tactics: crafting a centrist solution based on the recommendations of an expert government commission, building support among elites, and following traditional legislative procedure. They failed first amid Rep. Roybal's unorthodox "filibuster by amendment" strategy, and again in 1984, due to unforeseen issues like initially uncontroversial antidiscrimination provisions, adoption of an expansive guestworker program, and a dispute about money. Together with Peter Rodino they succeeded the third time around, they said, because they "outlasted" the opposition.[19] But in this telling, they succeeded only by giving up many of their policy goals, often under duress, from forces and conditions they initially had not contemplated would be decisive. Perhaps the most important of those forces were the policy objectives, strategies, and tactics deployed by The Group.

In 1981, as IRCA was being drafted on the heels of the Select Commission report, those that eventually coalesced into The Group faced challenges that seemed unwinnable. They had to try to defeat or mitigate employer sanctions and expanded guestworker programs. They opposed cuts in legal immigration and further restrictions on asylum seekers. They sought a generous legalization program and hoped to address "push factors" in source countries. And, they wanted to build a powerful field of Latino and immigrant advocates in the process. They had few resources, especially with the Leadership Conference on Civil Rights, the preeminent institutional voice for minorities, sitting out the debate. The core group's resources were dwarfed by those of agricultural growers, organized labor, anti-immigrant groups, and big business. They had few so-called boots on the ground. And their policy objectives were, as a rule, decidedly unpopular, indeed far less popular than they are today.[20]

The Group failed to stop employer sanctions, though they did obtain some mitigating protections. They succeeded almost everywhere else. IRCA's legalization program provided permanent legal residence to nearly 1.6 million people, many more than might've been legalized under the original bill. Another 1.1 million obtained lawful status through the SAW program included in IRCA instead of a guestworker program. Other programs in the 1986 bill—the Cuban–Haitian program and advancement to 1972 of the "registry date," essentially a statute of limitations—legalized another one hundred thousand undocumented people.[21] They won funding for the required English courses for legalization applicants, positioning many to naturalize and vote. The "family unity" provisions in the Immigration Act of 1990 protected perhaps another million ineligible family members from deportation, paving the way for them to eventually acquire legal status. The 1990 Act protected family visas, did not include a hard cap on legal immigration, and kept the asylum process largely intact, all while eventually doubling legal entries from abroad. And it ensured Temporary Protected Status and other relief for perhaps a million Central Americans and others facing civil strife or natural disaster in their home countries.

How did The Group do it? While a small coalition by DC standards, The Group was almost ideally constituted for a sustained legislative battle. Like the early chaos theorists, they were a multidisciplinary crew, including visionaries, technical experts, and veteran lobbyists with an unusual "feel" for the legislative process. They were augmented by rookies and junior staffers, who used their lower status as motivation to work that much harder. The Group was racially diverse, and in networker extraordinaire Phyllis Eisen, it had unusual insight into the thinking of virtually every other interest in the debate. The Group included team players and iconoclasts, front-of-the-stage stars and back-room actors, research-types and those inclined to pursue gut instincts; overall, as Joe Treviño said years later, the people in The Group "completed each other."[22] Others who came in and out of The Group added different perspectives, and what many of them saw and heard within The Group's deliberations shocked them. Individuals in The Group were capable of bitter, even violent disagreement as they rigorously debated tactics and strategy; one sometime participant said decades later that they "challenged each other in a way I'd never seen before and haven't since."[23] But they also managed an unusual degree of cohesion, best exemplified by Wade Henderson's oft-repeated dictum of the standard of behavior expected of The Group: "If any one of us is in the meeting, we're *all* in the meeting."

The Group pursued all of the traditional lobbying tactics but were dogged and persistent in ways that aren't terribly common in the modern era. They visited virtually every congressional office. They developed decent working relationships with their opponents and competing interests, a practice rarely seen today, where often the only communication between policy adversaries occurs via social media. The Group "camped out" in allied congressional offices, often for days, where they got to know staff and members of those offices' neighbors, committees, and caucuses. These highly personal interactions built highly personal relationships, making it more difficult for wavering lawmakers and staff to later disappoint someone they actually knew, which may well have made the difference between success or failure on numerous votes on amendments that often passed or were defeated by the slimmest of margins.

The Group also engaged in strategies and tactics that were unorthodox by the standards of the period, notably the "filibuster by amendment" that killed the bill in 1982, their close and direct lines of communication with congressional leadership, drafting "their" own bill with direct access to legislative counsel in 1983–1984, direct consultation with the parliamentarian's office leading to additional and lengthier sequential referrals of the bill in 1986, and encouraging Rep. Moakley to move his bill through the Rules Committee—a panel usually limited to producing procedural motions—positioning it to be added first to IRCA and then to the 1990 Act. The advocacy on safe haven relied heavily on the ACLU's then-innovative computer technology to document deaths of deported Salvadorans. The Group also complemented their focus on Capitol Hill's inside game, with an outside game, closely coordinating with Bert Corona and other community organizers as well as their own grasstops networks of Latino leaders, civil libertarians, the Catholic Bishops, and Protestant "church people."

The Group worked closely with business to raise controversy about the bill in 1984 and with pro-immigrant "supply siders" to protect legal immigration. They worked on framing a sympathetic narrative in conventional media, at the same time "narrowcasting" messages to the base via the Spanish International Network. Their successors then consciously shifted away from ethnocentric messaging by broadcasting less threatening, multiracial appeals to the public during the successful post-1996 benefits restoration campaigns. Although they had far less political clout than today, they leveraged every ounce of their limited power when LULAC blatantly engaged in partisan politics in 1984 at the party conventions and held Iowa's representative Harkin accountable for supporting guestworkers, and again when Michael Myers deployed a political opponent to pressure Rep. Rodino to clear the way for the Cuban–Haitian bill in 1986.

Going right up to—and arguably even over—the line of conventional legislative tactics wouldn't have been possible but for the autonomy The Group's supervisors afforded them. The National Immigration Forum's board tolerated Rick Swartz's tendency to test the organization's mandate that it not lobby or take policy positions. LULAC presidents Ruben and Tony Bonilla, Arnoldo Torres's first supervisors, intentionally delegated lobbying strategy and tactics to their staff.[24] NCLR's Raul Yzaguírre's principle that decisions "should be devolved to the lowest level possible" afforded his staff enormous leeway.[25] He later told a subordinate, "I didn't always know what you were up to, and maybe it was good that I didn't know."[26] Few lobbyists had more discretion than Wade Henderson, whose boss Mort Halperin consciously gave his staff "a lot" of autonomy. "And whatever they did," he said, "I would back them up."[27] This autonomy was essential as The Group tested and pursued multiple, even internally inconsistent strategies that, as with the first chaos theorists, violated fundamental tenets of conventional disciplines.

The Group's approach demanded considerable personal and professional sacrifice. All worked ridiculously long hours and perhaps as a result few of their marriages or romantic relationships survived the era.[28] Professionally, LULAC's Arnoldo Torres arguably lost his job over his willingness to stretch the limits of conventional lobbying tactics. MALDEF's Antonia Hernández and Richard Fajardo knew that their hard-line opposition to the bill could lead to a diminished role inside the Beltway, but pursued it both as a matter of principle and as a stratagem to keep pressure on The Group's "left flank."[29] Early in the debate NCLR's leaders knew that its moderation risked it being labeled a sellout, so they tacked left to join The Group, and then worked with Rep. Esteban Torres to help shape an IRCA compromise. Later, NCLR was willing to stress its relationship with its key ally Rep. Torres to take a harder line to retain its "standing" to continue to challenge employer sanctions.[30] The Latino groups all faced major, even existential fiscal constraints in the IRCA era, but all devoted substantial resources to advance pro-immigrant positions that would've been seen as heresy just a generation earlier.

The Group quickly adopted policy innovations that may not have reflected their formal organizational positions yet advanced their interests. By embracing the Special Agricultural Worker program in 1986, they helped break the gridlock between pro- and anti-guestworker lobbies, paving the way for enactment of

IRCA on its third try. The Group also pursued unique policy ideas of their own. Faced with what they believed was an inadequate legalization program, instead of concentrating on advancing the program's eligibility cutoff date—the highest-profile change they could've made—they won a dozen smaller amendments to the program's "substructure," and made them stick through implementation. The bill's antidiscrimination provisions were modeled originally on a labor statute, not a civil rights one. The State Legalization Impact Assistance Grants program required the unorthodox combination of an authorization and appropriation in one bill. The Immigration Act of 1990 included the "pierceable cap" on legal immigration devised by AILA's Warren Leiden to protect family immigration and the Moakley-DeConcini bill, which created Temporary Protected Status, an entirely new immigration category, the original version of which was banged out on a typewriter by the ACLU's Mort Halperin. To be sure, some of The Group's innovations weren't actualized: their "targeted" version of employer sanctions fell by the wayside, the Roybal bill's alternative to employer sanctions, enhanced labor law enforcement, was included in IRCA but wasn't backed by appropriations, and the International Commission on Migration's recommendations weren't pursued.[31] But they saw each as a potential butterfly that could alter future events.

In sum, The Group didn't approach the challenge of either killing or making radical changes to the heralded Simpson-Mazzoli bill as a "puzzle" to be solved solely via conventional strategies and tactics. Confronted with a popular bill sponsored by a highly capable bipartisan team and almost universally supported by the media and establishment elites, the rational course would've been to "speak truth to power": oppose the legislation on principle but invest scarce resources elsewhere, the legislative equivalent of "checking the box." Instead, beginning in 1982 they approached each successive challenge—first stopping the bill, then offering an alternative, later improving it incrementally, and finally helping it pass—as a mystery. Solving a mystery, paraphrasing Malcolm Gladwell, requires absorbing massive amounts of information received from the environment for clues, testing a wide variety of potential answers, while never being bound by the limits of conventional thinking.[32] Over hundreds of hours of weekly meetings The Group gamed out multiple scenarios and tried to be prepared for each conceivable outcome, an exercise analogous to meteorologists' "ensemble forecasting" method—developing multiple computer models each using a slightly different variable—which has made weather prognostication more accurate over the past several decades.[33]

As an observer of The Group later noted, its members "never accepted it at face value when the conventional wisdom says something just can't be done."[34] Instead, driven by a sense that "we were righting historical wrongs," Phyllis Eisen recalls, "We *believed* we could win. We *knew* there was an answer. We just had to be more clever" than opposing interests.[35] Faced with a proverbial storm, The Group's members didn't try and track down every butterfly whose wing-drying could be shaping it, nor did they throw up their hands and stick with conventional positions and tactics, reassuring themselves that the weather is unpredictable anyway. Instead, they tried to model the storm's likely paths, envisioned multiple approaches to reshape its course, and developed and tested plans for each plausible scenario. In this sense The Group shared some of the sensibilities of early chaos theorists, seeing a path forward that traditional science would've said simply didn't exist.[36] As Rick Swartz observed years later, collectively The Group had a certain "mindset" that they would do everything in their collective power, and never anything less, to advance their priorities.[37] Their successors maintained this mindset through IRCA implementation, passage of the Immigration Act of 1990, and four successive restorations of benefits to legal immigrants.

Lawmakers associated with the bill also took steps that made reform possible. Al Simpson, a commanding figure in the "world's greatest deliberative body," made numerous concessions to the opposition at key points in the process to move bills forward, cementing his distinctive place as one of the master legislators of the modern era. Many advocates found Ted Kennedy's role puzzling, but unable to endorse the bill he did the next best thing, which was to work behind the scenes to facilitate its improvement. As Arnoldo Torres acknowledged, "Looking back now, I see the value of the role that Kennedy played. Even though he couldn't support it, Kennedy helped Simpson pass the bill. Three million people were legalized as a result."[38]

Ron Mazzoli might've been all but forgotten by history after he selflessly asked Peter Rodino to assume chief sponsorship of the House bill in 1985, later allowing it to pass in 1986 even after adoption of a Special Agricultural Worker program he abhorred. It's perhaps fitting that a review of recent major policy achievements, along with the Americans with Disabilities Act (1990) and the expansion of the Earned Income Tax Credit (1993), listed the "Simpson-*Mazzoli* immigration act of 1986" as one of the few "serious accomplishments" of the 1980s and 1990s.[39] Even when they disagreed, lawmakers Hamilton Fish, Barney Frank, and Dan Lungren worked closely with their counterparts at every stage of the process at a time of growing partisan polarization.

The bill would never have passed in anything resembling its final form but for hard-line opponents Ed Roybal and Robert Garcia, who delayed the measure until it could be improved, and then Esteban Torres, who broke from his elders' orthodoxy to negotiate and deliver the votes to enact those improvements. Peter Rodino's refusal to accede to legislation he was uneasy with, and his decision to deputize Howard Berman to handle farmworker issues prevented adoption of a guestworker program and helped kill the bill in 1984. Berman rewarded this confidence by negotiating, together with Leon Panetta and Chuck Schumer, the Special Agricultural Worker program that paved the way for IRCA. Berman later helped manage the Immigration Act of 1990, in doing so becoming the single most effective pro-immigrant lawmaker of the twentieth century. And the skills, energy, and persistence that later elevated Chuck Schumer to become the Democratic leader of the Senate were all on full display in the IRCA era.

LESSONS

One might ask whether lessons from enactment of a bill thirty-plus years ago are even remotely applicable today, with the increasing salience of race in the debate and growing hyper-partisanship. But it would be a mistake to assume these factors weren't relevant in the late 1980s and the early 1990s when IRCA and the Immigration Act of 1990 were enacted. In fact, it's striking how omnipresent race has been as a factor shaping immigration policy, literally from the beginning of the existence of our southern border. The concept of Mexican, and by extension Latino, inferiority began as a blaring soundtrack behind major immigration developments in the post-Mexican–American War and pre-civil rights eras, but it's never truly disappeared. It often seemed like elevator music—rarely noticed but always in the background—playing softly behind discussions about immigration, before coming to the forefront of debates.

It's true that the spirit of bipartisanship on immigration was more common in the IRCA era than it is today, and that Democrats and Republicans increasingly are identified with pro- and anti-immigrant positions, respectively. But even a glance at the partisan voting breakdowns on key bills and amendments in 1986 and 1990 suggests that bipartisanship was somewhat overrated then. It is noteworthy that even when the volume of the racial background music was turned up and, even if not fully appreciated, the hard-line partisanship of the Newt Gingrich wing of the GOP was ascending rapidly, neither racial tensions nor partisanship precluded enactment of either IRCA or its follow-on bill in 1990.

At a time when pro- and anti-immigrant sentiments are increasingly divided along racial lines and between the political parties, some reformers might prefer to pursue a race-conscious, purely partisan approach, investing in electoral strategies designed to produce a more Democratic, immigrant-friendly administration and Congress. But exclusive reliance on this strategy cannot address the structural advantages that the GOP can expect for several decades. As Lee Drutman wrote, although Democrats won a majority of the popular vote in six out of the last seven presidential contests, "A Republican entered the White House after two of those defeats, thanks to the way the Electoral College favors rural and suburban voters." Drutman also noted that the GOP, in part due to gerrymandering, has held a majority in the House of Representatives in eighteen of the last twenty-four years.[40] Another benefit of the GOP's Electoral College advantage is how it also translates into overrepresentation in the Senate, where only forty votes can block movement of legislation. Immigration reform has twice passed the Senate in the past dozen years, but would this propensity last in an atmosphere of racialized hyper-partisanship?

Those inclined to put all of their eggs in a partisan electoral basket might also ask themselves whether and how long the Democrats' recent pro-immigrant incarnation would be sustained were they to assume power. As pollster Stanley Greenberg has noted, already many Democrats believe that the party risks being perceived as moving "from seeking to manage and champion the nation's growing immigrant diversity to seeming to champion immigrant rights over American citizens'."[41] Other research has shown that confronted with evidence of a majority-minority country, nearly half of white Democrats "expressed anger or anxiety."[42] Even among Latinos, the purported strongest pro-immigrant demographic, there is evidence that significant pluralities and even slight majorities support less partisan, balanced policies that include both more border security as well as protections against deportation for most unauthorized immigrants.[43]

One eminent political scientist believes that the body politic treats immigration as a "thermostatic" issue: once developments—like the country's impending majority-minority status—create a political environment perceived as too immigrant-friendly, public opinion then shifts in the opposite direction.[44] If true, the very act of electing a dominant pro-immigrant Democratic congressional majority could by itself trigger movement in the opposite direction within the party itself, while hardening the attitudes of the GOP opposition.

This author, for one, believes that pro-immigrant advocates shouldn't wait to push for reform until changing demographics produce a sweep of the presidency and Congress by unabashedly pro-immigrant Democrats. Bipartisan strategies inevitably require compromise, but they tend to have staying power; as one eminent journalist has noted, coherent reforms such as landmark civil rights bills, Medicare and Medicaid in the 1960s, and Reagan's 1980s tax cuts—and he might have added, the interstate highway system begun in the 1950s, the core environmental bills of the 1970s, and the Children's Health Insurance Program in the 1990s—were all bipartisan.[45]

History similarly suggests that the next set of successful, sustainable immigration reforms likely will be comprehensive and bipartisan in nature, with provisions addressing enforcement, legalization, and legal immigration. One reason noted by Doris Meissner, who has shaped and implemented immigration policy across six presidential administrations, is that notwithstanding changing political considerations, there has been a high degree of continuity of the outlines of proposed reforms over time, because immigration is ultimately a "good government" issue.[46]

Given growing hyper-partisanship on immigration policy, the notion that future reforms will reflect bipartisan compromises might appear oxymoronic to many. Yet that very polarization creates enormous incentives for partisans to resist their opponent's proposals unless they also get something in return. And any reforms enacted on a party line vote would almost certainly be reversed once the political winds changed. Paradoxical as it may seem, a bipartisan compromise approach, however difficult, might be the *only* way to overcome partisan gridlock.

And as much as many might prefer "leaner" or piecemeal reforms, absent a "Grand Bargain"—which history teaches us is always tenuous—the odds are stacked against enactment of bills that only address narrow interests by the legislative process itself. Once a bill appears to have a good chance of passage, factions whose interests aren't addressed will inevitably try and jump on the moving legislative train, and the record suggests that at least a few will succeed.

If these assumptions are correct, IRCA's history suggests that the next successful pro-immigrant reformers will have followed certain prescriptions.

First, they will have used all of the tools at their disposal: At least at the outset of the next successful campaign, pro-reform advocates should be prepared to deploy each of their major tools—new research, insider lobbying, strategic communications, field-based organizing, and an electoral strategy—without going "all-in" on any single approach, as it arguably did prior to 2006 with a DC-centric approach, or since with a heavily field-organizing model. If IRCA has any relevance to contemporary debates, it's that successful advocates pursue multiple, even competing, strategies simultaneously.

Second, they will have developed new messaging: This book suggests that race underlies much of the resistance to immigration, and explains how John Tanton's organizations contributed to the open racialization of the issues. Combatting such messaging is becoming an entire field unto itself, beyond the scope of this book. But pro-immigrant reformers might consider whether their own rhetoric contributes to "racializing" the debate.[47] Social scientists who study racial attitudes, such as Stanford's Alana Conner, have found that, "Telling people they're racist, sexist, and xenophobic will get you exactly nowhere. It's such a threatening message. . . . When people feel threatened, they can't change, they can't listen."[48] Toning down advocates' increasingly common conflation of immigration restriction with racism could well open some minds, and some doors.

Such moderate, unthreatening messaging has been criticized by some racial justice intellectuals as "respectability politics" that fails to "speak truth to power."[49] But new research affirms that the inclusive, nonviolent message of equality for all delivered by Martin Luther King and other leaders in the 1960s both changed minds and laid the groundwork for the civil rights legislation that followed.[50] More than five decades have passed since then, but if anything many whites feel more threatened by racial minorities today, a phenomenon described by scholar Robin DiAngelo as "white fragility."[51] Pro-reform advocates might do well to adapt the approach used in the post-1996 benefits restoration campaign, which consciously broadcast inclusive messaging to the general public while "narrow-casting" more aggressive messaging to "the base." Two steps taken by NCLR in 2017 may be instructive. The first was to change its name to UnidosUS, designed to send a more inclusive message.[52] The second was a new communications effort called Rise Above, urging Americans to rediscover the "ties that bind us as a country."[53]

Third, they will have built direct relationships with GOP and moderate Democratic lawmakers: In the IRCA era, advocates lobbied congressional offices in-person, over the telephone, and through lengthy letters. As email, social media, and other online communications technologies have advanced, advocates increasingly have turned to these more "efficient" tools. But it seems that as the quantity of communication with Congress has increased, its quality has diminished. Nonprofit managers, funders, and the news media often equate the size of a protest or the simple number of messages sent as the key "metric" of success, so some advocates seem to have largely abandoned grasstops strategies to persuade lawmakers through trusted community leaders. Even today's field-based grassroots strategies seem more focused on producing a large rally instead of the smaller, personal, face-to-face meetings that Bert Corona effectively deployed. Even lawmakers opposed to one's positions are human beings; pro-immigrant reformers might do well to think of them that way. Quaint as it may seem, with a closely divided legislature, old-fashioned one-to-one lobbying "within the system" may be the most effective strategy.

Fourth, they will have acknowledged the legitimacy of basic immigration enforcement. Every sovereign nation has the right to control its borders, which by definition means that some who wish to come to the US must be prohibited from entering, and that some here unlawfully will be returned to their home countries. Immigration advocates are quick to point out the inconsistencies, hypocrisies, and injustices of current immigration enforcement regimes, but rarely articulate enforcement policies they are prepared to support. As a result even those sympathetic to reform interpret pro-immigrant advocates' agendas as pushing "policies that approach an open border for all."[54] The GOP's post-2012 election autopsy was correct in observing that for many Latino and Asian voters immigration is a negative "gateway issue": if a candidate begins a speech by saying her goal is to deport their relatives, they'll stop listening to whatever follows. But just as "mass deportation" is an automatic nonstarter for Latinos and Asians, "open borders" may be a gateway issue that prevents swing-vote moderates from listening to pro-reform advocates the next time immigration reform is considered.

Fifth, they will have developed, tested, and accepted policy innovations: The broad outlines of comprehensive reform—tougher enforcement, legalization of the undocumented, maintenance of family-based preferences for legal immigration, and more visas for both permanent and temporary workers to satisfy business—have been essentially unchanged since the turn of the century. The same might've been said about IRCA, the outlines of which were set fifteen years before its enactment, yet that bill required a previously rejected innovation, the Special Agricultural Worker program, to catalyze its final passage. Future successful reformers will likely have accepted variants of proposals they previously rejected as well as completely new concepts that hadn't been considered before.

Sixth, they will have asserted greater independent leadership: Arnoldo Torres believes that Latino advocates should chart an independent course from many of the traditional interests in the debate.[55] Immigrant rights activists reflexively view virtually all newcomers as part of their constituencies, but two-thirds of Hispanics are native-born, and their interests may not always coincide with those who have yet to enter. So, for example, Latino advocates might reconsider the assumption that unfettered immigration is necessarily in their community's interest. After decades when high immigration has closely tracked falling wages, some neutral analysts have concluded, "Immigration has almost certainly contributed to the wage gap, particularly in low-wage occupations."[56] And while the Latino rank and file is generally pro-immigrant, a substantial portion of the population also supports more enforcement; in that context some of their future advocates, like their IRCA-era predecessors, will likely play roles in brokering and negotiating compromises that catalyze the next successful reforms.

A more independent course could include revisiting the longtime understanding that if business doesn't oppose legalization or family-based immigration then pro-immigrant advocates won't attack more visas for high-skilled workers or temporary worker programs. The formula failed in 2007 and 2013 when business couldn't deliver enough GOP support and going forward some believe that "the pro-immigration business coalition has lost its sway over the Republican Party."[57] Conversely, Latino leaders and organized labor may have common cause to consider restrictions on entry of large numbers of highly skilled workers, focusing instead on building on "ladders of opportunity" for upward mobility; as Janet Murguía has written, "Once employers know that their high-skilled jobs could be filled from abroad, why should they support improvements in our education system or investments in higher education?"[58] The immigrant–business alliance came close but failed to produce reform twice in the past dozen years; it's conceivable that to enact progressive reforms, Latinos and their major constituency of low-wage workers may need to come together with labor unions to form a "populist left" that succeeds in countering the "populist right" that forms the core of Trump's coalition.

Seventh, future successful reformers will almost certainly be required to exhibit considerable flexibility and sacrifice in negotiating the compromises required to enact sustainable policy. If, as this analysis suggests, the legislative process resembles the kind of "complex system" studied by chaos theorists, then almost by definition pro-reform advocates must prepare for the unexpected. Advocates' ability to respond quickly and effectively to such developments may well be the difference between success and failure. In the IRCA era the small, tight, disciplined, and quasi-autonomous members of The Group attained many of their policy goals by rapidly changing strategies and tactics; by comparison:

- Will the current, larger, and thus inherently more cumbersome infrastructure of pro-reform advocates and lawmakers be able to adapt to an ever-changing future political landscape?
- If the opportunity for compromise arises as in 1986 and 1990, when it was seized on by the advocates—and possibly in 2006 when they turned it down—will future reformers recognize the moment?
- When such compromise moments arise, will key advocates and lawmakers be willing to disrupt their personal lives, break with partisan orthodoxy, and even risk their professional futures to produce comprehensive immigration reform?
- And will they have built the kinds of personal bonds of trust among them that will allow compromise legislation to overcome inevitable assaults from the partisan extremes?

From the time of Machiavelli it's been known that advocates and policy makers that seek to upend the status quo and defy conventional wisdom confront formidable challenges: overcoming simple inertia, beating the considerable mathematical odds against major policy change, navigating a chaotic legislative process, and maintaining their momentum through the law's implementation. It is precisely for these reasons that even the successful IRCA-era reforms were declared dead on multiple occasions before they were revived.

As one influential analyst has written, "The metaphor for U.S. . . . policy on migration is a post at the border with two signs: one reads 'Help Wanted,' and the other reads 'Keep Out.' "[59] Where future leaders draw this line will say as much about American identity as any other question they might consider; no matter where the line is drawn, a significant plurality of Americans will disagree, although recent research suggests that public consensus on "a politics of immigration and citizenship that actually unites" the country may be less elusive than commonly believed.[60] Given inevitable but unpredictable developments here and abroad that could result in mass movements of people across borders, it's increasingly clear that immigration isn't a single problem that any single bill or even set of domestic policies will ever "solve."

Thus, we can expect ongoing debates about comprehensive immigration reform. Most reform proposals will be declared dead on arrival, and indeed most are destined for the morgue. But perhaps once a generation, due to skilled lawmakers, artful lobbying, a policy innovation, a new alliance, willingness to break from partisan orthodoxy, simple perseverance, or perhaps blind luck, the stars will align, the corpse will be jolted awake, and in the words of Al Simpson, "the big lug will get off the table and stagger off into the marshes." And once again, the nation will enact and implement comprehensive immigration reform, the corpse that will not die.

ACKNOWLEDGMENTS

Then statement that no single person produces a book is a cliché because it's indisputably true. This project began with a phone call to me from an adviser to an anonymous donor offering to help commission this book; I remain ever grateful to my unknown patron, whoever s/he is!

I owe a considerable debt to my colleagues at UnidosUS (formerly the National Council of La Raza), especially President and CEO Janet Murguía and Chief Operating Officer Sonia Pérez, for allowing me the flexibility to take the project on. Special appreciation to my too-numerous-to-name other colleagues at UnidosUS for accepting responsibilities I dumped on them, often unceremoniously, when I took on this adventure. My former bosses, Raul Yzaguirre, Emily Gantz McKay, Mark Van Brunt and Reyes Cortéz, all contributed in countless ways to my personal and professional development. Special thanks to Michael Cortés, Francisco Garza, Martha Escutia, Dan Purtell, Rose Briceño, Cecilia Muñoz, Emelda Medrano, Lissette Lopez, Wendy Young, Michelle Waslin, Flavia Jiménez, Joel Najar, Claudia Jasin, Lillian Hirales, Raul González, Melissa Lazarín, Clarissa Martínez De Castro, Felicia Escobar, Olga Medina, Elena Lacayo, Laura Vazquez, Albert Jacquez, Victoria Benner, Manuel Grajeda, and Carlos Guevara for their extraordinary work on immigration policy at NCLR/UnidosUS; I'd gladly share a foxhole with any of you again.

Thanks also to the crew at the Migration Policy Institute, particularly past presidents Demetrios Papademetriou and Michael Fix, for serving as the project's fiscal sponsor and providing work space on very generous terms. MPI president Andrew Selee, US Programs Director Doris Meissner, Communications and Public Affairs Director Michelle Mittelstadt, "Integrationist" nonpareil Margie McHugh, Finance and Administration Directors Ken Crognale and Gale Wright, HR and Administrative Manager Erik Lindsjo, Policy Analyst Faye Hipsman, Executive Assistant Violet Lee, and Events Manager extraordinaire Lisa Dixon were all invariably supportive, responsive, and helpful. I am particularly beholden to Muzaffar Chishti, director of MPI's New York office, for his early, enthusiastic support for this book project, extraordinary photographic memory, many thoughtful comments on portions of the manuscript, and most importantly for his decades-long friendship.

My deepest appreciation to publishers Robert Mandel and Irene Vilar, and the whole MV Press team, for delivering this baby into the world. Special thanks to my friend Rudy Arredondo, a warrior for social justice, for suggesting MV press as an option just as I was disseminating my book proposal. Deb Heimann brought her expert skills and considerable wisdom to the editing process. Many thanks to the W.K. Kellogg Foundation, Four Freedoms Fund, Raza Development Fund, Public Welfare Foundation, and UnBound Philanthropy for funding that enabled me to work part-time while writing the book, conduct multiple research trips, and support marketing efforts. I'm particularly grateful to Ramón Murguía, Alice Warner-Melhorn, Gerri Mannion, Margarita Rubalcava, Taryn Higashi, and Mary McClymont, for their forbearance over the many years it took to complete the effort. Special thanks to Tom Espinoza and Mark Van Brunt for their generosity and friendship.

Dr. Robert Trujillo and his staff at the Stanford University Libraries' Department of Special Collections, which houses among others the MALDEF and NCLR/UnidosUS records, helped this novice navigate the wonderful world of organizational archives; I hope the university's students and researchers realize what a treasure trove they have on campus. Thanks also to the staff at the Library of Congress for their assistance and professionalism. Special appreciation to Douglas Rivlin and Rep. Luis Gutiérrez for their help in accessing congressional floor debates and hearings from the pre-digitized era; they saved me literally hundreds of hours of work. The Romano "Ron" Mazzoli Oral History Project at the University of Louisville was an invaluable source of first-person accounts from the congressman, his former staff, and colleagues, and I deeply appreciate Mr. Mazzoli's courtesy in facilitating my access to those records. The online archives of several newspapers, especially Robert Pear's reporting in the *New York Times*, were a critical, indispensable reference. Nadine Cahodas kindly allowed me access to her personal collection of articles from *Congressional Quarterly Weekly Report*. Rick Swartz, Emily Gantz McKay, Maurice Belanger, Taryn Higashi, and Vanna Slaughter provided invaluable source materials not otherwise available in the public domain. I also relied heavily—as even a glance at the endnotes shows—on previously published works by Michael Barone and Grant Ujifusa, Michael Cortés, Ellis Cose, Louis Freedberg, Lawrence Fuchs, Doris Meissner and Demetrious Papademetriou, Harris Miller, Mae Ngai, David North and Anna Mary Portz, Rosanna Perotti, Shari Robertson and Michael Camerini, and Aristide Zolberg. I am indebted to all of them.

I am profoundly grateful to the many past colleagues and associates, especially my comrades in The Group, who submitted to (often multiple) interviews and innumerable follow-up requests; I've been humbled by their generosity. I'm particularly thankful to those that reviewed and provided corrections, encouragement, insights, and helpful comments on portions of the manuscript, including Muzaffar Chishti, Phyllis Eisen, Wade Henderson, Antonia Hernández, Cecilia Muñoz, Rick Swartz, Arnoldo Torres, Dr. Lauren Wolchok, Raul Yzaguírre, and several anonymous reviewers who provided cogent suggestions on earlier drafts. Monte Lake, Dan Maldonado, and Michael Myers also provided helpful comments and corrections. Of course, any errors of fact or logic that remain are solely my own.

My "co-pilot and navigator" Carol Wolchok has enriched my life immeasurably, accepted with (generally) good humor my frequent, lengthy absences while working on this project, and provided a number of rare materials from her personal "files." I'm grateful to Anthony Rogers, caretaker of my late mother's home where much of this book was written, for his reliable help. My father died just after IRCA passed. Since then I've met with presidents, famous lawmakers, award-winning scholars, and captains of industry, and my Dad is still the clearest thinker I've ever known. My late mother virtually reinvented herself after being widowed; her example inspired me to imagine what's possible when willing to venture beyond one's comfort zone. Both of my parents instilled in me a love of reading; I hope this product reflects even a fraction of their wisdom and grace. Thanks also to my extended family for their unfailing enthusiasm and encouragement; I just wish I had finished the book in time for my late Uncle Taka to read it.

This book is dedicated to the memory of four friends and mentors, all giants in the immigration reform field in the 1980s, who have since passed away: Michael Hooper, Wells Klein, Brenda Pillors, and Gary Rubin. The descriptions of their work in this book are but a glimpse of their enduring and oft-unheralded contributions to the field of immigration policy and practice. Each of them, in different ways, took me under their wing and taught me important lessons in the process. They helped make our country a better place for all, and we miss them still.

ENDNOTES

INTRODUCTION

1. Author interview with Mort Halperin, December 18, 2015.

CHAPTER 1

1. "The Group" was first described in the literature by Christine Marie Sierra in "Latino Organizational Strategies on Immigration Reform: Success and Limits in Public Policymaking," Roberto E. Villarreal and Norma G. Hernandez, eds., *Latinos and Political Coalitions* (Praeger Publishers, 1991).

2. Ben Zimmer, "The Unrestrained Speech of the 'Filterless,'" *Wall Street Journal*, June 27, 2015.

3. Author interview with J. Michael Treviño, October 2, 2012.

4. Author interview with Martha Escutia, November 1, 2012.

5. Author interview with Arnoldo Torres, November 1, 2013.

6. Michael Eduardo Cortés, *Policy Analysts and Interest Groups: The Case of Immigration Reform*, PhD dissertation, University of California-Berkeley, 1992, 396.

7. Lyle Saunders, "The Social History of Spanish-Speaking People in the Southwestern United States Since 1846," paper delivered at the 4th Regional Conference, Southwest Council on Spanish-Speaking People, January 23–25, 1950, cited in Julian Samora, *Los Mojados: The Wetback Story* (University of Notre Dame Press, 1971), 17.

8. For a contemporary version of this argument, see Richard Rothstein, *The Color of Law: A Forgotten History of How Our Government Segregated America*, Liveright, 2017. Rothstein, a distinguished journalist now associated with the left-leaning Economic Policy Institute, argued Hispanics were not systematically discriminated against by the government. As one critical reviewer noted, "First- and second-generation Hispanics live in segregated neighborhoods by choice, we are assured, not because they are forced to." See David Oshinsky, "A Powerful, Disturbing History of Residential Segregation in America," *New York Times*, June 20, 2017. Another variant of this view comes from "futurist" Joel Kotkin, who argued that Latinos resembled "Italians, an ethnic group who also came to this country largely poor and uneducated"; see Joel Kotkin, "The Future of Latino Politics," *Orange County Register*, July 24, 2016. Neither perspective can explain decades of discrimination against Hispanics that social science research suggests may be of the same order of magnitude as that facing African Americans, at least on certain key indicia like employment, housing, and education.

9. Charles Kamasaki and Raul Yzaguírre, "Black–Hispanic Tensions: One Perspective," *Journal of Intergroup Relations* 21, no. 4 (Winter 1994–95): 17–40.

10. Mae M. Ngai, *Impossible Subjects: Illegal Aliens and the Making of Modern America* (Princeton University Press, 2004): 132. Writing about the post–World War I era, Ngai notes: "Throughout the Southwest, and especially in Texas, all Mexicans suffered from a system of segregation that mimicked the Jim Crow practices of the South. Mexican Americans and immigrants alike lived in segregated *colonias*, were denied service in restaurants and drug stores that were patronized by whites, and were seated in separate sections in movie theaters. In Texas, poll taxes, and in some South Texas counties all-white primaries effectively kept Mexican Americans outside the polity."

11. William D. Carrigan and Clive Webb, "The Lynching of Persons of Mexican Origin or Descent in the United States, 1848 to 1928," *Journal of Social History* 37 (2003): 411, 413. See also, Richard Delgado, "The Law of the Noose: A History of Latino Lynching," *Harvard Civil Rights-Civil Liberties Law Review* 44 (2009).

12. Alejandro Portes and Ruben Rumbaut, *Legacies: The Story of the Immigrant Second Generation* (University of California Press, 2001).

13. See Marian Jean Barber, *How the Irish, Germans, and Czechs Became Anglo: Race and Identity in the Texas-Mexico Borderlands* (PhD dissertation, University of Texas, Austin, 2010).

14. It is a little incongruous that no "Anglo-Saxon" race exists, even by the loosest definition of the term "race." As chronicled by distinguished English historian Peter Ackroyd, the original peoples of the British isles included indigenous groups such as the Picts, the forerunners of the Scots, and the Silenes in Wales, whom the Roman historian Tacitus called "Celts." By the time of Julius Caesar's invasion of England in 55 BC, Britons, from Brittany in modern-day France, as well as Angles, Saxons, and other Germanic tribes, had been added to the native population. For the next millennium, England was invaded, conquered and occupied by Frisians from the Netherlands; Jutes and Danes from Denmark; Vikings from Norway; and in 1066 by William the Conqueror from Normandy, in France. Those who proudly called themselves "Anglo-Saxons" seven centuries later in the American Southwest were, in fact, the product of the mixture of dozens of indigenous peoples native to the British isles, immigrants from France and Germany, dozens of ethnicities represented among Caesar's legionnaires drawn not just from Italy but from the breadth of the Roman Empire, and invaders from northern Europe. As Ackroyd notes with some irony, the Anglo-Saxon people who viewed themselves during the nineteenth and twentieth centuries as the "empire race" had, for much of their formative history themselves been a "colonized and exploited people." See Peter Ackroyd, *Foundation: The History of England from Its Earliest Beginnings to the Tudors* (Thomas Dunne Books, 2011).

15. David R. Roediger, *Working Toward Whiteness: How America's Immigrants Became White, the Strange Journey from Ellis Island to the Suburbs* (Basic Books, 2005), 13.

16. Seth Sandronsky, "How America's Immigrants Became White," *Black Agenda Report*, posted April 15, 2007, http://www.blackagendareport.com/content/howamerica%E2%80%99s-immigrants-became-white, accessed May 3, 2014.

17. Stanley Lieberson, *A Piece of the Pie: Black and White Immigrants Since 1880* (University of California Press, 1981), 253–91.

18. Roediger, *Working Toward Whiteness*, 171–76.

19. This is, in fact, the principal thesis of Roediger's book. See also, Ta-Nehisi Coates, "The Case for Reparations, *The Atlantic*, June 2014.

20. Cybelle Fox and Thomas A. Guglielmo, "Defining America's Racial Boundaries: Blacks, Mexicans, and European Immigrants," *American Journal of Sociology* 118, no. 2 (September 2012): 352–53.

21. Rodolfo Acuña, *Occupied America*, 6th ed. (Pearson Longman, 2007).

22. David Montejano, "A Journey Through Mexican Texas, 1900–1930" (PhD dissertation, Yale University, 1982), cited in Alfredo Mirande, *Gringo Justice* (University of Notre Dame Press, 1987), 8.

23. See, for example, David Montejano, *Anglos and Mexicans in the Making of Texas: 1836–1986* (University of Texas Press, 1987), and Richard Flores, *Remembering the Alamo: Memory, Modernity, and the Master Symbol* (University of Texas Press, 2002).

24. Edward E. Telles and Vilma Ortiz, *Generations of Exclusion: Mexican Americans, Assimilation, and Race* (Russell Sage Foundation, 2008), 101.

25. Cynthia E. Orozco, *No Mexicans, Women or Dogs Allowed* (University of Texas Press, 2009), 30–31.

26. For an in-depth portrayal of the case, see the 2002 film, "*Mendez v. Westminster*: Desegregating California's Schools," WGBH Boston, described at http://www.pbslearningmedia.org/resource/osi04.soc.ush.civil.mendez/mendez-v-westminster-desegregating-californias-schools/, accessed May 9, 2014.

27. Gilbert C. Gonzalez, *Chicano Education in the Era of Segregation* (University of North Texas Press, 1990), 12, citing his own earlier work, "System of Public Education and its Function Within Chicano Communities" (PhD dissertation, University of California-Los Angeles, 1974).

28. For detailed history and analysis of Puerto Ricans in the US, one could not do better than to read the series of books by Clara E. Rodriguez, including *Puerto Ricans: Born in the USA* (Westview Press, 1989); *Historical Perspectives on Puerto Rican Survival in the U.S.* (Marcus Weiner Press, 1996) (with Virginia Sanchez Korrol); and for a broader view of Hispanic ethnicity, *Changing Race: Latinos, the Census, and the History of Ethnicity in the United States* (New York University Press, 2000).

29. See Mario Barrera, *Race and Class in the Southwest* (Notre Dame University Press, 1979), 10–12.

30. Numerous examples of such discrimination in this period can be found in Acuña, *Occupied America*; Cynthia E. Orozco, *No Mexicans, Women or Dogs Allowed*; and Ngai, *Impossible Subjects*, among many others.

31. "'Miracle at Donna' Director Works to Finalize Documentary," *Mid-Valley Town Crier*, April 13, 2014.

32. Mirande, *Gringo Justice*, 27–49.

33. Fox and Guglielmo, "Defining America's Racial Boundaries," 356–57.

34. Robert McKay, "Mexican Americans and Repatriation," *Handbook of Texas Online*, http://www.tshaonline.org/handbook/online/articles/pqmyk, June 15, 2010, accessed May 3, 2014.

35. Allan Englekirk and Marguerite Marin, "Mexican Americans," thinknowresearch.com, 2009, http://www.everyculture.com/multi/Le-Pa/Mexican-Americans.html, accessed May 9, 2014.

36. For a detailed account of the war, see: Michael J. Gonzales, *The Mexican Revolution: 1910–1940* (University of New Mexico Press, 2002).

37. T. R. Fehrenbach, *Lone Star: A History of Texas and Texans* (American Legacy Press, 1983), 690–91.

38. Mirande, *Gringo Justice*, 96–97.

39. Don M. Coerver, "Plan of San Diego," *Handbook of Texas Online*, June 15, 2010, http://www.tshaonline.org/handbook/online/articles/ngp04, accessed May 9, 2014.

40. McKay, "Mexican Americans and Repatriation."

41. Fehrenbach, *Lone Star*, 690–91.

42. Estimates cited in Mirande, *Gringo Justice*, 21.

43. Fehrenbach, *Lone Star*, 692.

44. See Don M. Coerver and Linda B. Hall, *Texas and the Mexican Revolution: A Study in State and National Border Policy, 1910–1920* (Trinity University Press, 1984), and Don M. Coerver, "Plan of San Diego," *Handbook of Texas Online*, June 15, 2010, http://www.tshaonline.org/handbook/online/articles/ngp04, accessed May 9, 2014.

45. "The History," *Refusing to Forget*, http://refusingtoforget.org/the-history/, undated, accessed March 7, 2016; see also Cindy Casares, "Texas Finally Acknowledges Rangers Killed Hundreds of Latinos," *Latina*, February 3, 2016, http://www.latina.com/lifestyle/our-issues/texas-rangers-kill-latinos, accessed March 7, 2016.

46. Mirande, *Gringo Justice*, 97.

47. For a detailed history of the immigration policy developments in this period, see Aristide R. Zolberg, *A Nation by Design: Immigration Policy in the Fashioning of America* (Harvard University Press & Russell Sage Foundation, 2008), 202–70.

48. Emilio Zamora, *The World of the Mexican Worker in Texas* (Texas A&M University Press, 1993), 35–49.

49. Abraham Hoffman, *Unwanted Mexicans in the Great Depression* (University of Arizona Press, 1974), cited in Mirande, *Gringo Justice*, 104.

50. Paul R. Ehrlich, Loy Bilderback, and Anne H. Ehrlich, *The Golden Door: International Migration, Mexico, and the United States* (Malor Books, 2008), 220.

51. Sarah Deutsch, *No Separate Refuge: Culture, Class and Gender on an Anglo-Hispanic Frontier in the American Southwest, 1880–1940* (Oxford University Press, 1987).

52. Acuña, *Occupied America*, 164.

53. *El Universal* newspaper, March 5, 1921, cited in Acuña, *Occupied America*, 164.

54. Since it is known that the Mexican-origin population was 500,000 in 1900, a reasonable estimate is that about 800,000 people of Mexican ancestry lived in the US as of 1921, after accounting for net immigration over two decades plus the large influx from the south during the Mexican Revolution. If approximately 150,000 of these people were indeed "repatriated" in 1921, it would have constituted about 18.75 percent of the total Mexican-origin population of the country at the time.

55. Acuña, *Occupied America*, 164.

56. Mae Ngai, "Immigration at the Turn of Two Centuries," remarks at conference on "The Changing Face of America: Inside the Latino Vote and Immigration Reform," University of California-Berkeley Journalism School, July 4, 2013.

57. Acuña, *Occupied America*, 173.

58. Francisco E. Balderrama and Raymond Rodriguez, *Decade of Betrayal: Mexican Repatriation in the 1930s*, rev. ed. (University of New Mexico Press, 2006), 70.

59. Acuña, *Occupied America*, 174.

60. Balderrama and Rodriguez, *Decade of Betrayal*, 210–11.

61. Balderrama and Rodriguez, *Decade of Betrayal*, 77.

62. *La Opinion*, July 13, 2004.

63. Balderrama and Rodriguez, *Decade of Betrayal*, 150.

64. "Entrada y Salida de Nacionales y Extranjeras Registradas, DAPP," *Revista de Estadistica* (Enero-Diciembre 1940).

65. Balderrama and Rodriguez, *Decade of Betrayal*, 151.

66. Balderrama and Rodriguez, *Decade of Betrayal*, 266.

67. Acuña, *Occupied America*, 173. A few other scholars' estimates are significantly lower. Abraham Hoffman, for example, estimated the total number of repatriates as "in excess of 415,000." Mexican scholar Fernando Saul Alanis Enciso's estimates, based on Mexican government records, is 425,000. See Hoffman, *Unwanted Mexican Americans in the Great Depression*, and Fernando Saul Alanis Enciso, " 'Cuantos Fueron': La Repatracion de Mexicanos en los Estados Unidos durante la Gran Depresion: Una Interpretacion Cuantativa, 1930–34," *Aztlan: A Journal of Chicano Studies* 32, no. 2 (Fall 2007).

68. Kevin R. Johnson, "The Forgotten Repatriation of Persons of Mexican Ancestry and Lessons for the War on Terror," *Pace Law Review* 26, no. 1 (2005).

69. Kasie Hunt, "Some Stories Hard to Get in History Books," *USA Today*, April 4, 2006.

70. Samora, *Los Mojados*, 50–51.

71. US Department of Justice, *Annual Report of the Immigration and Naturalization Service* (1947), 24.

72. The literature of the period and the few historical accounts that mention this incident include only passing references to the possibility that US citizens or legal residents may have been removed in the 1947 campaign.

73. American GI Forum of Texas and Texas Federation of Labor, *What Price Wetbacks?* (Allied Printing, 1954).

74. Juan Ramon Garcia, *Operation Wetback: The Mass Deportation of Mexican Undocumented Workers in 1954* (Greenwood Press, 1980), 157–59.

75. Ngai, *Impossible Subjects*, 227.

76. "Mexican Repatriation," Wikipedia, April 8, 2014, see http://en.wikipedia.org /wiki/Mexican_Repatriation, accessed May 3, 2014. See also Balderrama and Rodriguez, *Decade of Betrayal*.

77. See, for example, Hoffman, *Unwanted Mexicans in the Great Depression*.

78. Ngai, *Impossible Subjects*, 149.

79. Lyle Saunders and Olen Leonard, *The Wetback in the Lower Rio Grande Valley of Texas* (University of Texas Press, 1951).

80. Ngai, *Impossible Subjects*, 155.

81. Ngai, *Impossible Subjects*, 155–56.

82. Juan Gonzalez, *Harvest of Empire: A History of Latinos in America*, 3rd ed. (Penguin Books, 2011), 223.

83. Acuña, *Occupied America*, 226.

84. Leo Grebler, *Mexican Immigration to the United States: The Record and Its Implications*, University of California-Los Angeles, Mexican American Study Project, Advance Report no. 2 (1965): 34.

85. See, for example, Patricia Morgan, *Shame of a Nation: A Documented Story of Police-State Terror Against Mexican-Americans in the USA* (Los Angeles Committee for the Protection of the Foreign Born, 1954), 49–50.

86. "State Officials Thanked for Cooperation in Handling Local Immigration Problems," *Loomis News*, July 16, 1954, cited in Garcia, *Operation Wetback*, 194.

87. Natalia Molina, *How Race Is Made in America* (University of California Press, 2014), 132.

88. Garcia, *Operation Wetback*, 194.

89. Grebler, *Mexican Immigration to the United States*, 194, 215.

90. Molina, *How Race Is Made in America*, 135–37.

91. Nina Alvarez et. al., producers, *Latino Americans: The 500-Year Legacy that Shaped a Nation*, WETA documentary, 2013, the reference to Garcia's views on immigration at about 47:40 of disc 1 of the DVD version; for a detailed history of the organization, see Henry A. J. Ramos, *The American G.I. Forum: The Pursuit of the American Dream* (Arte Publico Press, 1998); for a powerful documentary film of the incident that birthed the group, aired on the Public Broadcasting Service, see John J. Valadez, *The Longoria Affair* (WGBH/Boston & Independent Television Service, 2010).

92. Acuña, *Occupied America*, 217; Ngai, *Impossible Subjects*,140–141.

93. Ngai, *Impossible Subjects*, 139.

94. Garcia, *Operation Wetback*, 237.

95. Ngai, *Impossible Subjects*, 139; Acuña, *Occupied America*, 218–19; see also Samora, *Los Mojados*.

96. Yolanda Vazquez, "Constructing Crimmigration: Latino Subordination in a 'Post-Racial' World," *Faculty Articles and Other Publications*, paper 254 (2015), 620, http://scholarship.law.uc.edu/fac_pubs/254, accessed June 10, 2015.

97. Alfredo Corchado, *Midnight in Mexico: A Reporter's Journey Through a Country's Descent into Darkness* (Penguin Press, 2013), 117.

98. Daniel Rothenberg, *With These Hands: The Hidden World of Migrant Farmworkers Today* (Harcourt Brace, 1998), 37.

99. On the bracero program generally, see Ernesto Galarza, *Merchants of Labor: The Mexican Bracero Story* (McNally and Loftin, 1964). See also, Samora, *Los Mojados*; Acuña, *Occupied America*; Ngai, *Impossible Subjects*; and Garcia, *Operation Wetback*.

100. Aviva Chomsky, *Undocumented: How Immigration Became Illegal* (Beacon Press, 2014), 56.

101. Letter from Bernando Blanco to Ed McDonald, cited in Ngai, *Impossible Subjects*, 143.

102. Susan Ferriss and Ricardo Sandoval, *The Fight in the Fields: César Chávez and the Farmworkers Movement* (Harcourt Brace & Company, 1997), 54.

103. Ngai, *Impossible Subjects*, 143.

104. Ferriss and Sandoval, *The Fight in the Fields*, 55.

105. David M. Reimers, *Still the Golden Door: The Third World Comes to America* (Columbia University Press, 1992), 57; Garcia, *Operation Wetback*, 112.

106. Acuna, *Occupied America*, 219.

107. Garcia, *Operation Wetback*, 84–85; Acuna, *Occupied America*, 219.

108. President's Commission on Migratory Labor, "Migratory Labor in American Agriculture," US Government Printing Office (1951), 152.

109. Samora, *Los Mojados*, 47–48; see also, Ngai, *Impossible Subjects*, 151.

110. Ngai, *Impossible Subjects*, 155.

111. Mirande, *Gringo Justice*, 113.

112. President's Commission on Migratory Labor, "Migratory Labor in American Agriculture," 38.

113. Samora, *Los Mojados*, 54–55.

114. Dale Maharidge, *The Coming White Minority: California, Multiculturalism, and America's Future* (Vintage Books, 1999), 75.

115. Ngai, *Impossible Subjects*, 146–52.

116. Samora and his colleagues made a particularly compelling case for this conclusion by comparing INS apprehensions and other indicators of unauthorized migration with authorized entries under the bracero program, demonstrating a positive correlation between them, instead of the negative relationship one would have expected had the program served as a substitute for otherwise illegal entries.

117. Mirande, *Gringo Justice*, 105–6.

118. Aristide R. Zolberg, *A Nation by Design: Immigration Policy in the Fashioning of America* (Harvard University Press & Russell Sage Foundation, 2008), 335.

119. Vazquez, "Constructing Crimmigration: Latino Subordination in a 'Post-Racial' World," 619. Vazquez's description drawn in part from Ngai, *Impossible Subjects*, 64–68.

120. Aviva Chomsky, *Undocumented: How Immigration Became Illegal* (Beacon Press, 2014), 57.

121. "The Foundation of LULAC," http://lulac.org/about/history/past_presidents/, accessed August 7, 2013.

122. Mario Barrera, *Beyond Aztlan* (Praeger Publishers, 1988), as cited in Benjamin Márquez, *LULAC: The Evolution of a Mexican American Political Organization* (University of Texas Press, 1993), 16.

123. "The Foundation of LULAC," http://lulac.org/about/history/past presidents, accessed August 7, 2013.

124. Márquez, *LULAC*, 17.

125. Ian Haney-Lopez, "Race and Erasure: The Salience of Race to Latinos/as," cited in Cybelle Fox and Thomas A. Guglielmo, "Defining America's Racial Boundaries: Blacks, Mexicans, and European Immigrants," *American Journal of Sociology* 118, no. 2 (September 2012): 367.

126. Cybelle Fox and Thomas A. Guglielmo, "Defining America's Racial Boundaries: Blacks, Mexicans, and European Immigrants," *American Journal of Sociology* 118, no. 2 (September 2012): 369.

127. Molina, *How Race Is Made in America*, 61–66.

128. For an overview, see Márquez, *LULAC*, and Craig A. Kaplowitz, *LULAC: Mexican Americans and National Policy* (Texas A&M University Press, 2005), 46–61; for achievements in education, see for example, Carolyn Hernandez, "LULAC: The History of a Grassroots Organization and Its Influence on Educational Policies, 1929–83" (PhD dissertation, Loyola University, 1995); Deirdre Martínez, *Who Speaks for Hispanics? Hispanic Interest Groups in Washington* (SUNY Press, 2009), and Guadalupe San Miguel, *Let All of Them Take Heed* (Texas A&M University Press, 2000).

129. See, for example, SER-National website: http://www.ser-national.org.

130. Annette Oliveira, "MALDEF: Diez Anos," Mexican American Legal Defense and Educational Fund, 1978, as cited in Márquez, *LULAC*, 74.

131. For more nuanced perspective on LULAC's views on immigration during this period, see Kaplowitz, *LULAC*, 46–61.

132. Márquez, *LULAC*, 29.

133. Juan Gomez-Quinones, *Roots of Chicano Politics, 1600–1940* (University of New Mexico Press, 1994), 366.

134. Roberto Villarreal, Norma G. Hernandez, and Howard Neighbor, *Latino Empowerment: Progress, Problems, and Prospects* (Greenwood Press, 1988), 19.

135. Márquez, *LULAC*.

136. See, for example, Armando Navarro, *Mexicano Political Experience in Occupied Aztlan* (AltaMira Press, 2005).

137. Arnoldo De León, "CHICANO," *Handbook of Texas Online*, Texas State Historical Association, modified June 3, 2013, http://www.tsaonline.org/handbook/online/articles/pfc02, accessed October 10, 2013.

138. Kaplowitz, *LULAC*, 130. Kaplowitz notes that LULAC and the activists made "similar demands on civic culture," meaning equality in voting, employment, government appointments, and other civil rights.

139. For more information on Puerto Rican activism of the period, see: Rodriguez, *Puerto Ricans: Born in the USA*; Clara E. Rodriguez and Virginia Sanchez Korrol, eds., *Historical Perspectives on Puerto Rican Survival in the U.S.* (Marcus Weiner Press, 1996); Sonia Song-Ha Lee, *Building a Latino Civil Rights Movement: Puerto Ricans, African Americans, and the Pursuit of Racial Justice in New York City* (University of North Carolina Press, 2014); and Darran Wanzer-Serrano, *The New York Young Lords and the Struggle for Liberation* (Temple University Press, 2015).

140. F. Arturo Rosales, *Chicano! The History of the Mexican American Civil Rights Movement* (Arte Publico Press, 1997), 132. For a slightly different account, see: Ferriss and Sandoval, *The Fight in the Fields*, 62.

141. Ignacio M. García, *Chicanismo, the Forging of a Militant Ethos among Mexican Americans* (University of Arizona Press, 1997), 30.

142. F. Arturo Rosales, *Testimonio, A Documentary History of the Mexican American Struggle for Civil Rights* (Arte Publico Press, 2000), 303.

143. Ferris and Sandoval, *The Fight in the Fields*, 243–44.

144. Author interview with Eliseo Medina, May 13, 2014.

145. Navarro, *Mexicano Political Experience in Occupied Aztlan*, 501–2.

146. García, *Chicanismo*, 34–35.

147. *El Plan Spiritual de Aztlan* as reproduced in Rosales, *Testimonio*, 362–63.

148. García, *Chicanismo*, 32–33.

149. For a detailed account of this episode and related events, see Richard Gardner, *Grito! Reies Tijerina and the New Mexico Land Grant War of 1967* (Bobbs-Merrill Company, 1970).

150. Rosales, *Testimonio*, 275.

151. García, *Chicanismo*, 35.

152. Todd S. Purdum, *An Idea Whose Time Has Come: Two Presidents, Two Parties, and the Battle for the Civil Rights Act of 1964* (Picador, 2014), 108–9.

153. David Halberstam, *The Best and the Brightest*, 4th ed. (Ballantine Books, 1992), 603–10.

154. Kevin B. Blackistone, "Asking Athletes About Politics Can Be a Good Question," *Washington Post*, December 20, 2015. See also, Manning Marable, *Malcolm X: A Life of Reinvention* (Penguin, 2011).

155. Joseph Epstein, "The First Talking Head," *Wall Street Journal*, August 15–16, 2015, C5.

156. Halberstam, *The Best and the Brightest*, 428.

157. Armando Navarro, *Mexican American Youth Organization: Avant Garde of the Chicano Movement in Texas* (University of Texas Press, 1995), cited in Rosales, *Chicano!*, 216

158. José Ángel Gutiérrez , "Formation of the Mexican American Youth Movement (MAYO)," interview with Jesus Treviño, National Latino Communications Center, January 27, 1992, reproduced in Rosales, *Testimonio*, 383.

159. Gutiérrez, "Formation of the Mexican American Youth Movement (MAYO)," 383.

160. Rosales, *Chicano!*, 218.

161. García, *Chicanismo*.

162. Author interview with Raul Yzaguirre, July 29, 2012; see also Rosales, *Chicano!*, 222.

163. Jaime Contreras, "Jose Angel Gutierrez, Still Angry After All These Years," utwatch.org, http://www.utwatch.org/archives/tejas/january1992_gutierrez.html, accessed August 30, 2013.

164. "Chicanismo, Youth, and La Raza Unida Political Party," in Rosales, *Testimonio*, p. 333.

165. Siobahn O. Nicolau and Henry Santiestévan, "Looking Back: A Grantee-Grantor View of the Early Years of the Council of La Raza," in Herman E. Gallegos and Michael O'Neill, *Hispanics and the Nonprofit Sector* (The Foundation Center, 1991), 54–61.

166. José Ángel Gutiérrez, "The Origins of the 'Eliminate the Gringo' Quote," reprinted in *Texas Civil Rights Review*, posted July 21, 2010, http://texascivilrightsreview .org/wp/480/j-a-gutierrez-on-the-origin-of-eliminate-the-gringo/, accessed September 10, 2013.

167. "MAYO Leader Warns of Violence, Rioting," *San Antonio Evening News*, April 10, 1969. See also Gutiérrez, "The Origins of the 'Eliminate the Gringo' Quote."

168. Search engine queries about Gutiérrez produce references to the "kill the gringo" statement from groups and individuals who express deep fears about illegal immigration as a precursor to a Latino take-over of the American Southwest. Nearly four decades after the original article appeared, when Gutiérrez was on the faculty of the University of Texas, Arlington, the college's media relations department issued a statement "in reference to comments attributed to" Gutiérrez, noting his first amendment right to express his views "outside the classroom." See statement: "Concerning Jose Angel Gutierrez," News Center, December 4, 2007, http://www.uta.edu/news/releases/2007/12/cocerning -jose-angel-gutierrez.php, accessed September 10, 2013.

169. "Henry B. González," Hispanic Americans in Congress 1822–1995, Library of Congress, http://www.loc.gov/rr/hispanic/congress/gonzalez.html, accessed September 8, 2013.

170. "Paul Houston," "Rep. González: He Packs a Punch When It Gets Tense," *Los Angeles Times*, July 15, 1990. See also: "Henry B. González: 1916–2000," http:// biography.jrank.org/pages/3372/Gonz-lez-Henry-B-1916-2000-Congressman--Henry-B .html, accessed September 8, 2013.

171. Jan Jarboe Russell, "Henry B. González," *Texas Monthly*, January 2001.

172. A very useful, somewhat more detailed, and highly personalized accounting of the events described herein can be found in Nicolau and Santiestévan, "Looking Back," 55–59.

173. Houston, "Rep. González: He Packs a Punch When It Gets Tense."

174. Laurence Stern and Richard Harwood, "Ford Foundation: Its Works Spark a Backlash," *Washington Post*, November 2, 1969.

175. Joint Committee on Internal Revenue Taxation and Committee on Finance, *Summary of H.R. 13270, The Tax Reform Act of 1969*, staff report, August 18, 1969, 17; see also: Emily Gantz McKay, *The National Council of La Raza: The First 25 Years*

(National Council of La Raza, July 1993), 12. See also, Nicolau and Santiestévan, "Looking Back."

176. See generally, McKay, *The National Council of La Raza*, and Nicolau and Santiestévan, "Looking Back."

177. Armando Navarro, *La Raza Unida Party: A Chicano Challenge to the U.S. Two Party Dictatorship* (Temple University Press, 2000), 50; Rosales, *Chicano!*, 222; Rosales, *Testimonio*, 336.

178. Daniel Pederson, "All These Guys Owe Willie," *Newsweek*, March 16, 1987, pp. 30–31.

179. Zaragosa Vargas, *Crucible of Struggle, A History of Mexican Americans from Colonia Times to the Present Era* (Oxford University Press, 2011), 349.

180. Rosales, *Chicano!*, 263.

181. As quoted in Armado Navarro, *La Raza Unida Party*, 251.

182. Rosales, *Chicano!*, 263.

183. Navarro, *La Raza Unida Party*, 251–252.

184. Compare Rosales's description that "the conference adjourned without reaching an accord" in, *Chicano!*, p. 263, with del Castillo and de Leon's contrary assertion in Richard Griswold del Castillo and Arnoldo de Leon, *North to Aztlan: A History of Mexican Americans in the United States* (Twayne Publishers, 1995), 135, and with Navarro's conclusion that "despite the disruptions, a ten-point plan . . . was endorsed," in Navarro, *La Raza Unida Party*, 252.

185. Navarro, *La Raza Unida Party*, 251–52.

186. See for example, Galarza, *Merchants of Labor* and *Spiders in the House: Workers in the Field* (University of Notre Dame Press, 1970); and Samora, *Los Mojados* and *La Raza: Forgotten Americans* (University of Notre Dame Press, 1971). In these classic works, both Galarza and Samora, two of the three cofounders of the Southwest Council of La Raza, following the accepted "neoclassical" economics model of the period, generally assume that increased numbers of foreign workers, through either guestworker programs or immigration, would be harmful to domestic Mexican American workers.

187. Navarro, *La Raza Unida Party*, 50–77.

188. Paul Andow, "Civil Rights Quid Pro Quo," unpublished essay, August 25, 1963, as quoted in Marquez, *LULAC*, 64.

189. Kaplowitz, *LULAC*, 91–100.

190. Brian D. Behnken, *Fighting Their Own Battles: Mexican Americans, African Americans, and the Struggle for Civil Rights in Texas* (University of North Carolina Press, 2011), 109.

191. Benjamin Marquez, "The League of United Latin American Citizens and the Politics of Ethnicity," in Roberto Villarreal, Norma G. Hernandez, and Howard Neighbor, eds., *Latino Empowerment: Progress, Problems, and Prospects* (Greenwood Press, 1988), 22–24.

192. García, *Chicanismo*, 22; for a deeper look at the ideological orientations of LULAC and other groups, see Mario T. García, *Mexican Americans: Leadership, Ideology and Identity, 1930–1960* (Yale University Press, 1989).

193. The issue concerns many within the organization even today; see for example, interviews of LULAC board and senior staff members cited in Deirdre Martínez, *Who Speaks for Hispanics? Hispanic Interest Groups in Washington* (State University of New York, 2009), 35–61.

194. Membership data from Marquez, *LULAC*, 87–88.

195. Marquez, *LULAC*, 89.

196. Luis Fraga, "Organizational Maintenance and Organizational Effectiveness: The League of United Latin American Citizens," paper presented at the Annual Meeting of the American Political Science Association, August 1980, pp. 82–83.

197. Marquez, *LULAC*, 88.

198. Author interview with Ruben Bonilla, September 27, 2012.

199. "LULAC Veers to the Left," Rosales, *Testimonio*, 404.

200. Bertram Levine, *Resolving Racial Conflict: The Community Relations Service and Civil Rights, 1964–1989* (University of Missouri Press, 2005), 140–43.

201. Author interview with Ruben Bonilla, September 27, 2012.

202. "Oral History Interview with Ruben Bonilla, 1996," September 26, 1996, Center for Mexican American Studies, University of Texas at Austin, http://library.uta.edu/tejanovoices/vml/CMAS_008.xml, accessed August 8, 2013.

203. Author interview with Ruben Bonilla, September 27, 2012.

204. Author interview with Arnoldo Torres, January 1, 2013.

205. Author interview with Ruben Bonilla, September 27, 2012.

206. Author interview with Arnoldo Torres, December 14, 2014.

207. Author interview with Arnoldo Torres, January 1, 2013.

208. Author interview with Ruben Bonilla, September 27, 2013.

209. Navarro, *Mexicano Political Experience in Occupied Aztlan*, 520.

210. Helen Rowan, "The Mexican American," paper prepared for the US Commission on Civil Rights, 1968, reprinted as Helen Rowan, *The Mexican American: A Paper Prepared for the U.S. Commission on Civil Rights* (Palala Press, 2015).

211. McKay, *The National Council of La Raza*, 6–7.

212. McKay, *The National Council of La Raza*, 7.

213. Nicolau and Santiestévan, "Looking Back," 52–53.

214. McKay, *The National Council of La Raza*, 6–7.

215. McKay, *The National Council of La Raza*, 8–9.

216. David S. Broder, *Changing of the Guard: Power and Leadership in America* (Penguin Books, 1980), 285.

217. Cited in Geoffrey Kabaservice, *The Guardians: Kingman Brewster, His Circle, and the Rise of the Liberal Establishment* (Henry Holt & Company, 2004), 344.

218. Herman Gallegos and Henry Santiestévan, "A Call to La Raza for a Personal Pledge to Non Violence," in *Board of Directors Orientation Binder*, National Council of La Raza, Fall 2002, copy on file with author.

219. Lawrence Stern and Richard Harwood, "Ford Foundation: Its Works Spark Backlash," *Washington Post*, November 2, 1969.

220. See Henry Santiestévan, "A Perspective on Mexican American Organizations," in Gus Tyler, ed., *Mexican-Americans Tomorrow* (University of New Mexico Press, 1975), 197–201; for a broader look at the field, see Roland V. Anglin and Susanna C. Montezelomo, "Supporting the Community Development Movement: The Achievements and Challenges of Intermediary Organizations," and related essays in Roland V. Anglin, ed., *Building the Organizations that Build Communities* (US Department of Housing and Urban Development, 2004).

221. McKay, *The National Council of La Raza*, 12.

222. *Southwest Council of La Raza*, annual report, undated but circa. 1973, 5; copy on file with the author.

223. *Southwest Council of La Raza*, report, undated but circa. 1973, 7; copy on file with the author.

224. Nicolau and Santiestévan, "Looking Back," 62.

225. McKay, *The National Council of La Raza*, 14.

226. For a detailed description of the controversy, see: Nicolau and Santiestévan, "Looking Back," 64–65.

227. McKay, *The National Council of La Raza*, 14.

228. Interview with Raul Yzaguírre by Emily Gantz McKay, January 26, 2005, transcript on file with the author. See also Nicolau and Santiestévan, "Looking Back," 63–65.

229. Resume of Raul Yzaguírre, attached to his application for the position of NCLR Executive Director, April 30, 1974, copy on file with the author.

230. McKay, *The National Council of La Raza*, 14–15; see also Resume of Raul Yzaguírre, attached to his application for the position of NCLR Executive Director.

231. Stern and Harwood, "Ford Foundation: Its Works Spark Backlash."

232. Author interview with Raul Yzaguírre, April 15, 2013.

233. Leslie R. Crutchfield and Heather McLeod Grant, *Forces for Good: The Six Practices of High-Impact Nonprofits* (Jossey-Bass, 2008), 165.

234. Author interview with Raul Yzaguírre, July 9, 2012.

235. "NCLR Unabridged Chronology," National Council of La Raza, rev. August 26, 2008, copy on file with author. See also Nicolau and Santiestévan, "Looking Back," 63–65.

236. Interview with Raul Yzaguírre by Emily Gantz McKay, January 26, 2005, transcript on file with the author; see also: Discussion with Michael Cortés, PhD, by Emily Gantz McKay, November 18, 2005; detailed notes on file with the author.

237. Vilma S. Martínez, "Hispanic Advocacy Organizations," in Gallegos and O'Neill, eds., *Hispanics and the Nonprofit Sector* (The Foundation Center, 1991), 80.

238. Author interview with Raul Yzaguírre, April 15, 2013.

239. Discussion with Michael Cortés, PhD, by Emily Gantz McKay, November 18, 2005; detailed notes on file with the author.

240. McKay, *The National Council of La Raza*, 16.

241. For a detailed and thorough examination of the sociological and policy significance of various ethnic and racial data collection frameworks, see Clara E. Rodriguez, *Changing Race: Latinos, the Census, and the History of Ethnicity in the United States* (New York University Press, 2000).

242. G. Cristina Mora, "Cross-Field Effects and Ethnic Classification: The Institutionalization of Hispanic Panethnicity, 1965 to 1990," *American Sociological Review* 19, no. 2 (February 2014): 183.

243. US Commission on Civil Rights, *Counting the Forgotten: The 1970 Census of Persons of Spanish-Speaking Background in the United States* (1974).

244. Broder, *Changing of the Guard*, 284.

245. Author interview with Raul Yzaguírre, December 12, 2012.

246. McKay, *The National Council of La Raza*, 20; see also broader discussion, 16–21.

247. Author interview with Angelo Falcon, December 17, 2012.

248. Author interview with Tommy Espinoza, July 8, 2012. Espinoza headed Chicanos Por La Causa, one of the NCLR-affiliated community development corporations. See: Nicolau and Santiestévan, "Looking Back," 64.

249. McKay, *The National Council of La Raza*, 20; see also broader discussion, 16–21.

250. Mora, "Cross-Field Effects and Ethnic Classification," 188. See also: G. Cristina Mora, *Making Hispanics: How Activists, Bureaucrats, and Media Constructed a New American* (University of Chicago Press, 2014).

251. Mora, *Making Hispanics*, 79; see generally, 50–82.

252. Author interview with Raul Yzaguírre, July 9, 2012.

253. Cortés, *Policy Analysts and Interest Groups*, 340.

254. Rodolfo de la Garza and Adela Flores, "The Impact of Mexican Immigrants on the Political Behavior of Chicanos," in Harley L. Browning and Rodolfo de la Garza, eds., *Mexican Immigrants and Mexican Americans: An Evolving Relation* (University of Texas, Center for Mexican American Studies, 1986); see also Rodolfo de la Garza, "Chicano Political Elite Perceptions of the Undocumented Worker: An Empirical Analysis," working paper no. 31, University of California-San Diego, 1981; and Lawrence Miller, Jerry L. Polinard, and Robert Wrinkle, "Immigration and the Undocumented: The Mexican American Perspective," paper presented at the Southwestern Political Science Association, April 1983.

255. Author interview with Michael Cortés, August 16, 2012. McKay agreed; she later observed that despite resource constraints, the immigration issue "was always on Raul's radar screen." Author interview with Emily Gantz McKay, August 21, 2012.

256. See: Michael Cortés, "Testimony Opposing Sanctions Against Employers of Undocumented Immigrants," submitted to the Committee on Employment and Economic Development, Government of the District of Columbia, March 1, 1978.

257. "Forging a Black-Hispanic Alliance," *Washington Post*, editorial, November 18, 1978.

258. Cortés, *Policy Analysts and Interest Groups*, 443.

259. Broder, *Changing of the Guard*, 331.

260. Cortés, *Policy Analysts and Interest Groups*, 442–43.

261. McKay, *The National Council of La Raza*, 21.

262. Broder, *Changing of the Guard*, 279–301.

263. Cortés, *Policy Analysts and Interest Groups*, 318.

264. McKay, *The National Council of La Raza*, 22.

265. Discussion with Michael Cortés, PhD, by Emily Gantz McKay, November 18, 2005; detailed notes on file with the author.

CHAPTER 2

1. There are many useful summaries of the history of US immigration laws. A very brief table can be found in Daniel Tichenor, *Dividing Lines: The Politics of Immigration Control in America* (Princeton University Press, 2002), 3–5 (Table 1.1). A lengthier summary through 1986, together with citations to statues and other source materials, is included as an Appendix in Cortés, *Policy Analysts and Interest Groups*, 598–612. Up-to-date and detailed listings can be found in Stanley Mailman, Steven Yale-Loehr, and Ronald Y. Wada, *Immigration Law and Procedure* (LexisNexis E-Books), available only via subscription, described at: http://www.lexisnexis.com/store/catalog/booktemplate /productdetail.jsp;jsessionid=3C1C9C52BA9D5B1B5189324215953897.psc1705_lnstore _001?pageName=relatedProducts&catId=&prodId=10420, accessed June 3, 2015.

2. Zolberg, *A Nation by Design*, 231.

3. James Fallows, "Immigration, How It's Affecting Us," *The Atlantic Monthly*, November 1, 1983.

4. Tichenor, *Dividing Lines*, 194.

5. David M. Reimers, "An Unintended Reform: The 1965 Act and Third World Immigration to the United States," *Journal of American Ethnic History* 3, no. 1 (Fall 1983): 9–28.

6. John F. Kennedy, *A Nation of Immigrants*, rev. ed. (Harper Perennial, 2008), 85.

7. A photograph of the signing ceremony can be seen at Jennifer Luden, "1965 Immigration Law Changed Face of America," National Public Radio, May 9, 2006, http://www.npr.org/templates/story/story.php?storyId=5391395, accessed June 11, 2015.

8. Zolberg, *A Nation by Design*, 332–33.

9. Kennedy, *A Nation of Immigrants*, 76.

10. Andrew Kohut, "50 Years Later, Americans Give Thumbs-up to Immigration Law That Changed the Nation," Pew Research Center, February 4, 2015, http://www.pewresearch.org/fact-tank/2015/02/04/50-years-later-americans-give-thumbs-up-to-immigration-law-that-changed-the-nation/, accessed June 11, 2015.

11. Daniel Rothenberg, *With These Hands: The Hidden World of Migrant Farmworkers Today* (Harcourt Brace, 1998), 139.

12. Douglas S. Massey, Jorge Durand, and Karen A. Pren, "Why Border Enforcement Backfired," *American Journal of Sociology* 125, no. 5 (March 2016): 1573.

13. See Louis Harrell and Dale Fischer, "The 1982 Mexican Peso Devaluation and Border Area Employment," *Monthly Labor Review*, October 1985; see also Marline Simons, "Mexican Peso Devalued for 2nd Time in 6 Months," *New York Times*, August 7, 1982.

14. Zolberg, *A Nation by Design*, 332–33.

15. Mirande, *Gringo Justice*, 127–28.

16. Joel Millman, *The Other Americans: How Immigrants Renew Our Country, Our Economy, and Our Values* (Viking, 1997), 62.

17. "Phyllis Schlafly: Today's Immigrants Are 'Not the Same Sort' as Europeans Who Contributed So Much," May 31, 2015, http://kstreet607.com/2015/05/31/phyllis-schlafly-today's-immigrants-are-not-the-same-sort-as-europeans-who-contributed-so-much/, accessed December 27, 2015.

18. Aviva Chomsky, *Undocumented: How Immigration Became Illegal* (Beacon Press, 2014), 44–45.

19. Mae M. Ngai, "How Grandma Got Legal," *Los Angeles Times*, May 16, 2006.

20. Mae M. Ngai, "Second Class Noncitizens," *New York Times*, January 30, 2014.

21. "Our People, Our Traditions," *Finding Your Roots*, Public Broadcasting Service, episode 207, first aired November 4, 2014.

22. Elahe Izadi, "Anne Frank and Her Family Were Also Denied Entry as Refugees to the U.S.," *Washington Post*, November 24, 2015, https://www.washingtonpost.com/news/worldviews/wp/2015/11/24/anne-frank-and-her-family-were-also-denied-entry-as-refugees-to-the-u-s/, accessed December 9, 2015.

23. "Biographical Note," The Peter Rodino Law Library, Seton Hall Law School, http://law.shu.edu/library/rodino/findingaid/historical-biographical-note.cfm, accessed September 30, 2013.

24. Bob Woodward and Carl Bernstein, *The Final Days* (Avon Books, 1976), 111.

25. Michael Barone and Grant Ujifusa, *The Almanac of American Politics, 1984* (National Journal, 1983), 751.

26. Rosanna Perotti, *Resolving Policy Conflict: Congress and Immigration Reform* (PhD dissertation, University of Pennsylvania, 1989), 83, footnote 3.

27. Michael C. LeMay, *Anatomy of a Public Policy* (Praeger Publishers, 1994), 29.

28. *Congressional Record*, May 3, 1973 at 14185 (Remarks of Rep. Rodino).

29. Author interview with Muzaffar Chishti, May 21, 2013; see also Perotti, *Resolving Policy Conflict*, 112.

30. Ben Zimmer, "The Double Life of 'Sanction,'" *Wall Street Journal*, November 29, 2010.

31. See: Definition of "contranym" at *Dictionary.com*, http://dictionary.reference.com/browse/contranym, accessed May 29, 2015.

32. Zolberg, *A Nation by Design*, 243.

33. *Congressional Record*, September 12, 1972, (Remarks of Rep. Yates and Rep. Badillo at 30167).

34. Lawrence Fuchs, "The Corpse That Would Not Die: The Immigration Reform and Control Act of 1986," in: *Revue Europennne de Migrations Internationals* 6, no. 1 (1990): 113.

35. Cited in Perotti, *Resolving Policy Conflict*, 85.

36. Edward M. Kennedy, *True Compass: A Memoir* (Twelve Books, 2009), 191–92.

37. LeMay, *Anatomy of a Public Policy*, 29–30.

38. *Congressional Record*, May 3, 1973, at 14190, citing a press release, "Diocesan Spokesmen Criticize House Bill on Illegal Aliens," Roman Catholic Diocese of Brooklyn, March 20, 1973 (remarks of Rep. Biaggi).

39. *Congressional Record*, May 3, 1973, 14207–8 (Remarks of Rep. White and Rep. Eilberg).

40. LeMay, *Anatomy of a Public Policy*, 29–30. See also Harris N. Miller, "The Right Thing to Do: A History of Simpson-Mazzoli," in Nathan Glazer, ed., *Clamor at the Gates* (Institute for Contemporary Studies Press, 1985).

41. Woodward and Bernstein, *The Final Days*, 512.

42. Barone and Ujifusa, *The Almanac of American Politics, 1984*, 750.

43. Michael T. Kaufman, "Peter Rodino Dies at 96, Led House Inquiry on Nixon," *New York Times*, May 8, 2005.

44. Robert V. Remini, *The House: The History of the House of Representatives* (Smithsonian Books and Collins, 2006), 438–39.

45. Woodward and Bernstein, *The Final Days*, 111, 112, 167.

46. Kaufman, "Peter Rodino Dies at 96."

47. Woodward and Bernstein, *The Final Days*, 248–50, 278–80.

48. "Garner J. Cline, 63," *Morning Call*, November 19, 1990, obituary, http://articles/mcall/1990-11-19/news/2770196_1_cline-garner-easton, accessed September 30, 2013.

49. Robert Pear, "Congress: On Immigration, a Power Behind the Scenes," *New York Times*, April 7, 1984.

50. Remini, *The House*, 441.

51. Richard Lyons and William Chapman, "Judiciary Committee Approves Article to Impeach President Nixon, 27-11," *Washington Post*, July 28, 1974.

52. Woodward and Bernstein, *The Final Days*, 321.

53. LeMay, *Anatomy of a Public Policy*, 30.

54. Perotti, *Resolving Policy Conflict*, 90.

55. Tichenor, *Dividing Lines*, 229–30.

56. Richard Lyons, "Seldom Active Senate Unit Drew $2 million in Decade," *New York Times*, September 29, 1975, cited in Perotti, *Resolving Policy Conflict*, 90.

57. LeMay, *Anatomy of a Public Policy*, 30.

58. The description of the "iron triangle" comes from Tichenor, *Dividing Lines*, 227–28.

59. Susan F. Martin, *A Nation of Immigrants* (Cambridge University Press, 2011), 191–92.

60. See Zolberg, *A Nation by Design*, 587, endnote 33, attributed to Reimers, *Ibid*.

61. Ellis Cose, *A Nation of Strangers*, William Morrow and Company, 1992, 114.

62. Zolberg, *A Nation by Design*, 343; see also Martin, *A Nation of Immigrants*, 192–93.

63. David M. Reimers, *Still the Golden Door: The Third World Comes to America* (Columbia University Press, 1992), 86.

64. Cose, *A Nation of Strangers*, 114–15.

65. See Zolberg, *A Nation by Design*, 344.

66. Reimers, *Still the Golden Door*, over several chapters.

67. Author interview with Arnoldo Torres, January 11, 2013.

68. Cose, *A Nation of Strangers*, 115.

69. Tichenor, *Dividing Lines*, 234.

70. Tichenor, *Dividing Lines*, 235.

71. Tom Curtis, "Will Success Spoil Leonel Castillo?" *Texas Monthly*, August 1976.

72. Broder, *Changing of the Guard: Power and Leadership in America*, 295.

73. Author interview with Raul Yzaguírre, July 9, 2012.

74. Tichenor, *Dividing Lines*, 235.

75. Fuchs, "The Corpse That Would Not Die," 114.

76. See Jimmy Carter, *White House Diary* (Farrar, Strauss and Giroux, 2010). The diary does contain references to the Cuban refugee crisis and one to the Haitian boatlift.

77. LeMay, *Anatomy of a Public Policy*, 34.

78. Anthony DePalma, "Rev. Theodore Hesburgh, 97, Dies; Lifted Notre Dame and Advised Presidents," *New York Times*, obituary, March 17, 2015.

79. Steven Kelman, *Making Public Policy: A Hopeful View of American Government* (Basic Books, 1987), 3–5. See also, "Public Trust in Government," Pew Research Center, November 3, 2015, http://www.people-press.org/2014/11/13/public-trust-in-government/, accessed November 24, 2015.

80. Martin, *A Nation of Immigrants*, 206.

81. Bryan Marquaerd, "Lawrence Fuchs: Professor Crafted Immigration Law Changes," *Boston Globe*, obituary, April 7, 2013.

82. See, for example, Testimony of Lawrence Fuchs, *Senate Hearings: Subcommittee on Immigration, Committee on the Judiciary*, October 22, 1996, where Fuchs argues, in pertinent part: "There has been a tendency in American public discourse to speak of group rights as if they were civil rights. Civil rights apply to individuals. We have no place in our constitutional system for group rights."

83. Lawrence H. Fuchs, "Immigration Reform in 1911 and 1981: The Role of Select Commissions," *Journal of American Ethnic History* 3, no. 1 (Fall 1993), 55–89.

84. Simpson quoted in Perotti, *Resolving Policy Conflict*, 129.

85. Robert Pear, "U.S. Immigration Panel Near an Agreement on New Policy Goals," *New York Times*, May 28, 1980; See also, Robert Pear, "Immigration Old and New," *New York Times*, December 11, 1980.

86. Robert Pear, "Alien Identification Cards Called Civil Rights Threat," *New York Times*, June 17, 1980.

87. Perotti, *Resolving Policy Conflict*, 135.

88. Robert Pear, "Immigration Panel to Meet in Private," *New York Times*, November 23, 1980.

89. Perotti, *Resolving Policy Conflict*, 134.

90. *U.S. Immigration Policy and the National Interest*, Committees on the Judiciary, House of Representatives and United States Senate, Joint Committee Print, August 1, 1981 (Final Report of the Select Commission on Immigration and Refugee Policy).

91. Fuchs, "Immigration Reform in 1911 and 1981," 64.

92. As quoted in Robert Pear, "Panel Asks Rise in Immigration, with Tighter Law Enforcement," *New York Times*, February 27, 1981.

93. "Excerpts from Final Report of Commission on Immigration and Refugee Policy," *New York Times*, February 27, 1981; Pear, "Panel Asks Rise in Immigration."

94. Robert Pear, "First Reviews on Immigration Proposals: Encouraging Words, Uncertain Prospects," *New York Times*, February 28, 1981.

95. John Kingdon, *Agendas, Alternatives, and Public Policies*, 2nd ed. (Harper Collins, 1977).

96. Norman L. Zucker and Naomi Fink Zucker, *Desperate Crossings: Seeking Refuge in America* (M.E. Sharpe, Inc., 1996).

97. Martin, *A Nation of Immigrants*, 232. See also, Steven R. Weisman, "Refugee Crisis: Shift in Views," *New York Times*, May 16, 1980.

98. "The Plight of the Haitian Refugees," National Coalition for Haitian Refugees, undated but circa. 1985.

99. Zucker and Zucker, *Desperate Crossings*, 46. See also, Martin, *A Nation of Immigrants*, 233–36.

100. "The Plight of Haitian Refugees," National Coalition for Haitian Refugees, undated but circa. 1985.

101. Martin, *A Nation of Immigrants*, 235.

102. Heather Reynolds, "Irreconcilable Regulations: Why The Sun Has Set on the Cuban Adjustment Act in Florida," *Florida Law Review* 63 (2011): 1020.

103. Cuban Adjustment Act, Public Law No. 89-732, 1966, 8 U.S.C. at 1255; see also Reynolds, "Irreconcilable Regulations," 1013–20.

104. "The Cuban Adjustment Act of 1966: Mirando por los Ojos de Don Quixote o Sancho Panza?" *Harvard Law Review* 114 (2001): 907.

105. Naomi Fink Zucker, "The Haitians versus the United States: The Courts as Last Resort," *Annals of the American Academy of Political and Social Science* 467 (May 1983): 154.

106. Rebecca Hamlin and Phillip E. Wolgin, "Symbolic Politics and Policy Feedback: *The United Nations Protocol Relating to the Status of Refugees* and American Refugee Policy in the Cold War," *International Migration Review* 46, no. 3 (Fall 2012): 610.

107. Zucker, "The Haitians versus the United States," 156.

108. Author interview with Rick Swartz, July 30, 2012.

109. Michael Barone and Grant Ujifusa, *The Almanac of American Politics, 1982* (Barone & Company, 1981), xvii; see also Dudley Clendenin, "Carter Is in Trouble with Voters in Two Major Sections of Florida," *New York Times*, October 19, 1980; Hedrick Smith, "Reagan Given Edge in 'Big 9' Battleground States," *New York Times*, September 14, 1980.

110. Perotti, *Resolving Policy Conflict*, 143.

111. Remini, *The House*, 453–54.

112. Barone and Ujifusa, *The Almanac of American Politics 1982*.

113. Marvin Caplan, *Farther Along: A Civil Rights Memoir* (Louisiana State University Press, 1999), 233.

114. Caplan, *Farther Along*, 246.

115. Charles and Barbara Whalen's *The Longest Debate: A Legislative History of the 1964 Civil Rights Act* (Seven Locks Press, 1985), for years the definitive account of the bill from the legislators' perspective; it includes twenty-two direct references to the Leadership Conference, not including references to key individual LCCR figures such as Joe Rauh, Clarence Mitchell, and other LCCR members in their individual or organizational capacities. See also Caplan, *Farther Along*, 235. Caplan refers to passage of the 1964 Act as a "triumph for the kind of coordinated lobbying—between grassroots and Washington—that the Leadership Conference sought to exemplify," at p. 231. See also Todd S. Purdum, *An Idea Whose Time Has Come* (Picador, 2014), and Clay Risen, *The Bill of the Century* (Bloomsbury Press, 2014), both of which also include extensive references to LCCR's role.

116. Caplan, *Farther Along*, 235. Caplan also describes early LCCR discussions involving how the coalition might refuse membership to some of these organizations which, after much "soul searching" were finally admitted.

117. Author interview with Ralph Neas, November 5, 2012.

118. Ari Berman, *Give Us the Ballot: The Modern Struggle for Voting Rights in America* (Farrar, Straus and Giroux, 2015), 110.

119. Email from Raul Yzaguírre to Charles Kamasaki, April 2, 2015.

120. Caplan, *Farther Along*, 235.

121. See, for example, Acuña, *Occupied America*, 62–66 (on resistance in Texas), 85–87 (on resistance in New Mexico); 103, 120 (on union organizing in California); see also Orozco, *No Mexicans, Women or Dogs Allowed*, 65–91 (summarizing pre-LULAC activism).

122. James Thomas Tucker, "Enfranchising Language Minority Citizens: The Bilingual Election Provisions of the Voting Rights Act," *Legislation and Public Policy* 10, no. 195 (2006): 195–260.

123. Caplan, *Farther Along*, 190–198.

124. Author interview with Raul Yzaguírre, April 15, 2013.

125. See for example, "Statement of Raul Yzaguírre," Leadership Conference on Civil Rights 40th Anniversary Dinner, May 8, 1990; see also, Kamasaki and Yzaguírre, "Black–Hispanic Tensions."

126. William Taylor, *The Passion of My Times: An Advocate's Fifty-Year Journey in the Civil Rights Movement* (Carroll & Graff Publishers, 2004), 131–44.

127. National Forum on Immigration and Refugee Policy, "A Proposal to Establish a National Forum on Immigration and Refugee Policy," undated but circa December 1981. The last entry in a chronology included in the proposal is the first formal meeting of the Forum's Board of Directors in November 1981, which among other things authorized Acting President Rick Swartz to raise funds for the organization.

128. Author interview with Rick Swartz, July 30, 2012.

129. Email exchange with Rick Swartz, March 10, 2013.

130. Pear, "First Reviews on Immigration Proposals."

131. Ira J. Kurzban, *Kurzban's Immigration Law Sourcebook* (American Immigra-

tion Council, 2014); see: http://agora.aila.org/product/detail/1848?utm_source=MKT
-PUB&utm_medium=print&utm_campaign=KURZBANS14, accessed July 18, 2014.

132. "In Memoriam: Ira Gollobin, a Haitian Refugee's Best Friend Since 1972,"
National Coalition for Haitian Rights, June 22, 2008; interview with Rick Swartz, July
30, 2012.

133. Zucker, "The Haitians versus the United States."

134. Hamlin and Wolgin, "Symbolic Politics and Policy Feedback," 609.

135. Author interviews with Rick Swartz, July 30, 2012, and August 7, 2012, and
author interview with Muzaffar Chishti, January 19, 2013.

136. Author interviews with Rick Swartz, July 30, 2012, and August 7, 2012.

137. Louis Freedberg, "The Role of Philanthropy in the U.S. Immigrant Rights Movement," Report to the Ford Foundation, undated but circa 2009.

138. Freedberg, "The Role of Philanthropy in the U.S. Immigrant Rights Movement,"
and author interview with Muzaffar Chishti, January 19, 2013.

139. See, for example, "New Basis Urged for Immigration," New York Times,
November 2, 1963, describing the proceedings of an AICC conference; "Immigration
Conference Elects Keating President," New York Times, March 6, 1965, announcing the
election of former US Senator Frank Keating as president of the organization; "Immigration Snag Found in 1965 Act, New York Times, May 21, 1966, reporting on a keynote
address by Senator Kennedy; and "Migration Unit Will Be Assisted at Theatre Here,"
New York Times, March 23, 1962, discussing a theater performance benefitting AICC,
with an event committee listing a "who's who" of high society figures in the city.

140. Author interview with Rick Swartz, April 3, 2015; email exchange with Rick
Swartz, March 7, 2013.

141. Dan Shiffman, Rooting Multiculturalism: The Work of Louis Adamic (Fairleigh
Dickinson University Press, 2003), 85.

142. Eleanor Roosevelt, "The Democratic War Effort," Common Ground, 1942, and
"1940–1949 archives of Common Ground, www.unz.org/Pub/CommonGround, accessed
March 28, 2013.

143. Gerald Meyer, "The Cultural Pluralist Response to Americanization," Journal
of the Research Group of Democracy and Socialism (November 2008): 19–51.

144. Author interview with Henry Cisneros, October 5, 2012.

145. John Heilemann, "Do You Know the Way to Ban Jose?" Wired, August 1, 1996.

146. Author interview with Muzaffar Chishti, December 17, 2012.

147. Author interview with Muzaffar Chishti, December 17, 2012. For examples of
Piore's work, see his faculty CV, May 5, 2015, posted at http://economics.mit.edu/faculty
/mpiore/cv, accessed July 7, 2015. Examples of Waldinger's work may be viewed at his
faculty webpage: http://www.sscnet.ucla.edu/soc/faculty/waldinger/, accessed July 7,
2015.

148. James Fallows, "Immigration: How It's Affecting Us," The Atlantic Monthly,
November 1, 1983.

149. For one prominent articulation of this view, see: Vernon M. Briggs Jr., Mass
Immigration and the National Interest, 4th ed. (Routledge Press, 2003).

150. For a brief introduction see: Michael Reich, David M. Gordon, and Richard C.
Edwards, "Dual Labor Markets: A Theory of Labor Market Segmentation," American
Economic Review 63, no. 2 (May 1973): 359–65. For a specific application to immigra-
tion, see: Michael C. Piore's classic book, Birds of Passage: Migrant Labor and Industrial
Societies (Cambridge University Press, 1980).

151. Sol C. Chaikin and Phil Comstock, "Toward a Rational Immigration Policy," *The Journal of the Institute for Socioeconomic Studies* 7, no. 1 (Spring 1982), 246–59.

152. Author interview with Muzaffar Chishti, January 19, 2013.

153. "Ruth Zagat Murphy Casselman: Led Immigrant Groups," *Los Angeles Times*, obituary, April 15, 1989.

154. Author interview with Muzaffar Chishti, January 19, 2013.

155. Minutes of the Board Meeting, National Forum on Immigration and Refugee Policy/American Immigration and Citizenship Conference, June 28–29, 1982.

156. See, for example, Keely's work, *U.S. Immigration: A Policy Analysis* (Population Council, 1979), one of the more widely read publications by lay people, including congressional staff and advocates, at the beginning of the Select Commission's deliberations.

157. Author interview with Christine Gaffney, January 16, 2013.

158. Author interview with Frank Sharry, August 16, 2012.

159. "Introduction: Guide to the Microfilm Collection, Immigration and Refugee Services of America, 1918–1985," Immigration History and Research Center, College of Liberal Arts, University of Minnesota, vii.

160. Audrey Singer and Jill H. Wilson, "Refugee Resettlement in Metropolitan America," *Migration Information Source*, Migration Policy Institute, March 1, 2007, 2; see also Donald Kerwin, "International Migration," US Immigration Law and Civil Society, Scalabrini International Migration Network, 6.

161. *Congressional Record*, February 9, 1994, S1275 (Statement of Senator Kennedy, tribute to Wells Klein).

162. Author interview with Christine Gaffney, January 16, 2013.

163. Nan Robertson, "At the 'Auction' for Refugees from Southeast Asia," *New York Times*, August 10, 1979.

164. Author interview with Christine Gaffney, January 16, 2013.

165. Robertson, "At the 'Auction' for Refugees from Southeast Asia."

166. Author interview with Muzaffar Chishti, December 17, 2012.

167. Elaine Woo, "Wells C. Klein; Helped Resettle Thousands of Refugees," *Los Angeles Times*, June 10, 2001 (obituary).

168. During his first ACNS Board of Directors meeting in 1987, the author was stunned to see that ACNS's $7 million in unrestricted net assets (almost $16 million in 2017 dollars), three times larger than NCLR's entire annual budget.

169. Author interview with Christine Gaffney, January 16, 2013; author interview with Frank Sharry, August 16, 2012.

170. Freedberg, "The Role of Philanthropy in the U.S. Immigrant Rights Movement."

171. Author interview with Rick Swartz, July 30, 2012.

172. Author interview with J. Michael Treviño, October 2, 2012.

173. Author interview with Michael Myers, December 17, 2012.

174. Mark Tooley, "Rededicating New York's 'God Box,'" *The American Spectator*, June 1, 2010.

175. "History," Church World Service home page, undated, http://www.cwsglobal .org/who-we-are/history.html, accessed March 26, 2013.

176. "Michael Myers, Former Staff Director and Chief Counsel, Senate Health, Education, labor and Pensions (HELP) Committee (1998–2010)," *Washington Post*, undated, http://www.washingtonpost.com/politics/michael-myers/gIQAvERGAP_/topic.html, accessed March 26, 2013; Author interview with Michael Myers, December 17, 2012.

177. *National Council of Churches et al. v. Shenefield*, US District Court, Southern

District of Florida, case no. 79-2959-CIV-ALH; *National Council of Churches v. Michael J. Egan*, US District Court, Southern District of Florida, case no. 79-2959-CIV-WMH; Author interview with Michael Myers, December 17, 2012.

178. Author interview with Arnoldo Torres, January 1, 2013.

179. Dan Martin, "Sponsors Now Make Life, Death Difference," *Baptist Press*, August 21, 1978.

180. See for example, "Haiti: Human Rights Under Hereditary Dictatorship," National Coalition for Haitian Refugees, October 1985, reporting on a fact-finding mission to Haiti by Hooper, Aryeh Neier of Americas Watch, and Brenda Pillors of the Congressional Black Caucus.

181. Author interview with Rick Swartz, July 30, 2012.

182. "Michael S. Hooper: His Quest for Haitian Democracy and Freedom," National Coalition for Haitian Rights, December 2000, http://www.nchr.org/nchr/hrp/jando/life _of_hooper.htm; Author interview with Rick Swartz, August 7, 2012.

183. For a listing of the coalition's executive committee, see Testimony of Michael S. Hooper, *House Hearings*, Subcommittee on Immigration, Refugees and International Law, Committee on the Judiciary, May 9, 1984.

184. Author interview with Muzaffar Chishti, December 17, 2012.

185. Barone and Ujifusa, *The Almanac of American Politics, 1984*, 811.

186. Don Swaby, "Shirley Chisholm: A True Revolutionary," *The Huffington Post*, February 19, 2008, http://www.huffingtonpost.com/donn-swaby/shirley-chisholm-a-true -r_b_87378.html, accessed October 4, 2013.

187. "Who Is the Most Underrated Politician in U.S. History?" *The Atlantic*, January/ February 2015, 15.

188. Michelle Garcia, "Shirley Chisholm, the First Black Woman to Run for President, Just Got the Presidential Medal of Freedom," *Vox*, November 25, 2015, http://www .vox.com/2015/11/25/9796730/shirley-chisholm-presidential-medal-freedom, accessed December 9, 2015.

189. Ellen Fitzpatrick, "The Radical and the Racist," *The Atlantic*, October 2016.

190. Mathew Murray, "Asthma Attack Claims Rep. Towns' Chief of Staff," *Roll Call*, June 15, 2005; "Brenda Elaine Pillors, Congressional Chief of Staff," *Washington Post*, June 23, 2005, obituary.

191. *Congressional Record*, June 17, 2005, E1270 (Remarks of Rep. Barbara Lee).

192. Author interview with Wade Henderson, March 8, 2013.

193. Ari Goldman, "Jewish Group Faces Reorganization," *New York Times*, February 13, 1990.

194. Oscar Handlin, "The American Jewish Committee, A Half-Century View," *Commentary*, January 1, 1957.

195. Marianne Sanua, *Let Us Prove Strong: The American Jewish Committee, 1945–2006* (Brandeis University Press, 2007), 235–58.

196. Author interview with Frank Sharry, August 16, 2012.

197. Author interview with Rick Swartz, July 30, 2012.

198. Bio of Phyllis Eisen, http://ed.gov/about/offices/list/ovae/pi/hs/eisenbio.doc, undated, accessed March 26, 2013.

199. Paul Sabin, *The Bet: Paul Erlich, Julian Simon, and Our Gamble over Earth's Future* (Yale University Press, 2013), 57–58.

200. Author interview with Phyllis Eisen, September 19, 2012.

201. Author interview with Rick Swartz, July 30, 2012.

202. Author interview with Phyllis Eisen, April 3, 2014.

203. Remini, *The House*, 445.

204. Author interview with Phyllis Eisen, April 3, 2014.

205. Oliveira, *MALDEF: Diez Anos*, 74.

206. Matt S. Meier and Feliciano Ribera, *Mexican Americans/American Mexicans: From Conquistadors to Chicanos*, rev. ed. (Hill and Wang, 1993), 228.

207. Maggie Rivas-Rodriguez, *Texas Mexican Americans & Postwar Civil Rights* (University of Texas Press, 2015), 85–89.

208. David A. Badillo, "MALDEF and the Evolution of Latino Civil Rights," Institute for Latino Studies, University of Notre Dame, Research Reports, vol. 2 (January 2005), 7.

209. Stephen H. Wilson, "Brown over 'Other White': Mexican Americans' Legal Arguments and Litigation Strategy in Desegregation Lawsuits," *Law and History Review* 21, no. 145 (2003), 193.

210. Teresa Palomo Acosta, "Mexican American Legal Defense and Educational Fund," Handbook of Texas Online, Texas State Historical Association, http://www.tshaonline.org/handbook/online/articles/jom01, accessed October 7, 2013.

211. Broder, *Changing of the Guard*, 282–83.

212. Georgia Wralstad Ulmschneider, "Mexican American Legal Defense and Educational Fund (MALDEF)," in David Schultz, ed., *Encyclopedia of American Law* (Facts On File, Inc., 2002), http://www.fofweb.com/activelink2.asp, accessed October 11, 2013. See also, Karen O'Connor and Lee Epstein, "A Legal Voice for the Chicano Community: The Activities of the Mexican American Legal Defense and Educational Fund, 1968–82," *Social Science Quarterly* 65, no. 2 (June 1984): 246–49.

213. For an in-depth understanding of "impact litigation" strategy, see generally, Stephen L. Wasby, *Race Relations Litigation in an Age of Complexity* (University of Virginia Press, 1995).

214. O'Connor and Epstein, "A Legal Voice for the Chicano Community," 25.

215. Oliveira, *MALDEF: Diez Anos*, 9, 11.

216. Deirdre Martínez, *Who Speaks for Hispanics?, Hispanic Interest Groups in Washington* (State University of New York Press, 2009), 94, citing in part internal reports from the Ford Foundation.

217. James A. Regalado, "Latino Representation in Los Angeles," in Roberto E. Villarreal, Norma G. Hernandez, and Howard D. Neighbor, eds., *Latino Empowerment, Progress, Problems, and Prospects* (Greenwood Press, 1988), 95–102; and Martínez, "Hispanic Advocacy Organizations," 77.

218. Robert Brischetto, "Today's Politics Not Willie Velasquez's," *San Antonio Express News*, May 8, 2014.

219. Badillo, "MALDEF and the Evolution of Latino Civil Rights," 7.

220. Carlos R. Soltero, *Latinos and American Law* (University of Texas Press, 2006), 79–80.

221. O'Connor and Epstein, "A Legal Voice for the Chicano Community," 251.

222. Maureen T. Hallinan, *Frontiers in Sociology of Education* (Springer Science + Business Media, 2011), 66; see also, Joseph T. Henke, "Financing Public Schools in California: The Aftermath of *Serrano v. Priest* and Proposition 13," *University of San Francisco Law Review* 21, no. 1 (1986–87).

223. Acosta, "Mexican American Legal Defense and Educational Fund."

224. Greg Moses, "Robin Hood Lives! MALDEF Claims Victory in Texas," *Texas*

Civil Rights Review, December 1, 2004, http://www.texascivilrightsreview.org/phpnuke /index.php, accessed October 7, 2013.

225. Michael A. Olivas, "The Story of *Plyler v. Doe*, The Education of Undocumented Children and the Polity," Institute for Higher Education Law and Governance Monograph, University of Houston, 2004, also included in David A. Martin and Peter H. Schuck, eds., *Immigration Stories* (Foundation Press, 2005). Olivas's monograph is viewed by many as the definitive story of the case; see for example, Hiroshi Motomura, "Forward to the Past: The Many Meanings of *Plyler v. Doe* on Its 25th Anniversary," paper presented at "The 25th Anniversary of *Plyler v. Doe*: Access to Education and Undocumented Children," Warren Institute, UC Berkeley School of Law, May 7, 2007, http://www.law.berkeley.edu/2913.htm, accessed October 7, 2013. Olivas has since published a book, *No Undocumented Child Left Behind* (New York University Press, 2012), that expands on his original monograph.

226. Douglas Martin, "William Wayne Justice, Judge Who Remade Texas, Dies at 89," *New York Times*, obituary, October 16, 2009.

227. Olivas, "The Story of *Plyler v. Doe*," 4–9.

228. Author interview with Rick Swartz, August 7, 2012.

229. Olivas, *No Undocumented Child Left Behind*, 17–18.

230. Jeffrey Toobin, *The Oath: The Obama White House and the Supreme Court* (Anchor Books, 2013), 107.

231. Olivas, "The Story of *Plyler v. Doe*," 16.

232. Stuart Taylor, "U.S. Bars Challenge to a Law Restricting Schooling for Aliens," *New York Times*, September 9, 1981.

233. Olivas, *No Undocumented Child Left Behind*, 112 (endnote 39).

234. Barbara Belejack, "A Lesson in Equal Protection: The Texas Cases That Opened the Schoolhouse Door to Undocumented Immigrant Children," *Texas Observer*, July 13, 2007, 14.

235. "Linda Greenhouse, "Justices Rule States Must Pay to Educate Illegal Alien Pupils," *New York Times*, June 16, 1982.

236. Soltero, *Latinos and American Law*, 123.

237. As cited in Hiroshi Motomura, *Immigration Outside the Law* (Oxford University Press, 2014), 20–30.

238. Linda Greenhouse, "Court's Ruling On Illegal Aliens A Doubtful Precedent," *New York Times*, June 17, 1982.

239. Michael Olivas, "Holding the Line: Implementation of *Plyler v. Doe* at 25," paper presented at "The 25th Anniversary of *Plyler v. Doe*: Access to Education and Undocumented Children," Warren Institute, UC Berkeley School of Law, May 7, 2007, http://www.law.berkeley.edu/2913.htm, accessed October 7, 2013.

240. Raul Reyes, " 'No Mas Bebes' Looks Back at LA Mexican Moms' Involuntary Sterilizations," *nbcnews.com*, February 1, 2016, http://www.nbcnews.com/news/latino /no-m-s-beb-s-looks-back-l-mexican-moms-n505256, accessed February 2, 2016.

241. Alexandra Minna Stern, "Sterilized in the Name of Public Health," *American Journal of Public Health* 95, no. 7 (July 2005): 1128–38.

242. See Aaron Flanagan et al., *The Quinacrine Report: Sterilization, Modern-day Eugenics, and the Anti-Immigrant Movement* (Center for New Community, 2013).

243. Reyes, " 'No Mas Bebes' Looks Back at LA Mexican Moms' Involuntary Sterilizations."

244. See documentary footage at Renee Tajima-Pena, *No Mas Bebes*, Public Broad-

casting Service, Independent Lens, premiered February 1, 2016, http://www.pbs.org /independentlens/films/no-mas-bebes/, accessed February 2, 2016.

245. Author interview with Antonia Hernández, October 30, 2012.

246. Malcolm Gladwell, *David and Goliath: Underdogs, Misfits, and the Art of Battling Giants* (Little, Brown, & Company, 2013), 107–12.

247. *Notable Hispanic American Women, Book II*, Gale Biography Resource Center, 1999; http://www.gale.cengage.vom/free_resources/chh/bio/hernandez_a.html, accessed February 22, 2013, and Hernández interview, October 10, 2013.

248. Author interview with Antonia Hernández, October 30, 2012.

249. Jocelyn Y. Stewart, "The Advocate: As President of the Mexican American Legal Defense and Educational Fund, Antonia Hernández Speaks for Millions," *Los Angeles Times,* September 12, 1999.

250. "Antonia Hernández: Working for Latino Causes With Soft-Spoken Determination," *Los Angeles Times*, December 13, 1992.

251. Stewart, "The Advocate."

252. Author interview with Wade Henderson, March 8, 2013.

253. Carlyle Murphy, "FAIR Leader Fights for Immigration Curbs," *Washington Post*, November 29, 1983.

254. Ann Cooper, "In Person: John Tanton: Immigration Reformer Stirs the Melting Pot," *National Journal*, May 17, 1986, 1210.

255. James Fallows, "Immigration: How It's Affecting Us."

256. Murphy, "FAIR Leader Fights for Immigration Curbs."

257. Author interview with Roger Conner, February 11, 2013.

258. Murphy, "FAIR Leader Fights for Immigration Curbs."

259. "Roger Conner, Part 2," Cutting Edge Law, uploaded January 28, 2011, https://www.youtube.com/watch?v=JuCG1IZdK5k, accessed July 3, 2015.

260. Murphy, "FAIR Leader Fights for Immigration Curbs."

261. Michael Eduardo Cortés, *Policy Analysts and Interest Groups*, 225.

262. Tichenor, *Dividing Lines*, 237.

263. Fallows, "Immigration: How It's Affecting Us"; see also: Isaiah Thomson, "Unfair," *Miami New Times*, June 7, 2007.

264. Cortés, *Policy Analysts and Interest Groups*, 247–84.

265. See for example, FAIR press packet dated October 5, 1982 (copy on file with author).

266. Cortés, *Policy Analysts and Interest Groups*, 228.

267. For a useful listing of the groups, see Flanagan et al., *The Quinacrine Report*, 10.

CHAPTER 3

1. Dan Balz, "Hispanic League's Gathering Hears Mondale Plea to Wield Ballot Power," *Washington Post*, July 3, 1982.

2. Herbert H. Denton, "Reagan EEOC Nominee Under Attack," *Washington Post*, November 4, 1981.

3. Herbert H. Denton, "Reagan Picks Black Lawyer for EEOC," *Washington Post*, February 13, 1982.

4. Author interview with Muzaffar Chishti, May 21, 2013.

5. Author interview with Phyllis Eisen, September 19, 2012.

6. Author interview with Michael Myers, December 17, 2012.

7. Cose, *A Nation of Strangers*, 157.

8. Author interview with Arnoldo Torres, February 21, 2014.

9. Author interview with Rick Swartz, July 30, 2012.

10. Author interview with Rick Swartz, August 7, 2012.

11. Author interview with Christine Gaffney, January 16, 2013.

12. Author interview with Muzaffar Chishti, May 21, 2013.

13. Author interview with Warren Leiden, April 26, 2013.

14. Andrea Sevetson, "Hearings and the LexisNexis Congressional Hearings Digital Collection," LexisNexis White Paper, 2007, accessed December 12, 2013, http://www.amdev.net/docs/congressional/Hearings_White_Paper.pdf, 1–3.

15. Miller, " 'The Right Thing to Do'," 58–59.

16. Eric Redman, *The Dance of Legislation* (Simon and Schuster, 1973), 169.

17. Interview with Alan Simpson, Romano "Ron" Mazzoli Oral History Project, September 30, 2010.

18. "Summary of Hearings Held by the Senate Judiciary Committee on Immigration and Refugee Policy, July 1981–April 1982," Congressional Research Service, April 1983.

19. Miller, " 'The Right Thing to Do'," 57–60.

20. Richard D. Lyons, "William French Smith Dies at 73; Reagan's First Attorney General," *New York Times*, October 30, 1990.

21. Remarks of Kenneth Starr, "Fifth Annual William French Lecture," Pepperdine University Law School, October 11, 2011, accessed November 21, 2013, http://www.youtube.com/watch?v=UXvia9bqcXw.

22. Author interview with Ralph Neas, November 5, 2012.

23. Task Force papers cited in Daniel J. Tichenor, *Dividing Lines: The Politics of Immigration Control in America* (Princeton University Press, 2002), 256–57.

24. Miller, " 'The Right Thing to Do'," 60.

25. See, for example, Smith's strong advocacy for the bill in: Richard L. Strout, "Controversial Immigration Reform Gets New Hearing in Washington," *Christian Science Monitor*, March 1, 1983.

26. Miller, " 'The Right Thing to Do'," 60.

27. Robert Pear, "It's Time for Immigration Law Reform—or Is It?" *New York Times*, January 3, 1982.

28. Perotti, *Resolving Policy Conflict*, 195.

29. Miller, " 'The Right Thing to Do'," 60–61.

30. Kelman, *Making Public Policy*, 162; see also, Jeffrey Pressman and Aaron Wildavsky, *Implementation* (University of California Press, 1973).

31. Cited in Bernard Avishai, "The Trouble with Israel," *Harper's*, August 2015, 29.

32. Jeffrey H. Birnbaum, *The Lobbyists: How Influence Peddlers Get Their Way in Washington* (Times Books, 1992), xiii–xv.

33. Zolberg, *A Nation by Design*, 357–58.

34. For an explanation of how "flexible cap" would result in major cuts to legal immigration, see Zolberg, *A Nation by Design*, 358.

35. See Congressional Research Summary and text of H.R. 5872, accessed May 23, 2012, http://thomas.loc.gov/cgi-bin/bdquery/D?d097:2:./temp/~bdp3Uw::|/home/LegislativeData.php?n=BSS;c=97|.

36. Lawrence Fuchs, "The Search for a Sound Immigration Policy: A Personal View,"

in Nathan Glazer, ed., *Clamor at the Gates: The New American Immigration* (Institute for Contemporary Studies Press, 1985), 17–48.

37. Alan K. Simpson, *Right in the Old Gazoo: A Lifetime of Scrapping with the Press* (William Morrow and Company, 1997), 72.

38. Miller, " 'The Right Thing to Do'," 57.

39. Nadine Cahodas, "Committees Plan Fast Action on Major Immigration Bill," *Congressional Quarterly Weekly Report*, April 10, 1982, 808.

40. "Not Nativist, Not Racist, Not Mean," *New York Times*, editorial, March 18, 1982, and "Turning Mean on Immigration," *New York Times*, editorial, August 9, 1982.

41. Michael Barone and Grant Ujifusa, *The Almanac of American Politics, 1982* (Barone & Company, 1981), xxvii.

42. Peter S. Canellos, ed., *Last Lion: The Fall and Rise of Ted Kennedy* (Simon and Schuster, 2009), 181–82.

43. Barone and Ujifusa, *The Almanac of American Politics, 1982*, xxx.

44. Nadine Cahodas, "Sen. Eastland: Last of a Vanished Breed," *Congressional Quarterly Weekly Report*, February 22, 1986, 478.

45. John Newhouse, "Taking It Personally," *New Yorker*, March 16, 1992, 65.

46. Barone and Ujifusa, *The Almanac of American Politics, 1982*, 1203.

47. Broder, *Changing of the Guard*, 350.

48. Newhouse, "Taking It Personally," 56.

49. Remarks of Senator Simpson in "Let 'Er Rip,' Reflections of a Rocky Mountain Senator," Conversations with History series, Institute of International Relations, University of California-Berkeley, September 17, 1997, http://globetrotter.berkeley.edu /conversations/Simpson/.

50. Cited in Cose, *A Nation of Strangers*, 154.

51. Fuchs, "Immigration Reform in 1911 and 1981," 81.

52. Martin, *A Nation of Immigrants*, 210.

53. Donald Loren Hardy, *Shooting from the Lip: The Life of Senator Al Simpson* (University of Oklahoma Press, 2011), 35–36.

54. Simpson, *Right in the Old Gazoo*, 66–67.

55. Remarks of Senator Simpson in "Let 'Er Rip,' Reflections of a Rocky Mountain Senator."

56. Fuchs, "Immigration Reform in 1911 and 1981," 82.

57. Canellos, *Last Lion*, 147–79.

58. David Broder, "Ted Kennedy Back in Business, with New Issue and New Voice," *Washington Post*, April 26, 1982.

59. Robert A. Caro, *The Passage of Power: The Years of Lyndon Johnson* (Vintage, 2013), 34.

60. Barone and Ujifusa, *The Almanac of American Politics, 1982*, 487.

61. Canellos, *Last Lion*, 204–5.

62. Barone and Ujifusa, *The Almanac of American Politics, 1982*, 485.

63. Canellos, *Last Lion*, 240–41.

64. Phillip Rucker, "Late Senator's Staff Became the Other Kennedy Family," *Washington Post*, August 28, 2009.

65. Canellos, *Last Lion*, 191–97.

66. Barone and Ujifusa, *The Almanac of American Politics, 1982*, 485.

67. Canellos, *Last Lion*, 236.

68. Martin, *A Nation of Immigrants*, 227–30.

69. Edward M. Kennedy, *True Compass: A Memoir* (Twelve Books, 2009), 192–93.

70. Author interview with Tom Castro, July 7, 2012.

71. Fuchs, "The Corpse That Would Not Die," 117.

72. Perotti, *Resolving Policy Conflict*, 89.

73. See for example, Amit Pandya, Vivian Berzinski, and Douglas L. Parker, *Illegal Immigration: An Alternative Perspective* (Institute for Public Representation, Georgetown University Law Center, undated but published 1981). The analysis argues that employer sanctions will be ineffective, undermine labor law enforcement, and cause substantial employment discrimination, among other problems.

74. Author interview with Antonia Hernández, October 30, 2012.

75. Miller, " 'The Right Thing to Do'," 62; Fuchs, "Immigration Reform in 1911 and 1981," 83–84.

76. Kennedy, *True Compass*, 487.

77. Author interview with Antonia Hernández, October 30, 2012.

78. Simpson, *Right in the Old Gazoo*, 69–70.

79. David Frum, "Blame Yesterday's Reforms for Today's Gridlocked Congress," CNN Opinion, March 1, 2010, http://www.cnn.com/2010/OPINION/03/01/frum.smoke.filled.congress/index/html.

80. Donald R. Wolfensberger, "A Brief History of Congressional Reform Efforts," Bipartisan Policy Center and Woodrow Wilson Center, February 22, 2013.

81. Christopher J. Dearing and Steven S. Smith, *Committees in Congress* (Congressional Quarterly Press, 1997).

82. Remini, *The House*, 462–63.

83. Dearing and Smith, *Committees in Congress*.

84. Todd S. Purdum, *An Idea Whose Time Has Come, Two Presidents, Two Parties, and the Battle for the Civil Rights Act of 1964* (Picador, 2014), 163.

85. Wolfensberger, "A Brief History of Congressional Reform Efforts."

86. Norman J. Ornstein, "The Open Congress Meets the President," in Anthony King, ed., *The New American Political System* (American Enterprise Institute, 1978), 203, cited in Steven Kelman, *Making Public Policy: A Hopeful View of American Government* (Basic Books, 1987), 52.

87. "Interview with Vin Weber," from "The Long March of Newt Gingrich," *Frontline*, Public Broadcasting Service, six-part documentary television series aired December 2011, http://www.pbs.org/wgbh/pages/frontline/newt/newtintwshtml/weber.html.

88. Remini, *The House*, 462.

89. Robert S. Walker, "The Right to Object," March 25, 2009, http://www.reservingtherighttoobject.com/2009/03/right-to-object.html.

90. Nicole Hemmer and Bryant Cebul, "They Were Made for Each Other," *New Republic*, July 11, 2016.

91. Remini, *The House*, 464.

92. Hemmer and Cebul, "They Were Made for Each Other."

93. Mathews, *Tip and the Gipper*, 294–95.

94. Ronald Brownstein, "Return of the Revolutionary," *National Journal*, January 26, 2012.

95. "Interview with Vin Weber."

96. Barone and Ujifusa, *The Almanac of American Politics, 1982*, 329.

97. David Broder, "House Can't Hold Onto LaHood," *Washington Post*, August 1,

2007; Mickey Edwards, "Bob Michel Feels a Nipping at His Heels," *Los Angeles Times*, August 31, 1993.

98. Barone and Ujifusa, *The Almanac of American Politics, 1982*, xxxix.

99. Barone and Ujifusa, *The Almanac of American Politics, 1982*, 411.

100. Interview with Romano "Ron" Mazzoli, May 14, 2010, Romano (Ron) Mazzoli Oral History Project.

101. Interview with Romano "Ron" Mazzoli, May 14, 2010.

102. Nicholas Dawidoff, "The Riddle of Jimmy Carter," *Rolling Stone*, February 1, 2011.

103. Interview with Romano "Ron" Mazzoli, May 4, 2010, Part One.

104. Interview with Romano "Ron" Mazzoli, May 4, 2010, Part Two.

105. Interview with Romano "Ron" Mazzoli, May 24, 2010, Part One.

106. Barone and Ujifusa, *The Almanac of American Politics, 1982*, 414.

107. Interview with Romano "Ron" Mazzoli, May 25, 2010.

108. Cose, *A Nation of Strangers*, 153.

109. Interview with Romano "Ron" Mazzoli, May 25, 2010.

110. Interview with Harris Miller, July 8, 2010, Romano (Ron) Mazzoli Oral History Project.

111. Nadine Cahodas, "Immigration Bill Moving Amid Intensive Lobbying," *Congressional Quarterly Weekly Report*, May 15, 1982, 1103.

112. Miller, " 'The Right Thing to Do'," 63.

113. Cahodas, "Immigration Bill Moving Amid Intensive Lobbying," 1103–5.

114. Senate Judiciary Committee Transcripts, May 18, 20, 25, and 27, 1982, cited in Perotti, *Resolving Policy Conflict*, 157f8.

115. "Turning Mean on Immigration," *New York Times*, editorial, August 9, 1982.

116. Sen. Alan Simpson, "Illegal Aliens," *New York Times*, letter to the editor, August 10, 1982.

117. Robert Pear, "Senate Opens Debate on Immigration," *New York Times*, August 13, 1982.

118. Associated Press, "Senate Defeats Effort to Dilute Aliens Bill," *Washington Post*, August 14, 1982.

119. Barone and Ujifusa, *Almanac of American Politics, 1982*.

120. *Congressional Record*, August 13, 1982, 21052 (Remarks of Senator Simpson).

121. *Congressional Record*, August 17, 1982, 10631 (Remarks of Senator Baker).

122. *Congressional Record*, August 17, 1982, 10631–10634 (Remarks of Senators Sarbanes, Grassley, Kennedy, and Hart).

123. Newhouse, "Taking It Personally," 56.

124. *Congressional Record*, August 13, 1982, 10631–32 (Remarks of Senator Simpson).

125. Miller, " 'The Right Thing to Do'," 62.

126. Barone and Ujifusa, *The Almanac of American Politics, 1982*, 143.

127. Interview with Daniel Lungren, Romano "Ron" Mazzoli Oral History Project, September 30, 2010.

128. Interview with Harris Miller, Romano "Ron" Mazzoli Oral History Project, July 8, 2010.

129. Miller, " 'The Right Thing to Do'," 62.

130. Interview with Harris Miller, Romano "Ron" Mazzoli Oral History Project, July 8, 2010.

131. Fuchs, "The Corpse That Would Not Die," 118.

132. Author interview with Rick Swartz, September 30, 2012.

133. Miller, " 'The Right Thing to Do'," 62.

134. Dan Balz, "Hispanic League's Gathering Heals Mondale Plea to Wield Ballot Power," *Washington Post*, July 3, 1982.

135. "Summary of Hearings Held by the Senate Judiciary Committee on Immigration and Refugee Policy, July 1981–April 1982." Over this period, Doris Meissner, acting commissioner of the Immigration and Naturalization Service (INS), Diego Asencio, assistant secretary of state for consular affairs, and Alan Nelson, deputy commissioner/commissioner of the INS were the witnesses to appear most often at the hearings, with eight, seven, and five appearances, respectively. Among Latino organizations during this period, LULAC testified five times, with Torres representing the organization on four occasions; MALDEF testified three times; and NCLR testified twice.

136. Per website of the American Immigration Lawyers Association, accessed December 15, 2015, http://aila.org/about.

137. Leslie C. Levin, "Specialty Bars as a Site of Professionalism: The Immigration Bar Example," *University of St. Thomas Law Journal* 8, no. 2 (2011), 201–9.

138. Author interview with Warren Leiden, April 26, 2013.

139. Levin, "Specialty Bars as a Site of Professionalism," 201.

140. John P. Heinz et al., *Urban Lawyers: The New Social Structure of the Bar* (2005), cited in Levin, "Specialty Bars as a Site of Professionalism," 223.

141. Michael S. Serrill, "Law: A Booming but Tainted Specialty," *Time*, July 8, 1985.

142. Remarks of Warren Leiden, "Reflecting on the Immigration Reform and Control Act of 1986," [Panel Presentation at Migration Policy Institute], January 30, 2014.

143. Among them were Ira Gollobin, called by Muzaffar Chishti the "Godfather of the Immigration Bar," Ira Kurzban, a Miami-based attorney who served as lead counsel in the Haitian Refugee Center case and a close friend of Rick Swartz, and Robert Juceam, a partner in the prestigious DC-based firm, Fried Frank, and a powerful player in the American Bar Association who would be instrumental in organizing major law firm and bar association support for pro-immigrant causes for several decades.

144. Author interview with Wade Henderson, February 26, 2013.

145. Author interview with Wade Henderson, March 8, 2013.

146. For a detailed accounting of the Palmer Raids see Robert K. Murray, *The Red Scare: A Study in National Hysteria, 1919–1920* (University of Minnesota Press, 1955) and Christopher M. Finan, *From Palmer Raids to Patriot Act: A History of the Fight for Free Speech in America* (Beacon Press, 2007).

147. Harlan Grant Cohen, "The Unforgivable Judgment of History," *New York University Law Review* 78 (2003), 1431.

148. "The Red Assassins," *Washington Post*, January 4, 1920, as cited in "Palmer Raids," *Wikipedia*, last modified April 7, 2014, http://en.wikipedia.org/wiki/Palmer_Raids.

149. Murray, *The Red Scare*, 250–51.

150. Author interview with Wade Henderson, December 19, 2012.

151. Author interview with Wade Henderson, March 8, 2013.

152. Author interview with Wade Henderson, February 26, 2013.

153. Author interview with Wade Henderson, December 19, 2012.

154. Author interview with Wade Henderson, February 26, 2013.

155. Author interview with Wade Henderson, December 19, 2012.

156. Author interview with Wade Henderson, December 19, 2012. There is a rich literature on the Great Migration, including Nicholas Lemann, *The Promised Land: The Great Black Migration and How It Changed America* (Vintage Press, 1991); James N. Gregory, *The Southern Diaspora: How the Great Migrations of Black and White Southerners Transformed America* (University of North Carolina Press, 2007); and especially, Isabel Wilkerson, *The Warmth of Other Suns: The Epic Story of America's Great Migration* (Random House, 2010).

157. Author interview with Wade Henderson, December 19, 2012.

158. Author interview with Rick Swartz, July 30, 2012.

159. Author interview with Antonia Hernández, October 30, 2012.

160. Author interview with Arnoldo Torres, January 17, 2013.

161. Author interview with Warren Leiden, April 26, 203; Author interview with Wade Henderson, February 26, 2013.

162. "Edward R. Roybal," *Hispanic Americans in Congress, 1822–1995*, Library of Congress, accessed January 24, 2014, http://www.loc.gov/rr/hispanic/congress/roybal .html.

163. "FEPC Battle in Council Revived," *Los Angeles Times*, June 8, 1956. See also, Katherine A. Diaz, "Congressman Edward R. Roybal: Los Angeles Before the 1960s," *Caminos* 4, no. 7 (July–August 1983).

164. "Edward R. Roybal."

165. Jack Rosenthal, "Latin Americans Sue U.S. on Rights," *New York Times*, October 23, 1971.

166. See for example, National Institute for Latino Policy, "Positive Movement on Addressing Latino Underrepresentation in Federal Jobs," *The NiLP Network on Latino Issues*, December 16, 2013, describing advocacy activity on the issue by the National Hispanic Leadership Agenda (NHLA), a coalition of the thirty-six leading national Latino civil rights organizations. Six weeks later, a subsequent NiLP posting included a letter to President Obama listing "Latino Inclusion in Federal Government" as one of the Hispanic community's top seven priorities; see "Latino Issues Issue Policy Priorities for State of the Union Speech," *The NiLP Network on Latino Issues*, January 28, 2014.

167. James T. Wooten, "President Seeks Legal Status for Many Aliens," *New York Times*, August 5, 1977.

168. "Edward R. Roybal," *Hispanic Americans in Congress, 1822–1995*.

169. "Disciplinary Actions by the House," *New York Times*, July 27, 1990. See also: "Edward R. Roybal," *Hispanic Americans in Congress, 1822–1995*, and interview with Dan Maldonado, August 15, 2012.

170. Barone and Ujifusa, *The Almanac of American Politics, 1982*, 125.

171. Author interview with Dan Maldonado, August 15, 2012.

172. Author interview with Warren Leiden, April 25, 2013.

173. Author interview with Jorge Lambrinos, November 14, 2012.

174. Author interview with Dan Maldonado, August 15, 2012.

175. Author interview with Henry Cisneros, October 5, 2012.

176. Author interview with Albert Jacquez, November 5, 2012.

177. Author interview with Skip Endres, November 8, 2012.

178. Author interview with Lynnette Conway Jacquez, September 14, 2012.

179. See: Miller, " 'The Right Thing to Do'."

180. Author interview with Phyllis Eisen, April 3, 2014.

181. Author interview with Skip Endres, November 8, 2012.

182. Author interview with Arnoldo Torres, February 21, 2014.

183. Author interview with Phyllis Eisen, April 3, 2014.

184. Author interview with Wade Henderson, March 8, 2013.

185. Author interview with Rick Swartz, July 30, 2012.

186. See for example, Kamasaki and Yzaguírre, "Black–Hispanic Tensions: One Perspective," 17–40.

187. Barone and Ujifusa, *The Almanac of American Politics 1986* (National Journal, Inc., 1985), 1327–28.

188. Author interview with Arnoldo Torres, February 21, 2014.

189. Author interview with Michael Myers, May 21, 2013.

190. Author interview with Arnoldo Torres, February 21, 2014.

191. Barone and Ujifusa, *The Almanac of American Politics, 1984* (National Journal, 1983), 144.

192. Author interview with Antonia Hernández, October 30, 2012.

193. Barone and Ujifusa, *The Almanac of American Politics, 1984*, 1156.

194. "Eligio 'Kika' De La Garza II," Hispanic Americans in Congress, Library of Congress, accessed April 10, 2014, http://www.loc.gov/rr/hispanic/congress/delagarza.html.

195. Matt S. Meier and Feliciano Ribera, *Mexican Americans/American Mexicans: From Conquistadors to Chicanos* (American Century, 1994), 222.

196. Barone and Ujifusa, *The Almanac of American Politics, 1984*, 1155.

197. Author interview with Antonia Hernández, October 30, 2012.

198. Author interview with Dan Maldonado, August 15, 2012.

199. Mathews, *Tip and the Gipper*, 60.

200. Jeffrey H. Birnbaum and Alan S. Murray, *Showdown at Gucci Gulch: Lawmakers, Lobbyists, and the Unlikely Triumph of Tax Reform* (Vintage Books, 1988), 166.

201. Author interview with Arnoldo Torres, February 21, 2014.

202. Mathews, *Tip and the Gipper*, 153.

203. Author interviews with Arnoldo Torres, January 17, 2013, and February 21, 2014.

204. Remini, *The House*, 451–52.

205. Barone and Ujifusa, *The Almanac of American Politics, 1982*, 1078.

206. Author interview with Arnoldo Torres, February 21, 2014.

207. Author interview with Rick Swartz, August 7, 2012.

208. Caplan, *Farther Along*, 217.

209. Remini, *The House*, 402.

210. Caplan, *Farther Along*, 217–18.

211. Author interview with Rick Swartz, August 7, 2012.

212. Author interview with Phyllis Eisen, April 3, 2014.

213. "Two Defective Immigration Proposals," *New York Times*, August 24, 1982, letter to the editor.

214. Author interview with Rick Swartz, August 7, 2012.

215. "Guerilla War on Immigration," *New York Times*, August 27, 1982, editorial.

216. See, for example, "Immigration Policy," in Annelise Anderson and Dennis L. Bark, eds., *Thinking About America: The United States in the 1990s* (Hoover Institution Press, 1988); "Illegal Aliens and Employer Sanctions: Solving the Wrong Problem," Hoover Essays in Public Policy, The Hoover Institution, 1986; and "U.S. Immigration

Policy in a Post-187 Era: Enforce the Law, But Preserve Civil Liberties," *Stanford Daily*, January 31, 1995.

217. Associated Press, "House Panel Takes Up Immigration Measure," *New York Times*, September 15, 1982.

218. Robert Pear, "House Committee Backs Penalties for Those Who Hire Illegal Aliens," *New York Times*, September 16, 1982.

219. Robert Pear, "House Panel Progressing on Immigration Bill," *New York Times*, September 17, 1982.

220. Readers interested in the details of some of these battles could do worse than to read Philip G. Schrag's *A Well-Founded Fear: The Congressional Battle to Save Asylum in America* (Routledge, 2000). Shari Robertson and Michael Camerini's outstanding documentary film, *Well-Founded Fear*, also released in 2000, shows how policies actually play out in practice, see: http://epidavros.org/well-founded-fear/.

221. Perotti, *Resolving Policy Conflict*, 157.

222. Robert Pear, "House Unit Backs Immigration Bill," *New York Times*, September 23, 1982.

223. Marjorie Hunter, "Congress: A One-Issue Session on 'Money, Money, Money," *New York Times*, August 20, 1982.

224. Miller, " 'The Right Thing to Do'," 62.

225. Barone and Ujifusa, *The Almanac of American Politics, 1984*, 242.

226. Pear, "House Unit Backs Immigration Bill."

227. Miller, " 'The Right Thing to Do'," 62.

228. Perotti, *Resolving Policy Conflict*, 15.

229. Author interview with Arnoldo Torres, February 21, 2014.

230. Author interview with Dan Maldonado, August 15, 2012.

231. Perotti, *Resolving Policy Conflict*, 158.

232. Pear, "House Unit Backs Immigration Bill."

233. Author interview with Arnoldo Torres, January 17, 2013.

234. Perotti, *Resolving Policy Conflict*, 240.

235. Miller, " 'The Right Thing to Do'," 63.

236. "Why Break the Immigration Clock?" *New York Times*, editorial, December 3, 1982.

237. Remarks of Tip O'Neill, *The Speaker from Texas*, KERA Television, documentary, 1987.

238. Birnbaum and Murray, *Showdown at Gucci Gulch*, 162.

239. Robert Pear, "Immigration Bill Is Cleared for House Debate," *New York Times*, December 9, 1982.

240. Author interview with Dan Maldonado, August 15, 2012.

241. Author interview with Warren Leiden, April 26, 2013; author interview with Arnoldo Torres, February 21, 2014; author interview with Antonia Hernández, October 30, 2012; see also, Nadine Cahodas, "Immigration Reform Measure Dies in the House," *Congressional Quarterly*, December 25, 1982, 3097.

242. Pear, "Immigration Bill Is Cleared for House Debate."

243. Cahodas, "Immigration Reform Measure Dies in the House," 3097.

244. LeMay, *Anatomy of a Public Policy*, 41.

245. *Congressional Record*, December 16, 1982, H10081 (Remarks of Rep. Mazzoli).

246. *Congressional Record*, December 16, 1982, H 10084 (Remarks of Rep. Roybal).

247. *Congressional Record*, December 16, 1982, H 10069 (Remarks of Rep. Rodino).

248. *Congressional Record*, December 16, 1982, H 10080–10083 (Remarks of Rep. Mazzoli).

249. *Congressional Record*, December 16, 1982, H 10083 (Remarks of Rep. Fish).

250. *Congressional Record*, December 16, 1982, H 10084 (Remarks of Rep. Roybal).

251. *Congressional Record*, December 16, 1982, H 10087 (Remarks of Rep. Mazzoli).

252. *Congressional Record*, December 16, 1982, H 10083–10086 (Remarks of Rep. Roybal).

253. *Congressional Record*, December 16, 1982, H 10089 (Remarks of Rep. González).

254. *Congressional Record*, December 16, 1982, H 10090 (Remarks of Rep. Mazzoli).

255. Pear, "Debate Is Heated over Immigration."

256. *Congressional Record*, December 17, 1982, H 10230 (Remarks of Rep. Lujan).

257. *Congressional Record*, December 17, 1982, H 10236–10237 (Remarks of Rep. de la Garza).

258. *Congressional Record*, December 17, 1982, H 10239–10242 (Remarks of Rep. García).

259. *Congressional Record*, December 17, 1982, H 10245–10261 (Remarks of Reps. Morrison, Erlenborn, and Lungren).

260. Miller, " 'The Right Thing to Do'," 63.

261. *Congressional Record*, December 18, 1982, H 10319 (Remarks of Rep. Wright and Announcement from the Speaker).

262. *Congressional Record*, December 18, 1982, H 10326 (Remarks of Rep. Hawkins).

263. *Congressional Record*, December 18, 1982, H 10236–10330 (Remarks of Reps. Mazzoli, Fish, Kazen, García, de la Garza, Rodino, Miller, and Conyers).

264. *Congressional Record*, December 18, 1982, H 10330 (Remarks of Rep. Lungren).

265. *Congressional Record*, December 18, 1982, H 10335–10336 (Remarks of Rep. Shaw).

266. *Congressional Record*, December 18, 1982, H 10336 (Remarks of Rep. Mazzoli).

267. Author interview with Arnoldo Torres, February 21, 2014.

268. Barone and Ujifusa, *The Almanac of American Politics, 1984*, 204–305.

269. *Congressional Record*, December 18, 1982, H 10350–10351 (Remarks of Reps. Hyde, de la Garza, and García).

270. Miller, " 'The Right Thing to Do'," 63.

271. Robert Pear, "What the House Said in Not Voting an Immigration Bill," *New York Times*, December 27, 1982.

272. Nadine Cahodas, "Immigration Reform Measure Dies in the House," *Congressional Quarterly*, December 25, 1982, 3098.

CHAPTER 4

1. Barone and Ujifusa, *The Almanac of American Politics 1984*, 1297–98.

2. Interview with Alan Simpson, Romano "Ron" Mazzoli Oral History Project, September 30, 2010.

3. Robert Pear, "Immigration Reform Is Alive and Well," *New York Times*, May 22, 1983.

4. Miller, " 'The Right Thing to Do'," 64.

5. Robert Pear, "New Drive Underway in Congress to Revamp U.S. Immigration Law," *New York Times*, February 22, 1983.

6. "Time to Turn the Illegal Tide," *New York Times*, editorial, February 21, 1983.

7. *House Hearings*, Subcommittee on Immigration, Refugees, and International Law, Committee on the Judiciary, March 1, 2, 9, 10, 14, and 16, 1983.

8. Milton Coleman, "Hispanics Hit Immigration Revision," *Washington Post*, February 26, 1983, A9.

9. Pear, "New Drive Underway in Congress to Revamp U.S. Immigration Law."

10. Author interview with Rick Swartz, August 7, 2012.

11. Donald Loren Hardy, *Shooting from the Lip: The Life of Senator Al Simpson* (University of Oklahoma Press, 2011), 76.

12. Perotti, *Resolving Policy Conflict*, 147.

13. Barone and Ujifusa, *The Almanac of American Politics 1984*, xxxvi–xlii.

14. "Forum Information Bulletin," vol. II, no. 3, National Immigration, Refugee & Citizenship Forum, newsletter, April 19, 1983.

15. Perotti, *Resolving Policy Conflict*, 252.

16. Robert Pear, "Senate Panel Backs Revisions in Immigration Law," *New York Times*, April 20, 1983.

17. *Congressional Record*, April 28, 1983, p. S 5531 (Remarks of Sen. Simpson).

18. *Congressional Record*, May 17, 1983, p. S12561 (Remarks of Sen. Simpson).

19. See generally, Ngai, *Impossible Subjects*, 152–66.

20. *Congressional Record*, May 17, 1983, pp. S12559–12561 (Remarks of Sen. Wilson).

21. *Congressional Record*, May 17, 1983, pp. S12561–12565 (Remarks of Sens. Simpson and Kennedy).

22. *Congressional Record*, May 17, 1983, p. S12580 (Roll Call vote no. 94).

23. *Congressional Record*, May 17, 1983, pp. S12557–12558 (Roll Call votes nos. 91, 92, and 93).

24. Author interview with Arnoldo Torres, October 8, 2014.

25. Barone and Ujifusa, *The Almanac of American Politics, 1982*, 520–21.

26. *Congressional Record*, May 17, 1983, p. 12585 (Remarks of Sen. Hart).

27. Author interview with Morton Halperin, December 18, 2015.

28. *Congressional Record*, May 17, 1983, 12586 (Letter from Michael N. Martinez to William A. Webb, May 5, 1983).

29. "The Immigration Reform Bill (S. 529) and Existing Protections Against Discrimination Based on Alienage," American Law Division, Congressional Research Service, May 12, 1983, memorandum, *Congressional Record*, May 17, 1983, 12588.

30. Perotti, *Resolving Policy Conflict*, 253.

31. "Forum Information Bulletin," vol. II, no. 4, National Immigration, Refugee & Citizenship Forum, newsletter, June 20, 1983.

32. Perotti, *Resolving Policy Conflict*, 204.

33. *Congressional Record*, May 18, 1983, p. 12840 (Roll Call no. 99).

34. Robert Pear, "Senate Approves Immigration Bill with Hiring Curb," *New York Times*, May 19, 1983.

35. *Congressional Record*, May 18, 1983, p. 12865 (Remarks of Sen. Simpson).

36. "Forum Information Bulletin," vol. II, no. 3, National Immigration, Refugee & Citizenship Forum, newsletter, April 19, 1983.

37. "Forum Information Bulletin," vol. II, no. 4, National Immigration, Refugee & Citizenship Forum, newsletter, June 20, 1983.

38. Nadine Cahodas, "Peter Rodino Turns Judiciary into a Legislative Graveyard," *Congressional Quarterly Weekly Report*, May 12, 1984, pp. 1097–1102.

39. Robert Pear, "Immigration Reform Is Alive and Well," *New York Times*, May 22, 1983.

40. Robert Pear, "U.S. and a Catholic Group Set Alien Amnesty Program," *New York Times*, May 21, 1983.

41. Pear, "Immigration Reform Is Alive and Well."

42. Pear, "Immigration Reform Is Alive and Well."

43. Charles F. Hemphill Jr. and Phyllis D. Hemphill, *The Dictionary of Practical Law* (Prentice Hall, 1979), as cited in Perotti, *Resolving Policy Conflict*, 209.

44. Author interview with Arnoldo Torres, January 17, 2013.

45. Perotti, *Resolving Policy Conflict*, 237.

46. Library of Congress, "Bill Summary and Status, 97th Congress (1981–1982), H.R.6514, All Congressional Actions," http://thomas.loc.gov/cgi-bin/bdquery/D?do97:3:./temp/~bdQsNa@@@X/home/Legislation, accessed April 23, 2012.

47. "Unabridged Chronology," internal NCLR document, revised August 26, 2008.

48. Alicia A. Garza, "WESLACO, TX," *Handbook of Texas Online*, Texas State Historical Association, June 15, 2010, http://www.tshaonline.org/handbook/online/articles/hew04, accessed May 30, 2014.

49. Author interview with Raul Yzaguírre, July 9, 2012.

50. Christine Marie Sierra, "Latino Organizational Strategies on Immigration Reform: Success and Limits in Public Policymaking," in Roberto E. Villarreal and Norma G. Hernandez, *Latinos and Political Coalitions* (Praeger, 1991), 66.

51. Dale Maharidge, *The Coming White Minority: California, Multiculturalism, and America's Future* (Vintage Books, 1996), 75.

52. Author interview with Martha Escutia, November 1, 2012.

53. Maharidge, *The Coming White Minority*, 12.

54. Author interview with Martha Escutia, November 1, 2012.

55. Edward Kostner, "Price of Fame," *Wall Street Journal*, book review, June 13, 2014.

56. Ben Zimmer, "Politicians Never Seem to Tire of 'Baloney,'" *Wall Street Journal*, May 23–24, 2015.

57. See: Sylvia Jukes Morris, *Price of Fame: The Honorable Clare Boothe Luce* (Random House, 2014).

58. William Raspberry, "An Awful Interview," *Washington Post*, August 25, 1982.

59. Raspberry, "An Awful Interview."

60. To put this grant in perspective, according to its audited financial statements, in 2013 the Henry Luce Foundation had net assets in excess of $840 million, including amounts left to it by Clare Boothe Luce valued at $155 million, and it awarded about $33.5 million in grants. A $40,000 grant in 1983, equivalent to about $93,500 in 2013, would have been a tiny fraction of the foundation's grant making even in the 1980s. See Henry R. Luce Foundation, Inc. Financial Statements, December 31, 2013, at: http://www.hluce.org/files/documents/luceaudit2013signed.pdf, accessed July 3, 2014.

61. "Hearing on Employment Discrimination and Immigration Reform, *House Hearings*, Subcommittee on Employment Opportunities, Committee on Education and Labor, May 19, 1982.

62. "Immigration Reform and Control Act of 1983," *House Hearings*, Committee on Agriculture, June 15, 1983, Serial No. 98-14, 94.

63. The initial portion of the hearing was presided over by the next-ranking Democrat, Rep. James Scheuer (D-NY); see "Immigration Reform and Control Act of 1983,"

House Hearings, Subcommittee on Health and the Environment, Committee on Energy and Commerce, June 17, 1983, 1–3.

64. See statements and subsequent discussion of Anthony J. Pellechio and Charles Seagrave in "Immigration Reform and Control Act of 1983," *House Hearings*, Subcommittee on Health and the Environment, Committee on Energy and Commerce, June 17, 1983, 193–211.

65. Statement of David S. North, "Immigration Reform and Control Act of 1983," *House Hearings*, Subcommittee on Health and the Environment, Committee on Energy and Commerce, June 17, 1983, 214.

66. Author interview with Michael Myers, December 17, 2012.

67. "Forum Information Bulletin," vol. III, no. 1, National Immigration, Refugee & Citizenship Forum, March 19, 1984.

68. Perotti, *Resolving Policy Conflict*, 204.

69. MALDEF had been an especially vigorous proponent of these arguments, prior to, during, and after the IRCA debate. See Wendy Fox, "Aliens and the Right to Work: Congress Comes to Terms with the Problem of Employment Discrimination Against Aliens," *Washington University Law Review*, vol. 65, no. 1, January 1987, for a good historical overview; see also "Written Testimony of Thomas A. Saenz, MALDEF," National Origin in Today's Workplace, Meeting of the US Equal Employment Opportunity Commission, November 13, 2013, for a more contemporary discussion, http://www.eeoc.gov/eeoc/meetings/11-13-13/saenz.cfm, accessed July 9, 2015.

70. "Forum Information Bulletin," vol. II, no. 5, National Immigration, Refugee & Citizenship Forum, August 19, 1983.

71. Miller, " 'The Right Thing to Do'," 65.

72. Fuchs, "The Corpse That Would Not Die," 119.

73. Milton Coleman, "Hispanics' Issues: Cutbacks, Clout," *Washington Post*, June 30, 1983.

74. Coleman, "Hispanics' Issues: Cutbacks, Clout."

75. Cose, *A Nation of Strangers*, 163.

76. Steve Reisman, "Enthusiastic Coast Hispanic Groups Hear President Defend Record," *New York Times*, August 26, 1983.

77. Francis X. Cline, "If This Is Washington, It Must Be 'Hispanic Week,' " *New York Times*, September 16, 1983.

78. Author interview with Arnoldo Torres, December 20, 2013.

79. Author interview with Richard Fajardo, October 30, 2012.

80. Author interviews with Rick Swartz, July 30 and August 7, 2012.

81. Author interview with Antonia Hernández, October 30, 2012.

82. Author interview with Antonia Hernández, October 30, 2012; Author interview with Richard Fajardo, October 30, 2012.

83. Author interview with Richard Fajardo, October 30, 2012.

84. Author interview with Martha Escutia, November 1, 2012.

85. Author interview with Richard Fajardo, October 30, 2012, and author interview with Martha Escutia, November 1, 2012.

86. Author interview with Martha Escutia, November 1, 2012.

87. Author interview with Richard Fajardo, October 30, 2012.

88. Author interview with Richard Fajardo, October 30, 2012, and author interview with Martha Escutia, November 1, 2012.

89. Author interview with Martha Escutia, November 1, 2012.

90. Cose, *A Nation of Strangers*, 164.

91. Author interview with George Slover, February 22, 2013.

92. Author interview with Richard Fajardo, October 30, 2012.

93. Charles Kamasaki and Martha Escutia, "Effectiveness of Labor Law Enforcement in Deterring Illegal Immigration," NCLR Issue Brief, March 1984.

94. Charles Kamasaki and Martha Escutia, "Critique of HHS and CBO Cost Estimates of Legalization," NCLR Issue Brief, June 1, 1984.

95. Author interview with Richard Fajardo, October 30, 2012.

96. Author interview with Rick Swartz, July 30, 2012.

97. Author interview with Martha Escutia, November 1, 2012.

98. Carlyle Murphy, "FAIR Leader Fights for Immigration Curbs," *Washington Post*, November 29, 1983.

99. Cortés, *Policy Analysts and Interest Groups*, 254.

100. Murphy, "FAIR Leader Fights for Immigration Curbs."

101. V. Lance Tarrance and Associates and Peter D. Hart Research Associates, "Hispanic and Black Attitudes Toward Immigration Policy: A Nationwide Survey Conducted for the Federation for American Immigration Reform," V. Lance Tarrance & Associates, June-July 1983.

102. Cited in Cose, *A Nation of Strangers*, 166.

103. William Raspberry, "Black v. Brown? Not Necessarily," *Washington Post*, September 16, 1983.

104. "The Speaker, on the Border," *New York Times*, September 25, 1983.

105. Cited in: Cose, *A Nation of Strangers*, 166–67.

106. Cortés, *Policy Analysis and Interest Groups*, 284.

107. Frank Sotomayor, "The Times Poll: Most Latinos Back Amnesty for Illegal Aliens," *Los Angeles Times*, 1983, cited in Cose, *A Nation of Strangers*, 166.

108. David Reimers, *Still the Golden Door: The Third World Comes to America* (Columbia University Press, 1992), 243.

109. Barone and Ujifusa, *The Almanac of American Politics, 1984*.

110. Miller Center, "Interview with Annelise Anderson," University of Virginia, December 17, 2002, http://millercenter.org/president/reagan/oralhistory/annelise -anderson, accessed July 24, 2014.

111. Glenn Garvin, "Documenting America," *Chicago Tribune*, October 11, 1995; see also, Richard Reeves, *President Reagan: The Triumph of Imagination* (Simon and Schuster, 2005), 76.

112. Fuchs, "The Corpse That Would Not Die," 120.

113. Robert Pear, "Aliens' Farm Wage Divides U.S. Aides," *New York Times*, August 13, 1983.

114. Robert Pear, "O'Neill Says Bill on Illegal Aliens Is Dead for 1983," *New York Times*, October 5, 1983.

115. National Immigration, Refugee & Citizenship Forum, "Forum Information Bulletin," vol. II, no. 5, August 19, 1983, p. 1.

116. Miller, " 'The Right Thing to Do'," 65.

117. "Let the House Vote on Immigration Bill," *Christian Science Monitor*, July 25, 1983.

118. Cose, *A Nation of Strangers*, 163.

119. Cline, "If This Is Washington, It Must Be 'Hispanic Week.' "

120. Miller, " 'The Right Thing to Do'," 65–66.

121. Fuchs, "The Corpse That Would Not Die," 120.

122. Author interview with Dan Maldonado, August 15, 2012.

123. Dick Kirshten, "The Hispanic Vote—Parties Can't Gamble That the Sleeping Giant Won't Awaken," *National Journal*, November 19, 1983, and interview with Dan Maldonado, August 15, 2012.

124. "The Speaker, on the Border," *New York Times*, editorial, September 25, 1983.

125. T. R. Reid, "Suspects Double-Cross: O'Neill Exercises Power, Bars Immigration Bill," *Washington Post*, October 5, 1983, as cited in Cose, *A Nation of Strangers*, 167.

126. Pear, "O'Neill Says Bill on Illegal Aliens Is Dead for 1983."

127. Miller, "'The Right Thing to Do'," 67.

128. Pear, "O'Neill Says Bill on Illegal Aliens Is Dead for 1983."

129. Robert Pear, "Immigration and Politics," *New York Times*, October 6, 1983.

130. Reid, "Suspects Double-Cross," 167.

131. Author interview with Dan Maldonado, August 15, 2012.

132. Pear, "O'Neill Says Bill on Illegal Aliens Is Dead for 1983."

133. "Immigration Reform, O'Neill Style," *New York Times*, October 9, 1983.

134. Miller, "'The Right Thing to Do'," 66.

135. "The Speaker as Gravedigger," *Boston Globe*, editorial, October 5, 1982.

136. Miller, "'The Right Thing to Do'," 66.

137. Perotti, *Resolving Policy Conflict*, 270.

138. Strout, "Reagan Pledges Support for Stalled Immigration Bill."

139. Perotti, *Resolving Policy Conflict*, 161 and footnote 20.

140. Cose, *A Nation of Strangers*, 168.

141. Remini, *The House*, 463.

142. David Broder, *Washington Post*, April 22, 1982, cited in Mathews, *Tip and the Gipper*, 199.

143. David Rogers, "Immigration Bill Promised," *Boston Globe*, November 23, 1983.

144. Cose, *A Nation of Strangers*, 168.

145. Fuchs, "The Corpse That Would Not Die," 120.

146. Cose, *A Nation of Strangers*, 168.

147. Martin Tolchin, "O'Neill Now Favors Revision of Immigration Laws," *New York Times*, November 30, 1983; see also, Rogers, "Immigration Bill Promised."

148. Associated Press, "O'Neill to Allow Vote in '84 on Immigration Bill," *Boston Globe*, December 1, 1983.

149. "Bordering on Immigration Reform," *New York Times*, December 11, 1983.

150. Caplan, *Farther Along: A Civil Rights Memoir*, 203.

151. Author interview with Warren Leiden, April 26, 2013.

152. Author interview with Warren Leiden, January 30, 2014.

153. Author interview with Richard Fajardo, October 30, 2012.

154. Author interview with Michael Myers, December 17, 2012.

155. Email exchange with Rick Swartz and Muzaffar Chishti, November 4–17, 2014.

156. Title IV: National Commission on Immigration, "Immigration Reform Act of 1984," H.R. 4909, 98th Congress.

157. Ida A. Brudnick, "Support Offices in the House of Representatives: Roles and Authorities," Congressional Research Service, February 5, 2013, 4.

158. Kris Kitto, "Drafting History," *The Hill*, September 21, 2009.

159. Robert Pear, "It Should Be Called the Grossman Health Care Bill," *New York Times*, November 26, 1993.

160. Pear, "It Should Be Called the Grossman Health Care Bill."

161. Pear, "It Should Be Called the Grossman Health Care Bill."

162. Author interview with Arnoldo Torres, January 17, 2013.

163. Author interview with Rick Swartz, July 30, 2012.

164. Author interview with Arnoldo Torres, January 17, 2013.

165. Raul Yzaguírre, "Immigration Reform: An Appeal to Common Sense," National Council of La Raza, November 1983.

166. See letter from Richard Day to Raul Yzaguírre dated December 27, 1983, in *NCLR Records*, Series M744, Box 141, folder 2, and letter from Raul Yzaguírre to Richard Day dated January 10, 1984, *NCLR Records*, Series M744, Box 141, Folder 5.

167. Author interview with Raul Yzaguírre, September 7, 2013.

168. Author interview with Richard Fajardo, October 30, 2012.

169. Author interview with Arnoldo Torres, January 17, 2013.

170. Francis X. Clines, "Reagan Says His Opponents Risk Central America Influx," *New York Times*, June 21, 1983.

171. "The Monroe Doctrine (1823)," Internet Archive, undated, http://web.archive.org/web/20120108131055/http://eca.state.gov/education/engteaching/pubs/AmLnC/br50.htm, accessed January 29, 2016.

172. Andrew J. Bacevich, "American Imperium," *Harpers*, May 2016, 31.

173. See generally, Walter LeFeber, *Inevitable Revolutions: The United States in Central America* (W. W. Norton and Company, 1993).

174. Bacevich, "American Imperium," 31.

175. Mark Robert Schneider, *Joe Moakley's Journey: From South Boston to El Salvador* (Northeastern University Press, 2013), 127.

176. Juan Gonzalez, *Harvest of Empire: A History of Latinos in America* (Penguin Books, 2011), 131, and "United States of America Gross GDP Per Capita, 1980," http://data.worldbank.org/indicator/NY.GDP.PCAP.CD?page=6, accessed January 29, 2016.

177. Schneider, *Joe Moakley's Journey*, 128.

178. Gonzalez, *Harvest of Empire*, 133.

179. LeFeber, *Inevitable Revolutions*, 218–20.

180. Russell Crandall, *America's Dirty Wars: Irregular Warfare from 1776 to the War on Terror* (Cambridge University Press, 2014), 310–11.

181. LeFeber, *Inevitable Revolutions*, 243–44.

182. José Napoleón Duarte, *Duarte: My Story* (Putnam, 1986), cited in Crandall, *America's Dirty Wars*, 313.

183. LeFeber, *Inevitable Revolutions*, 245.

184. Schneider, *Joe Moakley's Journey*, 128.

185. Crandall, *America's Dirty Wars*, 314.

186. LeFeber, *Inevitable Revolutions*, 250.

187. Schneider, *Joe Moakley's Journey*, 129.

188. LeFeber, *Inevitable Revolutions*, 255.

189. Schneider, *Joe Moakley's Journey*, 129.

190. LeFeber, *Inevitable Revolutions*, 278–79.

191. Calculations by the author based on data in LeFeber, *Inevitable Revolutions*, 362.

192. Gonzalez, *Harvest of Empire*, 129.

193. National Immigration, Refugee, & Citizenship Forum, "Legalization," background paper, June 1983, p. 10.

194. National Immigration and Alien Rights Project, *Salvadorans in the United States: The Case for Extended Voluntary Departure* (American Civil Liberties Union, April 1984), 4.

195. LeFeber, *Inevitable Revolutions*, 316–17.

196. *Refugee Problems in Central America,* Staff Report prepared for the use of the Subcommittee on Immigration and Refugee Policy, Committee on the Judiciary, US Senate, September 1983, US Government Printing Office, 1984, reference to human rights on p. 16, reference to lack of evidence that returnees were harmed on p. 29.

197. Letter from William French Smith to Rep. Moakley, July 19, 1983.

198. For an unusually lucid, contemporaneous, nontechnical explanation of the issues involved, see: Robert Pear, "Q&A on Asylum: Some of the Ins and Outs of Who Gets In," *New York Times*, May 26, 1985.

199. National Immigration and Alien Rights Project, *Salvadorans in the United States: The Case for Extended Voluntary Departure*, 6–7.

200. Barone and Ujifusa, *The Almanac of American Politics 1984*, 561.

201. Schneider, *Joe Moakley's Journey*, 125–127.

202. Robert Pear, "Stockman Warns Immigration Bill Too Costly," *New York Times,* January 19, 1984.

203. Author interview with Arnoldo Torres, January 17, 2013.

204. Author interview with Jorge Lambrinos, November 14, 2012.

205. Author interview with Warren Leiden, April 26, 2013.

206. Michael Barone and Grant Ujifusa, *The Almanac of American Politics 1986*, National Journal, 1985, 880.

207. Author interview with Arnoldo Torres, October 8, 2014.

208. Author interview with Rick Swartz, July 30, 2012.

209. Robert Pear, "Congress: On Immigration, a Power Behind the Scenes," *New York Times*, April 7, 1984.

210. Robert Pear, "Immigration Bill Is Hardly Home Free," *New York Times*, April 8, 1984.

211. Victoria McGrane, "George Dalley: Rep. Charles B. Rangel's Chief of Staff Savors Third Tour," *Politico*, April 24, 2008.

212. Associated Press, "Mondale Accepts Support of AFL-CIO in Campaign," *New Hanover-Brunswick News*, October 7, 1983.

213. Cose, *A Nation of Strangers*, 169.

214. Juan Williams, "Hispanic Leaders Attack Mondale for Skipping Their Conference," *Washington Post*, April 19, 1984.

215. McGrane, "George Dalley: Rep. Charles B. Rangel's Chief of Staff Savors Third Tour."

216. Robert Pear, "O'Neill to Delay Debate on Aliens," *New York Times*, May 3, 1984.

217. Robert Pear, "The Hesitant House," *New York Times*, May 7, 1984.

218. "Hispanic Votes vs. Public Interest," *New York Times*, editorial, April 27, 1984.

219. Author interview with Dan Maldonado, August 15, 2012.

220. Pear, "O'Neill to Delay Debate on Aliens."

221. Perotti, *Resolving Policy Conflict*, 161.

222. Cose, *A Nation of Strangers*, 171.

223. Cited in Perotti, *Resolving Policy Conflict*, 184.

224. Phil Gailey, "Sen. Tower Says He Won't Run for Seat in '84," *New York Times*, August 24, 1983.

225. David Frum, "Righter Than Newt," *The Atlantic online*, March 1995, http://www.theatlantic.com/past/politics/policamp/gramm.htm, accessed August 17, 2014.

226. Wayne King, "Texas Politicians Are Scrambling to Succeed Tower in Senate," *New York Times*, January 30, 1984.

227. Wayne King, "Rivals Preparing for Texas Runoff," *New York Times*, May 20, 1984.

228. Richard Dunham, "Ten Biggest Texas Political Comebacks of the Past Half-Century," *Texas on the Potomac*, posted August 2, 2012, http://blog.mysanantonio.com/texas-on-the-potomac/2012/08/ten-biggest-texas-political-comebacks-of-the-past-half-century/, accessed August 8, 2014.

229. Frum, "Righter Than Newt."

230. Patricia Kilday Hart, "Not So Great in '78," *Texas Monthly*, June 1999.

231. Scott Crass, "Kent Hance Beat Bush for Congress in 1978," *The Moderate Voice*, posted June 11, 2013, http://themoderatevoice.com/18297/hance-beat-bush-for-congress-in-1978/, accessed September 29, 2013.

232. Hart, "Not So Great in '78."

233. J. H. Hatfield, *Fortunate Son: George W. Bush and the Making of an American President* (Soft Skull Press, Third Edition, 2002), 63.

234. King, "Rivals Preparing for Texas Runoff."

235. "Conservative Holds Lead in Texas Senate Primary," *New York Times*, June 3, 1984.

236. "Tom O'Donnell, Co-Founder and Managing Partner, Gephardt Government Affairs," Gephardt Government Affairs bio, http://www.gephardtdc.com/bios/gga_bio_todonnell.pdf, undated, accessed August 15, 2014.

237. Associated Press, "Doggett, Hance Lock Horns at Convention," *Victoria Advocate*, May 13, 1984.

238. At the congressman's request, Kamasaki arranged for Hance to meet with Samuel Sanchez, a former NCLR affiliate executive director and an up-and-coming elected official in his native South Texas later that year.

239. Perotti, *Resolving Policy Conflict*, 264.

240. "The Speaker from Texas," KERA-TV, documentary, aired February 3, 1987.

241. John Korry, "TV Review: 'Speaker from Texas,' on Jim Wright, *New York Times*, February 3, 1987.

242. "Staring at Immigration," *New York Times*, editorial, June 6, 1984.

243. Robert Pear, "House Girds to Take Up Touchy Immigration Bill," *New York Times*, June 8, 1984.

244. Steven V. Roberts, "Roybal Digs in His Heels on Immigration," *New York Times*, June 10, 1984.

245. *Congressional Record*, June 11, 1984, p. H 5529-10 (Remarks of Rep. Pepper).

246. Miller, "'The Right Thing to Do'," 66.

247. "Weather History for Washington, DC," Weather Underground, http://www.wunderground.com/history/airport/KDCA/1984/6/11/DailyHistory.html?req_city=NA&req_state=NA&req_statename=NA, accessed September 5, 2014.

248. Barone and Ujifusa, *The Almanac of American Politics 1986*, 119.

249. *Congressional Record*, June 11, 1984, p. H 5536 (Remarks of Rep. Schroeder).

250. Robert Pear, "House to Debate Immigration Bill Despite Pleas of Hispanic Groups," *New York Times*, June 12, 1984.

251. Author interview with Michael Myers, May 21, 2013.

252. Steven Greenhouse, "Evelyn DuBrow, Labor Lobbyist, Dies at 95," *New York Times*, June 22, 2006.

253. Author interview with Muzaffar Chishti, January 19, 2013.

254. Greenhouse, "Evelyn DuBrow, Labor Lobbyist, Dies at 95."

255. Christine Marie Sierra, "Latino Organizational Strategies on Immigration Reform: Success and Limits in Public Policymaking," in Roberto E. Villarreal and Norma G. Hernandez, eds., *Latinos and Political Coalitions* (Praeger, 1991), 63.

256. Mark Arax, "MALDEF Attorney to Join Policy Group," *Los Angeles Times*, June 14, 188.

257. Cose, *A Nation of Strangers*, 181.

258. For background on the National Network, see: http://www.nnirr.org/drupal/; Tamayo's bio can be found at: http://www.pli.edu/Content/Faculty/William_R _Tamayo/_/N-4oZ1z12g9c?ID=PE234659, accessed August 28, 2014.

CHAPTER 5

1. Barone and Ujifusa, *The Almanac of American Politics 1986*, 528.

2. Interview with Romano "Ron" Mazzoli, May 14, 2010, Romano (Ron) Mazzoli Oral History Project.

3. Interview with Lynnette Conway Jacquez, Romano "Ron" Mazzoli Oral History Project, October 1, 2010, part 2.

4. *Congressional Record*, June 12, 1984, H5617–24 (Remarks of Rep. García).

5. National Immigration, Refugee & Citizenship Forum, "Forum Information Bulletin," vol. III, no. 1, March 19, 1984, 9.

6. Perotti, *Resolving Policy Conflict*, 205.

7. The Forum's usually highly perceptive newsletter failed to mention Frank's amendment; see: National Immigration, Refugee & Citizenship Forum, "Forum Information Bulletin," vol. III, no. 1, March 19, 1984, and cover memorandum dated April 4, 1984.

8. *Congressional Record,* June 12, 1984, 5642.

9. Barone and Ujifusa, *The Almanac of American Politics 1986*, 1290–91.

10. *Congressional Record,* June 12, 1984, 5643–44 (remarks of Reps. Erlenborn, Bartlett, and McCain).

11. *Congressional Record,* June 12, 1984, 5645 (Remarks of Rep. Hall).

12. *Congressional Record,* June 12, 1984, 5445–51 (Remarks of Reps. Hall, Mazzoli, Bartlett, Lungren, Berman, de la Garza, Glickman, Evans, Gramm and Wright).

13. *Congressional Record*, June 12, 1984, 5658 (Roll Call vote no. 30).

14. *Congressional Record*, June 13, 1984, 5681 (Remarks of Rep. Mazzoli).

15. *Congressional Record*, June 13, 1984, 5683 (Remarks of Rep. Lungren).

16. *Congressional Record*, June 13, 1984, 5694 (Remarks of Rep. Schroeder).

17. *Congressional Record*, June 13, 1984, 5698 (Remarks of Rep. Mazzoli).

18. *Congressional Record*, June 13, 1984, 5702 (Roll call No. 231).

19. Mazzoli's requests for a time agreement and objections by Reps. Boxer, Richardson, and García can be found at *Congressional Record*, June 13, 1984, 5705–6.

20. *Congressional Record*, June 13, 1984, 5716 (Roll Call No. 232).

21. Joyce Vialet, "Immigration Issues and legislation in the 98th Congress," Issue

Brief Number IB83087, Library of Congress, Congressional Research Service, Updated December 2, 1983, 8–9.

22. *Congressional Record*, June 13, 1984, 5735–38 (Remarks of Reps. Ottinger, Mazzoli, McCollum and Rodino).

23. *Congressional Record*, June 13, 1984, 5738–39 (Remarks of Rep. McCollum).

24. *Congressional Record*, June 13, 1984, 5738–43 (Remarks of Reps. McCollum, Richardson, Rodino, Ottinger, and Fish).

25. *Congressional Record*, June 13, 1984, 5748 (Remarks of Reps. Mazzoli, Coleman, Lungren, and Ottinger).

26. *Congressional Record*, June 13, 1984, 5776 (Remarks of Reps. García, Mazzoli and Lungren).

27. *Congressional Record*, June 13, 1984, 5778–83 (Remarks of Reps. Frank and Rodino and supplementary material).

28. Author interview with Rick Swartz, August 7, 2012.

29. See, for example, "Dissenting Comment" by William Ong Hing in Doris Meissner, Deborah Myers, Demetrios G. Papademetriou, and Michael Fix, *Immigration and America's Future*, Report of the Independent Task Force on Immigration and America's Future, Spencer Abraham and Lee H. Hamilton, Co-Chairs, Migration Policy Institute, September 2006, 151–52.

30. *Congressional Record*, June 14, 1984, 5810–14 (Remarks of Reps. Morrison, Miller, and Berman).

31. *Congressional Record*, June 14, 1984, 5825–37.

32. See, for example, discussion in Deirdre Martínez, *Who Speaks for Hispanics?* (SUNY Press, 2009), 137–145.

33. Barone and Ujifusa, *The Almanac of American Politics 1986*, 117.

34. Tom Hale, president of the Farm Labor Alliance, cited in Perotti, *Resolving Policy Conflict*, 215–16.

35. "Panetta, Leon Edward," *Biographical Directory of the United States Congress, 1774–Present*, http://bioguide.congress.gov/scripts/biodisplay.pl?index=P000047, accessed May 10, 2015.

36. Patrick Quinn, executive vice president of the National Council of Agricultural Employers, cited in Perotti, *Resolving Policy Conflict*, 216.

37. Referring to Morrison's 31 percent rating by the Consumer Federation of America, 29 percent by the League of Conservation Voters, and 42 percent by the League of Women Voters, cited in Barone and Ujifusa, *The Almanac of American Politics 1986*, 1243.

38. *Congressional Record*, June 14, 1984, 5839 (Remarks of Rep. Panetta).

39. *Congressional Record*, June 14, 1984, 5841–42 (Remarks of Rep. Morrison).

40. National Immigration, Refugee & Citizenship Forum, *Forum Information Bulletin*, vol. III, no. 1, March 19, 1984, 11–12.

41. *Congressional Record*, June 14, 1984, 5843 (Remarks of Rep. Frank).

42. *Congressional Record*, June 14, 1984, 5815–16 (Remarks of Rep. González).

43. *Congressional Record*, June 14, 1984, 5866 (Remarks of Rep. Torres).

44. Barone and Ujifusa, *The Almanac of American Politics 1986*, 121 (Lehman) and 1040 (Goodling).

45. *Congressional Record*, June 14, 1984, 5869 (Remarks of Rep. Mazzoli).

46. *Congressional Record*, June 14, 1984, 5869–70 (Roll Call No. 241).

47. *Congressional Record*, June 15, 1984, 5907 (Remarks of Reps. Owens, Roybal, Mazzoli, and Fish).

48. Barone and Ujifusa, *The Almanac of American Politics 1984*, 158.

49. See for example, Kevin Johnson, *The Huddled Masses Myth: Immigration and Civil Rights* (Temple University Press, 2003), 94–108.

50. Text of the Brown amendment in *Congressional Record*, June 15, 1984, 5908.

51. *Congressional Record*, June 15, 1984, 5908–10 (Remarks of Reps. Brown, Mazzoli, Lungren and Fish).

52. *Congressional Record*, June 15, 1984, 5911 (remarks of Reps. Waxman and Mazzoli).

53. Barone and Ujifusa, *The Almanac of American Politics 1984*, 527.

54. *Congressional Record*, June 15, 1984, 5911–13 (remarks of Reps. Mitchell, Mazzoli, Fascell, and Roybal).

55. Charles D. Thompson Jr. and Melinda F. Wiggins, *The Human Cost of Food* (University of Texas Press, 2009), 266.

56. *Congressional Record*, October 8, 1994, E2187–88 (Remarks of Rep. Ford).

57. *Congressional Record*, June 15, 1984, 5914 (Remarks of Reps. Ford, Lungren, and Mazzoli).

58. *Congressional Record*, June 15, 1984, 5915.

59. Perotti, *Resolving Policy Conflict*, 259.

60. *Congressional Record*, June 15, 1984, 5917 (Remarks of Rep. Mazzoli).

61. Robert Pear, "Backers Studying Immigration Bill," *New York Times*, June 16, 1984.

62. Miller, " 'The Right Thing to Do'," 64.

63. Under the so-called "King of the Hill" procedure, unless otherwise specified by the rule the last amendment adopted in a section would trump previously adopted amendments.

64. *Congressional Record*, June 19, 1984, 6033 (Remarks of Rep. Lungren).

65. Letter from Attorney General William French Smith to Rep. Hamilton Fish, June 19, 1984, included in *Congressional Record*, June 19, 1984, 6050.

66. Barone and Ujifusa, *The Almanac of American Politics 1986*, 304.

67. *Congressional Record*, June 19, 1984, 6045 (Remarks of Rep. Frank).

68. *Congressional Record*, June 19, 1984, 6060 (Roll Call No. 245) and 6064–65 (Roll Call No. 246).

69. Interview with J. Michael Treviño cited in Perotti, *Resolving Policy Conflict*, 264.

70. *Congressional Record*, June 19, 1984, 6076–77 (Roll Call No. 247).

71. *Congressional Record*, June 19, 1984, 6078 (remarks of Rep. Mazzoli).

72. Author interview with Martha Escutia, November 1, 2012.

73. Christopher Beam, "Cool Whip, What Does a Congressional 'Whip' Actually do?" *Slate.com*, March 30, 2010, http://www.slate.com/articles/news_and_politics /explainer/2010/03/cool_whip.html, accessed May 11, 2015.

74. Author interview with Martha Escutia, November 1, 2012.

75. *Congressional Record*, June 20, 1984, 6088–90 (Remarks of Reps. Mineta, Lungren, McCollum, and Mazzoli).

76. The so-called "enforcement first" posture is also known as "attrition"; see, for example, Daniel Strauss, "Chris Christie Signals Support for Ted Cruz's Immigration Strategy," *Politico*, January 19, 2016, http://www.politico.com/story/2016/01/chris -christie-ted-cruz-immigration-217996, accessed January 20, 2016.

77. *Congressional Record*, June 20, 1984, 6092–93 (Remarks of Rep. McCollum).

78. *Congressional Record*, June 20, 1984, 6115–16 (Remarks of Rep. Torres).

79. *Congressional Record*, June 20, 1984, 6116 (Remarks of Rep. Kemp).

80. *Congressional Record*, June 20, 1984, 6123 (Roll Call No. 249).

81. See "Cuban–Haitian Adjustment Act," *Forum Information Bulletin*, vol. III, no. 1, March 19, 1984, 15–16; Author interview with Rick Swartz, July 30, 2012.

82. Author interview with Michael Myers and Muzaffar Chishti, December 17, 2012.

83. Author interview with Muzaffar Chishti and Michael Myers, May 21, 2013.

84. Stephen Kurczy, "5 Reasons Why Haiti's Jean Claude Duvalier Is Infamous," *Christian Science Monitor*, January 20, 2011.

85. Elizabeth Abbott, *Haiti: The Duvaliers and Their Legacy* (McGraw-Hill, 1988).

86. Kurczy, "5 Reasons Why Haiti's Jean-Claude Duvalier Is Infamous."

87. Chuck Leddy, "The Only Successful Slave Revolt in the World," *Christian Science Monitor*, March 23, 2004.

88. Albert Prago, *The Revolutions in Spanish America* (McMillan Company, 1970), 194.

89. *Congressional Record*, June 20, 1984, 6123–24 (Remarks of Rep. Rodino).

90. *Congressional Record*, June 20, 1984, 6128 (Remarks of Rep. González).

91. Sec. 501(a) of National Commission on Immigration, in *Congressional Record*, June 20, 1984, 6135–37.

92. *Congressional Record*, June 20, 1984, 6136–37 (Remarks of Reps. Roybal, Mazzoli, and Lungren).

93. Interview with Romano "Ron" Mazzoli, Romano "Ron" Mazzoli Oral History Project, February 2, 2011, part 1.

94. Cose, *A Nation of Strangers*, 171–72.

95. Interview with Romano "Ron" Mazzoli, Romano "Ron" Mazzoli Oral History Project, February 1, 2011, part 1.

96. Nadine Cahodas, "House Passes Immigration Bill by Five Votes," *Congressional Quarterly Weekly Report*, June 23, 1984, 23.

97. Perotti, *Resolving Policy Conflict*, 165.

98. Cose, *A Nation of Strangers*, 172.

99. Interview with Lynnette Conway Jacquez, Romano "Ron" Mazzoli Oral History Project, October 1, 2010, part 2.

100. Cose, *A Nation of Strangers*, 172.

101. Douglas Martin, "Mario Obledo, Hispanic Rights Leader, Dies at 78," *New York Times*, August 20, 2010.

102. Author interview with Arnoldo Torres, September 16, 2013.

103. Author interviews with Arnoldo Torres, January 17, 2013, and September 16, 2013.

104. Author interview with Arnoldo Torres, September 16, 2013; author interview with Rick Swartz, August 7, 2012.

105. Author interview with Henry Cisneros, October 5, 2012.

106. America Rodriguez, "Spanish International Network," Museum of Broadcast Communications, http://www.museum.tv/eotv/spanishinter.htm, 2014, accessed September 11, 2014.

107. G. Cristina Mora, *Making Hispanics: How Activists, Bureaucrats and Media Constructed a New American* (University of Chicago Press, 2014), 134–35.

108. Gary Libman, "Danny Villanueva, President of KMEX-TV: He Gets His Kicks Serving Latino Community," *Los Angeles Times*, September 29, 1985.

109. Cose, *A Nation of Strangers*, 173.

110. Jesus Rangel, "Hispanic Leader Urges a Boycott of Convention's First Vote," *New York Times*, June 23, 1984.

111. Author interview with Arnoldo Torres, September 16, 2013.

112. "Maximum Turnout Is Democrats' Goal," *Washington Post*, July 21, 1984.

113. David S. Broder, "Zigzagging in Search of Identity," *Washington Post*, July 15, 1984. See also Dan Balz, "Hard Campaign Fleshed Out Mondale Image," *Washington Post*, July 15, 1984.

114. Balz, "Hard Campaign Fleshed Out Mondale Image."

115. David S. Broder and Paul Taylor, "Mondale Assumes Control of Democratic Convention," *Washington Post*, July 18, 1984

116. Author interview with Henry Cisneros, October 5, 2012.

117. "Immigration Bill Gain Ends Hispanic Threat," *New York Times*, July 19, 1984.

118. "Democrats in San Francisco; Mondale Promises Caucus He'll Fight Immigration Bill," *New York Times*, July 18, 1984. The *Times* story reported a 39–39 vote; the *Washington Post* reported a 38–38 deadlock; see Broder and Taylor, "Mondale Assumes Control of Democratic Convention."

119. "We Must Forgive Each Other, Redeem Each Other and Move On," excerpts from prepared text of Jesse L. Jackson's address to the Democratic National Convention, reprinted in the *Washington Post*, July 18, 1984.

120. Author interview with J. Michael Treviño, October 2, 2012.

121. Paul Taylor, "Unity Boogie Wasn't Just a Party Going Through the Motions," *Washington Post*, July 20, 1984.

122. Cose, *A Nation of Strangers*, 175.

123. Margaret Shapiro and David Hoffman, "Reagan Defends Immigration Legislation as Fair," *Washington Post*, July 7, 1984.

124. Cose, *A Nation of Strangers*, 174.

125. Author interview with Henry Cisneros, October 5, 2012.

126. Cose, *A Nation of Strangers*, 174.

127. Robert Pear, "Immigration Measure Is Put into Doubt," *New York Times*, July 26, 1984.

128. Perotti, *Resolving Policy Conflict*, 256.

129. Robert Pear, "Senate May Be Asked to Accept House Version of Immigration Bill," *New York Times*, July 25, 1984.

130. Robert Pear, "Immigration Measure Is Put into Doubt"; see also Shapiro and Hoffman, "Reagan Defends Immigration Legislation as Fair."

131. Paul Anderson, "Immigration Bill Unlikely to Survive Political Season," *Miami Herald*, July 29, 1984.

132. Author interview with Wade Henderson, March 8, 2013.

133. Bill Keller, "Obscure Western Farm Groups Won Foreign Worker Program," *New York Times*, July 21, 1984.

134. Elaine Woo, "Harry Kubo, 84: Farm Leader Was a Defender of Private Property Rights," *Los Angeles Times*, December 12, 2006.

135. Garcia, *From the Jaws of Victory*, 170.

136. Leland T. Saito, *Race and Politics: Asian Americans, Latinos, and Whites in a Los Angeles Suburb* (University of Illinois Press, 1998), 133.

137. Woo, "Harry Kubo, 84."

138. Garcia, *From the Jaws of Victory*, 169.

139. Woo, "Harry Kubo, 84."

140. Garcia, *From the Jaws of Victory*, 174–77.

141. Keller, "Obscure Western Farm Groups Won Foreign Worker Program."

142. Author interview with Monte Lake, October 23, 2012.

143. Carl P. Leubsdorf, "Dallas' Bob Strauss, Former Democratic Party Chairman, Dies at 95," *Dallas Morning News*, http://www.oas.org/en/sedi/desd/psf/speakers/R_Mosbacher.pdf, updated March 20, 2014.

144. Keller, "Obscure Western Farm Groups Won Foreign Worker Program."

145. Author interview with Arnoldo Torres, October 8, 2014.

146. Author interview with J. Michael Treviño, October 2, 2012.

147. Author interview with Robert García, November 28, 2012.

148. Author interview with J. Michael Treviño, October 2, 2012.

149. The origins of the meeting are disputed. NCLR's Escutia remembers setting it up, while LULAC's Torres claims credit, but both agree on what transpired.

150. Perotti, *Resolving Policy Conflict*, 239–40.

151. Author interview with Martha Escutia, November 1, 2012.

152. Author interview with Arnoldo Torres, September 16, 2013.

153. Robert Pear, "Backers Studying Immigration Bill," *New York Times*, June 16, 1984.

154. Barone and Ujifusa, *The Almanac of American Politics 1986*, 160.

155. Author interview with Howard Berman, March 5, 2013.

156. Author interview with Bari Schwartz, December 20, 2012.

157. Author interview with Mark Schacht, January 25, 2013.

158. Alma Guillermoprieto, "Simpson-Mazzoli Aliens Bill Criticized," *Washington Post*, July 25, 1984.

159. Dan Perrin, "Hail to Robert Pear of the *New York Times*," posted March 4, 2008, HSA Coalition, http://www.hsacoalition.org/issue-analysis/hail-to-robert-pear-of-the-new-york-times/, accessed July 9, 2015.

160. Robert Pear, "Federal Regulations Pare Requirements for Bilingual Ballots," *New York Times*, September 10, 1984.

161. Author interview with Martha Escutia, November 1, 2012.

162. The text of the resolution can be found at *House Hearings*, Subcommittee of Immigration, Refugees and International Law, Committee on the Judiciary, April 12, 1984, 26.

163. See for example, letter from Attorney General Smith to Rep. Moakley, July 19, 1983; and letter from Assistant Secretary of State Elliott Abrams to Rep. Barney Frank, July 18, 1983.

164. Author interview with Frank Sharry, August 16, 2012.

165. "Morton Halperin, Senior Advisor, Washington Office," Open Society Foundations, undated, https://www.opensocietyfoundations.org/people/morton-halperin, accessed February 27, 2016.

166. Jacob Heilbrunn, "The Hollow Man," *The New Republic*, March 21, 1993, https://newrepublic.com/article/62966/the-hollow-man, accessed February 27, 2016; another reference to McNamara's "whiz kids" at Ford can be found at David Halberstam, *The Best and the Brightest*, 229–30.

167. For a description of the complex issues involved in the case, see "National Secu-

rity Wiretaps: Civil Liberties Affirmed by Appeals Court," *First Principles*, vol. 5, no. 1, Center for National Security Studies, September 1979.

168. See the Center's website at www.cnss.org for more information about the organization.

169. Author interview with Mort Halperin, December 18, 2015.

170. Author interview with Carol Wolchok, December 18, 2015.

171. Bob Sipchen and Garry Abrams, "The Elusive Jackie Jackson: Articulate and Charismatic, She Balances Keeping Her Identity and Living in His Shadow," *Los Angeles Times*, May 18, 1998.

172. Author interview with Carol Wolchok, December 18, 2015.

173. Author interview with Mort Halperin, December 18, 2015.

174. Author interview with Carol Wolchok, December 18, 2015.

175. Author interview with Maurice Belanger, July 30, 2015.

176. National Immigration and Alien Rights Project, *Salvadorans in the United States: The Case for Extended Voluntary Departure* (American Civil Liberties Union, April 1984), appendix III.

177. Letters from Elliott Abrams to Rep. Mazzoli, June 5, 1984, and an undated letter apparently sent about two weeks later.

178. Political Asylum Project, "The Fates of Salvadorans Expelled from the United States," American Civil Liberties Union Fund of the National Capital Area, September 5, 1984, 3 and attachment II.

179. Schneider, *Joe Moakley's Journey*, 170.

180. Susan Gzesh, "Central Americans and Asylum Policy in the Reagan Era," Migration Policy Institute, April 1, 2006.

181. See for example, "In Support of Salvadoran Refugees," A Resolution Approved by the General Synod XIII, United Church of Christ, 1981.

182. Author interview with Carol Wolchok, December 18, 2015.

183. "Agenda," A Working Conference on International Refugee Protection and Care, National Immigration, Refugee & Citizenship Forum, August 4–5, 1983.

184. Schneider, *Joe Moakley's Journey*, 133.

185. Robert Pear, "Reagan Raises New Obstacle to House Bill on Immigration," *New York Times*, August 9, 1984.

186. Robert Pear, "Chief Sponsor Moves to Rescue Immigration Bill," *New York Times*, August 4, 1984.

187. Pear, "Reagan Raises New Obstacle to House Bill on Immigration."

188. Fuchs, "The Corpse That Would Not Die,"121.

189. Pear, "Reagan Raises New Obstacle to House Bill on Immigration."

190. Cose, *A Nation of Strangers*, 177.

191. Fuchs, "The Corpse That Would Not Die," 121.

192. Nadine Cohodas, "Immigration Bill Conference to Begin," *Congressional Quarterly Weekly Report*, September 8, 1984, 2223.

193. According to Kamasaki's desk calendar, the meeting was held on September 4, the day before Congress reconvened.

194. Perotti, *Resolving Policy Conflict*, 263–64.

195. Jeffrey Toobin, *The Nine: Inside the Secret World of the Supreme Court* (Anchor Books, 2008), 131.

196. Laura Blumenfeld, "The Nominee's Soul Mate," *Washington Post*, September 10, 1991.

197. Perotti, *Resolving Policy Conflict*, 166.

198. United Press International, "Mondale Asked to Follow Up on Vow to Fight Bill on Aliens," *New York Times*, September 12, 1984.

199. "Dear Friend" letter from Polly Baca, Harry Pachon, Helen C. Gonzales, Arnoldo S. Torres, and Raul Yzaguirre, August 31, 1984.

200. Fuchs, "The Corpse That Would Not Die," 121.

201. Jeffrey H. Birnbaum and Alan S. Murray, *Showdown at Gucci Gulch: Lawmakers, Lobbyists, and the Unlikely Triumph of Tax Reform* (Vintage Books, 1987), 253–55.

202. Author interview with Skip Endres, November 8, 2012.

203. Author interview with Kathy Kiely, October 23, 2012.

204. Cose, *A Nation of Strangers*, 176.

205. Author interview with Skip Endres, November 8, 2012.

206. Robert Pear, "Conferees Agree on Sanctions in Immigration Bill," *New York Times*, September 13, 1984.

207. Author interview with Kathy Kiely, October 23, 2012.

208. Pear, "Conferees Agree on Sanctions in Immigration Bill."

209. Author interview with Kathy Kiely, October 23, 2012.

210. Simpson, *Right in the Old Gazoo*, 74–75.

211. Robert Pear, "Accord in Congress Sets '81 Cutoff Date for Alien Amnesty," *New York Times*, September 17, 1984.

212. United Press International, "Ford, Carter Assist Push for Illegal Alien Amnesty," *Deseret News*, September 19, 1984.

213. Robert Pear, "Immigration Bill Is at an Impasse," *New York Times*, September 20, 1984.

214. Robert Pear, "Immigration Bill Conferees Reach a Major Compromise," *New York Times*, September 22, 1984.

215. Author interview with Mark Schacht, January 25, 2013.

216. Author interview with Howard Berman, April 12, 2013.

217. Author interview with Howard Berman, April 12, 2013.

218. Robert Pear, "Conferees Approve a Reprieve for Farmers on End of Hiring Illegal Aliens," *New York Times*, September 25, 1984.

219. Robert Pear, "Immigrants Bill Conference Deadlocks on Alien's Rights," *New York Times*, September 26, 1984.

220. Robert Pear, "No Meetings Seen on Aliens Measure," *New York Times*, September 27, 1984.

221. Pear, "No Meetings Seen on Aliens Measure."

222. "Man-made Mountain on the Border," *New York Times*, editorial, September 28, 1984.

223. Barone and Ujifusa, *The Almanac of American Politics 1982*, 763.

224. Perotti, *Resolving Policy Conflict*, 168.

225. Cose, *A Nation of Strangers*, 176.

226. Perotti, *Resolving Policy Conflict*, 168.

227. Author interview with Albert Jacquez, November 14, 2012.

228. Robert Pear, "Conferees on Alien Bill Again Fail to Compromise," *New York Times*, October 10, 1984.

229. Pear, "Immigration Conferees Reach a Major Compromise."

230. Pear, "No Meetings Seen on Aliens Measure."

231. Author interview with Rick Swartz, July 30, 2012.

232. Author interview with Dianne Stewart, September 25, 2012.

233. Debbie Mauldin Cottrell, "Helen Jane Rehbein Farabee," *The Handbook of Texas*, www.tshaonline.org/handbook/online/articles/ffa33, accessed September 27, 2013.

234. Mary Anne Connolly, "Liz Carpenter 1920–2010," In Memoriam, *Austin Woman*, April 2010, 70. According to The American Presidency Project, Johnson's first public statement following the assassination was as follows: "This is a sad time for all people. We have suffered a loss that cannot be weighed. For me, it is a deep personal tragedy. I know the world shares the sorrow that Mrs. Kennedy and her family bear. I will do my best. That is all I can do. I ask for your help—and God's." See http://www.presidency.ucsb.edu/ws/index.php?pid+2576, accessed May 15, 2015.

235. Author interview with Dianne Stewart, September 25, 2012.

236. The legislation barred legalization recipients from receipt of most federal cash assistance programs; see Title II, Sec. 201(h) in "Immigration Reform and Control Act of 1986, Conference Report," Committee on the Judiciary, House Report 99–1000, October 14, 1986, 35–37.

237. Author interview with Dianne Stewart, September 25, 2012.

238. Paul Burka, "The Coup Against Dew," *Texas Monthly*, October 2013, p. 314

239. For a bio of Rob Mosbacher Jr., see: http://www.oas.org/en/sedi/desd/psf/speakers/R_Mosbacher.pdf; author interview with Dianne Stewart, September 25, 2012.

240. Author interview with Rick Swartz, July 30, 2012.

241. Author interview with Dianne Stewart, September 25, 2012.

242. Pear, "Conferees on Alien Bill Again Fail to Compromise."

243. Cose, *A Nation of Strangers*, 177.

244. Pear, "Conferees on Alien Bill Again Fail to Compromise." Accounts differ on the vote count on the funding issue. The accounting cited herein relies on the *Times*'s contemporaneous article and the author's own recollection.

245. Simpson, *Right in the Old Gazoo*, 76.

246. Cose, *A Nation of Strangers*, 176.

247. Robert Pear, "Amid Charges, Immigration Bill Dies," *New York Times*, October 12, 1984.

248. Cose, *A Nation of Strangers*, 177.

249. Author interview with Rick Swartz, April 3, 2015.

250. Nadine Cahodas, "Art of Negotiation as Applied to Immigration," *Congressional Quarterly Weekly Report*, May 10, 1986, 1036.

251. Author interview with Arnoldo Torres, August 4, 2017.

252. Cose, *A Nation of Strangers*, 177.

253. Author Interview with Carl Hampe, September 10, 2012.

254. Author interview with Arnoldo Torres, August 4, 2017.

CHAPTER 6

1. "1984 Presidential Candidate Debate: President Reagan and Walter Mondale—10/21/84," The Ronald Reagan Presidential Foundation; the debate can be seen in its entirety at: https://www.youtube.com/watch?v=EF73k5-Hiqg#t=32m55s, accessed July 31, 2015.

2. Barone and Ujifusa, *The Almanac of American Politics 1986*, xxxix.

3. Author interview with J. Michael Treviño, October 2, 2012.

4. Author interview with Martha Escutia, November 1, 2012.

5. From the back cover of the VHS version of *Repo Man*, Universal City Studios, 1984.

6. Resume of Norman V. Lourie, updated March 1984, copy on file with the author.

7. "Norman V. Lourie," NASW Social Work Pioneers, http://www.naswfoundation .org/pioneers/l/lourie.html, accessed January 2, 2016.

8. Author interview with Rick Swartz, August 7, 2012.

9. Britt Peterson, "Private Social Clubs Try to Delay Their Doom," *Washingtonian*, April 29, 2015.

10. Associated Press, "All-Male Club in Washington Ends Policy Against Women," *New York Times*, June 19, 1988.

11. Barone and Ujifusa, *The Almanac of American Politics 1986*, 1483.

12. Simpson, *Right in the Old Gazoo*, 94.

13. "Alan Simpson Quotes," *InspirationalStories.com: Inspirational Quotes, Words, Sayings*, http://www.inspirationalstories.com/quotes/alan-simpson-its-going-to-be-an -extraordinary-debate/, accessed August 6, 2015.

14. Simpson, *Right in the Old Gazoo*, 94.

15. Robert Pear, "Senate Will Get Immigration Bill," *New York Times*, April 18, 1985.

16. Robert Pear, "Senate Gets New Version of Immigration Bill," *New York Times*, May 24, 1985.

17. In the Republican presidential debate on January 23, 2012, Romney described his alternative to mass deportations of unauthorized immigrants as "self-deportation." See story and video at: Lucy Madison, "Romney on Immigration: I'm for 'Self-deportation,'" *CBS News.Com*, January 24, 2012, http://www.cbsnews.com/news/romney-on -immigration-im-for-self-deportation/, accessed September 24, 2015.

18. See, for example, Daniel Strauss, "Chris Christie Signals Support for Ted Cruz's Immigration Strategy," *Politico*, January 19, 2016, http://www.politico.com /story/2016/01/chris-christie-ted-cruz-immigration-217996, accessed January 20, 2016.

19. Pear, "Senate Gets New Version of Immigration Bill."

20. Select Commission on Immigration and Refugee Policy, *U.S. Immigration Policy and the National Interest*, Committees of the Judiciary, House of Representatives and United States Senate, Ninety-Seventh Congress, First Session, August 1981, 74.

21. Statement of Joseph M. Treviño, *Senate Hearings*, Committee on the Judiciary, Subcommittee on Immigration and Refugee Policy, "Immigration Reform and Control Act of 1985," June 17–24, 1985, 99th Congress, First Session, 97.

22. Author interview with Carl Hampe, September 10, 2012.

23. "The Simpson-Nobody Bill," *New York Times*, May 24, 1985.

24. Pear, "Senate Gets New Version of Immigration Bill."

25. Nadine Cahodas, "New Immigration Bill Introduced in the Senate," *Congressional Quarterly Weekly Report*, May 25, 1985, 1025.

26. Barone and Ujifusa, *The Almanac of American Politics 1986*, 467–68.

27. "Frank McCloskey—Top 10 Contested Officeholders," *Time*, January 7, 2009, http://content.time.com/time/specials/packages/article /0,28804,1870059_1870058_1870003,00.html, accessed April 16, 2015.

28. Steven V. Roberts, "House Refuses to Order Special Indiana Election," *New York Times*, May 1, 1985.

29. "Frank McCloskey—Top 10 Contested Officeholders."

30. Interview with Romano "Ron" Mazzoli, Romano "Ron" Mazzoli Oral History Project, February 1, 2011, part 1.

31. See: "GOP Reps Stage Walk-Out in Protest of Ballot Recount Giving Election Win to Democrat Frank McCloskey," NBC News, May 1, 1985, http://www.nbcuniversalarchives.com/nbcuni/clip/5112528934_s03.do, accessed April 17, 2015; and Roberts, "House Refuses to Order Special Indiana Election."

32. Cose, *A Nation of Strangers*, 178.

33. Perotti, *Resolving Policy Conflict*, 312.

34. Cose, *A Nation of Strangers*, 178.

35. Author interview with Skip Endres, November 8, 2012.

36. Cose, *A Nation of Strangers*, 179.

37. Author interview with Skip Endres, November 8, 2012.

38. Perotti, *Resolving Policy Conflict*, 313.

39. Cahodas, "New Immigration Bill Introduced in the Senate," 1024.

40. Peter Applebome, "The Texas Six-Pack," *Texas Monthly*, June 1985.

41. Perotti, *Resolving Policy Conflict*, 300.

42. Navarro, *Mexicano Political Experience in Occupied Aztlan*, 520.

43. Author interview with Arnoldo Torres, January 22, 2013; Márquez, *LULAC*, 92.

44. Author interview with Rick Swartz, April 3, 2015.

45. Author interview with Arnoldo Torres, January 22, 2013.

46. Márquez, *LULAC*, 95.

47. Navarro, *Mexicano Political Experience in Occupied Aztlan*, 520.

48. Author interview with Arnoldo Torres, January 22, 2013.

49. Gary Scharrer, "LULAC President Reaches Out to Corporate America," *El Paso Times*, June 21, 1985.

50. Author interview with Arnoldo Torres, January 22, 2013.

51. Author interview with Arnoldo Torres, January 22, 2013.

52. Some accounts inaccurately state that Torres resigned in 1984, when his separation occurred in 1985 (see Navarro, *Mexicano Political Experience in Occupied Aztlan*, 521 and Matt Moffett, "LULAC, Hispanic Advocacy Group Turns Away from Liberal Traditions under New Leadership," *Wall Street Journal*, March 19, 1986). Torres himself publicly claimed he resigned as a matter of principle (see "Torres Resigns, Plans New Group," *Nuestro*, vol. 9, no. 5, 1985). However, he later seemed acknowledge that the LULAC board of directors passed a resolution terminating him at its Spring 1985 meeting (author interview with Arnoldo Torres, January 22, 2013).

53. Author interview with J. Michael Treviño, October 2, 2012.

54. Nancy Hicks, "Antioch Law School Offers a New Breed of Lawyer," *New York Times*, May 21, 1975.

55. Author interview with J. Michael Treviño, October 2, 2012.

56. Author interview with Arnoldo Torres, January 22, 2013.

57. Author interview with Martha Escutia, November 1, 2012.

58. Zohlberg, *A Nation by Design*, 342.

59. "Torres Resigns, Plans New Group," *Nuestro*, Vol. 9, No. 5, 1985, cited in Márquez, *LULAC*, 94.

60. Christine Marie Sierra, "Organizational Strategies on Immigration Reform," in Roberto E. Villarreal and Norma G. Hernandez, eds., *Latinos and Political Coalitions: Political Empowerment for the 1990s*, Praeger Publishers, 65.

61. Author interview with J. Michael Treviño, October 2, 2012.

62. Author interview with Rick Swartz, April 3, 2015.

63. Sierra, "Organizational Strategies on Immigration Reform," 65.

64. "Torres Resigns, Plans New Group."

65. Simpson, *Right in the Old Gazoo*, 68.

66. Remarks of Senator Simpson, *Senate Hearings*, Committee on the Judiciary, Subcommittee on Immigration and Refugee Policy, "Immigration Reform and Control Act of 1985," June 17–24, 1985, 99th Congress, First Session, 159.

67. "Statement of Arnoldo Torres," *Senate Hearings*, Committee on the Judiciary, Subcommittee on Immigration and Refugee Policy, "Immigration Reform and Control Act of 1985," June 17–24, 1985, 99th Congress, First Session, 101. The relevant passage states, "We ask you not to respond affirmatively to the race-baiters, the merchants of immigrant fear."

68. Donald Loren Hardy, *Shooting from the Lip: The Life of Senator Al Simpson* (University of Oklahoma Press, 2011), 78.

69. John Newhouse, "Taking It Personally," *The New Yorker*, March 16, 1992, 60.

70. Robert Pear, "Administration Reported Set to Back New Immigration Bill," *New York Times*, June 14, 1985.

71. Nadine Cahodas, "Action Starting on Immigration Legislation," *Congressional Quarterly Weekly Report*, July 20, 1985, 141.

72. Mary Thornton, "Senate Panel Approves Major Immigration Bill," *Washington Post*, July 31, 1985.

73. Statement of Raul Yzaguírre, *Senate Hearings*, Committee on the Judiciary, Subcommittee on Immigration and Refugee Policy, "Immigration Reform and Control Act of 1985," June 17–24, 1985, 99th Congress, First Session, 69.

74. Author interview with Rick Swartz, July 30, 2012.

75. Author interview with Lynnette Conway Jacquez, September 14, 2012.

76. Interview with Harris Miller, Romano "Ron" Mazzoli Oral History Project, July 8, 2010.

77. Author interview with Arnoldo Torres, September 30, 2015.

78. Interview with Lynnette Conway Jacquez, Romano "Ron" Mazzoli Oral History Project, October 1, 2010, part 1.

79. Author interview with Albert Jacquez, November 14, 2012.

80. Stephen Engelberg, "Rodino to Propose Immigration Bill in the House," *New York Times*, July 19, 1985.

81. "Peter Rodino Rides to the Rescue," editorial, *New York Times*, July 21, 1985.

82. "Pulitzer Prizes," New York Times Company website at: http://www.nytco.com/pulitzer-prizes/, accessed August 21, 2015.

83. Michael S. Teitelbaum, "Right vs. Right: Immigration and Refugee Policy in the United States," *Foreign Affairs*, vol. 59, no. 1, Fall 1980.

84. Simpson, *Right in the Old Gazoo*, 70–71.

85. Author interview with Roger Conner, February 11, 2013.

86. Frank del Olmo, "Real Chance for Immigration Reform: New Rodino Bill, with Simpson Measure, Finally Offers Hope," *Los Angeles Times*, July 26, 1985.

87. Claudia Luther, "Times Editor Was a Voice for Latinos," *Los Angeles Times*, obituary, February 20, 2004.

88. Del Olmo, "Real Chance for Immigration Reform."

89. Memorandum from Charles Kamasaki to Raul Yzaguírre, National Council of La Raza, February 11, 1985.

90. Perotti, *Resolving Policy Conflict*, 307, footnote 42.

91. Author interview with Dan Maldonado, August 15, 2012. See also Perotti, *Resolving Policy Conflict*, 307, footnote 42.

92. "Representative Roybal Introduces Sanctions-Free Comprehensive Immigration Reform Bill," *AILA Monthly Mailing*, American Immigration Lawyers Association, June 1985, 285.

93. Charles Kamasaki's memorandum of February 11, 1985, to Raul Yzaguírre references a then-active alternative bill drafting efforts by The Group, which never came to fruition as no such bill was ever introduced.

94. Barone and Ujifusa, *The Almanac of American Politics 1986*, 180–1.

95. Author interview with Ruben Bonilla, September 27, 2012.

96. Barone and Ujifusa, *The Almanac of American Politics 1986*, 885.

97. Interview with Lynnette Conway Jacquez, Romano "Ron" Mazzoli Oral History Project, October 1, 2010, part 1.

98. Author interview with Raul Yzaguírre, September 7, 2013.

99. Author interview with Albert Jacquez, November 14, 2012.

100. Perotti, *Resolving Policy Conflict*, 305–6.

101. Perotti, *Resolving Policy Conflict*, 304–5.

102. Cose, *A Nation of Strangers*, 179.

103. "House Judiciary Looks to Post-Rodino Era," *Congressional Quarterly Weekly Report*, June 7, 1986, 1307.

104. Memorandum from Paul Peterson (of the Brookings Institution) to Bruce Williams (of the Rockefeller Foundation) re: The National Council of La Raza's Policy Analysis Program, 31 October 1985, copy on file with the author.

105. Cose, *A Nation of Strangers*, 180.

106. Author interview with Carl Hampe, September 10, 2012.

107. Perotti, *Resolving Policy Conflict*, 308–10.

108. Cose, *A Nation of Strangers*, 180.

109. Tom Gjelten and Marisa Penaloza, "Built By Immigrants, U.S. Catholic Churches Bolstered by Them Once Again," *National Public Radio*, September 9, 2015.

110. Margaret Hornblower, "Charities Criticize Snags in Aiding Cubans," *Washington Post*, May 29, 1980.

111. Peggy Osberger Wilder, "Report on Chicago Symposium on a 'Catholic Policy Toward Immigration Reform,'" *Crisis Magazine*, May 1, 1983.

112. Gustav Niebuhr, "Public Lives: Bishop, from Experience, Smooths Way for Immigrants," *New York Times*, November 18, 2000.

113. Most Reverend Nicholas DiMarzio, PhD.D.D., "Thoughts on US Immigration Reform With Special Reference to New York City," Conference on U.S. Immigration Reform With Special Reference to New York City, Center for Migration Studies in cooperation with The Levin Institute, SUNY, 3 March 2011.

114. Author interview with Demetrios Papademetriou, September 7, 2015.

115. Niebuhr, "Public Lives."

116. Author interview with Michael Myers, May 21, 2013.

117. Author interview with Wade Henderson, December 19, 2012.

118. "Resolution on Immigration Reform," a resolution passed by the National Conference of Catholic Bishops, November 14, 1985, copy on file with the author.

119. Author interview with Rick Swartz, April 3, 2013. For a specific example, see:

Letter from Rev. Msgr. Nicolas DiMarzio to Arthur P. Endres dated August 15, 1986, *NCLR Records*, Series M744, Box 343, Folder 10.

120. Author interview with Roger Conner, February 11, 2013.

121. FAIR fundraising letter from John H. Tanton, MD, November 28, 1984.

122. Letter from Rep. Barney Frank to John Tanton, December 6, 1984.

123. "Temporary Safe Haven for Salvadorans," *Senate Hearings*, Subcommittee on Immigration and Refugee Affairs, Committee on the Judiciary, June 18, 1987, Serial No. J-100-26, 164–69.

124. Author interview with Roger Conner, February 11, 2013.

125. From US English website: http://www.usenglish.org/view/2, accessed March 3, 2016.

126. Marcia Chambers, "California Braces for Change with English as Official Language," *New York Times*, November 26, 1986.

127. Jay Mathews, "Immigrant Dominance Spurring a Backlash," *New York Times*, May 10, 1986.

128. "California English-Only Law Faces Court Tests," letter to the editor from Antonia Hernández, *New York Times*, November 25, 1986.

129. Chambers, "California Braces for Change with English as Official Language."

130. Lydia Chávez, "Leaders Ready for Fight Over English-Only Bill," *New York Times*, December 6, 1986.

131. Birnbaum and Murray, *Showdown at Gucci Gulch*, 4.

132. Larry Margasak, "Senate Again Takes Up Immigration Legislation," Associated Press, September 11, 1985.

133. Philip G. Schrag, *A Well-Founded Fear: The Congressional Battle to Save Political Asylum in America* (Routlege, 2000), 252.

134. "Q&A: Alan Simpson; 1986 Immigration Reform Legislation," *San Diego Union-Tribune*, May 28, 2006.

135. Anonymous Wilson aide quoted in Perotti, *Resolving Policy Conflict*, 326.

136. Karen Tumulty, "Senate Votes to Allow Aliens at Harvest Time: Reversal Backs Wilson Amendment for Hiring Large Numbers of Workers for Perishable Crops," *Los Angeles Times*, September 18, 1985.

137. Anonymous Wilson aide quoted in Perotti, *Resolving Policy Conflict*, 326–27.

138. Tumulty, "Senate Votes to Allow Aliens at Harvest Time."

139. Fuchs, "The Corpse That Would Not Die," 122.

140. Robert Pear, "Senate Alien Bill Draws Criticism," *New York Times*, September 19, 1985.

141. Hardy, *Shooting from the Lip*, 80.

142. Simpson, *Right in the Old Gazoo*, 76.

143. Rules were changed in 1975 to increase the number of votes required to sustain a filibuster in the US Senate from 34 to 41; see: "Filibuster and Cloture," US Senate, http://www.senate.gov/artandhistory/history/common/briefing/Filibuster_Cloture.htm, accessed October 15, 2015.

144. Pear, "Senate Alien Bill Draws Criticism."

145. "Giving Immigration the Business," *New Yok Times*, September 22, 1985.

146. Pear, "Senate Alien Bill Draws Criticism."

147. Robert Pear, "The Institutionalization of the Illegal Alien," *New York Times*, September 29, 1985.

148. Schneider, *Joe Moakley's Journey*, 143.

149. "Statement of Morton H. Halperin, Wade J. Henderson, and Carol Leslie Wolchok," *Senate Hearings*, Subcommittee on Immigration, Committee on the Judiciary, April 22, 1985, 4.

150. Cited in Schneider, *Joe Moakley's Journey*, 145.

151. "Update on Temporary 'Safe Haven' Proposals for Central Americans," *AILA Monthly Mailing*, American Immigration Lawyers Association, June 1985, 284.

152. "Statement of Morton H. Halperin, Wade J. Henderson, and Carol Leslie Wolchok," 6, 11, and 20.

153. Larry Margasak, "ACLU Says Some Deported Salvadorans Murdered," Associated Press, April 23, 1985, http://www.apnewsarchive.com/1985/ACLU-Says-Some-Deported-Salvadorans-Murdered, accessed March 26, 2013.

154. Larry Margasak, "'Invasion of Feet People' Predicted If Salvadorans Not Deported," Associated Press, April 22, 1985, http://www.apnewsarchive.com/1985/-Invasion-of-Feet-People-Predicted-if-Salvadorans-Not-Deported, accessed March 26, 2013.

155. Schneider, *Joe Moakley's Journey*, 144.

156. "Q&A: Alan Simpson; 1986 Immigration Reform Legislation," *San Diego Union-Tribune*, May 28, 2006.

157. Author interview with Mort Halperin, December 18, 2015.

158. Author interview with Emily Gantz McKay, August 21, 2012.

159. National Immigration and Alien Rights Project, *Salvadorans in the United States: The Case for Extended Voluntary Departure* (American Civil Liberties Union, April 1984).

160. Minutes of the meeting of the NCLR Board of Directors, April 12, 1985, Houston, TX. The board was also briefed by Rick Swartz of the National Immigration, Refugee, and Citizenship Forum.

161. Charles Kamasaki and Dan Purtell, "Issue Update: Suspension of Deportation for Salvadoran Refugees," National Council of La Raza, February 26, 1986.

162. Author interview with Skip Endres, November 8, 2012.

163. Nadine Cahodas, "Art of Negotiation as Applied to Immigration," *Congressional Quarterly Weekly Report*, May 10, 1986, 1036–37.

164. Garcia, *From the Jaws of Victory*, 27–28.

165. "Dolores Huerta – Children's Activist, Civil Rights Activist," biography.com, http://www.biography.com/people/dolores-huerta-188850, accessed October 15, 2015; see also Daniel Rothenberg, *With These Hands: The Hidden World of Migrant Farmworkers Today* (Harcourt Brace & Company, 1998), 259.

166. See "Dolores Huerta," https://en/wikipedia.org/wiki/Dolores_Huerta, accessed October 15, 2015.

167. Garcia, *From the Jaws of Victory*, 233.

168. Perotti, *Resolving Policy Conflict*, 350.

169. Author interview with Rick Swartz, August 7, 2012.

170. Author interview with Raul Yzaguírre, July 9, 2012.

171. Garcia, *From the Jaws of Victory*, 233.

172. Perotti, *Resolving Policy Conflict*, 329–30.

173. "Immigration Reform and Control Act of 1983," *House Hearings*, Committee on Agriculture, June 15, 1983, Serial No. 98-14, 94.

174. Author interview with Monte Lake, October 23, 2012.

175. Fuchs, "The Corpse That Would Not Die," 123.

176. Perotti, *Resolving Policy Conflict*, 330.

177. Nadine Cahodas, "Rodino Says He'll Move Immigration Bill," *Congressional Quarterly Weekly Report*, March 1, 1986.

178. Perotti, *Resolving Policy Conflict*, 348.

179. Bob Secter, "Rodino Postpones Immigration Bill: Backers Say Measure Is Near Death Because of Long Delay," *Los Angeles Times*, May 2, 1986.

180. Robert Pear, "Immigration Bill Is Still at Sea," *New York Times*, May 4, 1986.

181. Interview with Lynnette Conway Jacquez, Romano "Ron" Mazzoli Oral History Project, October 1, 2010, part 2.

182. Author interview with Albert Jacquez, November 14, 2012; see also Perotti, *Resolving Policy Conflict*, 307.

183. Perotti, *Resolving Policy Conflict*, 310.

184. Author interview with Muzaffar Chishti and Michael Myers, December 17, 2012.

185. Navarro, *Mexicano Political Experience in Occupied Aztlan*, 644.

186. Mario T. García, *Memories of Chicano History: The Life and Narrative of Bert Corona* (University of California Press, 2004), 126–29.

187. "Lyndon B. Johnson," BrainyQuote.com, Xplore Inc, http://www.brainyquote.com/quotes/quotes/l/lyndonbjo137075.html, accessed October 1, 2015.

188. Sergio Munoz, "Guided by a Vision: How Bert Corona Met the Challenges of Latino Leadership," *Los Angeles Times*, October 9, 1994.

189. García, *Memories of Chicano History*, 249.

190. García, *Memories of Chicano History*, 305.

191. Author interview with J. Michael Treviño, October 2, 2012.

192. For detailed insights into the relationships and dynamics between DC-based lobbyists in the Leadership Conference on Civil Rights and the field-based protest groups like the Southern Christian Leadership Conference, the Student Nonviolent Coordinating Committee, and the Congress for Racial Equality during the struggles to pass historic civil rights legislation in the 1960s, see Nick Kotz, *Judgment Days: Lyndon Baines Johnson, Martin Luther King, Jr., and the Laws That Changed America* (Mariner Books, 2005), Todd S. Purdum, *An Idea Whose Time Has Come: Two Presidents, Two Parties, and the Battle for the Civil Rights Act of 1964* (Picador, 2014), and Clay Risen, *The Bill of the Century: The Epic Battle for the Civil Rights Act* (Bloomsbury Press, 2014).

193. Author interview with Arnoldo Torres, September 4, 2015.

194. Nadine Cahodas, "Immigration Bill Stalls Over Farm Labor Issue," *Congressional Quarterly Weekly Report*, June 21, 1986, 1411–12.

195. See, for example, Statement on the Immigration and Naturalization Service: Implications for Hispanics, Statement of Raul Yzaguírre, *House Hearings*: Subcommittee on Immigration, Refugees, and International Law, Committee on the Judiciary, March 27, 1981.

196. Hamilton Fish Jr., *Hamilton Fish: Memoir of an American Patriot* (Regnery Publishing, 1991).

197. American Heritage Editors, "Ten Best Secretaries of State . . . ," *American Heritage*, vol. 33, Issue 1.

198. Barone and Ujifusa, *The Almanac of American Politics 1986*, 955.

199. Fuchs, "The Corpse That Would Not Die," 118.

200. Author interview with Christine Gaffney, January 16, 2013.

201. Letter from Charles Kamasaki to Dan Lungren and Kevin Holsclaw, June 26, 1986, *NCLR Records*, Series 5, Box 141, Folder 3.

202. Perotti, *Resolving Policy Conflict*, 328–38.

203. Cahodas, "Immigration Bill Stalls Over Farm Labor Issue," 1411–12.

204. Perotti, *Resolving Policy Conflict*, 331.

205. Author interview with Monte Lake, October 23, 2012.

206. Perotti, *Resolving Policy Conflict*, 385.

207. Nadine Cahodas, "House Panel Breaks Deadlock, Sends Immigration Bill to the Floor," *Congressional Quarterly Weekly Report*, June 28, 1986, 1479.

208. Perotti, *Resolving Policy Conflict*, 332–33.

209. See Cahodas, "House Panel Breaks Deadlock, Sends Immigration Bill to the Floor," 1479–80; see also Robert Pear, "House Panel Approves a Comprehensive Measure on Immigration, *New York Times*, June 26, 1986 and Perotti, *Resolving Policy Conflict*, 332–33.

210. Pear, "House Panel Approves a Comprehensive Measure on Immigration."

211. Cahodas, "House Panel Breaks Deadlock, Sends Immigration Bill to the Floor," 1480.

212. Pear, "House Panel Approves a Comprehensive Measure on Immigration." See also Cahodas, "House Panel Breaks Deadlock, Sends Immigration Bill to the Floor," 1479.

213. Robert Pear, "Congress: Wither the Immigration Bill," *New York Times*, July 14, 1986.

214. Perotti, *Resolving Policy Conflict*, 360.

215. Overview of the Office of the Parliamentarian, http://www.house.gov/content/learn/officers_and_organizations/parliamentarian.php, accessed April 4, 2013.

216. Author interview with Wade Henderson, March 8, 2013; Remarks of Charles Kamasaki, "African Americans, Civil Rights, and Immigration: A Legacy of Inspiration and Leadership," American Immigration Council Awards Presentation, March 26, 2010.

217. Remarks of Kamasaki, "African Americans, Civil Rights, and Immigration."

218. For a detailed account of how the process works in the corporate context, see Jeffrey H. Birnbaum, *The Lobbyists* (Times Books, 1992).

219. Bill Summary and Status, 99th Congress (1985–1986), H.R. 3810, http://thomas.loc.gov/cgi-bin/bdquery/D?d099, 2–3. Two committees—Banking, Housing and Urban Affairs and the Select Committee on Aging—held a hearing on August 6, 1986, a day after the supposed extended deadline.

220. Sonia Ospina, William Diaz, and James F. O'Sullivan, "Negotiating Accountability: Managerial Lessons from Identity-Based Nonprofit Organizations," *Nonprofit and Voluntary Sector Quarterly*, vol. 31, no. 1, March 2002, 22.

221. Kamasaki's desk calendar recorded the meeting with Murguía at 2:00 p.m. on September 24, 1986.

222. Author interview with Monte Lake, October 23, 2012.

223. Schneider, *Joe Moakley's Journey*, 146.

224. Jay Mathews, "El Salvador's Economic Refugees," *Washington Post*, September 9, 1986.

225. Paul Glickman, "How Genuine Are Refugee Claims of Persecution?" *Christian Science Monitor*, September 25, 1986, http://www.csmonitor.com/1986/0925/aref-f.html, accessed September 24, 105.

226. "Dear Representative" letter from Wade Henderson, American Civil Liberties Union, July 28, 1986; see also Jay Mathews, "El Salvador's Economic Refugees," *Washington Post*, September 9, 1986.

227. See International Organization on Migration's mission at its website: http://www.iom.int.mission.

228. "Women the World Should Know," *National Review*, March 8, 2006, http://www.nationalreview.com/article/216995/women-world-should-know-nro-symposium, accessed September 24, 2015.

229. See: Minutes of the Board Meeting of the National Forum on Immigration and Refugee Policy/American Immigration and Citizenship Conference, June 28–29, 1982, 2.

230. Nadine Cahodas, "Immigration Bill Resurrected; Conferees Begin Negotiations," *Congressional Quarterly Weekly Report*, October 11, 1986, 2573.

231. Barone and Ujifusa, *The Almanac of American Politics 1986*, 318–19.

232. Robert Pear, "House Refuses to Consider Broad Bill on Immigration," *New York Times*, September 27, 1986.

233. Nadine Cahodas, "House Kills Immigration Bill, Little Chance for Resurrection," *Congressional Quarterly Weekly Report*, September 27, 1986, 2267.

234. Pear, "House Refuses to Consider Broad Bill on Immigration."

235. Fuchs, "The Corpse That Would Not Die," 123–24.

236. Jordan Fabian and Ted Hesson, "Call Immigration Chuck Schumer's Legacy-Defining Issue," ABC News, May 5, 2013, http://abcnews.go.com/ABC_Univision/Politics/chuck-schumers-role-immigration-reform-define-legacy-undo/story?id=18960039, accessed September 3, 2013.

237. "To Control Aliens, Control Partisans," *New York Times*, editorial, September 29, 1986.

238. Perotti, *Resolving Policy Conflict*, 333.

239. Nadine Cahodas, "Refusal to Give Up Brings Dead Bill Back to Life," *Congressional Quarterly Weekly Report*, October 11, 1986, 2572.

240. See Perotti, *Resolving Policy Conflict*, 333–35, and Cahodas, "Refusal to Give Up Brings Dead Bill Back to Life," 2572.

241. For example, over fifty House members missed the vote on the rule on September 27, 1986, nearly two dozen more than had missed comparable votes in the previous session.

242. See John F. Matlock, Jr., *Reagan and Gorbachev: How the Cold War Ended* (Random House, 2004), for a detailed discussion of the Reykjavik negotiations.

243. Cahodas, "Refusal to Give Up Brings Dead Bill Back to Life," 2572.

244. Perotti, *Resolving Policy Conflict*, 358.

245. Cahodas, "Immigration Bill Resurrected; Conferees Begin Negotiations," 2571.

246. Author interview with Lynnette Conway Jacquez, September 14, 2012.

247. "The Speaker from Texas," KERA-TV, documentary, aired February 3, 1987.

248. Author interview with Albert Jacquez, November 14, 2012.

249. Perotti, *Resolving Policy Conflict*, 343.

250. *Congressional Record*, October 9, 1986, 29975–81 (remarks of Reps. Roybal, González, García, Sensenbrenner, Daub, Mazzoli, Lott, Rodino, and Fish, and record vote no. 4481, 29983).

251. *Congressional Record*, October 9, 1986, 30038–45.

252. *Congressional Record*, October 9, 1986, 30045–48 (Remarks of Rep. Frank).

253. *Congressional Record*, October 9, 1986, 30048–51 (Remarks of Reps. Rodino, Mazzoli, and Fish).

254. *Congressional Record*, October 9, 1986, 30066 (Record vote no. 455).

255. *Congressional Record*, October 9, 1986, 30074–75 (Record vote no. 456).

256. *Congressional Record*, October 9, 1986, 30075 (Remarks of Rep. O'Neill).

257. Cahodas, "Immigration Bill Resurrected; Conferees Begin Negotiations," 2573.

258. *Congressional Record*, October 9, 1986, 30075–76 (Record vote no. 457).

259. Cahodas, "Immigration Bill Resurrected; Conferees Begin Negotiations," 2571.

260. Robert Pear, "Conferees on Immigration Bill Pressing to Reconcile Differences," *New York Times*, October 10, 1986.

261. Nadine Cahodas, "Congress Clears Overhaul of Immigration Law," *Congressional Quarterly Weekly Report*, October 18, 1986, 2595.

262. Author interview with Skip Endres, November 8, 2012.

263. Author interview with Bob García, November 28, 2012.

264. Author interview with Angelo Falcon, December 17, 2012.

265. Ronald Smothers, "Rep. García: Bronx Figure with Following That's National," *New York Times*, April 11, 1985.

266. Perotti, *Resolving Policy Conflict*, 376.

267. Pear, "Conferees on Immigration Bill Pressing to Reconcile Differences."

268. Cahodas, "Congress Clears Overhaul of Immigration Law," 2595.

269. Hardy, *Shooting from the Lip*, 82.

270. Simpson, *Right in the Old Gazoo*, 77.

271. "Q&A: Alan Simpson; 1986 Immigration Reform Legislation," *San Diego Union-Tribune*, May 28, 2006.

272. Perotti, *Resolving Policy Conflict*, 311.

273. Author interview with Rick Swartz, December 30, 2015.

274. Hardy, *Shooting from the Lip*, 83.

275. Perotti, *Resolving Policy Conflict*, 296.

276. Schneider, *Joe Moakley's Journey*, 148.

277. Cose, *A Nation of Strangers*, 184.

278. Simpson, *Right in the Old Gazoo*, 78–79.

279. Hardy, *Shooting from the Lip*, 83.

280. For a more detailed explanation of budget rules, see: Bill Heniff Jr., "Overview of the Authorization-Appropriations Process," Congressional Research Service, November 26, 2012, http://www.senate.gov/CRSReports/crs-publish.cfm?pid='0DP%2BPLW%3C%22%40%20%20%0A, accessed January 30, 2016.

281. Author interview with Dianne Stewart, September 25, 2012.

282. Author interview with Skip Endres, November 8, 2012.

283. Robert Pear, "House Approves Compromise Bill on Illegal Aliens," *New York Times*, October 16, 1986.

284. Ed O'Keefe, "Warren Rudman's Legacy Laid Groundwork for 'Fiscal Cliff' Negotiations," *Washington Post*, November 20, 2012.

285. Robert Pear, "Reagan Said to Favor Signing New Aliens Bill," *New York Times*, October 17, 1986.

286. Cahodas, "Congress Clears Overhaul of Immigration Law," 2595.

287. Perotti, *Resolving Policy Conflict*, 379–80.

288. Author interview with Roger Conner, February 11, 2013.

289. Fuchs, "The Corpse That Would Not Die," 124.

290. Cortés, *Policy Analysts and Interest Groups*, 429; see also 421, noting that the AFL-CIO's political arm was not mobilized to support IRCA and 431, observing that organized labor supported IRCA "in a calculatingly bland fashion."

291. Sierra, "Organizational Strategies on Immigration Reform," 64. It might be

noted that Sierra's characterizations of NCLR's and LULAC's official positions on the bill are odds with the documentary evidence and recollections of several of the principals.

292. Author interview with Mort Halperin, December 18, 2015.

293. Author interview with Albert Jacquez, November 14, 2012.

294. Perotti, *Resolving Policy Conflict*, 375.

295. Cortés, *Policy Analysts and Interest Groups*, 357.

296. Robert Pear, "Congress, Winding Up Work, Votes Sweeping Aliens Bill, Reagan Expected to Sign It," *New York Times*, October 18, 1986. The statement also singled out Representatives Peter Rodino, Howard Berman, Charles Schumer, and Esteban Torres for praise, describing Torres's role as "statesmanlike and constructive." The full statement was reprinted as an op-ed in a number of smaller news outlets; see "The National Council of La Raza on New Immigration Legislation," *City Terrace Comet*, October 23, 1986.

CHAPTER 7

1. Robert Pear, "President Signs Landmark Bill on Immigration," *New York Times*, November 7, 1986.

2. Simpson, *Right in the Old Gazoo*, 79–80.

3. Email from Nadine Cahodas to the author, March 8, 2013.

4. A video of Lehrer performing the song is at: https://www.youtube.com/watch?v=_YcGRNmkB00.

5. Email from Nadine Cahodas to the author, March 8, 2013.

6. Author interview with Rick Swartz, August 5, 2017.

7. "National Coalition Formed on Implementation of the 1986 Immigration Act," press release, November 6, 1986, *NCLR Records*, Series M744, Box 379, Folder 1.

8. Russell Crandall, "The Academic Divide: Notes from the Inside," *America's Quarterly*, vol. 9, no. 1, Winter 2015, 88.

9. Eric Lindland et al., *"Just Do It": Communicating Implementation Science and Practice* (Frameworks Institute, 2015), 6.

10. As the eminent immigration practitioner Maurice "Maury" Roberts noted, "No other country has attempted an amnesty program of this magnitude before." Robert Pear, "Amnesty Begins; U.S. Meets Immigrants on Uneasy Terms," *New York Times*, May 3, 1987.

11. Bill Ong Hing, "The Immigration and Naturalization Service, Community-Based Organizations, and the Legalization Experience: Lessons for the Self-Help Immigration Phenomenon," vol. 6, *Georgetown Law Journal*, 1992, 424.

12. Crandall, "The Academic Divide: Notes from the Inside," 90.

13. Ben Goad, "Obama's Rush to Regulate," *The Hill*, February 24, 2014, http://thehill.com/regulation/pending-regs/198999-obamas-rush-to-regulate, accessed February 24, 2014.

14. The statute required that the legalization application period begin "not later than 180 days" after enactment. See: "Immigration Reform and Control Act of 1986, Conference Report," House Report 99-1000, Committee on the Judiciary, October 14, 1986, 28, 11–12.

15. "General Support Proposal," National Immigration, Refugee and Citizenship Forum, undated but circa August 1984, 13.

16. Rick Swartz, "Immigration and Refugees: Issues, Politics & Democratic Pluralism," Rick Swartz & Associates, March 1985.

17. Author interview with Christine Gaffney, January 16, 2013.

18. Author interview with Muzaffar Chishti, May 21, 2013.

19. Documents from the period assign various names to this entity. Because the name "Ad Hoc Coalition for Immigration Reform Implementation" appears on a formal stationary letterhead, this name is used throughout this text. See: "Minutes of the Ad Hoc Coalition Meeting, October 5, 1989," Ad Hoc Coalition on Immigration Reform Implementation, November 8, 1989.

20. Author interview with Muzaffar Chishti, May 21, 2013.

21. "Minutes of the Meeting of the Outreach and Public Education Task Force, Ad Hoc Coalition on Implementation of the Immigration Bill," November 25, 1986, NCLR Records, Series M744, Box 379, Folder 3.

22. Author interviews with Carlos Murguía, July 9, 2012, and with Cris Medina, July 7, 2012.

23. Author interview with Muzaffar Chishti, May 21, 2013; see also "Minutes of the Meeting of the Outreach and Public Education Task Force, Ad Hoc Coalition on Implementation of the Immigration Bill," November 25, 1986, NCLR Records, Series M744, Box 379, Folder 3.

24. In particular, later formal coalition documents carry the "A task force of . . ." language; also, author interview with Muzaffar Chishti, May 21, 2013.

25. Author interview with Rick Swartz, June 30, 2016.

26. Author interview with Rick Swartz, August 7, 2012; see also, National Immigration, Refugee & Citizenship Forum, Forum Information Bulletin, vol. VI, no. 2, February 19, 1987, and attached "Master List of Documents Available," NCLR Records, Series M744, Box 344, Folder 1.

27. Author interview with Warren Leiden, April 26, 2013; see also National Immigration, Refugee & Citizenship Forum, Forum Information Bulletin, vol. VI, no. 2, February 19, 1987, and attached "Master List of Documents Available," NCLR Records, Series M744, Box 344, Folder 1.

28. National Immigration, Refugee & Citizenship Forum, Forum Information Bulletin, vol. VI, no. 2, February 19, 1987, and attached "Master List of Documents Available," NCLR Records, Series M744, Box 344, Folder 1.

29. Author interview with Rick Swartz, June 30, 2016.

30. Author interview with Muzaffar Chishti, May 21, 2013.

31. Author interview with Phyllis Eisen, September 19, 2012.

32. John E. Hansan, "American Public Welfare Association," The Social Welfare History Project, Virginia Commonwealth University Libraries, undated, http://socialwelfare.library.vcu.edu/public-welfare/aamerican-public-welfare-association-, accessed July 21, 2016.

33. Author interview with Carol Wolchok, December 15, 2015.

34. Cortés, Policy Analysts and Interest Groups, 353.

35. Author interview with Warren Leiden, April 26, 2013.

36. See organizational background material on the American Immigration Council website at: http://www.americanimmigrationcouncil.org/about-us, accessed July 21, 2016.

37. David S. North and Anna Mary Portz, The U.S. Alien Legalization Program, Trans Century Development Associates, June 1989, 41–42.

38. Author interview with Wade Henderson, December 19, 2012.

39. Author interview with Mary McClymont, September 23, 2012.

40. Jack Hansan, "Catholic Charities USA," The Social Welfare History Project, Virginia Commonwealth University Libraries, http://socialwelfare.library.vcu.edu/religious /catholic-charities-usa/, accessed August 10, 2016.

41. Doris M. Meissner and Demetrios G. Papademetriou, *The Legalization Countdown: A Third Quarter Assessment* (The Carnegie Endowment for International Peace, February 1988), 71.

42. Author interview with Vanna Slaughter, June 12, 2013.

43. "Legalization and Application Fees," Migration and Refugee Services, U.S. Catholic Conference, undated but circa January 1987, *NCLR Records*, Series M744, Box 344, Folder 9.

44. See reference at *Dictionary.com*, undated, http://www.dictionary.com/browse /darkie, accessed June 15, 2015.

45. Letter from Romano Mazzoli to President Reagan, January 9, 1987, in *NCLR Records*, Series M744, Box 341, Folder 3, "the Act does not state or imply . . . that the legalization program was meant to be self-funded from fees collected."

46. Charles Kamasaki's desk calendar notes this meeting took place on February 19, 1987.

47. Author interview with Warren Leiden, April 26, 2013.

48. North and Portz, *The U.S. Alien Legalization Program*, 89–90.

49. Email to the author from Cecilia Muñoz, January 3, 2018.

50. Meissner and Papademetriou, *The Legalization Countdown*, 61.

51. Hing, "The Immigration and Naturalization Service, Community-Based Organizations, and the Legalization Experience," 426.

52. Press Release, Immigration and Naturalization Service, January 20, 1986, in: *NCLR Records*, Series M744, Box 344, Folder 1.

53. American Immigration Lawyers Association, "Summary of Coalition Comments to INS Preliminary Draft Regulations Relating to Legalization," undated but circa February 15, 1987, NCLR Records, Series M744, Box 379, Folder 9.

54. Memorandum to Interested Parties from Michael Myers, December 29, 1986, *NCLR Records*, Series M744, Box 344, Folder 9.

55. National Immigration, Refugee & Citizenship Forum, *Forum Information Bulletin*, vol. VI, no. 2, February 19, 1987, and attached "Master List of Documents Available," *NCLR Records*, Series M744, Box 344, Folder 1.

56. National Immigration, Refugee & Citizenship Forum, *Forum Information Bulletin*, vol. VI, no. 2, February 19, 1987, and attached "Master List of Documents Available," *NCLR Records*, Series M744, Box 344, Folder 1.

57. Meissner and Papademetriou, *The Legalization Countdown*, 61–66.

58. Hing, "The Immigration and Naturalization Service, Community-Based Organizations, and the Legalization Experience," 447–451.

59. Meissner and Papademetriou, *The Legalization Countdown*, 40–43.

60. North and Portz, *The U.S. Alien Legalization Program*, 14–16.

61. Hing, "The Immigration and Naturalization Service, Community-Based Organizations, and the Legalization Experience," 449–52.

62. North and Portz, *The U.S. Alien Legalization Program*, 22.

63. Robert Pear, "Aliens Facing $185 Fee on Amnesty," *New York Times*, March 16, 1987.

64. "Selected Immigration Bill Implementation Issues," National Council of La Raza, April 6, 1987, and cover memorandum of same date endorsed by NCLR and twelve other national organizations.

65. Robert Pear, "US Issues Rules Making It Easier for Aliens to Obtain Legal Status," *New York Times*, May 1, 1987.

66. Author interview with Muzaffar Chishti, May 21, 2013.

67. Author interview with Arnoldo Torres, January 17, 2013.

68. Author interview with J. Michael Treviño, October 2, 2012.

69. Deirdre Martínez, *Who Speaks for Hispanics? Hispanic Interest Groups in Washington* (State University of New York Press, 2009), 35–48.

70. Marcia Chambers, "Hispanic Rights Leader Gets Post Over Ex-Governor of New Mexico," *New York Times*, March 2, 1987. See also George Ramos, "Judge Holds Up Latino Group Leader's Firing," *Los Angeles Times*, January 23, 1987.

71. Author interview with Raul Yzaguírre, July 9, 2012.

72. Agenda for NCLR Immigration Consultation, February 16–17, 1987, *NCLR Records*, Series M744, Box 379, Folder 3.

73. Author interview with Christine Gaffney, January 6, 2013.

74. Memorandum from Rose Briceño and Arnoldo Resendez to Selected NCLR Affiliates, April 7, 1987, *NCLR Records*, Series M744, Box 341, Folder 8.

75. Cortés, *Policy Analysts and Interest Groups*, 353.

76. Howard Kurtz, "Groups Call INS Proposals Onerous," *Washington Post*, February 10, 1987.

77. Author interview with Dianne Stewart, September 25, 2012.

78. Letter to Charles Kamasaki from Kirke Wilson of the Rosenberg Foundation, undated but circa late August 1987, *NCLR Records,* Series M744, Box 142, Folder 11.

79. See: Statement of Charles Kamasaki, "Review of the Early Implementation of the Immigration Reform and Control Act of 1986," *Senate Hearings*, Subcommittee on Immigration and Refugee Affairs, Committee on the Judiciary, April 10, 1987, 62–71.

80. Author interview with Michael Myers, May 21, 2013.

81. Author interview with Christine Gaffney, January 16, 2013.

82. Author interview with Cris Medina, July 7, 2012.

83. Kelly Phillips Erb, "I'm from the Government and I'm Here to Help," *Forbes*, October 21, 2011, http://www.forbes.com/sites/kellyphillipserb/2011/10/21/im-from-the-government-and-im-here-to-help/#6c0a577336f7, accessed July 30, 2016.

84. For a brief video excerpt of Reagan delivering the line, see: https://www.youtube.com/watch?v=xhYJS80MgYA, posted August 11, 2011, accessed August 2, 2016.

85. Author interview with Cris Medina, July 7, 2012.

86. Extrapolated from "Estimated Pre-1982 Population Eligible to Legalize, by State" Memorandum to Mark Everson, Executive Associate Commissioner from Office of Plans and Analysis, Immigration and Naturalization Service, October 31, 1986, Table 1.

87. Author interview with Cris Medina, July 7, 2012, and author interview with Carlos Murguía, July 7, 2012.

88. Author interview with Artúro Lopez, June 10, 2013.

89. Meissner and Papademetriou, *The Legalization Countdown*, 67–68.

90. Robert Pear, "Amnesty Begins: U.S. Meets Immigrants on Uneasy Terms," *New York Times*, May 3, 1987.

91. Lisa Hoffman and David Pasztor, "Amnesty May 5—'We're Not Ready,'" *Dallas Times-Herald*, April 22, 1987.

92. Mary Thornton, "Critics Predicting Chaos in Alien Amnesty Effort," *Washington Post*, May 4, 1987.

93. Robert Pear, "Facts on Amnesty for Illegal Aliens in the U.S.," *New York Times*, May 5, 1987.

94. Memorandum to Mark Everson, Executive Associate Commissioner from Office of Plans and Analysis, Immigration and Naturalization Service, October 31, 1986, Table 1.

95. Meissner and Papademetriou, *The Legalization Countdown*, 80–88; see also Hing, "The Immigration and Naturalization Service, Community-Based Organizations, and the Legalization Experience," 469–72.

96. Hing, "The Immigration and Naturalization Service, Community-Based Organizations, and the Legalization Experience," 469–72.

97. North and Portz, *The U.S. Alien Legalization Program*, 32 graphed from INS data.

98. Gilbert Bailon, "The DWI Penalty," *Dallas Morning News*, May 30, 1987.

99. David Pasztor, "Amnesty," *Dallas Times-Herald*, July 28, 1987.

100. Peter Applebome, "Amnesty Program for Illegal Aliens Gaining Momentum," *New York Times*, August 3, 1987.

101. Marvine Howe, "Strong Fears Remain Over New Immigration Law," *New York Times*, August 2, 1987.

102. Applebome, "Amnesty Program for Illegal Aliens Gaining Momentum."

103. Louis Freedberg, "The Role of Philanthropy in the U.S. Immigrant Rights Movement," Report to the Ford Foundation, undated but circa 2009, 23.

104. Meissner and Papademetriou, *The Legalization Countdown*, 65.

105. Author interview with Christine Gaffney, January 16, 2013, and author interview with Cris Medina, July 7, 2012.

106. North and Portz, *The U.S. Alien Legalization Program*, chart on p. 32 graphed from INS data.

107. Meissner and Papademetriou, *The Legalization Countdown*, 22–39.

108. Applebome, "Amnesty Program for Illegal Aliens Gaining Momentum."

109. North and Portz, *The U.S. Alien Legalization Program*, 28–30; Meissner and Papademetriou, *The Legalization Countdown*, 54; and Applebome, "Amnesty Program for Illegal Aliens Gaining Momentum."

110. "Immigration Reform: Implementation of Legalization Program," Statement of Arnold P. Jones, Senior Associate Director, General Government Division, U.S. General Accounting Office, GAO/GGD-T-88-27, April 14, 1988, 2.

111. Author interview with Muzaffar Chishti, May 21, 2013.

112. Author interview with Mary McClymont, September 23, 2012.

113. Author interview with Vanna Slaughter, June 12, 2013.

114. See for example, "Summary of January 28 National Coordinating Agencies Meeting," letter from US Catholic Conference and seven other agencies to Richard Norton, February 2, 1988, *NCLR Records*, Series M744, Box 351, Folder 2.

115. Author interview with Muzaffar Chishti, May 21, 2013.

116. Meissner and Papademetriou, *The Legalization Countdown*, 77.

117. Author interview with Vanna Slaughter, June 12, 2013.

118. Gilbert Bailon, "Group Warns of Little-Known Amnesty Clauses," *Dallas Morning News*, March 18, 1987.

119. David Fritze, "INS Not Informing Aliens of Their Rights, Group Says," *Dallas Times-Herald*, May 30, 1987.

120. David Fritze, "Aliens Flooding Charity Office Seeking Amnesty Advice," *Dallas Times-Herald*, April 8, 1987.

121. Author interview with Vanna Slaughter, June 12, 2013.

122. John Gonzalez, "Area Leads in Amnesty Filings," *Dallas Morning News*, May 15, 1987.

123. Meissner and Papademetriou, *The Legalization Countdown*, 42.

124. Author interview with Vanna Slaughter, June 12, 2013.

125. Author interview with Vanna Slaughter, June 12, 2013; see also, for example, David Maraniss, "For Some, No Refuge from Fear of INS Law," *Washington Post*, May 3, 1987, part of a series entitled "On the Edge of America."

126. See for example, "The Immigration Scramble," *Dallas Times Herald*, March 22–25, special section.

127. Author interview with Lisa Hoffman, September 12, 2012.

128. Author interview with Vanna Slaughter, June 12, 2013.

129. Author interview with Muzaffar Chishti, May 21, 2013.

130. Author interview with Carol Wolchok, December 18, 2015.

131. Meissner and Papademetriou, *The Legalization Countdown*: see chart on 25–26 and accompanying text.

132. Mary Thornton, "Immigrant AIDS Tests to Start Dec. 1," *Washington Post*, August 29, 1987.

133. David Fritze, "INS Agents Return to Old Ways," *Dallas Times Herald*, November 15, 1987.

134. David Fritze, "INS Arrests Immigrant Who Qualifies for Amnesty," *Dallas Times Herald*, November 5, 1987.

135. Zita Arocha, "Paper Chase Is Difficult for Immigrants Seeking Amnesty," *Washington Post*, December 28, 1987.

136. Zita Arocha, "Many Illegal Aliens Wary of Amnesty," *Washington Post*, October 21, 1987.

137. Robert Pear, "U.S. May Let Some Illegals Stay If Relatives Qualify for Amnesty," *New York Times*, October 22, 1987.

138. Zita Arocha, "No Blanket Policy Set for Ineligible Spouses of Amnesty Aliens," *Washington Post*, October 22, 1987.

139. Doris M. Meissner, "A Better Fate for Split Families: INS, Tangled in Rules, Misses the Purpose of Amnesty," *Los Angeles Times*, November 5, 1987.

140. North and Portz, *The U.S. Alien Legalization Program*, chart on 32 graphed from INS data, and text on preceding pages 29–30.

141. Pear, "U.S. May Let Some Illegals Stay if Relatives Qualify for Amnesty."

142. North and Portz, *The U.S. Alien Legalization Program*, chart on 32 graphed from INS data.

143. Author interview with Warren Leiden, April 26, 2013.

144. Meissner and Papademetriou, *The Legalization Countdown*, 10.

145. Author interview with Tom Castro, July 7, 2012.

146. Meissner and Papademetriou, *The Legalization Countdown*, 10–11.

147. Author interview with Tom Castro, July 7, 2012.

148. Hing, "The Immigration and Naturalization Service, Community-Based Organizations, and the Legalization Experience," 438.

149. "Summary of Empirical Studies of Why Legalization Eligibles Have Not

Applied," Fact Sheet, National Council of La Raza, undated but circa. March 1988, *NCLR Records*, Series M744, Box 344, Folder 16.

150. Meissner and Papademetriou, *The Legalization Countdown*, 10–18.

151. Several of the most important cases are summarized in North and Portz, *The U.S. Alien Legalization Program*, 61–66. In subsequent litigation the courts ultimately decided that while they could rule on the eligibility questions, after the program ended they lacked the power to order a "judicial extension" of the amnesty application period; see: "Illegal Immigrants Who Missed Amnesty Period Lose Suit Again," *New York Times*, May 4, 1997.

152. "Extend and Expand" outline, National Immigration, Refugee and Citizenship Forum, undated but circa January 1988.

153. See text of "Dear Colleague" letter from Rep. Charles Schumer, February 10, 1988, *NCLR Records*, Series M744, Box 349, Folder 4.

154. Robert McG. Thomas Jr., "Alan Nelson, 63, Who Led Immigration Overhauls for U.S. and California," *New York Times*, obituary, February 6, 197.

155. Alan C. Nelson, Commissioner, Immigration and Naturalization Service, "Press Conference Statement," January 13, 1988, IRCA Update, in *NCLR Records*, Series M744, Box 344, Folder 15.

156. See: Memorandum to Mark Everson, Executive Associate Commissioner from Office of Plans and Analysis, Immigration and Naturalization Service, October 31, 1986, Table 1. The memo's author, Robert Warren, head of the INS Statistical Analysis Branch, later wrote that his estimate of 1.3–2.7 million potential eligibles was deemed "too low" by INS management which publicly projected 2—4 million legalization applicants; email from Robert Warren to Charles Kamasaki, December 10, 2014.

157. See North and Portz, *The U.S. Alien Legalization Program*, 53–54; see also Meissner and Papademetriou, *The Legalization Countdown*, 83.

158. Martin Tolchin, "Amnesty for Aliens Might Be Extended," *New York Times*, January 23, 1988.

159. Martin Tolchin, "Aliens Get Extension for Amnesty Proof," *New York Times*, March 19, 1988.

160. "Dear Colleague" letter from Rep. Charles Schumer, February 10, 1988, *NCLR Records*, Series M744, Box 349, Folder 4.

161. Letter from Reps. Albert Bustamante, Esteban Torres, and Bill Richardson to Rep. Peter Rodino, February 24, 1988, *NCLR Records*, Series M744, Box 349, Folder 4.

162. See "Action Needed Immediately on Extension of Legalization," Action Alert, National Council of La Raza, February 22, 1988; see also "Summary of Empirical Studies of Why Legalization Eligibles Have Not Applied," undated but circa April 1988, *NCLR Records*, Series M744, Box 349, Folder 6, and "Fact Sheet on Extension of Legalization," National Council of La Raza, undated but circa April 1988, *NCLR Records*, Series M744, Box 349, Folder 6.

163. "Doris Meissner, Senior Fellow and Director, U.S. Immigration Policy Program," Migration Policy Institute, http://www.migrationpolicy.org/about/staff/doris-meissner, undated, accessed March 31, 2017.

164. See the Endowment's website at: http://carnegieendowment.org/about/, accessed March 31, 2017.

165. Meissner and Papademetriou, *The Legalization Countdown*, 143.

166. "Demetrios G. Papademetriou, President of MPI Europe and President Emeritus

of MPI," Migration Policy Institute, http://www.migrationpolicy.org/about/staff /demetrios-g-papademetriou, undated, accessed March 31, 2–17.

167. Meissner and Papademetriou, *The Legalization Countdown*, xviii–9.

168. See the Institute's website at: www.migrationpolicy.org. In the interest of full disclosure, the author serves as a fellow at MPI, which provided extensive support for this book.

169. "Dear Representative" letter from US Catholic Conference and other organizations, March 2, 1988, *NCLR Records*, Series M744, Box 349, Folder 4.

170. "Dear Senator" letter from AFL-CIO and fifteen national organizations, April 22, 1988, *NCLR Records*, Series M744, Box 349, Folder 7.

171. "House Panel Votes to Extend Time for Aliens to Seek Legal Status," *New York Times*, April 1, 1988.

172. Doris Meissner, "The Alien Amnesty Should Be Extended . . . Despite the Good Job that INS Has Done," and Joe W. Pitts and Vanna Slaughter, "The Alien Amnesty Should Be Extended . . . Because of the Poor Job that INS Has Done," *Christian Science Monitor*, April 11, 1988.

173. "Immigration Reform: Implementation of Legalization Program," Statement of Arnold P. Jones, Senior Associate Director, General Government Division, U.S. General Accounting Office, GAO/GGD-T-88-27, April 14, 1988, 4.

174. Associated Press, "House Passes Extension of Amnesty Deadline for Illegal Aliens," *New York Times*, April 21, 1988.

175. Author interview with Albert Jacquez, November 14, 2012.

176. Peter Applebome, "Time for Amnesty? Congress' Debate on Extending Plan Rehashes Original Issues," *New York Times*, April 26, 1988.

177. Associated Press, "Chance of Amnesty Extension Appears Dead," *New York Times*, April 29, 1988.

178. North and Portz, *The U.S. Alien Legalization Program*, 32.

179. Meissner and Papademetriou, *The Legalization Countdown*, 10.

180. North and Portz, *The U.S. Alien Legalization Program*, 31.

181. Hing, "The Immigration and Naturalization Service, Community-Based Organizations, and the Legalization Experience," 458.

182. North and Portz, *The U.S. Alien Legalization Program*, 30.

183. "Immigration Reform: Implementation of Legalization Program," Statement of Arnold P. Jones, Senior Associate Director, General Government Division, U.S. General Accounting Office, GAO/GGD-T-88-27, April 14, 1988, 10. See also extended discussion in: Meissner and Papademetriou, *The Legalization Countdown*, 50–54.

184. Donald Kerwin and Charles Wheeler, *The Case for Legalization, Lessons from 1986, Recommendations for the Future* (Center for Migration Studies of New York, 2004), 18–19.

185. Author interview with Cecilia Muñoz, December 20, 2016.

186. Zita Arocha, "Amnesty's Gate to Swing Shut This Week for Illegal Aliens," *Washington Post*, May 2, 1988.

187. Richard R. Aguirre, "Agents Round Up 21 Aliens," *Dallas Times-Herald*, May 6, 1988.

188. North and Portz, *The U.S. Alien Legalization Program*, 30–33.

189. Muzaffar Chishti and Charles Kamasaki, "IRCA in Retrospect, Guideposts for Today's Reform," Policy Brief, Migration Policy Institute, January 2014, 6. The calculation comes from comparing the 1.6 million ultimately approved for Lawful Per-

manent Resident Status reported by various INS Statistical Yearbooks to the 1.767 million total applicants. See Don Kerwin, "More Than IRCA: US Legalization Programs and the Current Policy Debate," Policy Brief, Migration Policy Institute, December 2010, 2.

190. Wayne King and Warren Weaver Jr., "Washington Talk: Briefing; Immigration Battles," *Washington Post*, December 30, 1986.

191. North and Portz, *The U.S. Alien Legalization Program*.

192. See Paul Sabin, *The Bet: Paul Erlich, Julian Simon, and Our Gamble Over the Earth's Future* (Yale University Press, 2013).

193. Author interview with Roger Conner, February 11, 2013.

194. James Crawford, *Hold Your Tongue* (Addison-Wesley, 1992), 152–53, and author interview with Roger Conner, February 11, 2013.

195. Jason DeParle, "The Anti-Immigrant Crusader," *New York Times*, April 17, 2011.

196. Crawford, *Hold Your Tongue*, 152–53.

197. Cortés, *Policy Analysts and Interest Groups*, 214–35, and James Crawford, "English Issue Hides Immigration, Population Agendas," *Mesa Tribune*, October 21, 1988.

198. Jessica Weinberg, "Guilt by Association," *The American Prospect*, May 2, 2010; see also James Crawford, "What's Behind Official English?" in James Crawford, ed., *Language Loyalties: A Source Book on the Official English Controversy* (University of Chicago Press, 1992), 171.

199. Crawford, *Hold Your Tongue*, 153–54.

200. "IRLI Beginnings," Center for New Community, April 15, 2015.

201. "Immigration Rights Leader Rick Swartz Discusses His Battles Against the Anti-Immigrant Movement," *Intelligence Report*, Southern Poverty Law Center, June 18, 2002.

202. Crawford, *Hold Your Tongue*, 154.

203. Memorandum to WITAN IV Attendees from John Tanton, October 10, 1986, copy on file with the author, available on-line via https://www.splcenter.org/fighting -hate/intelligence-report/2015/witan-memo-iii, accessed June 17, 2016.

204. Jason DeParle, "The Anti-Immigrant Crusader," *New York Times*, April 17, 2011.

205. Crawford, "English Issue Hides Immigration, Population Agendas," and James Crawford, "Official English Attracting Bizarre Followers," *Mesa Tribune*, October 22, 1988. See also Crawford, "What's Behind Official English?" Crawford documented $2.5 million in contributions from Cordelia Scaife May to Tanton groups, a figure he later increased to $5.8 million after collecting more data; see Crawford, *Hold Your Tongue*, 158.

206. Joseph Tanfani, "Late Heiress' Anti-Immigration Efforts Live On," *Los Angeles Times*, July 25, 2013.

207. Crawford, "English Issue Hides Immigration, Population Agendas," and Crawford, "Official English Attracting Bizarre Followers."

208. Linda Greenhouse, "Supreme Court Roundup: Appeal to Save English-Only Law Fails," *New York Times*, January 12, 1999.

209. Crawford, "What's Behind Official English?" 171–72.

210. Jason DeParle, "The Anti-Immigrant Crusader," *New York Times*, April 17, 2011.

211. "The Puppeteer," *Intelligence Report*, Southern Poverty Law Center, June 18, 2002, 48.

212. Crawford, *Hold Your Tongue*, 163–65.

213. Crawford, *Hold Your Tongue*, 161–62.

214. DeParle, "The Anti-Immigrant Crusader."

215. Author interview with Roger Conner, February 11, 2013.

216. Barfield, "Immigration Perils U.S., Group Fears"; see also "Immigration Rights Leader Rick Swartz Discusses His Battles Against the Anti-Immigrant Movement," *Intelligence Report*, Southern Poverty Law Center, June 18, 2002.

217. DeParle, "The Anti-Immigrant Crusader."

218. Author interview with Roger Conner, February 11, 2013.

219. "Immigration Reform and Control Act: Report of the Legalized Alien Population," US Department of Justice, immigration and Naturalization Service, 1992, cited in: Kerwin and Wheeler, *The Case for Legalization, Lessons from 1986, Recommendations for the Future*, 20.

220. Meissner and Papademetriou, *The Legalization Countdown*, 83.

221. Martin, "The SAW Legalization Program," Appendix I, 115–32.

222. See discussion in North and Portz, *The U.S. Alien Legalization Program*, 46–51 and 76–89.

223. See extended discussion in Martin, "The SAW Legalization Program," Appendix I, 115–32.

224. North and Portz, *The U.S. Alien Legalization Program*, 52.

225. Martin, "The SAW Legalization Program," Appendix I, 115–32. See also North and Portz, *The U.S. Alien Legalization Program*, 80–82.

226. Associated Press, "U.S. Amnesty Ends for Farmworkers," *New York Times*, December 1, 1988.

227. Associated Press, "Fraud Charged in Program Giving Amnesty to Illegal Farm Workers," *New York Times*, December 22, 1988.

228. North and Portz, *The U.S. Alien Legalization Program*, 76–89.

229. North and Portz, *The U.S. Alien Legalization Program*, 89–93.

230. "INS Adjudications from the 19th to the 21st Century," *Interpreter Releases*, vol. 66, no. 9, March 6, 1989, 249.

231. North and Portz, *The U.S. Alien Legalization Program*, 94.

232. Chishti and Kamasaki, "IRCA in Retrospect, Guideposts for Today's Reform," 6. The calculation comes from comparing the nearly 1.1 million approved for Lawful Permanent Resident Status reported by various *INS Statistical Yearbooks* to the 1.3 million applicants. See Kerwin, "More Than IRCA: US Legalization Programs and the Current Policy Debate," 2.

233. Kerwin, "More Than IRCA: US Legalization Programs and the Current Policy Debate," chart on 2 and discussion on 4.

234. Studies conducted relatively soon after the legalization programs ended are cited in Chishti and Kamasaki, "IRCA in Retrospect, Guideposts for Today's Reform," 6. Several more recent studies are cited in Maria E. Enchautegui, "Legalization Programs and the Integration of Unauthorized Immigrants: A Comparison of S. 744 and IRCA," *Journal on Migration and Human Security*, vol. 2, no.1, 2014, 1 and 4.

235. Author interview with Vanna Slaughter, June 12, 2013.

236. Author interview with Martha Escutia, November 1, 2012.

237. Author interview with J. Michael Treviño, October 2, 2012.

238. Author interview with Richard Fajardo, October 30, 2012.

239. When informed that MALDEF had opposed IRCA, one member of the group's board of directors in the 1980s "could not believe it"; author interview with Tom Castro, July 7, 2012.

240. Author interview with Howard Berman, March 5, 2013.

241. Q&A: Alan Simpson; "1986 Immigration Reform Legislation," *San Diego Union-Tribune*, May 28, 2006.

242. Larry Richter, "Mexicans Crowd a Last Opening to the U.S.," *New York Times*, June 20, 1988.

243. See Frank D. Bean, Barry Edmonston, and Jeffrey Passel, eds., *Undocumented Migration to the United States* (Rand Corporation and Urban Institute, 1990), 238.

244. Pierrette Hondagreu-Sotelo and Angelica Salas, "What Explains the Immigrant Rights Marches of 2006?," in Rachel Buff, ed., *Immigrant Rights in the Shadow of Citizenship* (New York University Press, 2008), 214.

245. Author interview with Wade Henderson, December 19, 2012.

246. Kerwin and Wheeler, *The Case for Legalization, Lessons from 1986, Recommendations for the Future*, 18.

247. Sara Campos, "The Influence of Civil Society in U.S. Immigrant Communities and the U.S. Immigration Debate," in *International Migration, U.S. Immigration Law, and Civil Society: From the Pre-Colonial Era to the 113th Congress* (Scalabrini International Network, 2014), 150.

248. See discussion in: Meissner and Papademetriou, *The Legalization Countdown*, 88–95.

249. Author interview with Frank Sharry, August 12, 2012.

250. Louis Freedberg, "The Role of Philanthropy in the U.S. Immigrant Rights Movement," Report to the Ford Foundation, undated but circa 2009, 26.

251. "About Us: Who We Are," undated, http://www.thenyic.org/who-we-are, accessed May 30, 2016.

252. See the group's website at: http://miracoalition.org/about-us, accessed May 30, 2016.

253. "Boston Plans Help for Illegal Aliens," *New York Times*, October 11, 1987.

254. Author interview with Cecilia Muñoz, December 20, 2016.

255. "Our Story," undated, http://www.chirla.us/our-story, accessed September 6, 2016.

256. Ruth Milkman, Joshua Bloom, and Victor Narro, *Working for Justice: The L.A. Model of Organizing and Advocacy* (Cornell University Press, 2010), 76.

257. See "Los Pineros," http://lospineros.com/, undated, accessed August 12, 2016. See also: Brinda Sarathy, *Pineros: Latino Labour and the Changing Face of Forestry in the Pacific Northwest* (University of British Columbia Press, 2012).

258. Sarathy, *Pineros: Latino Labour and the Changing Face of Forestry in the Pacific Northwest*, 110–11.

259. "History of PCUN," http://www.pcun.org/about-pcun/history-of-pcun/, undated but circa 2014, accessed August 10, 2016.

260. Sarathy, *Pineros: Latino Labour and the Changing Face of Forestry in the Pacific Northwest*, 111.

261. Author interview with Larry Kleinman, June 12, 2013.

262. Author interview with Larry Kleinman, June 12, 2013.

263. "History of PCUN," http://www.pcun.org/about-pcun/history-of-pcun/, undated but ca. 2014, accessed August 10, 2016.

264. Author interview with Larry Kleinman, June 12, 2013.

265. Gary D. Bass, David F. Arons, Kay Guinane, and Mathew F. Carter, *Seen But Not Heard: Strengthening Nonprofit Advocacy* (Aspen Institute, 2007).

266. Memorandum to the Board of Directors and Members of the National Immigration, Refugee and Citizenship Forum from Board Chair Pat Craig, June 18, 1986, and accompanying "Summary of Board Resolutions and Actions."

267. Author interview with Vanna Slaughter, June 12, 2013.

268. Memorandum to the Board of Directors and Members of the National Immigration, Refugee and Citizenship Forum from Board Chair Pat Craig, June 18, 1986, and accompanying "Summary of Board Resolutions and Actions."

269. Author interview with Muzaffar Chishti, January 19, 2013.

270. Author interview with Cecilia Muñoz, December 2, 2016.

271. Rinku Sen with Kekkak Mandouh, *The Accidental American, Immigration and Citizenship in the Age of Globalization* (Berret-Koehler Publishers, Inc., 2008), 56–57.

272. Author interview with Cecilia Muñoz, December 2, 2016.

273. Letter from Charles Kamasaki to Scott Nielson, John D. and Catherine T. MacArthur Foundation, September 10, 1999.

274. "The Missing Link: Community-based Organization Participation in ESL-Civics Classes," National Council of La Raza Memorandum, March 1989.

275. American Council for Nationalities Service and the National Council of La Raza, "ESL Civics: Planning and Implementing English and Civics Programs, A Handbook," American Council for Nationalities Service, 1988; and American Council for Nationalities Service and National Council of La Raza, "SLIAG Advocacy Packet: A Guide for Community Base Organizations," National Council of La Raza, April 1989.

276. "Issue Update: Immigration and related issues," National Council of La Raza, undated but circa March 1988, 8.

277. American Immigration Council, "Reagan-Bush Family Fairness: A Chronological History," December 9, 2014, https://www.americanimmigrationcouncil.org/research/reagan-bush-family-fairness-chronological-history, accessed May 30, 2016.

278. Summarized in Cecilia Muñoz, *Unfinished Business: The Immigration Reform and Control Act of 1986* (National Council of La Raza, 1990), endnotes 32 and 33.

279. Zita Arocha, "In Shift, INS Backs Family Unity," *Washington Post*, May 24, 1988.

280. Muñoz, *Unfinished Business: The Immigration Reform and Control Act of 1986*, conclusions and recommendations on legalization on 49–51.

281. Scott McConnell, "The New Battle Over Immigration," *Fortune*, 1988, republished in: http://fortune.com/2013/06/16/the-new-battle-over-immigration-fortune-1988/, June 16, 2013, accessed June 17, 2013.

282. George T. Silvestri and John M. Lukasiewitcz, "Occupational Employment Projections: The 1984-95 Outlook," *Monthly Labor Review*, 1985, cited in Chishti and Kamasaki, "IRCA in Retrospect, Guideposts for Today's Reform," 10.

283. General Accounting Office, "The Future Flow of Legal Immigration to the United States," GAO/PEMD-88-7, January 1988, 3.

284. Miriam Jordan, "Diversity Visa Lottery: Inside the Program That Admitted a Terror Suspect," *New York Times*, November 1, 2017.

285. Michael E. Miller, "Diversity Visa Lottery, Criticized after New York Terrorist Attack, Was Invented to Help the Irish," *Washington Post*, November 1, 2017.

286. Neil A. Lewis, "Washington at Work; Wyoming's Folksy Senate Orator, Sharp-Tongued Ally of the President," *New York Times*, October 24, 1990.

287. Gary E. Rubin and Judith Golub, "The Immigration Act of 1990: An American Jewish Committee Analysis," American Jewish Committee, 1990, 11.

288. Zita Arocha, "In Shift, INS Backs Family Unity," *Washington Post*, May 24, 1988.

289. "Statement of the Honorable Peter W. Rodino, Jr.," attached to "Action Alert," National Immigration, Refugee & Citizenship Forum, August 1, 1988.

290. "Rep. Berman Introduces Bill to Reform Legal Immigration Procedures," news release, Office of Congressman Howard Berman, September 16, 1988.

291. Author interview with Warren Leiden, April 26, 2013.

292. Author interview with Cecilia Muñoz, December 2, 2016.

293. Carolyn Wong, *Lobbying for Inclusion, Rights Politics and the Making of Immigration Policy* (Stanford University Press, 2006), 102.

294. Cited in Tichenor, *Dividing Lines*, 269.

295. Author interview with Cecilia Muñoz, December 2, 2016.

296. Letter from Reps. Bustamante, Mineta, Towns, Torres, Matsui, Roybal, Dellums, and Dymally to Rep. Rodino, September 23, 1988.

297. Author interview with Cecilia Muñoz, December 2, 2016.

298. Douglas L. Martin, "Jack Brooks, Former Texas Congressman, Dies at 89," *New York Times*, December 5, 2012.

299. Martin, "Jack Brooks, Former Texas Congressman, Dies at 89."

300. Timothy R. Smith, "Jim Wright, House Speaker Who Resigned Amidst an Ethics Investigation, Dies at 92," *Washington Post*, May 6, 2015.

301. Robin Toner, "Wright Drama Is Officially Open and Democrats Play Many Roles," *New York Times*, April 18, 1989.

302. Cahodas, "House Judiciary Looks to Post-Rodino Era," 1307.

303. Interview with Romano "Ron" Mazzoli, Romano "Ron" Mazzoli Oral History Project, August 6, 2010.

304. Cose, *A Nation of Strangers*, 89.

305. "METRO DATELINES; Congressman Joins Race for Governor," *New York Times*, January 10, 1990.

306. Lee May, "Senate Panel Backs First Cap on Immigration," *Los Angeles Times*, June 9, 1989.

307. Stella Pope Duarte, *Raul H. Yzaguirre, Seated at the Table of Power* (Latino Book Publisher, 2016), 294.

308. Prepared statement of Cecilia Muñoz, National Council of La Raza, for the Subcommittee on Immigration and Refugee Policy, Committee on the Judiciary, United States Senate, March 3, 1989, 13.

309. Author interview with Cecilia Muñoz, December 2, 2016.

310. Cose, *A Nation of Strangers*, 195–203; see also, Wong, *Lobbying for Inclusion, Rights Politics and the Making of Immigration Policy*, 103–4.

311. May, "Senate Panel Backs First Cap on Immigration."

312. Email from Cecilia Muñoz to the author, January 3, 2018.

313. Readers can view a YouTube video of a typical mid-1980s episode of the program here: http://www.mclaughlin.com/video.htm?i=2134, accessed June 23, 2017.

314. Author interview with Cecilia Muñoz, December 2, 2016.

315. Vote No. 107, Roll Call Vote 101st Congress-1st Session, https://www.senate .gov/legislative/LIS/roll_call_lists/roll_call_vote_cfm.cfm?congress=101&session=1& vote=00107, accessed June 23, 2017.

316. Wong, *Lobbying for Inclusion, Rights Politics and the Making of Immigration Policy*, 103.

317. Vote No. 109, Roll Call Vote 101st Congress-1st Session, https://www.senate .gov/legislative/LIS/roll_call_lists/roll_call_vote_cfm.cfm?congress=101&session=1& vote=00109, accessed June 23, 2017.

318. Cose, *A Nation of Strangers*, 203.

319. Vote No. 110, Roll Call Vote 101st Congress-1st Session, https://www.senate .gov/legislative/LIS/roll_call_lists/roll_call_vote_cfm.cfm?congress=101&session=1& vote=00110, accessed June 23, 2017.

320. Roll Call No. 113, 101st Congress-1st Session, https://www.senate.gov /legislative/LIS/roll_call_lists/roll_call_vote_cfm.cfm?congress=101&session=1& vote=00113, accessed June 23, 2017.

321. Author interview with Cecilia Muñoz, December 2, 2016.

322. Author interview with Warren Leiden, April 26, 2013.

323. Wong, *Lobbying for Inclusion, Rights Politics and the Making of Immigration Policy*, 105.

324. Susan Rasky, "Senate Votes to Ease Immigration for Professionals and Europeans," *New York Times,* July 14, 1989.

325. "Testimony on Legal Immigration Reform, S. 358, H.R. 672, H.R. 2448," prepared statement of Cecilia Muñoz, National Council of La Raza, before the House of Representatives, Subcommittee on Immigration, Refugees and International Law, September 27, 1989.

326. "Summary: H.R.3374—101st Congress," https://www.congress.gov/bill/101st -congress/house-bill/3374?q=%7B%22search%22%3A%5B%22H.R.+3374 %2C+101st+Congress%22%5D%7D&r=7, accessed June 29, 2017.

327. American Immigration Council, "Reagan-Bush Family Fairness: A Chronological History," December 9, 2014, https://www.americanimmigrationcouncil .org/research/reagan-bush-family-fairness-chronological-history, accessed May 30, 2016.

328. American Immigration Council, "Reagan-Bush Family Fairness: A Chronological History."

329. Marvin Howe, "New Policy Aids Families of Aliens," *New York Times*, March 5, 1990.

330. American Immigration Council, "Reagan-Bush Family Fairness: A Chronological History."

331. "Amnesty and Compassion," *Washington Post*, February 6, 1990; http://pqasb .pqarchiver.com/washingtonpost/doc/307234315.html?FMT=ABS&FMTS=ABS:FT& date=Feb+6%2C+1990&author=&desc=Amnesty+and+Compassion, accessed May 30, 2016.

332. Howe, "New Policy Aids Families of Aliens."

333. "Metro Datelines; Congressman Joins Race for Governor," *New York Times*, January 10, 1990.

334. Zolberg, *A Nation by Design*, 378–79.

335. Wong, *Lobbying for Inclusion, Rights Politics and the Making of Immigration Policy*, 104–5.

336. Cose, *A Nation of Strangers*, 205.

337. H.R.4300—Family Unity and Employment Opportunity Immigration Act of 1990, 101st Congress, https://www.congress.gov/bill/101st-congress/house-bill/4300/all-actions?q=%7B%22search%22%3A%5B%22H.R.+4300+101st+Congress%22%5D%7D&r=14&overview=closed#tabs, accessed June 29, 2017.

338. Kirk Johnson, "Underdog to Front-Runner in Connecticut," *New York Times*, April 5, 1990.

339. Letter from Bruce C. Navarro, Deputy Assistant Attorney General to Rep. Hamilton Fish, Ranking Minority Member of the Judiciary Committee, July 30, 1990.

340. Memorandum from Michael Hill, US Catholic Conference, to Family Immigration Coalition, July 20, 1990.

341. Author interview with Cecilia Muñoz, December 2, 2016.

342. Memorandum from Rick Swartz to Jim McGovern, September 26, 1990.

343. The Judiciary Committee reported the bill out to the House on August 1, 1990; see: https://www.congress.gov/bill/101st-congress/house-bill/4300/all-actions?q=%7B%22search%22%3A%5B%22H.R.+4300+101st+Congress%22%5D%7D&r=14&overview=closed#tabs, accessed June 29, 2017.

344. Michael C. Ybarra, "House Judiciary Committee Votes Major Immigration Reform," *Washington Post*, August 2, 1990.

345. Kirk Johnson, "Connecticut Victory Shows Tax Fears, Morrison Says," *New York Times*, September 13, 1990.

346. Author interview with Rick Swartz, August 7, 2012; see also, Memorandum from Rick Swartz to Charles Kolb, September 26, 1990, and a fax sent the following day, on September 27; hard copies in author's files.

347. Letter from Bernard Cardinal Law, Archbishop of Boston to White House Chief of Staff John H. Sununu, September 27, 1990.

348. Statement of Administration Policy, H.R. 4300—Family Unity and Employment Opportunity Immigration Act of 1990, Executive Office of the President, Office of Management and Budget, September 26, 1990.

349. "Arena Profile: Rep. Dan Lungren," *Politico*, http://www.politico.com/arena/bio/rep_dan_lungren_.html, accessed July 2, 2017.

350. Cose, *A Nation of Strangers*, 205.

351. "H.R. 4300—Family Unity and Employment Opportunity Immigration Act of 1990," 101st Congress, https://www.congress.gov/bill/101st-congress/house-bill/4300/all-actions?q=%7B%22search%22%3A%5B%22H.R.+4300%22%5D%7D&r=1&overview=closed#tabs, accessed June 29, 2017.

352. "Final Votes Results for Roll Call 406," http://clerk.house.gov/evs/1990/roll406.xml, accessed June 29, 2017.

353. Nathaniel C. Nash, "Immigration Bill Debated in House," *New York Times*, October 3, 1990.

354. "Issue Update: Legal Immigration Reform," National Council of La Raza, October 31, 1990. See also Lee May, "Immigration Bill Survives Latino Attack," *Los Angeles Times*, October 27, 1990.

355. Cose, *A Nation of Strangers*, 206–7.

356. "Bill Summary and Status 101st Congress (1989–90) S. 358, "All Congressional

Actions with Amendments," http://thomas.loc.gov/, accessed March 11, 2013 ("Thomas" queries are now redirected to www.congress.gov).

357. Robert Pear, "Congress Sets Tentative Pact on Immigration Rise," *New York Times*, October 20, 1990.

358. "The Golden Door, Ajar," *New York Times*, October 13, 1990.

359. Robert Pear, "Lawmakers Agree on Immigration Rise," *New York Times*, October 21, 1990.

360. Edgardo Ayala, "Declassified Docs Shed Light on Jesuits' Murders," Institute for Policy Studies, November 27, 2009, https://web.archive.org/web/20101203223753/http://www.ipsnews.net/news.asp?idnews=49447, accessed July 7, 2017.

361. Clifford Krauss, "Washington at Work; Religion and Politics Become Fused in Congressman's District, and Heart," *New York Times*, August 23, 1990.

362. Author interview with Rick Swartz, August 12, 2012.

363. Muzaffar Chishti and Steven Yale-Loehr, "The Immigration Act of 1990: Unfinished Business a Quarter-Century Later," Issue Brief, Migration Policy Institute, July 2016, 2.

364. John Newhouse, "Taking It Personally," *The New Yorker*, March 16, 1992, 67.

365. Author interview with Frank Sharry, August 16, 2012.

366. Author interview with Frank Sharry, August 16, 2012.

367. Carol L. Wolchok, "Extensive Revision of Statute Will Have Broad Consequences," *The National Law Journal*, vol. 13, no. 38, May 27, 1991, 23.

368. Susan Gzesh, "Central Americans and Asylum Policy in the Reagan Era," *Migration Information Source*, Migration Policy Institute, April 1, 2006, 6.

369. Muzaffar Chishti and Steven Yale-Loehr, "The Immigration Act of 1990: Unfinished Business a Quarter-Century Later," Issue Brief, Migration Policy Institute, July 2016, 7. They note that despite the prohibition many TPS beneficiaries have qualified for green cards through family or employer visas.

370. *Congressional Record*, October 26, 1990, S17108-9 (Remarks of Sen. DeConcini).

371. Author interview with Cecilia Muñoz, December 2, 2016.

372. "Congressional Reaction to Immigration Act," *c-span.org*, October 26, 1990, https://www.c-span.org/video/?14719-1/congressional-reaction-immigration-act, accessed June 29, 2017.

373. See Wolchok, "Extensive Revision of Statute Will Have Broad Consequences," 25.

374. Philip J. Hilts, "Landmark Accord Promises to Ease Immigration Curbs," *New York Times*, October 26, 1990.

375. Cose, *A Nation of Strangers*, 206.

376. "All actions H.Res.531—101st Congress (1989–1990)," https://www.congress.gov/bill/101st-congress/house-resolution/531/all-actions?overview=closed&q=%7B%22roll-call-vote%22%3A%22all%22%7D, accessed July 20, 2017.

377. May, "Immigration Bill Survives Latino Attack."

378. Cose, *A Nation of Strangers*, 206.

379. "Bill Summary and Status 101st Congress (1989–90) S. 358, "All Congressional Actions with Amendments," http://thomas.loc.gov/, accessed March 11, 2013 ("Thomas" queries are now redirected to www.congress.gov). See also Robert Pear, "Major Immigration Bill Is Sent to Bush," *New York Times*, October 29, 1990.

380. "Statement on Signing the Immigration Act of 1990," November 29, 1990, http://www.presidency.ucsb.edu/ws/?pid=19117, accessed December 18, 2012.

381. Kirk Johnson, "The 1990 Elections: Connecticut—Battle for Governor; Weicker Triumphs Narrowly as a Loner in a 3-Way Race," *New York Times*, November 7, 1990.

382. Warren R. Leiden and Davis L. Neal, "Highlights of the Immigration Act of 1990," *Fordham International Law Journal*, vol. 14, no. 1, 100, 328–30.

383. Pear, "Major Immigration Bill Is Sent to Bush."

384. Cose, *A Nation of Strangers*, 207.

385. Wong, *Lobbying for Inclusion, Rights Politics and the Making of Immigration Policy*, 105, and "Rita Simon Interview," *The First Measured Century*, Public Broadcasting Service, http://www.pbs.org/fmc/interviews/simon.htm, July 2, 2017.

386. Gary E. Rubin and Judith Golub, "The Immigration Act of 1990: An American Jewish Committee Analysis," American Jewish Committee, 1990, 1.

387. "Issue Update: Legal Immigration Reform," National Council of La Raza, October 31, 1990, 1–3.

388. Navarro, *Mexicano Experience in Occupied Aztlan*, 527.

389. Author interview with Warren Leiden, April 26, 2013.

390. Author interview with Cecilia Muñoz, December 2, 2016.

391. Crawford, *Hold Your Tongue*, 162.

392. Ed Mendel, "Prop. 187 Opponents Question FAIR Funding," *San Diego Union-Tribune*, September 4, 1994.

393. Tucker Carlson, "The Intellectual Roots of Nativism," *Wall Street Journal*, October 2, 1997.

394. See the official website at: http://www.thesocialcontract.com/info/about_the_social_contract.html, accessed June 29, 2016.

395. "The Puppeteer," *Intelligence Report*, Southern Poverty law Center, June 18, 2002, 47; see also "White Nationalist Hired to Manage Anti-Immigrant PAC," *Imagine 2050*, Center for New Community, February 12, 2014.

396. Crawford, *Hold Your Tongue*, 161.

397. Jason DeParle, "The Anti-Immigration Crusader," *New York Times*, April 17, 2011.

398. Heidi Beirich, *The Nativist Lobby: Three Faces of Intolerance*, Southern Poverty Law Center, January 31, 2009, https://www.splcenter.org/20090201/nativist-lobby-three-faces-intolerance, 11, accessed June 17, 2016.

399. *Village Voice*, August 17, 1993, cited in Letter from Grover Norquist, Americans for Tax Reform, to US Senators, February 28, 1996.

400. "The Puppeteer," 45–46.

401. Cited in Jill Garvey, "Rick Oltman: Environmentalist or White Supremacist?, *Imagine 2050*, April 30, 2009, Center for New Community, http://imagine2050.newcomm.org/2009/04/30/rick-oltman-environmentalist-or-white-supremacist/, accessed June 2, 2016.

402. Center for New Community, *Protect Arizona Now Selects White Supremacist Leader to Chair National Advisory Board*, Center for New Community Special Report, August 2004, 4.

403. "The Puppeteer," 48–51.

404. Ron Russell, "The Greening of Hate," *New Times*, March 12, 1998.

405. Jim Motavalli, "Birth Control or Border Patrol?" *ASAP*, Earth Action Network, July 17, 1998.

406. John H. Cushman Jr., "Sierra Club Rejects Move to Oppose Immigration," *New York Times*, April 26, 1998.

407. Motavalli, "Birth Control or Border Patrol?"

408. Cushman, Jr., "Sierra Club Rejects Move To Oppose Immigration."

409. Tucker Carlson, "The Intellectual Roots of Nativism," *Wall Street Journal*, October 2, 1997.

410. David Welch, "Where Have You Gone, Bill Buckley?" *New York Times*, December 3, 2012.

411. Zolberg, *A Nation by Design*, 397.

412. Bruce Webber, "Paul Weyrich, 66, a Conservative Strategist, Dies," *New York Times*, December 18, 2008.

413. Morton Kondracke and Fred Barnes, *Jack Kemp: The Bleeding Heart Conservative Who Changed America* (Sentinel, 2015).

414. Author interview with Rick Swartz, July 30, 2012.

415. Ben Wattenberg, *Jewish World Review*, April 25, 2000.

416. John B. Judis, *New Republic*, June 2000, cited in "Is FAIR Unfair?" Anti-Defamation League, 2000, 14.

417. "FAIR's Fear Tactics," *Detroit News*, March 26, 2000.

418. "Welcome to Washington: News from the Nation's Capital," *The Ethnic News Watch Forward*, vol. CIV, no. 31, May 5, 2000, 5.

419. "Is FAIR Unfair?" 14.

420. See, for example Keith Bradsher, "The 2000 Elections: Michigan; Congresswoman Unseats a Senator," *New York Times*, November 9, 2000.

421. Crawford, *Hold Your Tongue*, 161–62.

CHAPTER 8

1. Alan C. Nelson, "Press Conference Statement," January 13, 1988, IRCA Update, in *NCLR Records*, Series M744, Box 344, Folder 15.

2. Louis Freedberg, "The Role of Philanthropy in the U.S. Immigrant Rights Movement," Report to the Ford Foundation, undated but circa 2009, 27.

3. Frank D. Bean and Georges Vernez, *Opening and Closing the Doors: Evaluating Immigration Reform and Control* (Rand Corporation and Urban Institute, 1989).

4. Roberto Suro, "Traffic in Fake Documents Is Blamed for New Rise in Illegal Immigration," *New York Times*, November 26, 1990. See also Karen A. Woodrow and Jeffrey S. Passel, in: Frank D. Bean, Barry Edmonston, and Jeffrey S. Passel, eds., *Migration to the United States: IRCA and the Experience of the 1980s* (Rand Corporation and Urban Institute, 1990), 66.

5. See for example, Douglas S. Massey et al., "Effects of the Immigration Reform and Control Act of 1986: Preliminary Data from Mexico"; Jorge Bustamante, "Undocumented Migration from Mexico to the United States: Preliminary Findings of the Zapata Canyon Project;" and Wayne A. Cornelius, "Impacts of the 1986 U.S. Immigration Law on Emigration from Rural Mexican Sending Communities," all cited in: Bean et al., eds., *Migration to the United States: IRCA and the Experience of the 1980s.*

6. Larry Richter, "Immigration Law Is Failing to Cut Flow from Mexico," *New York Times*, June 24, 1988.

7. Roberto Suro, "1986 Amnesty Law Is Seen as Failing to Slow Alien Tide," *New York Times*, June 1989.

8. Zolberg, *A Nation by Design*, 375–76.

9. Suro, "1986 Amnesty Law Is Seen as Failing to Slow Alien Tide."

10. Richard W. Stevenson, "Jobs Being Filled by Illegal Aliens Despite Sanctions," *New York Times*, October 9, 1989.

11. Richard W. Stevenson, "Fight Is Intensified on Fake Documents for Aliens," *New York Times*, August 4, 1990; see also: Suro, "Traffic in Fake Documents Is Blamed for New Rise in Illegal Immigration."

12. Zolberg, *A Nation by Design*, 375.

13. Suro, "Traffic in Fake Documents Is Blamed for New Rise in Illegal Immigration."

14. See Kathleen Sullivan and Cecilia Munoz, *Racing Toward Big Brother, Computer Verification, National ID Cards, and Immigration Control* (National Council of La Raza, State of Hispanic America, 1995); and Associated Press, "Experts: Legal Status Check Systems Can Be Easily Exploited," *New York Times*, August 22, 2018.

15. Suro, "1986 Amnesty Law Is Seen as Failing to Slow Alien Tide."

16. Doris Meissner et al., "Immigration Enforcement in the United States: The Rise of a Formidable Machinery," Migration Policy Institute, Report in Brief, 2013, 3 (fig. 1).

17. Cindy Carcamo, "Trump's Crackdown Focuses on People in the U.S. Illegally—but Not on the Businesses that Hire Them," *Los Angeles Times*, March 20, 2017.

18. Cited in Tichenor, *Dividing Lines*, 262.

19. Peter Brownell, "The Declining Enforcement of Employer Sanctions," *Migration Information Source*, Migration Policy Institute, September 1, 2005.

20. Michael Fix, ed., *The Paper Curtain: Employer Sanctions Implementation, Impact, and Reform* (Urban Institute Press, 1991), 322–23.

21. Richard W. Stevenson, "Jobs Being Filled by Illegal Aliens Despite Sanctions," *New York Times*, October 9, 1989.

22. "The Non-Issue of Immigration," *Fortune*, July 23, 1984, cited in Richard R. Hofstetter, Immigration Reform: Crisis and Compromise," *Boston College Third World Law Journal*, vol. 5, no. 97 (1985), 116.

23. See, for example, Michael Grabell, "Cut to the Bone," *The New Yorker*, May 8, 2017.

24. Kathleen Sharp, "For Migrant Workers, Legality Lowers Wages," *New York Times*, December 3, 1989.

25. Jason DeParle, "The Nation: New Rows to Hoe in the 'Harvest of Shame,'" *New York Times*, July 28, 1991.

26. Tim Henderson, "More Employers May Be Using Temps to Skirt Immigration Laws," Huffington Post, August 16, 2017, https://www.huffingtonpost.com/entry/more-employers-may-be-using-temps-to-skirt-immigration_us_59944f62e4b0afd94eb3f662, accessed September 20, 2017.

27. See, for example, Robert Pear, "Employers of Illegal Aliens Facing Stronger Action," *New York Times*, August 1, 1991.

28. Elizabeth Grieco, "Unauthorized Immigration to the United States," Migration Policy Institute, Fact Sheet, October 2003.

29. Chishti and Kamasaki, "IRCA in Retrospect," 5.

30. See, for example, Charles Kamasaki and Martha Escutia, "Effectiveness of Labor Law Enforcement in Deterring Illegal Immigration," National Council of La Raza, Issue Brief, March 1984, 5.

31. Jay Mathews, "Job Bias Cases Tied to Immigration Act," *Washington Post*, November 6, 1989.

32. These studies are summarized in Muñoz, *Unfinished Business*, 38–41.

33. See, for example, Cynthia Bansak and Steven Raphael, "Immigration Reform and

the Earnings of Latino Workers: Do Employer Sanctions Cause Discrimination?" Discussion Paper 98-20, University of California-San Diego, August 1998.

34. "Immigration-Related Discrimination," Remarks of Senator Kennedy, *Congressional Record*, April 26, 1990 (reprinted excerpt is not paginated), in: *NCLR Records*, Series M744, Box 337, Folder 1.

35. Muñoz, *Unfinished Business*, 38–41.

36. Robert Pear, "Study Finds Bias, Forcing a Review of 1986 Alien Law," *New York Times*, March 30, 1990.

37. Michael Isikoff, "GAO Says 1986 Law Led to Hiring Discrimination Against Hispanics, Ethnics," *Washington Post*, March 30, 1990.

38. The exchange is reported in Muñoz, *Unfinished Business*, 41.

39. "Immigration-Related Discrimination," *Congressional Record*, April 26, 1990 (Remarks of Senator Kennedy, reprinted excerpt is not paginated), in: *NCLR Records*, Series M744, Box 337, Folder 1.

40. Letter from Raul Yzaguírre to Ralph Neas, March 22, 1990, in *NCLR Records*, Series M744, Box 337, Folder 16.

41. Raul Yzaguírre, "Employer Sanctions Don't Work," *Washington Post*, April 3, 1990.

42. Carlos Sanchez, "Hispanic Groups, Labor Split in Rights Coalition," *Washington Post*, May 13, 1990.

43. Sam Fulwood III, "Rights Group Avoids Split with Latino Organizations," *Los Angeles Times*, May 9, 1990.

44. Sanchez, "Hispanic Groups, Labor Split in Rights Coalition."

45. Author interview with Raul Yzaguírre, February 28, 2015.

46. Sanchez, "Hispanic Groups, Labor Split in Rights Coalition."

47. Fulwood, "Rights Group Avoids Split With Latino Organizations."

48. "Statement of Raul Yzaguírre [at] LCCR 40th Anniversary Annual Dinner," May 8, 1990, hard copy in possession of the author.

49. Hector Tobar, "NAACP Calls for End to Employer Sanctions," *Los Angeles Times*, July 12, 1990.

50. Author interview with Mort Halperin, December 18, 2015.

51. Paul Houston, "Bill Targets Immigration Law's Employer Sanctions," *Los Angeles Times*, September 21, 1991.

52. Author interview with Wade Henderson, January 30, 2014.

53. Nicole Hemmer, "Republican Nativism Helped Turn California Blue. Trump Could Do the Same for the Whole Country," *Vox*, updated January 20, 2017, https://www.vox.com/the-big-idea/2017/1/20/14332296/reaction-trump-democrats-organize-hispanic-turnout-prop187, accessed February 27, 2017.

54. Author interview with Frank Sharry, August 16, 2012.

55. Hemmer, "Republican Nativism Helped Turn California Blue."

56. Author interview with Frank Sharry, August 16, 2012.

57. Ricardo Sandoval and Susan Ferriss, "The Dilemma of Immigration: How Should Hispanic Policymakers Respond to Proposition 187?" *Hispanic Business*, February 1995, 18–21.

58. Patrick J. McDonnell, "Prop. 187 Found Unconstitutional by Federal Judge," *Los Angeles Times*, November 15, 1997; and Martha Montero-Sieburth and Edwin Melendez, *Latinos in a Changing Society* (Praeger, 2007), 13.

59. Nicole Hemmer, "Republican Nativism Helped Turn California Blue."

60. Andrew Glass, "Congress Runs into 'Republican Revolution': November 8, 1994," *Politico*, November 8, 2007, https://www.politico.com/story/2007/11/congress-runs-into-republican-revolution-nov-8-1994-006757, accessed October 31, 2017.

61. Mickey Edwards, "Bob Michel Feels a Nipping at His Heels: The Newt Gingrich Brand of House Republicanism May Be Driving Him Out," *Los Angeles Times*, August 31, 1993.

62. Freedberg, "The Role of Philanthropy in the U.S. Immigrant Rights Movement," 39.

63. Robert Pear, "Clinton Embraces a Proposal to Cut Immigration by a Third," *New York Times*, June 8, 1995.

64. The story of the legislation's origins, introduction, and movement through the Congress is covered in detail, albeit with a heavy emphasis on refugee- and asylum-related provisions, in Philip G. Schrag, *A Well-Founded Fear: The Congressional Battle to Save Political Asylum in America* (Routledge, 2000).

65. Email to the author from Cecilia Muñoz, January 3, 2018.

66. John Heilemann, "Do You Know the Way to Ban Jose?" *Wired*, August 1996.

67. Author interview with Frank Sharry, August 16, 2012; see also Freedberg, "The Role of Philanthropy in the U.S. Immigrant Rights Movement," 39.

68. See, generally, Schrag, *A Well-Founded Fear.*

69. Eric Schmitt, "House Approves Ending Schooling of Illegal Aliens," *New York Times*, March 21, 1996. See also William Branigan, "House Backs State Option to Bar Illegal Immigrant Children from Public School," *Washington Post*, March 21, 1996.

70. Schrag, *A Well-Founded Fear*, 141–42.

71. Dara Lind, "The Disastrous, Forgotten 1996 Law that Created Today's Immigration Problem," *Vox*, updated April 28, 2016, https://www.vox.com/2016/4/28/11515132/iirira-clinton-immigration, accessed September 17, 2017.

72. William Branigan, "Education Clause Delays Illegal Immigration Bill," *Washington Post*, August 3, 1996.

73. Freedberg, "The Role of Philanthropy in the U.S. Immigrant Rights Movement," 40-41.

74. Alex Nowrasteh, "Removing the 3/10 Year Bars Is Not Amnesty," *Cato at Liberty*, April 23, 2014, https://www.cato.org/blog/removing-310-year-bars-not-amnesty, accessed September 21, 2017.

75. These studies are nicely summarized in Douglas S. Massey, "The Causes and Consequences of America's War on Immigrants," Julian Simon Lecture Series, No. 8, IZA Annual Migration Meeting, May 2011, http://conference.iza.org/conference_files/amm2011/massey_d1244.pdf#page=29, accessed September 12, 2017.

76. Massey's research and other data synthesized in Nowrasteh, "Removing the 3/10 Year Bars Is Not Amnesty." See also Lind, "The Disastrous, Forgotten 1996 Law that Created Today's Immigration Problem."

77. For one detailed analysis of the program, see Randy Capps, Muzaffar Chishti, Marc Rosenblum, and Cristina Rodriguez, *Delegation and Divergence: 287(g) and State-Local Law Enforcement* (Migration Policy Institute, January 2011).

78. See Jessica Vaughn, "Attrition Through Enforcement," Center for Immigration Studies, April 1, 2016; https://cis.org/Attrition-Through-Enforcement, accessed November 16, 2017.

79. Capps et al., *Delegation and Divergence*, findings summarized on 2–3.

80. See, for example, "The 287(g) Program: An Overview," American Immigration Council, Fact Sheet, March 15, 2017, https://www.americanimmigrationcouncil.org/research/287g-program-immigration, accessed November 16, 2017.

81. Alana Semuels, "The End of Welfare as We Know It," *The Atlantic*, April 1, 2016, https://www.theatlantic.com/business/archive/2016/04/the-end-of-welfare-as-we-know-it/476322/, accessed November 2, 2017.

82. Freedberg, "The Role of Philanthropy in the U.S. Immigrant Rights Movement," 37–38.

83. Sonia M. Pérez, "Testimony on the Impact of Welfare Reform on the Hispanic Community," Subcommittee on Human Resources, Committee on Ways and Means, US House of Representatives, February 2, 1995, 4.

84. Author interview with Frank Sharry, August 16, 2012; see also Isabel Anadon, "Immigration Reform: Whatever Happened to 'Fixing '96?'" http://www.latinopolicyforum.org/blog/immigration-reform-whatever-happened-to-fixing-96/, accessed September 10, 2012.

85. Email to the author from Cecilia Muñoz, January 3, 2018.

86. Author interview with Cecilia Muñoz, December 2, 2016.

87. Audrey Singer, "Immigrants, Welfare Reform, and the Coming Reauthorization Vote," *Migration Information Source*, Migration Policy Institute, August 1, 2002.

88. Alicia Epstein Korten, *Candid Stories of Foundations Maximizing Results Through Social Justice* (John Wiley & Sons, 2009), 107; see also Freedberg, "The Role of Philanthropy in the U.S. Immigrant Rights Movement," 41–43.

89. Author interview with Cecilia Muñoz, December 2, 2016.

90. "Create the Landscape in Which Policy Makers Will Do What We Want Them to Do" in Deirdre Martínez, *Who Speaks for Hispanics? Hispanic Interest Groups in Washington* (State University of New York Press, 2009), 75.

91. Author interview with Frank Sharry, August 16, 2012.

92. Freedberg, "The Role of Philanthropy in the U.S. Immigrant Rights Movement," 33. See also Korten, *Candid Stories of Foundations Maximizing Results Through Social Justice*, 101.

93. Letter from Charles Kamasaki to Scott Nielson, John D. and Catherine T. MacArthur Foundation, September 10, 1999.

94. Letter from Charles Kamasaki to Scott Nielson, John D. and Catherine T. MacArthur Foundation, September 10, 1999.

95. See, for example, footage of Sharry-led training sessions in Shari Robertson and Michael Camerini, "The Game Is On," *How Democracy Works Now*, Film 1, Epidoko Pictures, 2010–2013.

96. Freedberg, "The Role of Philanthropy in the U.S. Immigrant Rights Movement," 33.

97. These and other stories collected in Alyce P. Miller, *From Immigrants to Activists: Immigration, Nativism, Welfare Reform, and the Mobilization of Immigrant Voters in the Late Nineteenth and Late Twentieth Centuries*, PhD dissertation, University Of North Carolina at Greensboro, 2012, 225–228.

98. Tim Weiner, "Many Laotians in U.S. Find Their Hopes Betrayed," *New York Times*, February 14, 1997.

99. Judith Havemann, "Noncitizen Immigrants Retain Aid in Budget Bills, Disability Benefits Restored by the House," *Washington Post*, July 1, 1997.

100. "Some Welfare Benefits Restored," *Migration News*, vol. 4, no. 7 (1997): 1.

101. Michael Fix and Karen Tumlin, *Welfare Reform and the Devolution of Immigrant Policy* (Urban Institute, October 1, 1997).

102. Author interview with Frank Sharry, August 16, 2012.

103. Author interview with Dianne Stewart, September 25, 2012.

104. Duarte, *Raul H. Yzaguirre*, 294.

105. Robert Pear, "Bush Plan Seeks to Restore Food Stamps for Noncitizens," *New York Times*, January 10, 2002. See also Singer, "Immigrants, Welfare Reform, and the Coming Reauthorization Vote."

106. Aaron Sorkin, producer, "Debate Camp," *The West Wing*, Season 4, Episode 5, aired October 16, 2002.

107. Polls of Latino leaders in the 1990s conducted by *Hispanic Business*, for example, consistently found that "NCLR is by all counts the most effective Hispanic organization," cited in McKay, *The National Council of La Raza*, 34.

108. Jim Collins, *Good to Great: Why Some Companies Make the Leap and Others Don't* (HarperBusiness, 2001).

109. Leslie R. Crutchfield and Heather Grant, *Forces for Good: The Six Practices of High-Impact Nonprofits* (Jossey-Bass, 2008), 44.

110. "Former National Hispanic Leader Found Guilty of Immigration Fraud," US Department of Justice press release, May 9, 1995; https://www.justice.gov/archive/opa/pr/Pre_96/May95/262.txt.html, accessed August 23, 2013; see also, "Rights Leader Charged in Immigration Fraud," *New York Times*, April 7, 1994.

111. "LULAC Rejects Old Guard; Incumbent Concedes Before Vote," Associated Press, July 20, 1994; http://www.apnewsarchive.com/1990/LULAC-Rejects-Old-Guard-Incumbent-Concedes-Before-Vote/, accessed August 23, 2013.

112. George Ramos, "INS Raids Latino Group's Office in Alleged Fraud; Amnesty: Immigration Consultant Reportedly Filed Only 17 of Nearly 800 Applications," *Los Angeles Times*, November 21, 1990.

113. There is a noticeable gap in the list of past LULAC presidents between Oscar Moran, elected in 1986, and Belen Robles, elected in 1994; see: http://lulac.org/about/history/past_presidents/, accessed August 23, 2013.

114. Martínez, *Who Speaks for Hispanics?*, 140–48.

115. David M. O'Brien, "Why Many Think that Ronald Reagan's Court Appointments May Have Been His Chief Legacy," *History News Network*, April 4, 2005, http://historynewsnetwork.org/article/10968, accessed November 2, 2017.

116. Nadine Cahodas, "Reagan Leaving Conservative Mark on Courts," *Congressional Quarterly Weekly Report*, November 1, 1986, 2727–29.

117. See, generally, Nancy Scherer, *Scoring Points: Politicians, Activists, and the Lower Federal Court Appointment Process* (Stanford University Press, 2005).

118. Author interview with Antonia Hernández, October 30, 2012.

119. Duarte, *Raul H. Yzaguirre*, 245.

120. "Management Letter to NCLR Board of Directors for Fiscal Year 1988," Arthur Anderson & Company, April 12, 1989.

121. Author interview with Raul Yzaguirre, July 9, 2012.

122. Author interview with Raul Yzaguirre, December 12, 2012. See also, "Management Letter to NCLR Board of Directors for Fiscal Year 1993," Arthur Anderson & Company, December 10, 1993.

123. Urban Institute research cited in Korten, *Candid Stories of Foundations Maximizing Results Through Social Justice*, 114.

124. Hemmer, "Republican Nativism Helped Turn California Blue."

125. Associated Press, "Anti-immigration Group Loses Sierra Club Vote," April 21, 2004.

126. Terence Chea, "Sierra Club Voting on Immigration Limits," *Boston Globe*, April 1, 2005.

127. "White Nationalist Hired to Manage Anti-Immigrant PAC," Imagine2050, February 12, 2014, http://imagine20150.newcomm.org/2014/02/12/prominent-white -nationalist-to-manage-anti-immigrant-pac/, accessed June 20, 2016.

128. Leah Nelson, "How Do We Know FAIR Is a Hate Group? Let Us Count the Ways," *Hatewatch*, August 10, 2012, https://www.splcenter.org/hatewatch/2012/08/10 /how-do-we-know-fair-hate-group-let-us-count-ways, accessed August 25, 2016.

129. See, for example, Anti-Defamation League, "Immigrants Targeted: Extremist Rhetoric Moves into the Mainstream," 2010, http://archive.adl.org/civil_rights/anti _immigrant/fair.html#.V8M79aNTF1s, accessed August 25, 2016; see also, Anti-Defamation League, "Anti-Immigrant Front Groups Used in Fight Against Immigration Reform," May 3, 2013, http://www.adl.org/civil-rights/immigration/c/anti-immigrant -front-groups.html#.V7-Jc6NTF1s, accessed August 25, 2016.

130. Bill Berkowitz, "Nativists Declare Open Season on Undocumented Immigrants," *Hispanic Vista*, May 6, 2005; and Heidi Beirich, "The Teflon Nativists," *Intelligence Report*, Southern Poverty Law Center, December 17, 2007.

131. Heidi Beirich, *The Nativist Lobby: Three Faces of Intolerance* (Southern Poverty Law Center, January 31, 2009), 13.

132. Jeffrey M. Berry and Sarah Sobieraj, "Understanding the Rise of Talk Radio," *PS, Political Science and Policy*, vol. 44, no. 4 (October 2011).

133. Press release for FAIR's 10th annual event in June 2016: http://www.prnewswire .com/news-releases/hold-their-feet-to-the-fire-2016-50-talk-radio-hosts-from-across-the -country-to-broadcast-from-washington-dc-discussing-immigration-policy-june -22-and-23-300286698.html, accessed August 25, 2016.

134. Media Matters staff, "FAIR Hosts Extremist Rally to Denounce 'Disease-Ridden' 'Racist' Immigrants," April 5, 2011, http://mediamatters.org/blog/2011/04/05 /fair-hosts-extremist-rally-to-denounce-disease/182902, accessed August 25, 2016.

135. Linda Chavez, *Out of the Barrio: Toward a New Politics of Hispanic Assimilation* (Basic Books, 1992).

136. Linda Chavez, "The Company You Keep," *National Review*, June 11, 2007.

137. Excerpt from Mission Statement of the Council on Equal Opportunity, undated, http://www.ceousa.org/about-ceo/mission, accessed August 28, 2016.

138. Linda Chavez, "Lighten Up on Political Correctness," February 24, 2012, https:// www.creators.com/read/linda-chavez/02/12/lighten-up-on-political-correctness, accessed August 25, 2016.

139. Linda Chavez, "The Realities of Immigration," *Commentary*, July 1, 2006.

140. Linda Chavez, "Latino Fear and Loathing," *Townhall.com*, May 25, 2007, http:// townhall.com/columnists/lindachavez/2007/05/25/latino_fear_and_loathing, accessed August 27, 2016.

141. Linda Chavez, "Latino Fear and Loathing, Part II," May 31, 2007, https://www .creators.com/read/linda-chavez/05/07/latino-fear-and-loathing-part-ii, accessed August 25, 2016.

142. Linda Chavez, "The Company You Keep," *National Review Online*, June 11, 2007, http://www.nationalreview.com/article/221234/company-you-keep-linda-chavez, accessed August 28, 2016.

143. Robert Pear, "Little-Known Group Claims a Win on Immigration," *New York Times*, July 15, 2007.

144. Molly Ball, "The Little Group Behind the Big Fight to Stop Immigration Reform," *The Atlantic*, August 1, 2013.

145. Kate Zernike, *Boiling Mad, Inside Tea Party America* (Times Books and Henry Holt and Company, 2010), 4–7.

146. Matt A. Barreto et al., "The Tea Party in the Age of Obama: Mainstream Conservatism or Out-Group Anxiety," *Political Power and Social Theory*, vol. 22 (2011).

147. Zernike, *Boiling Mad, Inside Tea Party America*, 8–9.

148. Theda Skocpol and Vanessa Williamson, *The Tea Party and the Remaking of Republican Conservatism* (Oxford University Press, 2012), 47–72.

149. Devin Burghart and Leonard Zeskind, *Tea Party Nationalism* (Institute for Research and Education on Human Rights, 2010).

150. Barreto et al., "The Tea Party in the Age of Obama."

151. Zernike, *Boiling Mad, Inside Tea Party America*, 190–91.

152. Zernike, *Boiling Mad, Inside Tea Party America*, 190–91.

153. Kim Messick, "The Tea Party's Paranoid Aesthetic," *Salon*, August 10, 2013, http://www.salon.com/2013/08/10/the_tea_partys_paranoid_aesthetic/print, accessed September 2, 2013.

154. Skocpol and Williamson, *The Tea Party and the Remaking of Republican Conservatism*, 57–58.

155. Ronald P. Formasino, *The Tea Party, A Brief History* (Johns Hopkins University Press, 2012), 10–11.

156. Chishti and Kamasaki, "IRCA in Retrospect," 9.

157. Deborah Waller Meyers, "U.S. Border Enforcement: From Horseback to High Tech," *Insight*, No. 7, Migration Policy Institute, November 2005, 10, https://www.migrationpolicy.org/research/us-border-enforcement-horseback-high-tech, accessed November 16, 2017.

158. Jeffrey S. Passel, "Size and Characteristics of the Unauthorized Migrant Population," Pew Hispanic Center, March 7, 2006, Fig. 1 and Fig. 2 on 2 and 3, respectively, https://web.stanford.edu/group/scspi/_media/pdf/Reference%20Media/Passel_2006_Citizenship%20and%20Civil%20Rights.pdf, accessed November 17, 2017.

159. Author interview with Frank Sharry, August 16, 2012; see also footage of Sharry-led training sessions in Robertson and Camerini, "The Game Is On." Readers are advised to watch the entire twelve-part documentary film series for a detailed, insider, *cinema verite*-style series chronicling the 2001–2007 immigration debate, and beyond; for trailers and more information, see www.howdemocracyworksnow.com, accessed December 2, 2013.

160. Author interview with Cecilia Muñoz, December 2, 2016.

161. Doris Meissner et al., *Mexico-U.S. Migration.*

162. Freedberg, "The Role of Philanthropy in the U.S. Immigrant Rights Movement," 47.

163. Eric Schmitt, "Bush Aides Weigh Legalizing Status of Mexicans in U.S.," *New York Times*, July 15, 2001.

164. "Bush to Weigh Residency for Illegal Mexican Immigrants," *Los Angeles Times*, September 7, 2001, cited in Freedberg, "The Role of Philanthropy in the U.S. Immigrant Rights Movement," 48–49.

165. Prepared statement of Raul Yzaguírre, Senate Committee on the Judiciary, September 7, 2001, available at: http://publications.unidosus.org/handle/123456789/1336, accessed November 1, 2017.

166. Robertson and Camerini, "The Game Is On."

167. Johanna Moriariu, Katherine Athanasiades, and Veena Pankaj, *Advocacy, Politics, and Philanthropy* (Innovation Network, May 2015), 27.

168. See, for example, Marc R. Rosenblum, *US Immigration Policy since 9/11: Understanding the Stalemate over Comprehensive Immigration Reform* (Woodrow Wilson International Center for Scholars and Migration Policy Institute, August 2011), 10–11.

169. See a partial listing at "Immigrants' Rights Coalitions," National Immigration Law Center, undated, https://www.nilc.org/get-involved/links/ircoalitions/, accessed September 7, 2016.

170. See for example, websites of the Services, Immigrant Rights, and Education Network (SIREN) covering the California Bay Area at: http://www.siren-bayarea.org/, accessed September 7, 2016 and the Long Beach Immigrant Rights Coalition at: http://lbirc.org/, accessed September 7, 2016.

171. Mark Leach and Laurie Mazur, "Creating Culture: Promising Practices of Successful Movement Networks," *Nonprofit Quarterly*, December 23, 2013, https://nonprofitquarterly.org/2013/12/23/creating-culture-promising-practices-of-successful-movement-networks/, accessed January 13, 2014.

172. See: http://wearecasa.org/who-we-are/awards/, undated, accessed November 18, 2017.

173. Leach and Mazur, "Creating Culture: Promising Practices of Successful Movement Networks."

174. Adapted from various sources, including "Core Dilemmas of Organizing: What Is Community Organizing? What Isn't Community Organizing?" *educationaction*, March 22, 2008, http://www.educationaction.org/core-dilemmas-of-community-organizing.html, accessed April 28, 2008.

175. See, for example, Stephen Brobeck, ed., *Encyclopedia of the Consumer Movement* (ABC-CLIO, 1997), 120–22.

176. Larry Parachini and Sally Covington, *Community Organizing Tool Box* (Neighborhood Funders Group, April 2001), 16–19.

177. David Walls, "Power to the People: Thirty-five Years of Community Organizing," undated, http://web.sonoma.edu/users/w/wallsd/community-organizing.shtml, accessed November 18, 2017.

178. See Gary Delgado, *Beyond the Politics of Place: New Directions in Community Organizing in the 1990s* (Applied Research Center, 1994).

179. "Core Dilemmas of Community Organizing: How Do You Replicate Local Success?" May 12, 2008, *educationaction*, http://www.educationaction.org/core-dilemmas-of-community-organizing.html, accessed April 28, 2008.

180. Mike Miller, "Alinsky for the Left: The Politics of Community Organizing," *Dissent*, Winter 2010, https://www.dissentmagazine.org/article/alinsky-for-the-left-the-politics-of-community-organizing, accessed November 12, 2017.

181. Cited in Ruth McCambridge, "Exploring Barriers to Movement-Building," *Nonprofit Quarterly*, September 21, 2001, https://nonprofitquarterly.org/2001/09/21/exploring-the-barriers-to-movement-building/, accessed November 17, 2017.

182. See: "The CCC Story," undated but circa 2012, https://www.communitychange.org/real-power/45th-anniversary-timeline/, accessed November 17, 2017.

183. "Deepak Bhargava," *Huffington Post*, undated, https://www.huffingtonpost.com/author/deepak-bhargava, accessed November 17, 2017.

184. See Deepak Bhargava, "Director's Report," *Poverty and Race*, March/April, 2002, http://www.prrac.org/full_text.php?text_id=746&item_id=7788&newsletter_id=61&header=Race+%2F+Racism, accessed November 17, 2017.

185. See, for example, Caitlin C. Patler, "Alliance-Building and Organizing for Immigrant Rights: The Case of the Coalition for Humane Immigrant Rights of Los Angeles" in Ruth Milkman, Joshua Bloom, and Victor Narro, eds., *Working for Justice: The LA Model of Organizing and Advocacy* (Cornell University Press, 2010), 71–88.

186. Author interview with Cecilia Muñoz, December 2, 2016; email from Cecilia Muñoz, January 3, 2018.

187. "2003: Immigrant Organizing Committee Evolves into FIRM," undated but circa 2012, https://www.communitychange.org/real-power/immigration-timeline/, accessed November 17, 2017.

188. "Center for Community Change Applauds Appointment of Cecilia Muñoz as Director of the Domestic Policy Council," Center for Community Change, press release, January 10, 2012, https://www.communitychange.org/page/center-for-community-change-applauds-appointment-of-cecilia-munoz-as-director-of-domestic-policy-council/, accessed November 17, 2017.

189. Walter J. Nicholls, *The DREAMers: How the Undocumented Youth Movement Transformed the Immigrant Rights Debate* (Stanford University Press, 2013), 4–5.

190. Julia Preston, "House Backs Legal Status for Many Young Immigrants," *New York Times*, December 8, 2010.

191. See Section 5 of the Illegal Immigration Reform and Immigrant Responsibility Act of 1996.

192. "Student Adjustment Bills Side-by-Side," August 31, 2001; hard copy in author's files.

193. "Student Adjustment Bills Side-By-Side," July 21, 2003, hard copy in author's files, and author interview with Melissa Lazarín, November 14, 2017.

194. Author interview with Raul Yzaguírre, July 9, 2012.

195. Author interview with Melissa Lazarín, November 14, 2017.

196. Nicholls, *The DREAMers*, 32.

197. "NCLR Lauds Passage of Immigrant Student Bill in Senate Judiciary Committee," National Council of La Raza, press release, June 20, 2002.

198. Shari Robertson and Michael Camerini, "Marking Up the Dream," *How Democracy Works Now*, Film 6, Epidoko Pictures, 2010–2013.

199. Frank Sharry, "How Did We Build an Immigrant Movement? We Learned from Gay Rights Advocates," *Washington Post*, March 22, 2013, https://www.washingtonpost.com/opinions/how-did-we-build-an-immigrant-movement-we-learned-from-gay-rights-advocates/2013/03/22/8a0d2b9a-916e-11e2-bdea-e32ad90da239_story.html?utm_term=.3f246254bf08, accessed November 17, 2017.

200. For one typical DREAMer rally, see Robertson and Camerini, "Marking Up the Dream." See also Nicholls, *The DREAMers*, 66.

201. Author interview with Melissa Lazarín, November 14, 2017; see also Nicholls, *The DREAMers*.

202. United We Dream, "Our History," https://unitedwedream.org/about/history/, undated, accessed September 8, 2017.

203. Ruben Navarrette Jr., "DREAMers Are Pushing Their Luck," *CNN.com*,

December 19, 2012, http://www.cnn.com/opinion/navarette-dreamers/, accessed September 8, 2017.

204. The precise level of support—measured by the exit polls at 44 percent—was highly contested. See National Council of La Raza, "How Did Latinos Really Vote in 2004?" memorandum updated January 1, 2005, https://issuu.com/nclr/docs/file_nclr _how_did_latinos_really_vote_in_2004_revi/6, accessed November 17, 2017.

205. Doris Meissner, Deborah W. Meyers, Demetrious G. Papademetriou, and Michael Fix, *Immigration and America's Future: A New Chapter* (Migration Policy Institute, September 2006).

206. For an intimate, behind-the-scenes accounting of the drafting of the bill, see Shari Robertson and Michael Camerini, "Brothers and Rivals," *How Democracy Works Now*, Film 10, Epidoko Pictures, 2010–2013.

207. See William L. Galston, "Why the 2005 Social Security Initiative Failed, and What It Means for the Future," Brookings Institution, September 21, 2007, https://www .brookings.edu/research/why-the-2005-social-security-initiative-failed-and-what-it -means-for-the-future/, accessed November 19, 2005.

208. Susanne Jonas, "Reflections on the Great Immigration Battle of 2006 and the Future of the Americas," *Social Justice*, vol. 33, no. 1 (2006).

209. Freedberg, "The Role of Philanthropy in the U.S. Immigrant Rights Movement," 57–58.

210. "Arena Profile: Eliseo Medina," *Politico*, undated, https://www.politico.com /arena/bio/eliseo_medina.html, accessed November 21, 2017.

211. Cited in Freedberg, "The Role of Philanthropy in the U.S. Immigrant Rights Movement," 58.

212. Moriariu et al., *Advocacy, Politics, and Philanthropy*: for CCIR's structure see 19–20, for partial listing of Atlantic Philanthropies' immigration grantees, see tables on 48–52.

213. Author interview with Wade Henderson, December 19, 2012.

214. Shari Robertson and Michael Camerini, "The Senate Speaks," *How Democracy Works Now*, Film 11, Epidoko Pictures, 2010–2013.

215. Meissner et al., *Immigration and America's Future: A New Chapter*, estimate on undocumented population on xv.

216. Rachel L. Swarns, "Senate, in Bipartisan Act, Passes Immigration Bill; Tough Fight Ahead," *New York Times*, May 26, 2006.

217. For a brief and highly readable assessment of the "state of play" of immigration over this period, see Rosenblum, *US Immigration Policy since 9/11*.

218. Thomas E. Mann, "How to Think About the November 2006 Congressional Elections," Issues in Governance Studies, No. 5, Brookings Institution, July 2006, https:// www.brookings.edu/wp-content/uploads/2016/06/07election_mann.pdf, accessed November 21, 2017.

219. Shari Robertson and Michael Camerini, "The Last Best Chance," [also referred to in some iterations as "The Senators' Bargain"], *How Democracy Works Now*, Film 12, Epidoko Pictures, 2010–2013.

220. See commentary throughout Moriariu et al., *Advocacy, Politics, and Philanthropy*; passages in quotes from 18.

221. Author interview with Cecilia Muñoz, December 2, 2016.

222. "Democrats Take Congress," America Votes 2006, *CNN*, November 9, 2006 and

updated through 2007, http://www.cnn.com/ELECTION/2006/, accessed November 17, 2017.

223. Rosenblum, *US Immigration Policy since 9/11*, 12.

224. Muzaffar Chishti and Charles Kamasaki, "Grand Bargain or Grand Collapse: The Case of Immigration Reform," in Maximillian Angerholzer III, James Kitfield, Christopher P. Lu, and Norman Ornstein, eds., *Triumphs and Tragedies of the Modern Congress, Case Studies in Legislative Leadership* (Center for the Study of the Presidency and Congress and Praeger, 2014), 163–71.

225. Robertson and Camerini, "The Last Best Chance."

226. Chishti and Kamasaki, "Grand Bargain or Grand Collapse: The Case of Immigration Reform," 168.

227. Robertson and Camerini, "The Last Best Chance."

228. Molly Ball, "The Little Group Behind the Big Fight to Stop Immigration Reform," *The Atlantic*, August 1, 2013.

229. "The Grand Collapse," *New York Times*, editorial, June 30, 2007.

230. Robertson and Camerini, "The Last Best Chance."

231. Robert Pear and Carl Hulse, "Immigration Bill Fails to Survive the Senate, *New York Times*, June 28, 2007.

232. Chishti and Kamasaki, "Grand Bargain or Grand Collapse: The Case of Immigration Reform," see footnote 22 on 354.

233. See generally, Thomas E. Mann and Norman J. Ornstein, *It's Even Worse Than It Looks: How the American Constitutional System Collided with the New Politics of Extremism* (Basic Books, 2013). In the immigration policy context specifically, see Chishti and Kamasaki, "Grand Bargain or Grand Collapse: The Case of Immigration Reform," 68–70.

234. Author interview with Frank Sharry, August 16, 2012.

235. See Moriariu et al., *Advocacy, Politics, and Philanthropy*.

236. Occupy Wall Street, Black Lives Matter, the 2017 Women's March on Washington, the 2010 Tea Party Protests, or even the "Arab Spring," to cite just a few examples, suggest a growing inclination toward large demonstrations as a central advocacy tactic.

237. Zeynep Tufekci, "Does a Protest's Size Matter?" *New York Times*, January 27, 2017, https://www.nytimes.com/2017/01/27/opinion/does-a-protests-size-matter.html ?_r=0, accessed January 27, 2017; see also Zeynep Tufekci, "Twitter and Tear Gas: How Social Media Changed Protest Forever," *Wired*, May 22, 2017, accessed October 8, 2017.

238. Nick Srnicek and Alex Williams, *Inventing the Future: Postcapitalism and a World Without Work* (Verso, 2015), cited in Nathan Heller, "Out of Action, Do Protests Work?" *The New Yorker*, August 21, 2017, 70–71.

239. Shom Mazumder, "Yes, Marches Can Make a Difference. It Depends on These Three Factors," *Washington Post*, January 27, 2017, https://www.washingtonpost.com /news/monkey-cage/wp/2017/01/27/yes-marches-can-really-matter-these-three-factors -make-the-difference/?utm_term=.6aa25370462a, accessed January 27, 2017.

240. Heller, "Out of Action, Do Protests Work?" 70–77.

241. See, generally, Moriariu et al., *Advocacy, Politics, and Philanthropy*.

242. "The Big Sort," http://www.thebigsort.com/home.php, undated, accessed November 22, 2017. See also Bill Bishop, *The Big Sort: Why the Clustering of Like-Minded America Is Tearing Us Apart* (Mariner Books, 2009).

243. Mazumder, "Yes, Marches Can Make a Difference."

244. Robby Soave, "New Poll: Left-Wing Protestors Drive People into Arms of Donald Trump," *Reason.com*, March 14, 2016, http://reason.com/blog/2016/03/14/new-poll-left-wing-protesters-drive-peop, accessed August 26, 2016. For a historical example, see David Mislin, "Anti-War Protests 50 Years Ago Helped Mold America's Modern Christian Right Wing," *The Conversation*, May 2, 2018, http://theconversation.com/anti-war-protests-50-years-ago-helped-mold-the-modern-christian-right-90802, accessed May 2, 2018.

245. Moriariu et al., *Advocacy, Politics, and Philanthropy*, 38.

246. Reuters staff, "Obama to Tackle Immigration Reform This Year: Report," April 9, 2009, https://www.reuters.com/article/us-obama-immigration-times/obama-to-tackle-immigration-reform-this-year-report-idUSTRE5380MU20090409, accessed November 21, 2017.

247. For a highly critical but detailed account of Obama's economic policy strategy, see Noam Scheiber, *The Escape Artists* (Simon and Schuster, 2012).

248. One insider version of the battle over the Affordable Care Act can be found in Richard Kirsch, *Fighting for Our Health* (Rockefeller Institute Press, 2012).

249. See useful chronology in Moriariu et al., *Advocacy, Politics, and Philanthropy*, 27–28.

250. See Marc Rosenblum and Kristen McCabe, *Deportation and Discretion: Reviewing the Record and Options for Change* (Migration Policy Institute, October 2014), for a fair-minded review of Obama's deportation record.

251. Gretchen Gavit, "Cecilia Muñoz: Even Broken Laws Have to Be Enforced," *PBS Frontline*, October 88, 2011, http://www.pbs.org/wgbh/frontline/article/cecilia-munoz-even-broken-laws-have-to-be-enforced/, accessed November 22, 2017.

252. Matt Barreto and Gary M. Segura, *Latino America: How America's Most Dynamic Population Is Poised to Transform the Politics of the Nation* (Public Affairs, 2014), 151.

253. Sharry, "How Did We Build an Immigrant Movement?"

254. Gaby Pacheco, "Such Stuff as Dreams Are Made On," Letter to the Editor, *The Nation*, March 2016.

255. Julia Preston, "Young Immigrants Say It's Obama's Time to Act," *New York Times*, November 30, 2012.

256. An excellent DACA overview can be found at Dara Lind, "DACA, Explained: Why Donald Trump Holds the Fate of a Generation of Immigrants in His Hands," *Vox*, August 25, 2017, https://www.vox.com/policy-and-politics/2017/8/25/16202344/daca-trump-deferred-action-end, accessed November 22, 2017.

257. Excerpt from Garance Franke-Ruta, "What You Need to Read in the RNC Election-Autopsy Report," *The Atlantic*, March 18, 2013, https://www.theatlantic.com/politics/archive/2013/03/what-you-need-to-read-in-the-rnc-election-autopsy-report/274112/, accessed December 1, 2017.

258. David Nakamura and Ed O'Keefe, "The Rise and Fall of Immigration Reform," *Washington Post*, June 26, 2014, https://www.washingtonpost.com/news/post-politics/wp/2014/06/26/timeline-the-rise-and-fall-of-immigration-reform/?utm_term=.92954673461f, accessed November 22, 2017.

259. See summary by Muzaffar Chishti and Faye Hipsman, "As Immigration Reform Stalls in Congress, Activists Take a Page from the Civil Rights Movement," *Policy Beat*, Migration Policy Institute, October 17, 2013.

260. Shari Robertson and Michael Camerini, "Immigration Battle," *How Democracy Works Now*, Film 13, October 20, 2015, streaming at: http://www.pbs.org/wgbh /frontline/film/immigration-battle/, accessed November 17, 2017.

261. Faye Hipsman, "Top 10 of 2014—Issue #2: Obama Breaks Immigration Impasse with Sweeping Executive Action" Migration Policy Institute, December 18, 2014, https:// www.migrationpolicy.org/article/top-10-2014-issue-2-president-obama-breaks -immigration-impasse-sweeping-executive-action, accessed November 22, 2017.

262. Muzaffar Chishti and Faye Hipsman, "Supreme Court DAPA Ruling a Blow to Obama Administration, Moves Immigration Back to Political Realm," *Policy Beat*, Migration Policy Institute, June 29, 2016, https://www.migrationpolicy.org/article /supreme-court-dapa-ruling-blow-obama-administration-moves-immigration-back -political-realm, accessed November 22, 2017.

263. James Hohman, "DACA Reaction Shows How Immigration Has Become a Litmus Test for Democrats," *Washington Post*, September 6, 2017, https://www .washingtonpost.com/news/powerpost/paloma/daily-202/2017/09/06/daily-202-daca -reaction-shows-how-immigration-has-become-a-litmus-test-for-democrats /59af142730fb04264c2a1ced/?utm_term=.339601f72f73, accessed September 6, 2017.

264. Gerald F. Seib, "How to Break Free of Washington's Conventional Wisdom," *Wall Street Journal*, September 29, 2017.

265. Adrienne LaFrance, "The Intolerant Left," *The Atlantic*, November 14, 2017, https://www.theatlantic.com/entertainment/archive/2017/11/the-intolerant-left/545783/, accessed November 14, 2017.

266. Clio Chang, "How Democrats Gave Us Trump's Immigration Nightmare," *New Republic*, August 17, 2017, https://newrepublic.com/article/144378/democrats-gave-us -trumps-immigration-nightmare, accessed September 17, 2017.

267. New York Immigration Coalition, "Secretary Hillary Clinton to Address National Immigrant Integration Conference," press release, December 10, 2015, http:// www.thenyic.org/PR-niic-hrc, accessed November 21, 2017.

268. See "Hillary Clinton Receives Endorsement of New York Immigrant Rights Coalition and Unveils New Policies to Help Immigrant Families," undated but issued December 14, 2015, http://partnershipfornewamericans.org/wp-content /uploads/2016/04/%E2%80%8BClinton-Immigrant-Integration.pdf, accessed November 21, 2017.

269. Thomas B. Edsall, "How Immigration Foiled Hillary," *New York Times*, October 5, 2017.

270. There are many variations of the phrase sprinkled throughout the literature by and about Alinsky; see, for example, Michael Gecan, "Back of the Yards, Lessons from a Community Organizer on Building Power," *Boston Review*, January 4, 2017, http:// bostonreview.net/politics/michael-gecan-back-yards, accessed November 21, 2017.

271. Miranda Blue, "The Tea Party Letter Signers' Other Advice on Immigration Reform," May 22, 2013, *Right Wing Watch*, People for the American Way, http://www .rightwingwatch.org/content/tea-party-letter-signers-other-advice-immigration-reform, accessed September 3, 2016.

272. Miranda Blue, "Center for Immigration Studies Echoes Schlafly, Urges GOP to Focus on Turning Out White Voters," May 30, 2013, *Right Wing Watch*, People for the American Way, http://www.rightwingwatch.org/content/center-immigration-studies -echoes-schlafly-urges-gop-focus-turning-out-white-voters, accessed September 3, 2016.

273. Patrick J. Buchanan, "Requiem for a Grand Old Party," *WND.com*, May 9, 2013, http://www.wnd.com/2013/05/requiem-for-a-grand-old-party/, accessed September 5, 2013; see also, Miranda Blue, "Buchanan Calls for Renewed Southern Strategy, This Time Against Immigrants," *Right Wing Watch*, People for the American Way, May 20, 2013, http://www.rightwingwatch.org/content/buchanan-calls-renewed-southern-strategy -time-against-immigrants, accessed, September 3, 2016.

274. Miranda Blue, "White Nationalists Demand Credit for Another Idea That's Gone Mainstream in the GOP," *Right Wing Watch*, People for the American Way, April 21, 2014, http://www.rightwingwatch.org/content/white-nationalists-demand-credit -another-idea-s-gone-mainstream-gop, September 5, 2016.

275. Karthick Ramakrishnan, Kevin Easterling, and Michael Neblo, "Illegality, National Origin Cues, and Public Opinion on Immigration," June 2014, https://polisci .osu.edu/sites/polisci.osu.edu/files/NebloNatOrgCues063014_0.pdf, accessed October 7, 2016.

276. Lee Drutman, "How Race and Identity Became the Central Dividing Line in American Politics," *Vox*, August 30, 2016, http://www.vox.com/polyarchy /2016/8/30/12697920/race-dividing-american-politics, accessed September 1, 2016.

277. Marisa Abrajano and Zoltan L. Hajnal, *White Backlash, Immigration, Race, and American Politics* (Princeton University Press, 2015), 201–16.

278. Dara Lind, "One Chart that Shows Why the Republican Party Was Ready for Donald Trump," *Vox*, May 3, 2016, http://www.vox.com/2016/5/3/11571444/republican -democrat-anti-immigrant, accessed June 13, 2016.

279. David Weigel, "What's the Alt-Right? A Primer," *Washington Post*, August 24, 2016, https://www.washingtonpost.com/news/post-politics/wp/2016/08/24/whats-the -alt-right-a-primer/, accessed August 25, 2016.

280. James Crawford, *Language Loyalties: A Sourcebook on the Official English Controversy* (University of Chicago Press, 1992), 174.

281. Weigel, "What's the Alt-Right? A Primer."

282. Heidi Beirich, *The Nativist Lobby: Three Faces of Intolerance* (Southern Poverty Law Center, January 31, 2009), 7–11.

283. Benjamin Welton, "What, Exactly, Is the Alt Right? A Taxonomy," *Weekly Standard*, December 21, 2015, http://www.weeklystandard.com/what-exactly-is-the -alternative-right/article/2000310, August 27, 2016.

284. Evan Osnos, "The Fearful and the Frustrated," *The New Yorker*, August 31, 2015, http://www.newyorker.com/magazine/2015/08/31/the-fearful-and-the-frustrated, accessed August 1, 2016.

285. Clifford Young, "It's Nativism: Explaining the Drivers of Trump's Popular Support," June 1, 2016, *Ipsos.com*, http://spotlight.ipsos-na.com/index.php/news/its -nativism-explaining-the-drivers-of-trumps-popular-support/, accessed July 11, 2016.

286. Alan I. Abramowitz, Ronald Rapoport, and Walter Stone, "Why Donald Trump Is Winning and Why His Nomination Could Shatter the Republican Party," *Larry Sabato's Crystal Ball*, March 10, 2016, http://www.centerforpolitics.org/crystalball/articles /why-donald-trump-is-winning-and-why-his-nomination-could-shatter-the-republican -party/, accessed July 11, 2016.

287. German Lopez, "The Real Reason for Donald Trump's Rise, in Two Charts," *Vox*, June 7, 2016, http://www.vox.com/2016/6/7/11875964/donald-trump-racism-charts, accessed August 12, 2016.

288. Dara Lind and Mathew Yglesias, "Donald Trump and Immigration, Explained," *Vox*, August 22, 2016, http://www.vox.com/2016/8/22/12552082/donald-trump -immigration, accessed August 23, 2016.

289. Peter Wehner, "Can We Find Our Way Back to the Party of Lincoln?" *New York Times*, July 16, 2016.

290. Zack Beauchamp, "A Republican Intellectual Explains Why the Republican Party Is Going to Die," *Vox*, July 25, 2016, http://www.vox.com/2016/7/25/12256510 /republican-party-trump-avik-roy, accessed June 27, 2016.

291. Ron Brownstein, "How Much Will Trump Cost the Republican Party?" *The Atlantic*, June 9, 2016, http://www.theatlantic.com/politics/archive/2016/06/trump -gop-demographics/486320/, accessed June 9 2016.

292. Betsy Woodruff, "Anti-Immigration Extremists Love Trump," *The Daily Beast*, August 8, 2015, http://www.thedailybeast.com/articles/2015/08/18/anti -immigration-extremists-heart-trump.html, accessed September 3, 2016.

293. Jeet Heer, "Why Donald Trump's Conservative Enemies Are Praising Him This Week," *The New Republic*, September 2, 2016, https://newrepublic.com/article/136512 /donald-trumps-conservative-enemies-praising-week, accessed September 3, 2016.

CHAPTER 9

1. Harold Evans, "On the Brink, 'The Sleepwalkers' and 'July 1914,'" *New York Times*, Sunday Book Review, May 9, 2013.

2. James A. Warren, "Barbara Tuchman's 'The Guns of August' Is Still WWI's Peerless Chronicle," *The Daily Beast*, September 29, 2014, http://www.thedailybeast.com /articles/2014/09/29/barbara-tuchman-s-the-guns-of-august-is-still-wwi-s-peerless -chronicle.html, accessed April 6, 2015.

3. Thomas Laquer, "Some Damn Foolish Thing," *London Review of Books*, December 20, 2013.

4. Evans, "'On the Brink,' 'The Sleepwalkers' and 'July 1914,'" reviewing Sean McMeekin, *July 1914: Countdown to War* (Basic Books, 2013).

5. "The War that Ended Peace: The Road to 1914," *Publishers Weekly*, reviewing Margaret MacMillan, *The War that Ended Peace: The Road to 1914* (Random House, 2013), http://www.publishersweekly.com/paper-copy/reviews/single/978-1-4000-6855-5, undated, accessed April 9, 2015.

6. Laquer, "Some Damn Foolish Thing."

7. From excerpts of reviews printed in the paperback edition of Max Hastings, *Catastrophe 1914: Europe Goes to War* (Vintage Books, 2013), i–ii.

8. Warren, "Barbara Tuchman's 'The Guns of August' Is Still WWI's Peerless Chronicle."

9. Chishti and Kamasaki, "Grand Bargain or Grand Collapse: The Case of Immigration Reform," 171.

10. From a proverb of thirteenth or fourteenth century origin; this formulation is attributed by some to author James Baldwin; see: http://www.mainlesson.com/display .php?author=baldwin&book=people&story=nails, accessed August 31, 2017.

11. Meissner et al., "Immigration Enforcement in the United States: The Rise of a Formidable Machinery," 9.

12. Muzaffar Chishti and Faye Hispman, "Now that the Senate Has Passed Land-

mark Immigration Legislation, All Eyes Are on the House," *Policy Beat*, Migration Policy Institute, July 3, 2013, http://www.migrationpolicy.org/article/now-senate-has-passed-landmark-immigration-legislation-all-eyes-are-house, accessed August 31, 2017.

13. Moriariu et al., *Advocacy, Politics, and Philanthropy*.

14. Stanley Greenberg, "The Democrats' 'Working Class Problem,'" *The American Prospect*, June 1, 2017.

15. Malcolm Gladwell, *What the Dog Saw* (Back Bay Books, 2009), 250.

16. Frank R. Baumgartner et al., *Lobbying and Policy Change, Who Wins, Who Loses, and Why* (University of Chicago Press, 2009), 190–214.

17. The so-called "butterfly effect" was perhaps first described scientifically by meteorologist Edward Lorenz; see Peter Dizikes, "When the Butterfly Effect Took Flight," *MIT Technology Review*, February 22, 2011, https://www.technologyreview.com/s/422809/when-the-butterfly-effect-took-flight/, accessed October 13, 2017.

18. See, generally, James Gleick, *Chaos: Making a New Science* (Penguin Books, 2008).

19. Perotti, *Resolving Policy Conflict*, 267.

20. See trendline in chart posted at Gallup News, "Immigration: In-Depth A to Z," undated but circa July 2017, http://news.gallup.com/poll/1660/immigration.aspx, accessed November 28, 2017.

21. Just under forty thousand and a little over fifty thousand people adjusted under IRCA's Cuban–Haitian and "Registry" programs, respectively; see Donald M. Kerwin, "More Than IRCA: US Legalization Programs and the Current Policy Debate," Migration Policy Institute, Policy Brief, December 2010, chart on 12–13.

22. Author interview with J. Michael Treviño, October 2, 2012.

23. Author interview with Dianne Stewart, September 25, 2012

24. Author interview with Ruben Bonilla, September 27, 2013.

25. Author interview with Michael Cortés, August 16, 2012.

26. Author interview with Raul Yzaguírre, July 9, 2012.

27. Author interview with Mort Halperin, December 18, 2015.

28. Of the members of The Group and close associates over the 1982–1986 period, Henderson, Leiden, Myers, and Treviño were married; only Henderson's marriage survived. Chishti, Eisen, Escutia, Kamasaki, Purtell, and Torres had more or less steady relationships in the Simpson-Mazzoli era; only Purtell married his then-partner. But other romantic pairings emerged from the debate: Rep. Torres's staffer Albert Jacquez later married Mazzoli aide Lynn Conway, the ACLU's Amit Pandya and NCLR's Cecilia Muñoz married, Muzaffar Chishti wed Helene Lauffler of ACNS Affiliate Travelers and Immigrants Aid of New York, Michael Myers later married Church World Service staffer Kay Bellor, and NCLR's Charles Kamasaki paired up with the ACLU/American Bar Association's Carol Wolchok.

29. Author interview with Richard Fajardo, October 30, 2012.

30. Author interview with Raul Yzaguírre, July 9, 2012.

31. The final version of the Commission provision was sponsored by Rep. John Bryant, a Democratic centrist who worked often with The Group although he was decidedly less pro-immigrant than they were. Chaired by veteran diplomat Diego Asencio, the Commission for the Study of International Migration and Cooperative Economic Development published its final report, *Unauthorized Migration: An Economic Development Response*, in 1990.

32. Gladwell, *What the Dog Saw*, 172.

33. Michael Lewis, *The Fifth Risk* (W.W. Norton & Company, 2018), ebook edition 152–53.

34. Author interview with Dianne Stewart, September 25, 2012.

35. Author interview with Phyllis Eisen, April 3, 2014.

36. Many of these characteristics are described in Gleick, *Chaos: Making a New Science*; see especially Gleick's descriptions of early chaos theorists in his prologue on 1–8.

37. Author interview with Rick Swartz, August 5, 2017.

38. Author interview with Arnoldo Torres, August 4, 2017.

39. Michael Tomasky, "The Money Fighting Health Care Reform," *New York Review of Books*, April 8, 2010. It's notable that both of the other policy victories listed—the Earned Income Tax Credit and the Americans with Disabilities Act—were bipartisan in nature.

40. Lee Drutman, "It's the Culture, Stupid," *New Republic*, October 9, 2017, https://newrepublic.com/article/144964/culture-stupid-identity-politics-problem-democrats-solution, accessed October 9, 2017.

41. Cited in Thomas B. Edsall, "The Democratic Party Picked an Odd Time to Have an Identity Crisis," *New York Times*, August 2, 2018, https://www.nytimes.com/2018/08/02/opinion/democrats-midterm-identity-crisis.html, accessed August 2, 2018.

42. Thomas B. Edsall, "Who's Afraid of a White Minority?" *New York Times*, August 30, 2018, https://www.nytimes.com/2018/08/30/opinion/america-white-minority-majority.html, accessed September 4, 2018.

43. See: Mark Hugo Lopez, Ana Gonzalez-Barrera, and Jens Manuel Krogstad, "Chapter 5: Hispanics and Their Views of Immigration Reform," *Hispanic Trends*, Pew Hispanic Center, October 29, 2014; http://www.pewhispanic.org/2014/10/29/chapter-5-hispanics-and-their-views-of-immigration-reform/, accessed October 23, 2018; and Steve Taylor, "Telemundo Poll: Hispanics Oppose Border Wall, SB 4, and 'Zero Tolerance,'" *Rio Grande Guardian*, September 8, 2018, https://riograndeguardian.com/telemundo-poll-texas-latinos-oppose-border-wall-sb-4-and-zero-tolerance/, accessed September 11, 2018.

44. Theodore Kupfer, "Immigration Restriction in the Era of Trump," *National Review*, August 20, 2018; https://www.nationalreview.com/2018/08/immigration-restriction-cause-trump-helping-or-hurting/, accessed August 20, 2018.

45. Sam Tanenhuas, "The Promise of Polarization," *The New Republic*, October 29, 2018, https://newrepublic.com/article/151612/promise-polarization-book-review-sam-rosenfeld-the-polarizers, accessed October 29, 2018.

46. Cited in Perotti, *Resolving Policy Conflict*, 147.

47. Nicholas Kristoff, "Forget Excuses. What Counts Is Winning Elections," *New York Times*, November 7, 2018.

48. Cited in German Lopez, "Research Says There Are Ways to Reduce Bias. Calling People Racist Isn't One of Them," *Vox*, August 14, 2017, https://www.vox.com/identities/2016/11/15/13595508/racism-trump-research-study, Accessed August 14, 2017.

49. See, for example, Frederick C. Harris, "The Rise of Respectability Politics," *Dissent*, Winter 2014, https://www.dissentmagazine.org/article/the-rise-of-respectability-politics, accessed December 22, 2016.

50. Shom Mazumder, "Yes, Marches Can Make a Difference. It Depends on These Three Factors," *Washington Post*, January 27, 2017, https://www.washingtonpost.com

/news/monkey-cage/wp/2017/01/27/yes-marches-can-really-matter-these-three-factors
-make-the-difference/?utm_term=.6aa25370462a, accessed January 27, 2017.

51. Robin DiAngelo, "White Fragility," *International Journal of Critical Pedagogy*, vol. 3, no. 3, (2011): 54–70.

52. See "We Are UnidosUS," UnidosUS press release, July 10, 2017, https://www
.unidosus.org/about-us/media/press/releases/071117-Rebranding-Release; see also video featuring Janet Murguía, undated but posted circa July 10, 2017; https://www.unidosus
.org/about-us/who-we-are/; both accessed November 30, 2017.

53. See "Diversity Is Our Strength," UnidosUS, blogpost, October 2, 2017, http://
blog.unidosus.org/2017/10/02/diversity-is-our-strength/, accessed November 30, 2017.

54. "Immigration for All?" *Washington Post*, editorial, March 12, 2016. See also: Robert Draper, "The Democrats Have an Immigration Problem," *New York Times Magazine*, October 10, 2018.

55. Author interview with Arnoldo Torres, August 4, 2017.

56. See Meissner et al., *Immigration and America's Future: A New Chapter*, 9–11.

57. Margaret E. Peters, "None of Their Business," *New Republic*, November 6, 2017, https://newrepublic.com/article/145419/none-business-how-powerful-support
-immigration-lost-influence-over-republican-party, accessed November 7, 2017.

58. Janet Murguía, "Don't Abandon Families," *USA Today*, March 28, 2017.

59. Ruth Ellen Wasem, "Temporary Professional, Managerial, and Skilled Foreign Workers: Policy and Trends," Congressional Research Service, January 13, 2016, 18.

60. John Sides, "What Makes Someone a 'Real' American" 93% of Americans Actually Agree on This," *Washington Post*, July 14, 2018, reporting on results from the 2016 View of the Electoral Research (VOTER) Survey.

INDEX